Henry Purcell, 1659–1695
HIS LIFE AND TIMES

Henry Purcell, 1659–1695

HIS LIFE AND TIMES

Second, revised edition

Franklin B. Zimmerman

University of Pennsylvania Press

PHILADELPHIA   1983

Frontispiece: Henry Purcell, ca. 1690
(National Portrait Gallery, London)

A version of Appendix Three originally appeared
in *Organ and Choral Aspects and Prospects*,
ed. by Max Hinrichsen (London, 1958).

Library of Congress Cataloging in Publication Data

Zimmerman, Franklin B.
  Henry Purcell (1659–1695)

  Bibliography: p.
  Includes index.
    1. Purcell, Henry, 1659–1695.   2. Composers—England
—Biography.   I. Title.
ML410.P93Z5   1983   780'.92'4 [B]   82-40485
ISBN 0-8122-7869-0
ISBN 0-8122-1136-7 (pbk.)

Printed in the United States of America

Contents

Contents

Plates

Preface to the First Edition

THIS BOOK IS ADDRESSED TO the general public and, more especially, to those keenly interested in Purcell's musical legacy. Discussion of Purcell's life and times is accompanied by brief analysis and description of his most interesting and important works. Because of discontinuity in the Purcellian chronology and lacunae in sources of biographical data, certain dates, and the indicated relationships between individual works and Purcell's life story are sometimes hypothetical.

For these reasons I have delved somewhat further into historical and sociological backgrounds than the study of a musician's life and works might warrant, music being generally conceived of as an art above, or at least removed from, such material considerations. Here I have entered upon seeming digressions from a purely (or puristic) musical view, not to eke out an account otherwise too slender—new data have come to light—but rather to support my conviction that music in Restoration London was both a function and an expression of seventeenth-century English life, and ought therefore to be studied in context. Such relationships cannot always be clearly delineated, but they can surely be shown to have existed. At any rate, it is my hope that the view of Purcell against so broad a backdrop as that projected here will furnish perspectives as interesting and instructive to the reader as they have seemed to me.

We may never know fully the complex processes that produced the "British Orpheus"—a sobriquet, be it noted, which Purcell had earned already in his own day. But this need not diminish our interest in Purcell's legendary reputation, which is so adequately substantiated by his music. In entrusting his trio-sonatas of 1683 to his contemporaries, and to a larger posterity than he can have imagined, Purcell expressed "his hearty wishes that his book . . . fall into no other hands but theirs who carry musical souls about them." This valedictory carried both admonition and challenge to his contemporary musicians and music-lovers, whom he led into a new golden age of English music. That age knew no parallel in England until fairly recent times, when modern

English composers, often inspired by his example, turned away from continental models to mine the riches of their own traditions and to develop the musical propensities of their native language. After three centuries, the challenge still stands.

Explanation

Details relating to incidents in Purcell's life and musical activities are drawn mainly from seventeenth and eighteenth-century documents, all of which have been modernized without any indication other than the conventional symbol (. . .) for ellipsis and square brackets for editorial restorations of missing syllables or words. To supplement these, Appendix One contains relevant documentary information pertaining to each known member of the families of Thomas and the elder Henry Purcell—uncle and father, respectively, of the composer. This appendix also contains as fairly complete an anthology of contemporary Purcellian poems (or sections of poems) as I have been able to discover. Abbreviations for bibliographical references are listed on pp. xxxv−xxxvi.

Acknowledgments

FIRST EDITION

FIRST OF ALL, thanks are due Mr. Edward Croft-Murray and his wife, Jill, for all their warm hospitality. As keeper of prints and drawings at the British Museum, Mr. Croft-Murray lent valuable advice on all illustrative matter in this book, and, with the trustees of the British Museum, graciously gave permission to reproduce the Kneller portrait, the two broadsides, "Titus Tell-Troth" and "The Protestants' Joy," and the monument for William and Mary. Mr. Croft-Murray also told me of "The Cabal," for the reproduction of which I am grateful to Nostell Priory, Notts., for permission to publish.

I owe thanks for expert assistance with parish records and other documents to Mr. Donovan Dawe, assistant archivist at the Guildhall Library, and to the trustees of that institution for permission to quote from these.

I am grateful to Professor Vincent Duckles, music librarian at the University of California at Berkeley, and to his assistant, Mrs. Harriet Nicewonger, for placing at my disposal the rich resources of the remarkable collection they take care of.

For permission to reproduce "The magnificent Form usually Observed in the Procession to the Coronations of the Kings and Queens of England," "The Ground-plot of the Collegiate Church of St. Peter in Westminster," "The Grand Procession of the Sovraigne and Knights Champions," and the "Proceeding to the coronation . . . of King William and Queen Mary," I am grateful to Miss Mary Dunbar, former assistant archivist at Westminster Public Library, Buckingham Palace Road. She also provided me with valuable advice on Westminster rate books and residences.

To Professor Theodore M. Finney, chairman of the Department of Music at the University of Pittsburgh, and to Professor Halsey Stevens, chairman of the Department of Composition, University of Southern California, I am indebted for wise advice in all these matters and, more especially, for their undertaking the heavy task of reading critically the whole typescript. Without it the book was scarcely publishable.

My thanks are also due to:

Dr. Nigel Fortune, who told me of the references in the Ashtead Accounts, for which Mr. A. C. Lowther provided me with further information, and to the trustees of the Guildford Museum and Muniment Room for permission to quote.

To Miss Phyllis M. Giles, librarian, and to the syndics of the Fitzwilliam Museum, Cambridge, for allowing me to reproduce Purcell's autograph inscription from MS. 88.

To the curator of the Holburne of Menstrie Museum of Art in Bath for permission to reproduce the miniature of Colonel Edward Purcell.

To Lady Susi Jeans of Cleveland Lodge, Dorking, whose disinterested scholarly liberality and assistance with the records at Mickleham parish church have been most helpful.

To Dr. Neil Ker, librarian, and Mr. T. S. R. Boase, president of Magdalen College, Oxford, as well as to Mrs. Rosamund McGuinness for assistance with the Magdalen College records.

To Macmillan & Co. Ltd., to Mr. Harry Cowdell, and particularly to Miss Phyllis Hartnoll and Miss Elizabeth Ellem for careful criticisms.

To the trustees of the Bodleian Library, Oxford, for permission to reproduce "The Inthronization of Their Majesties King James the Second and Queen Mary"; "A Perfect description of the Firework in Covent Garden that was performed at the Charge of the Gentry and other inhabitants of that Parish for the joyful return of his Majesty from his Conquest in Ireland, 10 September 1690"; and "The Robin-Red-Breast Famous for singing every day on the Top of Queen Mary's Mausoleum Erected in Westminster Abbey."

To Dean Lawrence Powell and his gracious staff at the William Andrews Clark Memorial Library in Los Angeles for letting me reproduce the illustrations from Sandford's *The History of the Coronation of . . . James II . . .* and for other kindnesses too numerous to list here.

To the Public Record Office, Chancery Lane, London, for permission to reproduce Purcell's will and to quote various documents on the Purcell family.

To Mr. Harold Purcell, managing director of L.P.E. Television Ltd., London, for generous provision of unique genealogical data.

To the Royal Society of Musicians in London for permission to publish the putative portrait of Daniel Purcell.

To Miss Alice Stanley of the Literary Department of the Probate Registry, Somerset House, London, for services beyond official requirements, and to that institution for permission to quote various testamentary documents and transcripts.

To Mr. Lawrence E. Tanner, C.V.O., F.S.A., keeper of the Muniments and Library, Westminster Abbey, for granting reproduction of the Purcell coat-of-arms and quotation from the Treasurer's Accounts; and to him and to Mr. N. H. Mac-Michael, assistant librarian, for various aids, as well as to the dean and chapter of Westminster Abbey for permission to cite from the Westminster Abbey Precentor's Books.

To Mr. J. E. Thomas, F.L.A., city librarian, Cardiff Libraries, who, through the good offices of Lady Susi Jeans, provided me with information on the Purcells of Cardiff.

To Dr. Virginia Tufts of Los Angeles for advising me of the frontispiece in P. de Cardonnel's *Complementum Fortunatarum Insularum*, and to the Henry E. Huntington Library, San Marino, California, for allowing reproduction of the same.

SECOND EDITION

I am particularly grateful to Malcolm Call, associate director of the University of Pennsylvania Press, and to the Press's manuscript editor, Lee Ann Draud, without whose expert and diligent collaboration I dare say the book would never have gone to press. I am also grateful to the following institutions and persons for permission to reproduce the illustrations:

To the Bodleian Library, Oxford, for permission to reproduce plates 8, 30, and 37.

To the trustees of the British Museum for permission to reproduce plates 9, 10, 31, 32, 33, 36, II.D, II.E, III.G, III.I, III.J, III.K, III.L, III.M, III.N, IV.U, and V.X.

To Jill Croft-Murray, for her kind permission to reproduce plate IV.S.

To the Fitzwilliam Museum Library, Cambridge, for permission to reproduce plate 14.

To the Holburne of Menstrie Museum, University of Bath, for permission to reproduce plate 43.

To the Henry E. Huntington Library, San Marino, California, for permission to reproduce plate 7.

To the Master and Fellows, Magdalene College, Cambridge, for permission to reproduce plate 5.

To the National Portrait Gallery for permission to reproduce plates 17, 18, 20, 21, 26, 27, 29, III.F, III.H, III.O, IV.P, and V.V.

To the Nostell Priory for permission to reproduce plate 12.

To the Royal Society of Musicians of Great Britain for permission to reproduce plate V.X.

To the Archives Department, Westminster City Libraries, for permission to reproduce plates 1, 2, 3, 4, 6, 22, 23, 24, and 25.

To the Dean and Chapter of Westminster for permission to reproduce plate 13.

Preface to the Second, Revised Edition

OF ALL OBJECTIVES A biographer may strive to attain, none is more vital than to breathe life into his subject. With Henry Purcell, finding the inner man, getting even a fleeting glimpse of his personality is very difficult indeed. Virtually all extant records relating to him concern only the professional musician, on whose activities we are fairly well informed. But verifiable data relate only to the official actions he undertook, whereby Purcell emerges as a flat, two-dimensional figure, no matter how one tries to see him in the round. The mythology of the "Orpheus Britannicus," which had developed somewhat eponymously, even before his death, only blurs the issue. And various fictive presentations, however interesting, have only served to increase our difficulty in finding the real person.

Certain facts about Purcell's life are known. He was born of Henry and Elizabeth Purcell, probably in Westminster, in the latter part of the year 1659. His father died in August 1664, possibly a victim of the plague. He was schooled in Westminster and apprenticed at the Chapel Royal, where he sang as a choir boy. Thus orphaned at age five or six, Purcell was reared by his widowed mother and paternal uncle, Thomas.

Beyond these basic facts, we know almost nothing of his boyhood. As a scholar, he gained the respect of Richard Busby, famed schoolmaster at St. Peter's, Westminster, and enjoyed a "Bishop's Boy" scholarship there, in the place of his cousin Charles, from 1678 onward, regularly receiving his stipend even after his debut as a professional musician. He married at twenty-one or twenty-two; quite early in the marriage, and frequently thereafter, he fathered children, seven in all, of whom only two survived infancy.

Further, we know only that during his tragically brief creative span of fifteen years, Purcell was extraordinarily active as composer, editor, instrument-maker, musical consultant, music teacher, organ judge, and performer; that he was employed by three monarchs; that he may have been suspected of Catholic sympathies; and that he died at the early age of thirty-six, having established a splendid reputation as England's most prominent composer for court, church, theater, and public concert.

Beyond this we know scarcely anything about Purcell as he really was, outside official spheres and public life. Our small store of information relating to his personal attributes and his character may be described at best as anecdotal, at worst as mere gossip. On such scanty knowledge, how, then, can one bring this figure to life?

Purcell himself left almost nothing in the way of clear, unambiguous information contributing to a satisfactory description of himself as a person. Apart from his musical compositions, the earliest matter from his own hand dates back only to his twenty-second or twenty-third year, when he wrote the mystifying inscription in the flyleaf of Fitzwilliam MS 88, a fair copy-book of scored anthems and other music:

"God bless Mr. Henry Purcell, September 10th, 1682."

We really do not know what this may mean. Such inscriptions are not common in manuscripts of the period, and so far as is known, Purcell made no similar entry elsewhere. The note reveals that he may have been devout but gives no hint of the significance of this little prayer to Purcell's life story. Were these words written in memory of his father's death twenty years before? Did they record his grief for his firstborn son, whom he had buried about this time? Or might the phrase have commemorated the recent death of his foster father and uncle, Thomas Purcell? None of these questions can be answered at present. Possibly Purcell may have been concerned over difficulties in his career that began five years before, on 10 September; or perhaps, as Reinhold Sietz has suggested, he was merely jotting down a memorandum for his own birthday. This last suggestion seems most plausible. But at present none of these conjectures can be proven one way or another.

Chronologically, the next extant document from Purcell's hand is the Sacrament Certificate, reproduced as plate 16, below, which raises the interesting question as to whether or not Purcell belonged to the Roman Catholic faith. For abundance of stated opinions and lack of solid evidence, this stands as one of the most frustrating questions in Purcell research. The certificate itself verifies that on 2 February 1683 Purcell took the Sacrament of Communion according to the rite of the Church of England, before witnesses who testified to the fact next day in court. This demonstration that he was faithful to the Anglican

Church may or may not have been genuine. Perhaps taking the test was only a formality, since after the *First Test Act of 1673*, and especially after the second of 1678, which reinforced the terms of the first, all civil and military officers and all court personnel were required to take the test. On the other hand, the statute was most rigidly observed where Catholic sympathies were suspected, and it is possible that Purcell's connections with Matthew Locke, John Dryden, and John Baptist Peters may have brought him under suspicion. Just at that time Whigs and Parliamentarians were determined that there would be no return to the days of '41, particularly while a Stuart still occupied the throne.

Most court officials had to face the test at one time or another. John Blow and Nicholas Staggins both took communion in public as did others who had no Catholic sympathies. The evidence for Purcell's alleged Catholicism is all circumstantial and mainly based on rumor. The romantic tale of his having sought refuge from the strictures of an official religion not his own in company with his friend John Dryden in the tower at St. James Palace must be dismissed as mere fiction. Purcell also was friendly with other notable Catholics, such as Sir Robert Howard, Nicola Matteis, G. B. Draghi, and other Italian musicians. Moreover, as noted above, he seems to have married the daughter of J. B. Peters, an avowed Papist. However, this evidence also is not conclusive, and the fact that James II withheld confirmation of Purcell's appointment as composer until late in his reign outweighs all these circumstances and rumors. This king seldom overlooked members of the Catholic faith when showing his generosity or awarding preferments among the faithful at court. In sum, Purcell probably adhered to the Anglican faith throughout his life, however many Catholic friends, acquaintances, or Italophile tendencies he may have had.

Turning again to information originating with Purcell himself, one of the most interesting sources is the preface to the *Sonatas of Three Parts*, which he published in 1683. Together with his advertisements for this, his first published opus, these reveal to us that Purcell was meticulous in attention to detail and knowledgeable about Italian conventions, styles, and terminology. Furthermore, he was punctual and responsible in his business dealings, both with the public and with printers. It is clear from his statements that Purcell was quite taken with the expressive powers of Italian compositions, which caused him to "imitate the most fam'd Italian masters," as he styled them. From Purcell's own transcriptions and remarks, we know that he admired Monteverdi, Gratiani, Carissimi, and Lelio Colista. Other sources identify as his favorites also Niccolo Matteis, Alessandro Stradella,

Siface, and even a few lesser-known Baroque masters, such as Carlo Caproli, Bernardo Pasquini, Ercole Bernabei, and others who had worked closely with Siface in the musical establishment of Maria of Modena. This celebrated castrato entered service under Mary after her coronation as the consort of James II in 1686, as did many other former employees at Modena. Purcell surely was in frequent contact with these men during the years 1686 through 1688. Although we know from his carefully scored copies of the works of William Byrd, Thomas Tallis, Orlando Gibbons, and other Renaissance English masters that Purcell was devoted to music of his native isle, his familiarity with contemporary Italian works shows that his musical horizons were not limited. Like Bach he was a cosmopolitan, well in tune with his times and eager to keep abreast of the latest developments in his art. He proved an apt pupil of masters, both foreign and domestic, and soon surpassed his models.

Further along in the same preface, Purcell reveals diffidence about his education, an attitude that encourages us to wonder what his intellectual aspirations and attainments may have been. Was his schooling under Richard Busby at St. Peter's such as to cause him afterward to think nostalgically of those inspiring times? Or was the stipend he received as a "Bishop's Boy" merely the result of an administrative device to tide him over the difficult period between the time his voice broke and he became a fully self-sufficient professional musician? (In any case, his first professional appointments, as composer in 1677 and as organist in 1678, were awarded while he was still in school, and the regrets expressed in the above-mentioned preface were probably genuine.) Or perhaps he was merely being modest, as would befit a young composer seeking broad public support for his first publication. Without further evidence, one can merely speculate.

Nevertheless the preface, taken in its entirety, enhances our sense of Purcell's character and personality, especially if we are willing to read between the lines he addressed to the "Ingenuous reader":

> Instead of an elaborate harangue on the beauty and charms of music (which after all the learned encomions [*sic*] that one can contrive commends itself best by the performance of a skillful hand, and an angelical voice:) I shall say but a very few things by way of Preface, concerning the following book, and its author: for its author, he has faithfully endeavoured a just imitation of the most famed Italian masters; principally to bring the seriousness and gravity of that sort of music into vogue, and reputation among our countrymen, whose humor, 'tis time now, should begin to loathe the levity, and balladry of our neighbours: The attempt

he confesses to be bold, and daring, there being pens and artists of more eminent abilities, much better qualified for the employment than his, or himself, which he well hopes these his weak endeavours, will in due time provoke, and enflame to a more accurate undertaking. He is not ashamed to own his unskilfulness in the Italian language; but that's the unhappiness of his education, which cannot justly be accounted his fault; however he thinks he may warrantably affirm, that he is not mistaken in the power of the Italian notes, or elegancy of their compositions, which he would recommend to the English artists. There has been neither care, nor industry wanting, as well in contriving as revising the whole work; which had been abroad in the world much sooner, but that he has now thought fit to cause the whole thorough bass to be engraven, which was a thing quite beyond his first resolutions. It remains only that the English practitioner be informed, that he will find a few terms of art perhaps unusual to him, the chief of which are these following: *Adagio* and *Grave*, which import nothing but a very slow movement: *Presto Largo, Poco Largo,* or *Largo* by itself, a middle movement: *Allegro* and *Vivace,* a very brisk, swift, or fast movement: *Piano,* soft. The author has no more to add, but his hearty wishes, that this book may fall into no other hands but theirs who carry musical souls about them; for he is willing to flatter himself into a belief, that with such his labours will seem neither unpleasant nor unprofitable.

In this well-conceived, well-written preface, Purcell's expressions are those of a man humble enough about other accomplishments, but proud of his musical abilities. His literary style, elegant and clear, though casual after the new fashion set by Dryden, carries enough professional sheen to warrant the suspicion that he may have turned to this great literary innovator as a model. Some eight years later Purcell actually allowed Dryden to serve as ghostwriter for the preface to *Dioclesian,* which reveals another small facet of Purcell's character: He was not one to stand on ceremony in such matters. The fact that Dryden did not mind supplying the office tells us that by 1690, the friendship, which had begun only two years earlier during their collaboration in the production of *Amphytrion,* had ripened quickly.

Purcell's next revealing written matter is to be found in his letter to the dean of Exeter Cathedral, dated 2 November 1686. This represents his last-ditch attempt, after several letters to a Mr. Webber, to collect £27 owed him for lessons, boarding, and other necessaries he had provided for a boy named Hodg, apparently one of his earliest and least rewarding pupils. From this letter, clear and to the point, we learn that Purcell could be most persistent in pursuing what was due him, and also that he was fair and altruistic in his judgment. Purcell made it obvious that he needed and wanted the money but also exhibited a strong sense of responsibility where the rights of other creditors might be involved.

The letter, which tells us a little about Purcell, might reveal more if we knew something of the character of his pupil. It seems that he stayed at Purcell's house in Bowling Alley East for more than six months, being fed, instructed, and provided for. As to what Purcell may have taught him, again, there is no information. We may imagine that he would have used the beautifully graduated, meticulously detailed methods outlined in his edition of the Third Part of John Playford's *Introduction to the Skill of Music* (12th edition, 1694), and this simple but effective method shows something of Purcell's skill as a teacher. He may have instructed young Hodg in the art of figured bass realization, perhaps using the comprehensive yet simple method devised by his own teacher, John Blow. He probably tried also to teach the boy the art of keyboard improvisation, in which he himself had been coached by Christopher Gibbons. He may even have attempted to teach him to repair, tune, and maintain instruments, as he had learned from John Hingeston and from his own experiences in that official capacity. The tone of Purcell's letter suggests that the relationship was not successful. One wonders what Mrs. Purcell must have thought of the arrangements, whereby young Hodg was given all this for a mere £3 per month—especially since the money was not forthcoming.

Purcell was more fortunate with other pupils, all of whom, so far as records show, he took on during the last few years of his life. According to actual records, these included Katherine Shore, daughter of the famous trumpeter, John; Katherine Howard, daughter of Sir Robert and Lady Katherine; and John Weldon, then at Eton, later moderately famous as a London composer. The list probably also should include Jeremiah Clarke, William Croft, Henry Needler, and others, who later claimed Purcell as their teacher.

At present, no other documents originating with Purcell himself are extant. However, several incidents in his life may be reconstructed rather fully from official records. Some show how he reacted to complications and stresses in musical life under the first three post-Restoration monarchies. For instance, there is the notorious "Organ-Loft Incident," occurring during the coronation of William and Mary on 11 April 1689. In collaboration with Stephen Crespion, cantor and succentor of the Abbey, Purcell exercised a perquisite observed by former organists at the Abbey by selling tickets to seats in the organ loft to spectators, who paid handsomely for the privilege of viewing proceedings from that vantage point. Less than a week later, he and Crespion received peremptory orders from John Needham to turn over all ticket revenues to the dean and chapter of Westminster Abbey. Though summarily brought to the book thus for alleged peculation, Purcell was not badly treated in the end. He received more than half the sum taken in, from which he had already retained his expenses and "poundage" (fee for promotion). Had it been thought that Purcell was dishonest in these dealings, surely he would not have been given such generous terms.

The language of the order was stiff, and Needham behaved like a bad-tempered, bullying bureaucrat. But Purcell emerged £35 richer for the experience, his reputation intact, and his professional status unharmed. Having a great many more details relating to this contretemps than Hawkins found, we can entertain a more balanced view than the great pioneer music-historian's gossip might give us. We see Purcell as a resourceful and successful young musician playing the hard game of survival among London's professional musicians. It was a game that required of its practitioners pluralism in all musical spheres, perpetual financial opportunism, and infinite sagacity in pecuniary matters. It is a thousand pities that Purcell was compelled to play this game, but there is some satisfaction that his reprimand was mildly disciplinary rather than punitive. Ironically, from the same document we learn that Purcell's regular salary was a month in arrears just then. It is clear from other records that he had to wait nearly a year to be reimbursed for expenses incurred in preparing the organ for the coronation. Faced with such fiscal irresponsibility, Purcell did well to study his perquisites carefully, following profitable precedents by selling as many tickets as he could. We are informed by the incident of much we would otherwise not know, but the information need not be damaging. Purcell obviously was not an adept "organization man." But that fault, shared with many a creative personality, need not reflect unfavorably on his basic character.

Other extant records of the period do not yield inferences so readily or provide new insights. However, in the Vestry and Poor-Rate Books for the Parish of St. Margaret's, Westminster, several hitherto unnoticed entries shed new light on Purcell's personal life. When he moved with his family to Marsham Street in the spring of 1692, he did not relinquish ownership of the property in Bowling Alley East, where he had lived since 1686. In the Vestry-book for 1692, Purcell still was entered as the owner of two houses, which thereafter were occupied by Anne Peters, possibly an in-law, and five unattached women, all exempted from the poll tax levied in support of the war in France on the grounds that they earned too little money and were not married.

Careful research has not revealed what the relationship of these women to Purcell may have been, if anything. But he was clearly moving up in the world, residing now in the more fashionable neighborhood around Marsham Street and at the same time enjoying his income from the houses in Bowling Alley East.

Far less important, though interesting, is the question of Purcell's supposed doctorate. P. Motteux's advertisement of Matthew Prior's *Hymn to the Sun* "set to music by Dr. Purcell," which appeared in *Gentleman's Journal* for January 1694, seems the earliest mention of the degree. A similar reference is to be found in the eighteenth edition of *Angliae Notitiae*, but it is well to be wary of information about musicians in this source, for in the seventeenth edition, Purcell had been mistakenly identified as "Master of the Children of the Chapel Royal." After Purcell's untimely death on 21 November 1695, the *Post Boy* twice listed him as "Dr. Purcell" in its obituary notices. About that same time John Evelyn recalls having heard some of Dr. Purcell's songs at Mr. Pepys's house.

All these references seem erroneous. Records from Cambridge, Canterbury, Dublin, Lambeth, and Oxford list no conferral of a doctoral degree upon Purcell, and no other known sources refer to him by that title. Most contemporary sources list him simply as "Mr. Purcell," a style that is probably correct.

Turning to more general records, there are disappointingly few anecdotes on Purcell in journals, diaries, and music histories of the eighteenth century. Sir John Hawkins, who published *A General History of the Science and Practice of Music* in 1776, originated most of the traditional anecdotes, some of which are based on mere rumor. It was he who first indicted Purcell for his alleged peculation in the organ-loft incident. It was Hawkins also who recorded that Purcell, like Charles II, hated the viola da gamba. His dislike supposedly is reflected in the humorous catch, "Of All the Instruments That Are," which lampoons John Gostling's delight in that instrument. Hawkins also compares Purcell to Thomas Brown, reputed to be a carouser and frequenter of taverns such as The Hole in the Wall (characterized at length in D'Urfey's *A Fool's Preferment*), or such as Baldwin's Gardens or Owen Swan's Cobweb Hall in Bartholomew Lane. Supposedly Purcell also frequented The Purcell's Head Tavern in Wych Street, which boasted a full-length portrait of him in dressing gown and brown wig as its tavern sign. The owner of this tavern, one Kennedy, was bassoonist in the opera band and undoubtedly knew Purcell. (See Appendix Three, Iconography.) Upon rumors of Purcell's carousing in these places, Hawkins built what is perhaps his most pernicious gossip regarding the composer:

> There is a tradition that his death was occasioned by a cold which he caught in the night, waiting for admittance to his own house. It is said that he used to keep late hours, and that his wife had given orders to his servants not to let him in after midnight. Unfortunately he came home heated with wine from a tavern at an hour later than that prescribed him, and through the inclemency of the air contracted a disorder and died.

Hawkins's account, however, is weakened by his statement that Purcell was intimately acquainted with Tom Brown, whereas the latter informs us in the dedicatory poem to Playford's *Harmonia Sacra* that he did not know Purcell at all. Moreover, Hawkins's mention of servants strikes an odd note, for it does not seem that Purcell was so affluent at that time to afford the luxury. The tale itself, implying as it does a very bad relationship between Purcell and his wife, relates in this particular to another sample of gossip about Purcell reflecting less of fact than of Hawkins's jaundiced eye.

When Purcell was told of Alessandro Stradella's assassination by the estranged husband of his mistress, he is reported to have said that he would have forgiven Stradella an injury of that kind if only because he admired him so much as a musician, "which those who remember how lovingly Mr. Purcell lived with his wife, or rather what a loving wife she proved him, may understand without further explication." The tale itself and the gross innuendo may be discounted even though it is probably true that Purcell lamented Stradella exceedingly and openly admired his music. Such warmhearted praise and generous sympathy for a fellow musician accord well with what we know of Purcell's character, while the rest somehow does not.

In addition to a large public following, Purcell had many warm and intimate friends, and the mere number of these tells us a lot about his character. John Blow, John Dryden, John Dolben, Christopher Wren, Matthew Locke, and Richard Busby have left ample testimony of their regard for him, both as artist and friend. Among the slightly less famous, there were many more, including Henry Hall, a fellow pupil under Blow, Stephen Crespion, John Gostling, John Lenton, Matthias and John Shore, Moses Snow, Richard Tomlinson, and numerous others, including one Jacob Talbot, former owner of a copy of the original edition of Purcell's score for *Dioclesian*, which passed into the library of William H. Cummings and thence into the Nanki Library in Japan.

This exemplar bears the inscription "Ex dono carissimi desideratissim-que Autoris Henrici Purcell Musarum Sacerdotus: Qui Anno Domini 1695 Pridie Festi Stae Cecilia Multis Flebilis occidit, Nulli flebelior quam Amico suo atque Admiratori Jacobo Talbot."

Purcell's love for music, so simple and straightforward, and his genteel humility in personal relationships with friends and colleagues also reflect in the last three anecdotes that figure in this essay. Apparently he was a frequent, welcome guest at the home of the great and powerful family of the Norths, with whom he often performed chamber music, at the invitation of Lord Francis North, keeper of the Great Seal. Even though his fellow musicians were amateurs, he performed with them graciously, often bringing his own compositions. According to Roger North (*Roger North on Music*, p. 307), perhaps the most musical member of the family and certainly one of the most erudite musicians of his time: "Then rose up the Noble Purcell, the Jenkins of his time, or more. He was a match for all sorts of designs in musick. Nothing came amiss to him. He imitated the Italian sonata, and (bating a little too much of the labour) outdid them. And raised up opera and music in the theatres, to a credit even of fame as far as Italy, where Sig^r Purcell was courted no less than at home. . . ."

This splendid compliment bears all the more weight because the North family had had the good judgment to support and encourage John Jenkins in similar fashion a generation earlier. The general admiration of the North family reflects a very pleasant light on Purcell, revealing him to be not only one of the most highly admired musicians of his age, but a beloved person as well. This image shows clearly in Roger North's remarks on the "Art of Gracing" (i.e., melodic ornamentation), especially in the passage lamenting the fact that after the death of Purcell, "who has given us patterns of all the graces music can have," there were no masters who could teach this art. Roger North, like most contemporary musicians, looked upon gracing not as the addition of superficial decorations to music, but as a central and essential creative act of performance, or, in his own words, that "The grace of the hand is no other than a voluntary expression of the graces of the descant or of the composition" (ibid., p. 150).

These remarks relate to one of the most revealing of all Purcellian anecdotes. Jemmy Bowen, a precocious boy soprano quite famous in Purcell's day, was preparing for a public performance, as we know from Anthony Aston's "A Brief Supplement to Colley Cibber's, An Apology for the Life of Mr. Colley Cibber, Comedian" (London, 1889): "He, when practicing a song set by Mr. Purcell, some of the music told him to grace and run a division in such a place. *O let him alone* said Mr. Purcell; *he will grace it more naturally than you, or I can teach him.*" This little scene reveals a generous, humble devotion to the art of music that, particularly because it is so unassuming, endears him to us immediately.

One last glimpse of Purcell's personality may be gained from a playful "Rebus on Mr. Henry Purcell's name," as written by Richard Tomlinson and set to music by John Lenton, both of whom were lifelong colleagues of Purcell's, among court musicians with whom he had collaborated throughout his career. Neither the literary content of the rebus, which is minimal, nor the musical setting tell us much about Purcell. But the waggish, punning manner of the verses, and the playful rhyming translation into bad Latin, which is an anomaly, because all the punning syllables are found only in English, tells us something of the fond familiarity his fellow musicians felt for this fine fellow, "Harry Purcell," who also happened to be England's greatest and most renowned musician:

> The Mate to a Cock, and Corn tall as wheat
> Is his Christian name, who in music's compleat;
> His surname begins with the grace of a cat,
> And concludes with the house of a hermit, note that;
> His skill and performance each auditor wins,
> But the poet deserves a good kick on the shins.

> Galli marita par tritico seges
> Praenomen est ejus, dat chromati leges,
> Instrat cognomen,—blanditiis cati,
> Exit eremi in aedibus stali,
> Expertum effectum omnes admierentur
> Quid merent Poetae? ut bene calcentur.

So much for the glimpses of Purcell's character that may be gleaned from official records and anecdotes. These give us at least a preliminary sketch of his personal character, which may be highlighted by another, perhaps subtler, source of inferences, namely, his music. Admittedly we here enter on grounds even more conjectural than those ventured upon in the foregoing passages. Hence all evidence of the musical sort must be scrutinized and weighed most carefully, if it is to have any objective value.

One of the most attractive general features of Purcell's personal musical style lies in the obvious good humor with which he approached some of his compositions. We have already mentioned his little catch on the viola da gamba, in which he wittily poked fun at John Gostling, his close friend of long standing and fellow member of the Gentlemen of the Chapel Royal. The anonymous text, perhaps written by Purcell himself, is an example of comic, nonsensical verse at its best:

> Of all the instruments that are,
> None with the viol can compare:
> Mark how the strings their order keep,
> With a whet whet whet and a sweep sweep sweep;
> But above all this still abounds,
> With a zingle zingle zing, and zit zat zounds.

It is Purcell's delightful setting of this nonsense that gives rise to the suspicion that he may also have created the text, which, with its alliteration, assonance, and silly rhymes, lends itself beautifully to the canonic working out of the melodic motivs in a veritable symphony of characteristic viol sounds, which combine to achieve delicious comic effects.

Most of Purcell's best humorous musical moments were written thus, tongue in cheek. The ludicrous witches in *Dido and Aeneas*, with their comic peals of fiendish laughter contrasting effectively with the mock-sinister utterances of the sorcerer; the stiff and frozen Cold Genius and his shivering Cold People thawing and growing nimble under the warming ministrations of Cupid in *King Arthur*; the slow-witted, stuttering Drunken Poet surrounded by light-footed, teasing fairy-folk in *The Fairy Queen*; and the hissing, venomous trio sung by Envy and his followers in *The Indian Queen* in a remarkable allegory of villainy— all these display a delightful, good-humored musical wit and show Purcell to have been one of the most effective masters of the comic vein ever to compose. The attentive listener cannot help but smile or even laugh aloud at some of these scenes.

Another facet of his comic talent is to be seen in his bawdy catches, where in setting texts no more risqué than many set by his contemporaries, he outdoes them with an erotic realism that makes one blush even today. The ending of "Sir Walter Enjoying His Damsel One Night" is perhaps the most suggestive passage in all of Purcell's catches. It is a dialogue catch, and the damsel has the floor: "Sweet Sir Walter, sweet Sir Walter, switter, swatter, switter swatter, switterswatter. . . ." But the ribald catches "Young John the Gard'ner" and "Tom Making a Mantua" are nearly as bawdy, though perhaps showing less verisimilitude. Obviously, Purcell did not mind hitting near the knuckle. But Hawkins and others are not therefore justified in characterizing him as a man of loose morals, any more than such a judgment would be justified for Mozart, who set his pen to equally salacious subject matter from time to time.

Purcell's ready musical wit is apparent in other instances. Though it seems from the following anecdote that Purcell at the age of about thirty-four was not at all stuffy about "serious music," he did take pride in his craft. (Here again, Hawkins is our source, *vide* II, 564n.) Having eulogized the Scots air "Cold and Raw," Hawkins recounts the following tale of Purcell's encounter with Queen Mary's somewhat plebeian musical tastes:

> This tune was greatly admired by Queen Mary. . . . Having a mind one afternoon to be entertained with music, [she] sent to Mr. Gostling, then one of the chapel and afterwards subdean of St. Paul's, to Henry Purcell and Mrs. Arabella Hunt, who had a very fine voice, and an admirable hand on the lute, with a request to attend her; they obeyed her commands; Mr. Gostling and Mrs. Hunt sang several compositions of Purcell, who accompanied them on the harpsichord; at length the queen beginning to grow tired, asked Mrs. Hunt if she could not sing the old Scots ballad "Cold and Raw," Mrs. Hunt answered yes, and sang it to her lute. Purcell was all the while sitting at the harpsichord unemployed, and not a little nettled at the queen's preference of a vulgar ballad to his music; but seeing her majesty delighted with this music, he determined that she should hear it upon another occasion: and accordingly in the next birthday song, *viz.*, that for the year 1692, he composed an air to the words "May her bright example chace Vice in troops out of the land," the bass whereof is the tune "Cold and Raw. . . ."

The anecdote provides a delightfully human picture of Purcell, and it is pleasant to know that he would act so genuinely, and, in the end, with such good humor in what might have been a very awkward situation. It is interesting, too, to see how he escaped losing face while really not backing down before the royal will. Earlier, when he was about twenty-eight, Purcell had used another popular tune for a bass, in composing the fifth movement of the ode for King James II, "Ye Tuneful Muses, Raise Your Heads" (Z344). Purcell's humor here, if intended as political commentary, might have been dangerous. Just at that time the same tune was being heard on the streets as a broadside ballad "The Popish Tory's Confession; or, an Answer to the Whig's Exaltation." The opening lines "Down with the Whigs, we'll now grow wise," were safe enough in the sphere of James II and his court but scarcely the sort of thing to endear Purcell to the very powerful Whiggish opposition.

Nor was Purcell's comic vein limited to secular compositions. The opening vocal solo of his spirited anthem "They That Go Down to the

Sea in Ships" begins with a realistic two-octave descending scale—it was designed for Gostling, of course—in which the rocking motion of the boat is mimicked in the dotted rhythms of the melody. Later, when the text describes "staggering like a drunken man," the tune literally staggers, while the rhythm lurches most realistically. Here again, Purcell's imagination was stimulated by an actual event, for the anthem was a thanksgiving piece commemorating the miraculous salvation of Charles II, James, duke of York, and John Gostling from shipwreck during an outing on the royal yacht "The Fubbs," so named because of its broad beam, a feature it shared with the duchess of Portsmouth, along with this sobriquet.

These examples of Purcell's humor and wit, as expressed in certain musical passages, bring us about as far as it is possible to go in correlating personal with musical characteristics. We may perhaps be allowed to form certain opinions about Purcell the man on the basis of what we know about his meticulousness, his thoroughness, his comprehensiveness, and his unconventionality as a composer. But these facets of character, if indeed they are such, are far too abstract to be interpreted as traits of personality. As for those qualities in his music that speak most eloquently to us, such as the nobility of expression, the urgent creative energy, the beauty of melodic lines and word-setting, the imaginative illustrations of text and scenario, the fascinating contrapuntal ingenuity, and, perhaps more than anything else, his highly personal tender pathos and moving melancholy—all these qualities speak not so much to our erudition or even our understanding as to our feelings.

As for biographical interest, these qualities are of no use whatsoever. However well we may know his music or understand his form, techniques, and style, our musical intuitions bring us no closer to an understanding of Purcell as a private individual. To enhance our knowledge and understanding here, we must turn to other sources, of which there are only two remaining: his portraiture and the eulogies of those who knew him directly. (Anyone interested in the dubious evidence to be gleaned from his handwriting may find food for thought in the excellent article on this subject by A. Hughes-Hughes, "Henry Purcell's Handwriting," in *The Musical Times* for February 1896.) As for the other resources, both eulogies and portraits are included in the main body of this study, in Appendixes One and Three, respectively. The evidence afforded by these is highly heuristic at very best, and thus may be most advantageously interpreted by the individual reader.

The writer's own image of Purcell shows him to be a warm and open man of genius, serious by nature, but witty, warm, and humorous, and given to ready laughter. It would be easy to believe from what little evidence we have that he was ambitious, but difficult to imagine him elbowing aside competitors or treating anyone ungently as he climbed the ladder of success. In short, he was one of the best-liked musical personalities of his time—a man who gave a great deal to his public and his large circle of friends but took very little in return—a generous, gentle person with a very musical soul.

A Postscript
to the First Edition

THE FIRST EDITION OF this biography of Henry Purcell was in fact a second version of the narrative that follows, its predecessor having been stolen by an automobile thief in Hampstead Heath the night before it was to have been delivered to the publishers. This second version, written away from the sources, was widely reviewed, rather more favorably on one side of the Atlantic than on the other. The distance of those same sources persuaded me not to answer criticisms at that time but to wait for the opportunity provided by a second edition. Most of the points at issue have been disposed of tacitly at appropriate places in the narrative. However, one or two questions may be more conveniently argued here.

In one instance I was called to task for describing John Playford the Elder as a printer, citing as I did Ellen Playford's advertisement of the sale of the "Printing House of the late John Playford in Little Britain" (see 1st ed., p. 137). A more persuasive advertisement might have been cited:

> An ancient printing-house, in Little Britain, late in possession of Mr. John Playford, Printer deceased, well known and ready fitted and accommodated with good presses, and all manner of Letter for choice work of music, mathematics, navigation and all Greek or Latin books, with a fair and convenient dwelling-house, and convenient rooms for warehouses; all of which are to be sold as they are ready standing, or let by lease or yearly rent. Enquire of Mrs. Ellen Playford at the said house over against the Globe in Little Britain. (*London Gazette* No. 2135, 3–6 May 1686)

Charles Burney in volume 2 of his *History* (p. 330) describes Playford as "the most intelligent printer of music during the last century"; and Sir John Hawkins in the same volume (p. 736) states that he contributed "to the art of printing music from letter-press types." Fully aware that various authorities might disagree, I have decided to let my original statement stand.

A second criticism must be roundly repudiated. Mr. Robert Donington, adopting an essentially negative view, stated: "There is a good deal of straight English history mainly culled I suppose from Traill and Trevelyan." Nothing could be further from the truth than his supposition. Although these two authors appear in the bibliography, nothing was borrowed from either. Virtually all points of the historical narrative were drawn from documents relating to the lives and actions of musicians and their colleagues working in and around the court and churches in Westminster during Purcell's lifetime. All sources are cited, and secondary books on the subject were consulted mainly for verification and study. Although this narrative of Purcell's life and times was written by one who is not, alas, a historian, the facts presented are those drawn from the sources indicated and not from the two standard histories mentioned, which happen to be those I consulted least.

In closing, the author is persuaded that he can bravely stand his ground in all but one or two insignificant instances.

Abbreviations

TITLES OF BOOKS frequently referred to in text and notes have been abbreviated to author's surname, or other catchwords only. Fuller information appears below, where the author's full name and the abbreviated title appear. These same items will be found in the bibliography, where author, title, place, and date of publication are shown, each item there marked by an asterisk.

Add. MS. / Additional MS (with shelf number) in the British Library

Analytical Catalogue / F. B. Zimmerman. *Henry Purcell 1659–1695: An Analytical Catalogue of His Music*

Baker / Baker, Sir Richard. *A Chronicle of the Kings of England*, 4th ed.

Bodleian / Bodleian Library, Oxford

Boswell / Boswell, E. *The Restoration Court Stage 1660–1662*

Bryant / Bryant, Arthur. *King Charles II*

Burney / Burney, Charles. *A General History of Music*

Cal. S. P. Dom. / *Calendar of State Papers, Domestic Series*

Cal. Tr. Bks. / *Calendar of Treasury Books*

Cal. Tr. Papers / *Calendar of Treasury Papers*

Chester / See *Westminster Abbey Registers*

Cheque-book / Rimbault, E. F. *The Old Cheque-Book, or Book of Remembrance of the Chapel Royal, from 1651 to 1744*

Cummings / Cummings, W. H. *Purcell*

Day and Murrie / Day, Cyrus L. and Murrie, Eleanor Boswell. *English Song-Books, 1651–1702*

DNB / *Dictionary of National Biography*

Downes / Downes, John. *Roscius Anglicanus*

Evelyn / Evelyn, John. *Diary* (ed. E. S. de Beer)

Genest / Genest, J. *Some Account of the English Stage . . . 1660–1830*

Grove IV / *Grove's Dictionary of Music*, 4th ed.

Grove V / *Grove's Dictionary of Music*, 5th ed.

Grove VI / *Grove's Dictionary of Music*, 6th ed.

Hawkins / Hawkins, Sir John. *A General History of the Science and Practice of Music*

Highfill / Highfill, Philip H.; Burnim, Kalman A.; and Langhans, Edward A. *A Biographical Dictionary of Actors, Actresses, Musicians, Dancers, Managers and Other Stage Personnel*

HMC / *Historical Manuscripts Commission*

Husk / Husk, William H. *An Account of the Musical Celebrations on St. Cecilia's Day*

KM / Lafontaine, Henry Cart de. *The King's Musick*

Langbaine / Langbaine, Gerald. *The Lives and Characters of English Dramatic Poets*

Langhans / cf. Highfill

Laurie / Laurie, A. Margaret. *Purcell's Stage Works*

The London Stage / Lennep, William van, ed. *The London Stage*

Luttrell / Luttrell, Narcissus. *A Brief Historical Relation of State Affairs*

MGG / *Die Musik in Geschichte und Gegenwart* (ed. F. Blume)

Maitland / Maitland, William. *The History of London*

McGuiness / McGuiness, Rosamond. *English Court Odes*

Moore / Moore, Robert E. *Henry Purcell and the Restoration Theatre*

Nicoll / Nicoll, Allardyce. *A History of Restoration Drama*

OED / *Oxford English Dictionary*

PCC / Prerogative Court of Canterbury

PCW / Peculiar Court of Westminster

PMA / *Proceedings of the Musical Association*

PMLA / *Publications of the Modern Language Association*

PRMA / *Proceedings of the Royal Musical Association*

Pepys (W) / Pepys, Samuel. *Diary* (ed. H. B. Wheatley)

Pepys (M) / *Memoirs of Samuel Pepys* (ed. R. Latham and W. Matthews)

PRO / Public Record Office

Pulver / Pulver, Jeffrey. *A Biographical Dictionary of Old English Music*

RMA / Royal Musical Association

Scholes / Scholes, Percy A. *The Puritans and Music*

Secret Services / Akerman, John Y. *Moneys Received and Paid for Secret Services*

SIMG / *Sammelbände der internationalen Musikgesellschaft*

Squire, W. B. / Squire, William Barclay. "Purcell's Dramatic Music"

Term Catalogues / *Term Catalogues*

Tilmouth / Tilmouth, Michael. "English Chamber Music 1675–1720"

WAM / Westminster Abbey Muniments

WA Tr. Accts. / Westminster Abbey Treasurer's Accounts

Westminster Abbey Reg. / Chester, J. L. *The Marriage, Baptismal, and Burial Registers of the Collegiate Church or Abbey of St. Peter's, Westminster*

Westrup / Westrup, J. A. *Purcell, 1965*

Wood / Wood, Anthony à. *The Life and Times of Anthony Wood, antiquary of Oxford, 1632–1695, described by Himself*

Henry Purcell, 1659–1695
HIS LIFE AND TIMES

The Purcells of Westminster

Too little is known of Henry Purcell's boyhood to provide for a substantial account of his early life. However, various chronicles of events in London during the first decade of Charles II's restored monarchy can help to piece out the social and cultural environment that produced this Restoration genius. He was well-named the *Orpheus Britannicus* and may be compared in historical importance with such famous Englishmen of his own time as John Dryden, John Locke, Isaac Newton, and Christopher Wren, the first and last of whom were close personal acquaintances. In the face of difficulties that in the end proved insuperable, he carved for himself a musical career and created works that would ensure his renown as the greatest composer England could claim as her own for more than two centuries after his death, if not, indeed, for all time.

Nevertheless, biographical information is so scarce that Purcell's activities can only be surmised up to 1673, when his name first appears on extant records. Conjecture, guided by inferences drawn from available contemporary literature and official records, must all too often figure in the story of his early years. For later periods, information is only slightly less scant. But for the period after Purcell had entered upon his mature career, from about 1678 onward, his life story may be projected against social and historical backgrounds with clearer focus and greater certainty. This is possible because of evidence provided by manuscript and published sources of his works, and by official descriptions of his responsibilities at court and Abbey.

Confusion as to the identity of Purcell's father has been cleared by the uncovering of significant new evidence. The most important document discovered is the will of John Hingeston, which states definitely that Purcell was son to Elizabeth, and therefore may reasonably be assumed to have been the son of Henry, not of Thomas (see Appendix Two). The identification of Katherine Redmond and various other kinds of new evidence presented in Appendix Two leave little ground for the alternative case, which would establish Thomas Purcell as father not only of Matthew, Edward, Charles, Elizabeth, Katherine, Francis, and Thomas, but of another Edward, another Charles, Henry the composer, Joseph, and Daniel as well. This arrangement would have us believe that Thomas fathered thirteen children, while his brother, Henry, had only one, and that Thomas actually christened two each of his children Charles and Edward. We would also have to believe that he christened two of his sons "Henry," and that John Hingeston knew two Henry Purcells but did not bother to distinguish between them in his will. We would have to explain away a similar oversight on the part of Dr. Busby, who left Purcell a mourning ring, as we know from Frances Purcell's will, proved some eleven years after the death of her famous husband, Henry.

The establishment of the family tree in which Henry remains the son of Henry, which, though traditional, seems the true one, fixes the city and liberties of Westminster as the most probable place for the composer's birth. However, in the frequently quoted entry on Henry Purcell from his manuscript notes on English musicians, Anthony à Wood has added the following: "Born in London,"[1] which may mean merely that he was somewhat overgeneral in his reference or that Purcell actually was born in one of the London parishes. In any case, his birth record still remains to be found. Until it is, we are unlikely to know either the date or the circumstances of Purcell's birth.

From 1659 onward, the elder Henry's family lived in one of the houses on the south side of the Great Almonry, a residential area just south of Tothill Street and a few hundred yards west of Westminster Abbey. Most probably it was there that young Henry was born, even though W. H. Cummings, without presenting his evidence, has named a house in St. Ann's Lane, Old Pye Street. Although young Purcell did live in that street for a brief period after his marriage in 1680 or 1681—again, the actual document remains to be found—there seems little possibility that he was born in the house that, long since torn down, has so frequently been pictured as his birthplace. There is no record showing that his parents ever lived there. There is, however, proof that the family home was in the Great Almonry, where the elder Henry Purcell's payment of 1s. 6d. for the poor-rates suggests that he was poorer than most of his neighbors, who were taxed more heavily. Cummings, in his article on Purcell's birthplace for *Musical Times* (November 1895), adds that the Almo(n)ry (from Eleemossnary) had been an Alms House, but was turned into lodgings for singing men. Very likely, Henry Purcell was born there.

The probability that Purcell was born in Westminster is also supported by one of the stipulations of the scholarship he was later to enjoy as a "Bishop's Boy" at St. Peter's College, Westminster. According to Bishop Williams's deed of 26 April 1624, this scholarship was reserved for boys who came either from Wales or from the Diocese of Lincoln. If there were no acceptable candidates from these places, scholars might be chosen from one of the liberties of Westminster, as is known from provisions made for four scholarships Bishop Williams had founded at St. John's, Cambridge. These were reserved for the "Bishop's Boys" from St. Peter's, Westminster, and the letters of patent (drawn earlier than the above-mentioned deed, 30 December 1623) make it clear that the scholars from St. Peter's might include boys from Westminster, if there were insufficient applicants from Wales or Lincolnshire. Extensive but futile searching of these records in Wales, carried out by A. K. Holland and myself, and the absence of any evidence in Lincolnshire archives suggested that Purcell may have qualified for the scholarship under the third of these provisions.

This probability is further strengthened by positive evidence in favor of the theory that the elder Henry Purcell was living in Westminster about the time young Henry was born. Even though no birth or baptismal records have been found, the absence of any records in churches elsewhere in Westminster or London tends to endorse Jeffrey Pulver's suggestion that young Henry Purcell may have been christened within the precincts of the Abbey itself. Pulver very definitely places the elder Henry Purcell's residence in Westminster in 1659,[2] and since records now available for the years 1661 to 1664 list him as dwelling in the house that had been occupied until 1658 either by William Crane or by Captain Hickes, it is fairly certain that Henry and Elizabeth had moved to that address with their three-year-old son, Edward, in 1659, the year in which the younger Henry was born. There they lived, next door to Mr. Babington—later Captain Babington—on one side and Henry Lawes on the other. (After Lawes's death in October 1662, his house was occupied by Mr. Swettenham.) Some time after August 1664, when the elder Purcell died, Christopher Gibbons moved into the building, presumably becoming Purcell's mentor, as per Anthony à Wood's entry.[3] The widow Purcell soon moved to Tothill Street.

The elder Henry, married to Elizabeth some time before 1656 when their first son, Edward, was born, is named for the first time in the dramatis personae for William D'Avenant's *The Siege of Rhodes*, Part I, first staged, rather informally, it seems, that same year; then produced more magnificently shortly after the restoration of King Charles II, about 28 June 1661, with "new scenes and decorations, being the first that e'er were introduced into England. . . . All parts being justly and excellently performed; it continued acting 12 days without interruption with great applause," as we know from John Downes's enthusiastic report.[4] There he is mentioned as having alternated with Thomas Blagrave in the role of Mustapha, although there is no documentation (see Appendix One, XII, i). At present writing, we cannot be certain as to which production may have been the first to include the elder Henry Purcell.[5] In any case, it is clearly established that he was in London at the end of the Commonwealth period, and that he was professionally associated with a group of musicians living in Westminster, some of whom were later to be his neighbors.[6]

A precise date of birth for his third son,[7] Henry, is impossible to establish. Reinhold Sietz's guess that 10 September might have been his birthday is certainly worth considering.[8] But it is merely a guess, based on Purcell's enigmatic inscription on the flyleaf of the Fitzwilliam Museum autograph MS. 88, "God bless Mr. Henry Purcell / 1682 September the 10th." It is possible that this cryptic inscription may be otherwise significant. For instance, this date coincides with the fifth anniversary of Purcell's appointment as composer-in-ordinary to the king—perhaps Purcell was merely worried over possible discontinuance of his employment. Or perhaps, as suggested earlier, he was griefstricken over the death of his son, John Baptista Purcell.

That Purcell himself was born before 20 November may be safely inferred from the inscription on his memorial tablet in Westminster Abbey, which records that he died on 21 November 1695, in his thirtyseventh year. But the statement that he must have been born some time after June cannot be taken entirely at face value. It is based on the engraved frontispiece to the *Sonnatas of III Parts of 1683*, where the reader is informed that Purcell was twenty-four at the time the engraving was made.

These sonatas were eventually published in June but had been some time in preparation, as we know from notices published in the *London Gazette*, and from the explanation Purcell himself gave in the preface: "There has been neither care, nor industry wanting, as well in contriving, as revising the whole work; which had been abroad in the world much sooner, but that he has now thought fit to cause the whole thorough bass to be engraven, which was a thing quite besides his first resolutions."[9] The words "has now thought fit" suggest that everything but the thorough-bass was done, and that Purcell had even written most of the preface before coming to the decision to postpone. Furthermore, licensing, correcting, binding, and stitching must have taken some time. In the absence of any precise date for the completion of engraving and annotation, the evidence afforded by the portrait shows only that it was struck not later than June 1683 but possibly as much as a month or so earlier, since the works would normally have been in the press for about that length of time, at least.

At any rate, Purcell was born a year, or slightly more, after Evelyn had recorded on 3 September 1658: "Died that archrebel Oliver Cromwell, called protector," perhaps about the time his less forceful son Richard Cromwell (alias "Tumbledown Dick") retired from office. Absolutely nothing is known of Purcell's childhood, about which very little can be drawn from the records of his father's activities during the early years of the Restoration. Though strengthened by circumstantial evidence drawn from contemporary documents and accounts of major historical events, these remain nothing more than inference. His distinguished musical neighbors living in or near the Great Almonry during this period included the elder John Banister (in King Street, West);[10] Henry Lawes, who lived next door in the Great Almonry in 1661, but had moved into Dean's Yard before his death in 1662; Dr. Christopher Gibbons, who lived there also (as is known from later records); Captain Henry Cooke, in Little Sanctuary; Thomas Farmer, in New Palace; Dr. John Wilson, in Dean's Yard; and, perhaps as important as any, young Purcell's putative father-in-law, Captain John Peters, in New Palace. (See plates 1 and 2. Purcell's relationship to the Peters family cannot yet be proven, but the evidence for it is weighty, though circumstantial.)

Dr. Richard Busby also lived in the neighborhood and must frequently have been visited by some of his famous pupils. Here Busby trained John Dryden, John Locke, Robert South, and no less than sixteen bishops.[11] Busby's name appears frequently among the donors of benevolences in the "Overseers' Accounts" and the poor rate books for St. Margaret's Parish, Westminster, for the years he was registered as an inhabitant of the parish, that is, from 1628, when he received permission to "proceed bachelor of arts,"[12] until his death on 6 April 1695.[13]

John Dryden, a graduate of Cambridge, was already attracting universal attention at this time by his first three works (diametrically opposed to one another in the political loyalties they variously reflected): *Heroic Stanzas* (1659, a tribute to the memory of Oliver Cromwell) and *Astraea Redux* (1660), followed by *Panegyric on the Restoration* (1661), the last two dedicated to a restored monarchy. Other literary inhabitants or frequenters of Westminster included Samuel Pepys, who had married Elizabeth Marchant de Saint Michel at St. Margaret's,

Westminster, on 1 December 1655,[14] and the aging blind poet John Milton (married to Katherine Woodcock at St. Margaret's in 1656),[15] who had lived in Petty France at least until 1661. But if any of these took notice of the young Restoration genius, even after he had risen to fame, none troubled to record his views.

Pepys recorded a musical evening in which a Purcell took part, in the following oft-quoted entry of 21 February 1659/60. Whether this refers to Henry or to Thomas or to some other member of the family cannot be decided on evidence presently available.

> After dinner I back to Westminster Hall with him [Mr. John Crew, M.P.] in his coach. Here I met with Mr. Lock and Pursell, masters of music, and with them to the Coffee House, into a room next the water, by ourselves, where we spent an hour or two till Captain Taylor came to us, who told us that the House had voted the gates of the City to be made up again, and the members of the City that are in prison to be set at liberty; and that Sir G. Booth's case be brought into the House tomorrow.
>
> Here we had variety of brave Italian and Spanish songs, and a canon for eight voices, which Mr. Lock had lately made on these words: "Domine salvum fac Regem," an admirable thing.

Lord Braybrooke in his edition[16] renders the second sentence quoted above as follows: "Here I met with Mr Lock and Pursell, Master of Music. . . ." Use of the title in the singular would argue that Pepys was referring to the elder Henry Purcell, for his name was entered frequently as "Master of the Choristers" in the Westminster records.[17] Neither Matthew Locke nor Thomas Purcell held such title yet. The argument is weak, however, for Henry the elder's official position did not begin until the following year, when both Henry and Thomas Purcell received official appointments soon after the Restoration ceremonies were over. Thomas became a tenor in the Chapel Royal, then was appointed one of the musicians for "lutes and voices, theorbos and virginals."[18] Henry was made musician-in-ordinary for violins in place of Angelo Notari.[19] He also shared an appointment as musician-in-ordinary for lutes and voices with Angelo Notari, as this retroactive warrant shows:

> 15 Nov. 1662
>   Warrant to admit Angelo Notari and Henry Purcell musicians-in-ordinary for the lutes and voices, with the yearly wages of £40, to commence from St. John Baptist 1660.[20]

The terse official records give no reasons for the sharing of an appointment and indeed are not altogether in agreement as to whether there was only one appointment. But Notari, whom Charles I had brought to England by 1625, was quite old by this time, and court officials may have thought to render his position rather honorary than fully active, reinforcing the office with the strength and energies of a younger man. Henry Purcell was also installed singing man and master of the choristers at Westminster Abbey on 16 February 1661:

> Mr. William Tucker, one of the Gentlemen of his Majesty's Chapel, and Mr. Jonas Caldecut were installed pettycanons: and with them Henry Purcell, Edward Bradock, William Hutton, Richard Adamson, and Thomas Hughes were installed singing men, the aforesaid Henry Purcell, Master of the Choristers also, by Philip Tynchare, Chanter. For whose installation the Chanter received of:

Mr. Will. Tucker	0 5 0
Mr. Jonas Caldecut	0 5 0
Mr. Rich. Adamson	0 5 0
Mr. Th. Hughes	0 5 0
Mr. Ed. Bradock	0 5 0
Mr. Hutton	0 5 0
Mr. Purcell, instead of money, this book.[21]	0 5 0

The pages of the Westminster Abbey Precentor's Book and Treasurer's Accounts for 1660–64 show various receipts, disbursements, and other transactions connected with the elder Purcell's official duties. These reveal that Abbey musicians then lived precarious existences indeed, their small official stipends being frequently augmented by much-needed incidental honoraria for singing at burial services and official inaugurations, and by other institutional fees, such as those taken from visitors who paid to see the "monuments," then, as now, housed in the Undercroft Museum. Here is the account of one such windfall for 30 March 1661:

> The Princess Royal, Mary, the King's eldest sister, mother of the Prince of Orange, was laid in a vault. And for the attendance of the choir was paid to the Chanter for the whole company of pettycanons and singing-men (although many of them were not then installed, but allowed only to do service in the church because as yet the Chanter was elected only but not installed, for which cause also the Chanter's peculiar fee was left out of the bill) the sum of £6. 13s. 4d., which was thus divided:

To Mr. Tynchare Chanter	7 4
To Mr. Gibbons Organist	7 4
To Mr. Hooper	7 4
To Mr. Tucker	7 4
To Mr. Caldicot	7 4

To Mr. Hazard	7 4
To Mr. Harding	7 4
To Mr. Chapman	7 4
To Mr. Purcell	7 4
To Mr. Bradock	7 4
To Mr. Hutton	7 4
To Mr. Adamson	7 4
To Mr. Hughes	7 4
To Mr. Ambler	7 4
To Mr. Shorter	7 4
To Mr. Corney	7 4

To Mr. Finnell and Mr. Dagnall. Mr. Dagnall paid 4d., Mr. Finell paid 4d., due more 8d.

To Mr. Fisher for his attendance and then expecting a place in the choir but afterwards lost it   7 4[22]

From 1662 onward the finances of Henry Purcell and other Gentlemen of the Chapel Royal were considerably improved by a general increase in all salaries, from £40 to £70 per annum.[23] Unfortunately, this gain was only promissory, being offset, if not indeed nullified, by arrears in salary that by this time had become customary at court. The lord chamberlain's accounts for the period are filled with complaints and demands having to do with overdue salary payments.[24] Small wonder that pluralism was the order of the day for court musicians, who no doubt found their living precarious enough even when enjoying proceeds from several appointments.

As the day for Charles II's coronation drew near—fittingly, it had been scheduled for St. George's Day, 23 April 1661—the elder Purcell was extremely busy, as indeed were most musicians employed either at Westminster Abbey or Whitehall or both.[25] Not only was there much to do in preparing choristers at the Abbey for festival services: the elder Henry Purcell had also taken on new duties as a singing man in the Chapel Royal just about that time, as we know from a list of gentlemen singers for the coronation.[26]

On the day before the coronation, Ogilby's lavish and complicated "Entertainment" brought out the citizens of London, who witnessed processions of nobility and pageants of various entertainers and heard many concerts (see plate 3). The elder Henry Purcell seems to have been one of a very few among well-known professional musicians who did not take an active part in the grand "Entertainment"—quite understandable in view of the elaborate ceremony to be performed at Westminster Abbey that same day as the culmination of the "Entertainment." In their diaries both Pepys and Evelyn described events almost ecstatically. To maintain the breathless excitement of Evelyn's vivid description, I have deleted some details, naming only the more important personages who figured prominently in the story of Purcell's life:

> Was the coronation of His Majesty Charles the Second in the Abbey Church of Westminster. . . . [On the 22nd] Was the splendid cavalcade of his Majesty from the Tower of London to Whitehall . . . but indeed his Majesty went till early this morning, and proceeded thence to Westminster in this order: first went the Duke of York's Horse Guards, Messengers of the Chamber. . . . 136 Esquires to the Knights of the Bath, each [Knight] having two, most richly habited: . . . Clerk of the Parliament, Clerk of the Crown; chaplains-in-ordinary having dignities 10; . . . secretaries of the French and Latin Tongue; gentlemen ushers; daily waiters; servers, carvers and cupbearers-in-ordinary, esquires of the body 4 . . . Chamberlain of the Exchequer; . . . Lord Chief Justice of England, Trumpets, Gentlemen of the Privy Chamber, Knights of the Bath, 68 in crimson robes exceeding rich, and the noblest show of the whole cavalcade (his Majesty excepted); . . . Trumpets, sergeant-trumpeter, . . . Lord Chancellor, Lord High Steward of England; two persons representing the Dukes of Normandy and Aquitaine (*viz.* Sir R. Fanshaw and Sir Herbert Price) in fantastic habits of that time; gentlemen ushers garter; Lord Mayor of London; the Duke of York alone (the rest by twos); Lord High Constable of England; the Sword born by the Earl Marshal of England. Lastly the King in royal robes and equipage; afterwards followed equerries, footmen, gentlemen pensioners; Master of the Horse. . . . This magnificent train on horseback, as rich as embroidery, velvet, cloth of gold and silver, and jewels could make them and their prancing horses, proceeded through the streets strewed with flowers, houses hung with rich tapestry, windows and balconies full of ladies, the London Militia lining the ways, and the several companies with their banners and loud music ranked in their orders: the fountains running wine, bells ringing, with speeches made at the several triumphal arches: at that of the Temple Bar (near which I stood) the Lord Mayor was received by the Bailiff of Westminster who in a scarlet robe made a speech: thence with joyful acclamations his Majesty passed to Whitehall [with] bonfires at night. . . .[27]

Pepys's description of the cavalcade of the twenty-second was similarly enthusiastic:

> . . . it is impossible to relate the glory of this day, expressed in the clothes of them that rid [*sic*], and their horses and horses-clothes. . . . Embroidery and diamonds was ordinary among them. The Knights of the Bath was [*sic*] a brave sight of itself; and their Esquires. . . . Remarkable were the two men that represent the two Dukes of Normandy and Aquitaine. . . . My Lord Monk rode bare after the King, and led in his hand a

spare horse, as being Master of the Horse. The King, in a most rich embroidered suit and cloak, looked most nobly. . . . The streets all grav-
elled, and the houses hung with carpets before them, made brave show,
and the ladies out of the windows, one of which over against us I took
much notice of. . . . So glorious was the show with gold and silver, that
we were not able to look at it, our eyes at last being so much overcome
with it.[28]

The ceremonies Evelyn and Pepys witnessed and the music they
heard were also described by Sir Richard Baker, who drew upon the
accounts given by Elias Ashmole in his *Observations and Collections*.[29]
The following paragraphs give an abstract of the coronation day's ceremonial proceedings:

Very early in the morning of the twenty-third, the king went by
barge along the Thames from Whitehall to Parliament stairs, going to a
room in the House of Lords to change, then on to Westminster Hall
(see plate 6). At 9:30 A.M. the nobility took their places, rank by rank;
then after a short ceremony with music provided by the choirs of the
Chapel Royal and Westminster Abbey, they departed through New Palace Yard Gate House, turning left along King Street to return through
the churchyard into the Abbey, their whole way laid out for them on a
carpet of brilliant blue. At last, the procession arrived at the west door,
continuing along the nave and into the choir, where all the musicians
remained on the north side, except for twelve men, four boys, and an
organist, these occupying a raised gallery on the south side.

As the king entered, the Westminster choir (on the north side) sang
an anthem, "I Was Glad." Then, after Charles II had been presented
to the people as their king, the Chapel Royal choir sang "Let Thy
Hand Be Strengthened." After the sermon, both choirs sang the hymn
"Come, Holy Ghost," and for the annointing of the king with holy oils
"Zadok the Priest," composed especially for the occasion by Henry
Lawes, another pre-Commonwealth composer who had returned to
take up a post at the Restoration.

The choirs next sang "The King Shall Rejoice in Thy Strength" (possibly by William Child, another pre-Cromwellian composer who returned to Whitehall with the Restoration) and then the "Te Deum" as
the king sat in the chair of St. Edward. When Charles II had granted a
general pardon and returned to his throne again, the Gentlemen of the
Chapel Royal sang the anthem "Behold, O Lord, Our Defender" in divided style, after the manner of Gabrieli. Performance was divided between the Gentlemen of the Chapel Royal in the south gallery and the
"violins and other instrumental music," who, in their scarlet mantles,

were seated in a gallery on the north side. The work is anonymous but may well represent the first anthem with Italianate instrumental ritornelli to be heard in England. (This is not to say that it was the first with instrumental ritornelli of any kind, since both Byrd and Orlando Gibbons had already introduced this feature long since in their respective anthems "Christ Rising" and "This Is the Record of John.") The first portion of the ceremonies closed with a brilliant flourish by trumpet and drums.

Both anonymous works (the "Te Deum" and "Behold, O Lord") may have been composed by Cooke himself, if a remark quoted by Baker (after Ashmole) may be taken at face value. At any rate, more music in Venetian style was heard. "The king then took off his crown, after which were heard the Epistle, the Gospel, the Nicene Creed (begun by the Bishop of London and sung by the Gentlemen of the Chapel to music by Captain Cooke, Master of the Children of the Chapel, and composer of the special music for this solemnity). Again the instruments played alternately."[30]

The choirs next sang "Let My Prayer Come Up into Thy Presence"—once more probably by Cooke[31]—after which the king was given the Mark of Gold, then the Blessed Sacraments, these actions being followed by another anthem, "O Harken unto the Voice of My Calling." After Communion everyone returned to Westminster Hall, where banqueting and musical entertainment continued far into the night.

With such a beginning, small wonder that music at the Abbey and at the Chapel Royal were important public attractions during the Restoration, as is shown by numerous references in the diaries and journals of the time. Pepys's frequent attendance at Westminster Abbey services was due largely to his enthusiasm for music—enthusiasm by no means dampened when on 19 December 1661 he was allowed to sing in the choir.

Musical activities were not limited to the Abbey and the Chapel Royal, however. Like his fellow musicians, both at the Abbey and at court, the elder Henry Purcell practiced his art before theater audiences and managed also to keep in the public eye by supplying a few compositions for London's growing music publishing trade. Just after the Restoration, as we have seen, he had taken second billing as Mustapha in the first part of D'Avenant's *Siege of Rhodes*, although whether he also sang in performances of the second part of the "opera" is not known.[32] No doubt he was quite busy both as composer and performer.

Apart from such general influences, however, nothing is known of young Henry Purcell's life during these times. He was scarcely old enough to have been affected by the excitement attending the arrival of Catherine of Braganza on 13 May 1662, or to have shared in the gossip about Charles II's manifest disappointment upon finding his royal bride much plainer than her portraits had promised. Her appearance was probably more realistically portrayed in the interesting drawing published as a frontispiece to Philip de Cardonnel's *Complementum Fortunatarum Insularum.*[33] She was no raving beauty.

Other events of the year influenced the Purcell family fortunes more directly. On 1 January Charles II had not only doubled the membership of his musical establishment, but also increased greatly his choirmen's salaries as well, raising them from £40 to £70 per annum. For Henry Purcell the elder and his family this was no doubt very welcome, particularly after the arrival of a new baby early in March in the person of Katherine Purcell, baptized on 13 March.[34] (However, as pointed out earlier, there was little certainty that salaries would be paid on time, if at all; hence many benefits may have been more apparent than real.) New honors were bestowed upon his uncle Thomas Purcell, who at the very beginning of the Restoration had been named as the first of ten musicians "that do service in the Chapel Royal whose salaries are payable in the Treasury of his Majesty's Chamber."[35] On 8 August Thomas Purcell was also appointed composer-in-ordinary for the violins[36]—at first he shared the position with Pelham Humfrey, but then came into full enjoyment of the same in the place of Henry Lawes on 15 November 1662—and on 10 November to the Private Music for lutes and voices.[37] His advancement was rapid, and before long he was one of the most influential and affluent musicians of the early Restoration, an achievement not without significance in the life of his nephew Henry, especially after the death of Henry's father in August 1664.

In 1663, the year of the insurrection of Venner and the "Fifth Monarchy Men," Purcell was four. Although perhaps not old enough to appreciate fully the new preferments his father and uncle[38] had received at court, he surely would have been aware of the arrival of another child in the household, if indeed the conventional, but as yet undocumented, assignment of Daniel Purcell's birthday to this period be correct.[39] This was also the year in which Hingeston's new official instrument-keeper's quarters were set up in Whitehall—quarters which young Henry was to know well a few years later when he took up his duties as apprentice harpsichord repairer there.[40] It was also the year of Thomas Baltzar's death (of the "French pox and other distempers")—

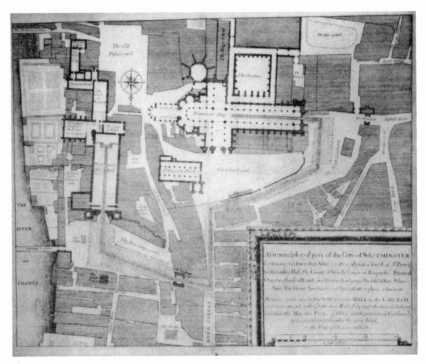

PLATE I. "A Ground-plot of part of the City of Westminster" (Archives
   Dept., Westminster City Libraries)

Baltzar, whose violin playing had done more, according to Anthony à
Wood,[41] to raise that instrument to respectability and popularity at
the English court than any other factor. At the end of the year, on
23 December, appeared a warrant from Treasurer Southampton to the
King's Remembrancer for remittances to various musicians, including
Thomas Purcell.[42] The name of Henry the elder is not listed here but
is entered under a warrant dormant on 27 February 1662 of £40 "for
his office and place of musician in ordinary to the King for lute
and voice."[43] Finally, ominously, came word from Amsterdam of the
dreaded plague.[44]

During the course of his fifth year, 1664, young Henry may have
gone along on occasion to the Abbey or to Whitehall with his father
and his uncle Thomas, who was busier than ever, now that he bore full
responsibility heretofore shared at court with Pelham Humfrey. Humfrey was now on the Continent absorbing the latest musical styles at
Versailles, Venice, Paris, Rome, and other musical centers of Europe.[45]

But all other events and activities of this year would have been blot-

PLATE 2. A view of Westminster Abbey, Westminster Hall, St. James's Palace, Pall Mall, and Conduit, ca. 1660. Wenceslaus Hollar (Archives Dept., Westminster City Libraries)

ted out in young Purcell's mind by family tragedy. His father, Henry the elder, died—quite suddenly it seems, since he is mentioned in the records right up to his death on 11 August[46]—and was buried at Westminster Abbey two days later, in the east cloister near Henry Lawes, who had been interred there less than two years earlier.

Shortly after this time, Elizabeth Purcell moved to Tothill Street South, for at this address her modest annual payment of four shillings for the poor rates is entered in the St. Margaret's, Westminster, "Overseers' Accounts"[47] every year from 1665 to 1699 when she died, within a few days of the anniversary of her husband's demise[48] and slightly less than four years after the death of her illustrious son Henry. There she lived, supporting her large brood of children on a slender widow's pension, eked out by various small sums granted her by the Westminster Abbey and chapter officials,[49] and by income from lodgers, such as Frances Crump, recorded as follows in St. Margaret's Vestry Books, No. 2416:[50]

Wednesay, 5 July 1676

Mrs. Purcell in Tothill Street made her application to the Vestry desiring some allowance may be made for her lodging of Frances Crump; it is ordered that that business be very well examined before any money be paid.[51]

Whatever her sources of income, it appears that Widow Purcell kept her five sons (Edward, Charles, Henry, Joseph, and Daniel) and her

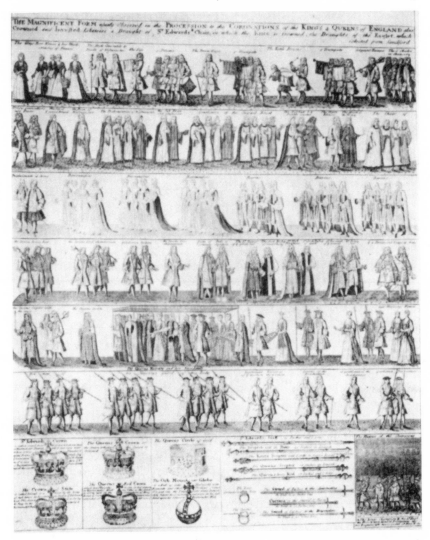

PLATE 3. "The Magnificent Form usually Observed in the Procession to the Coronations of the Kings and Queens of England. . . ." (Archives Dept., Westminster City Libraries)

daughter, Katherine, at home until places were found elsewhere. Edward probably had already begun his court career by 1676. Charles, we know, was a "Bishop's Boy" at St. Peter's, Westminster. Henry was already employed at least occasionally at Abbey and court and was to enjoy his first appointment as composer-in-ordinary upon the death of

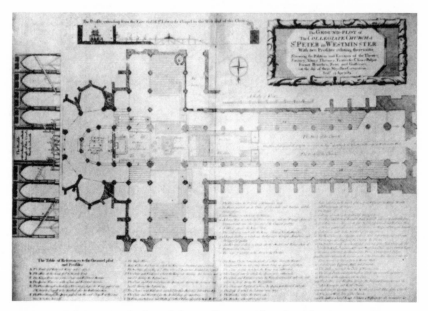

PLATE 4. "The Ground-plot of the Collegiate Church of St. Peter in Westminster . . . 23 April 1685" (Archives Dept., Westminster City Libraries)

Matthew Locke in the following year. Joseph, Daniel, and Katherine
probably remained at home.

As a musician, Thomas Purcell probably took greatest interest in the
careers of Henry and Daniel. However, he also enjoyed a well-paid
position as groom of the robes to Charles II, and may well have used
his influence to find a place for Edward Purcell as "gentleman usher
assistant; to come in upon the first vacancy" (see p. 274, below), which
place, we know from Chamberlayne, young Edward enjoyed as early as
1679. As for definite proof, we have only Thomas Purcell's letter to
John Gostling, which makes it clear that he was deeply involved in his
nephew's career as a composer.[52]

To return to our narrative, after administering her deceased husband's estate on 5 October 1664, Elizabeth Purcell ended the year in
mourning, sharing sorrow and bereavement with her immediate family, her relatives, and friends, and facing an uncertain future.

Boyhood

THE YEAR 1665 BROUGHT WOES on a national scale. On 14 April the unpopular war against the Dutch was declared,[1] despite which, by the end of the month the plague—said to have been carried from Amsterdam by ship—claimed the first of the more than 70,000 London inhabitants who were to be its victims. Pepys's entry for 30 April reflects general feelings the news aroused: "Great fears of the sickness here in the City, it being said that two or three houses are already shut up. God preserve us all!" Although not so heavily "visited" (the official euphemism for "infected") as other parts of London, Westminster soon felt the disastrous effects of the plague. According to Nathaniel Hodges, the pestilence had first broken out at the end of the summer of 1664 in Westminster. Quite possibly the elder Henry Purcell was one of its first victims:

> The plague, which we are now to give an account of, discovered the beginnings of its future cruelties about the close of the year 1664; for at that season two or three persons died suddenly in one family at Westminster, attended with like symptoms that manifestly declared their origin. Hereupon, some timorous neighbours, under apprehension of a contagion, removed into the City of London, who unfortunately carried along with them the pestilential taint; whereby that disease, which was before in its infancy, in a family or two, suddenly got strength and spread abroad its fatal poisons. . . .[2]

London's ecclesiastical and musical communities reflected the devastating influence of the pestilence immediately. Less than a month after his first entry on the plague, Pepys, going to the Chapel Royal on 28 May, reported that he heard little music. His inference was that staff and congregation were too small to sustain performances. Furthermore, Captain Henry Cooke's boys, Pelham Humfrey, John Blow, and John Blundeville had been released from active duty there on 17 May preceding, and others were absent.[3]

By June 1665 the number of "visited" had increased to 470 a week, a fact which "put the gentry and principal citizens on the wings of safety." This is yet another reason for doubting the anecdote of the incredibly quick composition of "I Will Always Give Thanks," the "Club Anthem," by Pelham Humfrey, John Blow, and William Turner for the celebration of the duke of York's victory over the Dutch at Lowestoft. No one would have wanted to attend a mass public celebration at such a time.[4]

By July the court had removed to comparative safety at Hampton Court, while a horror-stricken populace watched the march of red crosses on the doors of the "visited." These ominous symbols spread rapidly in all directions, as the fierce onslaught of the plague increased from day to day. On 12 July Pepys records that a solemn day of fasting had been ordained for "this Wednesday and the first Wednesday of every month during the visitation."[5] The wholesale mortality brought by the epidemic inspired universal terror, paralyzing entire communities. By the end of summer all Londoners were caught up in the macabre Saturnalia of the plague, the red crosses spreading like wildfire along the doorways of each neighborhood it invaded.

> In the months of August and September the contagion changed its former slow and languid pace, and having as it were got master of all, made a most terrible slaughter, so that three, four or five thousand died in a week, and once eight thousand. . . . In some houses carcases lay waiting for burial, and in others, persons in their last agonies: in one room might be heard dying groans, in another the ravings of a delirium, and not far off relations and friends bewailing both their loss and the dismal prospect of their own departure. Death was the sure midwife to all children, and infants passed immediately from the womb to the grave. Who would not burst with grief to see the stock for a future generation hang upon the breasts of a dead mother, or the marriage bed changed the first night into a sepulchre, and the unhappy pair meet with death in their first embraces. Some of the infected run about staggering like drunken men, and fall and expire in the streets; while others lie half-dead and comatose, but never to be waked but by the last trumpet . . . the number of sextons were not sufficient to bury the dead; the bells seemed hoarse with continual tolling, until at last they quite ceased; the burying places would not hold the dead, but they were thrown into large pits dug into waste grounds, in heaps, thirty or forty together; and it often happened that those who attended the funerals of their friends one evening were carried the next to their own long home . . . in the course of September, more than twelve thousand died in a week.[6]

The influence of all this upon the church is reflected in the somber scene described by an entry in the Westminster Abbey Precentor's

Book: "In the year 1665 by reason of God's visitation by the plague of pestilence, no wax lights or tallow candles were used in the church, but the service was daily performed by day-light, by Mr. John Tynchare, one of the petty canons, and by him alone from the beginning of July to almost the end of December."[7]

Henry Purcell celebrated his sixth birthday during these benighted times. At so impressionable an age he undoubtedly was left with un-forgettable memories of the Great Plague and its reign of terror. The frequent spectacle of the "visited" being carted off to the pest-houses by night and by day, the continual sound of the death knell and sex-tons' bells, the stench and the ugliness of death, indeed the whole mor-bid experience must have remained as one of the strongest of all memo-ries from his childhood.

Important occurrences also marked the year 1666 throughout Lon-don and England. Newton published his formulation of the law of gravitation and carried out his experiment with prisms and colors in light;[8] pestilence continued; the war with the Dutch went badly for the English; and during the night before 2 September dawned, the Great Fire broke out in Pudding Lane. Fanned by an unseasonable wind, in four days it reduced 450 acres of London to ashes and charred ru-ins. Altogether, 13,200 houses were destroyed by fire and demolition gangs, and two-thirds of London's populace were left without shelter.

If, as has been surmised, Purcell was born on 10 September, he would have celebrated his seventh birthday during the week of the Great Fire, which laid waste all the city about St. Paul's. Quite possibly he would have taken the short walk from Westminster along the Thames to the Tower just as Pepys had done on 2 September 1666, staring wide-eyed at the scene of conflagration and destruction to the northwest. This, too, would have remained as one of his most vivid childhood memories.

The disaster had an immediate and direct influence upon the affairs of London musicians, as several contemporary documents reveal. The following is typical:

> John Gamble, one of His Majesty's wind-instrument concert, pleaded for payment of £221 10s. 4½d, arrears of his salary over four and three-quarter years. All he possessed he had lost by the dreadful Fire, and he had contracted a debt of £120, for which one of his sureties had been sent prisoner to Newgate. Ruin awaited them and their families without this payment. Twenty-two musicians on the violin made similar plaint, having had houses and goods burnt in the Fire.[9]

By year's end all these calamities had run their courses. London citizens held a feast day on 10 October for the end of the Great Fire, and on 20 November following observed a general thanksgiving for the end of the pestilence.[10] In his entry for the latter date, however, Pepys added: ". . . but Lord! how the town doth say that it is hastened before the plague is quite over, there dying some people still, . . ." Such events, along with the thanksgiving for the victory over the Dutch at the mouth of the Thames (which had been celebrated at the Chapel Royal with Locke's anthem for the occasion, "The King Shall Rejoice"), no doubt created a happier atmosphere for all Londoners and Englishmen in general during the latter half of 1666. As if by divine providence, the naval victory had occurred on "St. James, his Day," 25 July, no doubt to the entire satisfaction of James, duke of York, to whom it was credited.

Certainly the atmosphere at court, with which young Purcell may by now have become officially acquainted as a Chapel Royal chorister, was happy enough. On 18 October Evelyn reported that Charles II had adopted the new "unfrenchified" dress he called "Persian," then penned a Jeremiad on the moral laxity symptomized by the introduction of women to the stage. For a special birthday treat for Queen Catherine on 15 November, the king preferred her over his "misses," according to Pepys:

> . . . I also to the ball, and with much ado got up to the loft, where with much trouble I could see very well. Anon the house grew full, and the candles light, and the King and Queen and all the ladies set—and it was, indeed, a glorious sight to see Mrs. Steward in black and white lace—and her head and shoulders dressed with diamonds. And the like a great many ladies more, (only the Queen none); and the King in his rich vest of some rich silk and silver trimming, as the Duke of York and all the dancers were, some of cloth of silver, and others of other sorts, exceeding rich. Presently after the King was come in, he took out the Queen, and about fourteen more couples there was, and began the Bransles. As many of the men as I can remember presently, were: the King—Duke of York—Prince Rupert—Duke of Monmouth—Duke of Buckingham—Lord Douglas—Mr. [George] Hamilton—Colonel Russell—Mr. Griffith—Lord Ossory—Lord Rochester. And of the Ladies—the Queen—Duchess of York—Mrs. Steward—Duchess of Monmouth—Lady Essex Howard—Mrs. Temple—Swedes [sic] Embassadress—Lady Arlington—Lord George Berkeley's daughter. And many others I remember not; but all most excellently dressed in rich petticoats and gowns, and diamonds—and pearl. After the Bransles, then to a Corant, and now and then a French dance; but that so rare that the Corants grew tiresome

that I wished it done. Only Mrs. Steward danced mighty finely, and many French dances, specially one called the New Dance, which was very pretty; but upon the whole matter, the business of the dancing of itself was not extraordinary pleasing.

Pepys does not indicate why he found the dancing so bad or why the branles and corants were not to be considered French dances. Perhaps the king's violins, having petitioned for arrears of salary just the week before, did not play with great enthusiasm: "Petition of the 22 musicians in the violins to the King, for payment of part of their arrears out of the £15,000 ordered for payment of his Majesty's servants; having attended His Majesty and the Queen in their progresses, besides daily attendance; and are 4 3/4 years in arrear, and have had houses and goods burned in the late fire."[11] Or perhaps the queen's feelings toward "la belle Steward" and other of the king's mistresses lent tenseness to the occasion. Further disquiet among orchestra members had arisen just three days earlier when Louis Grabu had been sworn in as master of the English Chamber Music,[12] much to the chagrin of John Banister, whose decline began officially, it seems, with the ". . . order that Mr. Banister and the 24 violins appointed to practise with him and all His Majesty's Private Music do from time to time, obey the directions of Louis Grabu, . . ."[13] As Anthony à Wood points out (vol. 2, 69), on 11 January 1666 Banister had already given a public concert at the "Schools in London . . . contrary to the rule in musick 30 years [ago] which was grave."

On 20 February the following year Pepys reported the latest court gossip, writing: "Here they talk also how the King's violin, Bannister, is mad that the King hath a Frenchman come to be chief of some part of the King's Music, at which the Duke of York made great mirth."

By 14 March Banister's complete disgrace was formalized by an order from the lord chamberlain transferring to Grabu Banister's former position as leader of the select band of twelve violins.[14] Grabu, it seems, had learned effective tactics from Lully's wily machinations before leaving the court of Louis XIV.

Before 1667 was over, the French vogue had reached its zenith. A splendid concert given at Whitehall on 1 October was attended and reported upon by the indefatigable Pepys, who was not pleased with the music itself, although impressed by the excellence of its performance:

. . . to Whitehall, and there in the boarded-gallery did hear the music with which the King is presented this night by Monsieur Grebus, the Master of his Music—both instrumental (I think twenty-four violins) and vocal; an English song upon Peace. But, God forgive me, I was never so little pleased with a concert of music in my life—the manner of setting of words and repeating them out of order, and that with a number of voices, makes me sick, the whole design of vocal music being lost by it. Here was a great press of people; but I did not see many pleased with it, only, the instrumental music he had brought by practice to play very just.[15]

In 1667, when he was approaching his eighth birthday, Purcell may have taken part as a chorister in the gala ceremonies for the Order of the Garter held on 23 April, the anniversary of Charles II's coronation. Evelyn has left a vivid account of the colorful ceremony, in which music played no small part:

In the morning His Majesty went to chapel with the Knights all in their habits and robes, ushered by the heralds. After the first service they went in procession, the youngest first, the sovereign last, with the Prelate of the Order and Dean, who had about his neck the book of the statutes of the Order, and then the Chancellor of the Order (old Sir H. de Vic.), who wore the Purse about his: then heralds and Garter King-of-Arms [Clarenceux], Black Rod: but before the Prelate and Dean of Windsor, went the Gentlemen of the Chapel, Choristers etc. singing as they marched, behind them two Doctors of Music in damask robes. This proceeding was about the Courts of Whitehall, then returning to their stalls and seats in the chapel, placed under each Knight's coat armour and titles. Then began second service, then the King offered at the altar, an anthem sung, then the rest of the knights offered [*sic*], and lastly proceeded to the Banqueting House to a great feast. The King sat on an elevated throne at the upper end, at a table alone. The Knights at a table on the right-hand, reaching all the length of the room; over against them a cupboard of rich gilded plate etc.: at the lower end the music; on the balusters above wind music trumpets and kettle-drums. The King was served by the Lords and pensioners, who brought up the dishes: about the middle of dinner, the Knights drank the King's health, then the King theirs. Then the trumpets, music, etc. played and sounded, the guns going off at the Tower. At the banquet came in the Queen and stood by the King's left hand, but did not sit. Then was the banqueting stuff flung about the room profusely. In truth the crowd was so great, that though I stayed all the supper the day before, I now stayed no longer than this sport began for fear of disorder: The cheer was extraordinary, each Knight having 40 dishes to his mess: piled up 5 or 6 high. The room hung with the richest tapestry in the world.[16]

The fact that it was one of the coldest Aprils on record[17] would only have added zest to the ceremony. But the choristers were probably glad that the weather had warmed up when they made their annual procession round the parish on Ascension Day, a few weeks later.

As a chorister Purcell may also have heard, on 28 July, the "strange, bold sermon of Dr. Creeton . . . before the King; how he preached against . . . adultery, over and over instancing how for that single sin in David the whole nation was undone; and of our negligence in having our castles without ammunition and powder when the Dutch came upon us. . . ." Or even if he had not yet taken his place in the Chapel Royal, he would have heard the talk which soon got round, as Pepys reported next day,[18] getting his information from Mr. Creed and his cousin Roger.

The comparison of Charles II to David was apt enough in other ways to be taken up later by Dryden in *Absalom and Achitophel* as a literary weapon against Charles II's enemies. Purcell later was to register this same parallel in an anthem or two, as did other Restoration composers. But this puritanical admonition had no noticeable effect on Charles II, who blithely continued to enjoy life as he saw fit. Perhaps the church's position of moral and righteous indignation had been weakened by further gossip that came Pepys's way—again cousin Roger was the source—telling it "as a thing certain" that the archbishop of Canterbury "do keep a wench, and that he is as very a wencher as can be." At any rate, on this same day the king demonstrated his unrepentant attitude by the dissolution of both Houses of Parliament, and having dismissed all members with scant apology for having called them to London to no purpose, went back to being "governed by his lust and women and rogues about him." [19]

In August 1667, just two months after the Dutch had blockaded the Thames and sailed up the Medway after burning the guardships there, all London was buzzing with news of the fall of Clarendon and the establishment of the Cabal, whose ministers (Clifford, Arlington, Buckingham, Ashley, and Lauderdale) wittingly or unwittingly did so much to further the cause of Catholicism in England during the next few years.[20] This, coupled with the machinations of Charles and the duke of York, led to the secret Treaty of Dover (1670), based upon quid pro quo measures to strengthen Catholicism in England and to bolster Louis XIV's position all over Europe; and by indirection to the Declaration of Indulgence of 1672; the second, very unpopular, war with Holland; and eventually to the Test Act of 1673, which Purcell himself later was to take, as a matter of public record.

What the convictions of the Purcell family may have been amidst all these actions and counteractions of the Catholic and Protestant parties cannot be known. If later, however, the younger Henry Purcell did entertain Catholic sympathies, as has been stated, it is certain that these faced him with serious decisions.

When the French vogue in music declined, that of the Italian musicians began to rise.[21] The decline was not slackened by Grabu's own musical ineptitude (later to become painfully apparent in a musical and political piece, *Albion and Albanius*, upon which he collaborated with Dryden) or by the attitude of young Pelham Humfrey, who returned from France in October 1667. According to Pepys, Humfrey's composition for the Sunday service at Whitehall was a good anthem, but he could not call it "anything but instrumental music with voice," nothing being made of the words.[22] After two more weeks (i.e., by 15 November 1667), Pepys's distaste for the young "monsieur" had grown to active dislike, mainly because of the latter's complete lack of respect for the Establishment, but particularly for his denigration of Grabu:

> . . . calling at my mercer's and tailor's, and there find, as I expected, Mr. Caesar and little Pelham Humphreys, lately returned from France, and is an absolute monsieur, as full of form, and confidence, and vanity, and disparages everything, and everybody's skill but his own. The truth is, everybody says he is very able, but to hear how he laughs at all the King's music here, as Blagrave and others, that they cannot keep time nor tune, nor understand anything; and that Grebus, the Frenchman, the King's master of the Music, how he understands nothing nor can play on any instrument, and so cannot compose: and that he will give him a lift out of his place; and that he and the King are mighty great! and that he hath already spoke to the King of Grebus, would make a man piss.

Purcell's connection with Humfrey was not to begin for several years—perhaps not until 15 July 1672, when the latter was appointed master of the children after Henry Cooke's death. But Humfrey's presence at court was undoubtedly important to the boy's musical development. Any affinity Purcell had for French or Italian music was undoubtedly strengthened by Humfrey's display of the latest styles of composition and performance from the court of Louis XIV and elsewhere in Europe.

The following year, 1668, was uneventful for musicians at Charles II's court. Nor, so far as the records show, did anything of importance occur within the Purcell family circle. Elizabeth continued to receive small sums from various officials at the court and Abbey from time to time,[23] but these were scarcely sufficient to provide her large family even with bare necessities. Edward Purcell, now about twelve, was probably already a page at court, for within a few years he was to emerge as a gentleman usher.[24] No doubt he was helped to that position by the good offices of his uncle Thomas Purcell, who was a groom of the robes. The responsibilities entrusted to Edward had been entrusted at least as early as 25 March 1673 and were not those that would have been given to an untried newcomer:

> Treasurer Latimer's subscription of a docket, dated 1673, Aug., of a warrant to the Treasurer of the Chamber to pay 100 marks *per annum* to Edward Purcell from Lady Day last; to be for preventing uncertain charges (by bills) which he shall be put to for His Majesty's service about making ready of standing houses and progress houses in the [King's] removes and other services as gentleman usher daily waiter assistant.[25]

Of Henry's second brother, Charles Purcell, later bursar of the English Royal Navy aboard HMS *Tyger*, in Barbados, nothing is known for this early period.[26] Daniel Purcell was too young to augment the family income in any way and probably did not begin as a chorister in the Chapel Royal for another six or eight years.[27] Katherine was six, and perhaps helpful about the house. On 20 May 1668 Elizabeth Purcell received £20 in a money warrant sent by the treasurer for her stipend as relict of Henry Purcell.[28]

A year later, on 24 May 1669—in Purcell's tenth year—Cosimo III, grand duke of Tuscany, saw in London a comedy-ballet based on the score of *Psyche*, when he attended a special performance at Drury Lane. It was a performance no doubt modeled after those being mounted about this time in France by Molière and by Lully, who already had an eye on the royal patent granted by Louis XIV to the Abbé Perrin, Robert Cambert, and the Marquis de Sourdéac for the establishment of an Académie de Musique in France on the eighteenth of that same month.[29]

The year 1670, which saw the granting of a charter to the Hudson's Bay Company, seems again to have passed fairly uneventfully for Purcell, who by now must certainly have shown signs of the extraordinary musical promise soon to make him famous. However, the secret Treaty of Dover with Louis XIV, wherein on 22 April Charles II traded a few religious and political scruples for enough hard cash to gain independence from Parliament, no doubt helped to ease the dire economic situation at court. As a chorister Purcell had been directly affected by the impoverishment of Charles II's coffers, which had kept the boys in rags for some time. In or before June 1670 Captain Cooke had found it necessary to submit the following petition to the king:

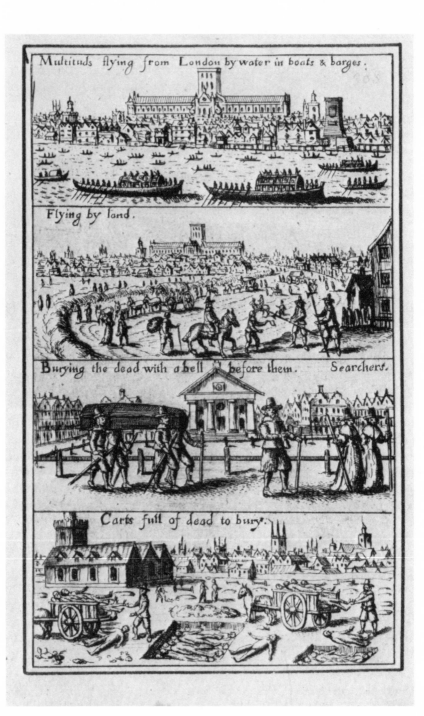

PLATE 5. The plague, from an anonymous broadsheet (Pepys Library 2973, p. 447, Magdalene College, Cambridge)

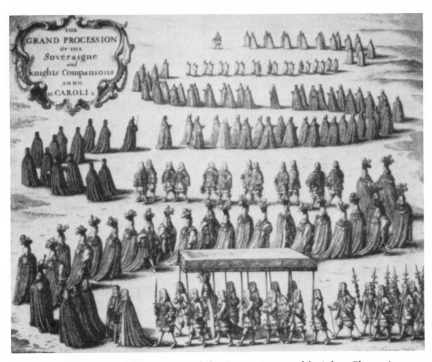

PLATE 6. "The Grand Procession of the Soveraigne and knights Champions. Anno 23 Caroli 2," 1672. Wenceslaus Hollar (Archives Dept., Westminster City Libraries)

> Petition of Henry Cooke, Master of the Children of the Chapel Royal, to the King. The children are not receiving their liveries as usual, are reduced to so bad a condition that they are unfit to attend His Majesty, or walk in the streets. Begs an order for their liveries, the charge not being great, and his Majesty having signified to the Bishop of Oxford that they should have their liberties continued.

On 30 June he received his answer: "Order of the above petition that the Children of the Chapel be for the future entertained and clothed as they were before the late retrenchments." After deliberation, something was done at last, and the following orders were issued on 6 and 12 July:

> Mr. Newport and Mr. Reymes called in with Captain Cooke about the clothes for the Children of the Chapel. Ordered: that the King will have them made as formerly. The officers of the Wardrobe say they have no money. My Lords desire Captain Cooke to furnish the money by loan on the funds on which the Wardrobe has orders; which he promised.

PLATE 7. "With Crowns of Peace and Love, kind Heavens on Katharin smile. . . ." Frontispiece engraved by I. A., for P. de Cardonnel's *Complementrum Fortunatarum Insularum*, 1662. (Henry H. Huntington Library, San Marino, Calif.)

Chapel boys; warrant for £214 4s. 0d. to complete £300. They have had £85 16s. To be employed and laid out for provision of liveries for the said children in full of the estimate dated 16 May last.[30]

Apparently Thomas Purcell had been similarly constrained to make a loan to the crown, for on 5 September 1670, when Henry Cooke was repaid, he received £173.7.3 in the Treasury Order (cf. Westminster Treasury Books, 5 Sept. 1670).

During this same period Purcell, it has been supposed, wrote his first occasional work for Charles II: the "Address of the Children of the Chapel Royal to the King, and Their Master, Captain Cooke, on His Majesty's Birthday, A.D. 1670, Composed by Master Purcell, One of the Children of the Said Chapel." The late Edward F. Rimbault, music fancier and antiquarian, claimed to own an autograph copy of the work.[31] But it is lost, and even though this manuscript may never come to light, it is tempting to speculate that such an address would have been in order, not only to wish the king "many happy returns of the day," but to bring to his attention the disgraceful state of the boys' clothing and equipment.[32]

That autumn new preferment came to Thomas Purcell's family. In the Westminster Abbey Treasurers' Accounts for Michaelmas 1670, Charles Purcell's name is entered among the "Bishop's Boys" who were recipients of the four scholarships founded by the Rev. John Williams, dean of Westminster, in 1624:

> Et in denariis solut. ad usum Scolasticor—xxv^li Decano Thesaur Ludo-magist et Coll. xxvis 8d ex dono Johanis Williams nuper Episcopi Lincoln et Decan. Westm. In toto pro hoc Anno . . . £26–6–8.

> (And from the money devoted to scholastic use, £25 from the Dean's Treasurer and Master of the College, and 26s. 8d. from the gift of John Williams, former Bishop of Lincoln and Dean of Westminster. In all for this year . . . £26 6s. 8d.)[33]

Charles Purcell held this scholarship until 1677, when he was replaced by his more illustrious cousin Henry, probably then attending St. Peter's College in a commoner's gown.[34]

The year 1671 saw the publication of Milton's *Paradise Regained* and also of his *Samson Agonistes*, a somber view of the era by this Restoration Tiresias who envisioned better times. It also saw the beginnings of theatrical developments that were to be of great importance to Purcell's career later on. On 9 November[35] the company of William D'Avenant, putatively the bastard son, certainly the godson, of William Shakespeare, opened the new theater at Dorset Garden where so many of D'Avenant's supposed father's works were to be bastardized, perhaps fittingly, in the coming decade. Among these were *Macbeth*, *The Tempest*, and *Timon of Athens*, of which later productions were to be connected with Purcell's name.[36]

For Henry Cooke this theatrical outlet occasioned yet another drain on the slender stock of talent available in the choristers of the Chapel Royal. Above and beyond their duties in Chapel, the boys were expected to participate in various stage performances requiring music, both at the Duke of York's Theatre in Dorset Garden and at the Theatre Royal in Drury Lane—this despite the express prohibition of such a practice in one of the original patents for "taking up boys" granted to Nathaniel Giles in 1626:

> Provided always, and we straightly charge and command that none of the said choristers of Children of the Chapel, so to be taken by force or this commission, shall be used or employed as comedians, or stage players, or to exercise or act any stage plays, interludes, comedies or tragedies; for it is not fit or decent that such as should sing the praises of God Almighty should be trained or employed in lascivious and profane exercises.[37]

However, neither Cooke nor any succeeding master of the choristers could refuse to obey frequent royal commands, explicitly calling the choristers out to play in the theaters.[38]

It was a trying year for Cooke. Beyond his usual chores—teaching Latin, mending clothes, and traveling to the provinces to look for new choirboys—he had also to attend to the needs of several boys who had been ill:

> 23 May 1671.
> The sum of £167 17s. 4d. to be paid to Captain Cook, Master of the Children of His Majesty's Chapel Royal, for learning the children on the organ, on the lute and theorbo, for fire and strings in the music room in the Chapel, for doctors, nurses, and for looking to several of the children when they were sick; for going to Westchester, Lichfield, Canterbury and Rochester to look for boys, and for other service for one year from Lady Day 1670 to Lady Day 1671.[39]

Worse yet, the Chapel Royal was reduced to chaos during this time, while enlargements were made and new fittings hung:

> 21 March 1670/1.
> Warrant to deliver to Captain Cooke, Master of the Children of His Majesty's Chapel Royal, three crimson damask curtains for the music room in the Chapel, the music room being enlarged.[40]

At the end of May, however, he took all his charges to Windsor for a fortnight,[41] remaining on with six of the boys until 25 July. (Whether Henry Purcell remained the whole time is not known. Surely, though, he was among the twelve who traveled down for the first two weeks.) The following year, 1672, a leap year, was on the whole a very good year for the Purcell family. Already Thomas Purcell headed the list of musicians in the Chapel, as may be seen in a great number of the lord chamberlain's records for the period.[42] On 10 January he and Pelham Humfrey were appointed composers, as assistants to George Hudson (then aged and infirm, who died before the year was out) to come in ordinary with fee "upon death or other avoidance."[43] Shortly there-after he also began to assume responsibility for annual payments to the king's musicians, the sum to be distributed amounting to about £400 at that time.[44] During this period he was also appointed marshal of the Corporation of Musicians, replacing Henry Cooke, who had "resigned office by reason of illness" and retired to Hampton Court, where he died on 13 July 1672.[45]

After Cooke's death his son-in-law, Pelham Humfrey, succeeded him, officially taking office on 15 July, and thus becoming official tutor to Henry Purcell, who was then about thirteen years of age.[46] Doubt-less, the close professional working relationship between Thomas Pur-cell and Pelham Humfrey had already resulted in a fairly close ac-quaintance between the new master of the choristers and the budding Restoration genius, whose talent as a composer already was known. In view of Pepys's irate remarks about Pelham Humfrey quoted above, one wonders whether Purcell would have accounted this to be an al-together fortunate new development. Perhaps "the absolute monsieur" had mellowed in the five years that had elapsed since Pepys's unflatter-ing commentary. Then, after Humfrey's death at Windsor on 24 July 1673, Thomas Purcell assumed all authority in the administration of the king's musicians.

Other members of the Purcell family also prospered. Daniel Purcell took up his new appointment as chorister in the Chapel Royal.[47] Cousin Charles Purcell's stipend as a Bishop's Boy at St. Peter's, Westminster, was confirmed. And Edward Purcell, brother or cousin to Henry and Daniel, received the unusual (and secret) honor of being trusted with 100 marks per annum, for which he alone was responsible.[48]

As the year ended, Henry Purcell, who was now fourteen years old, realized that his schooling and his days as a chorister of the Chapel Royal were ending. As suggested above, his unusual talents as a singer and instrumental performer had been recognized. But apart from the single composition written for Charles II's birthday in 1670—both existence and provenance of which are uncertain—there is no evidence that Purcell had as yet given anyone cause to believe that he was one of the most talented musicians of the age.

Nor, apparently, were many aware of the significance of the concert series that John Banister founded at the end of 1672, five years after his alleged peculation had brought about his fall from grace at court. The first of his concerts—probably one of the first professional chamber music concerts supported by box-office collections in Europe, Pepys's earlier mention of the post-office music-meeting notwithstanding[49]—was advertised as follows in the *London Gazette* for 26–30 December 1672: "These are to give notice that at Mr. John Banister's house now called the Music School, over against the George Tavern in Whitefriar's this present Monday [i.e., 30 December] will be music performed by excellent masters, beginning precisely at four of the clock in the afternoon, and every afternoon for the future precisely at that same hour."

Banister, motivated by the desire to repair his finances, as well as by the need to recoup his sadly deteriorated prestige and musical fortunes, had no way of knowing that he was setting an important historical precedent in thus launching one of the earliest public concert series. For many a Restoration musician, including Purcell himself, such concerts were to prove very useful, particularly during increasingly frequent seasons of economic distress at court.

3

Apprenticeship

WITHIN THE FIRST FEW WEEKS of the new year, Henry Purcell had further cause to reflect on what the future held for him, still a novice musician in the employ of the newly restored Stuart monarchy. On 17 January 1673 came down from the lord chamberlain's office a royal warrant dismissing Henry Hall, his friend, schoolmate, and fellow chorister in the Chapel Royal.[1] Hall's voice had broken just as the choir was preparing for the Christmas season,[2] and from that time forward until he became organist at Exeter a year later, he was kept and taught by Pelham Humfrey, who was paid £30 by the court, the usual sum where talented choristers were concerned.

Evidently Purcell's voice remained firm and true throughout most of that year, for a similar warrant for his dismissal did not appear until 17 December. His new stipend actually began at Michaelmas (29 September), by which time, surely, his voice had broken. The honorarium paid to Purcell is significant, if only because none is mentioned for Henry Hall. Clearly, Purcell's extraordinary musical talents already were recognized and valued in official circles.

> 17 Dec. 1673
>   Warrant to provide outfit of clothing for Henry Purcell, late child of his Majesty's Chapel Royal, whose voice is changed, and gone from the Chapel.
>   Warrant to pay to Henry Purcell, late one of the Children of His Majesty's Chapel Royal, whose voice is changed and gone from the Chapel, the sum of £30 by the year, to commence Michaelmas, 1673, last past.[3]

Apart from the annual stipend, Purcell's perquisites upon leaving were exactly the same as Henry Hall's had been: "two suits of plain cloth, two hats and hat bands, four whole shirts, four half shirts, six bands, six pairs of cuffs, six handkerchiefs, four pair of stockings, four pairs of shoes, and four pairs of gloves."[4] For Purcell, then, no period of adjustment, either awkward or welcome, intervened between the end of his chorister's duties and the beginning of his professional career as composer and organist. Nor was he so unfortunate as to be sent out to the provinces, as were many of his classmates. Six months before he left the Chapel as a singer, he had been assigned new duties there as assistant to John Hingeston, who was in charge of care and maintenance of the royal instruments. Purcell's new duties brought no further stipend, possibly because of his receiving £30 per annum as of the previous Michaelmas. He may have accepted these chores in good grace for a while but surely must have grown restive before the long, ten-year apprenticeship at last ended with Hingeston's death in 1683. Even then there was no mention of a stipend in the official warrant.

> 10 June 1673.
> Warrant to admit Henry Purcell in the place of keeper, maker, mender, repairer and tuner of the regals, organs, virginals, flutes and recorders and all other kind of wind instruments whatsoever, in ordinary, without fee, to His Majesty, and assistant to John Hingeston, and upon the death or other avoidance of the latter, to come in ordinary with fee.[5]

While improving under Hingeston his practical skills by taking apart, repairing, reassembling, and tuning all sorts of instruments, Purcell also studied composition and performance under Pelham Humfrey. Unfortunately, there is no description of the nature or manner of instruction. Just at this time Humfrey had the help of an "assistant instructor for viols and theorbos" in the person of John Lilly, which at least gives a hint as to the kind of instruction he did not find time for.[6] Presumably Humfrey coached his pupils in the art of descant, or, as it would now be termed, composition and counterpoint, particularly emphasizing those techniques and styles that he himself had so *recently* learned in France and Italy.

During the course of the year, London's theatrical musical traditions had taken a new, indeed a modernist, turn with the production in February of a "transmogrified" version of Shakespeare's *Macbeth*, with music by Locke. Locke also provided music for Settle's *Empress of Morocco* the following July, a month or so after Charles D'Avenant had undertaken the management of the company in the new theater in Dorset Garden on his father's death shortly before.[7]

Early in 1674, Thomas Purcell added yet another position to an already impressive list. Shortly after 22 February, when John Wilson died,[8] full of years and honored by all, Thomas Purcell succeeded him as musician-in-ordinary to His Majesty in the Private Music.[9] This brought to a total of at least five, perhaps six, the number of paid positions he held at court.[10] Small wonder that he was able to live in the most fashionable residential area in the vicinity of the court, and that he found it possible to leave his widow well off despite considerable arrears which the court owed him at his death in 1682.[11]

At the beginning of the year, Londoners witnessed the arrival of Robert Cambert, newly ousted from an exalted position in the Parisian musical community by Lully's machinations at the court of Louis XIV. His *Ariane, ou le mariage de Bacchus* (produced by the new Royal Academy of Music) was evidently successful, for it ran nearly a month after opening on 30 March 1674 at the newly restored Theatre Royal in Bridges Street.[12] Grabu no doubt helped with the production and musical performance, witness the warrant of 27 March, which ordered the persons responsible to deliver "to Monsieur Grabu, or to such as he shall appoint, such of the scenes remaining in the theatre at Whitehall as shall be useful for the French opera at the theatre in Bridges Street, and the said Monsieur Grabu to return them again safely after 14 days time, to the theatre in Whitehall."[13] One good thing led to another, it seems, and on 4 July next, twelve of the violins were ordered to report to Cambert at Whitehall at seven o'clock the following Wednesday morning (the eighth) for the royal entertainment to be performed at Windsor on Saturday, 11 July.[14] The pieces performed included *Pomone* (on the same libretto with which Cambert and Perrin had begun their unlucky enterprise in Paris three years earlier) and a *Ballet et musique pour le divertissement du Roy de la Grand-Bretagne*. The libretto for the latter was printed by "Thomas Nieucombe dans la Savoy" in London that same year.

Henry Purcell was not mentioned in the list of those who were paid riding charges to Windsor,[15] but since everyone else was there, and since the whole musical establishment had been transferred to Windsor for the summer season, he probably was among those who heard the music. What he or any other Englishman thought of the work has not been recorded. But from the fact that no further entertainments by Cambert and Grabu were scheduled, it may be assumed that the performance was not so successful as to demand repetition.

In fact, by the end of 1674 the decline of the vogue for French music mentioned previously now began in earnest. Perhaps the falling-off was not altogether due to musical weaknesses. Charles could no longer afford to employ openly at his court foreign musicians who were also prominent Catholics. As his impecunious condition placed him more and more at the mercy of Protestant enemies in Parliament, he would have had to be increasingly careful. The failure of the "Royal Academy of Music in Bridges Street, Covent Garden," which had undermined the joint venture of Cambert and Grabu, and the fall of the latter from

grace that same year may have been due also to political considerations. Cambert was doubly persona non grata to anti-Catholic Parliamentarians. They disliked him equally for the enormous expenses his
productions entailed, and for his being a very important person among
Catholics, having begun his career as a close friend of the papal nuncio
in Paris.[16]

Opportunities to hear other "fam'd Italian masters" had been plen-
tiful throughout the year. On 5 January Evelyn reported seeing "an
Italian opera in Music, the first that had been in England,"[17] and on 15
January J. B. Draghi's dances were performed in the production of
Shadwell's adaptation of Shakespeare's *The Tempest*.[18] In May another
performance of *The Tempest* included a song by Pietro Reggio,[19] which
Purcell may have heard from behind the footlights, since on 16 May
came down the order:

> It is His Majesty's pleasure that Mr. Turner and Mr. Hart or any
> other men or boys belonging to His Majesty's Chapel Royal that sing in
> *The Tempest* at His Royal Highness's Theatre do remain in town all the
> week (during His Majesty's absence from Whitehall) to perform that ser-
> vice, only Saturdays to repair to Windsor and to return to London on
> Mondays if there be occasion for them. And that [they] also perform the
> like service in the operas in the said theatre or any other thing in the like
> nature where their help may be desired upon notice given them thereof.[20]

Nicola Matteis was a stellar figure in London's concert season that
year, and remained in England as a permanent, active, and very influential musician. At any rate, on 19 November, John Evelyn reported in
such enthusiastic vein as to suggest that no Londoner who was at all
interested in music could have escaped hearing of him:

> I heard that stupendous Violin Signor Nicholao (with other rare musi-
> cians) whom certainly never mortal man exceeded on that instrument;
> he had a stroke so sweet, and made it speak like the voice of a man; and
> when he pleased, like a consort of several instruments . . . nothing ap-
> proached the violin in Nicholas hand: he seemed to be *spiritatoed*, and
> played such ravishing things on a ground as astonished us all.[21]

No document can be quoted to show that Purcell and Matteis actually did meet, as hinted by John Wilson in his book *Roger North on
Music*; consequently no influence on Purcell during this early period
can be proven conclusively. However, if Matteis did nothing more than
create new respect and popularity for the violin among England's musical public, he accomplished enough, thus paving the way for modern
Italianate style taken up by Purcell and other young English composers,

who would most certainly have been influenced by his splendid virtuoso playing.

Less than a fortnight after hearing Matteis, Evelyn reported on 2 December that he had "heard Signor Francisco on the harpsichord, esteemed one of the most excellent masters in Europe on that instrument: then came Nicholao with his violin and struck all mute, but Mrs. Knight, who sung incomparably, and doubtless has the greatest reach of any English woman: she had lately been roaming in Italy, and was much improved in that quality."[22]

Matteis's spectacular rise, and the new popularity enjoyed at the time by other Italian musicians in London, preceded by only a few weeks the eclipse of Grabu's star early in 1675. On 29 January, Nicholas Staggins replaced Grabu as master of the King's Music. As an indication of Charles II's change of musical policy about this time, the replacement is doubly significant. The appointment of an English musician pacified the xenophobes at court who, like Pelham Humfrey earlier, had little respect or love for the French composers and musicians the king had brought to Whitehall. Moreover, Staggins was an Italophile where music was concerned, and his period in office saw the rise of Italian music and the concomitant decline of French music at court.

On 14 July Pelham Humfrey died, quite suddenly it seems, of some unknown malady.[23] So, almost before he had gotten to know one teacher, Purcell found himself under the supervision of another, John Blow,[24] who was sworn into two of Humfrey's positions simultaneously,[25] a week after the latter was buried, on 17 July, in the cloisters of Westminster Abbey near the southeast door.[26]

Like Thomas Purcell, John Blow was an expert, seasoned pluralist. He had been one of the organists at Westminster Abbey since 1668, a musician for the king's virginals since 1669, and a gentleman of the Chapel Royal and composer in His Majesty's Private Music. Unquestionably, young Purcell had much to learn from his new master, even though there was actually but ten years difference in their ages.[27] Other disciples included Michael Wise, Henry Hall, and William Holder,[28] son of Rev. William Holder, sub-dean of the Chapel Royal, whom Michael Wise waggishly dubbed "Mr. Snub Dean," because he seemed such a martinet to the boys at the Chapel Royal.[29]

What Blow taught his youthful charges, apart from his role modeling on surviving as a musician, need not be left entirely to conjecture or reconstruction, for he compiled two pedagogical methods, which clearly demonstrate his principles of teaching music. One of these,

"Rules for Playing of a Through Bass upon Organ and Harpsicon" [*sic*],[30] represents the training Purcell would have had in accompanying various songs and instrumental pieces; and the other, "Rules for Composition," reveals some of the general principles and techniques of composition he learned.[31] For the most part, Blow's precepts are so simple, indeed so fundamental, as to give weight to Mr. Watkins Shaw's theory that he may have written them as a series of lessons for the young Henry Purcell.[32]

That Blow did teach Purcell is established by the commendatory verse in Blow's *Amphion Anglicus* (1700) by Henry Hall, who was also a pupil under Blow's instruction at this time and who had left the Chapel Royal only shortly before Purcell did:

> The Art of Descant, late our Albion's boast
> With that of staining glass, we thought was lost;
> Till in this work we all with wonder view
> What ever art with order's notes can do,
> Corelli's heights, with great Bassani's too;
> And Britain's Orpheus learned his art from you.

A warrant for a new felt hat "for Henry Purcell, a boy leaving the Chapel Royal" arrived at Michaelmas[33] to remind him of earlier days as chorister. But by this autumn Henry Purcell had begun, at least unofficially, his professional connection with Westminster Abbey, a connection that was to continue for the rest of his life. It was no doubt a matter of great pride to him to become a member of an establishment that could boast of the daily service of distinguished professional musicians such as, in addition to the men mentioned above, John Gostling, Thomas Blagrave, the hot-headed but very talented Michael Wise, William Turner, John Blow, and many others whose fame has already been sung by Sir Jack Westrup and other Purcell biographers.

But of his activities for the remainder of the year, nothing is known. Very likely he witnessed the elaborate preparations for Crowne's *Calisto*, for which Hall Theatre was gloriously refurbished. This was the last of a long tradition of self-contained English masques. Perhaps Purcell attended a rehearsal or two, as Evelyn had done, even though he may have been unable to attend the performance or participate in it himself.[34] What he may have thought of this lavishly expensive production is matter for conjecture. From a purely musical point of view, however, he would not have been impressed by Nicholas Staggins's feeble music. If the few surviving songs are representative, the performance would have been a waste of time, however impressive the spectacle or entertaining the dances.[35] His own masques, which were soon to be produced within operas, semioperas,[36] and stage plays, would establish new musical standards for this form, which he so thoroughly revised that it bore little resemblance to earlier specimens.

John Banister, who had stepped down for Grabu, played on as lowly fiddler in the king's band, even though his reputation among London chamber music lovers had risen considerably by this time.[37] His views on the fall of his old rival and on Staggins's new preferment have not been recorded. However, his reaction to this, as to other happenings at court, may be imagined from the attitude he exhibited in making so bold as to sell his livery allotment (presumably in perpetuity) for £40.[38] No doubt he needed the money, as did others of his colleagues at this time. But he was less patient than they.

Whether or not Staggins's appointment had any effect on Thomas Purcell's connection with the king's violins cannot be discovered. It may be significant that he is not listed among the nine musicians who accompanied Charles II to Newmarket for nineteen days, from 4 to 27 March. Nor does the name Purcell appear in the warrant of 27 May 1675 for musicians employed by Staggins for the "masque at Whitehall," although a very large and very interesting complement of French and English performers was called for the event.[39] However, he continued to collect each year his five liveries and, presumably, attendant fees, in addition to his stipend as groom of the robes.

Meanwhile, Purcell was finding his way into his new job as apprentice to John Hingeston. During those first months, his tasks as instrumental repairman and tuner for the court establishment were demanding and tedious, if at times challenging.[40] These duties no doubt served Purcell in good stead in his later career as a composer. In those times close acquaintance with all instruments was considered an important qualification for a composer, as we know from Pelham Humfrey's statements concerning Grabu, who, he said, did not know how to play any instrument and therefore could not compose.[41] He therefore no doubt profited much from his association with Hingeston, who not only repaired and tuned instruments, but also was a distinguished organist, violist, and composer. We may be sure that Purcell learned quickly, for in 1675, he was paid £2 for tuning the organ at Westminster Abbey, presumably on his own responsibility.[42]

About this same time Purcell also received £5 for "pricking out" some organ parts. Westrup quite rightly challenged the notion that this payment had anything to do with an official appointment of Purcell as copyist. Regular copyists were paid far more handsomely.[43] However, I think it is wrong to assume that this kind of work, like his slightly later work of copying Tudor anthems, was of small importance, either to the royal musical establishment or to Purcell himself. Sixteen years after the Restoration, Purcell was indeed copying the anthems of Elizabethan and Tudor composers, and, as even slight acquaintances with his own anthems will prove, learned a great deal in the process.[44]

Purcell's work in scoring anthems composed by earlier English masters was important to his growth as a composer for Abbey and Chapel Royal. No doubt it was also useful to the choir libraries of those institutions. Historically this activity and its results were far greater than such routine matters would imply. The scarcity of anthem scores in Purcell's day was the direct result of destructive actions, perpetrated on policy, by zealous Puritans during the civil war and its aftermath. When ransacking churches and chapels in search of symbols of Roman idolatry, they routinely visited choir libraries and organ lofts where artifacts of Catholic worship were certain to be found. Thus it was that organs in good repair and scores and parts for anthems and services were very much in demand throughout England, especially in London, when Charles II returned from his travels in 1660. Both as consultant in organ construction and as copyist, Purcell was a primary figure in the period of reconstruction of England's musical culture.

From 26 June until summer's end, Charles II retired to Windsor,[45] accompanied by his musical retinue, as may be seen by a warrant for payment of £410. 8s., which Thomas Purcell distributed to eighteen Gentlemen of the Chapel Royal and an organist, John Blow.[46] Neither Hingeston nor his apprentice, young Purcell, is mentioned on the list, an omission suggesting that Purcell and Hingeston did not go to Windsor until 15 August, although Staggins[47] and, presumably, the rest of the musical entourage had been there all summer. So for six weeks, Purcell would not have had his regular instruction from Blow.

It is impossible to say for certain what his activities may have been during this period. He may have used this time of relative calm and quiet to finish his annual tuning of the organ in Westminster Abbey—a task for which he received £2 again the following Michaelmas. It is fairly safe to assume that he would have spent as much time as could be spared from his duties under Hingeston to study and practice composition mainly on his own initiative, very likely through copying and studying old masters.

During this same time Henry Purcell found it necessary to adjust to a new fellow pupil in musical instruction. As mentioned above, John Blow had taken William Holder under his wing the previous September.[48] The new member of the circle was probably the son of William Holder, canon of St. Paul's and later sub-dean of the Chapel Royal. Young Holder may well have composed the two anthems preserved in the Tudway manuscripts,[49] which traditionally have been attributed to his father. As to what Holder, Purcell, and other pupils of Blow may have studied, no better guides could be suggested than the little treatises mentioned above.[50] For the most part Blow's precepts are so simply put and so fundamentally sound as to give great weight to Watkins Shaw's theory, as mentioned above.[51]

On 24 October the main event on the calendar at Westminster Abbey was the burial in the cloisters of Christopher Gibbons, last remaining son of Orlando.[52] His death, which occurred four days earlier, severed another of the few remaining strands connecting pre-Cromwellian musical traditions with those that had begun with the restoration of Charles II and his court. Christopher Gibbons, more famous as harpsichordist and organist than as composer, also influenced young Henry Purcell, whose main responsibilities as a practical musician were to be those he held as a keyboard artist. Christopher Gibbons had received his earliest training at the Chapel Royal while Orlando, his father, was organist there.[53] No doubt he was thoroughly grounded in the fundamentals of polyphonic music, both as regards actual composition and playing extempore. After his father's death on 5 June 1625, young Christopher, then just ten, is said to have been adopted by his uncle Edward (Orlando's elder brother), who was in charge of the musical establishment at Exeter Cathedral. There Christopher gained further training in traditional polyphonic style during his thirteen years of study, which presumably included a period of apprenticeship under his uncle's guidance.[54] The sequence of events, incidentally, was remarkably parallel to that which his pupil, Henry Purcell, was to undergo nearly forty years later.

Gibbons's presence at court and at Westminster Abbey thus established a definite link with the broad traditions of early Caroline and Jacobean music—a link that no doubt helped to provide Henry Purcell with the feeling for native English musical styles so manifest in all his works, early and late. How important this influence may have been for Purcell's development as a keyboard artist remains a moot point, because a large share of such influence would have been reflected in improvisatory techniques, of which no contemporary descriptions have come down to us.

However, several pieces of circumstantial evidence suggest that Gibbons may have been intimately acquainted with Purcell and his family circle. In 1661 Gibbons was in the orchestra for the performance of D'Avenant's *Siege of Rhodes* in which, as noted earlier, Henry Purcell the elder had taken the part of Mustapha.[55] From 1665 onward, the records show that Christopher Gibbons occupied the house in Great Almonry South in which the Purcells had lived up to the time of the death of Henry the elder in 1664. Furthermore, Orlando Gibbons's full anthems "Hosanna to the Son of David," "Lift Up Your Heads," and "Almighty and Everlasting God" are to be found among the few compositions dating from before the commonwealth, which Purcell copied shortly after this time. Presumably he had scored these for his own study, because these full scores would not have been otherwise useful.[56]

The influence of the Gibbons family also reached Purcell through Matthew Locke, who had gone to Exeter as a chorister in 1638, the year in which Christopher Gibbons had taken up his appointment as organist at Winchester. Locke's influence upon Purcell has been made much of, on documentary evidence that is at best circumstantial. The best evidence is to be found in a comparison of Locke's and Purcell's musical styles. Various affinities between Locke's and Purcell's idioms do indicate greater rapport than can be explained by their sharing a common tradition or similar professional standing in English music. But to date no specific evidence has been found to definitely establish a close relationship between the two men, though Locke, like Purcell's mentor, Christopher Gibbons, also studied with Edward Gibbons at Exeter.

The documentary evidence consists of the vague reference by Pepys mentioned earlier[57] and one letter from Matthew Locke to young Henry Purcell. For the existence of the letter, there is only the dubious testimony of E. F. Rimbault, as transmitted by Cummings, who wrote that he was "indebted to the late Dr. Rimbault for a copy":

> Dear Harry,—Some of the gentlemen of His Majesty's Music will honour my poor lodgings with their company this evening, and I would have you come and join them. Bring with thee, Harry, thy last anthem, and also the canon we tried over together at our last meeting. Thine in all kindness,
>   M. Locke.
> Savoy, March 16

Despite the inaccessibility of this manuscript and the careless manner in which it was first published,[58] the information it presents is worth considering. It is at least interesting enough, I think, to warrant begging the question of authenticity until such time as further evidence comes to light. If only because documents of any kind are extremely scarce for this period, the letter ought not to be dismissed, even though in the past, Rimbault and Cummings have not always proven the most reliable of authors.

The orthography and style of the letter seem authentic, and the allusions to Locke's circumstances are credible enough, even though the notion of his "trying over" an anthem in a private musical gathering (presumably held for enjoyment, as the tone of the invitation would suggest) seems without precedent.[59] Locke's interest in an anthem—the most "Anglican" of musical forms—would be hard to justify if Anthony à Wood's charge that he had "turned Papist" shortly after becoming organist to Queen Catherine of Portugal were true.[60] As to which of Purcell's anthems or canons Locke may have had in mind, nothing is known. None of Purcell's extant works may be dated so early with certainty. Nor can the date of the letter be ascertained, since only month and day are given. However, various deductions make 1676 seem the most likely year. By 16 March 1676 Locke would have gained firm enough control over the Chapel Royal band (over which he officiated, during Staggins's leave of absence for study in Italy)[61] for his invitation to "some of the gentlemen of His Majesty's music" to bear enough weight to bring them out.

Presumably it was during this period that Purcell composed his interesting "Stairre Case Overture," a piece clearly reflecting the adventurous influence of Matthew Locke. (For comments on evidence for such influence, as well as for specific information on sources, see Alan Browning's article "Purcell's 'Stairre Case Overture'" in *Musical Times* for December 1980, pp. 768–69.) The appearance of this little overture for string orchestra marked an important event in the career of the young composer, marking his debut into the concert and theatrical world.

Considering Locke's well-documented and long-standing relationship with the Purcell family,[62] the intimate relationship between himself and Henry the younger may well have existed. The extremely personal note struck in the text Purcell set (and possibly wrote) in memory of Locke's death further increases this possibility. It is unlikely, in view of suspicions about Matthew Locke's being a Papist, that he would have ventured into print with such an avowal as the following unless Locke had truly been his friend: "On the death of his worthy friend Matthew Locke, Music Composer-in-Ordinary to His Majesty, and Organist of Her Majesty's Chapel who died in August 1677."[63]

Locke's most important legacy to Purcell, however, may have been a conception of the strength and nobility of the English musical tradition—from which Purcell had already imbibed much (from his work with Humfrey and his duties as choirboy, copyist, organ novice, and so forth). However, it is also likely that Locke would have cultivated in young Purcell something of a taste for the vocal and instrumental styles of the great Italian schools, just then establishing undisputed preeminence in the musical world, what with the superior publications, performers, teachers, and composers these centers exported in such great quantities. English importation of all these in the latter half of the seventeenth century—a process paralleling the wholesale transplantation of the Italian madrigal in the first—was to become a significant factor in English musical life by the time Purcell came of age.

⤙ 4 ⤚

Professional Debut

Upon Matthew Locke's death, several musical positions fell open at court, as elsewhere in Westminster and London. He had held at least three royal appointments: as composer for the Private Music, for wind instruments, and for the violins. In addition, he was organist to Queen Catherine and also sustained various musical commitments to London theaters. Purcell, who succeeded him as composer-in-ordinary to the violins on 10 September 1677,[1] and who seems to have inherited some of his theatrical responsibilities as well, was the youngest of those who were advanced upon Locke's death.[2] That he was appointed composer-in-ordinary, though but eighteen, adds further weight to the conjecture that Locke may have been his mentor.

In these years court finances had become so shaky that many must have wondered what difference it made to be registered in the accounts either as "in-ordinary" or "extraordinary"—i.e., with or without a regular salary. About this time the gentlemen of the Chapel Royal banded together to petition for £877. 7s., owed to them since the summer of 1674, when they had traveled to Windsor. Despite the annotation "Resolution hereon: let something be done," matters were allowed to slide, and later the requested sum grew to the alarming total of £1422, and the gentlemen's complaints now had the support of a letter written by the bishop of London himself.[3]

Another musician who suffered from the court's insolvency was Louis Grabu, now in a very miserable state. Politically he had submitted to "grievous misfortune," even endured the king's "willingness to receive another person into his place during pleasure." But financial distress he could not face with such equanimity, and so submitted a series of abject petitions for aid.[4] Charles II dodged the immediate issue by asking for an itemized account, which Grabu drew up for Arlington to submit a month later. Arlington, then secretary of state, reported that Grabu was owed a total of £627. 9s. 6d., adding that he found his condition "to be very poor and miserable."[5] If the following letter written by Henry Savile to the earl of Rochester on 25 June 1678 may be credited at all, poor Grabu's situation must have seemed doubly hard, for Nicholas Staggins apparently lost no time in assuming full control:

> From the rising of the sun to the setting thereof, I see nothing that pleases my eyes or hear nothing but what grates my ears; only I am promised a moment's titillation by Mr. Staggins, who is come over with great credit and many new airs. His Majesty has already constituted him lord paramount over all music. He may reign there like a Great Turk and cut whose cat's-guts he please if the harmony be not to his liking. With what moderation he will use his absolute power, I leave it to fate and the immortal gods to determine.[6]

The French musical colony may have been dismayed by such maltreatment of a former chief, but their activities at court about this time reflect no general despondency. For the celebration of King Charles's birthday on 29 May, the French complement turned out in full array to perform Paisible's music for Madame de la Roche-Guilhen's *comédie-ballet, Rare-en tout*. In the wording of the order, as passed through Nicholas Staggins, or, he being absent, through Matthew Locke, there is the suggestion that royal command was felt to be needed to curb recalcitrance:

> 22 May 1677.
> That all His Majesty's musicians do attend to practises in the theatre at Whitehall at such times as Madame Le Roch and Mr. Paisible shall appoint for the practising of such music as is to be in the French comedy to be acted before His Majesty on the 29 May instant.[7]

Purcell, shortly to become an official composer in his own right, no doubt absorbed the experience as part of his musical education. However, it may have been from affairs such as this and from Grabu's music in particular that he gained the dislike for the "levity and balladry of our neighbours" of which he wrote in his preface to the trio-sonatas of 1683.

In such quasi-bankrupt times for musicians, Purcell no doubt was glad to receive on 13 February the benefits of a warrant for more clothing: "Warrant for payment for one and twenty ells, three quarters of holland, for four whole shirts, four half shirts, and for bands and cuffs for Henry Purcell, a child gone off from the Chapel."[8] Within eight months, however, with his appointment as a musician-in-ordinary and an annual livery allowance of £16. 2s. 6d., Purcell must have considered mere clothing warrants as part of his bygone boyhood. Already he had enjoyed an official, though as yet apparently unpaid, position as assistant to John Hingeston for some five years; for at least three years he had been de facto, if not official, organ-tuner and copyist at Westminster Abbey (where he was again paid £2 at Michaelmas 1677),[9] and, from 10 September, he had begun to enjoy the elevated status of a regular appointment at the Chapel Royal. Furthermore, his reputation as a composer was considerably enhanced by the appearance in print of five of his songs and by the recognition accompanying the performance of an anthem and two chamber works that took place in this period.[10]

On 13 September he finished the table of contents for a series of anthems he had scored in fair copy, presumably for his own study, since these scores would have been of little use in practical performance.[11] It can scarcely have been coincidental that twenty-two of these thirty-two anthems had been written by persons who had been his teachers and mentors. The list is small enough to be quoted in full:

Anon.	Instrumental movement à 4 in E minor		f.26ᵛ
Adrian Batten	Hear my prayer, O God	Full anthem	f.118(rev)
John Blow	Christ being risen	Verse anthem	f.93ᵛ(rev)
	Cry aloud	Verse anthem	f.28ᵛ
	God is our hope	Full, with V.	f.141(rev)
	My God, my soul	Verse anthem	f.108(rev)
	O God, wherefore art Thou	Full, with V.	f.138(rev)
	O Lord God of my salvation	Verse anthem	f.99(rev)
	O Lord I have sinned (For General Monk's burial, 1668)	Verse anthem	f.142ᵛ(rev)
	O sing unto the Lord	Verse anthem	f.9ᵛ
	Save me, O God	Verse anthem	f.134ᵛ(rev)
	Sing we merrily	Verse anthem	f.14ᵛ(bef.1674)
William Byrd	Bow Thine ear, O Lord	Full anthem	f.129(rev)

	O Lord, make Thy servant	Full anthem	f.125(rev)
	Prevent us, O Lord	Full anthem	f.126(rev)
William Child	Sing we merrily	Full anthem	f.114ᵛ(rev)
Orlando Gibbons	Almighty and Everlasting God	Full anthem	f.112(rev)
	Hosanna to the son of David	Full anthem	f.136(rev)
	Lift up your heads	Full anthem	f.124(rev)
Nathaniel Giles	O give thanks	Full anthem	f.119ᵛ(rev)
Pelham Humfrey	Lift up your heads	Verse anthem	f.23ᵛ(rev)
	Like as the hart	Verse anthem	f.7
	Lord, teach us to number	Verse anthem	f.21
	O Lord, my God	Verse anthem	f.4
	O praise the Lord	Verse anthem	f.1
Matthew Locke	I will hear what the Lord	Verse anthem	f.40ᵛ
	Lord, let me know mine end	Verse anthem	f.133ᵛ(rev)
	Sing unto the Lord	Verse anthem	f.31
	The Lord will hear thee	Verse anthem	f.38ᵛ
	Turn Thy face from my sins	Full, with V.	f.131(rev)
	When the son of man	Verse anthem	f.36ᵛ
William Mundy	O Lord, I bow the knee	Full anthem	f.122ᵛ(rev)
Thomas Tallis	I call and cry	Full anthem	f.127ᵛ(rev)
Thomas Tomkins	O Lord, I have loved	Full anthem	f.120ᵛ(rev)

(All those pieces marked with reverse foliation appear to have been copied in a later hand and may well be contemporary with or later than the date indicated in Purcell's autograph inscription on a flyleaf: "God bless Mr. Henry Purcell / 1682 September the 10th.")[12]

The wealth of evidence concerning his professional activity makes it all the more puzzling that the Westminster Abbey Treasurer's Account for 1678 should contain the earliest extant records to provide any information on Purcell's schooling. Until this year Charles Purcell (Henry's cousin) had been studying as a Bishop's Boy at St. Peter's College, Westminster, since 1670.[13] He was named (as "Carolo Pursell," the documents being drawn up in Latin) in the same entry each year down to 1678. Apparently the accountant entered it again that year, then, discovering an error or perhaps making a last-minute change, scraped off the name Charles from the vellum, replacing it with "Henrico" (later "Henrici" and even "Henri"), who continued to be named until 1680.[14]

In view of Purcell's age—by 1678 he was nineteen—and in consideration of the musical prominence he had already attained, this evidence of his having received a scholarship requires some explanation. There are really only two possibilities. Either there was another Henry Purcell at St. Peter's, Westminster, at that time—a remote possibility— or the regulations concerning the age and required studies and activities of Bishop's Boys were relaxed for Purcell.

The presence at Westminster of another promising student named Henry Purcell seems very doubtful in view of the lack of any contemporary mention of such a remarkable situation, so the second of these two possibilities seems most plausible. Furthermore, Dr. Richard Busby, the headmaster, was a friend of Purcell's, as evidenced by the gold ring he left him in his will.[15] Faced with a sudden vacancy in the list of Bishop's Boys—it is difficult to think of any other satisfactory explanation for the clumsy erasure of Charles's and substitution of Henry's name that spoil the tidy, professional appearance of the page —and concerned for the welfare of an extremely talented young friend, Busby may well have found it easy to temper any regulations that might have disqualified the young genius. Purcell, on the other hand, surely welcomed an opportunity to improve his education, which he still felt justified in depreciating publicly as late as 1683, when he wrote of himself in his preface to the trio-sonatas of 1683: "he is not ashamed to own his unskilfulness in the Italian language; but that's the unhappiness of his education, which cannot justly be accounted his fault. . . ."[16] Finally, the shortage of cash at court and the inordinate length of time

Purcell had spent waiting for an opening may have given Busby, or perhaps other officials, reason to extend this encouragement to Purcell. Whatever the cause or explanation, it is fairly certain that Purcell spent at least the first part of 1678 as a Bishop's Boy:

> Et in Denar. solut. ad Scholas Henrici. Purcell, Rogero Cooper, Edward Roberts et Sam. Langley xxv[li] et Reverendis. Decano Thesaur ad Ludi magister xx[s] ex dono Reverendis. Patris Johani Episcop Lincolnien. nup. Decan. Westmonastr. in toto hoc ano xxvi[li].[17]

> (And for money for the use of the scholars Henry Purcell, Roger Cooper, Edward Roberts, and Samuel Langley £25; and from the very Reverend Dean Treasurer to the Master of the School 20 shillings from the gift of the very Reverend Father, John, Bishop of Lincoln, formerly Dean of Westminster. For the whole of this year, £26.)

Whether with his increasing professional responsibilities Purcell was able to continue as full-time scholar, he did in fact continue to receive the same annual stipend until Michaelmas 1680, after which time his name disappeared from the records. His marriage about this time may have disqualified him to receive further stipends.[18]

A Bishop's Boy, or "Lord's Scholar," was one who held an exhibition under the benefaction of Rev. John Williams, bishop of Lincoln, and later archbishop of York, even before the Commonwealth, according to G. F. Russell Barker and Alan Stenning.[19] Elsewhere, these same authorities describe the founding of these scholarships as follows:

> In 1623, while Dean of Westminster, he [the Reverend John Williams] purchased 2 fee farm rents of £14 and £13. 6s . 8d., issuing respectively out of manors of Sudbury and Great Stanmore in the County of Middlesex. By a deed dated 26 April, 1624, he declared that the Dean and Chapter of Westminster should hold these rents in trust for four scholars of his own foundation, two of whom should be natives of Wales and two natives of the diocese of Lincoln, "to be educated and maintained in the Grammar School of St. Peter's College in Westminster and there to have free education until they shall be from thence elected and transplanted into St. John's Coll[ege], Camb[ridge]." . . . Adequate funds were not, however, provided to carry out the scheme, and though four boys, known first as Lord's Scholars and afterwards as Bishop's Boys, were annually elected at the School, but few of them were admitted to the scholarships at St. Johns.[20]

In addition to providing new evidence on Purcell's birthplace,[21] this award of scholarship sheds new light on Purcell's early schooling. As a Bishop's Boy, Purcell came under the supervision of Richard Busby, the

"Flogging Head" of Westminster School, whom his charges had privately dubbed "Sir Richard Birch-Hard." Whatever his reputation in this regard, no seventeenth-century English pedagogue commanded greater respect than he for fostering intellectual development among his pupils. Richard Steele, who lived long enough to assess Busby's teaching fairly, that is to say, by the accomplishments of his pupils, was only one of many who paid tribute to him as the English Chiron of his age: "I must confess (and I had often reflected upon it) that I am of opinion that Busby's genius for education had as great an effect upon the age he lived in as that of any ancient philosopher, without excepting one, had upon his contemporaries. . . . He had a power of raising what the lad had in him to the utmost height."[22]

Unfortunately, there is at present no way to discover what Purcell may have learned from this great pedagogue, who had taught John Dryden, John Locke, Christopher Wren, Henry Aldrich, and a great many other leading intellectual figures of the post-Restoration age. But there is proof that Busby regarded the young composer highly, for he willed him money for a gold mourning ring. There is no doubt that Purcell was the legatee, for Frances Purcell specifically mentioned "a mourning ring of Dr. Busby's" in her will, made out on 7 February 1706.

That Purcell was beyond the usual age for admission to St. Peter's College matters little. Busby was a rare academician, with enough imagination to see beyond bureaucratic regulations. Earlier he had admitted Charles Sackville, Lord Buckhurst, at age nineteen. Nor is there reason to wonder that Purcell should have passed his twenty-first birthday and already become famous before giving up his scholarship. Samuel Johnson said that it was known "to have been the practice of Dr. Busby to detain those youths long at school of whom he had formed highest expectations."[23]

Whatever his activities in gaining a general education, Purcell's musical development had not been neglected during those early years. Much of his practical training derived from the experiences he had had as Hingeston's apprentice and as parttime copyist and organist at Westminster Abbey. In view of his preferments to the highest posts in England open to organists and composers, it is safe to assume that he had worked diligently under Matthew Locke and John Blow, and perhaps under Pelham Humfrey and Henry Cooke as well. He may also have learned much from John Jenkins, who was replaced at court by John Moss on 14 October 1678, well after Purcell had begun to appear there frequently.[24] Both Jenkins and Purcell belonged to the circle of musicians and artists enjoying the hospitality of the North family, and it is unlikely that the young Restoration genius and the grand old man of English instrumental polyphony would not have become acquainted before the latter died, at age eighty-six, on 27 October 1678.[25]

With Jenkins's death, yet another important connection between the post-Restoration courtly establishment and England's musical past was severed—but not before young Purcell had had time to absorb something of the musical tradition that had culminated so impressively in Jenkins's works. Indeed this master of the English fancy, whose compositions have too long lain under the obloquy of Burney's stern obiter dicta,[26] created a magnificent corpus of chamber works of all varieties. On stylistic evidence alone, it is obvious that young Purcell learned from this body of music. In Jenkins's fantasies, particularly, were fulfilled those tendencies toward full dramatic and emotive expression, along with integrated thematic development, which had begun early in the century with Byrd, Orlando Gibbons, and their contemporaries.[27]

With the music of these masters, we come onto firm ground with regard to Purcell's actual musical education, for we have numerous copies of their compositions in Purcell's own hand. From these, it is clear that he studied his art by returning to the very heart of the great period of English polyphony under the Tudors and early Stuarts. To the list of compositions mentioned earlier must be added Pelham Humfrey's "By the Waters of Babylon," an anthem in British Library MS Add. 30932 reputed to have been rearranged by Purcell, in whose hand it appears. Another new autograph source, which belonged to the late R. Thurston Dart, includes four fantasias by Orlando Gibbons, several fantasias—actually suites—"for one basse & treble, both to the Organ," by Giovanni Coperario, and instrumental transcriptions of several madrigals by Claudio Monteverdi, which transcriptions represent, no doubt, the "Grave musicke, Fancies of 3, 4, 5, and 6 parts" mentioned by Thomas Mace in his *Musick's Monument,* where he refers to both Coperario and "one Monteverde, a Famous Italian author."[28]

These earliest masters of the fantasia had achieved technical emancipation from the rigid style of the old motet and ricercar by incorporating various techniques borrowed from madrigal composers, via instrumental transcriptions, and by pursuing variations techniques from early keyboard suites and compositions. Nevertheless, the fantasia retained its affinity for the grave style of the old motet, ornamenting, and, as it were, illuminating this with more expressive melodies, cast in the new harmonic mold of the seventeenth century, with broader perspectives of the new tonality.[29] Byrd and Gibbons had founded the new

PLATE 8. The beginning of Claudio Monteverdi's *Cruda Amarilli*, transcribed by Henry Purcell for viols (Bodleian Library)

style within the English tradition, where it had had a brief period of efflorescence among Jacobean consort composers before being driven from court, so to speak, during the Commonwealth.

The effects of this suppression did not last long, however.[30] John Jenkins, truly the "mirror and wonder of his age," as he was styled by Anthony à Wood,[31] wrote many pieces that strike the ear as somehow "Purcellian"—an eponymic prejudice soon dismissed, however, when one studies closely the fancies of the two composers. For now, it is enough to say that Purcell's study of the music of these masters of the fancy, a consciously antiquarian pursuit in post-Restoration England, was to result in a monumental collection of fancies that summarizes, as it ends, that tradition in magnificent climax.

Music and Restoration Politics

FROM 1678 THROUGH 1680, Charles II seemed to be having all conceivable kinds of difficulties on the political front. On 12 August 1678, one Christopher Kirkby warned the king of a "Popish Plot" to murder him so that his brother James, duke of York, might succeed to the throne. Kirkby had been urged on in this affair by Titus Oates, a miscreant with a bad reputation for opportunistic troublemaking. On 27 and 28 September, Oates and another fellow conspirator, Israel Tonge, were summoned to appear before the Privy Council, where Tonge produced a mysterious bundle of papers purporting to give details of this "Jesuit Plot," as it was also known. Then Oates alone was called in, and

> . . . as this strange creature—with neckless head and mouth set flat in the centre circle of his low brow and vast chin—told his story, the Council sat amazed. Gradually the wondrous tale unfolded: the Pope, the French King, the General of the Jesuits, the Provincials in England, Spain and Ireland, the Archbishops of Dublin and Tuam, and the Rectors of the Jesuit College, linked together in a mighty plot to kill the King, set up the Duke of York, plunge Ireland in blood, impose Catholicism by the sword, and destroy English commerce; the four Irish ruffians who were to do the bloody work at Windsor, the Lancashire incendiaries to fire London, and the three thousand cutthroats to massacre the sleeping citizens; the poisoners in attendance, who included Wakeman, the Queen's Physician, and Coleman, the Duchess of York's Secretary. It was a horrible conception, and one well attuned to Protestant fears.[1]

After Oates had stirred Parliament on 21 October, and especially after the spectacular murder of Edmund Godfrey, who had heard Oates's depositions, the Popish Plot was fully launched. At this juncture, some of Purcell's music became involved in the imbroglio when scurrilous anti-Whig broadsheets were circulated with the new texts fitted to the melodies. Three stage songs from *Theodosius* were particularly popular.[2] (See plate 11, where the tune of "Hail to the Myrtle

PLATE 9. Titus Oates (British Museum)

Shades" does service for the political text, "Hail to the Knight of the Post," a diatribe against Titus Oates.)

Battle lines were clearly drawn, and by the end of 1678, Charles II could see his Whig and Puritan enemies in open defiance. Their number and their political strength were such that he found it necessary to dissemble his Catholic sympathies, even to the extent of excluding James, duke of York, from his counsels and public affairs. He even went so far as to publish on 7 December "an order from the King and Council prohibiting his Majesty's subjects to resort to the chapels of her Majesty and foreign ministers where the Romish worship is celebrated, under severest penalties."[3] However, Charles held firm against Oates when he would have implicated the queen in a plot to poison her husband.

During all this time, the king may not have won many skirmishes in this, his lifelong cold war with the Whigs, but he displayed infinite resourcefulness in evasive delaying actions—as for instance with the postponement of the Yorkshire feast, which was to have been held on 12 November—while he quickly marshaled his own political forces.[4]

PLATE 10. Titus Oates (British Museum)

For such political purposes, Purcell's music was often pressed into service, as we have seen. In addition to the newly texted political broadsheet or "mock song," the catch provided a useful vehicle for political messages to the public. Since the time it had rivaled, if not replaced, the madrigal as the most popular social vocal form among English composers (about 1609, when Ravenscroft's *Pammelia* was published), the catch had had strong political associations. Again, Purcell's music reveals his awareness of England's traditions. The Popish Plot, for instance, is commemorated in one of the most successful of his political catches:

Now England's great council('s) assembled
To make laws for English-born freemen.
Since 'tis dang'rous to prate of matters of state
Let's handle our wine and our women.

Let's drink to the senate's best thoughts
For the good of the King and the nation.
May they dig in the spot as deep for the plot
As the Jesuits have laid the foundation.

A plague of all zealots and fools,
And each silly Protestant hater;
Better turn cat-in-pan and live like a man
Than be hang'd and die like a traitor.

Traditionally this piece has been assigned to the year 1676 because of its subtitle as published in *A Choice Compendium* in 1681: "A catch made in time of Parliament, 1676."[5] But there was neither a Jesuit plot nor a meeting of Parliament in 1676, Charles II having prorogued that body on 22 November 1675, not to call it again until 16 February 1677.[6] However, the parliamentary session alluded to in this catch may well have been that which began on 15 January 1678, or perhaps that of 21 October 1678, when Oates and Tonge were summoned to appear to substantiate the strange story they were spreading. Furthermore, it was about this time, according to Maitland,[7] that Charles II informed Parliament of the plot, whereupon Parliament "unanimously addressed His Majesty for removing all popish recusants out of the cities of London and Westminster."[8]

In such times even the anthem was not considered too sacred for enlistment in the royal cause. Under the king's patronage, this traditional English form had regained its earlier preeminence in the Anglican Liturgy. To Evelyn's disgust[9] and to Pepys's delight,[10] Charles had openly encouraged the production of anthems conceived in the style of the continental Counter-Reformation motet. From the very beginning of his reign, composers such as Captain Henry Cooke, Pelham Humfrey, and Matthew Locke had pleased both royal and public audiences by introducing into their anthems secular or even operatic features. The introduction of instrumental symphonies and ritornelli, the emphasis on soloists and solo vocal ensembles, contrasted with "full" and choral passages, and, particularly, the recitative-like affective style that became the norm—all these reminded contemporary listeners of the theater.[11] All these features increased the popularity of the anthem, at the same time widening its audience and insuring its effectiveness as a means for popularizing the court position. Faced with solid antagonism, even hostility, in Parliament, and beleaguered by the harsh budgetary policy of the Whig faction, Charles's political situation was such that he could not afford to overlook any opportunity to improve it.

Once again the English anthem, along with other Anglican forms, began to flourish, bringing even greater variety and virtuosity into play than in Elizabethan and Jacobean times. Just after the Restoration, while the ravages wrought during the Interregnum were to be repaired in English musical institutions, anthems and other service music by Tudor and early Stuart composers were revived. But very soon after the Restoration, composers like those named above set to work in earnest to reestablish English church music in something like its former glory.

As in earlier periods the choice of texts was dictated always by usage, which required certain psalms, hymns, and canticles for specific seasons. Within this "proper" repertory, there was scarcely any opportunity for topical allusion, although occasionally, by coincidence, a current event would run parallel to biblical narrative in a manner suitable for representation in an anthem. In such cases, it was possible to claim divine sanction for this or that political position on the basis of the biblical parallel.

At the same time, it should be pointed out that the Restoration anthem was not kept in a liturgical straightjacket, but rather was used as a vehicle for popularizing certain facets of state policy. With ceremonial anthems, whether royal or not, there was a great deal more scope for such usage. Freed from liturgical restrictions, composers could select and edit biblical texts according to the ends to be achieved. Sagacious politician that he was, Charles II did not neglect such opportunities to employ the anthem for communications that nowadays might be called propagandistic. Hence the Restoration anthem frequently represented Tory policy, and texts often were selected or edited so that they clearly reflected the Whig-Tory conflict. London was the main arena for political action, and it was for this arena that the topical anthem was called into service. Church authorities of Tory persuasion were convinced that such means furthered the ends of a divinely ordained monarch, and they suffered no qualms about misuse of Holy Scripture.

As a limited, though not like his father, a closely guarded monarch, Charles II needed to make use of every resource at his disposal to bolster the court's position. And if the texts prepared were always anti-Whig, what of that? He who paid the fiddler—or at least who had promised to pay—had the right to call the tune. Thus the Restoration anthem should be regarded as one of the most important musical ex-

Titus Tell-Troth:

OR,

The PLOT-FOUNDER Confounded.

A Pleasant New SONG. To the Tune of, *Hail to the Myrtle Shades.*

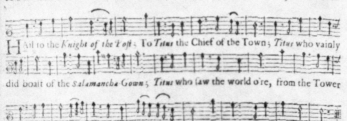

Hail to the *Knight of the Post*; To *Titus* the Chief of the Town; *Titus* who vainly did boast of the *Salamancha-Gown*; *Titus* who saw the world o're, from the Tower of *Valadolid*, Yet stood in the *White-horse* Door, and swore to it, like the *Creed.*

[2]
Titus at *Watton* in *May*,
 To *Titus* at *Islington*;
And *Titus* the self same day,
 Both Here and There again.
Titus who ever swore *Truth*,
 His politick *Plots* to maintain,
And never yet bawk'd an *Oath*,
 When call'd to the *Test* again.

[3]
Then *Titus* was Meekest of all,
 When *Never a Peny in's Purse,*
And oft did on *Pickering* call,
 His Charity to Imburse.
But when He swore *Damnable Oaths*,
 And *Lying* esteemed no Sin,
Then *Titus* was *One* of those
 Whom the *Devil* had entred in.

[4]
Then *Titus* the Frown of Heav'n,
 And *Titus* a Plague upon Earth;
Titus who'l ne'r be *Forgiven,*
 Curs'd from his *Fatal Birth*;
Titus the *Curse* and the *Doom*
 Of the Rich and the Poor Man too;
Oh *Titus*, thou *Shred of a Loom, Son of a Sh*
 What a plague dost thou mean to do?

[5]
Titus an *Orthodox Beast*,
 And *Titus* a *Presbyter Tall*;
Titus a *Popish Priest*,
 And *Titus* the shame of all;

Titus who ne'r had the skill
 The Wise with his *Plots* to deceive;
But *Titus* whose *Tongue* can kill;
 Whom Nature has made a Slave.

[6]
Titus the Light of the Town,
 Where *Zealots* and *Whigs* do resort;
Titus the Shame of the *Gown,*
 And *Titus* the Scorn of the *Court*;
Titus who Spew'd out the *Truth,*
 To Swallow the *Covenant*;
Yet never blush'd at an *Oath.*
 Whom *Lying* has made a *Saint.*

[7]
Yet *Titus* believed cou'd be
 Against any *Popish Lord*;
Whilst still against *S——y*
 The *Witness* and *Truth*'s abhorr'd;
So *Titus* got Credit and Gold
 For *Lying*, nor thought it a Sin;
But against *Dissenters* bold
 The *Truth* is not worth a pin.

[8]
Thus *Titus* Swore on apace,
 'Gainst those whom he never did see;
Yet *Titus* with brazen Face
 Wou'd our *Preserver* be.
But as *Titus* the foremost in Trust
 Discover'd this *Mystery*:
May *Titus* so be the *First*
 That leads to the *Triple-Tree.*

LONDON: Printed for *ALLEN BANKS*, 1682.

PLATE 11. "Titus Tell-Troth: or, The Plot-Founder Confounded" (British Museum)

PLATE 12. "The Cabal," ca. 1675. J. B. Medina (Nostell Priory)

pressions of post-Restoration society, especially during the reigns of
the last two Stuart monarchs. The importance of music lovers of this
part of the church service is underlined by many an entry in Pepys's
Diary, such as the following: "To my Lord, and with him to Whitehall
Chapel. . . . After sermon, a brave anthem of Captain Cooke's, which
he himself sung, and the King was well pleased with it."[12]

Like the court ode, the anthem was part of King Charles's public
relations activities. When it was an instrumentally accompanied anthem, there was really little difference between the two forms, musically speaking. At first the church's own annual cycle provided the occasions for which most anthems were written. But as the tradition
developed, it became more and more the custom for composers to find,
or even edit, biblical texts to fit occasions of state, particularly when
the sermon and anthem were part of a composite festive ceremony beginning in the church and ending in a neighboring banquet hall.[13]

Often a guild, society, or business fraternity sponsored such events, their members seeing no harm in mixing business with pleasure, with a dash of religion as well. Such a mixture was viable as long as one remembered that "Trade is one thing, religion another,"[14] such reminder being necessary if all elements were to be effective. As Tawney has pointed out in *Religion and the Rise of Capitalism*, such thinking was an important part of the whole Fabian transition from a Catholic aristocracy to a Protestant parliamentary monarchy, which took place in England between 1540 and 1688.[15]

As one of the most important musical genres of the Restoration, the anthem clearly reflected the conflict between two main factions, the Whigs and Tories.[16] Since Restoration anthem composers drew almost exclusively upon the *Book of Common Prayer* for texts,[17] opportunities for topical allusion would seem to have been limited. However, then as now, it was not only the devil who could quote scripture to his own ends; many of the situations described in the Psalms, as elsewhere in the Old Testament, could be adapted to reflect current events by a clever historiographer or court poet.[18]

Rebellious Puritans or a monarch on a tottering throne also could adapt scripture to their needs; witness the following exchange between Charles I and the Scottish preacher who, having reproached the king for his misgovernment, ordered that the congregation sing "Why dost thou, tyrant, boast thyself, thy wicked deeds to praise?". Thereupon, the king stood up and called for the psalm "Have mercy, Lord, on me I pray, for men would me devour." The congregation showed sympathy for the king by singing the latter.[19] If an embattled monarch could thus so adroitly extemporize from scripture, what wonder that Charles II, with a whole covey of divines, court poets, historiographers, and composers on hand would find means to use the anthem as a kind of sacred broadside to support his own policies and position.

Like many other composers at the post-Restoration court, Purcell set to music the Third Collect in the annual service of commemoration of the martyrdom of Charles I. If the singular musical expression he achieved in this anthem be a reliable guide to his feelings, Purcell was surely a Loyalist. There is no trace of the perfunctory approach to this text so often found in contemporary settings. Rather the music achieves a profound expression of poignant regret, which is most fitting for the sentiments expressed in the text:

> Turn Thou us, O good Lord, and so shall we be turned;
> Be favorable, O Lord, to Thy people which turn to Thee
> In weeping, fasting and praying.

For Thou art a merciful God, full of compassion,
Long suff'ring and of great pity. Thou sparest
When we deserve punishment, and in wrath thinkest upon mercy.

Spare Thy people, good Lord; spare them and let not
Thine inheritance be brought to confusion.
Hear us, O Lord, for Thy mercy is great,
And after the multitude of Thy mercies, look upon us.[20]

This text, incidentally, also appears as the penultimate prayer in the commination service, as set down in the *Book of Common Prayer*. Its association with established ritual no doubt held special meaning for those Anglicans especially sympathetic to the martyred king.

Young Henry Purcell composed his earliest anthem, "Lord, Who Can Tell" (Psalm 19:12–14)[21] some time in 1678. The text is prescribed for Christmas Day and also designated to be read regularly at Morning Prayer on the fourth day of each month. The meditative, melancholy mood of the verses Purcell selected would be incompatible with the joyousness of Christmas season. Probably the text was chosen for a special event—possibly for Sunday, 4 April, when the *London Gazette* proclaimed a general fast.

During the 1679–80 season, Purcell set another anthem suitable to the annual commemoration of Charles I's martyrdom:

Who hath believed our report?
And to whom is the arm of the Lord reveal'd?
He is despised and rejected of men,
A man of sorrow and acquainted with griefs;
And we hid as it were our faces from him;
He was despised, and we esteem'd Him not.
Surely He hath borne our griefs and carried our sorrows;
Yet did we esteem Him stricken and smitten of God, and afflicted.
But He was wounded for our transgressions,
He was bruised for our iniquities:
The chastisement of our peace was upon Him,
And with his stripes we are healed . . .
He is brought as a lamb to the slaughter,
And as a sheep before her shearers, dumb;
So op'neth He not his mouth. He was taken from prison to judgement:
Who shall declare His generation? For He was cut off out of the
Land of the living: For the transgressions of my people was He
    stricken.
All we like sheep have gone astray; We have turn'd ev'ry one to his own
    way;
And the Lord hath laid on Him the iniquity of us all.[22]

With the return of Charles II, who soon established a resplendent, though not unrestricted monarchy, the Anglican anthem was also restored but in entirely new guise. Its new manner, essentially secular in nature, reflected the king's experiences with the latest theatrical styles of church music as performed at Versailles, Paris, and elsewhere on the Continent where Jean-Baptiste Lully's manner prevailed. Very likely, the Lullian style along with Monteverdian second practice would have found its way into English musical life without Charles II's assistance. But the king's enthusiasm for the new and lively French music undoubtedly encouraged and quickened the process.

The widely popular works of the Gabrielis, of Monteverdi, and of Carissimi did not truly arrive in England until near the end of the century. At that time, they were very quickly accepted and became quite popular, as we have seen. Despite scruples of men like Evelyn and Thomas Mace, the new secular anthem, with its dramatic vocal accents and theatrical ritornelli and accompaniments, had come to England to stay. As in counter-Reformation centers, it was not that the church was invaded, but rather that it opened its doors to the secular world around it, on premises not unlike those advanced by Ignatius Loyola more than a century earlier.

Purcell had been busy early in 1679 composing a trial piece for John Gostling, the celebrated bass who at that time was still a singer at Canterbury Cathedral, as we know from the following letter written by his uncle Thomas Purcell:

> This for Mr John Gostling, Chanter of the choir of Canterbury Cathedral. London the 8th of February 1678/9.
> Sir,
> I have received the favour of yours of the 4th with the enclosed for my son Henry: I am sorry we are like to be without you so long as yours mentions: but 'tis very likely you may have a summons to appear among us sooner than you imagine: for my son is composing wherein you will be chiefly concerned. However, your occasions and ties where you are must be considered and your conveniences ever complied withall: in the meantime assure yourself I shall be careful of your concerns here by minding and refreshing our master's memory of his gracious promise when there is occasion. My wife returns thanks for the compliment with her service: and pray you give both our respects and humble services to Dr. Belk and his Lady, and believe ever that I am, Sir, your affectionate servant,
>
> T. Purcell
>
> Dr Perce is in town but I have not seen him since. I have performed your compliments to Dr. Blow, Will Turner, etc.
> F faut: and E lamy are preparing for you.[23]

Several new points of interest emerge from this letter, apart from the matter of Purcell's parentage as discussed above. What could Purcell have been composing wherein Gostling would be chiefly concerned? The wording leads us to believe that he was occupied with a sacred piece for bass solo. Presumably the good offices hinted at by Thomas Purcell had to do with Gostling's forthcoming appointment to the Chapel Royal, which he actually received before the month was out.[24] Although the letter does not mention the piece young Purcell was writing, it scarcely can have been other than his early solo anthem "I Will Love Thee, O Lord."[25] The careful selection of verses renders this a topical anthem for bass solo and chorus, precisely relevant to Charles II's predicament in August 1679. Just then the anti-Monmouth party had prevailed upon him to recall his brother, James, duke of York, from exile in Brussels, precipitating the first of Monmouth's rash conspiracies. The dynastic situation was so parallel to that between King David and his son Absalom as to require no editing, other than the selection mentioned above, to provide a very relevant corollary to the king's troubles and Monmouth's disgrace at the end of November. The verses selected, being numbers 1 through 6 and 16 through 18, reinforced the picture of King David, alias Charles II, as a lone and defenseless individual surrounded by vicious enemies. To avoid the "snares of death" that had been laid for him, his only recourse was to rely on divine protection according to his faith. The omission of all verses relating to King David's power and vengeance is as significant to the study of politics *temps* Charles II as is Purcell's setting of many of the omitted verses to the same science *temps* William III. In composing these verses for the anthem "The Way of God Is an Undefiled Way," Purcell celebrated the warlike figure of William III, amidst all his victories on various fields.[26]

To demonstrate that this kind of topicality is not being read into the texts, as it were, we need merely turn to John Dryden's then anonymous *Absalom and Achitophel*, where precisely the same parallel extends to cover all the main figures on England's political scene at that time. Dryden's political allegory is fully clarified by copious marginal notes in the hand of Narcissus Luttrell, court historiographer to Charles II,[27] which notes identify all the principal participants in England's political life in those times. Charles II is identified as King David, numerous progeny and all; Monmouth is represented as Absalom; Shaftesbury as Achitophel; the duke of Buckingham as Zimri; Titus Oates as Corah; and the duchess of Portsmouth as Bathsheba. Dryden's translation of the biblical history to seventeenth-century London could not have been clearer or more appropriate; and the same may be said of Purcell's anthem text, a point further strengthened by a contemporary paraphrase of Psalm 3, published ca. 1681.[28] Here are J. W. Ebsworth's introductory remarks and a few verses of the paraphrase:

> We believe that this undated Paraphrase of "A Psalm of David, when he fled from Absalom his son . . ." made its appearance before the excitement of Monmouth's rash attempt at insurrection, in the summer of 1685; certainly before Monmouth was butchered on the scaffold. The probable date seems to be between July, 1681, when Shaftesbury was a second time committed to the Tower, and the close of that year. Dryden's "Absalom and Achitophel" appeared anonymously on the 17th November, and was republished in the following month. The whole subject of the rebellion of Absalom against David, even before Dryden's poem was written, was familiarly compared with the disaffection of Monmouth against his father and his father's brother;[29]

> A Paraphrase on the Third Psalm, Entitled a Psalm
> of David, when he had fled from Absalom his son.
> Eternal Monarch, you who are
> The shield of injured *Kings*, and bear
> For all *Crown'd* Heads more than a *Common Care.*
> Behold how they increase who joyn
> To ruin me, how they combine
> 'Gainst Law Paternal, Regal and Divine,

John Dryden had painful cause to recall his use of these parallels at the end of the year, as we know from Anthony à Wood's memorandum for 16 December 1679 (vol. 2, 473): "John Dreyden the poet being at Will's Coffee House in Covent Garden was about 8 at night soundly cudgell'd by 3 men. The reason, as 'tis supposed, because he has reflected on certain persons in his 'Essay on the Satyr'—rather in 'Absalom and Achitophel'" (see also Luttrell, vol. 1, 30, where the duchess of Portsmouth is implicated).

About this time, Henry Purcell also set the above-mentioned Psalm 3 in its Latin version, "Jehovah, quam multi sunt hostes."[30] Whatever its possible relationship to religious and political life in the early 1680s, this motet stands as one of the most dramatic compositions of Purcell's entire career. Without documentation, it cannot be related to the climactic struggle between Whig and Tory in specific instance. But given the wide identification of Charles II as King David, and given the topical commentary on Psalm 3, there is little doubt that the work is timely. Everyone at court was aware of Charles II's difficulties and was caught up, willy-nilly, in the fray. Its Latin text, moreover, identifies the work as suitable to the Tory, High Anglican party.

Ostensibly, the controversy was political, since it was the royal succession at stake. The basic issues were both dynastic and religious, and the outcome in every instance depended on whether a Protestant or a pro-Catholic party gained supremacy.[31] Economically the conflict was between ancient landed aristocracy and the rising class of citizen shop-keepers. Finally, the conventional wisdom of the conservatives was pitted against the newly forming views and opinions of those of more liberal persuasion, to borrow an antithesis from Galbraith.[32] All these diametric oppositions are relevant to the topic at hand, for they clearly influenced general musical styles in England, but are reflected in texts of various other English anthems, as well as in those of birthday songs and welcome odes. Stage plays, dynastic operas, along with catches, songs, and other forms also reflect the highly polarized political situation between the parties. Similar topicality also may be seen in contemporary paintings, such as Verrio's "Julian Apostate," which though relating to the time of William and Mary, reveals clearly that the arts were drawn into the political conflict quite freely.[33]

In the winter of 1678, Oates and Tonge set in motion a wave of fear across the nation, producing reactions that were to make all kinds of difficulties for papists, as for the plans and ambitions of James, duke of York. Meanwhile, several important developments in public concert life had gotten underway. John Banister, who had done so much to launch the new tradition in London some six years earlier, and who in the period following his disgrace at court had had to turn to private teaching, now was flourishing. Diaries, journals, and newspapers refer constantly to numerous concerts and "music-meetings" for which he was responsible.[34]

On 18 November 1678, Banister moved his concerts to the Music School in Essex Buildings, the Strand. There he gave, on 22 November, a concert that may have been one of the earliest St. Cecilia celebrations in London: "On Thursday [*sic*] next, the 22nd of this instant November, at the Music School in Essex Buildings, over against St. Clements Church in the Strand, will be continued a consort of vocal and instrumental music, beginning at five of the clock every evening. Composed by Mr. John Bannister."[35] However, poor Banister did not live to repeat the event as an annual observation, for he died the following third of October.[36] His death came shortly after he had returned from the Continent, where he had gone on six months' leave beginning 23 May.[37] Historically his most significant achievement was that of having established the self-sustaining public concert of music played for its own sake and not just as an adjunct of religious service, courtly politics, or dramatic spectacle. The ideal of absolute music, presented as noble, serious entertainment, which Voltaire was to cite three quarters of a century later, found here an important beginning.[38]

Already another weekly concert series had begun in July the previous year in Clerkenwell Street, where Thomas Britton plied his trade "as small coals man." In the course of thirty-six years, this series became one of the most important features of London's musical life. Distinguished participants included the younger John Banister, son of the musician discussed above, Roger L'Estrange, Dr. Pepusch, Handel, John Hughs, Ned Ward, and various members of the nobility.[39] There is no actual evidence that Purcell attended any of these concerts in person; but certainly his music was heard there, for many of his pieces are to be found in autograph copy by Thomas Britton in a manuscript now in the British Library.[40] It would be odd, indeed, if Purcell had not attended any of these, or other early public concerts where his chamber works were frequently performed, though written for the court, where he had succeeded Matthew Locke as composer to the violins.[41] In view of Charles II's confessed dislike for the fantasia, it is unlikely that these little works were played frequently at court. For this we have Roger North's own testimony:

> King Charles the Second was a professed lover of musick, but of this kind only (i.e. French), and had an utter detestation of Fancys, and the less for a successless entertainment of that kind given him by Secretary Williamson, after which the Secretary had no peace, for the King (as his way was) could not forbear whetting his wit upon the subject of the fancy-musick, and its patron the Secretary. And he would not allow the matter to be disputed upon the point of meliority, but run all down by saying *Have not I ears?*[42]

Several of Purcell's songs, which appeared in print about this time, also were heard at concerts such as these. John Playford's *Second Book of Choice Ayres and Songs* included four of Purcell's light, amorous lyrics, along with an elegy "to his worthy friend, Matthew Locke" ("What Hope for Us Remains").[43] The title page for this collection, aside from confirming Purcell's new dignity as a gentleman of His Majesty's Music, indicated that these songs were "Sung at Court and the Public Theatres," being "the choicest new-mode songs . . . by several eminent masters of His Majesty's music." Therefore Purcell's music for *Theodosius*,[44] printed the following year, may not have represented the first of his theatrical ventures, as Downes claimed.[45]

As composer to the king's violins, Purcell no doubt took notice of the "Order directed to Mr. Nicholas Staggins, master of His Majesty's music, that His Majesty's four-and-twenty violins should attend His Majesty every night that a play is acted at court," which came down from the lord chamberlain on 18 February 1679.[46] Again, Purcell would have been involved with the theater before 1680.

Meanwhile Charles II's political difficulties continued. Indeed, by the beginning of 1679 the meddling of Louis XIV's agents had produced new "popish plots," which were now being revealed almost daily. Accomplishing little but to strengthen Whig opposition produced such complexities that Charles II, who played his own double games both at home and abroad, must have had great difficulty in telling friend from foe. He must have been wryly amused by some of the lines in John Blow's ode to celebrate New Year's day, 1679:

> While swell'd with Ambition and Boundless desires
> To Empire a turbulent Monarch aspires.
> His force like a deluge no border could find
> Till you to Restrain his fierce Torrent Inclin'd.
> But as soon as your mighty Resistance he found
> Tho both potent and proud, he flew back to his bound,
> Thus your Lustre the Light of his Sound did outvie
> And gave his *Nec pluribus impar* the Lye. . . .[47]

Within a few weeks King Charles was driven to desperate remedies by Whig impeachments of Catholic peers and by trials and indictments of several in the court party. His coffers empty, he applied to Louis XIV for assistance, then announced on 24 January the dissolution of Parliament as of 30 January. Master strategist that he was, Charles II would not have overlooked the fact that that date also marked the annual observance of the martyrdom of King Charles I. Although he was to lose in the general elections that followed in March, he certainly had simplified the situation for the time being. He had also saved the necks of a few loyal followers who had been awaiting Parliamentary pleasure in the Tower, among them Danby.[48]

Despite these difficulties Charles II continued to take care of his musicians as well as he could. The best he could do for Grabu, it seems, was to grant him a pass to France for his wife and three children.[49] His other court musicians received their salaries and other emoluments somewhat more regularly than during the early part of his reign, but always long after they were due. For instance, on 8 April 1679, the Gentlemen and Children of the Chapel Royal, among them Daniel and Thomas Purcell, were paid "riding charges and other expenses in their attendance on his Majesty at Windsor for forty-four days, from 14 August to 26 September 1678."[50] There is no mention of Henry Purcell in the list, which presumably means that he did not leave Westminster that summer.

All this while the king's position had continually worsened. Later in April a new Parliament voted an Act of Attainder against Danby, and on the twenty-seventh, the House of Commons censured the duke of York for recusancy, even though he had left England on the fourth of the previous month.[51] Lesser Catholics at court must have found themselves in the predicament of Melker Gold, who, like Grabu, fled the country, as we know from the following petition:

> . . . as a trumpet in His Majesty's troop of Guards ever since His Majesty's happy Restoration till last November, when he was dismissed for being a Roman Catholic and having had no allowance since November, is become so very poor, he cannot go into Suabia [*sic*], his native country, without some relief; there is £75 due him out of the fee-farm rents, £60 upon the law bill, and half a year's salary out of the Treasury Chamber, being £30, and he prays his Majesty to allow him wherewith to carry him home. The petition is referred to the Duke of Monmouth, his just demands to be satisfied.[52]

Though defeat seemed inevitable if he did not take action, Charles II held his hand until 26 May, when at last he found it necessary to prorogue both houses.[53] During one of the hottest summers of recent memory, the court's position gradually improved. Monmouth won an important victory against the Scottish Covenanters at Boswell Bridge, and the Whig party began to lose some of the momentum that had brought it such impressive victories the previous spring. Toward the end of June, Charles II apparently felt the situation was under control, for he ordered his musicians to Windsor on 30 June.[54] The wave of consternation that swept the country when his life was despaired of on 23 August (after a nearly fatal attack of "ague")[55] gave him a vote of popular confidence as great as he might have wished for.

Fantasia Year

PURCELL'S APPOINTMENT IN 1679 as organist at Westminster Abbey (about Michaelmas, or shortly after) marked the end of his basic apprenticeship, even though he continued as unpaid assistant instrument-keeper and repairer until December of 1683, when Hingeston died. Purcell is supposed to have succeeded as keeper of organs and musician for the viol, but there are no official records to show evidence that he actually did so. At any rate, with this practical experience, along with his education under Humfrey, Blow, and Locke, Purcell had finished his formal musical training. His efforts to master all styles of music were to continue to the end of his life—as North so perceptively was to observe in discussing Purcell's importance in the history of English music—but henceforth he was to be his own teacher. "Then followed the *Circe* and *King Arthur* by the *Orpheus Britannicus* Mr. H. Purcell, who unhappily began to show his great skill before the reform of music *al Italiana* and while he was yet warm in the pursuit of it, died. But a greater musical genius England never had." [1]

North reveals remarkable perceptivity here, but his intimation that Purcell had failed seems untenable. True, Purcell did not succeed in establishing a viable English operatic tradition—in these terms, one that was both profitable and fashionable—and therefore failed, in much the same way that Handel was to fail in establishing Italian opera in London. But the creative efforts of men like these cannot be so crudely measured. Nor are the results of these efforts subject to laws of progress. Purcell's inspired fantasias of 1680 [2] qualify as masterworks as fully as do *Dido and Aeneas* [3] and "Hail, Bright Cecilia." [4] Essential differences lie in proportions and compositional techniques, but not in inspiration. Purcell's creative forge burned as intensely in 1680 as in 1695, however much he had learned about forms and styles in the intervening years. These finely wrought fantasias reveal unmistakably that Purcell had become a master, leaving behind him both apprenticeship and journeymanship.

Early in June of 1680, he undertook the Herculean task of reviving the English fancy, or fantasia, which, as we know from Charles II's antipathy, was not a popular musical form at the Stuart court, and was considered quite old fashioned among English musicians. Why he turned to this task or how and for whom these pieces were performed are questions that cannot be answered at this writing. All we know is that he completed the first seven four-part fantasias with remarkable quickness, and that he composed all the fantasias systematically, exploring new technical problems in each, much as Bach was to do nearly half a century later in the two- and three-part inventions.

Probably Purcell had found a quiet retreat at Windsor, where Charles II had set up court on 19 April.[5] There was more free time for everyone that summer, for the king traveled very frequently to London to keep an eye on Whig intrigues from the vantage point of Whitehall. Just after publicly declaring on 8 June that he had never married Lucy Walters, thus affixing the royal seal to Monmouth's bastardy and totally ignoring the contents of the little black box that was supposed to hold the marriage certificate, the king departed on a three-day progress to Whitehall with James, duke of York. Tory solidarity, at least among the legitimate Stuarts, was clear to all.[6]

Purcell must have made the most of his free time, witness the speed with which he turned out more fantasias thereafter. He celebrated Corpus Christi Thursday, 10 June, by finishing the first four-part fantasia in G-minor. By the end of the following week he had composed five more and before the month was out another three. In August Purcell composed two more, longer fantasias, to end a most productive summer indeed.

The immediate benefit of Purcell's concentration on instrumental music in the summer of 1680 is readily apparent in his first large instrumental and vocal composition, "Welcome, Vicegerent,"[7] an ode to welcome Charles II back to Whitehall on 9 September. The disparity between his assured writing for instruments and his less confident treatment of the voices reflects the technical advance his preoccupation with instrumental forms had produced. While the vocal passages cannot be described as unskillful, they do not reveal the sureness of touch that characterizes his intrumental writing at this time.

Purcell's connection with the stage, heretofore only hinted at in the title pages of various song collections, also is definitely established for 1680, when he composed a masque scene and several act-songs for Nathaniel Lee's *Theodosius*. Here is vocal writing worthy of a master, which provides a hint as to how quickly Purcell was developing. Undoubtedly he had undertaken the new commission by summer's end, or shortly thereafter, for Lee's play was produced at Dorset Garden Theatre at least as early as October 1680, and published, with Purcell's music, very shortly thereafter. It was entered into the *Term Catalogues* for November.

Whatever the actual date of performance,[8] there can be no doubt that Purcell made his mark at the time of his introduction to London's public as a theatrical composer. Downes's entry on the event makes this abundantly clear: "All the parts in't being perfectly performed with several entertainments of singing; composed by the famous master, Mr. Henry Purcell (being the first he e'er composed for the stage) made it a living and gainful play to the company: the Court, especially the ladies, by their daily charming presence, gave it real encouragement."[9]

Three of the songs from *Theodosius*, namely, "Now the fight's done," "Hail to the myrtle shades," and "Ah! Cruel bloody fate," appeared in Playford's *Choice Ayres and Songs . . . Third Book*, 1681, which was ready for publication on 2 November 1680, although not advertised in the *London Gazette* until 16 December 1680. In fact, it was not published until the following year, as the epistle "To All Lovers of Music" explains. For the light it sheds on English song-composition at the outset of Purcell's career, this epistle is worth quoting in full:

> GENTLEMEN, This third book or collection of new ayres and songs had come to your hands some months sooner, had I not been prevented by long sickness; however I hope it will not now be unwelcome. I need not here commend the excellency of their composition, the ingenious author's names being printed with them, who are men that understand to make English words speak their true and genuine sense both in good humour and ayre; which can never be performed by either Italian or French, they not so well understanding the properties of our speech. I have seen lately published a large volume of English songs composed by an Italian master, who has lived here in England many years; I confess he is a very able master, but being not perfect in the true idiom of our language, you will find the air of his music so much after his country-mode, that it would suit far better with Italian than English words. But I shall forbear to censure his work, leaving it to the verdict of better musical judgments; only I think him very disingenious [*sic*] and much to blame, to endeavour to raise a reputation to himself and book, by disparaging and undervaluing most of the best English masters and professors of music. I am sorry it is (in this age) so much the vanity of some of our English gentry to admire that in a foreigner, which they either slight or take little notice of in one of their own nation; for I am sure that our English masters in music (either for vocal or instrumental music) are not in skill and judgement inferior to any foreigners whatsoever, the same rules in this

science being generally used all over Europe. But I have too far digressed, and therefore beg your pardon. This book being bound up with the two others formerly published, will make a complete volume. To conclude, I desire you to think, that I have herein as much studied your satisfaction as my own interest, and kindly to receive this collection, from GENTLE-MEN, Your Hearty Servant, JOHN PLAYFORD. (From my house in Arundel-Street, near the Thames side, Novemb. 2 1680.)

Here Playford referred to the collection of *Songs Set by Signior Pietro Reggio* advertised in the *London Gazette* for 11 March and again on 26 July and 9 December 1680. Reggio had dedicated his forty-six songs to the king, including among them a setting of "Arise Ye Subterranean Winds" for Shadwell's "operatic" adaptation of Shakespeare's *The Tempest*, which he had contributed to the original production in April 1674.[10] Other texts Purcell also was later to set include "She Loves and She Confesses Too" and "See Where She Sits."[11] Reggio's compositions to these texts are dull, worthy of neither the poet's nor the printer's arts, which are shown to such good advantage in the collection. Purcell's deliberate improvement of Reggio's originals cannot be looked upon as plagiarisms. Rather they should be seen as demonstrations of what might be done with these lovely and imaginative texts by a composer more sensitive to subtleties of the English language than Reggio.

In the passage quoted above, Playford touched upon a more serious problem, however, in his statements concerning the position of English masters vis-à-vis foreign competitors, who flocked to London throughout the seventeenth century. In speaking of its being the "vanity of some of our English gentry to admire that in a foreigner which they either slight or take little notice of in one of their own nation," Playford was but adding his own arguments for preferment of the native art to those of such men as Henry Lawes, Matthew Locke, Pelham Humfrey, and John Banister. Already the strength of the new English Baroque idiom had been established—a strength for which, be it noted, England had drawn upon her own magnificent polyphonic traditions. There wanted only a champion of Purcell's stature to demonstrate the essential strength of that English tradition.

Meanwhile Purcell had married. Again, as at so many important junctures in Purcell's life, the lack of any solid documentary evidence beclouds the event. The baptismal registers of All Hallows, London Wall reveal that one Henry, son of Henry and Frances Purcell, was baptized there on 9 July 1681, to be buried in the churchyard of the same parish a little more than a week later, on 18 July.[12] First of all, the identity of the two parents must be established. Is it possible to make certain that the composer Henry Purcell was indeed the man named here? Unfortunately not. However, it is significant that of the four Henry Purcells whom the records show to have been living in London or its environs at this time,[13] no other had a wife named Frances or seems to fit this particular situation in other ways. Hence it is quite probable, though not absolutely certain, that it is the composer who is named here. Second, it will be important to find an explanation for Purcell's having had a child christened at All Hallows, London Wall.

If Henry Purcell, musician, was the father of the child recorded, then his marriage must be moved back from the accepted date (1681)[14] by a year. Imperfect housing records do not help a great deal here, except in a negative way. For 1680–81 Purcell is not recorded in the rate-books as being a resident of St. Margaret's Parish, Westminster, where he apparently lived in 1682,[15] as John Baptista Purcell's birth is recorded in the Westminster Abbey accounts for that year. However, Purcell's name does appear in a list of "Persons entered after the assessment was made" (1681), where his payment of eight shillings is recorded. And for December 1682, there is an actual receipt for a rental allowance for the amount of forty shillings, signed by Purcell himself, as may be seen in plate 15, which reads: "December the 22^d 1682/ Rec^d then of Dr Onely, Treasurer, the sum of forty shillings being in full for a Quarters Rent due at Xmas. in lieu of a House, I say rec^d by me/ Henry Purcell."

Even the identification of Frances Peters as his wife is open to question. Arguing from evidence suggested by the Christian names of Purcell's second son, Westrup makes a good case for considering John Baptist Peters as Henry Purcell's father-in-law.[16] The case is further strengthened by the recent discovery of a photograph of an impaled coat-of-arms representing the Purcell and Peters family crests together.[17] The device suggests that the Purcell and Peters families were joined through the marriage of Henry and Frances. And indeed the photograph seems authentic.[18] However, until the original from which this was made can be found, it cannot be accepted as conclusive proof of anything. Finally, the baptism of Mary-Peters Purcell, daughter of Henry and Frances, at Westminster Abbey on 10 December 1693 adds yet further evidence favoring the hypothesis that Frances was a member of the Peters family.[19]

One further consideration remains: If the infant Henry Purcell was the first-born child of Henry and Frances, a possibility even more likely when it is remembered that most first-born sons were given their fathers' Christian names, then conventional reckoning back would estab-

PLATE 13. Putative impaled coat of arms for Henry Purcell and Frances (?) Peters. Origin unknown (Keeper of the Muniments and Library, Westminster Abbey)

lish the wedding day about 10 September 1680. This would provide yet another possible explanation for Purcell's cryptic entry in the Fitzwilliam Museum autograph, "God bless Mr. Henry Purcell / 1682 September the 10th."

If Mrs. Purcell was indeed Frances Peters before the wedding, and if "Beati omnes" [20] was indeed a wedding anthem, the Latin text can now be explained on new grounds. The Peterses were a famous family of London Catholics, and nothing would have been more natural than for the text of a wedding piece to have been written in Latin. Furthermore, the lighter, though very musical, manner of the piece might well be explained by the fact that Purcell had dashed it off hastily just before the ceremony. [21]

Another composition occupying Purcell's attention about this time

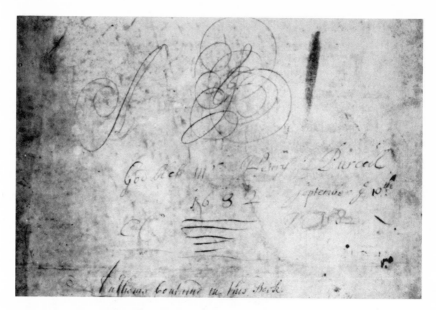

PLATE 14. "God bless Mr. Henry Purcell / 1682 September the 10th."
MS. 88 (autograph) flyleaf (Fitzwilliam Museum Library, Cambridge)

(as may be seen from its position in the same autograph)[22] may also have had topical associations. The somber hymn "Ah! Few and Full of Sorrows"[23] has for its text George Sandys's paraphrase of Job 14:1, that is, the funeral sentence "Man that is born of a woman." For mournful expressivity it bears comparison with the funeral sentences themselves.[24]

Although the work also survives only in fragmentary form, enough has been preserved to show that Purcell had conceived it as a composition of major importance—something, perhaps, designed as part of a memorial service for the death of some important person. If, as its position in the autograph suggests, it was written very late in 1680, no other event would have been so much in the minds of those at court as the funeral of William Howard, Viscount Stafford, which followed within three short weeks his unjust attainder in a trial that mocked justice. Charles, prevented from rescuing Stafford by his own policy of noninterference with the law, would have known no restraint in publicly mourning for him in commissioning such a work. And Purcell, a staunch friend of the Howard family, would have written music for the occasion, inspired by his own personal feelings, as well as by loyalty to the court.

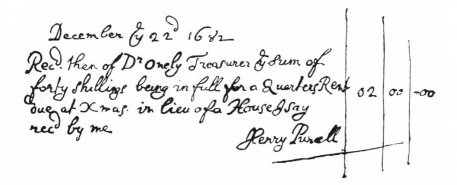

PLATE 15. Receipt for a rental allowance, signed by Henry Purcell. This document, which apparently has been lost, was reproduced in Bridge's "Purcell's Birthplace and Residences," p. 734.

Stafford's trial had another, less hypothetical, connection with Purcell's musical activity. On 11 December Nahum Tate's adaptation of Shakespeare's *Richard II* (with at least one song by Purcell, and perhaps some instrumental music) opened at the Theatre Royal, in Drury Lane.[25] Three days later, on the fourteenth, it was suppressed for political reasons—reasons undoubtedly connected with the trial of Stafford and with Shaftesbury's and Monmouth's truculent show of confidence and strength about town.[26] The year ended ignominiously for Charles II and his court.

It was an article of faith with Charles, however, not to allow political misfortune to dampen the pleasures of his *amour courtois*, a charmed circle, as it were, shut off from the harsh realities of the struggle for political power raging in the outside world. But even so, a major issue had arisen here also, and in this demimonde, the king's sybaritic courtiers drew up to do battle, no quarter asked or given, with no less determination than that shown by Whig and Tory protagonists. The issue revolved around Charles II's choice of the one to serve as chiefest of his amours. As always, Cupid was on the side of ampler charms,

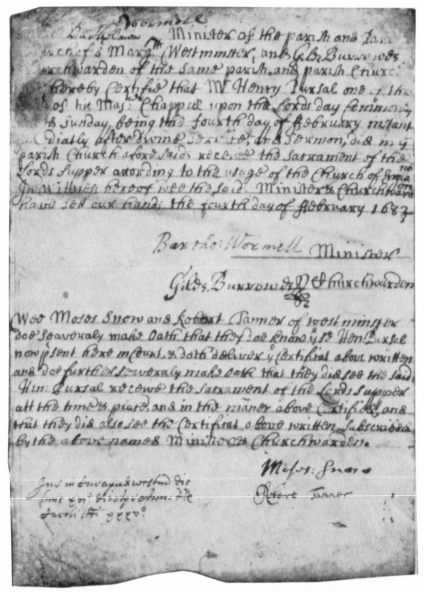

PLATE 16. Sacrament certificate, 4 February 1682/3 (Middlesex County
Records Office)

PLATE 17. Mary (Moll) Davis (National Portrait Gallery)

which alliance Charles straightforwardly acknowledged by abandoning Catherine of Braganza for the duchess of Portsmouth.[27]

Perhaps it was some such event as this that occasioned a courtly wag (who was sharp-witted enough to remain anonymous) to pen the words of a catch, "A Farewell to Wives," that Purcell set about this time:

Once in our lives
Let us drink to our wives. . . .[28]
(italics mine)

A much more complex musical event, John Blow's *Venus and Adonis* (composed ca. 1682), quite apart from its musical significance as the first English opera, provides interesting commentary on Charles II's charming "Court of Love." Chief characters in the masque were Venus, played by Mrs. Mary ("Moll") Davis, and Cupid, played by Lady Mary Tudor, her daughter by Charles II. "Moll" Davis had joined the ranks of Charles II's mistresses shortly after he had heard her singing on stage "My Lodging, It Is on the Cold Ground." Thereupon, the king "Rais'd her from her Bed on the Cold Ground to a Bed Royal," as Pepys wryly observed. As Charles II's mistress, Moll Davis had danced and sung in John Crowne's *Calisto* in 1675 and in various other pieces before appearing, together with her daughter, in *Venus and Adonis*. The libretto of the latter reflects everywhere the playfully amorous aura of Charles II's court, particularly in such lines as the following quaintly musical "spelling bee," sung by Cupid and a little band of followers at the beginning of Act 2. The scene begins as a dialogue between Cupid and his mother, Venus, before a band of little Cupids:

CUPID: You place with such delightful care
         The fetters which your lovers wear
         None can be weary to obey
         When you their eager wishes bless. (*pointing to little Cupids:*)
         The crowding Joys each other press
         And round you smiling Cupids play;
VENUS: Flattering boy, hast thou been reading thy lessons
         Thy lessons and refined arts—
         By which thou may'st set a-bleeding
         A thousand, thousand tender hearts?
CUPID: Yes, but mother, teach me to destroy
         All such as scorn your wanton boy.
VENUS: Fit well your arrows when you strike
         And choose for all what each may like
         But make some love, they know not why,
         And for the ugly and ill-humour'd die.
         Such as scorn Love's fire,
         Force them to admire.
CUPID: The insolent, the arrogant (*echoed by Little Cupids*)
         The M.E.R. Mer: C.E. Ce: Merce: (*echoed by Little Cupids*)
         N.A. Na R.Y. Ry, The mercenary (*echoed by Little Cupids*)
         The vain and silly. (*echoed by Little Cupids*)

The jealous and uneasy, (*echoed by Little Cupids*)
All, all such as tease ye. (*echoed by Little Cupids*)
Choose for the formal fool
Who scorns Love's mighty school,
One that delights in secret glances
And a great reader of romances.
For him that's faithless, wild and gay,
Who with Love's pain does only play,
Take some affected, wanton she (*echoed by Little Cupids*)
As faithless and as wild as he. (*echoed by Little Cupids*)[29]

Meanwhile, in less refined political spheres, the king's parliamentary opponents under Shaftesbury's leadership now went from strength to strength. Charles II, however, was not one to back down before a show of force. The text of Blow's New Year's ode for 1681, "Great Sir, the Joy of All Our Hearts," revealed the king's position in as favorable a light as possible, dwelling more particularly, it will be noticed, upon foreign than on domestic affairs:

Then Long may he Live and Long may he Reign
By whom we are blest with so happy a Chain.
By whose prudent conduct and peaceable Care
Our fortunate Isle thus flourishes
While our Neighbours are Left to the fortune of War. . . .

Your Friends unite, your Foes asunder Break;
For now Commences under Charles the Great
The Year of Wonder
Of this the Lucky Omen we
Receiv'd from that most happy Tree. . . .[30]

Despite the House of Commons's public resolution that whoever should advise a prorogation was a "betrayer of the kingdom, a promoter of Popery and a pensioner of France,"[31] Charles II gave orders on 10 January 1681 for the prorogation of a "fiery, eager and high-flying Parliament"[32] and had these carried out a week later, ordering it to reassemble at Oxford—still a Tory stronghold—on the twenty-first.[33] For professional musicians all this must have brought troubling reminders of 1641, when most of their predecessors had lost their livelihoods, especially when Charles II finally found it necessary to retrench by cutting down the salaries of those who served him at court. Worse still, he had to urge strict economy upon members of the royal family,[34] which meant, of course, that he was having the worst of it in both worlds.

On 30 January the court and the royal family, it may be stated with some certainty, turned their attention from all such pursuits, weighty or frivolous, to commemorate the martyrdom of the king's father. Falling as it did on a Sunday (Septuagesima), the occasion was no doubt celebrated with double solemnity. None of Purcell's works has been identified with the celebration, but both the text and the musical style of "Who Hath Believed Our Report" make it suitable to the occasion, and it is just possible that the anthem may have been composed for this year, rather than earlier.[35]

Meanwhile Purcell kept busy at the various tasks for which his several appointments made him responsible. Chief among these, we may be sure, despite complete absence of any kind of evidence, was that of developing as a composer. As to what kind of music he would have been composing, precise information again is lacking. However, in view of the fact that London concert life really began to flourish and to assume the character of a lasting institution about this time, it is a fair assumption that Purcell had taken notice of the new, potentially lucrative liaison between the composition, performance, and publication of chamber music. And since his twenty-two trio-sonatas (one a chaconne) were composed between 1680 and 1683, it is safe to assume that during the course of the year 1681, he devoted a fair amount of time to them. Indeed, comparing these to the fantasias in their stylistic and formal development, one sees that they are part of an unbroken stylistic continuum.

The thesis that Purcell would have had a great deal of spare time to devote to composition during the first seven or eight months of 1681 is supported by records revealing that Charles II and others at court were preoccupied with political affairs throughout this period. So busy was the king, indeed, that his former frequent visits to the theater appear to have been cut out altogether.[36]

During the Parliament he had convened at Oxford in March, Charles had to face the effrontery of both Monmouth (who rode in over Magdalen Bridge on the morning of 21 March when Parliament opened, his men armed with "Protestant flails")[37] and Shaftesbury, who tried to force the king to name Monmouth heir to the throne. Charles II's eventual reply was to dissolve Parliament once again, returning the same day (28 March) to Whitehall via Windsor.

April of 1681 saw the king busy, again negotiating with Louis XIV (and £400,000 richer afterward);[38] with the affairs of the Navy; with preparations for Roger L'Estrange's first issue of the *Observator* (Charles's new propaganda weapon); and with arrangements for the departure of the royal family and their entourage for Hampton Court for the summer.

Among numerous propaganda pieces published about this time may be mentioned *The Deliquiam: or, the Grievances of the Nation Discovered in a Dream*, a pamphlet "against those that appear against the Court." (Here marginalia identify Almanzor as the duke of York, Capriccio as Shaftesbury, Marcion as Monmouth, a Rogue as Dangerfield, a Son as Tonge, Towser as [Roger?] L'Estrange, and Hali as Halifax.)[39] The gist of another Tory tract may be gathered from the Whiggish reaction to it a shown in the following parody:

THE PROTESTANT DISSENTERS
Occasioned by a late Pamphlet called *The Royal Letany*

From Rome's tyrannizing o'er Kingdoms and Kings
From Religion that murder and massacre brings
From TREASON styl'd merit and such dreadful things
   Libera nos Domine.

From Plots and sham-plots good subjects to wrong
From those who to wade in our blood do think long
From Mass and from turning our Prayers to a song
   Lib. etc.

From fashions of France and their murdering arms
From secret impoisonings and mischievous charms
From Roman locusts, with which England swarms
   Lib. etc.

Printed for W. B. 1681[40]

May and June passed uneventfully, except for the business of Fitzharris's arraignment and bloody execution for his part in the "Irish plot" against the king, queen, and duke of York.[41] Then July brought the king unexpectedly back to London, where he quickly examined Shaftesbury and committed him to the Tower. For the rest of the month he was involved with the election of London's sheriffs (also, by implication, that of the lord mayor) and engaged in various negotiations with William, prince of Orange, against France and Spain. Charles was unsuccessful in the city election and had to hold his peace while a Whig-packed jury released Stephen College (author of the libelous anti-Tory pamphlets *The Raree-Show* and *The Protestant Tories*). The king's political fortunes still ran at low ebb but were soon to change for the better.

Purcell, whose musical activities during the period have been conjectured above, meanwhile saw several events that affected the fortunes of himself and his kinsmen. On 26 January one Richard Robinson was appointed instrument-keeper in the place of Henry Brockwell, who had surrendered his position for unknown reasons. The lack of any mention of Hingeston and Purcell prevents clear knowledge of what this may have meant for these two, who presumably still held joint duties under that same title.[42] On 11 February, one Francis Purcell was admitted as groom-in-ordinary to Charles II. The frankly nepotistic policy of the court in such appointments, and the fact that Thomas Purcell, in charge there as groom of the robes, may have been suffering serious illness, explains the preferment then given his son Francis, who was Henry Purcell's first cousin. Finding his son court employment was indeed a wise precaution, as may be seen from Francis's promotion at Thomas's death.[43] Thomas, who made his will on 4 June, may have been facing problems raised by his falling ill, and so would have been disposed to set up for the future as many of his kinsmen as possible.[44] Shortly afterward, on 8 June, a Mr. Purcell received £37. 10s. from the secret service funds. Probably this was Edward, who for some time now had held an important and responsible position at court as gentleman usher.[45] Then on 9 July at All Hallows the Less, the above-mentioned Henry Purcell, son of Henry and Frances Purcell, was baptized, possibly the first of the composer's numerous but, for the most part, short-lived offspring.[46]

At the beginning of August, if no earlier, Purcell must have been busy with a major work, a welcome ode. (The indefatigable Luttrell records the return of the court to Whitehall from Windsor, where Charles had evidently gone from Hampton Court during the course of the summer.) Purcell's next official responsibility was to compose the ode "Swifter, Isis, Flow"[47] for Charles II's homecoming.[48]

After the brutal execution two days later of Stephen College,[49] Charles was off at 5:00 A.M. to seek relaxation at Newmarket, "for some time," as Luttrell observed in his entry for 8 September 1681. Again life at court was relatively quiet, and Purcell very likely returned to projects for compositions that had absorbed his attentions earlier in the year. In addition to such works, however, he must also have been composing the B-flat major service and anthem,[50] for a payment of thirty shillings "for writing Mr. Purcell's service and anthem" is recorded in the Michaelmas accounts of Westminster Abbey.[51] In fact the dimensions of this great service make it probable that he had been working on it over an extended period.

One detail in the final version of the autograph score[52] affords an interesting insight into Purcell's stylistic development about this time. On the back of a correction sheet pasted over part of the benedicite appear the first eight bars of Monteverdi's "Cruda Amarilli" (see plate 8), the first madrigal in his famous publication of 1605, *Il quinto libro de madrigali* . . . (Venice, Riccardo Amadino). When it appeared in print, this madrigal was already famous because in 1600 Giovanni Maria Artusi had criticized it so severely in his *L'Artusi, ovvero, Delle imperfettioni della musica moderna*[53] for its unusual dissonance treatment throughout, which he felt was licentious in the extreme. The musical importance of this fragment may now be examined in detail, because the whole manuscript from which the correction slip was cut has come to light.[54] Discussion of the contents of this manuscript will appear in the musical portion of this series, in sections devoted to the influence of Orlando Gibbons, William Byrd, and Monteverdi, respectively.

Then, during August and September, Purcell must also have added to his musical responsibilities to the church, court, and chamber at least a few to the theater. Before Michaelmas he had also provided a song for D'Urfey's *Sir Barnaby Whigg*,[55] a very topical piece, which was recorded in the Michaelmas Term Catalogue and probably produced early in October.[56]

The year ended, as it had begun, with political strife. Shortly after Catherine of Braganza's birthday, which was lavishly celebrated with "ringing of bells, bonefires, &c; and at night there was a great play acted at Whitehall . . ." on 15 November,[57] Whiggish factions rose. For the anniversary of Queen Elizabeth's accession on 17 November, the Parliamentarians paraded London's streets all day, then at night held a great Protestant celebration, all by way of preparation for Shaftesbury's trial, which was held a week later. A packed jury returned "Ignoramus"—a term soon beating about their ears in street ballads and scurrilous poetry—and Shaftesbury was acquitted. But, as Bryant has pointed out, he was set free with two cans tied to his tail, one by Charles II (the trial), the other by Dryden (*Absalom and Achitophel*). As numerous ballads of the time forewarned, Achitophel's days of political power were nearly over.

7

Tory Composer

POLITICAL DIFFICULTIES CONTINUED into the New Year, coming to a head with Monmouth's ambitious expedition to the north and the subsequent arrest of Stafford. King Charles was beginning to see that Dryden's prophetic identifications in *Absalom and Achitophel* were not at all far-fetched. On the contrary, they were distressingly apt, although he may have felt momentarily encouraged by the sentiments of the poet—fortunately anonymous—who had cobbled together lines such as the following for Blow's New Year ode for 1682, "Arise, Great Monarch, Arise":

> See how our troubles vanish.
> See how the Tumultuous Tribes agrow.
> Propitious winds bear all our Griefs away
> And peace clears up the troubled day.
> Not a wrinkle, not a scar
> Of faction or Dishonest war;
> But Pomps and Triumphs deck the noble Kalendar.[1]

For those at court, times really had not yet improved markedly.

Prudently, Buckingham had retired from the scene and had broken with the Whigs earlier that same month. After the Tories had celebrated their usual observances on the martyrdom of Charles I on 30 January 1682, the Whigs replied by offering an "indignity" to the picture of the duke of York at the Guildhall.[2] At court, however, musicians were as yet little influenced by such events, being preoccupied with their own affairs. Evelyn comments on one of the most lavish celebrations in his description of the entertainment of the Moroccan ambassador at "the Duchess of Portsmouth's glorious apartment at Whitehall where was a great banquet of sweetmeats and music."[3]

Meanwhile Purcell had moved into new quarters in Great St. Ann's Lane, his name being listed with the annotation "new arrival," twenty-fourth on the roster for that street in the St. Margaret poor-rate books for 1682. Among his more famous neighbors were John Dryden's brother, Erasmus, in Bell Alley; Stephen Crespion, not only Purcell's colleague and friend at the Abbey, but his colleague as well; the publisher John Carr in Great St. Ann's Lane; Purcell's former master John Hingeston in Absey and Bowling; Thomas Shadwell in Tothill Street; and Claudius Le Grange, John Blow, and John Wilson in King Street. John Banister and Robert Ramsey seem to have suffered misfortune, for both appear among those "in arrear to the assessment for relief of the poor of this parish." Strangely enough, Widow Purcell's name is absent from the lists for this year.[4] Perhaps she was staying with her son Henry, who now lived a very short distance from the back entry to the Dean's Yard, Westminster Abbey—a time-saving convenience that he was no doubt glad of a few months later when he was appointed one of three organists of the Chapel Royal as successor to Edmund Lowe.[5]

On 17 May 1682 Purcell traveled to Windsor with sixteen other musicians. The complete list of musicians, with the sums paid to them, is given in the *Calendar of Treasury Books*:

> to 17 of the King's music attending the King at Windsor, viz., John Twist £23. 5s. 10½d., John Banister £11. 12s. 8½d., John Lenthall £11. 12s. 8½d., James Banister £11. 13s. 2d., Thomas Finall £11. 12s. 8½d., Richard Tomlinson £11. 13s. 2d., Henry Brockwell £27. 16s. 8d., John Myer £11. 12s. 8½d., Gyles Stevens £11. 13s. 2d., Fred Steffkins £11. 12s. 8½d., John Hingeston £15., Henry Gregory £11. 12s. 8½d., Dr. William Child £11. 12s. 8½d., Henry Purcell £11. 13s. 2d., Will Hall £14. 0s. 7½d., Edw. Howton £27. 10s. 0d., Jeff. Banister £11. 13s. 2d. [Total] £247. 7s. 11½d.[6]

Purcell probably wrote "What Shall Be Done in Behalf of the Man?"[7] (the third ode commissioned by the court) to celebrate the return of James, duke of York, from Scotland on 27 May as well as for Charles's birthday on the twenty-ninth.

James indeed felt welcomed by the London "mobile,"[8] which had turned out to greet him.

> The glory of the British line
> Old Jimmy's come again.[9]

For his first line the anonymous poet posed one of the burning questions of the day: "What shall be done in behalf of the man?" (namely, James, duke of York; the Whigs, whose banquet for Monmouth had been suppressed a short time earlier, probably had a ready answer). But the loyal poet—again probably Dryden—held to the party line, coming out strongly for James in the couplet:

> And now ev'ry tongue shall make open confession
> That York, royal York, is the next in succession.

Charles too was enjoying greater popularity than usual. The *True Protestant Mercury* (27–31 May) and the *Impartial Protestant Mercury* (26–30 May) recorded that the birthday was "kept very solemnly by all true lovers of the King," and the recovery of the king from a minor indisposition had "rendered the solemnity of this his birth- and Restoration-day much more glorious, the same having not for many years been celebrated with greater or more universal testimonies of duty and affection to so glorious a prince." [10]

For both of the brothers, this was the first time in twenty years that the menace of a too-solid opposition appeared less fearsome. Even the Westminster bell ringers, those perennial harbingers of England's happy occasions had reason to be pleased, since the king's journey to London gave them another day's profitable employment, as we know from the following entry from the Treasurer's Account:

> More to them for ringing on six holidays, vizt. 5th of November, Queen Katherine's birthday, Queen Eliza.'s birthday, St George's Day, the 29th of May, and the 8th of April, being the day the King and Duke came from Windsor.   £2. 3s. 4d. [11]

At any rate it was clear that the political pendulum had begun to swing back. Shaftesbury and Monmouth had already seen their followers dwindling the month before, when Charles II had found it very easy to suppress a meeting scheduled by the Monmouth faction for the day already appointed to celebrate the king's escape from the toils of the "Popish Plot." [12] Now, it became obvious, a crucial test of strength between the two parties would be called for by the Parliamentarians. The first skirmish of this new political combat was not long in coming. On 19 June 1682 John Moore, lord mayor of London, confirmed his choice of candidates for the two offices of London sheriffs in the traditional "Ceremony of Drinking to one of his fellow citizens; and accordingly, says my author (who at the very time published a true and impartial account of the Proceedings of the Common-Hall of the City of London at Guildhall, on the 24th of June, 1682, for electing of Sheriffs) at the Bridge-House Feast, the 18th of May last his Lordship was pleased to pass the compliment of drinking to Dudley North, Esq." [13]

Because his candidates were staunch Tories and also because control of London was essential to the control of England and Parliament, the Whigs had no option but to oppose, as forcefully as they could, Moore's nomination of Dudley North and Ralph Box. They campaigned in favor of their own candidates, Thomas Papillon and John Dubois. During the elections on Midsummer's Day (24 June), demonstrations and grave irregularities aborted the issue. This, at least, was the Tories' claim when the election was said to have fallen upon Dubois and Papillon after a show of hands that gave them a majority of between 1,000 and 1,200 votes. A new poll was demanded; but in the ensuing process, further irregularities called for another election. Finally Charles II entered the lists and yet another election followed, in which his candidates were duly—some said unduly—elected.

On 26 June Archibald Campbell, ninth earl of Argyle, was beheaded. Charles II seemed to move from strength to strength as one by one he destroyed or weakened his enemies. Throughout the summer of 1682, the royal party gradually gained the upper hand. Despite all Whig machinations, Tory sheriffs were finally placed in office by the end of the summer (not without a few of Charles II's deft touches, be it noted). The way was then clear for the election of the lord mayor, in which election the Tory party was again successful with its candidate, Sir William Pritchard (once more with the aid of discreet royal intervention). A month later, the new mayor was inaugurated with more than the usual gala municipal ceremonies. The election, however, was no mere "city" affair, but rather one in which the interests of both parties and the welfare of the king were at stake.[14] This is not the place for a further account of the rigged voting, the riots, the false ballots, and the political conniving, all of which show the elections of 1682 to have been the bitterest of all contests between Whig and Tory. Nor is it the moment to comment on the significance of the court party's victory in these elections, which also boded well for their future, as it concerned the Shaftesbury trial, the "Ignoramus" verdict, the quelling of the Scottish rebellions, indeed the whole broad design of Charles II's strategy. These events were of particular significance to Purcell, who was a close friend of the Norths.

It is appropriate to point out that the text of Purcell's anthem "Blow Up the Trumpet"[15] (Joel 2:15–17) was that proper to the twentieth Sunday after Trinity, which in 1682 coincided with the lord mayor's celebrations on 29 October. Furthermore, the text of the first lesson for matins for that Sunday had obvious bearing on the current political situation. Charles II was no doubt most gratified to discover in this lesson allusions to "elders," "congregations," "a Northern army," and a battery of sentiments that might easily be construed as anti-Presbyterian, therefore anti-Whig. No more appropriate text could have been found to celebrate his hard-won victory over the Whigs or to publicize the fact that "the King of England was King of London at last," as the newly appointed, but not yet infamously "bloody," Chief Justice George Jeffreys (see plate 27) observed at the time. However much this victory may have accelerated Whig efforts, bringing the narrowly averted Rye House Plot[16] in its wake, and hastening the "Glorious Revolution," it was the most significant political victory Charles had yet enjoyed. During this same period Charles II's return from Newmarket on 21 October occasioned Purcell's setting of the ode for the event, "The Summer's Absence Unconcerned We Bear."[17]

Nor was the summer of 1682 uneventful for the Purcell family. On 4 June Henry's cousin Charles Purcell had made his will, apparently just prior to his sailing for the Gold Coast on His Majesty's sloop *Le George*.[18] At the beginning of the following month, Henry Purcell was given the above-mentioned preferment at court, as is revealed by the entry in the Cheque-book for 11 July 1682: "Mr. Edw[ard] Lowe, Organist of his Ma[jes]ty's Chapel Royal, departed this life at Oxford the 11th day of July 1682, in whose place was sworn Mr. Henry Purcell, the 16th of September 1682, but to take place according to the date of his warrant, which was the 14th of July 1682."[19]

As is made clear by the following order, which is the sixteenth in the list of instructions set down by George Lord Bishop of Winton on 19 December 1663, Purcell's new position called for more than merely playing the organ. He had to sing as well:

> 16. Of the three Organists two ever shall attend, one at the organ, the other in his surplice in the quire, to bear a part in the psalmody and service. At solemn times they shall all three attend. The ancientest organist shall serve and play the service on the eve and day of the solemn feasts, viz: Christmas, Easter, St. George and Whitsuntide. The second organist shall serve the second day, and the third the third day. Other days they shall wait according to their months. (Cheque Book, p. 83)

Then, at the end of that month, the Purcell family encountered new grief. Thomas Purcell, who had been like a father to young Henry since the decease of the elder Henry in August of 1664, died on 31 July. Terse accounts in various records of the time neither mention a cause of death nor give other particulars. However, Thomas had been ill for some while, if Rimbault's annotation be correct, and probably had succumbed to a very serious, but not suddenly fatal, illness: a power of attorney was granted by Thomas Purcell[20] of St. Martin's Parish, authorizing his son Matthew Purcell to receive his salary as gentleman of the Chapel Royal:

> Know all men by these presents that I, Thomas Purcell, of the Parish of St. Martin's-in-the-Fields, in the County of Middlesex, one of the gentlemen of His Majesty's Chapel Royal, and servant to His Majesty,

have assigned, ordained, and made, by these presents do assign, ordain, and make my trusty and well beloved son, Matthew Purcell, my true and lawful Attorney for me and in my name, and to my use to ask, take, and receive all such arrears and sums of money as are due, and hereafter will become due and payable to me the said Thomas Purcell out of His Majesty's Treasury, Chamber Exchequer, Coffery Office, or any other place or office whatsoever, giving, and by these presents granting unto my said attorney my whole power and authority in and about the premises, and upon receipt of any such sums of money aforesaid, acquittance, or other discharges for me and in my name to make and give and for me and in my name to do and perform as fully and largely in every respect to all intents and purposes as I myself might or could do if I were there personally present, ratifying, confirming and allowing all and whatsoever my said attorney shall lawfully do or cause to be done in and about the premises aforesaid by virtue of these presents. In witness whereof I have hereunto set my hand and seal this 15th day of May in the three-and-thirtieth year of King Charles the Second over England, etc. Annoq. Domini 1681.

T. PURCELL

Sealed and delivered in the presence of
F. PURCELL.
Witt [*sic*] WALLEY.[21]

By 4 June of that previous year, it may have become apparent that Thomas's illness was very serious indeed, for it was at that time that he wrote his will. Nearly six weeks later he died on 31 July.[22]

Katherine finally proved the will on 8 November 1682. The long delay suggests that Thomas's last illness was a lingering one. Perhaps, as Westrup and others have suggested, he fell victim to the scourge of tuberculosis, which may have proved fatal to other members of the family, including young Henry himself.[23]

The extent of Thomas's influence at court may be seen in the number of successors appointed to fill his various positions, this number also affording testimony to his skill as a pluralist. On 6 August Josias Bouchier was appointed to fill his place as gentleman of the Chapel Royal,[24] and on 17 November John Goodwin succeeded him in the Private Music.[25] No record remains to reveal the disposition of his other musical positions, but the liveries listed opposite his name in the "Accounts for liveries for musicians" ending Michaelmas 1683 indicate that there were still some to be disposed of.[26] His son Francis replaced him as groom of the robes, assuming full responsibilities at Somerset House.[27] It is not known who may have succeeded him as marshal of the Corporation of Musicians, an office he held for a decade.

Exactly a week after Thomas was buried in the cloisters at Westminster Abbey (2 August), and only a short distance away, was baptized Henry's second son, John Baptista Purcell, whose initials would
have been exactly the same as those of his maternal grandfather if, as
Westrup holds, Frances Purcell was indeed related to J. B. Peters.[28] At
any rate, the new male heir must have been born within a few days of
his great-uncle Thomas's death, only to join him in the community
of cloister graves in Westminster Abbey after slightly more than
two months.[29]

The infant's death, or at least the illness that brought it about, offers
yet another possible explanation for the origin of the oft-quoted inscription Purcell wrote into a flyleaf of the Fitzwilliam Museum autograph: "God bless Mr. Henry Purcell / 1682 September the 10th."[30] Or
perhaps the severe illness of another son occasioned the remark.[31]
Other hypotheses are possible. Purcell may have been in some sort of
difficulty with regard to his appointment as composer-in-ordinary,
which had been made exactly five years earlier. (Interestingly enough,
Blow's appointment as private musician-in-ordinary also began on 10
September 1685.)[32] Or possibly there was some difficulty concerning
his formal appointment as Edward Lowe's successor, to which position
he was at last sworn in on 16 September.[33] Quite possibly this may have
been the day of his birthday, as Reinhold Sietz suggests,[34] but to my
knowledge no established custom existed for this kind of birthday inscription in post-Restoration England. At any rate, the day after the
king, the queen, their royal highnesses, and all members of the court
returned from Windsor,[35] Purcell (who must just then have been finishing the new welcome song, "The Summer's Absence") made this curious inscription, suggesting that he may have been at work on the autograph scores that make up this fine manuscript about this time.

At the end of the following month, Purcell was involved, at least by
authorship if not by political sympathy, in the grand civic festival surrounding the inauguration of William Pritchard, Charles II's successful
candidate for lord mayor of London that year.[36] However, it is incorrect to assume, as some have, that Purcell actually wrote any songs for
the occasion, whatever the truth may be concerning the anthem "Blow
Up the Trumpet" discussed above. For the secular festivities at the
Guildhall on 29 October, a number of Purcell's song-tunes that had
been used in earlier skirmishes between Whig and Tory were revived.
For instance, Matt Taubman's doggerel on the dissolution of Parliament, which had been sung to Purcell's "Now, now the fight's done"
(*Theodosius*) with the following text:

> Now, now the work's done and the Parliament set
> Are sent back again like fools as they met. . . .[37]

now gave way to the following words to the same tune:

> Now, now the time's come, noble Pritchard is chose,
> In spite of all people who would him oppose. . . .[38]

Thomas Jordan's account of *The Lord Mayor's Show: Being a Description of the Solemnity at the Inauguration of . . . Sir William Pritchard, Kt.*[39] also calls for tunes that may be Purcell's, including "Let the Traitors Plot On" and "Here's a Health to the King."[40] In fact the several "songs said to have been written for the inauguration of the Lord Mayor, Sir William Pritchard, on 29 October"[41] may be reduced to one catch, which was introduced as follows:

> Or this new song, which is set to an excellent
> Tune by Mr. Purcell

> Since the Duke is return'd we'll slight all the Whigs,
> And let them be hang'd for politic prigs;
> Both Presbyter Jack and all the old crew,
> That lately design'd Forty One to renew:
> Make room for the men that never denied.
> To "God save the King," "and Duke" they replied;
> Whose loyalty ever was fixt with that zeal
> Of rooting out schism and proud common-weal:
> Then bring up a bottle, each man in his place,
> 'Tis a health to the Duke, boy, give me my measure,
> The fuller the glass is, the greater the pleasure.[42]

Because the text is virtually the same as that appearing in later sources, it is quite likely that Purcell did compose the work for this occasion, and that the catch can be dated as having been first performed on 30 September 1682.

It is possible that more music than this may have been commissioned for the inauguration, which was important not only because of its political implications, but also, as Chamberlayne pointed out in *Angliae Notitiae*, because of the paramount importance of the office: "This great magistrate, upon the death of the King, is said to be the prime person of England."[43] The festival, as Chamberlayne described it, was sufficiently lavish to call for all sorts of music:

> . . . on the 29th of October [the Lord Mayor] goes to Westminster in his barge, accompanied with all the aldermen, all his officers, all the several companies or corporations, in their several stately barges, with their

arms, colours, and streamers, and having there in the Exchequer Chamber taken his solemn oath to be true to the King, returns in like manner to Guildhall, that is, the great common hall of guilds or incorporated confraternities, where is prepared for him and his brethren a most sumptuous dinner, to which many of the great lords and ladies, all the judges of the land, and oftentimes the lords of His Majesty's most honourable Privy Council; also foreign ambassadors are invited; and of late years the King and Queen's Majesty; the Duke of York, and Prince Rupert have been pleased to honour that feast with their presence.[44]

Mindful of the value of this political victory, and, perhaps, of its narrowness, Charles II kept a tight rein on all activities that might have gotten out of hand. Thus he suppressed all bonfires, public fireworks, and festivals for Guy Fawkes (5 November) and for Queen Elizabeth's Accession Day (17 November). Both days were traditional occasions for Protestant and Whig demonstrations, which Charles quite logically frowned upon just then.

Hence it was quite appropriate that the anonymous poet of Blow's New Year's ode for 1683 should begin:

> Dread Sir, Father Janus, Time's great Overseer;
> Abhorring the factious designs of the past,
> With a Loyal adress is come in post hast,
> To present you the Maidenhead of a new Year;
> Not debaucht with trait'rous Combinations. . . .

and end:

> The moveing Isle is fix'd and setled now,
> The Basis of its Empire Rests on you;
> In Gordian knots you've Ty'd the Royall Line;
> And made Succession as your Right Divine.
> For all your Suff'rings, all your Cares
> Designing owes you the Arrears
> Of steddy Joyes and numerous years;
> And when you Remove to be Crown'd above
> Shall never want one to sitt on your Throne. . . .[45]

Throughout this period Purcell evidently had been busy composing other vocal works, for eight new songs appeared in the fourth book of *Choice Ayres and Songs to Sing to the Theorbo-lute or Bass-viol.*[46] The collection was entered in the Term Catalogue for February 1683 and must surely have been in the press for the usual six months or more. At any rate, except for "Retir'd from any mortal's sight," which Purcell had set for the performance of Nahum Tate's transmogrification of Shakespeare's *King Richard II* on 11 December 1680, these pieces generally represent Purcell's song style at this period. The most striking of these are the beautiful "Sleep, Adam, Sleep," the "mad-song" "From Silent Shades" ("Mad Bess"), and the lovely "Song on a Ground" on Cowley's subtly erotic lyric, "She loves and she confesses too."[47]

By the beginning of February 1683, the political situation had grown quiet enough for Monmouth to be released on bail, despite his overt insubordination and clandestine complicity in various Whig machinations. The event was celebrated immediately by the usual publication of ballads in broadsheet form. As if for comic relief, the little "Battle of the Organs" between the Benchers of the Inner Temple and those of the Middle Temple began about this time. Both Bernard Smith and Renatus Harris had been asked to build instruments so that the Benchers might choose the better one for installation. It was a brilliant scheme for ensuring the construction of a good instrument and for bringing the societies much publicity. But it brought difficulties as well, and in the end gave rise to skulduggery.[48]

Also in February, Purcell had come to the notice of the authorities of Westminster Abbey. Perhaps it was because of his recent appointment as Lowe's successor, or perhaps because of suspicions of Catholic leanings on Purcell's part due to the religious persuasion of his wife, or perhaps it arose out of the general contention between Whig and Tory. Whatever the reason, on 4 February, a Sunday, Purcell took the sacrament in public according to the usage of the Church of England. And he did this before witnesses, as required by statute, in this case Moses Snow,[49] a fellow musician (both vocal and instrumental) at court; Robert Tanner, occupation unknown; Bartholomew Wormall, the minister; and Giles Borrowdell, a churchwarden:[50]

> [I,] Bartholomew Wormell, minister of the parish and pari[sh] church of Margaret's, Westminster, and Giles Burrowde[ll] churchwarden of the same parish and parish church [do] hereby certify that Mr. Henry Pursal, one of the [Gentlemen] of His Majesty's Chapel, upon the Lord's Day commonly [called] Sunday, being the fourth day of February instant [imme]diately after divine service and sermon, did in the parish church aforesaid receive the sacrament of the Lord's Supper according to the usage of the Church of England. In witness hereof we the said minister and churchwarden have set our hands the fourth day of February 1682/3.
>
> Bartho. Wormell, Minister
> Giles Borrowdell, Churchwarden

We Moses Snow and Robert Tanner of Westminster do severally make oath that they do know the said Hen. Pursal now present here in court, and doth deliver the certificate above written and do further severally

make oath that they did see the said Henry Pursal receive the sacrament
of the Lord's Supper at the time and place, and in the manner above certified, and that they did also see the certificate above written, subscribed
by the above-named minister and church warden.

Iur in Cur apud Westm.   Moses Snow
die Lune & vi di Apr.   Robert Tanner
Anno Regni Regis Caroli Scdi
xxxv

[Sworn in court at Westminster Monday, 16 April, in the thirty-fifth
year of the reign of our King Charles II.]

The unusual number of details given in the document[51] indicates
possible irregularities in Purcell's conduct. The suspicion that something may have been amiss is strengthened by an annotation at the bottom of the document recording that Moses Snow and Robert Tanner
were called into court at Westminster Hall on Monday, 16 April 1683,
to swear under oath that they had seen Purcell take the sacrament and
the minister and churchwarden sign the document. Such lengths seem
to signify suspicion of something calling for investigation. Perhaps he
had exhibited too much sympathy for John Dryden or for the Peters
family or for the Howards or for others who were suspect as Papists.
Or perhaps Purcell *did* himself adhere secretly to the Roman Catholic
faith.[52] Moreover, the breaking of the Rye House plot about this time
may have created a general attitude of wariness at court. Certainly, officials would have felt constrained to look more carefully into such matters after 23 March, when the plot was thwarted.[53]

On the other hand, this may have been merely one of the formalities
Purcell had to undergo as a result of his accession to Edward Lowe's
position in the Chapel Royal in the previous autumn or because of his
appointment as composer-in-ordinary to the "King's Musicke."[54] Or
perhaps because he was at last to succeed officially to two of John
Hingeston's positions—positions for which he had long since been
burdened with the chief responsibility. Although Purcell's appointments were not registered before the end of the year (when Hingeston died), it is safe to assume that he had taken over most of the work
long beforehand.[55]

Then in May, when all London was abuzz with political gossip
about the trial of fourteen citizens (including the unlucky aspirants
Dubois and Papillon) who had opposed Pritchard and his candidates in
the riotous summer elections, Purcell advertised in the *London Gazette* for 24–28 May his first instrumental publication:

These are to give notice to all gentlemen that have subscribed to the proposals published by Mr. Henry Purcell for the printing of his sonatas of three parts for two violins and bass to the harpsichord or organ, that the said books are now completely finished, and shall be delivered to them upon the 11th of June next. And if any who have not yet subscribed shall before that time subscribe, according to the said proposals (which is ten shillings the whole set), which are at Mr. William Hall's house in Norfolk street, or at Mr. Playford's and Mr. Carr's shops in the Temple; for the said books will not after that time be sold under 15s. the set.[56]

Promptly on 11 June another notice appeared in the *Gazette*, advising subscribers "to repair to his [Purcell's] house in St. Ann's Lane, beyond Westminster Abbey, or to send the proposal paper they received with the receipt to it when they subscribed . . . and they shall receive their books paying the remaining part of the money."[57] Apparently Purcell had not trusted Carr and Playford to collect and distribute for him but had decided to do everything himself—perhaps to save money, or perhaps because he had found several errors and wanted to correct them himself before the books got into circulation.[58]

At any rate by midsummer—when he was busy composing the ode for the marriage of George, prince of Denmark, and the future Queen Anne, which took place on 28 July[59]—he must have begun to reap the rewards of his labors. On 29 October that year he advertised in the *London Gazette* that "Subscribers" requirements having been met, further copies of the "Sonatas of III Parts" by Henry Purcell are to be sold by J. Playford, J. Carr, and H. Rogers.[60] As for the sonatas themselves, much—perhaps too much—has been written about their Italianate tendencies. Because Purcell himself claimed to have "faithfully endeavoured a just imitation of the most fam'd Italian masters," and because Roger North, among others, referred to their Italian style, there has been much concern over borrowed themes, formulas, and techniques, and all kinds of hypotheses as to who these famed masters may actually have been.[61]

To be sure, Purcell did profess interest in various Italian masters. And he demonstrated that interest in practical ways as concerns the music of Claudio Monteverdi, Giacomo Carissimi, Stradella, Graziani, and Lelio Colista. But only these are to be found among Italian composers whose music he either copied or edited. And of these, Purcell apparently felt that only Lelio Colista warranted analysis and discussion. Purcell commented on Colista's harmonic techniques specifically in part 3 of his edition of John Playford's *Introduction to the Skill of Music* and paid him the compliment of imitating his passage-work in one of the trio-sonatas. Being of a highly technical nature, these will be discussed more appropriately in a forthcoming volume devoted to style, technique, and form in Purcell's complete works. Here, it is enough to say that Purcell's ear evidently was caught by the freer attitude toward dissonance treatment noticeable in Colista's music, as in the works of the other Italian composers named above. This he emulated in his own work, but in his own way, combining these Italianate techniques with various kinds of free dissonance usage that had been characteristic of the native English tradition for more than a century. Musically, the results were most rewarding, as those familiar with the sonatas already know.

In taking up the trio-sonata, Purcell was, of course, imitating the Italians, because it was the latest new musical form to emanate from that highly musical nation. Even earlier, though, William Young and John Jenkins had also experimented with the trio-sonata, but their experiments, for some reason, had not attracted nearly so much attention as Purcell's. His renown within this rather slender tradition springs from his having acclaimed the Italian masters, then, borrowing their form, composed some of the most attractive trio-sonatas ever written. As for external labels, such as adagio, largo, presto, which he carefully defines in the preface to the sonatas, or some of the techniques and the overall texture, these sonatas do seem Italianate. But, with regard to their inner qualities, these are so like some of his later fantasias in style and expression as to show that here, as elsewhere in his music, he was his own master, and, above all, an English composer.

Furthermore, it had been a very common practice among English composers to pay lip service to Italian music for at least a century. Claims of allegiance to Italian ideals, as in Morley's published madrigals or in Henry Lawes's setting of an Italian table of contents, usually have very little to do with the spirit of the music itself—window dressing, rather than direct borrowing, one might say. Purcell wrote very clearly about Italian traits that appealed to him. But, in my opinion, his basically English, highly personal style flows forcefully and true, though evincing foreign influence in performance practices and new technical features, perhaps traceable to Italian virtuosi like Nicola Matteis. In discussing the latter's visit to London, North has discussed the same point, perhaps somewhat more negatively, in his "An Essay of Musical Ayre," fo. 78ᵛ. In discussing the consequences of Matteis's visit to London, he says: "Nothing in town had a relish without a spice of Italy, and the masters here began to imitate them, witness Mr. H. Purcell, in his noble act of sonatas, which, however, clogged with somewhat of an English vein—for which they are unworthily despised, are very artificial and good music." Arthur Bedford, in his *Great Abuse of Musicke* (p. 224), dwells upon the same quality in Purcell's trio-sonatas, again, more positively: "All concords in a song is like an entertainment consisting only of sweetmeats, which may surfeit, and yet not satisfy or fill the appetite; but discords, when well prepared for, and cleanly carried off, do introduce a pleasing variety. The Italian composition (especially their sonatas) is very eminent in this respect. From thence Mr. Purcell seems to have taken this his masterpiece, in which he hath been since inimitable."

In his oft-quoted preface to the trio-sonatas, Purcell implies that these were being performed as a matter of special interest to subscribers to the printed edition. The implication that publication went hand in hand with public performance and that profits from both were needed is most significant. One immediately wonders if Purcell may have followed a similar scheme to that discussed in connection with Kühnel's sonatas.[62] If so, there is no known record at present, but it is likely that Purcell had his eye on concert performances in publishing as well as in composing these sonatas in the first place. Apparently, he was quite willing to "hawk his wares" in person, for Roger North reports that Francis North, lord chancellor until his death in 1685, had "caused the divine Purcell to bring his Italian mannered compositions; and with him on the harpsichord, myself and another violin, we performed them more than once, of which Mr. Purcell was not a little proud, nor was it a common thing for one of his dignity to be so entertained."[63]

While composing these sonatas and seeing them through the press no doubt occupied Purcell during the first half of the year, it is clear that he would have been kept very busy composing odes during the second half. For in this time he finished no less than four, possibly even five. The first of these was a setting of "From Hardy Climes," on an anonymous text, for the marriage of Prince George of Denmark and the Lady Anne, who was one day to become Queen Anne. The bishop of London presided over the ceremony on 28 July 1683 at St. James's, Piccadilly, and it is safe to assume that London's beau monde turned out *tutti quanti* to witness the event and to hear Purcell's music.[64]

September was a happy month for those at court, what with the frustration of the Rye House plot being observed with the celebration of a special day of thanksgiving—probably the occasion for which Purcell wrote his ode "Fly, Bold Rebellion." But October was a month of mourning for almost everyone. First of all, the duchess of York miscarried of a male heir, thus dimming the hopes of the court party as far as the strength of orderly succession was concerned.[65] Then in October 1683, John Blow's wife died in childbirth, so that a good many of the musicians at court would have been actually, if not officially, in mourning.[66] Finally, on 20 October, Charles II returned from Newmarket, at which time, as Luttrell observed: "His Majesty and the Court are gone into close mourning for the death of Alphonso 6th, King of Portugal, her Majesty's brother."[67] The importance of the event is attested to by the fact that the Westminster Abbey bell ringers were paid a special stipend for their duties on this day.[68]

By 22 November Purcell had composed two, perhaps even three, odes to St. Cecilia. With two other odes to compose earlier in the year, and with the first book of trio-sonatas to see through the press, not to mention a large number of miscellaneous compositions, he must have been busy indeed. At any rate he had finished two of the works, "Laudate Ceciliam" and "Welcome to All the Pleasures,"[69] in time to rehearse them for the celebration on 22 November.

In addition to the odes and trio-sonatas, which had sold so well as to warrant a second impression, Purcell had also found time during the course of the year to compose a number of songs, both sacred and secular, and perhaps a few anthems as well. Several of the eight songs that Playford published in the fourth book of *Choice Ayres and Songs* were probably composed during 1683, while all seven in the fifth book were surely composed then, if not before, as Playford's "Note to all lovers and understanders of music" clearly reveals:

> Gentlemen, This fifth book of *New Songs and Ayres* had come sooner (by three months) to your hands, but the last dreadful frost put an embargo upon the press for more than ten weeks; and, to say the truth, there was an unwillingness in me to undertake the pains of publishing any more collections of this nature. But at the request of friends, and especially Mr. Carr, who assisted me in procuring some of these songs from the authors, I was prevailed upon. Yet indeed the greatest motive was to prevent my friends and countrymen from being cheated with such false wares as is [sic] daily published by ignorant and mercenary persons, who put musical notes over their songs, but neither minding time nor right places, turn harmony into discord: such publications being a scandal and abuse to the science of music, and all ingenious artists and professors thereof.

As the year came to a close after one of the coldest Decembers in living memory,[70] Purcell assumed yet another official position of responsibility at court. Hingeston, who had willed him £5 as a godson's share of his material wealth, left him also the responsibilities connected with the acquisition, construction, and repair of instruments at court. The first official notice came down from the lord chamberlain's office on 17 December, appointing "Henry Purcell to be organ-maker and keeper etc., in the place of Mr. Hingeston deceased."[71]

This meant another livery for Purcell, for which he would be paid each year £16. 2s. 6d. for clothing. As a regular annual stipend, he received another sum. The records do not show what this amounted to, but it would probably have been something more than the £30 Hingeston had received on 4 July 1663 and on other occasions for attendance at Windsor in his official capacity as "Keeper of the Organs."[72] Possibly his salary was part of the £60 per annum Purcell was allotted on 16 February the following year. Certainly the two offices were lumped together in the entry for Hingeston as "Tuner and Repairer of the Wind Instruments and Organs by patent under the Broad Seal, £60" recorded in the Treasury of the Chambers Office accounts for 1668.[73]

This account also records the interesting fact (which ought not to be overlooked) that Hingeston had a helper, one "Mr. Brockwell, keeper of the King's instruments," who received £18. 5s. for his services. When young Henry Purcell was appointed as another assistant to Hingeston on 10 June 1673,[74] it must have been because there was too much for one person with only one helper to accomplish. Certainly the extant accounts, by no means complete, show Hingeston to have been a very busy man.

Purcell had been shouldering these responsibilities for so long that this official appointment probably did not alter his daily routine at all, however much or little it may have improved his finances. Indeed, considering the various tasks to which he was committed, it is difficult to see how any further drain could have been made on his energy. The magnitude of his total responsibility during the next decade is astonishing. In fact the total burden of his labors suggests that he may actually have worked himself to death, whatever illness brought him at last to his deathbed.

～ 8 ～

London's Music
at the End of the Reign
of Charles II

As New Year 1684 dawned on a snowbound England, Charles II found himself at last in a position to enjoy the fruits of political victory. Consequently, cultural, musical, and social affairs at court were more frequent than ever before. Newfound solidarity and strength were celebrated by the anonymous poet who provided the text for Blow's New Year's ode: "My Trembling Song, Awake, Arise."

Meanwhile Purcell was extremely busy with his new responsibilities at court, all the while taking care of his former duties there and at Westminster Abbey. His work, which involved the upkeep of all kinds of instruments, no doubt provided him with useful practical experience. But it must have overloaded his schedule unmercifully. To shed light on Purcell's professional position at this time, Edward Chamberlayne's description of the court hierarchy may be quoted in full:

> *Of the King's Court, The Ecclesiastical, Civil, and Military Government thereof, with a Catalogue of the King's Privy-Councillors, or the King's Judges, Servants, &c.*
>
> The Court of the King of England is a monarchy within a monarchy, consisting of ecclesiastical, civil and military persons and government.
>
> For the ecclesiastical government of the King's Court there is first a Dean of the King's Chapel, who is usually some grave learned Prelate, chosen by the King, and who as Dean acknowledgeth no superior but the King. . . .
>
> By the Dean are chosen all other officers of the Chapel, viz. a Sub-Dean or Praecentor Capellae; thirty-two Gentlemen of the Chapel, whereof twelve are priests, and one of them is confessor to the King's

household, whose office is to read prayers every morning to the family, to visit the sick, to examine and prepare communicants. . . .

The other 20 gentlemen, commonly called the Clerks of the Chapel, are with the aforesaid priests to perform in the Chapel the Office of Divine Service in praying, singing, etc. One of these being well skilled in music, is chosen Master of the Children, whereof there are twelve in ordinary, to instruct them in the rules and art of music, for the service of the Chapel. Three other of the said clerks are chosen to be organists, to whom are joined upon Sundays, Collar-days,[1] and other Holy-days, a consort of the King's music to make the Chapel music more full and complete. . . . In the King's Chapel thrice every day prayers are read, and God's service and worship performed with great decency, order, and devotion, and should be a pattern to all other churches and chapels of England.

The King hath also his private oratory, where some of his chaplains-in-ordinary read divine service to the King on working days every morning and every evening. . . .

There are belonging to the King's Chapel three organists, viz.

Dr. William Child.

Dr. John Blow, who is also Master of the Children of the Chapel.

Mr. Henry Purcell.

All eminent for their great compositions and skill in music. Mr. Thomas Blagrave is Clerk of the Check [*sic*]. The rest of the Gentlemen of the Chapel are great masters also in the Science of Music and most exquisite performers, as

Mr. William Turner.	Mr. Thomas Heywood.
Mr. James Hart.	Mr. Alphonso Marsh.
Mr. ——— Goslin.	Mr. Stephen Crispins.
Mr. ——— Abel.	Mr. Leonard Woodson.

Musicians-in-ordinary, sixty-two, which are ranked in these three degrees, viz.

Private Music,

Wind Music, and

twenty-four violins.

Of all which, as also of the instrumental music of the Chapel, Dr. Nicholas Staggins is Master.

Trumpeters-in-ordinary are sixteen and one kettle-drummer, of whom Gervas Pryce, Esq., is the sergeant-trumpeter. John Maugridge drum-major, and four other drummers and a fife.[2]

Beyond his duties as organist, Purcell also had to repair other instruments, as specified in detail in the warrant for his appointment as "Keeper of Musical Instruments," which came through at last on 16 February. These duties, which were above and beyond those he had inherited from Hingeston as "organ-maker and keeper" on 13 December 1683, must have been onerous indeed. If we may believe that he carried out all his instructions, Purcell undoubtedly earned every penny of the £60 per annum his new appointment brought:

16 February 1683/4.

Henry Purcell appointed "keeper, maker, repairer and mender and tuner of all and every His Majesty's musical wind instruments; that is to say all regals, virginals, organs, flutes, recorders and all other kind of wind instruments whatsoever, in the place of John Hingston deceased." Wages £60 per annum, together with the money necessary for the "working, labouring, making and mending any of the instruments aforesaid." "And also licence and authority to the said Henry Purcell or his assigns to take up within the realm of England all such metals, wire, wainscot, and other wood and things as shall be necessary to be employed about the premises, agreeing, paying and allowing reasonable rates and prices for the same. And also in his Majesty's name and upon reasonable and lawful prices, wages and hire, to take up such workmen, artificers, labourers, work and store houses, land and water carriages and all other needful things as the said Henry Purcell or his assignes shall think convenient to be used on the premises. And also power and authority to the said Henry Purcell or his assigns to take up all timber, strings, and feathers, necessary and convenient for the premises, agreeing, paying and allowing reasonable rates and prices for the same, in as full and ample manner as the said John Hingston . . . formerly had."[3]

The kind of work Purcell was required to do is recorded in some of Hingeston's old accounts, such as the following:

3 November 1664.

Warrant to pay John Hingeston, keeper and repairer of His Majesty's organs, pedals, harpsichords and other instruments £90. 19*s*. 8*d*. for repairing the organs, harpsichords, pedals, and other instruments from 29 September 1664; bill signed by Mr. Nicholas Lanier.

29 January 1667/8.

Warrant to pay John Hingeston, keeper and repairer of His Majesty's organs, the sum of £111. 4*s*. 6*d*. for mending the organs at Hampton Court, St. James's, and Whitehall, and for strings for the pedals, harpsichords, and virginals, and for other services done by him from 29 September 1664 to 29th September 1667.[4]

Old accounts also give a general description of the workshop that was to be Purcell's. Probably this had not changed a great deal in the intervening decades:

20 August 1663.

Warrant to the Surveyor-General to make and erect a large organ loft by His Majesty's Chapel at Whitehall, in the place where formerly the great double organ stood, and to rebuild the rooms over the bellows room, two storeys high, as it was formerly, the lower storey for the Sub-Dean of His Majesty's chapel, and the upper storey with two rooms, one of them for the organist in waiting and the keeper and repairer of His Majesty's organs, harpsichords, virginals and other instruments, each room to have a chimney, and boxes and shelves for keeping the materials belonging to the organ and the organ books.[5]

The mechanical pursuits this new responsibility called for apparently did not cause Purcell to slacken his creative musical abilities. Early in 1684 he prepared for publication yet another composition with a preface written by himself, this to his "Musical Entertainment," "Welcome to All the Pleasures," performed in honor of St. Cecilia the previous November.[6] As an indication of new social forces already at work upon English music and musicians, Purcell's dedication is significant:

To the Gentlemen of the Musical Society, and particularly the Stewards for the year ensuing, William Bridgman, Esq.; Nicholas Staggins, Doctor in Music; Gilbert Dolben, Esq.; and Mr. Francis Forcer.

Gentlemen, Your kind approbation and benign reception of the performance of these musical compositions on St. Cecilia's Day (by way of gratitude) claim this dedication; which likewise furnishes the author with the opportunity of letting the world know the obligations he lies under to you; and that he is to all lovers of music, a real friend and servant, HENRY PURCELL.[7]

That Purcell had composed at least one other work for this occasion we know from an annotation in the largest of his autograph scores in fair copy, now housed in the British Museum as Royal Music MS. 20.h.8. After the title of "Laudate Ceciliam" on folio 190 (rev.), Purcell added the description: "A Latin song made upon St. Cecilia, whose day is commerated [*sic*] yearly by all musicians, made in the year 1683."[8] Nothing in this entry indicates that the piece was performed on 21 or 22 November. That it was written in honor of St. Cecilia in 1683 is evidence enough to show that it was part of these celebrations. Purcell may have intended to publish this work together with "Welcome to All the Pleasures"—hence his use of the plural in the preface mentioned above. As for "Raise the Voice,"[9] the third ode to St. Cecilia (which has been putatively assigned to this date on the basis of evidence in manuscripts now missing), nothing definite can be established, although the fact that it calls for the same instrumental complement as that required for "Laudate Ceciliam" suggests that these two may have been performed on the same program. That the *Ritornello Minuet* (section 6 in "Raise the Voice") appeared as a harpsichord transcription in *The Second Part of Musick's Hand-maid* (1689) proves little, because it merely provides a terminus ad quem some six years later.

Meanwhile, the court prepared for its annual summer stay at Windsor, leaving very early, according to Luttrell's entry for 5 April and to various notices in London newspapers.[10] Purcell undoubtedly went too. Although actual records are wanting to prove this, it is unlikely that he or any other important court musician would have been excused from the ceremonies held on 8 April at Windsor to solemnize the installation of Prince George of Denmark as a "Knight Companion of the Order of the Garter," to which he had been elected along with the dukes of Somerset and Northumberland, at the beginning of the year.[11] This Danish prince also had been involved in the failure of Betterton's plans to set up French opera in England.[12]

The old player had gone to Paris with high ambitions, but had "caught only the wretched Grabu," who published his equally wretched "Pastoral in French" with Hudgebut and Carr toward the end of the following month. To palliate his "frenchify'd" appetites, Charles settled instead for the prince's players, who went straight to Windsor, baggage and all, immediately after their arrival in England with "sixty-five trunks or packs of old clothes," on 26 May 1684.[13] However, these players could not possibly have satisfied Betterton's operatic aspirations, and their influence even upon the English stage play must have been slight, because they departed the following 11 December after a very short theatrical season at Whitehall. The "wretched Grabu" stayed on, of course, but his efforts to advance French opera in London were worse than negligible.

Purcell also may have been concerned with the theater about this time, it seems, for the next season saw a revival of Ravenscroft's *The English Lawyer*[14] (first produced in 1677 as an adaptation of a Latin comedy *Ignoramus* [1614], by George Ruggles), for which Purcell provided the catch "My Wife Has a Tongue as Good as E'er Twang'd."[15] This catch was probably introduced in the tavern scene just after one of the characters has said, referring to his wife: "Come give us a flourish . . . we'll sing her praises backwards." The catch, for three voices entering at the interval of seven bars, is certainly not one of Purcell's most impressive specimens. The poetry is neither pointed nor witty, and the composition is so short that there is no opportunity for the usual references of double meaning among the various voices. Perhaps its chief importance lies in its having been instrumental in starting the gossip concerning bad relations between Purcell and his wife. Hawkins did not have much more to go on in spinning his tale about Purcell's having caught his death of a cold because he was locked out late one night, too late for Mrs. Purcell's liking.

Another catch, "Come My Hearts," is even slighter and shorter, though polyphonically more interesting.[16] Its topical allusions to Tory policy (that is, loyalty to the king and the duke of York without benefit of the Test Act) probably represent its chief value, however:

Come, my hearts
Play your parts
With your quarts
See none starts
For the King's health is a drinking.

They that shrink
From their chink
From their drink
We will think
That of treason they are thinking.

Then to His Highness
See here the wine is
That has past the Test
Above the rest
For those healths deserve the best.

Toward the end of spring 1684, the battle of the organ-builders approached its decisive phase, as Renatus Harris asked the Benchers of the Inner Temple for permission to arrange a public hearing of his organ in Temple Church. Presumably Bernard Smith was given the same kind of permission about this time, if reports by Hawkins (after Tudway's letter to his son, now lost) and Burney be accurate.[17] By the summer both organists had their instruments ready for the contest, Harris's just south of the communion table, Smith's in the west-end gallery.

For some time Draghi (for Harris) and Purcell and Blow (for Smith) demonstrated the capabilities of the two instruments on alternate days. Then, as time wore on with no unanimous decision, all contestants played on the same day, presumably for ease of comparison. Even so, several years were to elapse before a decision was reached,[18] this being arbitrated at last in 1688 by Judge Jeffreys, who had by then achieved considerable renown as a man capable of making difficult judgments and decisions quickly. He bestowed the victor's laurels upon Smith, Blow, and Purcell, while Harris and Draghi had to be satisfied with a consolation award, their organ being sent partly to St. Andrews, Holborn (where Purcell's son Edward was one day to play upon it), and partly to Christ Church, Dublin.

When completed, Smith's organ in the Temple Church was one of the most modern yet constructed in England, what with its separate keys for B♭ and G♯ and A♭, D♯ and E♭ and its full and complex make-up. Here are the exact specifications of stops and pipes, along with a schedule submitted by Smith on 21 June 1688:

> 21 June 1688
> Mr. Bernard Smyth's bargain and sale of the organ
> in the Temple Church to both the societies of
> the Temples.

> Know all men by these presents that I, Bernard Smyth, of London, Gent., for and in consideration of one thousand pounds of lawful money of England to me paid, [to wit] five hundred pounds, part thereof, by the Treasurer of the Society of the Middle Temple, London, and the other moiety by the Treasurer of the Society of the Inner Temple, London, for which I have given several former acquittances, and in consideration of twenty shillings now paid to me by the Honourable Roger North and Oliver Montague, Esq., Benchers, and William Powlett, Esq., now Treasurer of the said Society of the Middle Temple, and by Sir Robert Sawyer, Knight, now Treasurer, and Charles Holloway and Richard Edwards, esquires, Benchers of said Society of the Inner Temple, have granted, bargained, and sold, and do hereby fully and absolutely grant bargain and sell unto the said Roger North, Oliver Montague, and William Powlett, and the said Sir Robert Sawyer, Charles Holloway, and Richard Edwards, esquires, all that organ which is now set up and standing in the organ-loft in the Temple Church belonging to the said two societies; and all stops and pipes and other parts and appurtenances of the said organ, and particularly the stops and pipes in the schedule hereunder written mentioned, and also the curtain rods and curtains—and all other goods and chattels being in or belonging to the said organ and organ-loft—To hold to the said Roger North, Oliver Montague, and Willm Powlett, and the said Sir Robert Sawyer, Charles Holloway, and Richd Edwards, esquires, their executors and administrators, in trust for and to the use of both the said societies of the Middle and Inner Temples. In witness whereof I the said Bernard Smyth have to these presents (a duplicate whereof I am to seal to the said Treasurer and Benchers of the Society of the Inner Temple) have set my hand and seal this one and twentieth day of June one thousand six hundred and eighty-eight.

The Temple Organ
The Schedule
Great Organ

1 pipes Prestand of metal	61 pipes 12 foot tone
2 pipes Holflute of wood and metal	61 pipes 12 foot tone
3 pipes Principal of metal	61 pipes 6 foot tone
4 pipes Quinta of metal	61 pipes 4 foot tone
5 pipes Super octavo	61 pipes 3 foot tone
6 pipes Cornet of metal	112 pipes 2 foot tone
7 pipes Sesqualtera of metal	183 pipes 3 foot tone
8 pipes Gedackt of wainscot	61 pipes 6 foot tone
9 pipes Mixture of metal	226 pipes 3 foot tone
10 pipes Trumpet of metal	61 pipes 12 foot tone
	948

Choir Organ

11 pipes Gedackt wainsecott	61 pipes 12 foote tone
12 pipes Holflute of mettle	61 pipes 06 foote tone
13 pipes A Sadt of mettle	61 pipes 06 foote tone
14 pipes Spitts flute of mettle	61 pipes 03 foote tone
15 pipes A Violl and Violin of mettle	61 pipes 12 foote tone
16 pipes Voice humane of mettle	61 pipes 12 foote tone
	366

Echos

17 pipes Gedackt of wood	61 pipes 06 foote tone
18 pipes Sup. Octavo of mettle	61 pipes 03 foote tone
19 pipes Gedackt of wood	29 pipes
20 pipes Flute of mettle	29 pipes
21 pipes Cornett of mettle	87 pipes
22 pipes Sesquialtera	105 pipes
23 pipes Trumpett	29 pipes
	401

With 3 full sets of keys and quarter notes.

BER. SMITH. (L.S.)

Sealed and delivered in the presence of
Geo. Miniett. Tho. Griffin. Richd. Cooke.[19]

Smith's organ was to become the pride of the church, with a range extending down to FFF, and the unusual tonal adaptability made possible by its "quarter notes," which, as a contemporary chronicler boasted, were rarities "no other organ in England hath; and can play any tune, as for instance the tune of the 119th Psalm (in E minor) and several other services set by excellent musicians; which no other organ will do."

The contest had been strenuous. North, who witnessed it, reported that the contestants had nearly ruined themselves with their extravagant competitiveness. And "old Roseingrave," according to Burney, saw some ungenteel conduct on the part of Harris and his crew, who were reported to have cut the bellows on Smith's instrument one night before a crucial contest. Nevertheless, as we have seen, Smith won the day, possibly because he had had the sagacity to employ Blow and Purcell as his performing champions.

As the summer of 1684 drew to an end, Purcell was busy with another welcome ode for Charles II's return from Windsor to begin the new season at Whitehall.[20] But before the celebration for which this was written could take place, the king and the duke of York set off on a small progress—"political fence-mending," a modern commentator would call it—touring from Winchester to London, where they arrived by 25 September to be greeted by Purcell's setting of Thomas Flatman's ode, "From Those Serene and Rapturous Joys."[21]

At the beginning of November, Charles Purcell sailed for Guinea, as captain of the sloop *Le George*,[22] and began the strange series of adventures that later were to lead the family into such a tangle of legal difficulties. Otherwise the records provide no hint of Purcell's activities during the rest of the month. Undoubtedly he was involved somehow in the elaborate preparations for the queen's birthday, which had begun on 10 November,[23] for Luttrell described it as one of the grandest affairs ever: "The 15th, being Her Majesty's birthday, was kept at Whitehall, and in the evening were very fine fireworks on the water before Whitehall, which lasted for about two hours; and at night was a great ball at Whitehall, where the Court appeared with much splendour and bravery."[24] For such unusual attention to the queen, Charles may have had ulterior motives. It can scarcely be coincidental that Monmouth slipped secretly back into England at this very time, or conceivable that his arrival in London was either unknown or unforeseen by the king. What better camouflage than a gala affair at court?[25]

In the week following the queen's celebration, Purcell was involved in the preparations for the St. Cecilia's Day celebrations for the evening of the twenty-first and the day of the twenty-second. This time, however, Purcell's activities would have been completely behind the scenes—

supervising the moving of instruments to and from the Stationers' Hall, perhaps making last-minute repairs or tuning the instruments. By contrast with the St. Cecilia's Day celebrations of the previous year (in which Purcell had been the star composer of the show, with two, perhaps even three, of his own works to see into performance), the 1684 affair was dull indeed. Its dullness was due in no small degree to Blow's offering for the occasion, "Begin the Song." This ode, after a rather promising overture (which Handel liked well enough to borrow lock, stock, and barrel for his oratorio *Susanna* in 1748),[26] sinks from depth to depth in musical banality. Musical cliches and platitudes inhabit every phrase.

Meanwhile Purcell had not whiled away time idly: witness the impressive number of his songs, dialogues, and catches appearing just then. In each of these genres, several works reveal an impressive growth of Purcell's individual style and expression, and a marked increase in technical facility and control.[27]

The New Year of 1685 found Charles II and his court happy, prosperous, and even better situated politically than the year before. Having won the battle for London, and therefore the struggle for control of England as well, Charles could afford to treat his enemies with benevolence, forgetting old injuries and issues. For the first time during his reign, his revenues seemed adequate, and there was relative tranquility in domestic and foreign affairs. Somehow he had managed better than any other Stuart monarch to wield the powers of an extremely strong, if not absolute, monarchy without resort to overviolent means of control in keeping the peace. In short, he had won a victory in a long and arduous campaign and was now in a position to enjoy its fruits.

Those of his more solemn subjects, who, like Evelyn, censured the king for the loose company he kept and the fast life he led, were seeing things too much in black and white. To be sure, he still enjoyed some lighter moments with his circle of ladies. At the same time it must be recognized that his accomplishments were far greater than any profligate could have boasted of, reckoning achievements alone. When cultural attainments also are considered, a true measure of his real stature begins to appear.

Although music and the arts had been virtually destroyed during the Interregnum, he had managed to re-create, against implacably fierce opposition, an environment in which creative personalities could flourish. Within two decades all the arts, and particularly music, had attained such excellence as to command respect all over Europe.

For Purcell and others like him, working conditions at court must have seemed propitious, despite the fact that the "wretched Grabu" had at last managed to get permission for a court production of his opera *Albion and Albanius*, as it was later to be called—a production forestalled only by Charles II's death on 6 February 1685. On the first day of the year, Edward Bedingfield had compromised his musical judgment as follows, in a letter to the countess of Rutland: "We are in expectation of an opera composed by Mr. Dryden, and set by Grabuche, and so well performed at the repetition that has been made before His Majesty at the Duchess of Portsmouth's, pleaseth mightily, but the rates proposed will not take so well, for they have set the boxes at a guinea a place and the pit at half. They advance £4,000 on the opera, and therefore must tax high to reimburse themselves."[28]

For the musicians the most important sign of the king's newly won solvency had been the unaccustomed promptness of payments of salaries and fees, for which they were duly grateful, their gratitude sharpening the grief they shared with the whole court when he died. He had indeed been a friend and an encouraging patron, and in the period just preceding his death had managed to improve court finances so that current salaries, at least, could be kept up no matter how heavily arrears weighed upon the books. Purcell spoke for them all in his elegy for the king, "If Pray'rs and Tears," which begins with a mournful, evocative C-minor recitative setting of the opening lines of these "Sighs for our late sovereign King Charles the Second," as the anonymous poet subtitled his elegy:

> If pray'rs and tears
> The shields the Church of England only bears
> In some great exigence of State
> Could those have warded off the blows of Fate
> We had not fallen, we had not sunk so low
> Under the grievous heavy weight,
> The pressures of this day's sad overthrow
> Oh how the first amazing blow
> Bowed down each loyal head. . . .[29]

Meanwhile Purcell had moved from Great St. Ann's Lane to Bowling Alley East, as may be seen in entries in the St. Margaret's, Westminster, Churchwarden's Accounts for 1684[30] and 1685. Apparently the move implied no advance in tax rating, for the amount collected still stood at fourteen shillings per annum, an amount reflecting a respectably high but not yet affluent position.[31] Quite possibly he moved merely to be nearer to the Abbey, perhaps finding his house through the good offices of Stephen Crespion, canon and succentor in the Abbey, and one of Purcell's closest and staunchest friends.[32] That Purcell moved just before the last quarter of 1684 is shown by the fact that he paid only three-fourths of his yearly rate. That is to say, he paid 10s. 6d., leaving 3s. 6d. remaining in the "arrears" column at the end of the book.

The move was no doubt accomplished under pressure. Apart from his regular duties he had recently become more and more involved in editorial tasks, a sign not only of his growing reputation as a composer, but also of the meticulousness that characterized every aspect of his musical work. The first two books of the *Theatre of Music* (which must have been in the press by about this time) and the dedication of these to "Dr. John Blow, Master of the Children, and one of the Organists of His Majesty's Chapel Royal and to Mr. Henry Purcell, Composer-in-Ordinary to His Sacred Majesty and one of the Organists of his Chapel Royal," reveal that Purcell had by this time attained first place among English composers, and that his achievements were recognized.

For New Year's Day 1685 the usual forces were assembled to perform the ode, "How Does the New-born Infant Year Rejoice," again set by Blow.[33] Then on 26 January ten of the king's musicians were rehearsing for a ball, which probably took place during the course of the next few days[34] (though not on 30 January, when the martyrdom of Charles I would have been commemorated). At any rate the month ended with much musical activity at court, as well as in London and Westminster. Evelyn commented upon this, explaining that on 27 January he had dined at Lord Sunderland's, where he was "invited to hear that celebrated voice of Mr. Pordage, newly come from Rome. . . . An excellent voice both treble and bass; Dr. Wallgrave accompanied it with this theorbo lute, on which he performed beyond imagination, and is doubtless one of the greatest masters in Europe on that charming instrument. Pordage is a priest as Mr. Bernard Howard told me in private."[35]

On the twenty-eighth he was invited to Lord Arundell's house, where he heard Pordage again, this time accompanied by "Signor Jo. Baptist" (Draghi) on the harpsichord, and also his (Evelyn's) daughter Mary, who sang "to the great satisfaction of both masters, and a world of people of quality present: as she also did at my Lord Rochester's the evening following, when we had the French boy so famed for his singing, and indeed he had a delicate voice and had been well taught." Evelyn commented, too, on hearing the loud-voiced Mrs. Packer and the "stupendous" bass Gostling.[36]

Then suddenly, on 2 February, a few days after Evelyn had heard the

PLATE 18. Eleanor Gwynn (National Portrait Gallery)

French boy again, "singing love songs in that glorious gallery," Charles II was stricken with apoplexy (2 February, ironically, was also Nell Gwynn's birthday).[37] He died four days later and the nation mourned. The event was announced in the *London Gazette* that came out the following Monday, 9 February, in the following laconic manner:

> Whitehall. 6 February 1684/5.
>   On Monday last in the morning our late gracious sovereign King Charles the Second was siezed with a violent fit, by which his speech and senses were for some time taken from him, but upon the immediate ap-

PLATE 19. Dutch engraved portrait of King Charles II

plication of fitting remedies he returned to such a condition as gave some hopes of his recovery till Wednesday night, at which time the disease returning upon him with greater violence, he expired this day about noon.

In the same journal, Charles II's obsequies were described with very little reference to music and scarcely any of the pomp usually attached to such occasions. On the secular scene numerous elegiac verses appeared by the chief poets at court,[38] for the most part neither worse nor better than the "Sighs for Our Late Sovereign King Charles the Second" mentioned earlier.

In the aftermath of the king's sudden death, the gloom naturally attendant upon the death of so popular a figure seemed immeasurably deepened by contrast to the bright gaiety, not to say profligacy, that had reigned at court a few days earlier. Evelyn's memento of the courtly scene of 25 January epitomizes the gaiety of Charles's love affairs, just as his entry for 6 February reveals the funeral woes that now weighed upon the king's erstwhile merry companions.

> I am never to forget the unexpressible luxury and profaneness gaming, and all dissolution, and as it were total forgetfulness of God (it being Sunday evening) which this day sennight, I was witness of; the King sitting and toying with his concubines Portsmouth, Cleaveland and Mazarine: a French boy singing his love songs in that glorious gallery, whilst about 20 of the great courtiers and other dissolute persons were at basset round a large table, a bank of at least 2,000 in gold before them. . . .[39]

The contrast is mirrored, somehow, in two other songs by Purcell, written at this time, "Love Is Now Become a Trade" and "Farewell All Joys, Now He Is Gone."[40]

Music and Theater in London
(Part 1)

WITHIN A FEW SHORT WEEKS preparations began for the coronation of the new monarch, who moved to St. James's palace early in April. Scandalmongers, eager to capitalize on rumors that Charles II had died by unnatural causes, repeated strange tales of nocturnal apparitions at Whitehall. Perhaps the anti-Catholic party had had a hand in an attempt to conjure up this ghost story, their phantom, like that of Hamlet's father, unquiet because of foul deeds; but Luttrell discredited everything, as he may have felt duty-bound to do, as official historiographer at court: "April 1685. There is a common report about town of some apparition that walks at Whitehall; and the King's removal to St. James's hath given many credulous persons the occasion to believe the same, tho' it was only for a little while, that the lodgings at Whitehall might be fitted up."[1]

For the credulous, and perhaps for wishful thinkers, another omen occurred at the coronation (23 April, St. George's Day), when the crown nearly toppled from James II's head. Since it was to do so in reality within a few years, superstition for once upheld its followers. Otherwise the coronation was a splendid and happy ceremonial event, nothing being omitted but the Holy Sacrament, to make it the equal of any pomp in Christendom. Luttrell, who made this observation, directed his readers to the "public prints" for particulars, the most important of these being, of course, Francis Sandford's *The History of the Coronation of the Most High, Most Mighty and Excellent Monarch James II.*

Sanford's account is too long and detailed to be reproduced or even summarized here. However, one or two quotations will be useful to lend vividness and verisimilitude to some of the scenes illustrated in plates 22–25, and perhaps to identify some of the chief participants in

PLATE 20. King James II, artist unknown (National Portrait Gallery)

PLATE 21. Queen Mary of Modena, by William Wissing (National Portrait Gallery)

PLATE 22. Children of the Chapel Royal (Archives Dept., Westminster City Libraries)

PLATE 23. Trumpeters and kettledrummers in the procession of the coronation of James II (Archives Dept., Westminster City Libraries)

the colorful ceremony. The first of the musicians to appear were a fifer, drummers, trumpeters, and a kettledrummer:

> A fife, in a livery coat of scarlet cloth, richly laced with gold and silver, and lined with shalloon, and His Majesty's cipher and crown on the back and breast, with his fife and banners nicely embroidered and trimmed with silver and gold fringe, viz.
>
> Clement Newth.

> Four drums, in the same livery as the fife, with His Majesty's arms depicted on the drums, with scarves of crimson taffeta fringed with silver, all in one rank, viz.

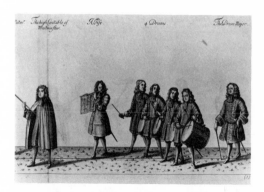

PLATE 24. A fife, four drums, the drum major (Archives Dept., Westminster City Libraries)

PLATE 25. "The Choir of Westminster in number 16; the Groom of the Vestry; the Organ Blower; Two Sackbuts, and a double Courtal" (Archives Dept., Westminster City Libraries)

1. Jacob Langley 2. John Skyrme 3. Devorax Clothier 4. Tertullian Lewis.

The drum-major, in a fine scarlet cloth coat, richly laced with gold and silver, and a crimson taffeta scarf about his waist, richly fringed with gold, viz.

Mr. John Mawgridge.

Eight trumpeters, all in rich liveries of crimson velvet, laced with gold and silver, with silver trumpets, having banners of crimson damask fringed about with gold and silver, with strings suitable and richly embroidered . . . viz.

1. Henrick Davent 2. Michael Maer 3. Peter Mounset 4. Hugh Fisher
5. Jervais Walker 6. Matthew Shore 7. William Bull
8. Benedict Ragway.

The kettle-drums, with their banners of crimson damask richly fringed
and embroidered with His Majesty's arms and supporters, and followed
by the kettle-drummer in the same livery as the trumpeters, viz.

Robert Mawgridge[2]

Then, after a number of other court functionaries had marched by,
four abreast in equally colorful attire, the Children and Gentlemen of
the Chapel Royal came along, in their midst the Westminster Choir
and "two sackbuts and a double curtall." Here, as above, Sandford's
complete list provides a roster of the most important musicians employed in these organizations:

> Children of the Choir of Westminster: 1) William Christian, 2) Thomas
> Price, 3) George Rogers, 4) William Morley, 5) John Bates, 6) John
> Walker, 7) John Howell, 8) William Williams . . . The Children of
> His Majesty's Chapel Royal: 1) Charles Allison, 2) Jeremiah Clarke,
> 3) Thomas Richardson, 4) James Townsend, 5) Simon Corbet, 6) Wil-
> liam Smith, 7) Jacob Wood, 8) George Rogers, 9) Richard Henman,
> 10) Charles Husbands, 11) Vaughan Richardson, 12) William Norris
> . . . (Each had two yards of scarlet cloth as their fee.)[3] . . . The Choir of
> Westminster in surplices, with music books in their hands: 1) Charles
> Green, Clerk, 2) Richard Cherington, Clerk, 3) Josias Boucher went as
> a Gentleman of the King's Chapel, 4) Robert Tanner, 5) Moses Snow,
> 6) Thomas Jennings, 7) Charles Taylor, 8) Morgan Harris went as a
> Gentleman of the King's Chapel, 9) Thomas Richardson went as a Gen-
> tleman of the King's Chapel, 10) Thomas Blagrave went as a Gentle-
> man of the King's Chapel, 11) Thomas Finell, one of the King's musi-
> cians, 12) Edward Braddock went as a Gentleman of the King's Chapel,
> 13) John Charole, a Petty Canon, went as a Gentleman of the King's
> Chapel, 14) Thomas Linacre, Clerk, a Petty Canon, 15) John Tynchare
> (alias Littleton), Clerk, a Petty Canon, 16) Stephen Crespion, Clerk, a
> Petty Canon, went as a Gentleman of the King's Chapel. (Such of the
> Choir of Westminster as were Gentlemen of the King's Chapel, went in
> that qualification, and the places here were supplied [by direction of the
> Dean of Westminster] with other persons skilled in music.) . . .

Gentlemen of His Majesty's Chapel Royal, in surplices, with mantles
over them, four a-breast, viz.

Counter-Tenors

1) Mr. Michael Wise, supplied by Edward Morton, 2) Mr. Thomas
Heywood, supplied by Dr. Uvedal, 3) Mr. John Abel, supplied by Aug.

Benford, 4) Mr. Josias Boucher, 5) Mr. William Turner, 6) Mr. Thomas Richardson, 7) Mr. John Goodgroom, 8) Mr. Nathaniel Watkins.

Tenors

9) Mr. Morgan Harris, 10) Mr. Alphonso Marsh, 11) Mr. Henry Frost, 12) William Powell, Clerk, 13) Mr. James Cobb, 14) Mr. Edward Braddock, 15) Henry Smith, Clerk, supplied by George Hart, 16) John Sayer, Clerk.

Basses

17) Richard Hart, 18) Samuel Bentham, Clerk, 19) Leonard Woodson, Clerk, 20) John Gostling, Clerk, 21) Henry Purcell, Organist of Westminster, 22) Nathaniel Vestment, 23) John Charole, Clerk, 24) Andrew Trebeck, Clerk, 25) George Bettenham, 26) James Hart, Clerk, 27) Blaze White, Clerk, 28) George Yardley, Clerk, 29) Thomas Blagrave, Clerk of the Check to the Gentleman of the Chapel, 30) Nicholas Staggins, Dr. in Music and Master of the King's Music, 31) John Blow, Dr. in music, Master of the Children of the Chapel and Organist, supplied by Francis Forcer, 32) William Child, Dr. in music, Eldest Gentleman of the Chapel.

(For Blow, the following marginal note: "Dr. Blow had also five yards of fine scarlet cloth for his mantle as composer.")[4]

These musicians, followed by other court and Abbey employees, all dignitaries of the city of London, and the entire English nobility formed the brilliant procession that moved "from Westminster Hall, through the New Palace Yard into King Street, and so through the Great Sanctuary, unto the West door of the Collegiate Church of St. Peter, the passage being railed in on both sides . . . and guarded by His Majesty's Horse and Footguards . . .":

> Two breadths of blue broad-cloth . . . spread from . . . the Hall . . . to the Choir . . . which cloth was strewed with nine baskets full of sweet herbs and flowers, by Mary Dowle, a Strewer of Herbs in Ordinary to His Majesty. . . . The drums beat a march, the trumpets sounded several levets and the choirs sang all the way from the Hall to the church, this anthem: . . . "O Lord, grant the King a long life." [Marginal note: "Composed heretofore by Dr. Child"][5]

It would be tedious to recount all the details of the coronation ceremony. It followed in the main the procedure outlined for Charles II's coronation. However, the whole affair had grown much more complicated, probably because Mary of Modena was present to be robed, anointed, crowned, and enthroned. Surprisingly, there seems to have been no notice taken of the fact that the royal pair originally had been married by proxy in September 1673 or that diplomats of Louis XIV had arranged the marriage. Nor, it seems, was anyone disturbed by his continued interest in domestic affairs at the Stuart court.[6]

All told, nine anthems were sung, most of these being performed—as were other incidental instrumental and vocal pieces—in the *cori spezzati* tradition that had been developing at San Marco's, Venice, for a century or more and in England, at least since the coronation of Charles II.[7] Sandford describes the performance of these anthems in detail,[8] beginning with the entrance of the king and queen into the Abbey, when the Westminster Choir went before them, singing Purcell's full anthem, "I Was Glad When They Said."[9] As the queen entered the choir, the King's Scholars of Westminster School sang "Vivat regina Maria, vivat Jacobus Rex" from the gallery adjoining the organ loft, after which came the acclamations, followed by Blow's full anthem, "Let Thy Hand Be Strengthened," sung by all choirs as "their majesties reposed themselves in their chairs of state."

The bishops of St. Asaph and Oxford then sang the litany, to which the choirs answered with the responses, this ceremony being followed by a sermon and the oath during which no music was heard. As a preface to the anointing, William Turner's setting of "Veni creator" ("Come, Holy Ghost, our souls inspire"), after which, just at half past two, the choirs then sang Henry Lawes's anthem:

> Zadok the Priest, and Nathan the Prophet
> Anointed King Solomon, and all the people
> Rejoiced and said GOD SAVE THE KING
> Long live the King, May the King live for ever.

Before the investing, Blow's short anthem "Behold, O Lord, Our Defender" was sung, and afterwards Turner's "Deus in virtute" ("The King shall rejoice in thy strength"), followed by William Child's "Te Deum," and then Blow's "God Sometimes Spake in Visions." After the coronation of the queen, the ceremony ended, as it had begun, with a composition of Purcell's. This final piece was "My Heart Is Inditing of a Good Matter,"[10] "performed by the whole consort of voices and instruments"—a splendid climax to the royal pageant.

If this last statement may be taken to mean exactly what it says, the usual way of performing this anthem must provide us with only a pale approximation of that original performance, which would have included not only a string orchestra accompanying eight-part solo and choral ensembles, but also the brilliant sounds of hautbois, trumpets, drums, and other instruments. A further hint of what may have been involved here is to be gained from the following account, which could scarcely apply to any but the last and most glorious work heard at the coronation, Purcell's "My Heart Is Inditing":

> 9 November 1686.
>   These are to pray and require you to pay unto Dr. Nicholas Staggins, Master of His Majesty's Music, the sum of £19. 11s. 6d. for fair writing of a composition for His Majesty's coronation day from the original score the 6 parts, for drawing the said composition into forty several parts for trumpets, hautboys, violins, tenors, basses, pricker's diet included, for ruled paper, pens, ink and chamber rent, and disbursed in providing several musicians for the coronation day who were not His Majesty's servants.[11]

The day following the coronation brought further festivities, culminating that night "with fireworks before Whitehall on the water" (in which, unluckily, three or four persons were injured) and a great ball afterward.[12] No account of the music performed has survived, but it is certain that many of the king's musicians were on hand for the event. Two days later, as if to mark both an end to official mourning for Charles II and an auspicious beginning to the reign of James II, the theaters were reopened.

Early in June Purcell received compensation from the authorities for his expenses and services in setting up the second organ in Westminster Abbey for the coronation of James II and Mary of Modena. In view of the dilatoriness they had shown on similar occasions in the past, they were remarkably prompt this time. The documents mention other earlier services that Purcell had rendered without specifying what they were:

> To Henry Purcell, for so much money by him disbursed and craved for providing and setting up an Organ in the Abbey Church of Westminster for the Solemnity of the Coronation, and for the removing the same, and other services performed in His said Majesty's Chapel since 25th of March 1685 according to a bill signed by the Bishop of London . . .
>
> £34. 12.[13]

Also on 3 June, Dryden's opera *Albion and Albanius* was at last performed, not at Whitehall as had been intended—Nicoll aptly described it as "a vast piece of royal flattery"—but at Dorset Garden.[14] Originally Dryden and Grabu had intended thus to pay tribute to Charles alone and had indeed even managed to get the production into rehearsal before the king's sudden death canceled all plans. It was June before libretto and score could be revised to refer to James II (Albanius) as well

PLATE 26. Duke of Monmouth, artist unknown (National Portrait Gallery)

as to his later brother (Albion). However, the run lasted for only six days, for on 9 June the sudden appearance of Argyll in Scotland and of the duke of Monmouth (see plate 26) at Lyme Regis in Dorset sent scurrying off the boards all these fictive heroes and their symbolic representatives: Thamesis (Thames), Archon (Monk), and Zelota (Zealots). So Dryden and the "wretched Grabu" had their hopes dashed

PLATE 27. Judge George Jeffreys, attributed to W. P. Claret (National Portrait Gallery)

again, while James II and his generals hurried off to make firm the foundations of the state, thus so arduously, if unprofitably, eulogized.

In little less than a month, Monmouth's hopes ended ingloriously at Sedgemore, he being taken prisoner at 7:00 A.M. on 8 July[15] and brought back to London to be beheaded hastily and unskillfully, though not unceremoniously, on 15 July. Purcell's interest in the affair is illustrated in his setting of D'Urfey's little allegory "A Grasshopper and a Fly,"[16] which, though published in the following year, was surely composed as a topical piece for performance at court about this time. The frankly double-edged satire in this dialogue was such, very likely, as to find little favor with King James II and Mary of Modena, who were not oversympathetic toward English musicians in any case. To celebrate their victory, they apparently turned for music not to an English composer in the Chapel Royal, but to an Italian, G. B. Vitali, whose work the queen had heard in her native Modena.[17] The great event was commemorated, probably in Italy, by his oratorio, *L'Ambizione debellata: ovvero, La Caduta di Monmouth*,[18] upon a libretto evidently produced rather quickly by the Venetian G. A. Canal, it being in print before the end of 1686.

This *azione drammatica* brought to the stage *Ragione* (Reason), *Fede* (Faith), and *Innocenza* (Innocence) to argue the royal cause against *Ambizione* (Ambition) and *Tradimento* (Treason), who represented Monmouth and his followers. The conclusion was foregone, having been announced in the title, and the libretto was therefore devoid of dramatic interest. The music itself, however, is often quite dramatic in its expression, and the overture and a few ritornelli and arias are quite worth hearing. Only the long and rather characterless recitative passages give any hint that Vitali may have been working with some haste.

It was also about this time that Purcell wrote incidental music for his fifth play, Tate's *Cuckold's-Haven*, given at the Theatre Royal, as were the four previous plays for which he had written music. Here, however, the connection between Purcell's song "How great are the blessings of government grown"[19] and the play is even more tenuous than is usual for the Restoration stage. In fact, the duet was sung (between the second and third acts of the play) rather as a tribute to James II, who happened to be present, than as an integral part of the play. (Hence, the editor of vol. 22 of the Purcell Society Edition was not altogether wrong in including the duet among the songs rather than with the dramatic music.)[20]

Quite possibly this performance took place about the time of the public thanksgiving that James ordered for 28 July. Two more of Purcell's theatrical compositions have been assigned to this year; however, neither can be dated for certain as belonging to 1685. The mad song in Lee's *Sophonisba*[21] not only appears for the first time in print at a suspiciously late date,[22] but also appears from a stylistic point of view to belong to Purcell's later period. The long fioriture for certain words and the echos are particularly uncharacteristic of this period in Purcell's stylistic development. Possibly he did write the song for a revival in 1691 or even in 1693.[23] His music for Charles D'Avenant's *Circe*[24] also seems more advanced in style than are most works that may be assigned to 1685 with certainty. Again, the long melismas and echo effects argue for a later date. Purcell perhaps supplied the music for the performance on 7 November 1690, for which Mrs. Barry was paid "£25 for 'Circe,' acted by command."[25] For all these reasons, I have considered it best to discuss these works in connection with his later years.

By the end of August, James II and his lord chamberlain had at last returned to some of the administrative tasks involved in setting the court's musical establishment in order. For although Staggins (on 25 March)[26] and a few others had had their positions confirmed, the official warrants had not been written. Thus it was probably with some relief that on 31 August thirty-four musicians (Purcell among them) found themselves at last being sworn in as His Majesty's musicians-in-ordinary. The lists of those named included twenty-three countertenors (the last two of whom, John Abell and William Turner, are listed inexplicably as "The vocal part" in the lord chamberlain's warrant); five basses (including Gostling and Bowman); one flautist by the name of Monsieur Mario; a tenor, Thomas Heywood; and a bass violinist, Coleman.[27] Purcell was named as a harpsichordist; Blow as a composer; Reading, Henry Eagles, and Mons. Le Rich as "Bases" (presumably instrumental); and Henry Brockwell as keeper of the instruments. During the two following months, these appointments were all confirmed by certificates[28] that indicate that two other musicians had also been appointed, Solomon Eccles and Francis Mariens. Clearly, Purcell had been demoted, losing in the process two prominent positions he had enjoyed under Charles II, namely, those of composer and organist to the Chapel Royal. This seems as powerful an argument as any to prove that Purcell was not a Catholic.

Of these thirty-six musicians, less than half were on hand for Her Majesty's birthday on 25 September, and for the "great rejoicings at Windsor and a ball at night, the court being there," which Luttrell recorded,[29] and which is registered also in the warrant for riding charges paid to Nicholas Staggins and the fifteen other musicians who made the trip. Purcell was not among these, possibly because he was busy preparing an ode for the king's birthday, proclaimed soon after the queen's, and observed on 14 October.

Purcell, who at the time was officially merely a harpsichordist, apparently was still expected to supply compositions, even though Blow was listed as official composer in the above-mentioned list. At any rate, Purcell composed one of his most original pieces—"Why Are All the Muses Mute?"[30]—for James II's fifty-second birthday, and Luttrell duly recorded the public demonstration of joy for the event.[31] On 10 October 1685 Samuel Pepys had written to Robert Southwell the following, as reproduced in *The London Stage*, vol. 1, p. 343: "Tonight we have a mighty Musique-Entertainment at Court for the welcoming home the King and Queen. Wherein the frequent returns of the words arms, beauty, triumph, love, progeny, peace, dominion, glory, &c had apparently cost our poet-prophet more pain to find rhimes than reasons." Neither "Why Are All the Muses Mute" nor *L'ambizione debellato* seem to fit this description. Most likely, the entertainment on 10 October was written by yet another composer, since Purcell was busy enough providing music for the king's birthday, and Draghi likewise was occupied with composing his magnum opus on the downfall of Monmouth. Evelyn, in turn, boastfully dropped royal names in his entry for the day following the celebration, i.e., 15 October (The conversation he mentions appears to have taken place during the performance, a distraction that no doubt endeared him to the composer and the musicians.): "Being the King's birthday, was a solemn ball at Court; and music of instruments and voices before the ball. At the music I happened (by accident) to stand very next to the Queen and the King, who talked with me about the music." The ode celebrated also the suppression of Monmouth's rebellion in the west, as is revealed by the lines describing the sending of the "threatening monster Rebellion back down to Hell." Monmouth's campaign, which came to a halt at Sedgemoor on 5 July, and brought him to the executioner's block at Whitehall ten days later, was the occasion for which Purcell provided the ode. (Hence, "Why Are All the Muses Mute" may be considered in a way an English companion-piece to the Italian oratorio *L'ambizione debellato: ovvero La Caduta di Monmouth*, upon which G. B. Vitali and his librettist, Canal, were no doubt already at work at this time.) Be this as it may, Purcell had had to compose the ode under the distressing, distracting circumstances of the aftermath of Jeffreys's "Bloody Assizes," in which James II relentlessly pursued all enemies, either his own or his church's. Only the day before his birthday he had pushed the prosecution of one Henry Cornish, former Whig sheriff who had persecuted papist plotters in 1680. James was quite satisfied to see the poor man convicted on the flimsiest of evidence and drawn and quartered ten days later.

The rest of the year 1685 passed uneventfully for musicians at court.

In fact the whole season must have seemed dull to the average Londoner. St. Cecilia's Day came and went without unusual stir. Nahum Tate's and William Turner's ode for the occasion ("Tune the Viol, Touch the Lute") sank even below the standard Blow had set the previous year with "Begin the Song."[32] In fact the affair turned out to be such a fiasco from the musical point of view that no celebration was held the following year.[33]

August Kühnel, a German musician who had come to England only shortly before, attracted attention about this same time by a new kind of musical venture, as advertised in the following announcement in the *London Gazette* for 19–23 November:

> Several sonatas, composed after the Italian way, for one and two bass viols, with a thorough-bass, being upon the request of several lovers of music (who have already subscribed) to be engraven upon copper plates, are to be performed on Thursday next, and every Thursday following, at six of the clock in the evening, at the Dancing School in Walbrook, next door to the Bell Inn, and on Saturday next, and every Saturday following, at the Dancing School in York Buildings. At which places will be also some performance upon the baritone, by Mr. August Keenall [Kühnel], the author of this music. Such who do not subscribe are to pay their half crown towards the discharge of performing it.[34]

This confirms the direct connection between the music publisher's trade and concert life in London that was hinted at in the account of Purcell's sonata publications two years earlier.

On 3 December Grabu returned again from Paris, having recovered from the ill effects of the previous summer's fiasco, almost to disappear from sight thereafter, although he lingered about the court for some time, and even managed to mount a concert (as advertised in the *London Gazette* for 15 November 1694).[35] For 18 December Evelyn reported a magnificent entertainment given at court for the Venetian ambassadors. He was almost carried away by his own description:

> I dined at the great entertainment his Majesty gave the Venetian ambassadors Signors Zenno and Justiniani, accompanied with ten more noble Venetians of their most illustrious families Cornaro, Maccenigo, etc., who came to congratulate their majesties coming to the crown, etc. The dinner was one of the most magnificent and plentiful that I have ever seen, at 4 several tables with music, trumpets, kettle-drums, etc., which sounded upon a whistle at every health. The banquet was 12 vast chargers piled up so high, as those who set one against another could hardly see one another, of these sweetmeats, which doubtless were some days piling up in that exquisite manner, the ambassadors touched not, but leaving

them to the spectators who came in curiosity to see the dinner, etc. were exceedingly pleased to see in what a moment of time, all that curious work was demolished and the comfitures etc. voided and table cleared. Thus his Majesty entertained them 3 days, which (for the table only) cost him 600 pounds as the Clerk of the Green-Cloth, Sir W. Boreman, assured me. . . .

London's musical life for the year ended on 31 December with a concert, alluded to (with annoying vagueness) in a letter from Peregrine Bertie to the countess of Rutland: "My cousins and the ladies have been in town. I had the good fortune to see them at a music meeting for about three minutes . . . the last music-meeting but one, was sung the song of young Dorinda, which I suppose your ladyship has heard of. The last meeting was sung this enclosed song, I need not name the author, because I am sure when I say nothing of the author your Ladyship may easily guess who it is."[36]

Soon after the beginning of the new year (celebrated with a new ode by Blow, "Hail, Monarch, Sprung of Race Divine"),[37] the French opera company returned to London, this time to perform Lully's *Cadmus et Hermione*, possibly, as W. J. Lawrence has suggested, to make up for the dismal failure of Grabu's *Albion and Albanius*.[38] Apparently the performance did not take shape as quickly as the producers had planned. At least Peregrine Bertie's references to the opera in three successive letters to the countess of Rutland indicate postponement and delay:

23 January 1685/6: Next week begins the French Opera.
28 January 1685/6: The French Opera will begin the week after next.
11 February 1685/6: Today was the French Opera. The King and Queen were there, the music was indeed very fine, but all the dresses the most wretched I ever saw; 'twas acted by none but French.[39]

Whatever the feelings of the two mediocrities, Cambert and Grabu, thus pursued by their nemesis Lully, Purcell may have liked the music enough to borrow the melody from Lully's "Entrée de l'Envie" for his own music for *The Tempest*[40] nearly a decade later. No one has yet speculated upon the ten-year gap between the opportunity to hear and the alleged borrowing of this tune or upon the absence of this or any other plagiarism in Purcell's hand.[41] On the face of the matter, it would seem strange that Purcell should borrow once, then never again, as far as is known—a consideration that lends additional weight to the argument of those who doubt Purcell wrote all the music for *The Tempest* that has been ascribed to him. It is therefore quite logical, as well as pleasant, to suppose that such rank plagiarism would have been uncharacteristic of Purcell, as is some of the music for *The Tempest*, though published in modern editions under his name. Moreover, as Peter Dennison points out in his article in Grove VI, p. 779, Purcell did quote and develop a phrase from Pelham Humfrey's *Song for Aeolus*, but this would have been seen in those times as a tribute, not a theft.

Meanwhile James II managed to clear up the arrears in salaries that had kept court musicians in a precarious hand-to-mouth situation almost from the time of the Restoration. William Child, for instance, was given liveries for the years 1662, 1665–67, and 1679–84. Others received similar reimbursements, which amounted to £16. 2s. 6d. for each year in arrears, but Purcell's name is nowhere mentioned. Either his payments had been met regularly or he was not one of those so fortunate as to receive redress.

March passed uneventfully, although Matthew Purcell's application for administration of the will of Charles Purcell caused some concern for the family.[42] On the following 6 May the will was at last proved. But Matthew and the rest of the Purcell family could scarcely have felt that the net results justified his efforts, because William Bayley's widow had by this time disposed of most of the stolen estate.[43] April seems to have brought little work for musicians at court, so far as extant records show. However, it is unlikely that St. George's Day (23 April) passed without some musical celebration, as it marked also the first anniversary of James II's coronation. Indeed, there might be some reason to suppose that the "Pastoral Coronation Song" ("While Thyrsis, wrapt in downy sleep")[44] may have found a sequel in the delightful little river song "Whilst Cynthia Sung,"[45] which appeared about this time in Henry Playford's and Richard Carr's *Theatre of Music*, book 3. Certainly, thematic resemblances in these two songs seem to indicate some such relationship, involving James and Mary in their own stylish circle of courtly love at Whitehall, which reflected, though palely, the more interesting circle that Charles II had kept revolving about himself.

About this time Purcell's purely instrumental pieces began to find their way into published collections, as they were to do henceforth with increasing frequency. He was not yet represented in John Playford's *The Dancing Master*, now in its seventh edition, but the famous old publisher's new volume, *The Delightful Companion or Choice New Lessons for the Recorder or Flute*, did contain a purely instrumental piece, "Lilliburlero,"[46] along with an instrumental transcription of the catch "Here's That Will Challenge All the Fair."[47] However,

"Lilliburlero" is printed anonymously in the collection and may have been associated with Purcell's name only two years later. At any rate, it was in 1688 that the tune appeared with the anti-Jacobite text by Thomas Wharton, which tune, as he put it, was to help William III to "whistle King James out of three kingdoms."[48] When Playford may have published this collection is not certain; but it undoubtedly had appeared some time before 6 May, when Mrs. Ellen Playford announced the "sale of the printing house of the late J. Playford in Little Britain."[49]

The early summer weeks passed uneventfully, Purcell going along to Windsor, it may be assumed, when the court moved there about 14 May. Then, some time before 3 August, he returned to Westminster Abbey to arrange for the burial of his son Thomas, probably the third child he had buried in these five years. Westrup assumes that the boy died in infancy, perhaps only a few days after birth. But there is no evidence to show that he may not have been considerably older. Again records are lacking—but their absence proves nothing either way.

Purcell did not remain with the court at Windsor until 1 October, when other musicians returned to London. He had earlier business there, as we know from an entry in the church records of St. Katherine Cree:[50] "The organ being now finished, it is ordered that Mr. Joseph Cox do procure Mr. Purcell, Mr. Barkwell, and Mr. Moses, masters in music, and Mr. White, organ master, or such others competent judges in music as may be prevailed with to be at our church on Thursday next, the 30th of this instant September, at two of the clock in the afternoon to give their judgments upon the organ. . . ."[51] A later paragraph from the same source, for 30 September, reads: "Doctor Blow, Mr. Purcell, Mr. Mosses, Mr. Fforcell this day appeared at our church, Mr. Purcell was desired to play and did play upon the organ, and after he had done playing they all reported to the vestry that in their judgments the organ was a good organ, and was performed and completed according to contract." Purcell then stayed on to hear the contestants for the organist's place, the procedure being carried on as follows:

> Mr. Niccolls, Mr. Beach, Mr. Snow, and Mr. Heath this day appearing and according to an order of the last Vestry did severally play upon the organ in the audience of the above Dr. Blow, Mr. Purcell, Mr. Mosse, and Mr. Fforcell and several parishioners of this parish. And the said Dr. Blow, Mr. Purcell, Mr. Mosse, and Mr. Fforcell after the said Mr. Niccolls, Mr. Beach, Mr. Snow and Mr. Heath had done playing reported to the Vestry that the third person that played (which fell out to be Mr. Snow) did in their judgements play the best and most skillfully of

them all, and that the first that played (which fell out to be Mr. Beach) played next best. And thereupon the Vestry proceeded to a choice of an organist, and the said Mr. Niccolls, Mr. Beach, Mr. Snow and Mr. Heath being put in nomination for an organist, and every person of the Vestry then present giving this vote by scratch of pen or scrutiny. The choice by majority of hands continued . . . fell upon Mr. Snowe who had eight hands and Mr. Beach but five hands, and Mr. Niccolls and Mr. Heath but one hand apiece. And the said Mr. Snowe being afterwards made acquainted with the said choice, gratefully accepted of the said place.[52]

Despite Purcell's finding that the organ was a good instrument, some difficulty must have arisen, for Bernard Smith, who built it, did not receive payment until 28 May 1687, when he was given £250 as per contract. From the rest of the account given above, it appears that Purcell and Smith were paid 14s. for their trouble and that Blow and Purcell received 5s. each for coach hire. Further sums laid out are recorded in the accounts audited for the same date:

Paid and spent at the Crown Taverne upon Dr. Blow and others when they approved of an organ and chose an organist	£008. 13s. 0d.
Paid Mr. Snow, organist, for one quarter salary due at Christmas	£005. 0s. 0d.
Paid Mr. Moses Snow for a quarter salary due at Lady Day	£005. 0s. 0d.[53]

From all this it is evident that the proving of the organist and the hearing of the candidates was a serious affair, involving probably several days' sojourn in the area, apparently far enough from Westminster to warrant travel and accommodation expenses. But on these points, as usual, the records are silent, leaving basis only for conjecture. The episode is rendered all the more interesting, however, by the fact that the minister at St. Katherine Cree at this time was none other than Nicholas Brady,[54] who was to provide the "Ode to St. Cecilia" ("Hail, Bright Cecilia"), which Purcell was to set with such brilliant and successful results a few years later.

By 14 October Purcell had to prepare yet another birthday "Ode for the King." For this occasion he composed "Ye Tuneful Muses, Raise Your Heads,"[55] in the text of which the anonymous poet took care to pay suitable and sufficient respect to the queen in the later stanzas of the ode. To add splendor to the day's events, James ordered four troops of guards to assemble in Hyde Park and, as a finishing touch, brought his mistress, Mrs. Sedley, out of retirement in Ireland.[56] One wonders if

Purcell may have introduced the raucous ballad tune "Hey, then up go we" as the bass to the chorus "Be lively then and gay" with tongue in cheek.[57]

Meanwhile Purcell had been losing time over a petty but annoying problem. His letter to the dean of Exeter reveals his impatience with the matter and also mentions one of his earliest pupils, of whose accomplishments no other word has reached us:

Westminster, November the 2nd, 1686

> I have wrote several times to Mr. Webber concerning what was due to me on Hodg's account and received no answer, which has occasioned this presumption in giving you the trouble of a few lines relating to the matter. It is ever since the beginning of June last that the money has been due: the sum is £27, *viz.* £20 for half a year's teaching and boarding the other a bill of £7 for necessaries which I laid out for him, the bill Mr. Webber has. Compassion moves me to acquaint you of a great many debts Mr. Hodg contracted whilst in London and to some who are so poor 'twere an act of charity as well as justice to pay 'em. I hope you will be so kind to take it into your consideration and also pardon this boldness from
>
>   Sir, your most obliged
>   humble servant
>   Henry Purcell[58]

Again, the outcome is in doubt. But what with a slender stipend at court, and a growing family at home, Purcell no doubt needed the money.

At the beginning of December the king "permitted Sir Charles Cotterell, master of ceremonies, to resign," as Luttrell put it, bringing his natural son, Mr. Fitzjames, back from Germany to reign in his stead.[59] Cotterell, incidentally, had been a very close friend of Mrs. Katherine Philips ("the matchless Orinda") and hence may have kept alive her memory at court. Purcell later was to set some of her poems in a most sensitive manner. Cotterell was by now seventy-four years old and no doubt happy to relinquish the responsibility of keeping the overserious monarch and his rather petulant wife sufficiently entertained.

As if to recoup his ailing fortunes, Grabu advertised publication of his opera *Albion and Albanius*, which was nearly ready, there remaining "no more to be printed but ten sheets in folio." It is significant that there was no mention of a performance or even of a request to Fitzjames that there be one.[60] Perhaps December was a bad month for theatrical productions, as John Dryden's *The Spanish Fryar* (for which Purcell was to compose a song several years later)[61] was suppressed by

King James II, even though Charles II had let it be performed and published six years before.[62]

The year closed quietly, although Purcell may have been upset by the fact that the money for house rent due to him at Christmas was not paid on time, in fact did not come to him until Michaelmas the following year. He may also have been apprehensive for his friend and colleague Bernard Smith, who was no doubt put out by the handsome commission to build a new organ at Whitehall, for which Smith's archrival, Renatus Harris, received £300 on 31 December, then £200 more on 18 October 1687, another £60 on the following 3 July, £137. 13s. on 3 April 1688, and at last a final and munificent £600 on 3 July 1688.[63] Having won the organ-builder's contest at Temple Church, Smith still lost his most lucrative commission.

The year of Newton's *Principia*, 1687,[64] saw Purcell engaged in a major project, composing sacred songs for *Harmonia Sacra*, book 1, upon which task, indeed, he may well have begun much earlier. March passed without any notable occurrence except the death of Lully on the twenty-second in Paris and the licensing of Grabu's published score of *Albion and Albanius*, which may have had a revival during the course of the month.[65] There is no record of the event, but James II's desperate political plight during this period was such as to lend credence to the possibility that the opera was trotted forth to forestall the designs of those who sought his overthrow. Then in April, as the Queen Dowager came out of mourning, the atmosphere at court became more lively, especially after 4 April, when James published the "Declaration of Indulgence," which, though William III was to countermand it, removed at least temporarily the necessity for all oaths and tests.[66] Evelyn heard Siface sing again (as he had done at the Chapel Royal on 27 January, a little less than three months before). Some of his remarks no doubt reflected the opinions of other Londoners:

> I heard the famous singer the eunuch Cifacca, esteemed the best in Europe, and indeed his holding out and delicateness in extending and loosing a note with that incomparable softness and sweetness was admirable. For the rest I found him a mere wanton, effeminate child; very coy and proudly conceited to my apprehension. He touched the harpsichord to his voice rarely well, and this was before a select number of some particular persons whom Mr. Pepys (Secretary to the Admiralty and a great lover of music) invited to his house, where the meeting was, and this obtained by peculiar favour and much difficulty of the singer, who much disdained to show his talent to any but princes.[67]

Siface, or Giovanni Francesco Grossi, as he was officially listed, had become acquainted with Queen Mary, it seems, during his tour of duty at Modena, or possibly, at San Marcello's in Rome,[68] where his name had been one of the most prominent on the list of those retained to perform the almost weekly oratorios given there. During this time he was also, apparently, a member of the papal choir until 1679, when he entered the service of the duke of Modena, there to find G. B. Vitali, still serving as assistant chapel-master.[69] As Siface's fame continued to develop, he appeared also in the Neapolitan opera house, in Florence, Venice, indeed, in almost all the important Italian cities of the day, Queen Christina of Sweden being one of his greatest admirers at this time.[70]

It was this international celebrity, then, whom Mary of Modena invited to join the Chapel Royal in London, where Siface appeared at the beginning of the year 1687. No doubt she and the king had him in mind for the new Chapel Royal musical establishment, which had been entrusted to James, duke of Ormonde, by royal warrant:

> Royal warrant to James, Duke of Ormonde, to pass, allow and pay the following establishment which the King has thought fit to order for the Royal Chapel which he has lately built in the Palace of Whitehall, viz. to a total of £2,042 per an. . . .

	[per an.]
[payments include:]	£
two sacristans at £50 each	100
two vergers at £50 each	100
six preachers at £60 each	360
four chaplains at £80 each	320
assistants	50
organist	100
assistant to the organist	20
seven chapel boys, for diet, washing, firing and servants' wages	300
to same, for clothes, linen, hats, shoes, stockings at £10 each	70
for a master to teach them	30
for house rent for them	40[71]

See also the entry in the same accounts for 5 July 1687, where the musicians are listed, along with their salaries:

Establishment for the music for the Chapel Royal:

	[per an.] £	
Seignr. Fede, Master	200	
Seignr. Grande	110	
Seignr. Sansoni	100	
Mr. Abell	60	
Mr. Pordage	60	
Mr. Analeau	60	£580 [!]

Gregorians

——— Master	50	
Mr. Nicholson	50	
Mr. Sherburne	50	
Mr. Reading	50	
Mr. Curkaw	50	
Mr. La Grange	50	
Mr. Desabaye	50	
Mr. Pawmester	50	
Mr. Arnould	50	
Seignr. Albricci	40	£490

Instruments

Mr. Hall	50	
Mr. Farmer	50	
Mr. Hooten	50	
Mr. Crouch	50	
Mr. Goodwyn	50	
Mr. Carr	50	
Mr. Peasable	50	
Mr. Finger	40	
Mr. Neydenhanger	40	£430
		£1500 [72]

How all this may have affected Purcell's life cannot be known. Apparently he had become acquainted with Siface, witness the little harpsichord piece (possibly satirical) that he wrote in the following year,[73] and through him may well have come to know of other "famed Italian masters" with whom the famous castrato had worked in Italy.[74] Again, however, the records give us nothing concrete to go on, and at present only conjecture is possible. Nevertheless, it does seem that Purcell, along with other English musicians, found himself participating less and less in musical life at court as more and more foreigners were brought in.

On 9 June 1687 a new son, named Henry, was baptized.[75] No doubt the physical (and audible) presence of another member of the family reminded Purcell that he still had a large sum of money owing to him for his contributions of time, energy, and materials to the coronation the year before. On the very next day he petitioned the king for payment of costs he had sustained in repairing musical instruments, asking not only for the £20. 10s. that he had already disbursed, but for an assurance of £60 per annum as well. The final outcome of all this is not known, but apparently this petition was at last graciously received by Edward Griffin (treasurer of the Chamber) who reported

> "that the petitioner's place of provider and repairer of organs and harpsichords for His Majesty's Chapel and Private Music for which he formerly had an allowance of £60 per an. is omitted in the establishment: and there being an absolute necessity for such a person and he hath hitherto supplied the same without any consideration, having disbursed £20. 10s. as by the bill annexed [missing] appears," therefore prays an order for payment thereof and that a provision be made for payment of what he shall disburse in the future.[76]

The fact that Purcell found it necessary even to submit such a petition, much less wait for an answer, is sufficient commentary on the musical enlightenment of the new court and on the kind of understanding and cooperation he could expect there.

Perhaps those who controlled such matters at court were too concerned with the general stir caused by James II's feud with Magdalen College, Oxford, to take notice of such small items of business.[77] Or it may have been the mourning imposed upon the whole court by the death of the queen's mother in Rome,[78] or perhaps merely that customary procrastination was prolonged by the progresses undertaken by their majesties in August.[79] Whatever the cause, Purcell's only recourse was to be patient. The necessity to petition must have seemed doubly onerous, what with his recent demotion at the time James II ascended the throne. He had enjoyed his position as organist to the Chapel Royal only a little more than three years and no doubt keenly felt the loss, both of dignity and income.

Music Under James II
and Mary of Modena

BY MID-SEPTEMBER 1687 Purcell's baby son Henry—perhaps the second he had so christened—had succumbed to an unknown illness.[1] Nevertheless, his obligations at court continued without respite, and he was soon very busy preparing another royal ode for James II's birthday, which fell on 14 October. This was the last celebration of this event the king was to enjoy in England, even though his anniversary was to come around once more before his final departure from Whitehall. For this occasion in 1687, Purcell set "Sound the Trumpet, Beat the Drum,"[2] an anonymous, somewhat cliché ridden, but musically suggestive poem, which he supplied with some of the best occasional music he had yet composed. In Purcell's creative development, this ode stands as the first of its kind, representing his attainment of a new style, which may be identified with that of many of his later works.

Meanwhile James II was having difficulty maintaining the kind of musical establishment he wanted for his new chapel at Whitehall. On 21 October an order issued from the lord chamberlain's office made it clear that more cooperation was required: "To Dr. Staggins, master of His Majesty's music. Whereas you have neglected to give order to the violins to attend at the Chapel at Whitehall where Her Royal Highness the Princess Ann of Denmark is present, these are therefore to give notice to them that they give their attendance there upon Sunday next and so to continue to do as formerly they did."[3]

James's and Mary's Roman Catholic policies were beginning to arouse antagonism in the sphere of music, as everywhere else. Evelyn voiced the general sentiments in his entry for 29 October that same year: "The K: Q: Invited to feast at Guildhall, together with Dadi, the Pope's Nuncio—O strange turn of affairs, that those who scandalized the Church of England, as favourers of Popery (the Dissenters) should publicly invite an emissary from Rome, one who represented the very person of their Antichrist!"

The occasion, as described in the original publication, is recorded in *The London Stage* (vol. 1, p. 360) as follows:

> LONDON'S TRIUMPH; or, The Goldsmith's Jubilee: Performed on Saturday, October XXIX. 1687. For the confirmation and entertainment of the Right Honourable Sir John Shorter, Kt. Lord Mayor of the City of London. Containing a description of the several pageants and speeches, made proper for the occasion, together with a song, for the entertainment of his Majesty, who with his royal consort, the Queen Dowager; their Royal Highnesses, the Prince and Princess of Denmark, and the whole Court honour his Lordship, this year, with their presence. All set forth at proper costs and charges of the Worshipful Company of Goldsmiths. By M. Taubman.

On 7 November Henry Playford's *Harmonia Sacra*, book 1, was at last advertised in the Term Catalogue. Viewed as a whole, the contents, both as to text and music, reveal a style that can best be described as very "high church." Had James II grasped the import of various straws in the wind, he might have saved his crown. His subjects were willing to go a long way toward achieving a ceremonial form and an outward show equal in dignity and pomp to that of the Roman Catholic church, but they would not convert to a foreign religion. Had he realized this, he might have averted the catastrophe that descended upon him the following year. Clearly their majesties were less concerned with matters so subtle as these than with less debatable means for strengthening their hold on the monarchy, as we know from Luttrell's announcement,[4] which speaks of the queen's physicians having let blood on 17 November in order to prevent a miscarriage.

Purcell had not only contributed a larger share than anyone else to *Harmonia Sacra*, book 1, but, as Henry Playford stated in a preface, "To the Reader," had taken upon himself the responsibilities of music editor as well. For this information, for its commentary on the current theological and aesthetic speculations on music and its functions, and for the interesting insight into a Restoration "Doctrine of the Affections" it affords, the passage merits quotation in full:

> TO THE READER. The approbation which has been given by those of the greatest skill in music, and the encouragement I have met with from a number of worthy subscribers do give me just reason to hope, that this collection of divine songs (tho' the first of this nature extant) will find a kind reception with the best of men. The youthful and gay have already

been entertained with variety of rare compositions, where the lighter sportings of wit have been tuned by the most artful hands, and made at once to gratify a delicate ear, and a wanton curiosity. I now therefore address to others, who are no less musical, though they are more devout. There are many pious persons, who are not only just admirers, but excellent judges too, both of music and wit; to these a singular regard is due, and, their exquisite relish of the former ought not to be palled by an unagreeable composition of the latter. Divine hymns are therefore the most proper entertainment for them, which, as they make the sweetest, and indeed the only, melody to a religious ear, so are they in themselves the very glory and perfection of music. For 'tis the meanest and most mechanical office of this noble science to play upon the ear, and strike the fancy with a superficial delight; but when holy and spiritual things are its subject, it proves of a more subtle and refined nature, whilst darting itself through the organs of sense, it warms and actuates all the powers of the soul, and fills the mind with the brightest and most ravishing contemplations. Music and poetry have in all ages been accounted divine and therefore they cannot be more naturally employed, than when they are conversant about heaven, that region of harmony, from whence they are derived.

Now as to this present collection, I need say no more than that the words are penned by such persons, as are, and have been, very eminent both for learning and piety; and indeed, he that reads them as he ought, will soon find his affections warmed, as with a coal from the altar, and feel the breathings of divine love from every line. As for the musical part, it was compos'd by the most skilful masters of this age; and though some of them are now dead, yet their composures have been reviewed by Mr. Henry Purcell, whose tender regard for the reputation of those great men made him careful that nothing should be published, which, through the negligence of transcribers, might reflect upon their memory. Here therefore the musical and devout cannot want matter both to exercise their skill, and heighten their devotion; to which excellent purposes that this book may be truly effectual is the hearty desire of your humble servant, Henry Playford.[5]

Playford's last few sentences make it quite clear that Purcell had assumed responsibility for the musical correctness of the whole. Something of his skill as a proofreader is to be seen in the emendations printed just after the preface.

Young Henry Playford did not yet have the reputation for being so skillful a publisher as old "Honest John," but he was certainly deep enough as a thinker on music and its ultimate significance. Writing at a somewhat later date, Roger North remarked upon the same concept (that is, the affections) as it existed within the secular sphere:

My thoughts are first in general that music is a true pantomime or resemblance of humanity in all its states, actions, passions, and affections. And in every musical attempt reasonably designed, human nature is the subject, and so penetrant that thoughts, such as mankind occasionally have, and even speech itself, share in that resemblance; so that an hearer shall put himself into the like condition, as if the state represented were his own. It hath been observed that the terms upon which musical time depends are referred to men's active capacities. So the melody should be referred to their thoughts and affections. And an artist is to consider what manner of expression men would use on certain occasions, and let his melody, as near as may be, resemble that. And if it be said that it is impossible to produce speech out of inanimate sounds, or give an idea of thought, as speech doth, I answer that whenever a strong genius with due application hath attempted it, the success hath been wonderful; as when the great Corelli used to say *Non l'intendite parlare?*[6]

In the same vein, though somewhat lighter, a little poem from the *Gentleman's Journal* for April 1693 changes the simile, but not the thought:

Man justly tuneful numbers may admire,
His soul is music, and his breast a lyre;
A lyre which, while its various notes agree,
Enjoys the sweets of its own harmony.
In us rough hatred with soft love is join'd
And sprightly hope with grovelling fear combin'd,
To form the parts of our harmonious mind.
Hence, since the soul to music is allied,
Unmatch'd by force 'tis by consent decoy'd;
Not were the strings of the soft lute design'd
As links to chain, but lines to guide the mind.
What ravishes the soul, what charms the ear,
Is music, tho' a various dress it wear.
Tho' none should lend an ear, tho' none a tongue,
Yet music still shall live in Waller's song.
Beauty is music too, tho' in disguise,
Too fine to touch the ear, it strikes the eyes,
And thro' 'em to the soul the silent stroke conveys.
The music's heav'nly such as in a sphere
We only can admire, but cannot hear.
Nor is the pow'r of numbers less below,
By them all humours yield, all passions bow,
And stubborn crowds are chang'd, yet know not how,
Let other arts o'er senseless matter reign;
Mimic in brass, or with mix'd juices stain:

Music the mighty artist man can rule
(As long as it has numbers, he a soul.)
As much as man can those mean arts control.[7]

The lighter musical charms referred to in this poem are reflected in a song collection that came out less than two weeks later. On 18 November the *London Gazette* announced publication of the first volume in a new songbook series, *Comes Amoris: Or, the Companion of Love*. This was printed by Nathaniel Thompson but published by John Carr, who had compiled a "choice collection of the newest scores now in use" in this rather nondescript songbook. With his five songs, Purcell shared pride of place with Samuel Akeroyde and "Anonymous." (One of Purcell's songs, "When First Amintas Sued for a Kiss,"[8] was printed anonymously here, indicating that Purcell probably did not have sufficient time for careful proofreading as that he had done for Henry Playford.) Other composers, including Thomas Shadwell,[9] Alexander Damascene, R. Courteville, Charles Green, William Turner, George Hart, Robert King, and Thomas Farmer, were represented by one, two, or three songs each. But they were definitely the lesser lights of the times, musically speaking, and so these songs show them to be.

Purcell's most prominent work in the collection is "Catch by Way of Epistle: To All Lovers of Music" (the usual publisher's announcement, set to music).[10] Although of negligible musical value, it is historically interesting, being, as far as I can discover, the first of that nauseous line of "advertisement" lyrics that has proliferated so vastly in modern times.

A few days later the *London Gazette* for 21–24 November 1687 announced the appearance of another secular collection in which Purcell figured conspicuously, with the fourth book of *The Theatre of Music*. This was the last of a series, apparently published after Henry Playford and Richard Carr had parted company, not on the best of terms, as a pointed reference to "new pretenders" who could be "disparaging of this book" indicates. Playford's remarks about his former partner are summed up in the following: "But I pass them over in charity with *Go on and prosper* not doubting but that (when it comes to the hands of judicious gentlemen and understanders of music) they will find the difference. . . ." Again, Purcell had a lion's share of the songs in the collection,[11] thus assuming corresponding responsibility for the musical quality:

> To all lovers and understanders of music, Gentlemen, this fourth and last book . . . will (I doubt not) be very acceptable to all the knowing gentle-

men in the skill of music, for several reasons I here mention. First that most of these songs and dialogues were composed by the eminent Dr. John Blow and Mr. Henry Purcell, my ever kind friends, and several other able masters, from whom I received true copies, which were by them perused, before they were put to the press.

Two days before publishing this collection, Playford launched a new series of his own, modeled after its immediate predecessor, as the following passage from the preface to *The Banquet of Music* reveals:

> To the Reader. Having already published a collection of this nature, entitled, *The Theatre of Music*, containing many excellent songs, in four books, I am encouraged to proceed to this second volume, called, *The Banquet of Music*, whereof you are here presented with the first book; hoping that both this and the following will receive the same favourable reception with the former, which will further encourage the endeavours of Your humble servant, H. Playford.

In this collection Playford sought the advantages of extreme variety, including in it settings both sprightly and serious, and including with actual songs, catches, dialogues, and even a small pastoral cantata with recorder ritornelli and accompaniments, "How Pleasant Is This Flow'ry Plain." [12]

Among Purcell's contemporaries and elders, such as Samuel Akeroyde, Moses Snow, John Banister, and John Blow, his brother Daniel seems to have been the youngest of the nine or ten composers who contributed to this collection. Two of Daniel's settings—"By What I've Seen" and "'Twas Night and All the Village"—are rather good songs. The musicianship they bespeak may be taken as evidence that his receiving the post of organist at Magdalen College, Oxford, that year was not due alone to his famous brother's influence.

This last publication almost coincided with the celebration of St. Cecilia's Day, being licensed on 19 November. The members of the London Society quite evidently had been marshaling their forces to regain ground lost in the fiasco of 1685, which apparently had undone any plans for 1686. [13] The society invited John Dryden to supply the poem for the celebration in 1687 (he complying with the unsurpassable lyrics of the ode "From Harmony, from Heavenly Harmony") and turned to Giovanni Battista Draghi for the musical setting. Was Purcell too busy composing and editing pieces for the first book of *Harmonia Sacra* and other collections? Or was he, perhaps, out of favor under a Catholic monarch, whose "papist" policy at court may have been reflected in the choice of these two prominent Catholics to provide the poetry and music for the celebration of 1687? For want of evidence, these questions cannot be answered. What is clear, though, is that Draghi's poetic sensibilities and musical powers were not such as to enable him to take full and imaginative advantage of the opportunity Dryden had provided. Now and then his setting strikes a happy grain of inspiration. But the full potential of the poem, which Purcell might have realized, was to remain more or less in limbo until Handel undertook to measure its musical capabilities more than half a century later, with his St. Cecilia ode for 1739, "From Heavenly Harmony."

For the Purcell family the year ended with several perplexing distractions. Toward the end of November, the miserable affair of Charles Purcell's estate had at last come into court, as Edward Purcell brought a suit against William Bayley's widow, Anne, who had made off with the goods of the late captain, Henry Purcell's cousin and former schoolfellow. The Chancery proceedings[14] were long and tedious and produced nothing but exasperating procrastinations, as far as extant records show. On 20 December Anne Bayley brought forth no satisfactory answers, but only tiresome evasions, denying any knowledge of any "goods and chattels," and questioning both Edward's authority as executor and Charles's former authority as captain. (In other words, she employed every delaying tactic she could think of.) It is difficult to imagine that the matter rested there; available records give no further information.

Another business matter was much nearer to Henry Purcell's own immediate interests. On 12 December Henry Guy, secretary to the treasurer, wrote to the bishop of Durham to report on the petition (now missing) in which Purcell had asked for payment of £20. 10s. for repairs to the king's organs and harpsichords. His additional request that funds be set aside to meet necessary expenses that might arise in the future indicates that he had in the past been forced to assume financial obligations he could not afford. As to whether or not his request was granted or even honored with an answer, again extant records are silent. At least some action had been taken on the matter before the year was out, whatever the final outcome.[15]

During or perhaps before the beginning of 1688, Purcell was busy with a new anthem, "Blessed Are They That Fear the Lord,"[16] which he was writing on royal commission for a thanksgiving ceremony for the queen's being with child, the child later to be the "Old Pretender," Prince James Edward. The "solemn and particular office," as Evelyn called it,[17] was celebrated in his church and in all churches within ten miles round on 15 January, then two weeks later all over England. For this event, as well as for the actual birth some six months later, an anthem was called for in the document published before the event.

The text of this anthem can be construed as special pleading for the maintenance of the established monarchial house, just as the annual celebration of the martyrdom of Charles I, observed on the following day, can be interpreted as both a caveat on the dangers of Protestant revolution and a plea for loyalty to the House of Stuart. Luttrell's recording of both celebrations at once, as reported by Luttrell and Evelyn, is probably not coincidental.[18]

It was upon this composition that Burney wrote his absurd pronouncement that "Purcell, who had so much distinguished himself in the former reign, does not appear, by the date or occasion of his exertions, to have produced any particular anthem, ode or drama, for the Church, Court, or stage, from the death of Charles II, his first royal master, till after the Revolution, except the anthem 'Blessed are they that fear the Lord,' which he composed by order of the Court in 1687, as a thanksgiving for the Queen's pregnancy."[19] Burney, perhaps misled by the old-style dating of the original document, not only got the date wrong, but was wrong in his general statement as well. As a glance at the *Thematic Catalogue* will show, Purcell wrote a great many anthems and sacred works in this period.

In fact Purcell may already have been busy early in the same year with his incidental music for a revival of Fletcher's and Massinger's *The Double Marriage*.[20] This revival may also have been prompted by James II's feelings of political insecurity, as Luttrell's comment might be construed to show: "The 6th was observed as a festival for joy of the King's coming to the crown; there was music at the chapel, cannons discharged at the Tower, and at night was a play at Court."[21] Both Nicoll[22] and Laurie,[23] as well as contemporary authorities Downes[24] and Langbaine,[25] all name February 1688 as the most likely date for the revival to which Purcell is supposed to have supplied incidental music. Judging from the style of the music itself, I feel that Purcell could not have been writing such awkward, unpolished music as late as 1688. A comparison of this piece with other Purcell compositions of 1688 suggests either that the music dates from a much earlier period or that it was not by Purcell at all.

Two weeks later, after nearly a year's bureaucratic temporizing, Purcell at last received notice that he was to be paid expenses and the instrument-keeper's stipend that he had petitioned for the previous season.[26] However, the royal warrant to the Board of the Greencloth (which produced, at last, the actual cash) was not entered in the accounts until early in the next month, by which time costs had mounted. The following stipulations were made: "And whereas it hath been represented unto us by the Bishop of Durham that £81 is due to Henry Purcell for repairing the organ and furnishing the harpsichords Christmas last and that it is necessary for that service to allow the sum of £56 per an.; these are to require you that the same be passed, allowed and paid accordingly."[27] On 2 April he also received £32 for providing organ and other necessaries, so Purcell must have felt quite well off for a change,[28] as far as returns from his instrument-keeping responsibilities were concerned.

During the course of this same month, he was probably also remunerated (though according to contemporary accounts not too handsomely) for the songs he wrote for Thomas D'Urfey's *A Fool's Preferment*,[29] a rehash of Fletcher's *Noble Gentleman* (first produced in 1626), except for one scene borrowed from an anonymous novel, *The Humours of Basset*. The play was licensed on 21 May,[30] complete with Purcell's music, and most likely therefore was performed the previous month, as Nicoll, Laurie, and others have argued. That the play was received coldly, as Nicoll says,[31] cannot be attributed to any shortcomings so far as the incidental music is concerned. Nor is it logical to assume that this would have been badly performed by William Mountfort, the ill-starred actor, singer, and playwright who took the part of Lyonel and probably sang the upper part in the dialogue as well, according to Dr. Laurie's convincing arguments.[32] In fact, as she also points out, the anonymous author of the satire *Wit for Money*[33] makes one of his characters say that "those scenes of Bassett which gave offence to a very Great Lady, were the ruin of it." Purcell's eight songs, in fact, are among the best that he had written up to that time and represent a remarkably complete representation of all the various kinds of theatrical songs he composed throughout his career.

Two new collections of songs appeared also in May, as if to reemphasize the fact that Purcell was now, by all odds, the foremost songwriter in England. The first of them to be announced in the *London Gazette* (for 7–10 May) was Henry Playford's second book of *The Banquet of Music*, in which he brought forth the "newest and best songs sung at Court and at public theatres." Apart from Purcell's four songs, the collection also contains an anonymous Italian song "Dite, O ciele" (so spelled) and Blow's "Eurydice My Fair," a dialogue between Orpheus and Eurydice that reminds one of Monteverdi in musical characteristics as well as subject matter.

Purcell was also represented by four songs in John Carr's *Vinculum*

Societatis, or The Tie of Good Company, advertised in another May issue of the *London Gazette*, which appeared on the twenty-fourth. As the title suggests, the styles of both music and poetry in the collection were suited more to the common taste than those of *The Banquet of Music*, which aspired to the beau monde. Carr's second book, *Comes Amoris; Or, the Companion of Love*, aimed at even lower, not to say lewder, tastes, as far as Purcell's contributions were concerned, there being three risqué catches with the separate title page *A Small Collection of the Newest Catches for 3 Voices.*[34]

The rest of May seems to have passed without incident for Purcell, except perhaps for the occasion at Whitehall Chapel, which he may have witnessed, when one of the singing men had to read James II's already much-contested Declaration of Indulgence after morning lessons.[35] Few even among those already opposing the declaration (such, especially, as Sancroft and Ken) realized what mischief the king had set in store for himself with this misguided attempt to lead at least two of his three kingdoms nearer to Catholicism. But all this, even if Purcell was present on that occasion, would have been erased from his mind by the birth of his daughter, Frances, on 30 May,[36] and the ceremony of her baptism at St. Margaret's, Westminster, on 1 June.[37]

A week later, however, the declaration would have been very much in Purcell's thoughts, as in those of most Englishmen at the time, as the famed seven bishops—Dr. Lloyd of St. Asaph, Dr. Ken of Bath and Wells, Dr. Turner of Ely, Dr. Lake of Chichester, Dr. White of Peterborough, Sir Jonathon Trelawney of Bristol, and Archbishop Sancroft of Canterbury—made of their opposition to the "illegal" declaration a national issue and were arrested and sent to the Tower. Purcell's own reactions to the affair are unknown, except as they might be guessed at from the lines of the jaunty little catch, "True Englishmen Drink a Good Health to the Mitre,"[38] apparently written the following year, or at least published then in the comparative safety of the reign of William and Mary:

> TRUE Englishmen, drink a good health to the Miter,
> Let our Church ever flourish tho' her enemies spight her;
> May their cunning and Forces no longer prevail,
> But their malice as well as their Arguments fail:
> Then remember the Seven, who supported our Cause,
> As stout as our Martyrs, and as just as our Laws.[39]

Events developed rapidly, and on 30 June the seven bishops were acquitted, to the well-demonstrated joy of London's inhabitants, who danced to the music of church bells around bonfires in the streets.

So great was the general excitement created by the acquittal that the sudden, and premature, birth of Prince James Edward on 10 June did not immediately arouse trouble, as John Evelyn had dourly prophesied it would in his entry on that date, which, interestingly enough, was Trinity Sunday. As if dissatisfied that this great occasion had not brought forth the general applause he had been expecting, the king sought to call his subjects' attention to the matter by ordering a day of thanksgiving on the seventeenth, ending with fireworks, and on the eighteenth a gala concert of water music, or, as Luttrell described it in his entry for the day, "an exercise of music, vocal and instrumental, by the King's music." The following week the royalist journal *Public Occurrences* came out on 26 June with a notice of the concert:

> Mr. Abel, the celebrated musician, and one of the Royal Band, entertained the public, and demonstrated his loyalty on the evening of 18th June 1688 by the performance of an aquatic concert. The barge prepared for this purpose was richly decorated, and illuminated by numerous torches. The music was composed expressly for the occasion by Signor Fede, Master of the Chapel Royal, and the performers, vocal and instrumental, amounted to one hundred and thirty. . . .
>
> Great numbers of barges and boats were assembled, and each having flambeaux on board, the scene was extremely brilliant and pleasing. The music being ended, all the nobility and company . . . gave three shouts; and all the gentlemen of the music went to Mr. Abel's house, which was nobly illuminated. . . . The entertainment lasted till three of the clock the next morning, the music playing and the trumpets sounding all the while. . . .[40]

The king, insensitive as ever to the mood of his subjects, could think of no better way to seek their support than to parade before them music and musicians, foreigners, and "papists," all as if designed to give them greater cause for discontent. Court musicians may well have felt injured as well as insulted when they received on 19 August the order that ". . . a number of His Majesty's musicians shall attend the Queen's Majesty's maids of honour to play whensoever they shall be sent to, at the homes of dancing, at such homes and such a number of them as they shall desire. And hereof the master of the music and the musicians are to take notice that they observe this order."[41] The peremptory style of the order hints, between the lines, that there may have been reluctance on the part of some musicians to provide such lowly service to play music they thought beneath them.

As far as the records show, the remainder of the summer passed uneventfully for Purcell and other musicians at court, most of whom attended the king at Windsor from 24 July until 20 September.[42] However, lack of mention of the two most prominent musicians in the records of the time lends substance to the stories that suggest that James's and Mary's foreigners were not above, indeed were quite successful in, intriguing against their most notable English colleagues. Relationships between the English and foreign contingents, representing as they did the larger Protestant and Catholic factions that divided the country, must have been extremely unpleasant at times.

Music and the Glorious Revolution

PURCELL EVIDENTLY WAS NOT commissioned to write any music for James II's fifty-fifth birthday celebration, his last in England. When 14 October came round again, it was obvious to everyone that practicing discreet silence was the court's wisest policy. So uneasy were the times that even the usual birthday salute of guns from the Tower was forbidden, as Evelyn remarked. He noted also that the sun had been eclipsed at its rising that morning, and that the day was "signal for the victory of William the Conqueror against Harold. . . ." Ominous signs, these, which no doubt impressed the superstitious as they did Anthony à Wood, who also reported later that month seeing a blazing star and hearing the story of two men seen fighting in the sky above Oxford about midnight.[1] Further auguries, and events foretold, were not long in appearing. Five days after the birthday of King James II, William of Orange sailed from Hellevoetsluis[2] for Tor Bay under a red flag, while Father Petre and many of his Catholic companions hastily packed their belongings. Within a few weeks, on 4 November, William III celebrated the anniversary of his own birth just off the English coast. Next day—another omen, since it was Guy Fawkes Day—he landed with his forces at Tor Bay. It must have seemed to everyone that the end of James II's reign had come.

During this period, when he had few official responsibilities at court, and when no St. Cecilia or theatrical commissions were in hand, Purcell evidently spent a little time on songs for publication, as we know from the fact that Henry Playford's third book of *The Banquet of Music* was licensed on 1 December 1688. Purcell furnished only two compositions for the collection: a catch, "If All Be True That I Do Think,"[3] and an interesting duo, "Were I to Choose the Greatest Bliss."[4] The latter was to achieve a certain popularity during the century after Purcell's death, appearing in no less than seventeen publications.

PLATE 28. King William III

For those in musical life, the Glorious Revolution brought a period of suspended animation. The "revolutionaries" had little time or use for the art of music apart from the "music" of trumpets, drums, and other military instruments that William had ordered to be sounded from the fleet before Dover, to strike awe into the hearts of his prospective subjects, no doubt. There was also the little tune "Lilliburlero,"[5] for which the prominent Whig Thomas Wharton provided an anti-

PLATE 29. Queen Mary II, adapted from a painting by William Wissing (National Portrait Gallery)

Jacobite text and Purcell the harmonization. The original tune[6] probably predates the Revolutionary period. As for the name of the tune, it may very well be associated with the harvest song from southeast Ireland, which was sung when one of the maids fell behind in binding sheaves:

PLATE 30. "A perfect Description of the Firework in Covent Garden that was performed at the Charge of the Gentry and other inhabitants of that Parish for the joyful return of His Majesty from his Conquest in Ireland, 10 September 1690." Mezzotint by Bernard Lens (Bodleian, Gough Maps 45.f.48ʳ)

> Lully by lero
> Lully by lero
> Lully by lero
> Help her along.[7]

By Christmas, James II was ruefully attending mass in Paris, while affairs in England were returning to normalcy, though of a new kind. The Glorious Revolution had produced a new attitude toward monarchy in England and a much clearer mandate to Parliamentarians than ever before. New policies were not long in forming. Charles Sedley spoke for a good many of the gentry when he said about this time that he "wished to make the King's daughter a Queen in return for his Majesty having made his daughter a Countess,"[8] but many in England had more sober reasons for welcoming William and Mary to the throne.

Moreover, London music concerts had begun again, as is known from the duke of Norfolk's notice that he had lost a muff at the music meeting held in York Buildings on 30 December.[9] The undeclared sus-

PLATE 31. "The Protestants Joy: or, An Excellent New Song on the Glorious Coronation of King William and Queen Mary, which in much Triumph was celebrated at Westminster on the 11th of this instant April" (Bagford Collection, vol. 2, p. 172, British Museum)

pension that seemed to suppress other musical activities persisted through January 1689 and early February, despite excellent opportunities for musical celebrations on 1 January, when a New Year's ode would ordinarily have been performed, and on 31 January when a "Day of Thanksgiving" was proclaimed for delivery of the nation from "Popery and slavery,"[10] and on 6 February, when both the prince of

Denmark's birthday and Parliament's declaration for William and Mary might have been observed with special (that is, musical) pomp.

Then, on 11 February 1689, a concert took place that Mr. Brattle and the American Puritan Judge Sewall went to Covent Garden to hear. This proved to be a harbinger of the very lively musical life that was to develop in London during the last decade of the seventeenth century and the first thirty or forty years of the eighteenth.[11] Two days later: "the Lords and Commons assembled at Westminster, came both houses to the Banqueting House at Whitehall, and there presented the Prince and Princess of Orange with the instrument agreed on for declaring them King and Queen . . . and the night ended with bonfires, ringing of bells, and great acclamations of joy."[12] Such an occasion must have called for music, even if only in the sounds of William III's beloved trumpets and drums. At present writing, however, no record has been found to indicate anything of a serious nature written for the joyous event. (It is probably symptomatic of the general state of musical affairs at the time that documents usually containing musical allusions make no mention of any events more important than those discussed above for the period between Christmas 1688 and early March 1689.)

Then, throughout March, the lord chamberlain's offices were filled with bustling preparations for the forthcoming coronation, and musical activities again assumed some importance. Significantly, the king's first order toward renovating his musical establishment, apart from authorizing a routine and belated warrant for winter clothes for Blow's Chapel Royal boys, was for equipment for the sergeant-trumpeter, sixteen trumpets, and a kettledrummer, with "the same for His Majesty's drum major, a drummer and a fife," three other kettledrummers being added to the list by a later warrant of 28 March.[13] Then on Lady Day (25 March) came down the list of His Majesty's thirty-nine musicians, all of whom had been provided with scarlet mantles—suitable dress for coronations—three days earlier. It is immediately apparent that the list had been pruned of the exotic foreign names that had ornamented James II's roster, which, in all but one or two cases, had been replaced by good English patronymics. It is clear also that the musical establishment had been reduced nearly by half. The significance of the high salary and top billing given Matthias Shore, the new sergeant-trumpeter, should be noted:

A list of such of the King's servants as receive their salaries in the Treasury of the Chamber's office, with an account of what was owing in arrears to each of them at Lady Day, 1689:

Mathias Shore, Sergeant-Trumpeter, £80
Dr. Staggins, Master of the Music, £100
Musicians, £30 each

H. Farmer,	Edward Hooton,
Charles Powell,	Henry Heale,
Edmund Flower,	Theophilus Fitz,
James Paisible,	Charles Staggins,
Thomas Fashon,	John Lenton,
Edward Greeting,	John Abel,
Samuel Akeroyde,	William Turner,
Robert King,	John Gostling,
John Crouch,	John Bowman,
John Bannister,	Francis Mariens,
William Clayton,	Charles Coleman,
William Hall,	John Blow,
Robert Carr,	Balthazer Redding,
Nathaniel French,	Francis Le Rich,
Richard Tomlinson,	Richard Lewis,
John Goodwynn,	Solomon Eccles.[14]

Equally noteworthy is the conspicuous absence of Henry Purcell's name. In fact no appointment seems to have been authorized for him until 22 July, when he was mentioned along with five rank-and-file musicians: "John Bannester (the younger), Robert Carr, Henry Heale, Charles Powell, Henry Purcell, musician composer, and Robert Strong, appointed musicians for the Private Music."[15] Extant records do not show that Purcell was in disgrace during the time just before William and Mary were crowned, as he most certainly was, unjustly, just afterward, due to the organ-loft incident at the coronation. Nevertheless, it seems obvious that he was not nearly so popular as he was later to be, either at the end of the reign of James II or at the beginning of William's and Mary's. Perhaps the infrequent appearance of his name in records of James II's court merely shows that as a staunch Anglican, preferments he might have had went to Catholic musicians. On the other hand, there may have been a suspicion that the Purcell family tended toward Catholicism, for years later Henry's son Edward strenuously denied any connection with the Roman church when competing for a position as organist at St. Andrew's, Holborn. Was he perhaps concerned over a traditional tendency in the Purcell family? Again, one can only surmise.

Yet there appears no other cause for those in power at court and in the Abbey to have mistreated their foremost musician, already universally acclaimed both at home and abroad. Like John Dryden, whose career also went into decline at this time, Purcell may have been a Catholic. (Certainly the absence of any official confirmation of an appointment to the Chapel Royal or the Abbey would suggest that any suspicion that may have been brewing would have had to do with religious matters.)

Evidence of Purcell's alleged Catholic persuasion is insufficient. It cannot be proven even that he held Catholic sympathies. As for references to the subject in modern publications, Douglas Newton's discussions in *Catholic London* are typical, being based on hearsay and conjecture, and not without wishful thinking.[16] How carefully Newton argues his case may be seen in his statement that Purcell "maintained his Catholic religion even in Elizabeth's Court." Other conjectures, less demonstrably false, are perhaps vaguely entertainable, though undocumented. Apparently Purcell was allowed full scope for his "Catholic talents":

> St. James stands as he, James II, and his line left it, and as we go down St. James's Street and see its lovely red brick gateway, we look direct on one Catholic memory. Above that gateway, in a suite of apartments reached by a winding stair case, in a clock tower, lived Purcell, the glory of English music. It was his sanctuary from a world whose religion was not his. Dryden often went up those winding stairs to visit him. Purcell allowed him to make the rooms a hiding place, too, but from his debts.

No mention of Mrs. Purcell and the children, who, presumably, as Newton would have it, were staying in Bowling Alley East, where Purcell continued to pay rates throughout the years until 1692, when he moved at last to Marsham Street.[17] But then, this does not destroy the possibility that Purcell may have had a "retreat" at St. James's. It would, of course, make it altogether unlikely that he later met his death from being locked out, as another unsubstantiated rumor would have it.

A thorough search of all accessible records having to do with a clock tower at St. James's and a sifting of the literature on Dryden's later days have been fruitless, producing no evidence to support Newton's bland assertion that Purcell was a Catholic. To be sure, Purcell's constant association with other such prominent Catholics as Matthew Locke, the Howards, the Peters family (into which he married), and a number of foreign musicians does provide circumstantial evidence. And the fact that he had to take the test in 1683 (to demonstrate his allegiance to the Anglican church) long after his appointment, as if doubts as to his religious probity might just have arisen, confirms the legitimacy of this evidence. Whether or not he was a Catholic, secretly or openly, cannot be determined; but at best, the possibility seems remote.

On 17 April 1689 extensive preparations for the coronation, which had long occupied everyone at court and half the gentry, were complete. There would be little point in tracing the "Form and Order" of the ceremonies observed. And, since musical arrangements were not recorded, there is little to relate beyond Luttrell's comment that "the coronation of their majesties was performed at Westminster, much in the manner the former was."[18]

Few events in Purcell's life, however, have been so well documented as has his altercation with the dean and Chapter of Westminster Abbey, which brought him to grief shortly after the royal event. Trouble arose over funds collected from those who viewed the coronation from the organ loft. In addition to documents published by earlier biographers, new records have come to light in the Abbey Muniments Room, where they have remained more or less hidden because some thrifty clerk used the backs of various sheets for records relating to events in the reigns of Queen Anne and the Georges, under whose names these have been indexed. The new information they contain does not entirely clear Purcell's name, for it seems that he was somewhat dilatory; but it does mitigate the case considerably, showing that his motivations and his conduct were quite honorable. By past precedents, both Purcell and Stephen Crespion had every reason to believe that the money they had collected from occupants of the organ loft during the coronation was rightfully theirs.

Right from the beginning of the post-Restoration period, the rules that governed the disposition of funds brought in from ticket sales to spectators at coronations were unclear. This we know from one of the earliest of such documents, a petition for royal intervention in the "business" of the coronation of Charles II, which took place on 29 May 1661:

> The Verger's Petition May 30, for money at the coronation: To the right Worshipful the Dean and Chapter of the Collegiate Church of St. Peters of Westminster.

> The humble petition of the Vergers, Sacrists, Bell-ringers and other the officers and the stewards to the same belonging. Showeth:
> That whereas your worships have been pleased upon some just and weighty consideration to order, and declare in Chapter that all such sums of money that shall be taken, and received by Adam Osgood, Clerk of the Works of the said Church, for any galleries, seats, or other places upon the solemn day of His Majesty's most happy coronations, and the

first day of this present parliament, should be brought in by the said Adam Osgood, and so distributed betwixt him and your petitioners, being all officers and servants to this church, after such manner and proportions as to your wisdom should be meet.

Your petitioners therefore humbly pray that (in pursuance of the said order and declaration) your worships would be pleased to cause the said Adam Osgood to bring in all such monies as he retained, to hear what can be said betwixt him, and your petitioners as to the greatness of the same, and after to divide the same as to your worships shall seem most agreeable to the rules of equity.

> And your pet[itioners] shall pray etc
> [unsigned] [19]

It is clear from this petition that the handling of the ticket receipts for the coronation was ill-regulated from the start. Even without knowledge of the outcome of this controversy between Osgood and his colleagues, it is obvious that official laxness had invited irregularities. From the very beginning, the division of coronation fees had been a bone of contention. Long before Purcell appeared on the scene, as the above-quoted petition and the following entry from the Precentor's Book reveal, "rules of equity" were so vaguely established as to call for royal arbitration:

In April 1661 a warrant was granted by the Rev. Dean to the Chanter and the rest of the Choir for the erecting of scaffolds in the Churchyard in respect of His Majesty's Coronation solemnized on St. George's Day. For which purpose agreement was made between the choir and the carpenter, that the profits thereof should be equally divided between them, the carpenter receiving the one half, he being at the whole charge of the scaffolds; excepting only that the choir paid for sail-cloths £0. 15s. 0. and the carpenter but 5s. and that the choir pay [sic] also for watching and other expenses equally with the carpenter £0. 14s. 0d. and given by the choir to the poor of St. Margaret's Parish £0. 16s. 0d. The sum received by the choir was £17. 9s. 0d. out of which . . . there remains to be divided into 16 equal parts £15. 4s. 0d. which was to every part £0. 19s. 0d. But the Vergers who should have had a part being left out, they had between them £0. 19s. 0. out of the money collected for the monuments. The organist being a good gainer by his organ loft and scaffolds being erected, had no share with the rest of the choir.[20]

Here the precedent for the organist's right to funds collected from visitors to the organ loft is clearly established. Apparently, the organist was given carte blanche to make his own terms with the carpenter, collect whatever entrance fees he could, and pocket them without further word to anyone, as long as he did not expect to have a share in the general income. Presumably this was the precedent Purcell later followed.

Any account of these matters that may have been kept among papers relating to the coronation of James II seems either to have been lost or to be too well hidden for easy discovery. However, two later documents refer to this coronation and shed at least some light on these proceedings, in which Purcell, as organist both for Westminster Abbey and for the Chapel Royal, must have taken part officially. One of these dates from the reign of George I and is "An account shewing in what parts of the Abbey the several scaffolds of the Dean and Chapter and their officers, etc. were erected at the coronations of King James, King William and Queen Mary, and Queen Anne":

> At the coronations of King James, King William and Queen Mary, and Queen Anne the Dean and Chap[ter] of Westminster had scaffolds built for their families and friends on the south side of the Choir from the pulpit to the place where the trumpets and drums are seated.
> The Chanter, minor Canons, Gentlemen of the Choir, and other officers of the same church by the Dean's leave did at those solemnities build scaffolds in all the aisles westward from the Choir and the South Cross of the Abbey till the Coronation of Queen Anne. When some days after a scaffold was built in the South Cross one Mr. Negus took possession of that scaffold under pretence on an order from the Earl Marshall tho' the same had been built in such manner as had been used at the cost and charges of the officers of the said church who were great losers thereby, being forced to compromise the matter not having time to apply for relief.
>
> James La Freese, Sgt. to Brigdar Stwd.
Scaffolds for the D[ean] and Preb[endary] etc.[21]

This reveals not only that scaffolds were built for the coronation of James II, but that the lack of any firm and authoritative policy (which led astray Osgood, Purcell, and, evidently with more profit, Negus) still obtained as late as 1714. Another petition, apparently written just before the coronation of William and Mary, shows the dean and Chapter of Westminster attempting to recover a "concession" of which they had been deprived at the coronation of James II. He, no doubt, had other ends in view when it came to the enrichment of any clergy that may have been in attendance:

> The Dean and Chapter's petition to the King and Queen for their fees due at their majesties' coronation. To the King and Queen their most excellent majesties. The humble petition of Thomas Bishop of Rochester, Dean of the Collegiate Church of St. Peter in Westminster and the Chapter of the same church

Showeth:

That your petitioners and their predecessors by right of their Charter and liber Regalia, have time out of mind at the coronation of the King and Queen of this realm, been used to claims and have (except at the coronation of King James the Second) several perquisites and advantages of very great value for their service and attendance at the said coronations. And your petitioners having put in their claims before the Right Honourable the Lord Commissioners appointed by Your Majesty to judge and determine of matters of that nature in your Courts of Claims. The said Commissioners have allowed of your petitioners' claims and as to the fees due to your petitioners, they are deferred to Your Majesty's good will and pleasure.

> Your petitioners do humbly pray Your Majesties, that you will be graciously pleased to allow unto them such compensation for their dues and services as in your princely wisdom shall serve. And your petitioners, as in duty bound, shall ever pray for the long continuance of Your Majesty's happy reign and government.[22]

A similar memorandum issued just prior to Purcell's troublesome embarrassment over coronation fees would have spared Purcell his chagrin had he known of its existence. Coming just after the above petition was submitted, the following order shows that the foregoing, or a similar request, was granted about three weeks before the ceremonial day:

25 March, 1689:

It is ordered that all such money as shall be raised for seats at the Coronation, within the church organ-loft or churchyard shall be paid into the hands of the Treasurer & distributed as the Dean of the Chapter shall think fit. And that all vacant places both in the church and churchyard which are not taken up and employed for the King's use be disposed of by the Dean and Chapter of Westminster as they shall think fit.[23]

Evidently Purcell and Crespion knew nothing of these arrangements, which seem clearly to have been aimed at the perquisites they were hoping to enjoy at the coronation of William and Mary. Following the precedent laid down at the coronation of Charles II, and possibly that of James II, they may well have fallen foul of the new regulations without knowing of their existence. It is hardly conceivable that they would have flouted royal will had they known it.

One can easily imagine the situation. Purcell, busy with his many other responsibilities at Westminster as well as at the Chapel Royal, would already have contracted with some local builder for scaffolding and other materials. By the time this petition had been granted, just eighteen days before the coronation itself, he would already have begun to draw up a list of those who were to be admitted to the organ loft and perhaps might already have collected some money. In the midst of all the urgent preparations going on throughout the rest of the Abbey, it would have been easy for someone who should have informed him of the new order to forget to do so. Or is it just possible, as Hawkins assumed, that "ignorance or malice" had some part in the affair? Having quoted another version of the order to Purcell given below, in which Purcell was referred to as the "organ-blower," he adds: "Upon which it may be observed that the penning of it is an evidence of great ignorance or malice, in that it describes him by the appellation of organ-blower who was organist of their own church, and in truth the most excellent musician of his time." [24] Furthermore, Purcell may have had something more to go on than a mere precedent set in Charles II's reign, for Dr. Barton, describing the coronations of James II, William and Mary, and of later monarchs, sent the following details in a letter to Charles Low, Esq., in 1714: "The choir men had the rest of the Abbey given to them from the West door to the door of the choir. The gallery below the organ on the same side was left to the King's Scholars and Doctor Knipes's boarders. The organ-loft itself the organist had and what was above the organ eastward some great folks had." [25]

For whatever reasons, and by whatever means, Purcell certainly did wander into difficulties over the loft. Within a week of the coronation (which took place on 11 April), he was confronted with the following:

> It was ordered that Mr. Purcell, the organist to the Dean and Chapter of Westminster, do pay to the hand of Mr. John Nedham, Receiver of the College, all such money as was received by him for places in the organ-loft at the coronation of King William and Queen Mary by or before Saturday next, being the 20th day of this instant April. And in default thereof his place is declared to be null and void. And it is further ordered that his stipend or salary due at our Lady Day last past be detained in the hands of the Treasurer until further order. [26]

This was drastic treatment, indeed. But within a very few days— presumably within the prescribed time—Purcell turned over the money he had collected, keeping only the amount allowed by authority, as we know from another account in Needham's hand:

> The account of the monies received at the coronation of King William and Queen Mary (and the payments thereof). The account of such monies as I have received from Mr. Crispyn and Mr. Purcell of the money received by them at the Coronation.

	£	s.	d.
Of Mr. Crispyn	423	16	7
Of Mr. Purcell his poundage and other expenses being deducted	78	04	6
Total is	492	01	1 [N.B. Total should be £502. 1s. 1d.]
Mr. Gregory's bill for erecting and pulling down the scaffolds for the use of the Dean and Chapter of Westminster	67	16	02
Paid to the woman for cleansing the effigies of King Charles the Second	10	00	00
Total	77	16	02
There will remain in my hand the sum of	414	04	11
The money received by myself, all charges being deducted	064	09	6
	478	14	5 [27]

In this context the accounts of Purcell's receipts could hardly have been made from any financial source other than that provided by spectators who paid to view the coronation proceedings from the organ loft. The exact meaning of "his poundage and other expenses" cannot be ascertained at present. "Poundage," according to *OED*, could have signified either "a payment of so much per pound sterling upon the amount of any transaction in which money passes" or "a percentage of the total earnings of any concern, paid as wages to those engaged in it, sometimes in addition to a fixed wage." On the face of it the latter seems to fit the situation under discussion most closely, particularly in the light of other records that are to follow. As for "other expenses," we can only suppose that these would have had to do with setting up the seats in the organ loft, tickets, and so forth. We have no way of judging Mr. Needham's probity in other matters, but it is certain that his arithmetic was not beyond criticism. The sum he arrived at is short of what it should have been by £10. What may have happened to the missing sum is anyone's guess, but it appears from this that no one watched the watchers. Moreover, the full bill for Mr. Gregory's services amounted to a larger sum, as the following receipt dated 17 May 1689 shows:

Rec'd of Mr. John Nedham by order of the Dean and Chapter of Westminster the sum of one hundred and five pounds being in full for the scaffoldings and work done in and about the Church at Westminster with relation to the Coronation either by order or by the order of the said Mr. Nedham

(signed) By me, Tho. Gregory

The entry referring to the effigies, which might seem somewhat irrelevant in a statement of proceeds and expenditure, is quite in order. The showing of the effigies, or "monuments" (as they are called in the Westminster Abbey Treasurer's Papers), provided another very profitable source of funds for the Abbey, these being divided up periodically among all interested parties. Although there seem to be no extant records after the reign of Charles II, the following account of May 1670 shows that the sums involved were not negligible: "Collected for the sight of the monuments £138. 06s. 03d."[28] For their part in the coronation of Charles II, it will be remembered, the vergers had had to be satisfied with nineteen shillings from the "monuments money," their share having been overlooked when coronation proceeds were divided up.

It has been supposed that this was the end of the matter, Purcell having kept his post, somewhat chastened by an official rebuke and seemingly poorer by nearly £80 than he had expected to be. Nevertheless, he was in good standing at Westminster Abbey, as elsewhere in his plurality of posts. There is no way of knowing how his reputation fared. But financially he did not do so badly as the above account would suggest. Another disbursement record reveals that he was given back nearly half the money he had turned over:

All necessary charges being deducted out of the money which Mr. Crespion and Mr. Purcell paid to Mr. Nedham there remaining

	£414	4	11
Whereof he is to pay by gift of the Dean and Chapter to:			
To Mr. Crespion as chanter and petty canon	24	00	00
To Mr. Tynchare as sacrist and petty canon	24	00	00
To the three other petty canons at £18 each	54	00	00
To the six senior choirmen at £15 each	90	00	00
To the next choirmen at £10 each	40	00	00
To the next choirman	8	00	00
To the two that supply the 12th place in the choir at £5 each	10	00	00
To Mr. Baggs the sacrist	6	00	00

To the two vergers at £14 each	28	00	00
To Mr. Purcell	35	00	00
To the four bell-ringers at £5 each	20	00	00
To Mr. Hawkes as porter	3	00	00
To Mr. Lake	10	00	00
To the 12 almsmen at 30s. each	18	00	00
To the 8 choristers at 20s. each	8	00	00
To the college butler	2	00	00
To the gardener	2	00	00
To the three choir widows. *viz.* Mrs. Tucker, Mrs. Godfrey and Mrs. Kettlewell 10s. each	1	10	00
To the three sweepers 10s. each	1	10	00
To the cloister-porter	1	10	00
	£387	10	00
The remainder of the fabric	£26	14	11

(signed) Tho. Rosten. Dec. Westmr[29]

On the reverse side of this page, these names and amounts appear again, each payment being countersigned by its owner, except for the sweeping-man, widows, almsmen, and choristers, some of whom may have been illiterate. For some obscure reason, Mr. Needham's receipts were not subject to such wide distribution among the Abbey personnel:

Mr. Needham's money	£64	9	6
To Mr. Needham	20	0	0
To Mr. Knipe	20	0	0
To Moor, a librarian	5	0	0
The remainder to the fabric			

(signed) Tho. Rosten[30]

Why were Needham and Knipe allowed to divide up their receipts between themselves (with a small allowance to Mr. Moor) when Purcell and Crespion had been called to book so peremptorily? And why were no sums or balances entered here? Surprise changes to suspicion with the discovery of another mistake in Mr. Needham's addition (again in his own favor) in the account of the funds set aside for "fabric money":

Fabric Money:			
Out of Mr. Crispyn's and Mr. Purcell's	£26	14	11
Out of Mr. Needham's	13	9	6
The Churchwarden's	10	—	—

Tho. Rosten[31]

There should have been £19. 9s. 6d. for the "remainder to the fabric" from Needham's account, not £13. 9s. 6d. as is entered here. What

happened to the missing £6 is anyone's guess. Such laxity suggests peculation. Might Crespion and Purcell have argued that their attempt to
retain their collections was justified both by past precedent and current
corruption?

Incomplete accounts of this affair have been unnecessarily damaging
to Purcell's reputation. At least there is room for the charitable supposition that he and Crespion thought in good conscience that they
were merely abiding by tradition, not flouting authority. Furthermore,
Purcell, like most English court musicians of his time, found it extremely difficult to collect his salary and reimbursements on time. Even
the injunction quoted above shows that Purcell's half-yearly stipend
was already a month overdue. How much longer he had to be patient is
again a matter for conjecture. Certainly though, court officials were
not overzealous in seeing that payments were met on time or that the
financial needs of their musicians were given very much thought. In
fact overdue payments of stipends and salaries had long since become
the rule rather than the exception, as may be seen from almost any
page of the lord chamberlain's treasury papers.[32]

Just before this time, Purcell had found himself considerably out of
pocket for repairing and keeping fit the organs and instruments of the
Chapel Royal and had had to wait for more than a year to be reimbursed the £81 he had spent on materials.[33] At the coronation of
James II, he had spent £34. 12s. on erecting an extra organ in the Abbey, and then had waited more than six months for payment.[34] History
repeated itself at the coronation of William and Mary, except that his
payment was delayed for more than a year, as we know from the following informative receipt, signed by Purcell himself:

> 1 Aug. 1690: Rec: for £32 for providing organ at coronation &c.: Rec'd
> of Wm Jephson, Esq., by me, Henry Purcell, the sum of two & thirty
> pounds in satisfaccion of so much money by me expended in providing
> an organ and other necessaries for the use of the Chapel Choir at their
> Majesties Coronation, April 11th 1689.
> I say rec'd . . . . (signed) Henry Purcell[35]
> (authentic signature).

Small wonder, then, if he should have adopted a catch-as-catch-can
policy where financial matters were concerned. His self-interest was
not only justified by earlier precedent; it was very probably demanded
by his immediate economic situation.

During the same period, his daughter, Frances, was born even while
he was occupied in preparing music for the production of Dryden's
The Spanish Fryar, which took place early in June of 1688. Purcell's

ornate and expressive setting of "Whilst I with Grief" was first heard with this play.[36] On 13 June, Purcell's music was heard again at the Queen's Theatre, when *Circe* was revived.[37] A week and a day after the coronation, a series of concerts began, as we know from an advertisement in the *London Gazette* for 15–18 April 1689. Quite probably Purcell was involved in some fashion.

During all these activities, including the sordid business of the organ-loft incident, Purcell was busy composing music for Thomas Shadwell's "Now Does the Glorious Day Appear," which he identified as "An Ode on the Queen's birthday, sang [*sic*] before their majesties at Whitehall. . . ."[38] Unlike his five other "birthday songs" for Queen Mary, this one is undated. Since 1689 was the only year for which no ode is specified and Shadwell's poem was published in 1690,[39] it seems probable that 1689 was the year for which Purcell composed the piece. By this time, without scarcely a doubt, Purcell had begun work on *Dido and Aeneas*, the first opera of the Glorious Revolution—indeed the first truly dramatic "English Opera" worthy of the name. Like the foregoing ode, it was to be a magnificent musical tribute paid to his employers and countrymen, whatever immediate, petty annoyances may have beset him.

Musical Life
Under William and Mary

MEANWHILE, TWO MUSICAL COLLECTIONS prominently displaying Purcell's name had appeared: the second part of *Musick's Handmaid* and *The Banquet of Music*, book 3; both were advertised in the Term Catalogue for May 1689. The latter, licensed on 1 December 1688, may be considered as belonging to Purcell's activities for the previous year. The first-named, however, dates from 1689. It links up with the first book, *Musick's Handmaid . . . Lessons for Virginals or Harpsycon*, which "Honest John" Playford had published in 1663. He reedited it in 1678, along with the second part, and published both jointly with his son Henry. The latter brought out the second book in yet another edition in 1689, relying upon Purcell for musical editing, as well as for the majority of the compositions, as he had done in several other instances: "The Second Part of Musick's Handmaid: CONTAINING The newest Lessons, Grounds, Sarabands, Minuets and Jigs, set for the virginals, harpsichord and spinet. London, Printed on copper-plates, for Henry Playford . . . 1689."

The engraved illustration on the title page of the second book shows that its basic purpose was the same as that of the first despite the archaic dichotomy between *musica theorica* and *musica practica* that ostensibly divided them. The little pieces these contained were written for the instruction of amateur musicians and hence were suitable for more or less talented daughters of rich or noble families who owned harpsichords and who could afford music masters.[1] The composer's task was to fill these little books with pretty pieces, not too difficult for the available time and talent of such aspirants. Purcell managed well, creating little pieces that were not mere trifles. But however well he may have discharged his duties as composer, he can be criticized for one interesting editorial slip. The first piece in the collection, an air in C major, is printed anonymously, even though it is a transcription from Purcell's welcome song for 1682, "The Summer's Absence Unconcerned We Bear" [Z. 337].

Purcell's connection with formal education about this time led also to his setting of "Celestial Music,"[2] a new ode performed "at the house of Mr. Maidwell, a school master."[3] This house in Westminster later became Maidwell's school.[4] But Purcell's reason for setting this text (by one of Maidwell's students) has not yet been discovered. Cummings was certainly wrong in stating that it was performed for the return of the prince of Denmark.[5]

Meanwhile, a much more significant school performance was being prepared at Josiah Priest's Boarding School for Young Ladies and Gentlewomen in Chelsea, where Purcell's *Dido and Aeneas* was first performed. By 1689, according to an advertisement in the *London Gazette* for 22–25 November 1680, Priest had been in Chelsea, then at some considerable distance from London, for nearly a decade: "Josiah Priest, dancing master, who kept a boarding school for gentlewomen in Leicester Fields, is removed to the great School House at Chelsea, which was Mr. Portman's. . . . There will continue the same masters, and others, to the improvement of the said school." As Michael Tilmouth has indicated, Priest had been thinking about the move some time earlier, having actually announced his intentions in the *London Gazette* for 25 November 1678.[6]

Priest's venture had numerous precedents, as various accounts of the time reveal, and under his predecessors' direction, there had been, in fact, an earlier musical stage work in 1676 at Chelsea School itself, as the following title reveals: "Thomas Duffett: *Beauties Triumph*, a Masque. Presented by the Scholars of Mr. Jeffrey Banister and Mr. James Hart. At their New Boarding-School for Young Ladies and Gentlewomen, kept in that House which was formerly Sir Arthur Gorges at Chelsea, Written by T. Duffet . . . London: Printed in the year MDCLXXVI."[7] Purcell was perhaps still in the shadow of official disfavor at court, where everyone was too preoccupied with William's anti-Jacobite campaign in the highlands and later in Ireland to think about much else. (His court appointment had at last been recorded on 22 July.) At any rate, the absence of any major events at court throughout the summer freed him for other commissions, making it possible for him to write the ode for Mr. Maidwell's school and to accept the much more important commission from Josiah Priest. Perhaps the impending arrival of a new son—Edward, who was to be baptized at Westminster on 6 September 1689[8]—caused him to receive gratefully any commission that paid well.

No later than October, and possibly as early as July 1689, Purcell's *Dido and Aeneas* was performed at Gorges House, Chelsea, the same house Josiah Priest had taken over for his school for young gentle-women. At least this is the approximate date usually agreed upon at present on the basis of evidence that seems solid, though much of it is circumstantial.[9] The only known copy of the libretto may have been printed solely for the audience at the first production, as nothing beyond the following is given on the title page: "An opera perform'd at Mr. Josias Priest's Boarding-school at Chelsea by young Gentlewomen."[10]

As for the actual performance, this statement scarcely represents the whole truth, because it is unlikely that the school would have provided sopranos capable of singing the parts of Dido and Belinda (not to men-tion Aeneas's tenor role, or the choral bass and tenor parts). Nor could a girls' school have provided the orchestral players and dancers re-quired. Hence Priest very likely would have invited as many London professionals as needed, although his young gentlewomen may have performed the dances. Not knowing how, or when, or even actually where at Gorges House it was performed, we are also completely igno-rant as to the reception *Dido and Aeneas* may have received. It seems improbable that such an important milestone in English music history would have gone unheeded at the time. But no source yet discovered mentions the original performance.[11]

That the opera was written to commemorate some aspect of the Glorious Revolution is clear; but apart from certain general correspon-dences that the plot bears to the contemporary royal situation, notice has been taken only of the hint in the following passage from D'Urfey's "Epilogue" (spoken by Lady Dorothy Burk):

> Rome may allow strange tricks to please her sons,
> But we are Protestants and English nuns,
> Like nimble fawns and birds that bless the Spring
> Unscarr'd by turning times we dance and sing.[12]

However, Tate's departures from Virgil's original story also suggest that he may have designed this little drama as a topical allegory relat-ing to the ascendance of William III, Mary II, and the parliamentar-ian party. As poet laureate he would normally have been expected to supply such a "dynastic" libretto for the reigning monarchs, just as Purcell, composer-in-ordinary, would have been expected to set it to music.

Certainly the parallels are there. Even in the prologue to *Dido and Aeneas* one need not look too far beneath the surface to find topical reference. The allusion to William and Mary as "Phoebus and Venus" is too obvious to call for further comment. Together with the reference to some special occasion (perhaps a royal birthday) in the line "To celebrate this genial day," the following eulogy confirms that the opera was produced for some event of special significance in the lives of William and Mary:

> NEREID: Look down ye orbs and see
> A new divinity
> PHOE: Whose lustre does outshine
> Your fainter beams and half eclipses mine . . .
> PHOE: Earth and skies address their duty
> To the sovereign Queen of Beauty . . .
> CHO: To Phoebus and Venus our homage we'll pay,
> Her charms bless the night, as his beams bless the day.

This unequal tribute to the two monarchs correlates with the political situation at the time of their accession to the throne. In fact these lines sound as if written to ease reconciliation of the "queen's party" to the terms of a joint sovereignty. More explicit use of the same twin metaphor in Blow's ode for King William's birthday, 1692, substantiates this notion:

> Secured by Hyde's Advice and Nassau's arm
> Our isle no threatening power can harm
> Britain shall all attempts withstand
> Whilst these two love to shield the land.

> Whilst he abroad does like the sun display
> His active beams and gives to others day
> She like the modest regent of the night
> Supplies his room but not with borrowed light. . . .[13]

All these factors, of course, have little to do with the continuous popularity of this well-paced, arresting musical drama, which until recently stood as the only seventeenth-century opera holding the boards right through to the present. To be sure, *Dido and Aeneas* is relatively easy and inexpensive to perform. But the same might be said of John Blow's *Venus and Adonis* or of Monteverdi's *Orfeo*, neither of which was frequently performed until well along in the twentieth century.

John Blow's little opera, which might be considered the first true English opera[14] despite rival claims for works by William D'Avenant,[15] Richard Flecknoe,[16] and Matthew Locke,[17] made its appearance just at the end of the reign of Charles II. As an aesthetic event, its first performance marked the successful conclusion to a series of attempts to establish "the recitativo style," which may be traced back well into the reign of James I. These various attempts had arisen from the general desire on the part of composers, performers, and potential auditors to naturalize the Italian "dramma per musica," then still a relatively recent innovation and great cultural attraction in Italian cities.

To return to the first performance of *Dido and Aeneas*, the actual date of which is still unknown, it is possibly significant that Queen Mary went "often in the evening to Chelsea reach in her barge" and was "diverted there with a consort of music."[18] Very likely it was her delight in music that brought back to court on 20 October a custom that had been in abeyance when "their majesties dined the first time publicly at Whitehall, with music, heralds, . . . etc., as their predecessors did."[19]

D'Urfey, who had written the epilogue to *Dido and Aeneas*, was also responsible for the ode celebrating William III's birthday on 4 November, "Cloudy Saturnia Drives Her Steeds Apace."[20] But if its three movements and chorus were ever set, no trace of the music remains. There was, however, a ball at the theater for the king's birthday, "with scenes and lights."[21] Apparently this affair, which fell on Thursday evening, preempted the services of a number of musicians who otherwise would have been playing at the weekly concerts in York Buildings, resumed earlier in April after disturbances attending the Glorious Revolution had subsided. On 28 October the *London Gazette* published an announcement to the effect that: ". . . the Bow Street Consort defer their performance in York Buildings until November 11 on account of the King's birthday. Thereafter to be given weekly."

Then, on the day of this concert, the same journal reported a merger of the Bow Street and York Buildings concert series, and the resumption of the regular season on Thursday, the fourteenth. What a busy fortnight London musicians had had, what with all the necessary rehearsals and performances these various events required. Something of the popularity of this sort of concert and the feeling of eagerness on the parts of some of the audiences that attended is reflected in the special license granted on 25 December 1689 to Robert King for the Vendu concerts:

> Whereas we do well approve of the abilities in music of Robert King, one of our musicians, and he having besought us to have our authority to set up a consort of music, and to have the sole government thereof, and that none force their way in without paying such prices as shall be set down. Our will and pleasure therefore is, and we do hereby license and authorize the said Robert King to set up a consort of music to be performed by

such as he shall appoint and as often as he shall think fit, and we require and command all persons to forbear rudely or by force to enter in or abide there during the time of performing the said music without observing such rules and paying such prices as shall be by him set down. And all our officers civil and military are required to be aiding and assisting herein. Given at our Court at Whitehall the 25th day of December 1689 in the first year of our reign.

By His Majesty's command
Shrewsbury [22]

The times had been too unsettled for the preparation of a concert celebrating St. Cecilia's Day,[23] but the musical activity at the Vendu and at York Buildings shows that London concert life had already regained its former vigor.

For New Year's Day, Luttrell[24] recorded that the ". . . King and Queen came to Whitehall, where many of the nobility and gentry came to wish them a happy New Year, and there was a great consort of music, vocal and instrumental, and a song composed by the poet laureate. The mayor, aldermen and sheriffs waited on their majesties to compliment them." Shadwell's song, "With Cheerful Hearts Let All Appear," as set by Blow could scarcely have furnished all the music performed for the occasion, but nothing else appears to have been recorded.

During the last weeks of 1689, Purcell must already have been occupied in composing his first work to celebrate the Glorious Revolution. Although the ode "Of Old When Heroes Thought It Base" [25] was not actually performed until later, the Society of Yorkshiremen in London had commissioned it for 14 February 1690. Supposedly Purcell would have had the work nearly completed when an announcement in the *London Gazette* for 7 February 1690 put off the performance until the twenty-seventh of the following month, after the parliamentary elections. These brought into power not the Whigs, who had placed William III on his throne, but the Tories. The new monarch demonstrated his political sagacity by promptly joining forces with the latter.[26]

Because of this postponement, or perhaps by Tory design, the first performance of Purcell's "Yorkshire Feast Song" very nearly coincided with the anniversary of the beginning of the reign of William and Mary, whose monarchy had been recognized a year and a day before, even though their coronation had not been celebrated until later, on 11 April. For such an occasion, the ode seems to have been quite lavish enough, as we know from the descriptive title given it by the poet, D'Urfey: "An ode on the assembly of the nobility and gentry of the City and County of York, at the anniversary feast, March 27th, 1690.

Set to music by Mr. Henry Purcell. One of the finest compositions he ever made, and cost £100 the performing." [27] D'Urfey's enthusiastic description of this ceremonial composition is confirmed by an advertisement in the *London Gazette* for 14 March 1690: "The Annual Yorkshire Feast will be held the 27th instant at the Merchant Taylors' Hall in Threadneedle Street, where will be a very splendid entertainment of all sorts of vocal and instrumental music." William's Whig supporters were no doubt resentful of all this Tory splendor, particularly since they had just been deserted. On the other hand, they must have joined their opponents in applauding these rousing lines in the final chorus that might have served as a battle song for the Glorious Revolution:

> Sound trumpets, sound, beat every drum
> Till it be known through Christendom;
> This is the knell of falling Rome. . . .

D'Urfey's rhymes and meter are by no means impeccable. But his grasp of the nation's mood could not be improved upon.

Those Whigs of quasi-Puritanical persuasion must have been pleased with William's and Mary's austere moral code, which regulated manners as well as morals at court and elsewhere. They not only proscribed "prophane swearing and cursing, prophaning the Lord's day, drunkenness and such immoralities," [28] but instituted a general fast "to be kept . . . the third Wednesday in every month sucessively during the present war, for supplicating God for pardon of our sins, imploring his blessing and protection in the preservation of His Majesty's person and prosperity of his arms in Ireland. . . ." [29]

As in Puritanical times, this proscriptive attitude evidently extended to certain musical practices that were forbidden on fast days: "Mr. Comptroller has complained to the Green Cloth against Mr. Story for keeping music and revelling in his house on the fast-day; and 'tis believed he will be turned out." [30] William's attitude toward any but martial music when not apathetic was negative. As Purcell and his fellow musicians were soon to learn, the court could no longer be looked upon as the center and home of English musical culture. Nevertheless Purcell was commissioned to produce more music for their majesties a little more than a month after the original performance of the "Yorkshire Feast Song." The occasion was again Queen Mary's birthday, and the poet again Thomas D'Urfey, who provided two poems for the same event: "Arise, My Muse" [31] and "High on a Throne of Glitt'ring Ore." [32]

The first of these, which was no worse than D'Urfey's usual stuff in quality, apparently was too much for Purcell in quantity. At any rate, he did not take the trouble to set D'Urfey's last two choruses, with the result that the ode ends proclaiming King William's brave deeds, rather than extolling Queen Mary's virtues, as the poet intended.[33] The queen cannot have been pleased, for the piece ends comically, with the chorus exhorting William ad infinitum to "Go on, go on, illustrious man," just after she has been portrayed entreating him to stay at home. If indeed Queen Mary was nettled by Purcell's setting of her birthday ode, her displeasure might well account for her deliberate slighting of Purcell's music in favor of the Scottish tune "Cold and Raw," as Hawkins recounted in his gossipy little anecdote (granted, of course, that the anecdote be true). (See the Preface to the Second Edition.)

Whether or not it was written for the same occasion as the foregoing, Purcell's sprightly setting of D'Urfey's "High on a Throne of Glitt'ring Ore" occupied a special place in the very happily conceived series that he composed for the queen. The text appeared in D'Urfey's *New Poems* of 1690, definitely labeled "An Ode to the Queen especially set to music by Mr. H. Purcell," and because the text referred to her having sat on the throne, the piece could only have been written for either 1689 or 1690, the latter year being the more likely.

Purcell provided for another event that was to have been part of the celebrations for Queen Mary's twenty-eighth birthday this same year in his songs and instrumental music for Dryden's *Amphitryon*. Boswell[34] lists a warrant to prepare the theater for a play on Wednesday, 30 April, being the queen's birthday. Nicoll[35] also records an entry in the lord chamberlain's accounts, which posted a box for the queen and another for the maids of honor for this same performance. However, the entry was canceled without explanatory note and another made for 21 October for a performance that the queen evidently did attend with her maids of honor, because a payment of £15 is recorded opposite that date.

Purcell's music for *Amphitryon* (including a full set: tripartite overture, act-tunes, and three songs) no doubt contributed a great deal to the general popularity of the play, which was to have fairly frequent revivals during the next decade. Dryden, whose musical sensibilities had been so underdeveloped that he had tolerated Grabu's dull music for his first opera *Albion and Albanius*, at last had seen the light. After allowing credit in the dedication to Plautus and Molière and the players for any excellence the play might have, Dryden continued, with further false modesty:

> But what has been wanting on my part has been abundantly supplied by the excellent composition of Mr. Purcell, in whose person we have at

length found an Englishman equal with the best abroad. At least my opinion of him has been such since his happy and judicious performances in the late opera. To all which, and particularly to the composition of the Pastoral Dialogue, the numerous choir of fair ladies gave so just an applause on the third day. I am sorry, for my own sake, that there was one star wanting, as beautiful as any in our hemisphere; that young Berenice, who is mis-employing all her charms on stupid country souls, that can never know the value of them; and losing the triumphs, which are ready prepared for her in this Court and town.

(Here Dryden alluded to Berenice, wife of Ptolemy III, who had dedicated a lock of her hair as a votive offering for her husband's return from an invasion into Syria. The parallel to Queen Mary's situation in the spring and summer of 1690 is too clear to need further explanation, in view of William's successful summer campaign in Ireland.)

The musical establishment at court had been growing, but around May it suddenly received a serious setback with the king's order "that the musicians be presently reduced to 24 performers and an instrument keeper, and that though there is provision made only for that number by the establishment, yet care will be taken for paying the rest for the time they have served. . . ."[36] The list for 25 March 1689 included thirty-four musicians from the former reign (at an aggregate salary of £1,140 per annum plus liveries, which would have amounted to an additional £548. 5s.). To these sums were to be added the stipends of the instrument-keeper, the salaries of twenty gentlemen of the Chapel Royal and of the master and boys of the Chapel, and stipends for sixteen trumpeters and kettledrummers, the latter apparently occupying a place very near to William's heart. Significantly, in the retrenched account for the following St. Andrew's Day, only twenty-six "musicians to the King and Queen" were named.[37]

All this reveals how profoundly the musical situation at court had changed since the seventies and eighties. Charles II had found ways to protect his musicians from similar orders, not enforce them, and the change in royal attitude after the Glorious Revolution is reflected in the reduction of the number of musicians in the king's employ, before and after the retrenchment. Here, perhaps, lies one explanation for the great rise of concert life in London about this time: Musicians were otherwise unemployed.

The relative infrequency of Purcell's name in official lists is significant and probably explains his having turned increasingly to the theater both for income and for a musical outlet. His increased involvement with theater music, possibly originating from adverse financial conditions at court, very likely explains the sudden upsurge of his popularity in theatrical circles about 1690, for which he had prepared the way with his earlier works for the stage. The above-mentioned retrenchment would have found him hard at work on music for Betterton's revision, "with alterations and additions after the manner of an opera," of Beaumont's and Massinger's *The Prophetess: or, the History of Dioclesian.*[38] The new production, which marked Purcell's professional debut on the operatic stage, was announced in the *London Gazette* for 16 June 1690. It is fairly certain that it was mounted at the Theatre Royal, Drury Lane, soon after the notice had appeared, for Carr and Playford were advertising for subscriptions for the publication of Purcell's music in the same journal for the following 7 July.

The plot of the opera is quite simple, and its topicality transparent, what with William III's having departed for Ireland just twelve days before the advertisement had appeared. In the original story, Delphia had prophesied to Diocles (later the Emperor Dioclesian) that he would become emperor upon killing a certain mighty boar. By happy coincidence, the murderer of the previous emperor was named Aper ("boar"), so that when Diocles had slain him, with the complicity of Niger, an honest Roman, he actually had carried out an act of divine justice. Charinus, current Roman emperor, was well pleased, and Aurelia provided added incentive by offering herself in marriage to the slayer of "the boar." Diocles therefore was acclaimed first as hero, then as emperor. (Though nothing is said here about Emperor Charinus, history reveals that he actually was quite complacent about sharing the emperorship not only with Dioclesian, but with Maximilian as well.) Topically as well as musically the work was well suited to the temper of the times and was most successful. As Downes pointed out ". . . being set out with costly scenes, machines and clothes: the vocal and instrumental music done by Mr. Purcell, and dances made by Mr. Jo. Priest, it gratified the expectation of Court and City; and got the author great reputation."[39] An anonymous "Epistle to the Rt. Hon. Charles, Earl of Dorset and Middlesex"[40] confirms the case for such topical uses of music and the operatic stage by conjectures as to what would happen if France had a William III:

> Their plays, their songs, would dwell upon this wound,
> And operas repeat no other sound;
> Boyne would for ages be their painters' theme.

Purcell's star as a theatrical composer was rising rapidly. As if Dryden's public recognition of the worth of his music for *Dioclesian*[41] had unleashed new forces in his favor, he suddenly found himself in continual demand, both at Drury Lane and at Dorset Garden. During the last few months of 1690, his music was being performed in connection with four, or perhaps even five or six, London productions, including Dryden's *Amphitryon* (as mentioned above) and Elkanah Settle's *Distress'd Innocence*[42] in October; "A New Play" mentioned for "Why My Daphne," which was published in the sixth book of *The Banquet of Music*—licensed on 2 December 1690;[43] *The Gordian Knot Unty'd*, possibly as early as December 1690;[44] *Sir Anthony Love*,[45] and (just possibly) *The Knight of Malta*.[46] All told, these had required thirty-five separate compositions, including the eleven (or twelve) that Purcell had probably finished in the previous spring. A regular theatergoer would have found it quite difficult *not* to hear Purcell's music in play after play that season, such was his popularity.

Something of a mystery surrounds the play *The Gordian Knot Unty'd*, written by an anonymous Francophile, as P. A. Motteux explained at the time: "You have asked me, who was the author of that play called *The Gordian Knot Untyd* and wondered with many more why it was never printed. I hear that gentleman who writ lately a most ingenious dialogue concerning women, now translated into French, is the author of that witty play, and it is almost a sin in him to keep it and his name from the world."[47] The author alluded to was almost without a doubt the same person who wrote *A Dialogue Concerning Women, Being a Defence of the Fair Sex Written to Eugenia*, also an anonymous work, although it has a preface signed by John Dryden.[48] The French version was also printed, under the title "*Défense du Beau Sexe. . . .* Écrit en anglais par une personne de qualité, et traduit en français par une Dame anglaise," the preface signed by "Jean Dryden."[49]

Dennis Arundell has identified one William Walsh as the author of the play, which he traced to Molière's *Monsieur de Porceaugnac*[50] (for which Lully had supplied music in France twenty years earlier). A reference in the 1691 edition of John Bancroft's *King Edward III* seems to indicate that *The Gordian Knot* was performed in 1690, some time before December.[51] However, the fact that Motteux speaks of the play as contemporary to the *Dialogue concerning Women*, published in 1691, makes the latter date equally probable. The identity of the "Dame anglaise" is still to be discovered.

On the political scene, September had brought William III back to England as the hero of the Boyne—very little was made then of Limerick—just as the musical season was getting under way in London. As usual there is no record of what music, if any, was performed for his arrival in London on the tenth after a four-day progress. Very likely he would have been more than content with fireworks and a flourish of trumpets and drums for this occasion as well as for the general thanksgiving proclaimed on the fourteenth in the city of London. The king's disregard for music may account for the existence of two odes for his fortieth birthday—Shadwell's "Welcome, Thrice Welcome" and Matthew Prior's "As Though Britannia's Raging Sea"— with no known musical setting for either.[52] Nor was the St. Cecilia celebration for 1690 an affair grand enough to excite either great interest or commentary worth recording. Perhaps the lack of any organized public performance for the years 1688 and 1689 put extraordinary difficulties in the way of the organizers of the celebration for 1690.[53] If so, these cannot have been alleviated, but only aggravated by the selection of the inept Shadwell as the poet for the occasion and the slight songwriter Robert King as composer. Apparently little care was taken to see the music preserved, for it cannot now be found—a fact that perhaps may be taken in lieu of any contemporary commentary on the composition.[54]

The tune "Lilliburlero," with its Purcellian associations, was again heard in the streets, as a new broadside ballad to this tune appeared about the time William III returned to share his victory with loyal Englishmen: "The Courageous Soldiers of the West; or The undaunted Countrymen's Resolution in taking up Arms in the defence of King William and Queen Mary, together with the Protestant Religion."[55] We have no way of knowing what William's reaction may have been to the pointed lack of reference to his own heroic exploits on the occasion or the even more pointed reference to:

> Marlborough both true and loyal
> now with the rest did add to the train.[56]

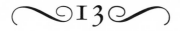

A Royal Excursion
Abroad

WILLIAM INSISTED ON IMPRESSIVE musical forces for a long postponed
return to his native land, crossing the channel in January 1691. The
king's first journey back to Holland since he had embarked there at the
end of 1688 to lead a successful expedition to topple James II from
his throne was not just a nostalgic voyage. On the contrary, he had
been "earnestly entreated by the States of Holland, and the confederate
Princes in Germany, etc. to meet at a general Congress at The Hague, in
order to concert military and economic forces for the next campaign." [1]
He acquiesced, of course, having always opposed Louis XIV's ambition to turn all of Europe into his own empire.

Contemporary accounts of ceremonies attending the "Congress of
the Allies," though indicating glories reminiscent of the Field of the
Cloth of Gold, are disappointing insofar as descriptions of musical
events are concerned. [2] William III, though slighting music domes-
tically, did appreciate its importance for good foreign policy, and he
took with him to Holland a large number of musicians. [3] Nothing is
known of the music they may have played, but the following lists make
it clear that he had transferred most of his musical staff to Holland for
the occasion, hiring a few new oboists as well.

Accounts of William III's voyage to Holland have been vague, if not
confused, with regard to the roster of musicians that actually accompanied him to take part in the celebrations in honor of the Congress of
the Allies at The Hague. In order to clarify this matter, we must examine in detail the various documents that record the activities of the musical participants. Altogether there are four lists. That published by Lafontaine in *King's Musick*, [4] which occupies the first column in the table
below, has been publicly known for the longest time. Following this, in
the second, third, and fourth columns are reproduced the three new
lists discovered by Lady Jeans, as mentioned above.

These lists reveal that two groups of musicians were under consideration. One, consisting of those who stayed behind attending Queen Mary, included nine orchestral players. The larger group included five oboists hired especially for this voyage, eight trumpeters, sixteen orchestral players,[5] and twelve in the vocal ensemble. In other words, the roster of musicians who went to Holland numbered forty-one, or perhaps just forty persons, for it appears that Edmond Flower had become too ill to attend some time before embarkation for the trip. Of these, thirty-five were regular court musicians, and five oboists, as mentioned above, were engaged only for this voyage and did not hold positions at court thereafter. These were "musicians extraordinary" in the language of court bureaucracy and were not on regular salaries.

The rubrics relating to oboists and "vocal musick" in the third and fourth lists are significant. It is important that we understand their implications. On the third of the documents shown above, the names of ten vocal musicians are listed more or less opposite the names of the nine orchestral musicians who stayed behind, but occupying a position opposite the names of the oboists as well. No rubric specifies their disposition. Then, directly beneath the names of the oboists, appear the names of "Dr John Blow and Hen: Purcell, Composers," who were considered a part of the "vocall musick" as we know from the annotation to the left.

The key to the meanings of all these groupings and annotations, however, is to be found on the fourth document listed above. Here again, the twenty-six regular members of the "Band of Violins" is divided into two groups, the larger of which went to Holland with the king. But on this list, the name of John Mosley has been transferred from its position alongside the names of Blow and Purcell, to be included with the musicians who stayed home. If the composers had stayed home, one could logically assume that their names also would have been moved into the list for their appropriate group.

The temporary status of the five oboists is doubly emphasized here. On the left we read "Hooboys that were in Holland: only for that voyage," and on the right "These are to be paid for their journey into Holland, & no longer." In column three of the document, there is only one annotation, but it too is significant: "Hoboys only for this voyage & not to be established but to be paid for attending His Ma.[y] into Holland." These annotations assume special significance when we read marginal instructions opposite the list of members of the "vocall musick." On the right is written, "Vocal Consort/to be added/Voyces."

I

A list of His Ma.^{ty's} servants above stairs who are to attend His Ma.^{ty} in his voyage unto Holland, and who are paid in the Treasury Chamber:

Trumpeters
Mathias Shore, Sgt.
William Bull
Thomas Barwell
Jarvis Walker
John Stevenson
John Shore
James Truelove
(this name crossed
   out and William Shore
   inserted)
John Maugridge,
   kettledrummer

Musicians
Dr. Nicholas Staggins,
   master
John Bannister (al-
   tered to Francis
   Cruys)
Robert King (altered
   to Henry Eagles)
Bingham
William Hall (altered
   to Samuel Akeroyd)
Robert Carr
John Goodwyn
Henry Heale
Edward Hooton
Christian Stephkins
Morgan Harris
Edmund Flower
Rickard Tomlinson
Frederick Stephkins
Solomon Eagles
John Lenton
Richard Lewin
Charles Powell
   and Five Hooboys
John Mosley, Keeper
   of the Instruments
William Brown, Cham-
   berkeeper to the Music

II

Musitians and Others who attended His Ma.^{ty} into Holland

(A partial list showing only those of string band and oboes who were alerted to go to Holland.)

Nicholas Staggins,
   master
Francis Cruys
Henry Eagles
Bingham
Samuel Akeroyde
Robert Carr
John Goodwyn
Henry Heale
Edward Hooton
Christian Stephkins
Morgan Harris
Edmund Flower
Richard Tomlinson
Frederick Stephkins
Solomon Eagles
John Lenton
Richard Levin
Charles Powell
Five Hoboys
Keeper of the Instru-
   ments: John Mosley
Chamberkeeper of
   Musick William
   Broune

III

These are to Certifie the Right Honble the Lord Chamberlaine of their Ma.^{ti's} Household that some of the Persons hereinafter named did attend his Ma.^{ty} into Holland do humbly beg your Ldship's favorable assistance towards the receiving the money which is ordered them in the Treasury Chamber which cannot be received till your Lordship does declare your pleasure therein.

	Nic.° Staggins, Master	These did go into Hol-
	John Goodwin	land & attend His
	Ed: Hooton	Ma.^{ty} in that voyage.
	Robt Carr	Nic.° Staggins
	Henry Heale	
	George Bingham	
	Morgan Harris	
	Christian Stefkins	
Violins 24	Fred: Stefkins	
	Richard Lewiss	
	Soll: Eaccles	
	Hen.^e Eaccles	
	John Lenton	
	Charles Powell	
	Francis Cruys	
	Edmond Flower nay sick	

These were left behind	John Bannister	Vocal Music
to attend on Her Ma.^{ty}	Robt: King	
	Wm Hall	Wm Turner
	Wm Clayton	Jo: Goslin
	Daniel Short	Jo: Bowman
	Robt Strong	Mr. Damascene
	Alexander Delature	Mr. Robert
	Charles Coleman	Leon. Woodeson
	Theo: Fittz	Mr. Richardson
		Mr. Marsch
		Mr. Bowger
		Mr. Snow

Hoboys, only for this	George Sutton
voyage, & not to be es-	La: Rich
tablished but to be	Granvell
paid for attending His	Bresong
Ma.^{ty} into Holland	Baptist

          Nic.° Staggins
          John Mosley: Instrument
                Keeper
vocall ⎰ Dr. John Blow ⎱ Composers
musick ⎱ Hen: Purcell ⎰

These are to certifie the Right Honble Ld Chamberlaine of their Maties Household, that the persons hereafter named did attend his Ma.^ty into Holland, who do humbly crave your Ldship's favorable assistance, towards the attaining the money that is ordered them in the Treasury Chambers, which cannot be received till your Ldship does declare your pleasure therein.

	Nic.° Staggins, Master	the part that attended
	John Goodwin	his Maj.^ty into Holland
	Edward Hooton	
	Hen.^e Heale	
	Robt Carr	
	George Bingham	
	Morgan Harris	
	Hen.^e Eaccles	
	Soll: Eaccles	
	Fred: Stefkins	
	Christ.^r Stefkins	
	John Lenton	
Band of Violins	Charles Powell	
	Richard Lewiss	
	Franciss Cruse	
	Edmond Flower	
	Robert King	The remaining part that
	John Bannister	Attended the Queen
	Wm. Clayton	
	Theop: Fittz	
	Wm. Hall	
	Daniell Short	
	Robt. Strong	
	Alixander Delature	
	Charles Coleman	
	John Mosely: Instrument Keeper	
Hooboys that were in Holland: only for that voyage	George Sutton	These are to be paid for their journey into Holland, & no longer.
	Francis Lari	
	_____ Brazong	
	_____ Baptist	
	_____ Granvell	
	John Blow: Composer	
	Hen.^e Purcell: Harpsicall	
Vocall Consort to be added Voyces	Wm: Turner	
	_____ Gozlin	
	_____ Bowman	
	_____ Damazen	
	_____ Robert	These to be continued
	Lenard Woodson	
	_____ Richardson	
	Alfanso March	
	Joseph Boucher	
	Moses Snow	

This annotation appears opposite the names of ten singers, which follow directly beneath two names, which are bracketed together, "John Blow, Composer; Hen: Pursell, Harpsicall." For the rubric identifying their status, we must look back to the third column, where they are classified as part of the "vocall musick." Obviously, the annotation "to be added/Voyces" was meant to clarify the ambiguous position of the singers on the previous list, whose names had been merely added in available blank space. Here it is clear that they were listed among those of the vocal music already scheduled to go to Holland, namely, Blow and Purcell. The identification of the latter brings to light one further point. If he did not go to Holland, then no official harpsichordist was listed—an omission that seems highly unlikely in view of the king's need to put his best foot forward at the Hague, musically as well as otherwise.

But it is the annotation to the right of the roster of the "vocall musick" that clinches matters: "These to be continued" tells us that, unlike the oboists who were hired to go to Holland and were employed for the voyage only, the vocal music, including Blow and Purcell, were regular employees who went to Holland and who were to be continued on the payroll as regular employees thereafter. That the "vocalists," Blow and Purcell, are not represented in the first column can be attributed to the fact that they were paid by another office. This would explain also the omission of their names on Staggins's list of those receiving riding charges.

As for circumstantial evidence, it is also significant that the Purcell chronology of works reflects very little activity for early 1691. The ode for Queen Mary's birthday, "Welcome, Welcome, Glorious Morn," was due for performance on 30 April. But Purcell could easily have finished this composition during the 103 days duration of the trip to Holland, if indeed he had not found occasion to compose it earlier. Moreover, John Blow wrote no New Year's ode for that year—an unusual omission. Except for the revolutionary year (1689) and the year of Queen Mary's death (1695), 1691 is the only year not celebrated with a New Year's ode between 1679 and 1696. A logical explanation would arise from the fact that Blow, who usually composed the New Year's ode, was abroad at that time.[6]

Other members of the "vocall musick" remain to be considered. Michael Tilmouth[7] has pointed out that William Turner,[8] one of the singers, was unlikely to have appointed Thomas Whitfield his "true and lawful attorney" if he were going abroad. But surely, his plan to go to Holland would have furnished his main reason for doing so. Certainly

Henry Heale, who traveled to Holland as a member of the king's orchestra at this time, had appointed Mary, his wife, for the same reason.[9] John Mawgridge, who traveled with King William III as "kettledrummer," also appointed his wife as executrix at the same time.[10]

Although their repertoire is still unknown, it is certain that the musicians were properly prepared and rehearsed for the great "Congress of the Allies," because they had gone to Holland some weeks before William himself made the trip. Many, if not all, of the musical band seem to have spent three and a half months in Holland, as can be seen from the records of their riding charges:

> Warrant to pay Dr. Nicholas Staggins, Master of His Majesty's music, Edward Hooton, John Goodwin, Robert Carr, Henry Heale, Henry Eagles, George Bingham, Morgan Harris, Christian Stephkins, Solomon Eagles, Francis Cruys, John Lenton, and Charles Powell, musicians-in-ordinary to his Majesty; La Rush, George Sutton, Greenville, Baptist and one more hautboy, the several sums following viz:
>
> To Dr. Staggins 5s. by the day for the space of 103 days, from 1 January 1690 to 13 April 1691 for his riding charges and other expenses in attending his Majesty unto Holland, amounting to £24. 15s., and to each of the said musicians and hautboys 3s. by the day for the said time, amounting to the sum of £15. 9s. each.[11]

No records have come to light to show when or where the English musicians performed. Certainly they took part in the pageantry of William's public entry into The Hague on 26 January, the triumphal arch surmounted by Fame sounding her golden trumpet, reminding Purcell and his colleagues of the by now well-known song from *Dioclesian* of the year before. They also probably took part in the earl of Devonshire's grand entertainment, as described by Luttrell.

Frequent public audiences, such as that granted to the elector of Brandenburg on 16 February or to the governor of the Spanish Netherlands, the marquis de Gastanaga, on 18 February, also provided opportunities for music. Indeed, for the public audience granted to the count of Winditzgratze on 24 February, the master of ceremonies managed the whole affair. On the following day a public demonstration called for even more elaborate ceremony. Then, suddenly, the besieging of Mons by the French armies put an end to these ceremonies. William III immediately assumed the role of the soldier and marshaled forces to save Mons. But he was too late, and the city capitulated on 9 April, three days after William had at last set out with his army to lift the siege.

With some forty of the royal musicians away, the records for Janu-

ary and February 1691 naturally reveal little important musical activity
in London and yield no direct references to Purcell, who apparently
had gone on the expedition as official composer and harpsichordist.
Perhaps the intense cold all over England, which Luttrell recorded in
his entry for 4 February, had reduced musical activities even further.
Nevertheless the lull in London concert life came to an end about 20
February 1691, as the following announcements from the *London Gazette* on 19 and 26 February 1690/1 reveal:

> 19 February 1690/1. The consort of music lately in Bow Street is re-
> moved next Bedford Gate in Charles Street, Covent Garden (where a
> room is newly built for that purpose), and by command, is to begin on
> Friday next the 20th instant, where it is afterwards to be continued every
> Thursday, beginning between 7 and 8 in the evening.

> 26 Feburary 1690/1. The new consort of music which began on Friday
> the 20th instant . . . will be performed at the aforesaid place this present
> Thursday the 26th instant, and so continue every Thursday beginning
> between 7 and 8 in the evening.

Just a month later—still some two or three weeks before the royal
musicians returned—Frank and Robert King advertised in the *London
Gazette* the resumption of their royally approved concerts at the Two
Golden Balls, inaugurated at the beginning of the previous season on
9 October.[12]

Then, in the *London Gazette* for 26 February to 2 March 1690/1
appeared good evidence that Purcell had not been idle. The music for
Dioclesian (as *The Prophetess* was now called) was ready for publication, and it seems that he had had no little trouble in preparing it: "The
book, containing all the vocal and instrumental music in *The Prophetess, or The History of Dioclesian* (composed by Mr. Henry Purcell) is
now finished; and will be delivered to the subscribers by John Carr at
his shop near the Middle Temple Gate, upon receipt of the remaining
part of the subscription money." A note, or "advertisement" inserted
in the printed edition explains why a work actually "in the press"
nearly a year before should only at this late date be ready for sale:

> In order to the speedier publication of this book, I employed two several
> printers; but one of them falling into some trouble, and the volume
> swelling to a bulk beyond my expectation, have been the occasions of
> this delay.
>   It has been objected that some of the songs are already common, but
> I presume that the subscribers, upon perusal of the work, will easily
> be convinced that they are not the essential parts of it. [Here Purcell

no doubt referred to several of Thomas Cross's engraved single-sheet songs, such as "Sound Fame" and "Tell Me Why," which had appeared in 1691.]

I have, according to the promise in the proposals, been very careful in the examination of every sheet and hope that the whole will appear as correct as any yet extant.

My desire to make it as cheap as possible [*sic*] I could to the subscribers, prevailed with me so far above the consideration of my own interest that I find, too late, the subscription money will scarcely amount to the expense of completing this edition.

The whole document is interesting, as much for explanations left out as for those given. How was it possible for Purcell's songs to have appeared in print without his knowledge? What was his arrangement with the publishers, whereby he could lose money even before the book had gone on sale to the public? The plaintive tone Purcell adopts in the last paragraph seems to indicate that he had little hope of adequate recompense but could not really afford any loss. Straitened financial circumstances, as here intimated, however, were to be his lot during his last five years, as were the overwork and overworry that this sort of debacle always brings on.

During the trip to Holland and for the next few weeks, Purcell was preparing a new ode for Queen Mary's birthday. For the celebration of this, the queen's thirty-third birthday, Purcell found himself burdened with the delightful verses of the anonymous ode "Welcome, Glorious Morn." Even while composing this ode, Purcell must also have been engaged in supplying music for Dryden's *King Arthur*,[13] his second major semi-opera for the London stage. Dryden had written the libretto first to celebrate the wisdom and sagacity of Charles II, altered it to eulogize James II, and modified it again to entertain William III. Poor Dryden! In his magnum opus for the musical stage, he found it necessary not only to make changes dictated by the rise and fall of monarchs, but also to submit to Purcell's demands for certain alterations, as the following lines from his preface reveal: "But the numbers of poetry and vocal music are sometimes are so contrary that in many places I have been obliged to cramp my verses, and make them rugged to the reader, that they may be harmonious to the hearer." Whatever the difficulties or the damage to Dryden's ego, this collaboration with Purcell produced a work unique in English music history, indeed without parallel anywhere. Though it is primarily an entertainment, it remains a unified work, unlike *The Fairy Queen*, and a truly poetic stage piece, unlike *Dioclesian*. In describing its essentially English character despite the taste for foreign styles displayed by both author and composer, Sir Jack Westrup got to the heart of the matter: "However Dryden might attempt to imitate the accents of the Italian tongue, he could not avoid the flavour of his native English. That flavour is to be found, too, in Purcell's melodies." [14] As Nicoll points out, the first production took place at Dorset Garden Theatre in 1691, possibly as early as May, a date indicating that Purcell must have been at work on *King Arthur* even before composing the queen's birthday ode. [15] Indeed, he had probably spent a great deal of time on this opera during the period of hectic activity discussed above. As a matter of fact, at least two pieces for the opera were written even earlier. Purcell wrote the first chaconne for the ode for King James of 1687, "Sound the Trumpet," [16] while he had already used the first overture to introduce a birthday ode he had written for Queen Mary in 1690, "Arise My Muse." [17] One of the most famous pieces may have had previous existence outside Purcell's music. Captain Walter Scot, in his *True History of Several Honourable Families of the Right Honourable Name of Scot* (1688), [18] describing preparations for a battle, wrote, "Meantime the trumpets sounded 'Come if you dare.'" [19] Purcell therefore may have borrowed this trumpet challenge from actual military practice.

As intimated above, Dryden had written his opera in 1683 or 1684, to be performed with some of the stage machinery used in the 1685 production of his *Albion and Albanius*. [20] Indeed the latter had grown out of the sung prologue that Dryden had conceived for *King Arthur*. [21] He must have had a great deal of revision to do in resurrecting *King Arthur* (now subtitled *The British Worthy*) after seven years, for an opera written to eulogize Charles II now had to be transformed into a fitting tribute to William III and all his military prowess—particularly that which he had just proven in the bogs and on the battlefields of Ireland. As Robert Moore pointed out, Dryden's direct reference to William in the final chorus is unmistakable, although what he hoped to gain by such left-handed compliments is hard to say. [22] Being out of favor at court, perhaps he followed Dryden's example in staying quite outside the circle of courtly flatterers:

> Our natives not alone appear
> To court his martial prize;
> But foreign kings adopted here,
> Their crowns at home despise.

The opera was very successful at its first performance and quite probably lived up to Dryden's conditional prognostication in the preface: "If it succeeds upon the stage it is like to be the chiefest entertainment of the ladies and gentlemen this summer." Downes, writing much later, after it had proven itself, described *King Arthur* in glowing terms, remarking that "it was excellently adorned with scenes and machines. The musical part set by the famous Mr. Henry Purcell; and dances made by Mr. Jo. Priest. The play and the music pleased the Court and City, and being well performed, 'twas very gainful to the company." [23] The work was successful enough to be revived and performed several times, probably about December or January, as is known from Motteux's remarks in his advance notice of *The Fairy Queen* in the *Gentleman's Journal* for January 1692. [24]

Even before he had seen these signs of success, Dryden demonstrated that his musical tastes had improved considerably since 1685, when he had written in the preface to *Albion and Albanius*: "When any of our countrymen excell him [Grabu], I shall be glad to confess my error; in the meantime let virtue be recommended though in the person of a stranger." Dryden's remarks in the preface to *King Arthur*, as revised for the 1691 production, although not an explicit confession, do reveal that he had seen the error of his old ways and had recognized the excellent musical countryman he had prophesied, though in a negative way, six years earlier: "There is nothing better than what I intended but the music; which has since arrived to a greater perfection in England than ever formerly; especially passing through the artful hands of Mr. Purcell, who has composed it with so great a genius that he has nothing to fear but an ignorant, ill-judging audience." This was high praise indeed, and it no doubt crowned for Purcell this his most successful season to date, giving him a foretaste of the universal acclaim that was to be his in full measure, if ever so briefly, before he died.

Meanwhile, Purcell was preoccupied with another matter that arose the same month. On 18 June his sister, Katherine Purcell, married suddenly, to the surprise of her family, who no doubt had long since given her up to spinsterhood. The marriage license in the vicar-general's office, which gave the lowest age warrantable for spinsterhood, improved upon the matter by mentioning her mother's consent: "20 June 1691. William Sale of Sheldwich, Kent, Clerk, Bach., abt 33 and Mrs Catherine Purcell, of St. Margaret's Westminster, aged 22, with consent of her mother; at St. Mary Magdalen, Old Fish Street, London." Although he gives 18 June as the date, W. H. Challen verifies the entry in his typescript list of marriages in Guildhall Library, London. That this was indeed Henry Purcell's sister—who must have been born before 1664, when Henry Purcell the elder died, and was therefore twenty-nine, not twenty-two—is attested by an entry in PCW Admon. for 7 September 1699, which shows that the estate of Purcell's mother, Elizabeth, was administered by "Katherine Purcell, wife of William Sale."[25]

The following week the lord chamberlain's office issued a warrant authorizing payment to Nicholas Staggins and his musicians for "riding charges and other expenses in attending his Majesty unto Holland," as we have seen.[26] Neither Purcell's nor Blow's name appears on this list, nor in that accompanied by another such warrant issued on 10 July following. Perhaps they did not stay for the whole period of 103 days cited in these documents. Whether they were back in England or merely paid separately we cannot know; these records are mute. On the other hand, the "vocall musick" probably were paid from another account.

The summer of 1691 found Purcell concerned with nothing of great moment, except, perhaps, his need for rest and preparations for various commissions for the following year. However, he wrote two catches celebrating historical events and perhaps even a third, of a more domestic nature, during this period. The two historical ones, "Let Us Drink to the Blades"[27] and "The Surrender of Limerick,"[28] celebrated respectively the siege and eventual surrender of Limerick. Thus, even though they were not published until some time later, the two works may be dated fairly accurately. The text of the first referred to the situation at Limerick some time before General Ginkel approached the city on 25 August, and the second to William's capture of that city on 3 October.

On the twenty-sixth of the same month, Ginkel returned victoriously to London to bask in the grateful admiration of the populace, the nobility, and the royal family. That evening, already marked on the calendar as the beginning of the Charles Street concerts,[29] the king, who had just arrived from Holland, and Ginkel met the lord mayor at a splendid dinner at the Merchant Taylors' Hall, both heroes being duly feted and acclaimed. The following week, while the joyful acclamations of the populace were still ringing in everyone's ears,[30] came another, two-day celebration for William's forty-first birthday (4 November) and the regular annual celebration of Guy Fawkes Day on the fifth, given special and official significance this year. Further reasons for celebration existed, at least in loyal Tory circles, because 5 November was also the fourteenth anniversary of the marriage of William and Mary, and the third anniversary of William's landing at Tor Bay. Luttrell, who called attention to this fact, described with obvious enthusiasm the resplendent scene at court:[31]

. . . the Court was all in their splendour, the Queen very rich in jewels; and all the great officers attended: the Archbishop of York preached before the House of Lords, Mr. Fleetwood before the House of Commons, and the Bishop of Salisbury before their majesties: after which their majesties dined publicly. The night concluded with a great ball and dancing at Court, bonfires and illuminations throughout the city, with ringing of bells, etc.

No specific musical compositions, however, are recorded for any of these events.

For the 1691 St. Cecilia celebration (which was held on 23 November, because the twenty-second fell on Sunday),[32] John Blow and Thomas D'Urfey pooled their talents for the ode "The Glorious Day Is Come." D'Urfey's handiwork is recorded for all to examine,[33] but Blow's music has been lost except for two duets preserved in his *Amphion Anglicus*,[34] "Couch'd by the pleasant Heliconian spring" and "Ah heav'n! What is't I hear." Neither of these pieces kindles sufficient interest to cause regret for the loss of the remaining portions of the ode, although the first part of "Ah heav'n!", a duet on a ground, resembles Purcell's "In vain the am'rous flute" from the St. Cecilia ode for the following year, and the second may have influenced "If so, your goodness may your pow'r" in the *Indian Queen*.[35]

Evidently Motteux was interested enough in the 1691 celebration not only to comment on the music and poetry, but also to describe something of the workings of the organization, in his issue for January 1691–92:

St. Cecilia's day is observed through all Europe by lovers of music. In Italy, Germany, France, and other countries, prizes are distributed on that day in some of the most considerable towns, to such as make the best anthems in her praise. . . . On that day, or the next when it falls on a Sunday as it did last time, most of the lovers of music, whereof many are persons of the first rank, meet at Stationers Hall in London: not through a principal of superstition, but to propagate the advancement of that divine science. A splendid entertainment is provided, and before it is always a performance of music by the best voices and hands in town, the words, which are always in the patroness's praise, are set by some of the greatest masters in the town. This year Dr. John Blow, that famous musician, composed the music, and Mr. D'Urfey, whose skill in things of that nature is well enough known, made the words. Six stewards are chosen for each ensuing year, four of which are either persons of quality or gentlemen of note, and the two last either Gentlemen of their majesties' music, or some of the chief masters in town. Those for the last year were, the Honourable James Saunderson, Esq.; Sir Francis Herd, Baronet; Sir

Thomas Samuel, Baronet; Charles Blunt, Esq.; Mr. John Goodwin; and
Mr. Robert Carr. And those chosen for the next: Sir Thomas Travel,
Bart.; Josias Ent, Esq.; Sir Charles Carteret, Bart.; John Jeffrys, Esq.;
Henry Hazard, Esq.; and Mr. Barkhurst. This feast is one of the gen-
teelest in the world; there are no formalities or gatherings like at others,
and the appearance there is always very splendid. Whilst the company is
at table, the hautbois and trumpets play successively. Mr. Showers hath
taught the latter of late years to sound with all the softness imaginable,
they played us some flat tunes, made by Mr. Finger, with a general applause, it being a thing formerly thought impossible upon an instrument
designed for a sharp key.[36]

Besides providing a catch for the revival of Fletcher's *The Knight of
Malta* (which can be assigned to this year only tentatively), Purcell also
wrote one rather longer song for a current revival of Dryden's sequel to
The Indian Queen, The Indian Emperor: "I looked and saw within the
book of fate."[37] The song is known in the Gresham autograph manuscript[38] and also in a single-sheet edition that identifies the singer as
Mr. Pate,[39] who played the part of "Kalib" in the shape of a woman.

Close on the heels of this production, came a revival of Southerne's
new comedy, *The Wives' Excuse*,[40] which apparently assumed too
frankly satirical a tone to go down well. Of the five songs mentioned in
or associated with the play, Purcell set four, two apparently written for
specific singers—Mrs. Butler and William Mountfort, respectively.

As for publicity among London's beau monde, 1692 began very
pleasantly for Purcell, because Peter Motteux published in the January
issue of the *Gentleman's Journal* a very flattering essay on his successful fusion of French and Italian musical styles, citing *Dioclesian* and
King Arthur as evidence not only of Purcell's mastery of these two foreign manners, but also of his successful attempts to capture an English
public with the "semi-opera," or "ambigue," which their own stage
traditions seem to have brought them to prefer: "Now I speak of music, I must tell you that we shall have speedily a new opera, wherein
something very surprising is promised us: Mr. Purcell, who joins to the
delicacy and beauty of the Italian way the graces and gaiety of the
French, composes the music as he hath done for *The Prophetess*, and
the last opera called *King Arthur*, which hath been played several times
the last month."[41] Even Arthur Bedford, in *The Great Abuse of Musick*,[42] had to admit that operatic music seemed more attractive, really
second only to sacred music:

The operas are a musical entertainment upon the stage, for the diversion
of such gentlemen and ladies, who are lovers of this science consisting of

acts and scenes, like a comedy or tragedy. The design thereof is not only to divert the hearer with such an amusement; but also to advance the science of music to the utmost perfection: and indeed, that which is divine being only excepted, this method seems most likely to accomplish the same.

Roger North, however, probably held the more sensible and balanced view when he wrote, in his *Memoirs of Musick*:[43] "[These semi-operas] were followed at first, but by an error of mixing two capital entertainments, could not stand long. For some that would come to the play hated the music and others that were very desirous of the music would not bear the interruption that so much rehearsal gave; so that it is best to have either by itself entire."

Motteux, however, had already explored this problem in much greater detail, going into some of the reasons for the English predilection for "semi-operas":

> Other nations bestow the name of opera only on such plays whereof every word is sung. But experience hath taught us that our English genius will not relish that perpetual singing. I dare not accuse the language for being over-charged with consonants, which may take off the beauties of the recitative part, though in several other countries I have seen their operas still crowded every time, though long and almost all recitative. It is true that their trios, chorus, lively songs, and recits with accompaniments of instruments, symphonies, machines, and excellent dances make the rest be born with, and the one sets off the other. But our English gentlemen, when their ears are satisfied, are desirous to have their mind pleased, and music and dancing industriously intermixed with comedy or tragedy. I have often observed that the audience is no less attentive to some extraordinary scene of passion or mirth, than to what they call *Beaux endroits*, or the most ravishing part of the musical performance. But had those scenes, though never so well wrought up, been sung, they would have lost most of their beauty. All this, however, doth not lessen the power of music, for its charms command our attention when used in their place, and the admirable consorts we have in Charles Street and York Buildings are an undeniable proof of it. But this shows that what is unnatural, as are plays altogether sung, will soon make one uneasy which comedy or tragedy can never do unless they be bad.[44]

As he had seen the old year out, Purcell saw the new year in with more music for the theater, writing a song or two for *The Marriage-Hater Match'd*,[45] by D'Urfey, who had just provided the text for Blow's New Year's ode, "Behold How All the Stars Give Way."[46] Motteux, writing of the play as a recent event in the *Gentleman's Journal*,[47] said it had a fairly successful run of six days, despite a bad start, caused by poor preparation on the part of the actors.

There is, however, some question as to how much music Purcell did write for D'Urfey's comedy. The duet "As soon as the chaos" is certainly his, for it appeared in *Orpheus Britannicus*, Book 1. As for the little soprano solo "How vile are the sordid intrigues of the town," justifiable doubt lingers as to Purcell's authorship because of conflicting contemporary ascriptions to both Purcell, in *Joyful Cuckoldom* (1693), and to D'Urfey, in *Comes Amoris*, book 4 (1693).

Had Purcell lived long enough to develop and unify the expressive means of the "semi-opera," he might have forged an English operatic style, founding a native English form that could have invoked the blessings of all three national muses: Italian *Euterpe*, French *Terpsichore*, and English *Thalia*. At any rate Purcell's major work for 1692, *The Fairy Queen*, a musical setting for Elkanah Settle's revision of Shakespeare's *A Midsummer Night's Dream*, reveals that he had made great progress toward the fusion and successful realization of all three genres.

Although no contemporary document has been found to prove such a hypothesis, circumstantial evidence strongly indicates that *The Fairy Queen*, like the Shakespearian play it adorned, was conceived as a tribute to the reigning feminine monarch of its time. References to Queen Mary as Gloriana were quite common in the lyric poetry of the Restoration period.[48] The parallel was obvious and intentional, as this was also the term by which Elizabeth's poets had referred to their queen. This fact becomes particularly significant in view of the fact that Queen Mary was the first truly popular queen since Elizabeth's reign.

The timing of *The Fairy Queen* also supports the notion that it may have been intended as a congratulatory piece to the queen. It was first announced in the *Gentleman's Journal* for March 1691–92, when she had taken up the reins of government, as Luttrell recorded: "On Sunday last the Queen assumed the government, on notice of the King's being sailed off at Harwich; the sword was carried before her to the Chapel in the morning by the Lord Westmoreland, and in the afternoon by the Lord Grand."[49] However, Luttrell did not record the actual performance of *The Fairy Queen* until two days before the queen's birthday (30 April), when he announced that it was to be acted on the following Monday (2 May), the "clothes, scenes and music" costing £3,000. The performance may well have coincided with the annual celebrations for the queen's birthday. Indeed, although Luttrell himself mentions no performance before this date, Nicoll gives April 1692 as the month in which it was first mounted at Dorset Garden.[50] Evidence that the play was performed at this time is found in the *Gentleman's Journal* for May 1692: "The opera of which I have spoken to you in my former hath at last appeared, and continues to be represented daily; it is called *The Fairy Queen*. The drama is originally Shakespeare, the music and decoration are extraordinary. I have heard the dances commended, and without doubt the whole is very entertaining." This evidence is further supported by the announcement of the publication of the first edition of the opera in the *London Gazette* for 5–9 May 1692: "The Fairy Queen: a new opera. Represented at the Queen's Theatre by their majesties' servants. Printed for Jacob Tonson, at the Judge's Head in Chancery Lane. Where complete sets of Mr. Dryden's works in 4 volumes are to be sold. The plays being put in the order they were written."

The anonymous adapter's share in this first edition was quite large, and Shakespeare's portion small indeed. Hence, the first production must have seemed a Restoration piece throughout. That these were not good times for Shakespeare is shown by the further diminishing of his representation in the second edition, which appeared the year after the first. Here the "opera" moved even further from the original pattern provided by *A Midsummer Night's Dream*, approaching masque and entertainment in style, as if the producer had withdrawn Shakespearean elements not pleasing to his audiences.

The bustle of affairs at the Queen's Theatre must have stepped up to a feverish pace about this time. One can imagine Purcell, Settle (or whoever the anonymous adapter may have been), and Josiah Priest doing all their errands and rehearsing one day, then rushing home to burn up several candles for the next. In spite of all the hasty preparations, the opening performance was a genuine success. The pecuniary hopes expressed in the last couplet of the prologue were evidently disappointed,[51] but this was not due to a poor reception by the public. On the contrary, the production was successful from every point of view except the financial, and, as Downes recorded,

> . . . in ornaments was superior to the other two; especially in clothes for all the singers and dancers, scenes, machines and decoration, all most profusely set-off; and excellently performed, chiefly the instrumental and vocal part composed by the said Mr. Purcel and dances by Mr. Priest. The Court and the town were wonderfully satisfied with it; but the expenses in setting it out being so great, the company got very little by it.[52]

By mid-June Purcell also had written a song and perhaps a drinking catch for John Crowne's *Regulus*,[53] a tragedy performed at Drury Lane "before the long vacation," as Motteux predicted in the May issue of the *Gentleman's Journal*, reporting the following month that the play had been produced on 17 June. In the August issue he published the song "Ah Me, to Many Deaths Decreed,"[54] describing it as "set by Mr. Purcell the Italian way" and paying both the song and the song-stress who first performed it pretty compliments: ". . . had you heard it sung by Mrs. Ayliff, you would have owned that there is no pleasure like that which good notes, when so divinely sung, can create."

This "Italianate style," in which no contemporary Italian composer was capable of writing with such mastery, characterizes most of Pur-cell's vocal works from this period, however frequently he may have cast his musical thoughts in the triadic "tonic-and-dominant" style, which had become popular after the accession of William III. Certainly the Italianate style figures very prominently in most of Purcell's florid theatrical songs written about this time. Upon closer examination, however, the style turns out to be not Italian at all, but rather Pur-cellian. The artful melodic sequences, the adroit fitting of fioriture and rhythmic figures to English prosody, and especially the graphic illustra-tion of the word and affective demonstration of the phrase are all char-acteristics for which Purcell could have found no worthy Italian model. He had by now demonstrated that he had no peer and very few equals as a composer of music for the stage. Despite the lack of any solid foundation for opera in England, he had created in *Dido and Aeneas* a work that no continental composer could surpass, however favorable the milieu in which he worked. Here, as in other works for the theater, he demonstrated so keen an ear for the language of the stage, whether for accents of tragedy or comedy, that he had no reason to model his style after that of any composer or nation.

But the court and the town had not devoted their musical attention solely to staged works in the first half of 1692. On the contrary, the year had begun with a great visitation of the nobility at court for which Luttrell recorded the observance of a "Happy New Year" followed on 6 January by a great ball at Kensington, during which, however, the dour Dutchman "His Majesty spent the evening in the Treasury."[55] It would be pleasant to suppose that his musical and poetic sensibilities were too refined for the coarse concoctions of Blow and D'Urfey (who had written music and poetry for the New Year's ode, "Behold How All the Stars Give Way"). But it is more likely that he was planning finances to sustain the campaign in the Low Countries, upon which he was to embark again in slightly more than two months' time.[56] On the evening of the seventh, as Luttrell reports, "The Queen and the Queen dowager went . . . to the play of Mr. Dryden's opera"—presumably *King Arthur*.

The atmosphere of ceremonial gaiety continued through January and February with the annual Twelfth Night gaming (which this year made King William £200 poorer, his porters that much richer); with another great ball at Kensington for Princess Anne's twenty-seventh birthday, celebrated two days late, on 8 February, so that it might not coincide with the anniversary of King Charles II's death on the sixth,[57] and a splendid entertainment mounted by the lord mayor on 27 February.[58]

March, on the other hand, was a month of royal leave-takings, some more genuinely sorrowful than others, it may be suspected; the queen bade good-bye first to her husband on 3 March and then, at the end of the month, to the Dowager Queen Catherine of Braganza. Both wept at the parting, which took place finally on 31 March after several postponements,[59] even though they had not been on the best of terms during the preceding year. March saw also the announcement in the *Gentleman's Journal*[60] of the long-postponed tragedy by Dryden and Southerne, *Cleomenes, the Spartan Hero*.[61] Then, in the April issue[62] Motteux had to announce that it had been suppressed by Queen Mary, perhaps for political reasons; mentioning it again in the May issue as follows: "Since that time the innocence and merit of the play have raised it several eminent advocates who have prevailed to have it acted and you need not doubt but it has been with great applause."[63] Luttrell on 16 April reports, however, that offensive passages had been expunged before the first performance,[64] for which Purcell provided a song, "No, No, Poor Suff'ring Heart." Then, at the end of the month, came the celebration of Queen Mary's birthday, which had become one of the chief musical events of the year. Again, Purcell was chosen to compose the ode, a setting of Sir Charles Sedley's "Love's Goddess Sure." If Hawkins's story concerning Purcell's use of the old Scottish melody "Cold and Raw"[65] can be accepted as true, Purcell must have been performing chamber music for some time before the queen, who perhaps had not forgotten his unpolitic treatment of D'Urfey's poem for her birthday ode in 1690.

As if all these musical duties had not been enough to occupy his time during the first few months of the year, Purcell had also taken the trouble to move his family to new quarters before Lady Day (25 March), when the parish overseers came around with the poor-rate assessment books. On page 80 of St. Margaret's Parish Accounts for this year occurs the marginal annotation "Gone" opposite Purcell's name, still among those of the residents of Bowling Alley East. Next to this is written "Ann Peters–2 houses." Ann Peters, possibly a member of his wife's family, apparently was the new resident. But this does not tell the whole story.

Another entry, in the St. Margaret's Parish Vestry Book for 1692,[66] reveals that Purcell did not relinquish ownership in the house in Bowling Alley East, but merely sublet it. At least the record in question still refers to the house as "Mr. Purcell's," then goes on to list four other female dwellers (not including Ann Peters): "28 April 1692. At Mr. Purcell's in Bowling Alley Mrs. Ann Davis, Mrs. Lucy Davis, Rebecca Davis, Letitia Davis to be summoned to appear to show cause why they should not be assessed £1 per quarter." And a little farther down the same page, a fifth (or, if Ann Peters lived there, a sixth) woman is named: "Madame Carhile at Mr. Purcell's to be summoned."

The book from which these entries came is entitled: "A true Duplicate of Schedule of the Assessment of the Several Wards and Divisions within the Parish of St. Margaret's, Westminster, in the County of Middlesex. Made by virtue of an Act of Parliament for raising money by a Poll payable quarterly for one year for carrying on Vigorous War against France." The collectors, some of whose names are familiar from the poor-rate books (e.g., Erasmus Dryden, William Read, William Carning, Francis Ayres), managed to collect a sum total "after all appeals determined" of £919. 15*s.* all from St. Margaret's Parish and signed, sealed, and delivered on May Day 1692 for the glory of England and William III. Appeals came mainly from those who had been advised that they might be let off if they could prove either that they were worth less than £300 or that they were "married women."

What dispositions were made in the cases of the five or more women living at Mr. Purcell's or on what basis their appeal may have been are moot points. (Certainly, considering the various Restoration usages of the term "Mrs.," that title alone would not have sufficed to prove that they were married women at all.) As must so often be said, here again the records tell us nothing more.

Whatever the situation in Bowling Alley East, Purcell apparently had found a more attractive dwelling in Marsham Street, not far away. His name appears in the "Overseers' Accounts" two years later as the tenant of the house inhabited until 1692 by one Ann Law.[67] Or perhaps during the two years in which he apparently paid rates neither in Bowling Alley East nor in Marsham Street, he may have taken up lodgings in the Dean's Yard (or elsewhere in Westminster Abbey precincts), where no secular records would have been kept.

The money collected upon this occasion evidently served its purpose well. Before the end of May, England had great occasion to rejoice when, aided by a second "True Protestant Wind," the Netherlands fleet sailed from the Dutch coast in time to join the English fleet and soundly trounce the forces of Tourville and the French, thus drowning James II's hopes for a victorious return to England in these "fatal Ides of May." [68] Purcell must have been proud of the fact that his tune "Let the Soldiers Rejoice" [69] (from *Dioclesian*) was chosen to celebrate the occasion, announced in a broadside brought out almost before the smoke of battle had cleared as:

> The Royal Triumph Or, The Unspeakable Joy of the three Kingdoms, for the glorious Victory of the FRENCH, by the English and Dutch Fleets; to the Joy and Comfort of all True Subjects. Tune is, Let the Soldiers Rejoice. . . .
>
> Valiant protestant boys
> Here's millions of joys
> And triumph now bro . . . ught from the ocean; etc.

As earlier discussions have revealed, Purcell's activities at court and in the theater kept him extremely busy during the early months of 1692. As church musician and composer, however, he appears to have had an easy time. No anthems appeared during this period, no services or other liturgical music. E. Chamberlayne records a rise in salary for Purcell in 1692 and a new position as well. [70] Whereas before Purcell had received only £70, as did other musicians, now he was paid the same as the other two organists, as the following extract shows:

The Organists Three

1. Dr. William Child	£100 per annum
2. Dr. John Blow	£100
3. Mr. Henry Purcell, Master of the Twelve Children	£100

It has been assumed that the annotation "Master of the Twelve Children" was a slip, for Blow is given this title in both the fifteenth and eighteenth editions of *Angliae Notitiae*. It scarcely seems possible that Purcell would have replaced him for the short period intervening. If Purcell did have this new responsibility, he would have been busy indeed. But if the entry is erroneous, his responsibilities as one of three organists would have been fairly light. The weight of evidence currently available indicates that Purcell *was* master of the Choristers for a time.

Thomas Ford so described him, as did Richard Busby in the fifth codicil to his will (see Appendix One; XIII, 3 and XIII, 7, respectively).

By the summer of 1692 he must already have been at work composing and collecting together the sacred songs and dialogues that were to appear in the second book of Henry Playford's *Harmonia Sacra* the following year. Each of these illustrated something new and original. "In Guilty Night,"[71] or "Saul and the Witch of Endor" (as it is subtitled in this collection and on many a program), is a dramatic little *scena*, which defies accurate classification solely as a cantata, oratorio, or sacred song. It partakes of the styles and techniques of all three and, indeed, reveals that Purcell's sacred compositions were not shut off from the extensive experience in writing music for the stage that he had had over the five years separating this collection from *Harmonia Sacra*, book 1.

In selecting the eighth to twentieth verses, the anonymous paraphraser had chosen the very passage from I Sam. 28 that would have come nearest to paralleling the circumstances of English monarchs, past and present, just after the Glorious Revolution. Saul, who had lost Jehovah's favor through royal misconduct, was in a situation very much like that of James II in Ireland. The parable is particularly close in the part of the story just before these chosen passages, where David had Saul in his power momentarily (28:7–17) but refused to "stretch forth his hand against the Lord's anointed." So William, at the Battle of the Boyne, refused Schomberg's very sound tactical suggestion to seal off James II's avenue of escape, presumably to avoid having the ex-king's blood on his hands. His relationship to the enemy king was that of son-in-law, not son, but this does not essentially weaken the parallel.[72]

After the Battle of the Boyne, James must have realized that his cause was lost, just as Saul had had his very accurate premonitions before the Battle of Gilboa. Certainly William III knew, for he returned to London at the end of the summer campaign, and, on the first day of October, issued a public proclamation for a general thanksgiving to be held on Sunday, the nineteenth of that same month. Possibly Purcell had composed "In Guilty Night" for a performance at the Chapel Royal; it is perhaps more likely that it was intended for Westminster Abbey, because no ensemble instrumental movements or passages are required.

The Italianate style discussed above is very much in evidence here, as it is also in the next major work upon which he had no doubt begun work during the summer and autumn of 1692, attempting the most

PLATE 32. Signed ticket for a St. Cecilia celebration, 1696
(British Museum)

PLATE 33. The Duke's Theatre, Dorset Gardens (British Museum)

ambitious musical project for St. Cecilia's Day yet undertaken by anyone in England. With "Hail, Bright Cecilia,"[73] he not only laid bare the
grey mediocrity of all the music written for celebrations between 1683
(when he had entertained the society with "Welcome to All the Pleasures") and 1692, but also revealed the enormous progress he had
made in mastering old and evolving new techniques of composition
during the course of these nine years. In every moment from the five-
part overture that opens the ode to the majestic choral da capo that
ends it, Purcell showed his genius in the richly inventive polyphonic
style, the delightfully imaginative turn of musical metaphor, the subtly
skillful clothing of the English language in musical dress, indeed all the
best attributes of his stylistic maturity. His consummate skill and astonishing variety are shown in the magnificent hymns of praise to St.
Cecilia (movements 2 and 13); the compositions dedicated "to music,"
of which art she was patron saint (movements 3, 4, 5, 6, and 12), and
to its instruments (movements 7, 8, 9, 10, and 11).

Purcell also demonstrated on this occasion musical skill other than
that normally expected of a composer, if Motteux's account may be

PLATE 34. The Duke's Theatre in Lincoln's Inn Fields, as it appeared in the reign of King Charles II

believed: "The following ode ['Hail, Bright Cecilia'] was admirably set to music by Mr. Henry Purcell and performed twice with universal applause, particularly the second stanza [beginning 'Tis Nature's Voice'], which was sung with incredible graces by Mr. Henry Purcell himself."[74] The strength of the immediate success the work achieved may be judged not only from the double performance given at its first hearing, but also from the frequent revivals given during the course of several ensuing decades.[75] A signed ticket for a St. Cecilia celebration in

PLATE 35. Inside of the Duke's Theatre in Lincoln's Inn Fields, as it appeared in the reign of King Charles II

1696, as shown in plate 32, reflects something of the lavish nature of these events.

Small wonder, in view of the strain this celebration must have placed on the musical resources at court, that William III's birthday had come and gone with scarcely a stir at the beginning of that same November. Blow may have composed "Welcome Genial Day" to commemorate the king's celebration and "Whilst He Abroad Does Like the Sun Display"[76] to compliment Queen Mary. But neither work, if indeed either or both were performed this year, attracted enough attention at court for Luttrell to consider them worth recording. At any rate, in his entry for 5 November, he records the celebration of the king's birthday but mentions no ode.[77]

14

Music and Theater in London (Part 2)

WITHIN LESS THAN A MONTH, all Londoners were shocked by news of two tragic deaths, suddenly ending the careers of Anthony Leigh, comedian, and William Mountfort, playwright, musician, and, as C. Cibber called him, "affecting lover in tragedy."[1] William Mountfort's violent death—some called it murder—climaxed a series of events that his skill in portraying an "affecting lover" may have set in motion. Among regular theatergoers at that time were two friends, Charles, fourth lord Mohun of Okehampton, about fifteen years old, and Captain Richard Hill, about twenty, just home from campaigns in Flanders and Ireland. Hill had conceived a strong passion for the beautiful but, according to contemporary reports, unusually virtuous actress-singer, Mrs. Bracegirdle. Because she repulsed his advances (he thought, mistakenly, because of a clandestine affair with Mountfort), Hill decided to abduct her. On 9 December, as she was leaving Gawen Page's house on Princes Street, he appeared with a hired coach and several ruffians to kidnap her. However, his plan was foiled by Page's courageous and adroit defense. Armed only with a walking stick, he managed to spoil the attempt. Frustrated and enraged, Hill wandered through the streets, naked sword in hand (having lost his scabbard or thrown it away in the scuffle) until late that night, when he and Mohun encountered Mountfort in Norfolk Street, returning home. Mohun and Mountfort, apparently friends, embraced and were discussing matters quietly when Hill took offense at something or other, boxed the actor's ears, ran him through, and fled. The wound proved fatal, and within a few hours London had lost one of its best and most engaging actors.[2]

Purcell had known Mountfort not only as an actor, but as playwright and singer as well. Mountfort had collaborated in the writing of two plays (*Distress'd Innocence* and *Henry the Second*), had played major roles in *A Fool's Preferment* (in which he took the part of Lyonel), in *The Wives' Excuse*, and perhaps a dozen others for which Purcell had supplied music. He had also sung songs for many of these plays and had written the words for "O How Happy's He" to a tune from Purcell's music for *Dioclesian*. But possibly the best evidence that the composer and actor were close friends appears in an anonymous preface to a nearly contemporary edition of *Six Plays Written by Mr. Mountfort:* "He was buried in the vault of St. Clement Danes in the Strand, Mr. Purcell performing the Funeral Anthem; a great many gentlemen attended his obsequies. . . ." A. S. Borgman[3] gives the following account, quoting Luttrell[4] as his source:

> On the night of Tuesday, the thirteenth, the unfortunate actor was laid to rest in the vault at St. Clement Danes. The funeral ceremonies were said to have been attended by a thousand persons among whom were a great many gentlemen, "who thus showed their respect for one whom they loved and esteemed." Royalty was not indifferent at the passing of a player, for the funeral anthem was sung by a group of choristers from Whitehall accompanied by Henry Purcell.

(Unfortunately, none of these sources identifies the specific anthem performed; presumably the choir would have sung Purcell's own early setting of the funeral sentences.) To this melancholy account, Anthony à Wood adds a superstitious note to the effect that the great bell of St. Clement Danes cracked as it was ringing the death knell for Mountfort.[5]

The excellence of the theatrical fare that London had enjoyed during the autumn of 1692 caused the period after the deaths of Mountfort and Leigh to seem all the more gloomy. Having been commissioned to write music for seven, perhaps even eight, plays that season, Purcell no doubt was keenly aware of the change, since the cessation of theatrical life would have had a direct bearing upon his income. For him, as well as for everyone else connected with the theater, the double tragedy in December marked the beginning of a period of inactivity, as Motteux pointed out in the *Gentleman's Journal:* "We are like to be without new plays this month and the next; the death of Mr. Mountfort, and that of Mr. Leigh soon after him, being partly the cause of this delay. The first that is promised us is a comedy by Mr. Southerne."[6]

Moreover, the court went into official mourning on 2 January 1693, for the death on 24 December of the electress of Bavaria.[7] Nahum Tate's New Year's ode, for which Blow provided music, must have seemed ironical with the incongruous optimism of the first line itself, "The happy, happy year is born."[8] All these events deepened the general gloom, from which the theatrical world did not begin to emerge until nearly spring of 1693.

Although not all stage productions or the revivals of these can be dated certainly, Purcell's theatrical commissions for the season probably included Shadwell's *The Libertine; or, The Libertine Destroyed;* Dryden's and Lee's *Oedipus*; Mountfort's and (?) Bancroft's *Henry the Second, King of England*; Southerne's *The Maid's Last Prayer*; Congreve's *The Old Bachelor*; Thomas Wright's *The Female Virtuosos*; D'Urfey's *The Richmond Heiress*; and possibly Shadwell's *Epsom Wells*.[9]

The Libertine, Shadwell's tragicomic version of the Don Juan legend, after Dorimon's *Le Festin de Pierre*—not Molière's *L'athée foudroyé* as has been supposed—was first produced at Dorset Garden on 12 June 1675 and revived there in 1682 and again about October 1692. (Dr. Laurie[10] argues that the latter revival took place in 1695, but this would have meant that the march and canzone for Queen Mary's funeral would have been introduced in a most inappropriate play while this beloved queen's memory was yet fresh in the public mind. In my opinion the traditional dating of this revival in 1692, when the text was reprinted, is the more likely.) Apart from the "supernatural" music in act 5, Purcell provided music for an opening masque ("Nymphs and shepherds come away"), a devils' song, and a trumpet song ("To arms, heroic prince"). As for the reception the play may have had, no contemporary account is known. But from the frequency of revivals, especially after Purcell's music had been heard, we may assume that it was quite successful.[11]

In the same month London theatergoers saw Dryden's and Lee's tragedy *Oedipus*,[12] also at Dorset Garden, and again heard Purcell's music (two solo songs and two "supernatural" choruses), probably on 13 October, for which date Luttrell records a revival.[13] The plot and trimmings of the play were such as would please London audiences to begin with—hence the frequent revivals—but Purcell's contribution added the pièce de résistance that made irresistible to London theatergoers that which their

> Palates relished most,
> Charm! Song! and Show!
> A murder and a Ghost.[14]

The play attracted enough attention to be noticed and recorded by Luttrell, who entered a note on the production for 13 October 1692.[15] The unusual success of the play might be sufficient evidence that the 1692 revival was that for which Purcell provided the music, even without Burney's straightforward, but unfortunately undocumented, statement to that effect: "He published the music to a masque sung in the tragedy of *Oedipus*, when it was revived in 1692."[16]

Henry the Second, the tragedy with comic overtones, probably represents the joint handiwork of Mountfort and Bancroft. It was first performed on 8 November as is known from a playbill for the second night, 9 November.[17] Purcell wrote only the song, "In vain 'gainst Love I strove" (for act 3), for this play. The Hornpipe sometimes attributed to *Henry the Second* clearly belongs to *King Arthur*.[18] The production was a decided success, as is known from Motteux's comments: "*Henry Second, King of England*, a new play by the author of that called *Edward the Third* . . . hath been acted several times with applause. It is a tragedy, with a mixture of comedy. . . . We are promised a comedy by Mr. Shadwell."[19] The piece referred to in the last line is *Epsom Wells*, which was revived in 1693, twenty-one years after its first production at Dorset Garden in 1672. The play calls for seven songs and three instrumental pieces altogether. Purcell's one contribution (the duet "Leave these useless arts in loving" in act 5) may have been commissioned merely to lend his name to the revival.[20]

Meanwhile Mountfort had been killed and Leigh had died. What with these deaths, the stabbing of Powell, and official mourning at court, no stage production with music by Purcell was mounted until some time in March 1693, when Southerne's comedy *The Maid's Last Prayer; or, Any Rather than Fail* was acted for the first time at Drury Lane.[21] In the January issue of the *Gentleman's Journal*—Motteux by now had fallen more than two months behind schedule, as he explained in the preface—the notice that "*The Maid's Last Prayer* was acted for the third time this evening and will be acted again tomorrow" reveals both that the play was performed about mid-March and that it was relatively successful. Anyway, it ran to at least four performances. Southerne's remark in the preface to the published version (advertised in the *London Gazette* for 9–13 March) seems to indicate that it had been performed at least once by then: "I think it had its beauties though they *did not* appear upon the stage" (italics mine). Although Southerne wrote the comedy itself, he provided the lyrics for only "Though you make no return to my passion,"[22] the first of the three songs that Purcell composed for the play. The poem for the second, "No, resistance is but vain,"[23] was written by Anthony Henley, while that of the third, "Tell Me No More," variously attributed to Southerne himself and also to William Congreve, probably the real author.[24]

Congreve's first play, *The Old Bachelor*, also appeared about this time, reaching a third printing by 23 March 1693.[25] The first performance of this extremely successful work followed immediately upon that of Southerne's play discussed above, and indeed may have driven it from the boards. Purcell's contribution consisted of a three-part overture, a full set of eight act-tunes, and two rather racy songs, "Thus to a ripe consenting maid" and "As Amoret and Thyrsis lay." His splendid music probably contributed significantly to the success of the production.

During the course of the next month or so, the less successful production of *The Female Virtuosos* was mounted at the Theatre Royal. Thomas Wright, who was also Betterton's stage machinist, had adapted the play from Molière's *Les Femmes savantes*. Motteux, writing favorably but guardedly, intimates that he had seen the performance but not read the play. Perhaps he attended a performance some time before 22 June, when the printed play was at last advertised for sale in the *London Gazette*: "We have had since May last a new comedy called *The Female Virtuosos*; something in it was borrowed from Molière's *Femmes savantes*; and as it hath wit and humour, it cannot but please in the perusal as in the presentation." Purcell wrote only one duet for the play, setting a song text by Anne, countess of Winchelsea, "Love, thou art best of human joys," not one of his best works.

For another play that was unsuccessful, at least initially, Purcell evidently took his responsibilities more seriously. His "Dialogue Between a Mad Man and Mad Woman," his catch "Bring the bowl and cool Nantz,"[26] and his song "How vile are the sordid intrigues"[27] indeed may have won a good portion of the success achieved by D'Urfey's *The Richmond Heiress* upon its revival after a first unsuccessful run, being "suffered but four days, and then kicked off for ever" as Dryden put it. But according to Gildon,[28] by altering the play D'Urfey managed to "please the town in reviving the play later."

Meanwhile, Purcell must have been hard at work on another ode for Queen Mary, who had resided at Whitehall in solitary splendor after William III had departed for more battle campaigns on the eve of Lady Day just previous.[29] This ode was a setting of a text by Nahum Tate, who supplied the lyrics in celebration of Queen Mary's thirty-first birthday, 30 April 1693. Tate began the ode with a grandiose terza rima, which, however, he abandoned after a few terzettos. On the whole it is not a bad poem, although the rhyme scheme sometimes gets in the way of sense. But it could not have provided much in the way of inspiration for Purcell. Luttrell's entry for 2 May that year leaves a description of the occasion that seems to associate the ode again with a ball: "Sunday last being the Queen's birthday, the guns were discharged at the Tower as usual; and the next day the nobility congratulated Her Majesty thereon; and at night was a great ball at Court." For the overture, Purcell transposed the first two movements of "Hail, Bright Cecilia," into C major, possibly because he had already written the vocal part of the ode in C major, with a soprano part that could be put no higher.[30] His falling back on a composition that had been heard so recently in London not only testifies to his own crowded schedule about that time, but also sheds light on the complaisant attitude of his public toward "borrowing" of musical matter. Interestingly, it also reveals that he felt quite free to deck out a work commissioned for the queen with an overture composed for another occasion.

During the first six months of 1693 very few demands on Purcell's time had been made by duties at the Chapel Royal, unless, perhaps, his compositions in *Harmonia Sacra*, book 2, had been intended for performance there. Nor is there any evidence that he wrote any chamber music during this period. However, the absence of any works for these two offices cannot be taken to indicate that he had written only for the theater.

On the contrary, a new musical outlet had appeared on the scene to challenge Berardi's tripartite classification, which categorized all music as written for church, chamber, or theater. Indeed, for a century and a half, these had provided all needed channels between musical supply and demand in Western music. But a new outlet, the public concert, already was to be reckoned with. Its original home was London, where it had passed from the management of amateurs, such as Pepys and the Norths, into the skilled hands of established if at times desperate, professionals such as Banister and, much earlier, Edward Chilmead. (The latter had lost his musical livelihood long before the Restoration with the parliamentary visitation to Oxford in 1648. Thereupon he was driven to setting up a series of concerts at the Black Horse in Oxford, where he carried on for six years.)

For these, amateur music was enjoyable stuff but apparently required nothing more in the way of concentration than could be achieved while drinks or food or both were being sold and consumed. Early concert life in London had had such humble bibulous origins. It is significant and revealing that the prosecution in 1658 of "Thomas Smith at the Music house at Blue Bell by the postern gate of London Wall" was intended to punish him for having "one puncheon of compounded and adulterated unwholesome drink fit to have the head beaten out,"[31] and not for having countenanced unwholesome music probably far worse than the drink, and less in conformity with Commonwealth principles, if the truth were known. Such a convivial attitude toward music sorely tried visiting virtuosos like Matteis and Baltzar, as various anecdotes reveal,[32] but the attitude prevailed all through the seventeenth century and into the eighteenth. (Indeed, one of the most widespread explanations of Purcell's death indicates overconviviality.) Ned Ward, though writing somewhat after these times, provides the sauciest, most detailed report on such activities in his description of the Mitre in Wapping in part 14 of his *London Spy:*

> Remembering we had heard of a famous amphibious house of entertainment, compounded of one half tavern and t'other *musichouse,* made us willing to dedicate half an hour to what diversion we might there meet with. . . . As soon as we came to the sign of the spiritual helmet, such as the high priests used to wear when they bid defiance to the devil, we no sooner entered the house, but we heard fiddlers and hautboys, together with a humdrum organ, make such incomparable music, that had the harmonious grunting of a hog been added to the bass to a ravishing concert of caterwauling performers, in the height of their ecstasy, the unusualness of the sound could not have rendered it, to a nice ear, more engaging. Having heard of the beauty and contrivance of the public *musicroom,* as well as other parts of the house, very highly commended, we agreed, first to take a view of that which was likely to be most remarkable. In order to which we ascended the grades, and were ushered into a most stately apartment. Dedicated purely to the lovers of musick, painting, dancing and t'other things too. No gilding, carving, colouring or good contrivance, was here wanting to illustrate the beauty of this most noble academy where a good genius may learn with safety to abominate vice and a bad genius as (with as much danger) to practice it. The room by its compact order and costly improvements looks so far above the use its now converted to, that the seats are more like pews than boxes; and the upper end, being divided by a rail, looks more like a chancel than a music-box; that I could not but imagine it was built for a fanatic meeting-house, but that they had for ever destroyed the sanctity of the place by putting an organ in it; round which hung a great many pretty whimsical pictures. . . . There were but a few companies in the room; the most remarkable person was a drunken commander, who plucking out a handful of money, to give the music sixpence, dropped a shilling, and was so very generous that he gave an officious drawer, standing by half a crown for stooping to take it up again. . . .[33]

Banister's loss of status (and salary) at court in 1667 undoubtedly influenced his decision to mount a regular series at Whitehall in 1672, even though he may have been involved in the Mitre concerts mentioned by Pepys in his entries for 21 January and 18 February 1660.[34]

At any rate, under his aegis concert-giving in London began to develop greater musical dignity, even though as yet unable to separate itself from its public-house origins. Here is Roger North's description of the Banister concerts:

> The next essay was of the elder Banister, who had a good theatrical vein, and in composition had a lively style peculiar to himself. He procured a large room in Whitefriars, near the Temple back gate, and made a raised box for the musicians, whose modesty required curtains. The room was rounded with seats and small tables, alehouse fashion. One shilling was the price, and call for what you pleased; there was very good music, for Banister found means to procure the best hands in town, and some voices to come and perform there, and there wanted no variety of humour, for Banister himself (*inter alia*) did wonders upon a flageolet to a thro'base, and the several masters had their solos. This continued full one winter, and more I remember not.[35]

There was no real concert life, however, and these concerts with their lack of order and decorum gave only gradual impetus to the growth of a public. Even as late as the 1690s Roger North was complaining about the lack of order:

> . . . the plan of this project was not so well laid as ought to have been, for the time of their beginning was inconsistent with the park and the playhouses, which had stronger attraction. And what was worse, the masters undertakers were a rope of sand, not under the rule or order of any one person, and everyone forward to advance his own talents, and spiteful to each other, and out of emulation subtracting their skill in performing; all of which scandalized the company, and poisoned the entertainment.[36]

Then, after Matteis—and before him, Baltzar and Becker—had created a certain awareness of proper musical etiquette, and after James II and William III had allowed London's musical center of gravity to shift from court to theater and concert hall, English public musical life began to develop apace. Or, to view the matter from another perspective, Matteis's discovery that "pistols did not walk so fast as guineas," to borrow Roger North's phrase,[37] was soon shared by lesser-known musicians. Even as late as 1713, Mattheson could point out in his *Das neu-eröffnete Orchestre*, that "He who in the present time wants to make a profit out of his music betakes himself to England."[38] At any rate, during the reigns of Charles II and James II, a great many foreign musicians flocked to London to give concerts.[39] Most had come to England as court musicians, engaging only incidentally in public concerts.

During the reign of William and Mary, however, more and more visiting artists came to profit from the new prosperity England was beginning to enjoy.

Native musicians also grasped the pecuniary advantages to be gained from concert ventures, and by the end of the century had given considerable impetus to the growth of the entrepreneurial public concert. Frequent entries in various journals and periodicals appearing during the first six months of 1693, for instance, testify to a flourishing musical activity in London, not counting concerts like those at York Buildings, in Charles Street, at Thomas Britton's in Clerkenwell Street, and at the Two Golden Balls, all of which were weekly affairs not advertised in the above-mentioned journals. Despite North's criticisms, quoted above, these concerts were providing serious competition to theatrical events, as were open-air entertainments held in various gardens during fine weather. Moreover, such affairs tended to pursue their own separate courses without regard for court polity or policy. At the beginning of 1693, for instance, Margarita l'Épine, who had been brought over from Italy by the German impresario Jakob Greber[40] sometime in 1692, after bridling at the English public, relented, letting it be announced in the *London Gazette* that: "The Italian lady, that is lately come over, that is so famous for her singing, has been reported that she will not sing no more in the consort in York Buildings—This is to give notice that next Tuesday, being the 10th instant, she will sing in the consort in York Buildings, and so continue during this season."[41]

In addition to weekly concerts given on Tuesday nights at "The Vendu," and others held at York Buildings, another series had begun the year before, set for Thursday nights at "Freeman's Yard in Cornhill, near the Royal Exchange."[42] Margarita l'Épine featured prominently in both series; but whether or not she participated in the activities of a third group, in Covent Garden, is unknown. Since her fellow countryman Pier Francesco Tosi played there from time to time, she may have done so.[43]

Events such as these, which indicated that commercial concerts were soon to become the mainstay of London's musical life, did not preclude musical activity at the royal court. For instance, Purcell himself, however much he may have been involved in York Buildings concerts, was very busy throughout the early portion of the 1693 season with revisions and additions to *The Fairy Queen*, which was again performed on 16 February for Queen Mary and the maids of honor at Dorset Garden.[44]

15

Purcell as Composer for Church, Court, Concert Hall, and Theater

DURING WILLIAM'S ABSENCE in the spring of 1693, Queen Mary had to cope with financial difficulties inherited from the reigns of her father, James II, and uncle, Charles II. A very serious problem arose from irregular payments to the vocal musicians, as revealed in the following complaint, submitted to the lords of the treasury on 24 May 1693: ". . . the vocal and instrumental music were joined in the late reigns of King Charles and King James, with an allowance of £40 per annum each . . . they were sworn in indifferently and directed to be paid to Lady Day 1690, since which the instrumental only had been paid."[1] Temporarily skirting the issue, she approved the minute ordering that the complaint be "respited till the establishment is altered,"[2] then continued "calling the tune" even though the piper, or, rather, the singers, had not been paid. Early in May, probably on May morning (i.e., the first of May), she ventured out to be entertained on board Mr. Shore's pleasure boat against Whitehall and to hear "a consort of music, vocal and instrumental."[3] Apparently nothing had been done by end of summer, witness "the petition of Dr. Nicholas Staggins, praying the King to settle upon him the allowance of £200 per annum . . . which he had received in the time of King Charles the second, as Master of Music."[4] From the end of April through the whole of May, Purcell had been extraordinarily busy with music at court and performances at the theaters. On Sunday, 30 April, his "Celebrate This Festival" had been performed at Whitehall. Then in quick succession came *The Prophetess* and *The Female Virtuosos*, both performed by the United Company. These events were followed immediately by preparations for Dryden's *The Spanish Fryar.*[5]

All these activities had to be worked into Purcell's regular schedule at court and Abbey. His sacred compositions must also have occupied a great deal of his time, for early that June, Purcell was putting finishing touches to the second book of *Harmonia Sacra*, as we know from Peter Motteux's announcement in the June issue of the *Gentleman's Journal:* "A music book intituled *Harmonia Sacra* will shortly be printed, for Mr. Playford. I need not say anything more to recommend it to you than that you will find in it many of Mr. Henry Purcell's admirable composures. As they charm all men, they are universally extoll'd, and ev'n those who know him no otherwise than by his notes, are fond of expressing their sense of his merit." In this last sentence Motteux referred to Thomas Brown's dedicatory poem, also appearing in this issue, which includes the verse: "Thus I unknown, my gratitude express."[6] This second book of *Harmonia Sacra* was at last licensed for printing on 1 July, and advertised for sale in the *London Gazette* for 6–10 July.

Purcell also was represented by an occasional song in *Gentleman's Journal*, the complete second volume of which was announced for publication on 13 July.[7] The song "We Now My Thyrsis" (Z427) is merely a slight revision of Purcell's setting of Bernard Howard's little love poem "I Lov'd Fair Celia," which the composer may have intended as an improvement upon Ralph Courteville's setting of the same. Indeed, the fact that Motteux supplied the new text for Purcell's setting may explain the appearance of the piece in this issue.

Certainly, as far as concerns publication or performance of his music, extant records reveal little activity on Purcell's part. During this somewhat quiet summer, it is fairly certain that he would have used any time left over from official duties to compose music for the new theatrical season, to commence the following autumn. Purcell's most impressive new composition for this milieu was his occasional suite for Congreve's comedy of manners, *The Double Dealer*. The play also was impressive, even to Dryden, as may be gathered from Motteux's reference to it in the November 1693 issue of *Gentleman's Journal:* "I need not say anything of Mr. Congreve's *Double Dealer* (the only new play since my last) after the character which Mr. Dryden was given of it. . . ." Dryden had written to William Walsh on 12 December, a letter containing the following interesting passage, which reaffirms his expression of good wishes and congratulations, as printed in the preface to Congreve's play:

> I have remembered you to all your friends; and in particular to Congreve; who sends you his play, as a present from himself, by this con-

veyance; and much desires the honour of being better known to you. His *Double Dealer* is much censured by the greater part of the town: and is defended only by the best judges, who, you know, are commonly the fewest. Yet it gets ground daily, and has already been acted eight times. The women think he has exposed their bitchery too much; and the gentlemen are offended with him for the discovery of their follies and the way of their intrigues under the notion of friendship to their ladies' husbands. My verses, which you will find before it, were written before the play was acted, but I neither altered them nor do I alter my opinion of the play.[8]

Purcell had little time, however, to ponder the vagaries of fortune that might sweep his music to fame or oblivion, whatever the merit of its vehicles. Even while composing the pieces for *The Double Dealer*, he was busy with his new song for Shadwell's *Epsom Wells:* "Leave these useless arts in loving" (Z579), revised for the season, according to William Barclay Squire.[9] He also revised his contributions to *The Richmond Heiress* (Z608), which, as Motteux points out, D'Urfey had altered and emended for another short run about this time. In that same paragraph, Motteux refers to the imminence of the premiere of *Don Quixote* (Z578/I), which indicates that Purcell had yet further work in hand to be completed before the theatrical season was underway.[10]

About this time, Purcell evidently was involved somehow in advancement of the career of a young musician, together with his former mentor, Dr. John Blow. The following letter from Roger Herbert to the earl of Rutland does not specify just what Purcell's part may have been in providing assistance to this underemployed musician, but it does furnish a new glimpse of his activities in a new context:

> 14 October 1693: Roger Herbert to the earl of Rutland (*H. M. C. Rutland*, vol. 2): I am now with Dr. Blow and Mr. Purcell and some other great masters of musick. The doctor presents his humble service to your Lordship and offers a gentleman to be your Lordship's organist, who is a German. . . . This German is a Roman Catholick. His name is Alberrix, his father was Master of the Chapel at Whitehall to King Charles the Second, and he has had very great salaries but will—if your Lordship be pleased to grant it to him—serve you for twenty pounds a year.[11]

As if all this were not enough, Purcell had also received an order from Dryden to provide a musical dialogue for his last play, *Love Triumphant*, already in rehearsal early in December, as we know from a letter to William Walsh written 12 December: "Your critique, by your description of its bulk, will be too large for a preface to my play, which is now studying, but cannot be acted till after Christmas is over. I call it *Love Triumphant; or: Nature will prevail. . . .*"[12] From John Evelyn's entry for 11 January 1694, it seems that the play was long in preparation, for he notes that it was "shortly to be acted." Thus between January and early June, when Purcell's successful transmogrification of the second part of *Don Quixote* was performed, Purcell had written music for no fewer than seven new plays. All told, he had provided some twenty-three songs and incidental instrumental pieces.

Dryden's play was a failure, as we know from an anonymous contemporary letter,[13] although Motteux expressed the wish that it not be, as reported, his last, kindly evading any sort of critical evaluation: "Whatever Mr. Dryden writes spreads so soon everywhere, that I can tell no news of his *Love Triumphant*."[14] His non sequitur, however, gives the truth of the matter.[15]

Purcell set only Carlos's sarcastic *Epithalamium*, which was actually written by Congreve, not Dryden, at the end of the subplot. Here Sancho, the befooled bridegroom, listens complacently while two children of his "virgin bride" sing:

> How happy's the husband, whose wife has been try'd!
> Not damn'd to the bed of an ignorant bride!
> Secure of what's left, he ne'er misses the rest
> But where there's enough, supposes a feast.

Purcell's setting may have included the instrumental dance by way of introduction, and the accompaniment specified by stage directions for this scene. At any rate, his "jig" on a bass fashioned from the popular "Lilliburlero tune," which he had composed for *The Gordion Knot Unty'd* (Z597), resembles the song in melodic cast and rhythmic organization. Both might well do duty for the missing music in this scene.[16]

Purcell's song was sung by Mrs. Ayliff, who accompanied the musicians hired by Carlos for the serenade. John Eccles's song, "Young I Am, and Yet Untried," on a text by Dryden, was sung by "The Girl," who appears to have made her debut with this play. Most probably she was "the young Gentlewoman of 12 years of age" mentioned in the *London Gazette* for 26 November that same year, in connection with the Charles Street concerts. During the next eighteen months, she sang Purcell's songs in a great many productions of operas and plays. Later, styled with greater dignity as "Mrs. Letitia Cross," she continued to appear as principal singer in various plays right up to the end of the century. Purcell was evidently impressed by her vocal and musical abilities, for he composed several songs specifically for her to sing, including "Celemene, pray tell me," in *Oroonoko* (Z584); "Dear, pretty youth," in *The Tempest* (Z631); "How happy is she," in *The Rival Sisters* (Z609)—the song is a companion piece to "How happy's the husband," except that it is in the minor; "I attempt from Love's sickness" and "They tell me," from *The Indian Queen* (Z630); "Man is for the woman made," in *The Mock Marriage* (Z605); "O lead me to some peaceful gloom," in *Bonduca* (Z574); and perhaps a few others. As to whether or not she actually was only twelve years of age, we can only note that from 1695 onward she was invariably styled as "Mrs Letitia Cross"—a curious usage for a young maid even then, when that title did not necessarily signify the married state, but rather the attainment of a certain age group.

For the above-mentioned plays, Purcell was only one composer among several—perhaps an indication that demand for his songs and incidental music for plays had outrun by far his capabilities for producing them on schedule. The number of commissions that came to him cannot be estimated accurately. But judging only from those he actually accepted, we may subscribe to the common observation then current that a song by Purcell provided best surety for the success of any new production in London at that time.

With the close of the calendar year upon them, those in charge of court affairs were planning celebrations for the new year all during this time. Having entrusted the New Year's ode to Nahum Tate and John Blow for the previous year, they took special pains to secure fine poetry and music for 1694, turning to Matthew Prior for the ode and to Purcell for the musical setting, as we know from a heading in *The Literary Works of Matthew Prior* (ed. H. B. Wright and M. K. Spears, vol. 2, pp. 125–28): "Concert. Hymn to the Sun. Set by Dr. Purcel, and sung before their Majesties on New Year's Day, 1694." Unfortunately, the music is lost, and we have no way of appraising Purcell's creative reaction to the poetry of this new colleague in lyrical collaboration.

Ten days later came the revival of *Dioclesian*, which had been resurrected about the time its publication appeared in May of 1693. The event of 10 January 1694 was politically important, as we know from the Newdigate Newsletters, 11 January 1693–94: "On Tuesday the Prince of Baden dined with the Duke of Linster [*sic*] and yesterday his Highness saw the new opera called Diaclessia [*sic*] acted at the King's Playhouse." This revival was probably the occasion for which Purcell wrote the new songs "When first I saw the bright Aurelia's eyes," "Since from my dear," "Let monarchs fight" (words by Betterton), and "Let the soldiers rejoice" (words by Betterton).[17]

In the March issue of the *Gentleman's Journal*, Motteux also paid his compliments to Southerne's new play, *The Fatal Marriage; or, The Innocent Adultery*,[18] which was "so kindly received" that this gentleman correspondent was by then "no stranger to its merit. As the world has done it justice. . . . and it is above my praise, I need not expatiate upon that subject." The play's great success, also noted by the contributor to Gerald Langbaine's seventeenth edition,[19] was probably due at least in part to the excellent novel upon which it was based, *The History of the Nun, or, The Fair Vow-taker*, by Aphra Behn. Purcell's music again contributed to the play's success, as we may judge from the frequency with which the two songs—"The danger is over" and "I sigh'd and owned my love" (595/1, 2)—were reprinted in London during the next few decades.[20]

During the same month,[21] Beaumont's and Fletcher's *Rule a Wife and Have a Wife* (Z587) saw another of its many revivals during Purcell's lifetime. The *Gentleman's Journal* for April 1694 included Purcell's song with the following annotation: "A song, the notes by Mr. Henry Purcell, the words fitted to the tune by N. Henley." [correctly identified as "A. Henley" in the table of contents] According to the single-sheet edition of the song in *Joyful Cuckholdom*, the only other contemporary print and also the only source identifying the song with the play, Mrs. Hudson sang at the revival in question, which as yet has not been dated precisely. That the song belongs to the spring of 1694 is fairly certain, because it appears just before an excerpt from "Come Ye Sons of Art Away," the Ode to Queen Mary for 30 April that year. Moreover, it appears just after "I sigh'd and owned my love" from *The Fatal Marriage*, as mentioned above.[22]

The presence of the piece in Purcell's song autograph—London, Gresham College MS VI.5.6., now in Guildhall Library—shows that he not only approved of Anthony Henley's mock-song, but actually participated in the revision of the music by transcribing the score, originally for strings, for the harpsichord.

Exactly when Dryden's *Aureng-Zebe* was revived in a production including music by Purcell also is unknown (see Z573), but 1694 is the most likely year, since the song "I See She Flies Me" was first published in *Comes Amoris*, Book 5, that year, and a reprint of the play also was then published. The text of the play does not refer specifically to the song, although it does call for "Soft music" for Aureng-Zebe's soliloquy in act 4, scene 1. But the engraved, single-sheet edition, published by Thomas Cross ca. 1695, definitely identifies the piece as belonging to the play, as do most later editions. British Library MS Add. 22099, f.69, also ascribes the song to Dryden's play; but on stylistic grounds alone, it is clear that the date given in the manuscript is wrong, even though the rest of the information given in the inscription may be correct: "'I see she flies me': Song from *Aureng-Zebe*, 1696."

The last three plays mentioned by Motteux for that season all were based on Cervantes's *Don Quixote*. D'Urfey's *The Comical History of Don Quixote* eventually grew to three parts, the first two of which appeared in May and July, respectively, of 1694. Even earlier, John Crowne's *The Married Beau, or The Curious Impertinent* (Z603) dealt, as the subtitle shows, with a popular tale in part 1 of the original *Don Quixote*. Purcell provided an overture, eight act-tunes, and one song—"See where repenting Celia lies" (Z603/10)—for the production of Crowne's play, which was quite successful, if we may believe the report in *Gentleman's Journal*: "We have had two comedies since my last and that call'd *The Married Beau, or The Curious Impertinent*, by Mr. Crown, already acted many times and impatiently expected, is to be the next play."[23] For once Motteux's journal appeared nearly on time, so it is clear that the play actually was performed some time in April.

Parts 1 and 2 of D'Urfey's "transmogrification" from Cervantes's original followed in quick succession, the production of the second being hastened by the success of the first. Nor were hopes disappointed with the second production, as Motteux explained in his next issue: "The first part of Mr. D'Urfey's Don Quixote was so well received, that we have had a second part of that Comical History acted lately, which doubtless must be thought as entertaining as the first; since in this hot season it could bring such a numerous audience." In these, as in part 3, which D'Urfey essayed in the following season, Cervantes's philosophical melancholy and deep insights into the human comedy are completely absent. Nevertheless, in their characterizations, as in the handling of plot and situation, these plays were far superior to anything he had written up to that time, or indeed, at any later time. One suspects that Motteux, who had published his own translation of *Don Quixote*, may have had more to do with the productions than merely to provide inspiration.[24] As far as their successes were concerned, a large measure of credit must be reserved for the abundance of very entertaining music Purcell composed for the plays. Even though the work had had to be fitted into one of the busiest times in Purcell's career, it is clear from the following table that he had contributed the lion's share of music for these productions:

The Comical History of Don Quixote. Part 1. D'Urfey. Late May 1694, D.G.

RUBRIC OR FIRST-LINE	COMPOSER	VOICES (SINGERS)
II. Drums and Trumpets sounding (March)		
II. Dance of Knights	–	
II. Sing all ye muses	Purcell	CT & B (Freeman & Reading?)
II. Young Chrysostome	Eccles	S
II. Dance		to following song?
II. Sleep poor youth	Eccles	B (Reading?)
III. When the world	Purcell	B (Reading?)
IV. Let the dreadful engines	Purcell	Bowman (DP)
IV. Dance of Slaves	–	
IV. 'Twas early	Eccles	Doggett (DP)
V. With this sacred	Purcell	Bowman (DP) & 2S
V. Antick Dance	–	
V. Dance of Furies	–	

The Comical History of Don Quixote. Part 2. D'Urfey. ca. June 1694.

RUBRIC OR FIRST-LINE	COMPOSER	VOICES (SINGERS)
I. Musick sounds		
I. If you will love me	anon.	S & T
I. Entertainment of Dancing	–	
II. Dance of Spirits	–	
II. Ye Nymphs	Eccles	Mrs. Ayliff (DQS)
II. Dance of Milkmaids	–	
III. Damon let a friend	Pack	Mrs. Hudson (DQS)
III. March to drum and fife	–	
III. Antick Dance	–	
IV. Since times are so bad	Purcell	Reading & Mrs. Ayliff (DQS)
IV. Dance of Spinsters	–	
V. Genius of England	Purcell	Freeman & Mrs. Cibber (text) Trumpet: J. Shore
V. I burn	Eccles	Mrs. Bracegirdle (DP)
V. Dance of 7 Champions	–	–
V. De foolish English	anon.	T
Lads and lasses	Purcell	Mrs. Hudson (TsM3) [25]

The foregoing impressive list of theatrical and occasional commissions Purcell had undertaken during these last few years of his life cannot be explained entirely on the assumption that he was merely responding to popular demand. Whatever he may have been paid for his works, he probably needed the income they brought quite urgently, for during this entire period, his name does not appear in the lists of king's musicians receiving salaries, riding charges, liveries, and other emoluments (as recorded in the lord chamberlain's accounts under William and Mary). Indeed, in available documents pertaining to musical life at court during their reign, Purcell's name appears only twice: once, quite belatedly when his appointments were at last recorded, and then a second time when his successors were named. Apparently, Purcell was unpopular at court, or at least so the records seem to indicate. Similar cases of royal displeasure had sent poor Louis Grabu packing during the reign of James II and had forced John Banister into the new and relatively untried paths of concert entrepreneurship.[26]

However, his diminished circumstances did not prevent him from implementing extensive repairs and improvements to the organ at St. Peter's, Westminster, which was, of course, the instrument upon which he practiced and performed daily. Throughout the summer and early autumn of 1694, Purcell must have invested a large share of time, energy, and concern in this matter, as is shown in the following entry in the Westminster Abbey Chapter Minutes, 1683–1714, fo. 47v (12 July 1694):

> Ordered that an agreement be made by Mr. Stephen Crispian, Chanter, and Mr. Purcell, Organist of the Collegiate Church of Westminster, for and on behalf of the Dean and Chapter of Westminster, with Mr. Bernard (Smith) Organ Maker, for the amending, altering and new making of the organ belonging to the said Collegiate Church, in such manner as the said Stephen Crispian and Henry Purcell shall direct, and that the said Mr. Smith shall have the sum of £200 for the performance thereof to be paid as shall be agreed. . . .
> Subscribed by the said Bernard Smith in the
presence of Steph. Crispian
Henry Purcell
John Needham.[27]

More evidence for Purcell's financial need are the pupils on organ and spinet he taught during this same period. At least six months before Michaelmas (25 September) 1693, he had given lessons to John Weldon at Eton College, as we know from the college account books:

1692–93	Allowed Mr. Walter by the College towards putting out Weldon the chorister for half a year at Michaelmas 1693	£5
1693	. . . Weldon for two quarters ending at Michaelmas 1693	£5
	. . . paid for Weldon (as part of £15. 11s. 6d) To Mr. Purcell	£1.10.0
1694	Item, allowed by the College to Mr. H. Purcell with Weldon, the chorister, for half a year, ended at Lady Day 1694	£5.0.0[28]

There is no record of Purcell's having traveled to Windsor, and it is unlikely that he did, as Queen Mary remained either at Whitehall or Kensington while William was away for most of the summer. And even after the king's return, his asthma kept the royal pair away from Windsor or any other place on the Thames.[29] It is possible that Purcell visited Eton from time to time but more likely that Weldon, who studied composition as well as performance, went to him. In any case, the lessons continued only a short while, for Weldon, who reached age eighteen in January of that year, was soon off to Oxford, where he had received an appointment at New College. He always spoke proudly of Purcell as his master. Others whom Purcell taught include Elizabeth Howard, Catherine Shore, daughter of the famous trumpeter John Shore, Jeremiah Clarke, and Henry Needler.

Another of Purcell's pupils during this period was richer in material means, though perhaps poorer in musical talent. The records at Ashtead Manor show that at least as early as 27 July 1693, the Howards had been entertaining the hope that their daughter, Katherine, would become proficient on the spinet. This is clear from the following transcript:

1693 July 27	Pd. Mr. Player for tuning Misses spinet	£(0)	10	0
1693/4 Feb. 8	Pd. Mr. Purcell for one month's teaching Miss on the Harpsichord	£2	3.	6.
1693/4 Mar. 5	Pd. Mr. Purcell for one month's teaching Miss on the Harpsichord	£2	3.	6.
1694/5 Feb. 12	Pd. Mr. Purcell for one month's teaching Miss 2 guineas [*sic*]	£2	6.	0.
1695 Apr. 19	Pd. Mr. Purcell in full	£2	10.	0.[30]

A final entry mentioning the name Purcell refers to a period, years later, during which Frances Purcell, by then a widow for eight years, had been a house guest at the mansion in Ashtead:

1703 13 Nov.   Given to Mrs. Purcell's maid   £(0)   5.   0.

Though ambiguous, indeed noncommittal, this entry reminds us of Frances Purcell's remarks in the dedication to *Orpheus Britannicus*, which appeared in 1698. This clearly identifies Lady Katherine as Purcell's pupil:

> To the Honourable, The Lady Howard. Madam, Were it in the power of music to abate those strong impressions of grief which have continued upon me ever since the loss of my dear lamented husband, there are few (I believe) who are furnished with larger or better supplies of comfort from this science than he has left me in his own compositions, and in the satisfaction I find, that they are not more valued by me (who much own myself fond to a partiality of all that was his) than those who are no less Judges than Patrons of his performances. I find, Madam, I have already said enough to justify the presumption of this application to your Ladyship, who have added both these characters to the many excellent qualities, which make you the admiration of all that know you. Your Ladyship's extraordinary skill in music, beyond most of either sex, and your great goodness to that dear person, whom you have sometimes been pleased to honour with the title of your master, makes it hard for me to judge whether he contributed more to the vast improvements you have made in this science, or your Ladyship to the reputation he gain'd in the profession of it: for I have often heard him say, that as several of his best compositions were originally design'd for your Ladyship's entertainment, so the pains he bestowed in fitting them for your ear, were abundantly rewarded by the satisfaction he received from your approbation, and admirable performance to them, which has best recommended both them and their author to all that have had the happiness of hearing them from your Ladyship.

Purcell's pieces in *Musick's Handmaid II* probably represent the kind of music young Katherine Howard had practiced. As she advanced, she might also have studied the pieces and the rules published by Henry Playford in *A Choice Collection of Lessons for the Harpsichord or Spinnet* (1696). These represent Purcell's teaching methods, still valid today for novice and intermediate keyboard artists:

> There will nothing conduce more to a perfect attaining to play on the harpsichord or spinet than a serious application to the following rules: In order to which you must first learn the gamut or scale of music, getting the names' of the notes by heart, and observing at the same time

what line and space every note stands on, that you may know and distinguish them at first sight, in any of the following lessons, to which purpose I have placed a scheme of keys exactly as they are in the spinet or harpsichord, and on every key the first letter of the note directing to the name, lines and spaces where the proper note stands.

Purcell's pedagogical method may be evaluated less conjecturally in another didactic work upon which he must have been engaged at the time, since the following year saw the publication of John Playford's twelfth edition of *An Introduction to the Skill of Music*, for which Purcell revised the third book, "A Brief Introduction to the Art of Descant: or, Composing Music in Parts." In recasting this section—inherited from Thomas Campion, Christopher Simpson, John Playford, and others—Purcell demonstrated that meticulous attention to detail that characterizes the born teacher. With exemplary brevity, he disposed of the fundamentals of music, coming after half a dozen pages to the essential problems of handling dissonance.

Here he displayed fully his extraordinary capacity for meticulous attention to significant detail in a logical and systematic manner—a very important capability for excellent instruction. His intuitive grasp of the necessity for gradual, though not dilatory, progress on the part of the pupil toward full development of needed skills and understanding is exemplary, particularly for advancement in the discipline of music. In his careful approach to various techniques of counterpoint—"Of Fuge, or Pointing"—in his succinct analysis of "the Italian manner," indeed, in the whole of this "Brief Introduction," Purcell set a model for all teachers of musical composition—a model that might be used profitably in the classroom even today.[31]

Meanwhile London's concert life had increased apace. Tosi's concerts were resumed on 30 October 1693 and continued each Monday throughout the winter season. The concerts at Charles Street and in York Buildings took place as usual on Tuesdays and Thursdays, respectively, and all the anniversary occasions usually celebrated with musical performance—i.e., St. Cecilia's Day, royal birthdays, and other commemorations—were observed as they occurred on the calendar. Purcell apparently wrote nothing for the St. Cecilia celebration in 1693, the honor for that commission falling upon Godfrey Finger, who set the eclectic verses of Theophilus Parsons's "Cecilia, Look Down and See,"[32] the music for which, alas, has been lost. That it was enjoyable to the London musical community may be assumed from the fact that it was performed twice more that same season, as the following entries from the *London Gazette* inform us: "In York Buildings on Monday next will be performed the last St. Cecilia song. beginning at the usual hour."[33] and: "At the consort in York buildings, on Monday next the 5th instant, will be performed, Mr. Finger's St. Cecilia Song, intermixed with a variety of new music at the ordinary rates."[34]

Henry Purcell's younger brother, Daniel, also became involved in the St. Cecilia tradition that season, setting Thomas Gilden's "Begin and Strike th' Harmonious Lyre" for celebration of the saint's day in Oxford.[35] Whether his work was actually performed, or merely commissioned, cannot be ascertained from records presently available.

As for Henry Purcell's connection with the tradition, the success of "Hail, Bright Cecilia," first performed on 22 November 1692, apparently was sufficient to warrant another performance on 26 January 1694, as we know from an advertisement in the *London Gazette:* "At the consort-room in York-buildings, on this present Thursday, at the usual hour, will be performed Mr. Purcell's Song, composed for St. Cecilia's Day in the year 1692, together with some other compositions of his, both vocal and instrumental, for the entertainment of his Highness Prince Lewis of Baden."[36] The *Gentleman's Journal* for January-February 1694 indicates that one of the songs was Purcell's "Scotch Song" for which Motteux had supplied the text, "Sawney Is a Bonny Lad" (Z412); and it is possible that the second version of "If Music Be the Food of Love" (Z379B), which appeared in *Comes Amoris* about this time, may have been one of the songs alluded to above. As for instrumental music that might have appeared on this program, nothing at all is known. There are, of course, the various instrumental suites composed for the theaters, as described above, which would have fit into the program quite well. It is even quite possible that Purcell's *Trumpet Sonata* (Z850) was performed at this time. If Michael Tilmouth's ingenious conjecture be well founded, the piece would have been heard already as the overture to Purcell's setting of Matthew Prior's *Hymn to the Sun* on 1 January, then revived for this concert some four weeks later.[37] (But here, I fear we pile conjecture upon conjecture!) In any case, the list of missing compositions cannot be too long, for the performance of "Hail Bright Cecilia" would have occupied nearly an hour, leaving little time for other large works.

Concerning the performance of "Hail Bright Cecilia," it may be assumed that many of those who had performed in November of 1692 were present on this later occasion. Purcell, conducting from the harpsichord, would have been surrounded by the same soloists: Woodson, Williams, and Damascene (basses); Turner (tenor); Bouchier, Howell, and Pate (countertenors); and Mrs. Ayliffe (soprano). Due to limitations of space in the York Buildings concert hall, it is unlikely that they were accompanied by the full band of twenty-four violins, even for this royal occasion. Representatives from His Majesty's "Wind Music" would have included players on two flutes and bass flute, two oboes and tenor oboe, two trumpets and a pair of kettledrums. As for the organ parts, Purcell may have changed instruments for the great ensemble movements or called in any one of a number of distinguished colleagues—John Blow, Giovanni Battista Draghi, or perhaps one of his pupils—if, indeed, an organ was available for the occasion. Some trebles and altos from the children of the Chapel Royal may have also joined forces, although their presence certainly would have crammed a lot of musicians into a relatively small amount of space.[38]

From the records, it is clear that this was a very busy time for Purcell. He not only had been involved in the commission for New Year's Day and the two performances mentioned above for January, but also had accepted a commission to compose an ode for the centenary celebrations for Founder's Day, 9 January 1694, at Trinity College, Dublin. Presuming that this work, "Great Parent, Hail" (Z327), was composed well beforehand, along with the New Year's ode, we can only imagine the intensity of Purcell's schedule throughout the winter months.

The celebration for Dublin was announced in the same issue of the *London Gazette* that announced the above-mentioned concert for Prince Louis of Baden at the end of January. However, the concert was entered as an event published with other general news rather than published as an advertisement:

> Dublin. Jan. 9. This day was celebrated in the University of this city, the secular day of their Foundation by Queen Elizabeth, being one hundred years since their first establishment; the solemnity began in the morning about 10, with prayers in the College Chapel. . . . The afternoon was taken up with speeches, verses, and music, both vocal and instrumental, in praise of their foundress and benefactors, of their majesties King William and Queen Mary under whose auspicious reign they were restored. . . .

John Dunton reports the same event in a contemporary journal, *Some Account of my Conversation in Ireland* (1699). Something seems amiss, however, with his chronology for the event, which somehow has become traditional. Elizabeth I founded Trinity College officially on 16 March 1592. Hence the centennial of Founder's Day should have fallen on 16 March 1692.[39] However, the records show that the first student had matriculated on 9 January 1592, and this was the historic moment that the college authorities had chosen to commemorate.[40]

Strictly speaking, then, we are discussing a "Matriculation Ode," not a Founder's Day composition. The text does make much of "Bless'd Eliza's day," "Thy Muses Second Jubilee," "Another Century Commencing," and so on. So the case is not clear cut, a condition that perhaps gives us cause to reconsider the importance of such close study of text and archival information. Perhaps the ostensible was not the only cause for celebration. It is clear that these festivities also honored recent victories of the English army in Ireland, as intimated by the following stanza, the seventh in the poem:

> But chiefly recommend to fame
> Maria and great William's name:
> For surely no Hibernian Muse
> Whose isle to him her freedom owes,
> Can her restorer's praise refuse
> While Boyne or Shannon flows.

We cannot hold Purcell accountable for "propagandizing" the royal position with his music, but it is clear that Nahum Tate was aware of the reference to the immediate political and military events the commemorative ode included, by reference, as it were. Earlier in the text, Tate had indicated that the celebration was intended for a time "after war's alarms repeated and a circling age completed"—which in the unfolding of events hinged upon the key date, 5 October 1691, when Limerick, last Jacobite stronghold in Ireland, capitulated to William III's forces.[41] Then followed a period of uneasy peace, as we know from Evelyn and other diarists, while James II and the French forces threatened new invasions from time to time. By 9 January 1694, however, it was clear that England had established a victorious peace, and that date was chosen as an appropriate occasion to celebrate the restoration of English hegemony over Ireland. The Glorious Revolution could now be accounted a success in most of all three kingdoms of Great Britain. Quite incidentally, as it seems, a celebration of Trinity College's centennial was also in order.[42] Nahum Tate, an alumnus of the college, was chosen as poet for the occasion and Purcell as composer. Samuel Fitzpatrick described the ceremony in some detail:

> On 9th(?) January 1693/4 the first centenary of the university was celebrated with great solemnity: *Preces tempore meridiano solenniosis (una cum cancione) in sacello habebuntur.* In the afternoon *Hora secunda pro meridiano, Post musicum instrumentorum concentum,* a Latin panegyric in honor of Queen Elizabeth was pronounced by Peter Browne, F.T.C.D., followed by a *carmen seculare* in Latin hexameters and laudations of King James I, Charles I, Charles II, and William and Mary. King

James II was, for obvious reasons, ignored, but the city of Dublin sensed a grateful recognition of the benefits conferred by her magistrates on the infant university. After a Latin debate and a *carmen seculare lyricum* recited by Anthony Dopping, son of the Bishop of Meath, Eugene Lloyd, Proctor of the University, closed the Acts *Discedentes pro sequitur perita musicorum manus.*[43]

Thus, Purcell had paved the way for Handel's musical adventure in Ireland nearly half a century later when, as Alexander Pope phrased it, the "Empress of Dullness . . . drove him to the Hibernian shore."[44] On the following day, in London, the Prince of Baden saw a performance of *Dioclesian*, given in honor of the same event.[45]

Purcell was very active in the second half of the London concert season, which, like the theatrical season, continued well into the summer despite sultry weather.[46] Although the concert on Monday, 7 May, was the last of the season at York Buildings, as announced in the *London Gazette* for 3 May, the Vendu in Charles Street continued its concerts until mid-June, without interruption even for renovations to the music room.[47] Purcell's name is not mentioned in any of the accounts of public concerts after those for the January revival of "Hail Bright Cecilia," but there are frequent references to revivals of plays for which he supplied music in the *London Gazette*, the *Gentleman's Journal*, the *Post Boy* and other journals, which mention *The Fatal Marriage*, *The Double Dealer*, *Love Triumphant*, *The Old Batchelor*, and *The Married Beau*, and the two parts of *Don Quixote* discussed above. In addition, events at court received due notice: On Monday, 30 April, Purcell's "Come, Ye Sons of Art Away" was performed for Queen Mary's birthday, an event apparently coinciding with one of the revivals of John Crowne's *The Married Beau*, as mentioned above, which in turn was followed in quick succession by *All for Love* and parts 1 and 2 of *Don Quixote*, then by *Theodosius*, all before the beginning of summer. It would have been difficult to miss hearing quite a lot of Purcell's music in any given week at court, theater, or church during this period.

The rest of the summer passed uneventfully, it seems, Purcell's schedule being filled with routine work, except for a few minor developments, such as publication of his little song "Celia's Fond" (Z364), with "words fitted to the tune" by Peter Motteux,[48] which appeared in the *Gentleman's Journal* for July. On the fifth of that same month, the *London Gazette* announced publication of Purcell's music for *Don Quixote*, an event that may have occupied more of his time. A week later Purcell was called in to help draw up and to sign an agreement between the dean and chapter of Westminster Abbey and Bernard Smith:

> 12 July, 1694. Ordered that an agreement be made by Mr. Stephan Crespian, Chanter and Mr. Purcell, Organist of the Collegiate Church of Westminster, for and on behalf of the Dean and Chapter of Westminster with Mr. Bernard (Smith) organ-maker for the amending and altering and new making of the organ belonging to the said Collegiate Church in such manner as the said Stephen Crespian and Henry Purcell shall direct, and that the said Mr. Smith shall have the sum of £200 for the performance thereof, to be paid as shall be agreed.[49]

The document itself was recorded as follows:

> That the same shall be viewed and approved of by Mr. Stephen Crespian, Clark Chanter of the Collegiate Church of St. Peters Westminster and Henry Purcell, Gentleman Organist of the said church; and what defaults shall be found by them or either of them in the composing and making of the said organ, shall be altered, amended and made good by the said Bernard Smith,
>
> Ber. Smith
>
> Subscribed by the said
> Bernhard Smith in the
> presence of Steph. Crespian
>   Henry Purcell
>   John Nedham[50]

Purcell signed, perhaps forgetful of his and Crespion's trouble with Needham over the "organ-loft incident" and not knowing that the day agreed upon for the second payment would follow his death by a week,[51] and unaware that he was destined never to play upon the newly renovated organ.

$\frown$ 16 $\frown$

The End of an Era

DURING THE SEASON OF 1694−95, which was the last Purcell was to finish, his work for the lyrical stage reached its climax. Between the performance of Edward Ravenscroft's *The Canterbury Guests*[1] in November and the revival of Beaumont's and Fletcher's *Bonduca*[2] about June or July the following summer, Londoners heard Purcell's music in no fewer than nine plays. In this same period, he was occupied with music for *The Tempest*,[3] *Timon of Athens*,[4] and, presumably, with preparations for *The Indian Queen*,[5] an operatic revival of the play by Sir Robert Howard and John Dryden, which Tom Betterton was supposed to be getting underway.[6]

All told, Purcell created some ninety individual pieces during this time, requiring effort on his part that must be seen as prodigious, in view of his official duties at court and Abbey, not to mention his private teaching. All of this must have told on his strength, and although the actual cause of his death early the following season is unknown, overwork was probably a contributing factor.

Of such melancholy considerations, though, not a hint is to be heard in the witty and comic dialogue "Good Neighbour, Why Look You Awry?", Purcell's first stage song to be heard in the new season, with the performance of *The Canterbury Guests*. This play evidently was intended for production in May of the previous season, as J. Genest remarks, since one of the characters in the play speaks of 3 May as "tomorrow."[7] What kind of reception the play may have had is not known, but Motteux's tactful avoidance of any mention in *Gentleman's Journal* for October-November (p. 276) may indicate that it was not successful: "I have only just room to tell you that we have had a new comedy by Mr. Ravenscroft, 'tis call'd *The Canterbury Jests* [*sic*]; *or, A Bargain Broken*." The setting of the dialogue, which fully demonstrates Purcell's extraordinary skill in capturing the accents and energy of plainspoken English invective, rises considerably above the general level achieved within the spoken portions of the play.

William III returned at last to London on 11 November, having landed at Margate on the previous day, arriving there after several months of campaigning in the Low Countries. The capture of Huy had been his most notable achievement, but, as far as we know, this event was not celebrated musically. However, Purcell had composed an anthem on his return, "The Way of God Is an Undefiled Way," on a text rendered topical by careful selection of the more militant verses of Psalm 18.[8] It is one of the ironies of history that most of the omitted verses should have been those chosen to depict Charles II's political situation back in 1679–80, when Purcell, in one of his earliest court anthems, had shown that monarch as a lone, vulnerable figure, surrounded by enemies.[9] In this new anthem, of which there is a fine copy in the newly discovered William Kennedy Gostling manuscript, bearing the annotation "King William then returned from Flanders" and the above date, the heroic military stance of the central figure could scarcely have been contrasted more sharply with the persecuted monarch revealed in Purcell's setting of "I Will Love Thee, O Lord" (N67).

On the following Thursday, 15 November, further musical celebrations for the king's return were in order, when his birthday observances were at last held, eleven days after the correct date, as Narcissus Luttrell explains:[10] "This day was a great ball at Whitehall, designed for the King's birthday, but put off by reason of his not being there." Nahum Tate had provided a mawkish text for the occasion—"Spring, Where Are Thy Flow'ry Treasures"—and Staggins composed the music. His attempt to catch the martial atmosphere so aptly illustrated in Purcell's anthem seems very lame by comparison.

Just a week and a day later, on 23 November, Purcell's new setting of the *Te Deum and Jubilate*[11] provided magnificent ceremonial music for the annual church service sponsored by the "Sons of the Clergy" for the observance of the St. Cecilia's Day tradition. According to Husk,[12] the author and composer of the St. Cecilia ode for this year are both unknown. However, one of the songs in *Thesaurus Musicus*, Book 5, printed in the following year, identifies one of its pieces as "Mr. Pickets' Song, sung at St. Cecilia's Feast by Mrs. Robart"[13] and provides a clue to at least one composition performed on that occasion. Purcell's new setting may have seemed to some inappropriate for a sacred occasion, what with its martial accompaniments, featuring trumpets and drums, and his careful avoidance of polyphonic settings for the traditional texts. However, Purcell was but following a tradition established by Giovanni Gabrieli at San Marco in Venice, by Zarlino for the victory of the Battle of Lepanto (in 1571) in that same city, and by Dufay, with his "Supremum est mortalibus" for the Peace of Viterbo in 1433.

Like these earlier composers, Purcell was merely linking an outstand-
ing occasion of church and state with brilliant, ceremonial motets,
frankly secular, even theatrical in expression. The victor at Huy, the
conqueror of Ireland, and the hero of the Glorious Revolution could
have had no more appropriate musical tribute or one more suited to
the spirit with which he and his beloved queen had reanimated the
British nation. As for the reputation of the piece itself, not to mention
Purcell's, it is a great pity that it was for long known to the public only
in William Boyce's misguidedly revised version, a performance of
which caused Felix Mendelssohn-Bartholdy to storm out of St. Paul's
Cathedral in disgust more than a century later.[14]

That William and Mary heard the *Te Deum and Jubilate* at least
once, and probably twice, is indicated in Luttrell's note for 11 December 1694: "Sunday last [i.e., 9 December] was performed before their
majesties in the Chapel Royal the same vocal and instrumental music
as was performed at St. Bride's Church on St. Cecilia's Day last."[15] St.
Cecilia's Day being 22 November, this passage raises the question of
whether the composition was performed on the twenty-second or on
the twenty-third. Perhaps Husk erred in assigning the latter date, for
John Evelyn's entry for the twenty-third records that "K. William had
two fits of an ague." It is extremely unlikely that King William would
have gone anywhere on that day.

Significantly, in light of future events, Evelyn also remarked that it
was "An extraordinary sickly time especially of the smallpox, of which
divers considerable persons died." It was indeed a bad autumn in this
regard, for smallpox had carried off 1,325 victims, as contrasted with
only 257 in the same three months of 1693. Moreover, no fewer than
eighty-five deaths had been recorded in the bills of mortality for just
one week, between 13 and 20 November.[16]

A month later it was generally feared that this terrible scourge had
reached the most considerable person in all of England—Queen Mary
herself. Luttrell[17] reported on the twenty-second that she was "somewhat indisposed and that the smallpox was feared," then wrote on the
twenty-fifth more hopefully, or at least wishfully:

> The Queen was taken ill on Saturday last, and 'twas feared to be the
> smallpox, but this morning her physicians perceived it to be the measles:
> she was this day prayed for in all the churches about this city: the King
> so extremely concerned at it, that he has ordered a bed in her Majesty's
> room at Kensington, and will not stir from her, but sees all things admin-
> istered to her himself; there are no ill symptoms appear, but is in hopeful
> way of recovery.

On the twenty-seventh, however, the truth could no longer be avoided, as Luttrell plainly stated before describing in detail the progress of the terrible disease. First came the onset of St. Anthony's Fire, with its macabre "blue spots," then the letting of blood and scarification of the forehead, then extreme unction, while a whole nation grieved. Finally, death came at about 1:00 A.M. on 28 December, the day of the Feast of the Holy Innocents.

The Privy Council meanwhile had decided that Queen Mary's funeral rites should be carried out privately, like those held ten years earlier for King Charles II,[18] but soon reversed its decision upon encountering public opinion. On 1 January 1695 that august body submitted to universal demands for a stately public funeral, which began with a formal period for "lying-in-state" on the following Sunday (6 January) and continued with preparations for an enormous funeral procession and highly ceremonial final rites, at which all the peers of the realm were to be in attendance. According to Luttrell, costs were estimated to exceed £100,000.[19]

For some reason—perhaps because the council had appointed a committee to administer the affair—none of the events came off on schedule. Lying-in-state did not begin until 21 February, as we know from Luttrell's dutifully detailed entry:

> This afternoon the queen began to lie in state in the bedchamber, all the officers of her household attending, according to their offices, under the direction of the Marquess of Winchester, her chamberlain; and the ladies of honour also attend, 4 of whom stand about the corpse, and are relieved by others every half hour; upon her head lies the crown, and over it a fine canopy; at her feet lies the sword of state, the helmet and her arms upon a cushion, the banners and scutcheons hanging round; the state is very great, and more magnificent than can be expressed: all persons are admitted without distinction: she is to lie so every day from 12 till 5 o'clock till she is interred.[20]

The general mood of mourning and the nation's love for its queen were perhaps best represented not by the pompous sermons and lachrymose elegies that poured forth at this time, but, if we may believe a very popular anecdote, by a robin that came to sing over her each day as she lay in state. At any rate this sentimental story soon achieved the status of a minor miracle, symbolizing the British nation's deep regard for its gentle queen, so tragically taken away. (See plates 36 and 37, where Grinling Gibbons's monument shares space with the picture and poem representing "The Robin-Red-Breast Famous for singing every day on the Top of Queen Mary's Mausoleum. . . .")

PLATE 36. Monument for William and Mary. Grinling Gibbons
(British Museum)

PLATE 37. "The Robin-Red-Breast Famous for singing every day on the Top of Queen Mary's Mausoleum Erected in Westminster Abbey, 1695." Drawn from life by F. Barlow, engraved by P. Tempest (Bodleian, Gough Maps 45.f.50)

Meanwhile Purcell, along with virtually every artist, musician, and poet in the nation, had been creating tributes to the queen, both for her final rites and as general memorials. Purcell had written four pieces for the funeral and two exquisite elegies; James Paisible composed "The Queen's Farewell"; and John Blow set "No, Lesbia, No," the text of which was an English translation of Henry Purcell's elegy *Incassum Lesbia*. Finally, on 5 March, all elaborate preparations were in order for the queen's interment, which "was performed with great solemnity, and all the shops throughout the city were shut. . . ." First came two hundred old women in long black gowns, each with a boy to her train.[21] What an awesome spectacle they must have formed, walking solemnly before the queen's funeral car, along graveled walks between black-wrapped handrails that Christopher Wren had erected all the way from Whitehall to Westminster Abbey.[22] John Evelyn, like almost everyone who witnessed the scene, was profoundly moved: "Was the Queen's funeral infinitely expensive, never so universal a mourning, all the Parliament men had cloaks given them, 400 poor women, all the streets hung, and the middle of the streets boarded and covered with black cloth: there was all the nobility, mayor, and aldermen, judges, etc."

The progression moved slowly along, to the solemn harmonies of Purcell's "March for the Queen's Funeral, Sounded Before Her Chariot," as intoned by a choir of "flatt trumpets."[23] The melancholy harmonies produced by these instruments were accompanied all the way by muffled drumbeats,[24] as the following entries from the lord chamberlain's accounts reveal:

> January, 1694/5: Account for 20 yards of black baise to cover five drum
> cases, at 3.d 6s. per yard   £3. 10s
> and for 8 yards ditto to cover one pair of kettle-drums at 3s. 6d.
> per yard   £1. 8s.
> 10 January, 1694/5. Warrants for the providing of mourning for the late
> Queen:
> To the first regiment of foot-guards, 25 covers for drums and 6 banners
> for the hautboys.
> To the 16 Gentlemen of the Chapel Royal.
> To the Sargeant Trumpeter, 16 trumpeters and a kettle-drummer.
> To Dr. Staggins, master of the music.

Furthermore, the official "Order and Form" specifically mentions "the Gentlemen of the Chapel and Vestry in capes and the Children of the Chapel singing all the way."[25] (Unfortunately, there is no record of what they may have sung.) As for the march, it was a sacred contrafactum that Purcell had salvaged from an earlier work, for he had first composed it as a setting for the supernatural scene in Thomas Shadwell's *The Libertine* when it was revived in 1692. The otherworldly sounds of the choir of sack-buts (i.e., "flatt-trumpets") were originally intended to express the feelings aroused by the "drawing near of ghosts." However inappropriate the original scenario, the supernatural quality and the deep seriousness of the piece lent themselves admirably to the queen's funeral rites. (It has been argued that Purcell's music for *The Libertine* must have been written after the funeral, since no one would have wanted to hear a theatrical piece used for her funeral. In my opinion, no one would have dared use the queen's funeral march on any stage after the public ceremony, while very few, if any, who attended that event, would have remembered the theatrical piece.)

The court in mourning, there was no New Year's ode for 1695; nor was there any celebration for Coronation Day on 11 April, being the day of burial for both the marquis of Halifax and Richard Busby, Purcell's former mentor.[26] Busby's gift of a mourning ring to Purcell is circumstantial evidence of Purcell's actual presence at the funeral ceremonies, corroborating as well his attendance as a scholar at St. Peter's, Westminster, nearly two decades earlier.

The death of the queen also put an end to the series of birthday odes Purcell had composed, brightening the last day of April for each of the preceding six years since 1690. That same anniversary seems to have been observed in 1695 by publication of Henry Playford's beautiful print of *Three Elegies Upon the Much Lamented Loss of Our Late Queen Mary*—the title page appropriately edged in black—containing poems and settings commissioned for the occasion. These elegies were entered in the Trinity Term Catalogue and advertised in the *London Gazette* for 6 May.

This handsome publication, a musical triptych in memory of the queen, presented as its centerpiece "The Queen's Epicedium," as set by Purcell of Mr. Herbert's Latin translation of his own English verses on the occasion, "No, Lesbia, No." This latter poem, as set by John Blow, opens the set. In sheer expressive depth and subtlety, Purcell clearly outshone his former teacher here. Nevertheless, comparison of the two settings provides for better understanding of each. Obviously, the texts run parallel, though the Latin version, being more specific in its allusions and figures of speech, presents the aspect rather of an original poem than of a translation. Here are the two texts, side-by-side, under the original title page:

THREE ELEGIES UPON THE MUCH LAMENTED LOSS OF OUR LATE
MOST GRACIOUS QUEEN MARY. THE WORDS OF THE TWO FIRST BY
MR. HERBERT. THE LATTER OUT OF THE OXFORD VERSE: AND SET
TO MUSIC BY DR. BLOW AND MR. HENRY PURCELL. LONDON.
Printed by J. Heptinstall, for Henry Playford, near Temple-Church; or at his
House over-against the Blue-Ball in Arundel Street, 1695.

The Queen's Epicedium. By Mr. Herbert. Latine Redditum

No, Lesbia, no, you ask in vain,
My harp, my mind's unstrung
When all the world's in tears, in
   pain:
Do you require a song?

Incassum Lesbia, incassum rogas
Lyra mea, Mens est immodulata;
Terrarum Orbe lacrymarum pleno,
Dolorum: rogitas tu cantilenam?

2

See, see how ev'ry nymph and swain
Hang down their pensive heads and
   weep!
No voice nor pipe is heard in all the
   plain;
So great their sorrows, they neglect
   their sheep.

2

En nymphas! En Pastores! caput
   omne reclinat
Juncorum instar! admodum fletur;
Nec Galatea canit, nec ludi Tityrus
   agris: [27]
Non curant oves. moerore perditi.

3

The Queen! the Queen of Arcadia
   is gone
Lesbia, the loss can't be exprest
Not by the deepest sigh, or groan,
Or throbbing of the breast.

3

Regina! heu! Arcadiae Regina
Periit! O! Damnum non
   exprimendum;
Non, non suspiriis, gemitis imis,
Pectoris aut queruli singultu turbido.

4

Ah! Poor Arcadius! how they
   mourn
O the delight, and wonder of their
   eyes
She's gone! and never must return
Her star is fixt, and shines before
   the skies.

4

Miseros Arcadas! O quam lugentes!
Suorum Gaudium Oculorum, Mirum
Abiit! hunques, O nunques reversum
Stella sua fixa coelum ultra lucet. [28]

The third elegy in the collections is Purcell's setting, also in C minor,
of "O dive Custos Auricae domus," a poem by Henry Parker of New
College, Oxford. In composing the piece for two sopranos, Purcell fell
back upon some of the latest Italianate techniques for pathetic expressions—the techniques of the trio-sonata, transferred to the vocal
idiom. Along with many other examples of this kind of performing en-

semble in Purcell's works, these might well be called "trio-cantatas," because they duplicate the texture of the trio-sonata in every way. And in these vocal models, Purcell demonstrated his ingenuity in as impressive a manner as that of the trio-sonatas, which he so successfully championed in England.

During the months in which these somber events transpired, new decisions faced at least two members of the Purcell family. Henry, busier than ever with an ever-increasing backlog of theatrical commissions, apparently decided that he needed assistance, for he was soon joined in London by his younger brother, Daniel. The latter had resigned as organist at Magdalen College, Oxford, and moved to London.[29] Tradition has it that his move was dictated by an urgent request from his brother for musical assistance, as if already Henry Purcell knew that his health was failing. Or perhaps he had summoned Daniel because he was already overtaxed in the current theatrical season and wanted to assure himself that he would not fall further behind in the next, and so made preparations well in advance. At any rate, Daniel appears to have been on hand for the remaining productions of the season, including *Pausanias*, *The Mock Marriage*, and perhaps *Timon of Athens* as well.

All this, of course, is conjectural. But it is certain that he acquired his new position as organist at St. Andrew's, Holborn, through the good offices of an Oxford friend, Henry Sacheverell, of Magdalen College.[30] As an illustration of Sacheverell's close relationship with the Purcell family, it is interesting that he failed in his attempt to get a living at St. Andrew's for yet another member of the college, the Rev. Robert Lyddel, incumbent at Wytham when Edward Purcell, Henry's elder brother, retired there early in the following century. This same Dr. Henry Sacheverell wrote a lively tribute to Henry Purcell and to John Blow upon the First and Second Books of *Harmonia Sacra*, which still stands as one of our best contemporary tributes to the two composers: "Hail, mighty pair; Of Jubal's art the greatest glory. . . ." All in all, the little circle seems close indeed.[31]

Whatever communication had been made to Daniel Purcell that spring, Purcell certainly had enough on his hands from the beginning of April 1695, when his music for *The Spanish Fryar* was performed, although he had enjoyed a period of respite, as far as theatrical commissions were concerned, since the previous 22 December when all acting had stopped during the period of mourning for the queen.[32] A performance of Thomas D'Urfey's *Cynthia and Endymion*, with the lovely song "Musing on cares of human fate" by Henry Purcell, had been planned for performance in late 1694, but it is possible that the performance was canceled, with the result that the play actually was first performed in December 1696.[33] Some time before 1 April 1695, Henry Purcell received a commission to provide an overture and eight act-tunes, with a song as well, for revival of Aphra Behn's *Abdelazer, or, the Moor's Revenge*, first performed in 1676. Betterton and several of the older, more experienced actors had broken away from Christopher Rich's tyranny—he was the original patent holder—during the respite offered by the period of mourning for Queen Mary. Thus Rich found himself with only a few inexperienced actors, decided to schedule ahead of his new opposition, and hurried the play into production on 1 April. The management had hoped to ensure success by commissioning music by Purcell, but they had not reckoned on the abysmal quality of the acting, which drove away the audience after one night. Purcell's music did not attain the full popularity it deserved until well into the twentieth century, when Benjamin Britten immortalized the Rondeau in his remarkable set of variations, *A Young Person's Guide to the Orchestra.*

The revival of *Abdelazer* was an important event in the history of the London theater, even though the production itself did not please the first audience in the Patentees' old theater, Drury Lane. At least, according to Colley Cibber, the first performance did not attract enough audience to warrant a second:

> Forces being thus raised, the war was declared on both sides, Betterton and his chiefs had the honour of an audience of the King, who considered them as the only subjects, whom he had not yet delivered from arbitrary power; and graciously he dismissed them, with an assurance of relief, and support—accordingly a select number of them were empowered by his royal licence to act in a separate theatre, for themselves. This great point being obtained, many people of quality came into a voluntary subscription of twenty, and some of forty guineas a-piece, for erecting a theatre within the walls of the tennis court in Lincoln's Inn Fields. But as it required time to fit it up, it gave the Patentees more leisure to muster their forces, who notwithstanding were not able to take the field till the Easter Monday in April following. Their first attempt was a revived play, called *Abdelazar, or the Moor's Revenge*, poorly written, by Mrs. Behn. The house was very full, but whether it was the play or the actors that were not approved, the next day's audience sunk to nothing.[34]

Purcell at this time may have been contemplating extensive music for a revival of Sir Robert Howard's and John Dryden's *The Indian Queen*, but it is fairly clear that he did not carry out his plan until well along in the following season, as we shall see a little later. Probably his next major undertaking was to write an overture, a few act-tunes, and a masque for the revival of a transmogrified *Timon of Athens*, after Shakespeare, if indeed he actually was the original author. That Purcell did not compose the F-Major act-tunes[35] was persuasively argued by the late Sir Jack Westrup, who first noted that the opening pieces had garbled in the Old Purcell Society Edition, and misattributed as well, as all are ascribed to James Paisible in a reliable near-contemporary manuscript.[36] The preceding four tunes in D major are also suspect—a fact that seems to indicate Purcell's inability to complete the commission alone and Paisible's consequent assistance. Since Daniel Purcell was already in London, it seems strange that Purcell would have called on a foreigner. Perhaps both Paisible's and J. W. Franck's compositions were written for an earlier revival.

Paradoxically, it seems that *Timon* had attracted the attention of foreign composers right from the beginning of its "transmogrified" career. When Shadwell first undertook to revise the play in January of 1678, he called upon the ill-fated Louis Grabu instead of finding a native-born composer to set Shakespeare to music.[37] Some fifteen years later, Motteux turned to J. W. Franck, a German, for musical settings of the independent masque scenes, three of which Purcell composed anew for the revival of early summer 1695. Finally, it seems that Paisible was brought into the affair.

Extant manuscript sources for these pieces do not reveal enough in the way of conclusive evidence for absolute certainty on any of these points. The element of doubt remaining is paralleled by confusion about the identities of the performers who took part in the earliest productions. Royal Music MS 24.e.13, for instance, contains an overture that is quite different from the one usually associated with *Timon*, being that for the ode "Who Can from Joy Refrain,"[38] with several harpsichord transcriptions, songs, and even the trumpet sonata.[39] Several times one encounters the names "Jacob" and "George," who probably sang the parts with which their names appear. In fact, these probably were the boy singers Jacob Wood, treble, and George Rogers, second treble.[40] Of the many "George's" whose names dot the musical records of the time, the latter, also listed as one of the children of the choir of Westminster, George Rogers, is probably the boy who took part in the music of *Timon*. It is unlikely, however, that this would have been the first production for which Purcell provided music, for "The Cares of Lovers," a song assigned to George in the manuscript, was published only slightly later as having been sung by "The Boy," alias

Jemmy Bowen, who had sung Purcell's new song "Lucinda Is Bewitching Fair" in the revival of Aphra Behn's *Abdelazer* performed earlier in the season.

On the other hand, the two names Jacob and George, both written into the royal manuscript in a later hand, may have been added for performers who took part in the revival announced in the *Daily Courant* for 1 January 1707–8, which stated that *Timon of Athens* would be performed "With all the original music. To which will be added a Masque composed by the late Mr. Henry Purcell, between Cupid and Bacchus, to be performed by Mr. Leveridge, Mrs. Lindsay and others." The possibility that the others might include Jacob and George is strengthened by the fact that Richard Leveridge's name also appears in the royal manuscript, added in the same hand that entered theirs.

Meanwhile the first posthumous anniversary of Queen Mary's birthday, 30 April, passed without official comment. By curious coincidence, this was the day on which Betterton's rebel theatrical crew at last had reached a level of organization sufficient for their debut as a separate company, performing William Congreve's comedy *Love for Love*. The play was a resounding success, even without Purcell's music, and the Patentees under Christopher Rich, who had not yet recovered from their failure with *Abdelazer*, felt totally defeated. Colley Cibber framed the matter metaphorically as a battle report, he being chief spokesman for the Patentees: "After we had stolen some few days march upon them, the forces of Betterton came up with in terrible order: In about three weeks following, the new theatre was opened against us with a veteran company and a new train of artillery; or in plainer English, the old actors in Lincoln's Inn Fields began with a new comedy of Mr. Congreve's, called *Love for Love*, which ran on with such extraordinary success that they had seldom to act any other play 'till the end of the season." [41]

William III's departure for the summer campaign in the Low Countries on 12 May seems to have ended activities, either musical or theatrical, at court. [42] At least, official records are silent throughout June and July. Elsewhere, the "Consort of Music" in Charles Street, Covent Garden, advertised in the *London Gazette*, 3–6 June 1695, that their last concert of the season would take place on 10 June. The usual records of theatrical activities also are silent, except for mention of a minor scandal arising when one "Phillips, a dancer in the playhouse" was committed to Newgate for being among those who robbed a large number of expensive costumes from the Dorset Garden Theatre.

Then throughout most of July, Henry Purcell was occupied with the task of composing an ode for the sixth birthday of the duke of Gloucester, which was performed 24 July 1695, six years after Princess Anne had been "safely delivered . . . at Hampton Court, to the joy of the whole court."[43] The text of the ode, "Who Can from Joy Refrain," remains anonymous, although W. H. Cummings, who edited the piece for the Purcell Society Edition in 1891, has stated that the verses were written by Nahum Tate, then poet laureate. Perhaps Tate was the author; but the awkwardnesses of rhythm and rhyme and the generally low quality of the writing point either to a less experienced writer or perhaps to hasty work on Tate's part.

Purcell also may have worked in haste, but of this there is not the slightest evidence in the music, which though virtually unknown, remains one of the most impressive of all the court odes he ever composed. The long final ground shows Purcell as the master of great ensemble climaxes, in pride of place which he yields only to Mozart. By the end of July, Purcell's work table seems already to have become overloaded, as may be deduced from the fact that he borrowed his own *Overture to Timon* for the ode. During late spring and early summer, he had had four important stage productions for which to compose music,[44] not to mention a large number of compositions to see through the press. During this same period, he had also traveled to Guildford, giving lessons to young Katherine Howard at Ashtead Manor in Surrey, not to mention carrying out other duties required by his various positions. On 19 August, Purcell may have been active as a performer, for the entire ode was performed again, between the acts of a play, probably Congreve's *Pyrrhus, King of Epirus*, which played at Lincoln's Inn Fields in a summer production advertised in the *London Gazette*, 22–26 August 1695. No other theatrical piece seems to have been acted in August, and no other music is known for this play.

On 29 August came an express from William, bringing to London happy news of the fall of the citadel and castle of Namur, against whose outworks the king had been preparing an assault during most of the summer. On the twenty-sixth, the French General Boufleurs had at last capitulated, bringing upon Louis XIV the most serious defeat he had suffered since his armies had overrun the Low Countries early in 1690. For William III the victory crowned unremitting efforts of an entire career; both as prince of Orange and as king of England he had directed all the forces he could muster against the French legions and their monarch. Quite understandably he felt that the victory called for an official thanksgiving on 8 September and yet another on Sunday, the twenty-second of the same month. The latter day included also celebrations for his victory over the French at Kassel.[45]

Some of Purcell's martial tunes for performance of an anonymous adaptation of Fletcher's *Bonduca*[46] were well attuned to the present temper of the English nation, whose military prowess under Marlborough was soon to lead to preeminence for British armies throughout Europe. The original play had no doubt been chosen because of its effectiveness as a vehicle for military glorification, which, indeed, the anonymous alterations considerably enhanced. But it was Purcell's music that really sounded the martial spirit of the times.

It is possible that King William had encouraged a revival of *Bonduca* just at this time, if only to lend brilliance to the celebrations mentioned above. In the dedication, George Powell speaks of unusual haste, pointing out that his "anonymous friend" had spent only four days revising the tragedy, and that the whole production had been "revised quite through, and likewise studied up in one fortnight." The manner in which this elaborate alibi is presented suggests that Powell himself had done the adapting and was not too pleased with his work. All this haste in turn points to the imposition of an early deadline by King William, perhaps that recorded by John Evelyn for 22 September, which he identifies as: "The Thanksgiving Day appointed for the success of the King and confederates against the French at Cassal and Namur." Furthermore, the period elapsing between Sunday, 8 September, when the capture of Namur was celebrated in church services throughout London, and the general thanksgiving is a fortnight—precisely the amount of time mentioned by Powell in the prologue to *Bonduca*.

Whether or not the military cast of the more popular pieces in *Bonduca* can be explained as Purcell's response to the well-known tastes of King William or whether merely due to the vogue then existing for this kind of music, the fact remains that this is some of the most martial music Purcell ever composed. Certainly, two of the tunes, "Britons, Strike Home" and "To Arms," were universally associated with recent exploits of British armed forces. These pieces were as important in England's growth as a world power, as Verdi's choruses "Va, pensieri" from *Nabucco* and "Si ridesti il Leon" from *Ernani* were to be nearly two centuries later in Italy's *risorgimento*.

Then, in quick succession, Purcell found himself involved in four other productions. He was commissioned to provide music for Robert Gould's tragedy *The Rival Sisters; or, the Violence of Love;*[47] Thomas Scott's comedy *The Mock Marriage;*[48] Thomas Southerne's tragedy

Oroonoko;[49] and Thomas D'Urfey's *The Comical History of Don Quixote, Part 3*.[50] For each of these plays, Purcell wrote only a little music, calling upon Blow, Courteville, Morgan, Ackeroyd, and others, to compose the bulk of the songs required.

Gould's tragedy may have been played in the summer, because the dedication mentions the absence of gentry and nobility from the town. Moreover, the play had been delayed, so it is quite possible that Purcell had written his three songs well before the tragedy was at last acted, probably in October 1695.[51] In any case, he wrote more music for *The Rival Sisters* than for any other stage play for which he was commissioned to work that season. However, although the script requires music for every act, Purcell produced songs only for the second and fourth acts, although he did supply an overture and eight act-tunes. If he supplied the songs and "horn music" called for in acts 1 and 3, respectively, these have been lost.

Evidence also is somewhat confusing with regard to the exact dating of another play given that season. The *London Gazette* for 14 October announced publication of *The Mock Marriage* as an accomplished fact at that time; and John Dennis stated very clearly, in a letter dated 26 October, that there had "just been a play acted called the *Mock Marriage*." Dr. Laurie, however,[52] reasons that Dennis was wrong, since at least three performances would have been necessary for the author to speak of the play as even a moderate success; as he spoke of it in glowing terms, there seems little question that Dr. Laurie is probably correct. It is not altogether clear which songs were actually written by Purcell. Purcell's authorship of "O how you solemnly protest" (act 2) and "Man is for the woman made" (act 3) is not subject to doubt. But the pedigree of the other song in act 3, "'Twas within a furlong of Edinboro town," lies under a cloud, being ascribed to Jeremiah Clarke in one manuscript, to Purcell in others, and in printed sources.[53]

For each of the last two theatrical commissions he was to undertake, Purcell wrote only one song each. Whatever the reason for this, Purcell seems to have been content that James Paisible should have written an overture and four act-tunes for *Oroonoko*,[54] while he contributed only one piece, a setting of D'Urfey's dialogue, "Celemene, Pray Tell Me." The text does not appear in the play; but there is little question that it was written for *Oroonoko*, for it was published in the fourth book of *Deliciae Musicae* in 1696 as belonging to the play, along with two songs by Courteville, "A Lass There Lives upon the Green" and "Bright Cynthia's Power."[55] As for the music, Purcell's setting reveals the extraordinary expressive power that he achieved in much of the music written just at the end of his life. Here there is not the slightest sign that his creative abilities were slackening.

Soon London theater audiences heard again from Thomas D'Urfey, who seemed to believe that they could never get too much of a good thing. He fashioned yet a third play from Cervantes's *Don Quixote*, and was surprised and openly displeased that it did not succeed like the former two parts. He blamed everyone but himself for its shortcomings, casting aspersions on singers, dancers, and puppeteers alike for failing to please the audience.[56] As far as is known, Purcell provided only one song for the play, "From rosy bow'rs," which is the key song in act 5. This little multisectional cantata is a tour de force of affective expressive techniques, and, as well, a marvelous study in abnormal musical psychology. Altisidora, as sung by Miss Cross, exhibits every kind of derangement that a woman crazed by love might undergo. At first she is melancholy-mad from the effects of frustrated love; then she is mirthfully mad; and then again mad in lethargic melancholy. From that state she goes into a passionate madness, and then into "swift frenzy":

> No, no, I'll run straight mad
> That soon my heart will warm;
> When once the sense is fled,
> Love has no power to charm.
> Wild through the woods I'll fly,
> And dare some savage boar,
> A thousand deaths I'll die,
> Ere thus in vain adore.

Purcell has caught every psychological nuance, not only in illustrating the sense of individual words and phrases, but in catching the mood of each stanza as well. Of all his mad songs, this is the most powerful vehicle for the expressive display of extraordinary emotions.

The exact date of the first performance of *The Indian Queen* as it had been newly composed into an opera during the last year of Purcell's life has never been definitely established. Several authorities have indicated that the operatic version of the play was first performed in mid-April 1695.[57] Dr. Margaret Laurie argues persuasively either for summer or for November of that year. The original production must have come after 1 April, because the members of the cast are exclusively those of the Theatre Royal, who remained loyal to Christopher Rich after Thomas Betterton, Anne Bracegirdle, and other seasoned actors and singers had seceded. It has been suggested that *The Indian Queen* had been projected long before the split for performance by the United Company, and that Betterton's procrastination, even after the production had been funded, was partial cause of the dissatisfaction that brought about the final rupture.[58] It has also been suggested that Betterton had intended to mount *The Indian Queen* as inexpensively as possible because of financial distresses brought on by the revival of *Bonduca* shortly before. But this argument is greatly weakened at the last octave of the epilogue (spoken by Montezuma), which indicates that expenditures had been lavish, if perhaps not so impressive as for *King Arthur* and *The Fairy Queen*:

> 'Tis true, y'have marks enough, the plot, the show,
> The poets scenes, nay, more, the painters' too;
> If all this fail, considering the cost,
> 'Tis a true voyage to the Indies lost;
> But if you smile on all, then these designs,
> Like the imperfect treasure of our minds,
> 'Twill pass for current wheresoe'er they go,
> When to your bounteous hands their stamps they owe.

Indeed, in view of the circumstantial nature of all evidence on *The Indian Queen*, any opinions as to the date of the first performance are of necessity imprecise and largely conjectural. The pirating of the songs by Heptinstall, Hudgebutt, and May has been presented as an unfeeling, cynical act, committed while he was on his deathbed.[59] But we have only a few circumstances to go on, which are scarcely sufficient to provide adequate basis for so harsh a judgment. It is not even safe to suppose that Daniel Purcell was called in at the last moment to finish the opera because his brother had died so unexpectedly, as we are led to believe by a note in British Museum Manuscript Additional 31453, f. 37ᵛ. The annotation is added in a later hand than the one that copied the music, and also the manuscript itself was written a full four years after Purcell's death.

Nor does the comparatively small measure of music he composed give us any clue as to the date of the origin of *The Indian Queen*, as those suggest who hold that the small amount of music he composed was due to his illness. Apart from the masque, which Daniel set, Purcell supplied music for everything required by the libretto. Furthermore, he was so exceedingly busy during the last five years of his life, and had so many commissions to fill that one cannot establish any meaningful relationship between quality and quantity. When we turn to the music itself, we are convinced that this is a masterwork from Purcell's riper years—a fitting final magnum opus—even though it is about half the size of *King Arthur* and *The Fairy Queen*, his two prior semi-operas.

The dating of Purcell's contributions to *The Tempest* is even more conjectural, for only the song "Dear, pretty youth"[60] was published in original version before the eighteenth century. This song appeared first in *Deliciae Musicae*, book 3, which was released in 1696 but probably printed about November 1695, about which time it also appeared in a single-sheet edition. The tune of the song "Come unto these yellow sands" also was printed early in the eighteenth century but with new words: "Now Comes Joyful Peace."[61] For the rest of the music in the play, evidence supplied by extant sources is so unsatisfactory, and the internal evidence supplied by the musical style so controversial as to occasion dispute about the authenticity of these works in the Purcell canon. There is no recorded evidence of performances of Shadwell's version of *The Tempest* between 2 February 1682 and 25 May 1697.[62] Quite possibly, Purcell's songs could have been written for the first of these, while the balance of the music, attributed to Weldon, may have been written for the performance given in 1697. It is also quite possible that Purcell had gotten the music ready for performance in 1695, about the time the songs appeared in *Deliciae Musicae*, only to find that the performance was postponed. Perhaps he supplied these songs, while Weldon wrote the doubtful pieces later on when the work was at last staged. On the strength of the annotation in *Deliciae Musicae*, however, it seems most likely that there was a performance in 1695, which somehow was not recorded, for "Dear Pretty Youth" clearly is headed: "A new song in *The Tempest* sung by Miss Cross to her lover, who is supposed dead." However, it does not necessarily follow that Purcell had composed the song just at that time. On stylistic grounds alone, this seems unlikely. Moreover, most of the songs he did compose in his last days bore some sort of rubric indicating that they were composed just before he died.

We know, for instance, that Purcell fell ill shortly after composing music for the quaint, allegorical poem "Lovely Albina's Come Ashore," which was originally described as "the last song that Mr. Purcell set before he died,"[63] but afterward printed in *Orpheus Britannicus* (1698) as "the last song the author set before his sickness." This latter rubric bears the authority of his widow, Frances Purcell, who oversaw publication. The very last song Purcell wrote appears to have been "From rosy bowers," as discussed above in connection with *Don Quixote*, Part 3, for in *Orpheus Britannicus* it appears under the rubric "the last song that Mr. Purcell set, it being in his sickness."

On 21 November 1695, Purcell made, or at least signed, his will, an uninformative document that tells us only that he left all his worldly goods to his loving wife, whom he appointed his sole executrix (see App. One, XIII, 7 and plate 38), an act that scarcely can be reconciled with the tale recounted by Hawkins, who says that he had caught his death because Mrs. Purcell locked him out of the house one cold night earlier that year. At any rate, he died that same day, upon the eve of the annual St. Cecilia celebrations, to which he had made such lively and imaginative contributions over the past dozen years.

The immediate cause of death is unknown, but Westrup's conjecture that he died of tuberculosis seems well taken. However, the fact that Purcell made no will until the day of his death indicates that his illness was probably less serious. Without identifying a source, Hawkins recounted the tale alluded to above, saying that Mrs. Purcell so disapproved of her husband's habitual carousing that she locked him out of doors one night, with the result that he caught cold, suffered complications, and died. We know from John Evelyn's remark that the weather had been mild throughout October up to 3 November, the date of the entry—a fact that greatly narrows the period during which Purcell might have caught his cold. Slightly later, however, we read in *The Flying Post* for 26–28 December 1695, that "Mr William Smith, a Gentleman, belonging to the Theatre Royal, who had acquired a considerable estate, and thereupon desisted from acting, was prevailed upon by the New Play house to remount the stage; but upon shifting his clothes in the last new play, took cold and died thereof this week." The new play was John Banks's *Cyrus the Great*, which apparently was acted about mid-December.[64] The weather, it seems, was too mild just before Purcell's death to support Hawkins's tale and quite severe enough just afterward. Incidentally, Hawkins does not help to clarify the matter when he suggests that Purcell died of a lingering and not a sudden illness, perhaps consumption.

Though evidence is by no means solid, it seems that Purcell had fallen sick some months before his death and had taken to his bed at least several weeks before, while composing the last two songs discussed above, and perhaps part of *The Indian Queen* as well. Because in 1696 Henry Purcell's widow advertised sale of the third edition of his "Lessons for the Harpsichord" at her house in Great Dean's Yard, it has been suggested that that was where he must have died. So weak an argument is further weakened by two pieces of evidence adduced by J. Frederick Bridge in his article "Purcell's Birthplace and Residences." These point to the house in Marsham Street as the place where he suffered his final illness. Not only were his rates recorded as paid up to

Easter 1696, well after his death, but Bridge found an actual audit from June and August 1695, with the entry: "To Mr. Purcell his acc! for a house for half a y: due Lady Day, £04–00–0."

Then, suddenly, he took a violent turn for the worse, which scarcely left him with time enough to prepare his will. At least, this seems the only possible explanation for the evident haste of the clerk, who scribbled out a common testamentary form, not even taking time to re-sharpen his quill, which very obviously had worn quite blunt even before he handed it to Purcell for his signature. Other evidence indicating extreme haste appears in the frequent omissions, hastily amended, and in the scribe's bad planning of the space into which the text was to be fitted (see plate 38). Also, it is clear that the annotation for calendar and regnal dates and the statement mentioning the witnesses, without which the legality of the will might have been in question, were crowded into the lower left margin as afterthoughts. The odd figures, *ꝛ𝔰* , just under Purcell's signature appear more naturally as *𝔇𝔲* when the page is turned upside down, in which position the quill strokes appear correctly placed and executed, and seem to be trial strokes for the letters "D" and "u" perhaps written just after the quill was sharpened. Again, there is evident haste, as if there had been no time to search for a piece of scrap paper.

Purcell's signature provides the most telltale evidence of all. This pitiful blurred scrawl, contrasting so tellingly with his usual robust and well-formed, round Italian hand represents his last signature, and, very likely, his last act as well, for its shapelessness gives mute testimony to the swiftness with which life's force was running out. He died before midnight.

Next day, the St. Cecilia Society met for its annual celebrations, beginning in the morning at St. Bride's with sacred music, prayers, and services, and continuing in the afternoon with secular music in a concert at Stationers' Hall. John Blow had composed the major works for both events. For St. Bride's he wrote a *Te Deum*, which like that composed the year before by Purcell, was in D major and utilized impressive instrumental forces. And for the secular concert, he composed a St. Cecilia ode, "Great Quires of Heaven." [65] One verse in particular must have painfully reminded all present of the irremedial loss their profession and their art had suffered on the previous night:

> While the musician served his saint
> What could she ask but Heaven would grant?
> When prayers on music's wings arise
> Heaven, granting, does but sympathize.

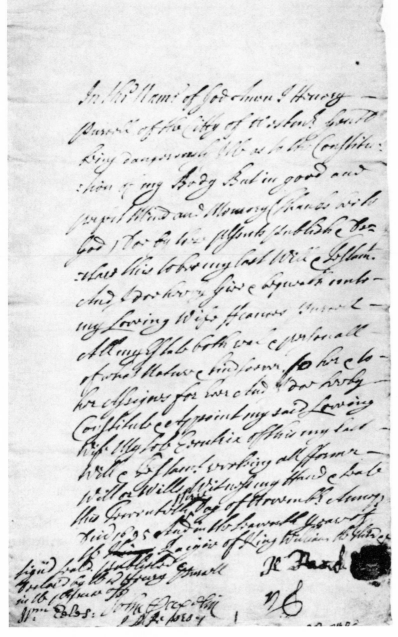

PLATE 38. Last will and testament of Henry Purcell, died 21 November 1695 (Public Record Office, London)

PLATE 39. Detail of seal, will of Henry Purcell (Public Record Office, London)

Purcell's burial in the Abbey took place on 26 November. But even before that date an anonymous journalist for the *Post Boy* had mourned the death of "this very great master of music."[66] Officials at Westminster Abbey also paid fitting tribute, unanimously voting that he be buried in the north aisle of the Abbey without expense to his heirs. According to Cummings,[67] John Dolben, in collaboration with Christopher Wren, took a death mask as he was lying in, from which the latter sculpted a bust. In the absence of these objects, or of firmer evidence that they actually existed, the account cannot be verified. However, it is certain that shortly after this time, Purcell's gravestone was carved, presenting to passersby in the Abbey the following verses until around 1722 when it became so worn as to be no longer legible:[68]

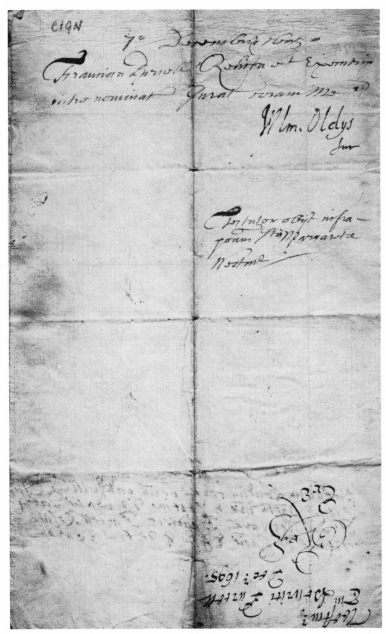

PLATE 40. Front, codicil to Henry Purcell's will (Public Record Office, London)

PLATE 41. Back, codicil to Henry Purcell's will (Public Record Office, London)

Plaudite, felices superi, tanto
  hospite; nostris
Praefuerat, vestris additur ille
  choris:
Invida nec vobis Purcellum terra
  reposcat,
Questa decus secli deliciasque
  breves.
Tam cito decessisse, modos cui
  singula debet
Musa prophana suos, religiosa suos,
Vivit, io et vivat, dum vicina organa
  spirant,
Dunque colet numeris turba canora
Deum.

Immortals, welcome an illustrious
  guest,
Your gain, our loss, yet would not
  earth reclaim
The many-sided master of his Art,
The brief delight and glory of his age:
Great Purcell lives, his spirit haunts
  these aisles
While yet the neighboring organ
  breathes its strains,
And answering choirs
Worship God in song.[69]

On a pillar nearby, Lady Dryden's memorial to Purcell reads simply: "Here lyes Henry Purcell, Esq., who left this life, and is gone to that blessed place where only his harmony can be exceeded. Obiit 21mo die Novembrs, anno aetatis suae 37mo, Annoq. Domini 1695" (see plate 42).[70]

It was Henry F. Turle, son of the well-known organist, who, according to W. H. Cummings, raised by subscription the funds needed to renovate Purcell's grave in 1876, at which time the following inscription in honor of his wife, Frances, was added:

> Francisca
> Henry Purcell Uxor,
> Cum conjuge sepulta est.
> xiv Feb. MDCCVI[71]

Although we know more of the circumstances of Purcell's death and burial than of any other sacramental event in his life, our knowledge still is limited. As may be judged from the sacrament certificate recording Purcell's compliance with the Test Act in 1683, Purcell was a member of the Anglican Church. Hence his entombment would have been conducted according to the simple rites described in the *Book of Common Prayer*: After the procession had entered the Abbey, moving to the strains of Purcell's own *March and Canzona*, the clergy and choir, led by his lifelong friend, Stephen Crespion, intoned the first three funeral sentences: "I am the resurrection," "I know that my redeemer liveth," and "We brought nothing into this world." These finished, the mourners and officials gathered in the north aisle where the burial was to take place. There around the open grave, the band of mourners listened as

PLATE 42. Tablet to the memory of Henry Purcell in Westminster Abbey

appropriate verses of Psalms 39 and 40 were read, followed by the funeral lesson, 1 Corinthians 15, after which, in preparation for the burial, soloists and choir sang the last four funeral sentences before interment, composed by Purcell himself: "Man that is born of a woman"; "In the midst of life we are in death"; "Yet, O Lord"; and the simple but extraordinarily expressive version of "Thou knowest, Lord, the secrets of our hearts," which had been sung for Queen Mary's elaborate funeral eight months before.[72] "I heard a voice from heaven," the last of the funeral sentences, was sung after earth was cast upon the coffin, and the rite concluded with the final collect.

This simple ceremony marked Purcell's passing from the city and liberty of Westminster and from London, whose citizens he had so enriched with his music. Indeed, the whole of England and music lovers on the Continent soon realized the loss of this singular musical genius who only then was beginning to gain the recognition he deserved. It is said that the famous Italian composer Corelli had planned a special trip to England to see Purcell and was deterred only by news of the latter's death.[73] With him passed the bright promise of a fully developed native English musical culture, particularly in the new dramatic art from Italy, which he had done so much to naturalize in England. In full consideration of all he achieved during the brief thirty-six years of his life, Purcell could have received no more fitting recognition than that accorded in the mythic title "The English Orpheus," a fitting memento of the magic of his music.

APPENDIX ONE

Documents

IN THIS APPENDIX ARE REPRINTED extracts from contemporary documents, papers, publications, and records that concern the various members of the Purcell family. For the most part only primary sources are registered. But when what has seemed to me important data can be obtained only from secondary sources, these also have been recorded.

The first portion of this appendix is arranged alphabetically, according to the first names of the various members of the family. Where several Purcells share the same first name, the order is chronological as far as possible. Under each name the arrangement is also chronological, where such arrangement is feasible. Extant poems or other literary pieces (such as puns, in the case of Daniel Purcell) are appended to each entry, arranged alphabetically by author's name, or alphabetically by first line under "Anonymous." Notes and commentaries by F. B. Zimmerman are bracketed throughout.

i CHARLES PURCELL (cousin)

1. Testamentum Caroli Purcell. PCC: 63 Lloyd (Somerset House).

In the name of God Amen. I, Charles Purcell, gentleman, of London in the County of Middlesex, being in good health and of sound and perfect mind and memory, praise be therefore given to Almighty God, do make and ordain this my present last Will and Testament, in manner and form following: that is to say, first and principally I commend my soul into the hands of Almighty God, hoping through the merits, death, and passion of my saviour Jesus Christ, to have full and free pardon and forgiveness of all my sins and to inherit everlasting life, and my body I commit to the earth to be decently buried, and as touching the disposition of all such temporal estate, as it hath pleased Almighty God to bestow upon me, I give and dispose thereof as followeth: First I will that all my debts be paid and discharged. *Item* I give unto my dear mother Katherine Purcell a mourning [ring] *Item* I give unto my loving sisters Elizabeth and Katherine Purcell each a mourning ring, and my wages that is [*sic*] due or shall become due, my goods and what money I have I give unto my loving brother, Edward Purcell, my full and sole executor of this my present last will and testament, and I do hereby revoke, disannul, and make void all former wills and testaments by me heretofor made as witness my hand this fourth day of June in the year of our Lord One Thousand six hundred eighty two,

Charles Purcell
Signed and sealed in the presence of
M. Purcell   Eli. Purcell   Sarah Fynes[1]

2. PCC: March Admon. 1686, p. 50.

Carolus Purcell secundo die emairt [*sic*] Commissario Mattheo Purcell ffrati naturali et legitimo Caroli Purcell nuper de parochia Sancti Martini in Campis in Comitatu Middlesex sed in Nave rocat Le George sloope in partibus de Guyney Celibis defuncti [nentis] &c. Ad Administrandum bona, jura, et credita dicti defuncti De bene &c. Jurat Catherina Purcell matre prius renuntiante

ult' Martij 1686.

Hae Litterae Aministracionis introduct et, renuntiat &c. Testamentum probat[um] mense Maij 1686.

3. PCC: March Admon. 1686 (abstract from B. Cooke, Esq.), 2 March 1685–86.

Charles Purcell late of St. Martin-in-the-Fields, Middlesex, but in the ship called *Le George* Sloope "in partibus de Guyney," bachelor. Admon. to Matthew Purcell, brother of deceased. This admon. renounced, will was proved in May 1686.

4. Chancery Proceedings, Bridges C5/90/90. 28 Nov. 1687. Parkyny.

To the Right Honourable George Lord Jeffreys Baron of Wem. Lord High Chancellor of England.

Humbly complaining sheweth unto your Lordship your orator Edward Purcell . . . of Mickleham in the County of Surrey, gentleman, brother and executor of the last Will and Testament of Captain Charles Purcell deceased. That the said Charles Purcell by commission from His M[ajesty], dated on or about the month of September in the year of our Lord one thousand six hundred and eighty and four, was appointed Captain and

---

1. This Sarah Fynes was, very likely, the member of the Fynes family of Buckinghamshire who was buried in the Wing parish church (near Claydon House and the Verney Estates) that same summer.

Commander of the good ship called the *George*, belonging unto the Royal African Company of England by which commission from his [. . .] Company's commission the said Captain Purcell had full authority to seize and take all ships and goods belonging unto any of his said Majesty's subjects that should be found trading to or from any parts of Africa from Sally[2] to Cabo de buena Esperanza. And your orator further [testifies that the said Captain] Purcell by virtue of his said commissions did take upon him the command of the said ship and within some short time after, that is to say about the month of November in the said year of our Lord one thousand six hundred and eighty and four, did sail from the port of London unto [Africa] and unto the Gold Coast of Guinea and Arda,[3] and other ports unknown unto the orator pursuant to his instructions given him by the said Royal Company. And your orator further shews that the said Charles Purcell did carry with him in the said ship of which he was Captain as a forf[eit] silver plate and other goods, chattels, and merchandises to the value of two or three hundred pounds and by traffic with his ready money at some of the said ports to which he arrived became lawfully possessed of and interested in diverse ounces of gold and other merchandises of great value and after [. . .] with about the month of November or thereabouts or some other time within the year of our Lord one thousand six hundred eighty and six, the said Charles Purcell, in the said ship and in his command as Captain thereof, died some time before his said voyage having made his Will is [. . .] due form published and attested and thereof made constituted and appointed your orator his sole executor and within some short time after your orator had notice of the said Charles Purcell's death your orator in due form as he is advised proved his said Will in the Prerogative Court of Canter[bury and] thereby is become intituled to all the goods and chattels, gold, silver plate, money and other things whatsoever whereof the said Charles Purcell died possessed or was interested in. But so it may please your lordship that upon the death of the said Charles Purcell all his said goods and chattels [. . .] plate money, wearing apparel, lining, and other merchandises and things did come to the hands and possession of William Bayley being mate of the said Captain Charles Purcell in the said ship or otherwise mate in the ship called *Orange Tree* who sailed in company with the said ship the *George*, unto which said ship called *Orange Tree*, some time before the death of the said Charles Purcell, all the goods and chattels of the said Purcell after his death were carried from [the *George*] the said William Bayley did possess himself of six ounces and upwards of gold and several gold rings, one large silver punch-bowl and stone fire-cup tipped and footed with silver, one fowling piece, one cane, all his wearing clothes and diverse quantities of linen, a great quantity of brandy, twelve half cases of spirits, amongst diverse other merchandises and goods unknown to your

2. Salli, or Salé, a seaport on the Atlantic coast of Morocco (*Encyclopedia Britannica*, 14th ed., vol. 19, p. 871).

3. Probably Ardrah, now Allada, Dahomoy, Africa (*Encyclopedia Britannica*, vol. 24, p. 80, E4).

orator which said particular goods and chattels above particularly specified were of the value of one hundred pounds or thereabouts and the said Bayley did sell the said silver punch-bowl unto one Mr. John Winder or some other person for sixteen pounds or some such like other greater sum of money and did likewise sell the said fowling piece and cane unto one John Cabes for five pounds or some other greater sum of money, and the said Charles Purcell's wearing apparel and linen was sold by the said William Bayley at the mast of the said ship called *Orange Tree* for twenty pounds or other sum of money, all which he had and received. . . . And your orator further shews that the said William Bayley having so possessed himself of the goods and chattels of the said Charles Purcell, and sold and disposed of some of them as aforesaid, the said Bayley, some time after came to England, and in his said voyage and before his arrival in England died [. . .] after whose decease, Anne Bayley, widow and relict of the said William Bayley either as executrix of him the said William Bayley, or by virtue of administration of his goods and chattels to her granted, hath now possessed herself not only of the personal estate of the said William Bayley, being of great value, but also of diverse goods and chattels which were the property, goods, and chattels of the said Charles Purcell [. . .] and now conceals the same from your orator, well knowing that your orator is altogether ignorant what the same goods and chattels were or wherein they did consist or the true values and also knowing that your orator's witnesses who could prove the same were all seamen and under officers of the said ships the *George* and the *Orange Tree*, and are now either all dead or else in remote places beyond the seas, for want of whose testimonies your orator is disabled to bring action at Common Law for the same against the said Anne Bayley, and only relievable in a Court of Equity by a full discovery upon oath of the said Anne Bayley, and the more is especially for that your orator hath been credibly informed that since her said husband's death she has possessed herself of her said husband's account books and papers or other books, memorandum, or writings wherein he had made entries of diverse goods and chattels of the said Charles Purcell's, which came to his hands and possession after the said Charles Purcell's death in specie, as likewise what goods, chattels, or other things of the said Purcell's he had exposed to sale, and for what sums of money he had received upon such sale and from whom which said account books or books, papers, memorandums, or writings manifesting the same, your orator prays she, the said Anne Bayley, may also set forth upon oath and bring into this honourable court to be inspected without defacing, altering or obliteration and may produce such leaves as she has taken or torn out of any such books in order to conceal the same from your orator's knowledge. In tender consideration of all which premises, your orator prays that the said Anne Bayley may set forth whether she is not executrix or administrix of her said husband, and whether, since her husband's death, she hath not possessed herself of his personal estate, and whether she did not likewise possess herself of diverse great quantities of gold as the same came from the Indies, frequently called dust gold, to the value of two hundred pounds and upwards, amongst which was the said six ounces and upwards of your orator's said brother's, together with diverse other goods and chattels which were the said Charles Purcell's at the time of his death, and brought back in the said ships or one of them, and that she may set forth in particular what the same were and of what value, and may set forth whether several of her said husband's account books, paper memorandums and writings after his death did not come to her hands, wherein were mentioned what goods and chattels, how many ounces of gold, and how many gold rings and other matters and things therein conjoined were the proper goods and personal estates of the said Charles Purcell, and whether she had not heard and been readily informed by some person or persons who went on the said voyage in the said ships or the one of them with the said Charles Purcell and her said husband, and did return home on the said ships or the one of them, that her said husband did sell the said silver punch-bowl, gun, and cane of the said Captain Purcell, and did likewise sell some part of the linen and wearing clothes and diverse other things after his death at the mast of the said ships or the one of them for a considerable sum of money, and whether amongst her said husband's account books, etc. [. . .] she did not find an account thereof . . . that she may give your orator satisfaction for the same, she having personal assets of her said husband's sufficient to pay all his debts and funeral expenses with great overplus [. . .] etc. And may your lordship grant your orator His Majesty's most gracious writ of subpoena directed to her the said Anne [Bayley] to retain etc. . . .

Memb. 2. Jurat 20 Die Decembris 1687. / The answer of Anne Bayley, widow defendant, to the Bill of complaint of Edward Purcell, gentleman, Complainant.

[Anne Bayley] denies any knowledge of anything . . . questions Edward Purcell's authority as executor and Charles Purcell's authority as Captain.

5. St. James's, Westminster: Overseers' Accounts.

1686: Hay Market Street: Charles Purcell   £0–12–0
1687: Hay Market Street: [no entry for Charles Purcell]
1688: Hay Market Street: Charles Purcell's house taken by Joseph Styles

[Since Charles, son of Thomas, died in 1686, these records seem to refer to him, and not to the other Charles Purcell mentioned under II, below.]

II CHARLES PURCELL (brother)

See genealogical table (p. 265). For yet another, earlier Charles Purcell, see parish records of St. Andrew's, Holborn, MS. 6667/4 (Guildhall Library, London), 18 Sept. 1657: Margaret, daughter of Charles Purcell and of Margaret, his wife, [born] in Mr. Greenbold's house at Holborn Bridge (baptized 27 Sept.).

I. WAM 33705 (Treasurer's Account, 1672), fo. 4.

Annual Reddit: "Et in Denarijs Solut ad usum Scholasticor Jacob Leisley, Johann Anthobus, Daniel de Lyne et Johni Cooper per dimd. Anni, *Carol* [*sic*] *Pursell*, et Wildebore Ellis per An°: integ Tot Stipend xxv^{li}. Et Reverendissimo Decano Thesaurar et Ludi Mag^{ro}: xx^{li} ex Dono Reverendissimi Patr. Johnis Episcopi Lincolniensis nuper Decani Westmonast in Toto hoc Anno . . . xxvi^{li}."

[Similar entries in 33706–10 (Rob^{to} Davies, Carolo Pursell, Wildbore Ellis, et Rogero Cooper), 33711 and 33712 (Charles Purcell is first on the list, followed by: Rogero Cooper, Wildbore Ellis, Edwardo Roberts.)]

III DANIEL PURCELL (brother)
(see plate v.x)

1. Bodleian, MS. Wood D 19(4), fo. 108.

Purcell, Daniel, organist of Magdalen College in Oxford, brother to Henry Purcell. [Wood originally had "son of," but altered—not necessarily "corrected"—the entry to read as above. Wood may have written "son of" before young Henry Purcell became famous, then changed the entry to read "brother of" when his fame was established. Neither correction nor entry would make sense if Henry Purcell the elder were not the father.]

2. Bodleian, MS. Mus.e.17, fo. 40.

Purcell (Daniel), brother to Henry, organist of Magdalen College, whence he moved to London.

3. *KM*, p. 339 (8 April 1679).

Paid £6. 12s. for summer's service as Royal Chapel choir boy at Windsor.

4. *A Register of the Presidents, Fellows, Demies . . . of St. Mary Magdalen College* (ed. J. R. Bloxam).

1689 Soloist Dr. Rogers nuper organistae	£30	
Mr. Purcell organistae	£36	13s.
1690 Soloist Mr. Mro. Morgan Transery Genty antiphonas	£8	
Mr. Harris reficienti organum per compositimen	£50	
Dr. Rogers nuper organistae	£30	
Mr. Purcell organistae	£40	
1691 Soloist Clements pro 70 formulis precatronem		11s.
Mr. Harris reficients organum	£50	
Dr. Rogers nuper organistae	£30	
Mr. Purcell organistae	£30	

1692 Soloist	Clements pro formantis organum	£15	
	Mr. Harris reficienti organum	£51	
	[Rogers and Purcell as before]		
	[Rogers and Purcell as before]		
	John Clements Bibliopolae pro. form precal	6s.	
	[Rogers and Purcell as before]		
1695	Mr. Harris reficienti et mundantr. organ per comp.	£10 0s. 6d.	
	Clements pro form prec	12s.	
1696 Soloist	Mr. Harris refic. et mundi organ. per comp.	£8	
	Jacob Duke organ, villin. gerenti ord. Pr. Pras	£2	
	Mr. Hecht et Purcell organ	£40	

[After this date Hecht alone.]

5. *A Register of the Presidents, Fellows, Demies . . . of Saint Mary Magdalen College* (ed. J. R. Bloxam), vol. 2, p. 203.

1688. Purcell, Daniel res. 1695. Son of Henry Purcell, Gentleman of the Chapel Royal (*obiit* 1718). He was brother of Henry Purcell, and from him derived most of that little reputation which as a musician he possessed.

6. Vicar-General Marriage Licences. 8 May 1705.

Daniel Purcell, gentleman, of St. Paul's, Covent Garden, and Elizabeth Torer of the same, spinster, aged 27, to take place at St. Paul's, Covent Garden.

[If this referred to Daniel Purcell the musician, apparently the marriage did not take place. See 7(*a*), below, where he is described as a bachelor.]

7(*a*). PCC: Jan. 1717/18, fo. 10.

Decimo Septimo die emavit Commissario Josephe Purcell fratri naturali et legitimo Danielis Purcell [nuper] paroche Sancti Andrewe Holborne London defuncti Celibis ha[b]entis &c Ad Administrandum bona jura et credita dicti defuncti De bene &c Jurat[e]

Ult. Jan. 1718

7(*b*). PCC: Admon. 17 Jan. 1717/18.

Daniel Purcell of the Parish of St. Andrew, Holborn, London, bachelor. Admon. granted to Joseph Purcell, natural and lawful brother of the deceased.

8. Bodleian, MS. Rawl. D 833.169 (referring to Daniel Purcell).

I was acquainted with him when [he was an] organist at Magdalen College: [all] allowed him the title of Punmaster General. . . .

[Cf. Bloxam, *A Register of Presidents*, vol. 2, pp. 204–5, who recounts several puns.]

9. Bodleian, MS. Mus. d. 226.

(Daniel Purcell—partial autograph—from the library of James Kent, anthems and solo songs.)

An Elegy on the Death of Mr. Dan. Purcell
by L. Man.

In softer accents or more tuneful lays
Other may mourn his death, or sing his praise
Yet none more truly can his fate bewail
But alas! will fruitless grief avail?
To paint in words the man, and faintly show
What once he was, is all we now can do.
His modest and obliging carriage gain'd
Him real friends, who always friends remain'd.
In him, two very rare perfections met,
Great skill in music, and a ready wit.
His wit, peculiar in the grace alone;
Pleas'd all who heard it, but offended none.
    In th'art of music, he perform'd so well
    That him, his brother only cou'd excell.

10. From the *Weekly Journal* of 29 June 1717. (Burney Coll., vol. 183b.)

A Punni-Musical Epistle to Mr. Daniel P—:
Or, a Letter in his own Way.
. . . . . . Thus I
In Baralypton Blunderbuss ye.

Ox. and Camb. Miscel. p. 189.
Cremona, 20 Nov. 1716.

Honest Dan.

I have beaten time so often at the overture of your resting place, without playing upon you at sight, that I perceive the tenor of your life to be chiefly in taverns, where you will never leave drinking a treble quantity, till your hand quavers. If this be any slur to your reputation, and you think me a Jew to harp upon a harsh string, I shall use no flourish or rondeau of words, but tell you plainly, that it frets me to the guts, that you are so hard to be found when a man is solo in an evening. I know sometimes you take some fugues into the country air, and I wish it prove no more than an opera pretium to you; if it does, I must needs say you manage your purse ill. I design to watch your ritornellos to town, and will strive to bring you more to my bow; and knowing we shall agree to an hair, I desire we may wet our whistles together, and make some recitativo's of the past crotchets of our long acquaintance. Time was we could both of us have played upon the virginals;

and particularly you have been a man of note for your many compositions upon them. I know you to be in alt, as to your religion; and should you continue to be above Ela in your politics, I shall never suffer myself, I assure ye, to be out of tune with my friend on such fiddlefaddle accounts.

If the sharpest of the critics should censure this letter as flat, they are entirely out of the key, and have not their fantasias screwed up to the present pitch of

Dear Dan,
Yours, from the merry violin to the
german flute and the recorder,
Signior Allegro

II. British Museum, $\frac{1855 \ \text{c.4}}{58}$ Broadsides, etc. 1682–1780.

John Jones [not dated]

Whereas it has been industriously and maliciously reported, that Mr. John Jones (now a candidate for the place of organist to the United Parishes of Allhallows, Bread Street and St. John the Evangelist) is a BUNGLER, etc.

This false report having already been a very great prejudice to Mr. Jone's [*sic*] interest, in relation to his being elected organist to the said parishes; therefore (in justice to the said Mr. Jones) 'tis thought fit to undeceive those gentlemen who have been thus imposed on, by such false and base insinuations, that the said Mr. Jones is a person fitly qualified and capable of playing on any organ, being very well recommended and approved; as appears by a certificate of several undeniable masters, who have given it under their own hands, and did it before an organ was put up (or designed so to be) in the said parish church. Any gentlemen desirous of seeing the original of the following certificate, may do it at Steel's coffee house in Bread Street. We, whose names are under written, do certify, that Mr. John Jones, brought up in the Cathedral Church of St. Paul's, is capable of playing (in any parish church in England) on the organ.

As witness our hands.

Richard Brind, organist of St. Paul's Church.
Master of the Boys of St. Paul's and organist of St. Bennet.
Daniel Purcell, organist of St. Dunstan's in the East and St. Andrew's, Holborn.
Charles Young, organist of Allhallows, Barking.
Peter Horwood, organist of Christ Church.
Benjamin Short, organist of St. Sepulchre and St. Dunstan, Stepney.
George Hayden, organist of St. Mary Magdalen, Bermondsey.
Maurice Greene, organist of St. Paul's, St. Andrew's, Holborn, and St. Dunstan's in the West.
Edward Henry Purcell, organist of St. Martin Orgar.

Gentlemen,

Your vote and interest is earnestly desired in favour of the said Mr. Jones, who has given full assurance of a constant attendance.

IV EDWARD PURCELL (brother) of St. Margaret's, Westminster (see plate 43)

1. Edward Chamberlayne, *Angliae Notitia*, 12th ed. (1679), part 1, p. 162.

   Mr. Edward Pursel, gentleman usher, assistant; to come in upon the first vacancy.

2. *Cal. Tr. Books*, 8 June 1681.

   To Mr. Purcell   £37. 10s.

3. Edward Chamberlayne, *Angliae Notitia*, 14th ed. (1682), part 1, p. 166.

   Mr. Edward Pursel, gentleman usher, assistant, to come in on first vacancy.

   [N.B. In the 15th ed. (1684), Edward Purcell does not appear to have "come in," since four new names appear. Perhaps he had gone off to the army by this time.]

4. *Cal. Tr. Books*, 2 Dec. 1682.

   To Edward Purcell, gent. usher   £20

5. Charles Dalton, *English Army Lists and Commission Registers 1661–1714* (London, 1892), vol. 2, p. 27.

   The Queen Consort's Regiment of Foot, Feb. 1685. Lt. Edward Purcell, commissioned 20 Feb. 1685 (5 companies served at Sedgemore in the King's Own Regiment).

6. Ibid., vol. 2, p. 135, n. 18.

   Lt. Ed. Purcell . . . Captain in the same: Nov. 1687.

7. Ibid., vol. 2, p. 208. (List of Commissions for 1688, signed 1 Dec. 1688.)

   Lt. Ed. Purcell to have Capt. Hayman Rooke's late captaincy as Grenadier Company in the Queen Consort's Regiment.

8. Ibid., vol. 5, p. 126.

   The Queen's own Regiment of Marines commanded by Brigadier-General William Seymour . . . Major Purcell to be Lt. Col. *vice* Lt. Colonel Rook, preferred 1 March 1704. [n. 4: Appointed major of Brigadier-

PLATE 43. Colonel Edward Purcell, brother of the composer (Holburne of
Menstrie Museum, University of Bath)

General Seymour's Regiment of Foot, 8 June 1702. Appears to have retained his company, as his name stands as senior captain of the regiment in 1715.]

9. Charles Dalton, *George the First's Army 1714–1727* (London, 1910), vol. 1, p. 140, and p. 141, n. 4.

Captain Edward Purcell. 1 May 1711. [n. 4: Appointed major of the Queen's Own Regt. 8 June 1702.] Served at Vigo and Cadiz, Regimental Lt.-Col. 1 March 1704. Appears to have sold his Lt.-Colonelcy to Kempenfelt, 1 May 1711; . . . left the regiment in May 1716.

[A certain Lt.-Col. Purcell died at Kingston upon Hull on 23 October. See under v, below.]

10. British Museum Add. MS. 28,888, fo. 225. (Catalogued as a letter from F. Purcell to J. Tucker, 1702, but certainly by Edward Purcell.)

May the 9th, 1702

Sir
   I have above a week been laid up with the stone, or I would have waited on you myself, to desire to know if you have any directions, to draw a commission for me as major to Col. Seymore, I desire your answer by the bearer, in which you will oblige

Sir, your most humble servant,
E. Purcell

11. Westminster Public Library, Account Book, no. 1660.

   A codicil or addition to the last Will and Testament of me, Edward Purcell, of the parish of St. Margaret's, Westminster, in the County of Middlesex, Esquire, which Will was duly executed by me and bears date the [. . .] day of [. . .] last past before the date hereof. I give, devise, and bequeath unto Mrs. Mary Mullins of the parish of St. Margaret's, Westminster, aforesaid widow all such plate, household goods, and furniture of what kind or quality soever books, linen and wearing apparel that I shall be possessed of at the time of my decease, and shall be in my new dwelling house in Great Dean's Yard in Westminster. In trust nevertheless to and for the use, benefit, and behoof of my niece Frances Welsted, when she shall come to the age of twenty years anything in my said Will contained to the contrary thereof notwithstanding, in witness whereof I have hereunto set my hand and seal the second day of October in the third year of the reign of our sovereign Lord George by the grace of God King of Great Britain, etc. In the year of our Lord one thousand seven hundred and sixteen.

E. Purcell

Signed, sealed, delivered, declared, and published by the said Edward Purcell, for and as a codicil or addition to his last Will and Testament in the presence of us, who have subscribed our names as witnesses thereunto in his presence. Thomas Prickard, Mary Williams, Edward Stephenson. (Probatim) Tertio die mensis decembris anno domini 1717mo emanavit commission Marie Williams solute curatrici legitime assignate France Welsted Minori Nepoti et universali legatario nominate in scedula testamentaria Edwardi Purcell nuper parochie supradicte defuncti ad administrandum bona etc. dicti defuncti cum ejus testamentaria schedula annexa in usum et beneficium et donec et quotienscumque dicta Franca Welsted Vicesimum primum aetatis sue annum compleverit de bene etc. prius iurate.

[Though recorded in the Archives Room, Westminster Public Library, Buckingham Palace Road, the actual will has been lost since being removed to safety during the Second World War. The codicil, which apparently served also as an envelope for the original will, can be seen. But several intensive searches on the part of the author for the will itself have failed.]

12. Wytham parish registers (in portion written by "Robertus Lydall, S.T.B. Coll. Magd. Oxon. Socius Rector" from 28 Aug. 1712 onward).

The Honourable Col. Ed. Purcell, died June the 20th and was buried in the Chancel the 23rd of the same month.

[For a drawing of Wytham Manor and the parish church in the time of Edward Purcell see Knyff's drawings (engraved by Kip), and Bodleian, MSS. Top. Berks. c. 51, no. 240, and Top. Oxon. b. 3 fo. 71v.]

13. Gravestone in the chancel, Wytham parish church, Berks.

Here lieth the body of Edward Purcell, eldest son of Mr. Purcell, Gentleman of the Royal Chapel, and brother to Mr. Henry Purcell, so much renowned for his skill in music. He was gentleman usher to King Charles the 2nd, lieutenant of Colonel Trelawney's regiment of foot; in which for his many gallant actions in the wars of Ireland and Flanders he was gradually advanced to the honour of lieutenant-colonel. He assisted Sir George Rook in the taking of Gibralter, and the Prince of Hesse in the memorable defence of it. He followed that prince to Barcelona, and was at the taking of Mountjoy, where that brave prince was killed: and continued to signalize courage in the siege, and taking of that city: in the year of Our Lord 1705. He enjoyed great service, until the much lamented death of his late Mistress Queen Anne; when decayed with age, and broken with misfortunes, he retired to the house of the right honourable the Earl of Abingdon. He died June 20th 1717. Aged 61 years.

[N.B. The transcript published by Hawkins in 1776 (vol. 2, p. 746) departs from the original in several details. The only error that has had mischievous results is that pertaining to Edward Purcell's age at death, which on the stone clearly reads "61" not "64." This Edward Purcell, then, was born sometime before June 1656, not in 1653.]

v Edward Purcell (cousin) of Mickleham

[For the earliest record of Edward Purcell's responsibilities as a gentleman usher daily waiter assistant, see under IV above. See also under I Charles Purcell (cousin), 4, and under XXV Samuel and Temperance Wall, 1–3, 7, 8. See also *The Gentleman's Magazine* for 23 October 1732, p. 1031, for an obituary notice of Lt.-Col. Purcel, an officer on half pay, at Kingston upon Hull. Dalton (*George the First's Army*, vol. 1, p. 140) associated the name with that of Lt.-Col. Edward Purcell.]

vi Edward Purcell (son)

1. *Westminster Abbey Reg.*, p. 74.

   Baptisms: 6 Sept. 1689.
   Edward, son of Henry and Frances Purcell.

2. St. Margaret's Westminster, Vestry Books, no. 2419 (1724–38), p. 61.

   Fri. 8 July 1726
   Upon reading the humble petition of Edward Purcell, Joseph Centliure, and a letter from Mr. John Robinson, praying to be admitted organist of this parish church in the room of Mr. John Isham, ordered that the said Edward Purcell be and is hereby chosen and appointed organist of this parish in the room of the said John Isham at the salary of thirty pounds per annum during the pleasure of this vestry, he paying the blower forty shillings per annum out of the same, and that twenty-two pounds, part of the said thirty pounds, be annually paid by the clerk of this parish as hath usually been paid to former organists, and the other eight pounds by the church wardens of this parish, and that the payment of the said salary do commence from Midsummer last.

3. Court Minutes at Office of Christ's Hospital, London.

   Peter Horwood elected music master 28 Jan. 1719 (120).
   Then the Court proceeded to the election of a music master for this house in the room of Mr. John Barrett late music master deceased. The petitioners for the said place were

   Mr. Peter Horwood   Mr. John Isham
   Mr. Edward Purcell   Mr. Charles King
   All masters of music.
   After they were severally called in and their petitions read, they were severally put up for the question and reduced to two, viz. Peter Horwood and Charles King, who being again severally put up, the majority fell (and so the President declared) on Mr. Horwood who is elected accordingly and he being called in and acquainted therewith returned the Court his hearty thanks and promised faithfully to discharge his duty; and the Court re-

ferred the taking of his charge to the Committee of Almoners who are to see he take it accordingly.

4. A. W. Hughes Clark, *The Register of St. Clement, Eastcheap, and St. Martin Orgar* (Harl. Soc. Reg. 68), p. 16.

4 July, 1740.
Edward Purcell, organist, buried near the organ gallery door.

VII Edward Henry Purcell (grandson)

1. PRO: LC "Miscellanea," 5/70, p. 175 (July 1739).

Edward H. Purcell, late Child of the Chapel allowance of clothes. Whereas the Sub-Dean of His Majesty's Chapel in the absence of the Dean, has certified the [*sic*] Edward Henry Purcell's voice is changed who was one of the Children of the Chapel, and therefore removed from the service of the Chapel, these are as to the said Edward Henry Purcell the usual allowance of one suit of plain cloth, one hat-band, two holland shirts, two cravats, two pairs of cuffs, two handkerchiefs, two pairs of stockings, two pairs of shoes, and two pairs of gloves. And etc. given etc. this 19th day of July 1739 in the 13th year of His Majesty's reign. Grafton.

2. According to an article in the *Musical Times*, June 1931, E. H. Purcell appears in a subscription list attached to Boyce's *Twelve sonatas for 2 violins, &c* (1747), as organist of St. Clement's, Lombard Street.

3. Greater London Council Record Office. P.79/JN.1./142.

Transcript of vestry minutes of St. John, Hackney.
11 Aug. 1753 (p. 198).
Agreed that the salary of the organist shall for the future be twenty pounds by the year and that for his said salary he shall attend on all Sundays in the year and on all days whereon a sermon shall be preached (fast-days excepted) and that on every Sunday throughout the year a voluntary shall be played after both the morning and evening service.

Saturday, 22 Sept. 1753 (p. 200/20).
At a vestry in order to choose an organist.
The question was put whether the vestry do now proceed to the choice of an organist of this parish and was carried in the affirmative.
The question was likewise put whether the persons who now appear as candidates for the said place be called in separately to hear the order of the last vestry read to them and was carried in the affirmative.
And the candidates were called in severally and the said order of the last

vestry was read to each of them, and they were severally asked what attendance they designed to give in the said office to which they severally answered as follows, viz:

Mr. Edward Henry Purcell proposed to attend personally every other Sunday throughout the year and during the winter half . . . viz. from Michaelmas to Lady Day he will also attend personally in the afternoon of each of the four intermediate Sundays. And he promised that at these times when he shall not attend personally, he will employ such a deputy to officiate for him as shall be to the satisfaction of the gentlemen of the vestry.

Mr. David Heureux proposed to attend personally every Sunday throughout the year both morning and afternoon without employing any deputy whatsoever (sickness excepted).

Mr. William Ward proposed to attend personally every Sunday throughout the year both morning and evening and declared that he hath no other place of organist nor will apply for any other if he shall be chosen into the place of organist of this parish.

Mr. Richard Low, Mr. Thomas Archer, Mr. Moses Patence proposed "to attend personally every Sunday, etc. without employing a deputy except in case of sickness."

Agreed that the method of this present election be by scratching for all at once. And that the person who hath the majority of votes shall be the person elected.

The gentlemen then proceeded to scratch for the said candidates and

Mr. Purcell, had	9 votes
Mr. L'Heureux, had	6
Mr. Ward, had	2
Mr. Low, had	0
Mr. Archer, had	1
Mr. Patence, had	0

The majority being for Mr. Edward Henry Purcell, he was declared duly elected . . . at the salary settled at the last vestry, to commence from Michaelmas next on condition that he perform his proposal and promise above mentioned.

4. A. W. Hughes Clark, *The Register of St. Clement, Eastcheap, and St. Martin Orgar* (Harl. Soc. Reg. 67), p. 51.

Baptisms: 17 May 1761.

Frances, daughter of Edward Henry and Abigail Frances Purcell (born April 12th).

5. Greater London Council Record Office. P.79/JN.1./142. Transcript of vestry minutes of St. John, Hackney.

Easter Tuesday, 24 April 1764 (pp. 555–56).
Complaint having been made against Edward Henry Purcell the present organist.
Resolved that the vestry clerk do write to the said Edward Henry Purcell and acquaint him that the vestry insists on his being regular in his attendance, and that he do give in the name of his deputy to the Churchwarden, and also give notice from time to time to the Churchwarden for the time being when he shall change him, and who he shall appoint in his stead.

[A note on the margin of this page reads: "Organist, wrote to him, he promised to send the name of his deputy" signed "R. D." (Richard Dann) "Vestry Clark."]

Resolved that the choice of an organist be deferred until the next vestry, and that Edward Henry Purcell the present organist do officiate until that time.

Monday, 30 April 1764 (p. 359).
The Vestry Clerk acquainted the vestry that he had wrote [sic] to Mr. Purcell the organist agreeable to the resolution of the last vestry, Mr. Purcell not attending this vestry.
Resolved that the choice of an organist be deferred until the next vestry, and that Mr. Purcell do officiate in the mean time.

Saturday, 3 Aug. 1765 (p. 411).
The Churchwarden declared a vacancy in the place of organist of this parish by the death of Mr. Purcell. . . .
Resolved that the Churchwarden be and is hereby desired to pay to Mrs. Purcell the widow of the late organist the salary which would have been due to her husband at Michaelmas last.

6. A. W. Hughes Clark, *The Register of St. Clement, Eastcheap, and St. Martin Orgar* (Harl. Soc. Reg. 67), p. 21.

Burials: 5 Aug. 1765.
Edward Henry Purcell, organist, buried near the organ gallery door.

VIII ELIZABETH PURCELL (mother)

1. Westminster Abbey Chapter Minutes, 1662–85. (31 Dec. 1669.)

Ordered that a lease be made to Mrs. Purcell of a tenement in Tothill Street for 40 years under the old rent and usual covenant.

2. St. Margaret's, Westminster, "Overseers' Accounts," 1665–66, p. 169.

> Widow Pursell, Tothill Street South: Assessed four shillings, collected four shillings, arrears nil.

[Similar entries in accounts up to 1682, when "Widow Pursell's" name is not in the list, or thereafter.]

3. WAM 61228A (Precentor's Book, 1660–71), folios 56*v*, 57*v*, 58, and 61.

> Various payments to "Mr. Purcell's widow" for August, September, October, and December 1664.

4. St. Margaret's, Westminster, Churchwardens' Accounts, vol. 80 (1699–1700).

> Money received for burials: 22 Aug. 1699.
> Elizabeth Purcell.

5. PCW: Admon. 7 Sept. 1699.

> Estate administered by Katherine Purcell, wife of William Sale.

IX FRANCES PURCELL (wife)

1. Richmond Town Hall: Parish Meeting Book, 1596–1735 (St. Mary Magdalene parish church, Richmond), p. 232.

> 19 May 1705.
> Mrs. Purcell and family with Mr. Rawlins in the gallery.

2. Kathleen Courtlander, *Richmond from Kew Green to Ham Common* (London, 1953), p. 89.

> Frances Purcell, widow of the composer, who acquired a house in the Royal Manor after her husband's death. She brought the deceased Henry's music manuscripts with her and made her will in the parlour of her last home.

[N.B. No documentary substantiation for any of this.]

3. Testamentum Nuncupativum Franciscae Purcell. PCC (Somerset House).

> 7 February, 1706.
> Memorandum that Frances Purcell, late of Richmond in the County of Surrey, widow, deceased, did whilst she lived and being of sound and disposing mind, memory, and understanding, and as she sat in a chair in the parlour of her dwelling house at Richmond aforesaid, utter and declare her last Will and Testament nuncupative in the words following [to wit] She

ordered and appointed Mr. Thomas Tovey to be her executor until Frances Purcell her daughter should attain the age of eighteen years, and upon her attaining to such age her said daughter to be her executrix. And that according to her husband's desire she had given her dear son good education, and she also did give him all the books of music in general, the organ, the double spinnet, the single spinnet, a silver tankard, a silver watch, two pair of gold buttons, a hair ring, a mourning ring of Dr. Busby's, alarum clock, Mr. Edward Purcell's picture, handsome furniture for a room and to be maintained until provided for, and all other her estate of houses, monies, and what she otherwise had she gave to her said daughter Frances Purcell, which said words or words to the same effect was uttered and spoken by the said deceased on Thursday the seventh day of February 1705/6, being then ill of the sickness of which she soon after died, as and for her last Will and Testament nuncupative in the presence of us who have subscribed our names as witnesses thereto whom she desired to bear witness or take notice of what she said.

Ann Ecles, Ann Pendelton, Amy Howlett

Tertio die mensis Aprilis 1706 dictae Anna Eeles, Anna Pendelton et Amata Howlett juratae fuerunt super veritate praemisorum coram me J. Exton Surrogate presente Wal. Hutchins. N.P.

Probatum fuit [huiusmodi] Testamentum apud London coram venti viro Georgio Paul Legum Doctore Surrogato [ventis] et Egregij viri Domini Richardi Raines Militis Legum etiam Doctoris Curiae Praerogativae Cantuariensis Magistri custodis sive commissarij legitime constituti Quarto die mensis Julij Anno Domini Millesime Septinge[simo] Sexto Juramento Franciscae Purcell Filiae dictae Defunctae et Executricis in dicto Testamento nominato cui commissa fuit Administratio omnium et singulorum bonorum jurium et creditorum dictae Defunctae de bene et fideliter administrando eadem ad sancta Dei Evangelia Jurat. Exam. Calendar of Grants of Probate and Administration of Commissary Court of Dean and Chapter of Westminster.

[Frances Purcell was born 30 May 1688, reaching the age of 18 on that date in 1706, more than a month before the will was proved on 4 July 1706. N.B. The Frances Peters whose birth is recorded for 5 Aug. 1669 in Herbert Westlake's transcription of *The Registers of St. Margaret's, Westminster* (Harl. Soc. Reg. 64, 1935), p. 90, would have been too young in 1679–80 to have married the younger Henry Purcell.]

4. *Westminster Abbey Reg.*, p. 257.

Burials: 14 Feb. 1705/6.

The widow of Mr. Henry Purcell. In the middle of the north aisle, near his monument.

x Frances Purcell (daughter)

Westminster Abbey Reg., p. 74.

Baptisms: 30 May 1688.
Frances, daughter of Henry and Frances Purcell.

[Recorded also at St. Margaret's, Westminster, but under 1 June, which was probably the date of baptism.]

xi Francis Purcell (cousin)

1. PRO: LC "Miscellanea," 5/53, fo. 50v.

   Francis Purcell, groom of the Privy Chamber to the King, his warrant dormant. . . . We will and command you that at the Feast of the Saints next coming you deliver unto our well-beloved servant Francis Purcell whom we have appointed to be one of the grooms of our Privy Chamber in ordinary . . . a livery . . . to be received yearly at the Feast of All Saints. [Warrant dormant 8 August 1673.]

2. Ibid., fo. 155 (ca. 29 Sept. 1682).

   We will and command you that immediately upon sight hereof you pay or cause to be paid unto our trusty and well-beloved servant [a livery] . . . Francis Purcell whom we have appointed to be one other groom of our robes in the place of his father, Thomas Purcell, deceased. . . .

3. PRO: LC "Miscellanea," 5/15, p. 12.

   Thomas and Francis Purcell, Somerset House keepers. These are to signify unto you His Majesty's pleasure that you prepare a bill fit for His Majesty's royal signature containing a grant to pay under the Great Seal of England unto Thomas Purcell and Francis Purcell and the larger [*sic*] liver of them of the office and place of under housekeeper, Wardrobe Keeper, and Keeper of the Privy Lodgings of His Majesty's Mansion House called Denmark House, otherwise Somerset House, otherwise Strand House in the Strand in the County of Middlesex, in ordinary without fee until the death, surrender, or avoidance of Henry Brown, now living. And then to have and enjoy the said places . . . with the yearly fee of one hundred and twenty pounds payable out of the Exchequer at the 4 usual feasts . . . 1st April 1674.

4. Ibid., p. 32.

   Whereas you have my warrant . . . for the place of Housekeeper and Wardrobe keeper of Somerset House to Thomas and Francis Purcell after

the death of Henry Browne. . . . These are therefore to require you to prepare and dispatch the same notwithstanding any caveat to the contrary, as
you will answer to the contrary at your peril, and this shall be your warrant . . . 30th August 1674.

5. PRO: LC "Miscellanea," 5/86, p. 1.

Liveries and fees payable out of His Majesty's Great Wardrobe this cur-
rent year, to end at Michaelmas 1675. . . .
At the Feast of All Saints:
Grooms of the Privy Chamber Assistant to the King

Richard Burns	£40 0 6
Francis Purcell	£40 0 6

Officers of the Robes to the King

. . .

Thomas Purcell, Groom	£40

6. Charles Dalton, *English Army Lists and Commission Registers 1661–
1714*, vol. 1, pp. 204 and 255.

King's Own Regiment of Dragoons: Cornet, Francis Purcell, Feb. 19th,
1678.
Francis Purcell, Cornet, June 11th, 1679.

7. PRO: *Cal. Tr. Books*, 26 June 1679.

£37. 15s. 0d. to Francis Purcell in full of all pay due to him as Cornet of
Dragoons, under Captain Edmund Chaffin.

8. *Cal. Tr. Books*, 27 June 1679.

Cornet Francis Purcell disbanded. Order No. 769.

9. PRO: S. P. Dom. Entry Books (S.P. 44) 51, p. 313.

Whereas we have been often petitioned by the grooms assistant of our
Privy Chamber concerning the disputes that have arisen about their succeeding into the places of our six grooms-in-ordinary for the determination
whereof we referred the same unto you, our Chamberlain of our Household, who have certified us, that since our Restoration the grooms assistant
have always succeeded to be grooms-in-ordinary upon vacancies, according
to their seniority of being sworn into those places. Our will and pleasure
therefore is for the settlement hereof for the future, that the present 3
grooms of our Privy Chamber assistant, by name James Davis, Francis Purcell, and St. John Mitton [or Milton] shall succeed and be admitted by
you . . . into the places of the six grooms-in-ordinary upon any vacan-

cies . . . given at our Court at Whitehall the 11th day of February 1679 [1679/80] in the 32nd year of our reign.

By His Majesty's Command. H.C.

10. PRO: Pipe Office Declared Account (E 351) 2836: "Account of Henry Sidney, Esq. to Charles II from Annunciation, 1681–2," fo. 4*v*.

Shoes, viz. for wearing shoes, tennis shoes, galoshes, boots and buskins, and for livery boots for Gilbert Spencer, David Graham, Francis Purcell, Gervaise Price, James Gibbons, and Tobias Rustat: £122. 4. o

11. PRO: H.O. Warrant Book 5, p. 51.

Passes for Francis Purcell and his servant James Boyce to go to Harwich for Holland and Flanders.

12. *Cal. S. P. Dom.* 30 June 1696.

Passes for Mr. Charles More, Robert Bolney, William Holforth, Richard Hunt and Francis Purcell to go from Gravesend to Portugal on the recommendation of Richard Purcell.

XII THE ELDER HENRY PURCELL (father)

1. D'Avenant, Sir William, *The Siege of Rhodes* made a representation by the art of prospective [*sic*] in scenes, and the story sung in recitative music, etc. (British Museum, 644.d.68. Pub. London, 1656; another edition, both parts, 1663).

The Story Personated

Solyman	(Captain Henry Cook)	
Villerious	{ Mr. Gregory Thorndel and Mr. Dubartus Hunt }	Double parted
Alphonso	{ Mr. Edward Coleman and Mr. *Roger Hill* }	Double parted
Admiral	{ Mr. *Matthew Lock* and Mr. *Peter Ryman* }	Double parted
Pirrhus	{ Mr. *John Harding* and Mr. Alphonso Marsh }	Double parted
Mustapha	{ Mr. *Thomas Blagrave* and Mr. *Henry Purcell* }	Double parted
Ianthe	{ Mrs. Coleman, Wife to Mr. *Edward Coleman* }	Double parted

The composition of Vocal Music
was performed

The	First Entry	by	Mr. *Henry Lawes*
	Second Entry		Capt. *Henry Cook*
	Third Entry		Capt. *Henry Cook*
	Fourth Entry		Mr. *Matthew Lock*
	Fifth Entry		Mr. *Henry Lawes*

The Instrumental Music was composed by
Dr. *Charles Coleman*, and Mr. *George Hudson*.
The Instrumental Music
is performed

by	Mr. *William Webb*
	Mr. *Christopher Gibbons* [sic]
	Mr. *Humphrey Madge*
	Mr. *Thomas Balser*, a German,
	Mr. *Thomas Baites*
	Mr. *John Banister*

2. WAM 33695 (Treasurer's Account, 1661).

fo. 1*v*. Payment to Henry Purcell of £10. 0. 0. as *cantator in choro*.

fo. 2. Payment to Henry Purcell of £7. 5. 0. as Master of the Choristers.

fo. 4*v*. Paid to Mr. Pursell for the Choristers' dinner for three quarters of a year ending Michaelmas 1661, at £5 per annum: £3. 15. 0.

fo. 5. To Henry Purcell for books of services for the choristers £1. 0. 0.

[Such payments recur in 1662, 1663, and 1664 more or less regularly. See his signatures for these on folios 15, 48, 48*v*, 19*v*, 50, etc.]

3. St. Margaret's, Westminster, Register of Baptisms, fo. 145.

13 March 1661/2.
Katherine, the daughter of Mr. Henry Purcell, was baptized.

4. *KM*, p. 151. (14 Nov. 1662).

. . . and Henry Purcell [appointed] musician-in-ordinary for lute and voice in the same place with Angelo Notari.

5. *KM*, p. 151. (15 Nov. 1662).

Warrant to admit Angelo Notari and Henry Purcell musicians-in-ordinary for the lutes and voices, with the yearly wages of £40, to commence from St. John Baptist 1660.

6. *KM*, p. 165. (10 Dec. 1663.)

[In list of] Gentlemen of the Chapel Royal.

7. *Cal. Tr. Books*, 27 Feb. 1663/4.

Money warrant dormant for the wages and fee of £40 per annum to Henry Pursell (Pussell) for his office and place of musician-in-ordinary to the King for the lute and voice.

8. J. P. Malcolm, *Londinium Redivivum* (1802–7), vol. 1, p. 246 (from the accounts of the Treasurer of Westminster Abbey for 1664).

Cantatoribus in choro pro stipend "et regard." Thomas Hazard, John Harding, Christopher Chapman, Henry Purcell, Edward Braddock, William Hatton, Owen Adamson, Thomas Hughes, Richard Mabler, Thomas Shorter, Thomas Carey, and Thomas Finnell. (£8 and 40s. each.)

9. *KM*, p. 170. (20 August 1664.)

John Goodgroome appointed to the Private Music for the lutes, viol, and voices, in the place of Henry Purcell.

(See also *Cal. S. P. Dom.* 28 Nov. 1664.)

10. Cheque-book, p. 13.

Mr. Henry Purcell, one of His Majesty's Gentlemen of the Chapel, died the eleventh day of August 1664, in whose place came Mr. Thomas Richardson.

11. Cheque-book, p. 212.

[Rimbault quotes the following document, of which a copy was in his possession:]

These are to certify that Mr. Henry Purcell, who succeeded Segnor Angello in his place of the Private Music; that the said Mr. Henry Purcell took possession of his place in the year 1663, upon St. Thomas's Day; deceased the 11th August 1664:

	Henry Cooke
There are to certify	Tho. Purcell
the death of Mr.	Alfonso Marsh
Henry Purcell	Gregory Thorndale
	Edward Colman

12. PRO: Patent Roll C66/3009.

Charles the Second . . . to the Treasurer and Undertreasurer of our Exchequer. . . . Whereas upon the humble request of Angelo Notari, one of the musicians-in-ordinary for the lute and voice, of [*sic*] his inabilities to execute that employment without an assistant, we have been graciously pleased in consideration of service done and to be done unto us, have given and granted . . . unto the said Angelo Notari and Henry Purcell, whom we have nominated his assistant, the said office and place of musician-in-ordinary to us for the lute and voice with the former annuity, wages and fee of forty pounds per annum. . . . To have and enjoy the said office and place of musician to us as aforesaid during their lives and the longer liver of them . . . the first payment to commence from the Feast of St. John Baptist which was in the year of our Lord 1660. . . .

13. *Cal. Tr. Books*, 20 May 1668.

Money warrant for £46. 10. 10 to Hannah, daughter of Clement Lanier [and for various other widows, orphans, and other dependants of deceased musicians, including an account for] £20.0.0 to Elizabeth, relict of Henry Purcell.

14. *Westminster Abbey Reg.*, p. 161.

Burials: 13 Aug. 1664.
Mr. Henry Purcell, one of the Gentlemen of the King's Chapel, and Master of the Children of this church; in the east cloister.

[According to *Westminster Abbey Reg.*, his estate was administered 7 Oct. 1664 by his widow; see also VIII: Elizabeth Purcell.]

15. *Westminster Public Library, Westminster Account Book and Calendar*, no. 5 (1664–66), vol. 5, p. 55.

Henrici Pursell: Septimo die mensis Octobris
     Adco 1664^0
Comiss fuit Dio monis et singularit bonor Jurium et creditum Henrici Purcell misi que Sta. Margareta in Civitate Westm. defunct Elizabethae Pursell vid Relice erit Qef-do bene et fide & jurat et salvo Jure & Jurem ejtum XX^{to} iii^b.

16. WAM 61228A (Precentor's Book, 1660–71), unfoliated pages at end.

Burials: 13 Aug. 1664.
Mr. Henry Purcell, one of the Gentlemen of His Majesty's Chapel Royal and master of boys of Westminster, was buried in the great cloisters near Mr. Lawes.

[N.B. The signature of one "Henry Purcell" in the front cover of the Sion Library copy of *The Faith, Doctrine, and Religion Professed and Protected in the Realm of England . . . thirty-nine Articles* (London, 1661: press mark A57.3/R63[2]) may be that of Henry Purcell the elder. However, the signature is so painstakingly copied that it is difficult to identify it with the various specimens in Westminster accounts, despite such similar features as the backward "e," the old inverse "r" and the very similar capital "H."]

XIII The Younger Henry Purcell

1. Anthony à Wood, Oxford, Bodleian, MS. Wood D 19(9) (S.C. 8568–69).

Born in London—He, Dr. Child, and Dr. Blow all organists to King William and Queen Mary.

PURCELL, HENRY, originally one of the Children in the King's Chapel. Bred under Dr. Chr. Gibbons, I think, afterwards organist to King Charles 2nd, William III. Organist at St. Peter's Church at Westminster.

He and John Blow . . . chief authors of the second part of *Harmonia Sacra.* [fo. 104]

His sonatas à 3 = See Dr. B. Rogers's sonatas in 4 parts. See Playford's account: catalogue 11.4.a and *bis*. [fo. 104*v*]

[Under entry for John Blow]: Dr. Rogers tells me that John Blow was born in London, and that he, Henry Purcell, and Dr. William Child are organists to King William and Queen Mary, and. . . . [fo. 22]

He [B. Rogers] said that John Playford died 1687 . . . soon after a Pastoral Elegy was made on his death; to which musical notes were set in two parts by Mr. Henry Purcell—printed in one sheet folio. Dr. Rogers has it. [fo. 101]

Purcell, Hen. living. [fo. 146: Table of Contents]

2. PRO: LC "Miscellanea," 5/86 [isolated section in middle of book, paged 1–8], pp. 1 and 3.

Ch. R: Musicians and Feasts
Great Wardrobe Anno R.R. Ch.II.27.
Liveries and fees payable out of His Majesty's Great Wardrobe this current year to end at Michaelmas 1675.
[Selections from lists:]

		£	s.	d.
At the Feast of All Saints				
Grooms of the Privy Chamber assistant to the King	Richard Binns	040	0	6
	Francis Purcell	040	0	6
Officers of the Robes to the King	Lancelott Thornton, Clerk	040		
	Tobias Rustat, yeoman	040		
	Tobias Rustat more	040		
	Thomas Purcell, Groom	040		
	Paul fferine, Groom	040		
	James Watson, Groom	040		
	Robert Rustat, Groom	040		
	Thomas Bocock	040		
At the Feast of St. Andrew				

[Erasures and names written alongside reproduced as they appear; the second set of names is in a different hand, as is "junior" after John Bannister.]

	£	s.	d.
~~Lewis Grabu~~ Master of the Music, Dr. Staggins	16	2	6
~~Thomas Purcell~~ John Goodwyn	16	2	6
Anthony Roberts	16	2	6
~~John Hingston~~ Robert Carr	16	2	6
William Gregory	16	2	6
~~Thomas Purcell~~ Nathaniell ffrench	16	2	6
Musicians ~~Humphrey Madge~~ Jeoffrey Aleworth	16	2	6
Thomas Lanier	16	2	6
~~John Smyth~~ Francis Cryne	16	2	6
John Gamble	16	2	6
~~John Jenkins~~ John Mosse	16	2	6
~~John Lilley~~ Edmund fflower	16	2	6
*John Harding John Bowman	16	2	6
John Bannister jun ʳ	16	2	6
Edward Hooton	16	2	6
*Mathew Lock Henry Purcell	16	2	6
~~Thomas Bates~~ William Gregory	16	2	6
~~Alphonso Marsh~~ John Abell	16	2	6 etc.

3. Thomas Ford, Bodleian, MS. Mus.e.17, "An account of Musicians &
their works . . . ," folios 39*v* and 40.

Here lies Hen. Purcell, Esq., who left this life and is gone to that blessed
place where only his harmony can be excelled. obb. 21. Nov. 1695.

Purcell, Henry. Son of Hen: Purcell, Gent. of Chapel, who died Aug. 11,
1664, scholar to Dr. Blow and to Dr. Christopher Gibbons, Master of the
Children and organist to Charles II and William III and organist of St. Peter's, Westminster. He died Nov. 21, 1695.

4. PRO: LC "Miscellanea," 5/64, fo. 83.

Clothes for a Chapel boy whose voice is changed. These are to signify
unto you His Majesty's pleasure, that you provide and deliver, or cause to
be delivered, unto Henry Purcell, late one of the Children of His Majesty's
Chapel Royal, whose voice is changed and is gone from the Chapel, two
suits of plain cloth, two hats and hat-bands, four whole shirts, four half
shirts, six bands, six pair of cuffs, six handkerchiefs, four pair of stockings,
four pair of shoes, and four pair of gloves. (17th Dec. 1673.)

5. WAM Treasurers' Accounts.

33709 (1675), fo. 5:
To Henry Pursel for tuning the Organ   £2.   0. 0

33710 (1676), fo. 5v:
To Henry Purcell for pricking out two books of organ parts £5.   o. o

33712 (1677), fo. 5:
To Henry Purcell for tuning the organs   £2.   o. o

33713 (1678), fo. 5:
[The same entry.]

33714 (1679), fo. 4:
[For an account of Purcell's scholarship at St. Peter's
  College, see pp. 52–56.]

33715 (1680), fo. 2:
Organistae: Et in Denarijs Solutis Henrico Purcell   £10. o. o

33716 (1681), folios 2 and 5:
[The same entry.]
To the organist in lieu of a house   £8. o. o

33717 (1682), passim and fo. 5:
[The same entries.]
Paid for writing Mr. Purcell's service and anthems   £o. 30. o

33718–20 (1683–85), passim:
[Similar entries.]

33721 (1687), fo. 5v:
Paid Mr. Purcell one quarter's rent for his house due
  Christmas 1686   £o. 40. o

33722 (1688), folios 2 and 5v:
Et in de denar Solutis Heno Purcell   £10. o. o
To Mr. Purcell the organist in lieu of a house   £8. o. o
Paid Mr. Purcell for making the service books   £o. 58. 6

33723 (1689), folios 2v and 5v:
Et in denar solutis Henro Purcell   £10. o. o
Paid Mr. Purcell the organist in lieu of a house   £8. o. o

33724–8 (1690–94), passim:
[Similar entries.]

6. St. Katherine Cree, Churchwarden's Accounts, 1650–91. 1686/7: List of
Subscribers.

An account of the moneys given, received, and paid for the erecting an
organ and building a gallery in the parish church of St. Katherine Cree.
£124. £77. £80. £44. received many subscriptions of £11. £105, 5, 6, 2,
1 etc.

Payments.

Paid Mr. Bernard Smith for making the organ as contract £250.0.0

Paid various sums for gallery £65 etc.

Spent on Mr. Pursell and Mr. Smith 14/–

Paid coach hire for Dr. Blowe and Mr. Pursell 5/–

For curtains and curtain rings £1.18.4d.

Altogether, a sum of £355.11.3d. was paid out.

7. Excerpt from the Fifth Codicil of Richard Busby, undated and unsigned (Busby died in April 1695). Quoted in G. F. Russell Barker, *Memoir of Richard Busby*, p. 145.

And to every of the King's Scholars belonging to the King's School at Westminster I give the sum of ten shillings for the like use. And to the Chaunter Petty Canons, Organist (Henry Purcell) and Master of the Choristers belonging to the Collegiate Church of Westminster aforesaid to every of them twenty shillings apiece. And to the rest of the gentlemen of the Choir of the said Church to every of them the sum of thirteen shillings and four pence. . . .

8. Testamentum Henrici Purcell. PCC: 243 Irby (Somerset House). Dec. 1695.

In the name of God Amen. I, Henry Purcell, of the City of Westminster, gentleman, being dangerously ill as to the constitution of my body, but in good and perfect mind and memory (thanks be to God) do by these presents publish and declare this to be my last Will and Testament. And I do hereby give and bequeath unto my loving wife, Frances Purcell, all my estate both real and personal of what nature and kind soever, to her and to her assigns for ever. And I do hereby constitute and appoint my said loving wife my sole executrix of this my last Will and Testament, revoking all former Will or Wills, witness my hand and seal this twenty-first day of November, Annoque Domini one thousand six hundred ninety five. And in the seventh year of the reign of King William the Third &c. H. Purcell.

Signed, sealed, published, and declared by the said Henry Purcell in the presence of William Eeles, John Chapelin, J. B. Peters.

Probatum fuit [huiusmodi] Testamentum apud London coram venerabili viro Willelmo Oldys Legum Doctore Surrogato [venerabilis] et egregij viri Domini Richardi Raines Militis Legum etiam Doctoris Curiae Praerogativae Cantuarensis Magistri Custodis sive Commissarij legitime constituti septimo die mensis Decembris Anno Domini millesimo sexcentimo nonagesimo quinto Juramento Franciscae Purcell Relictae dicti defuncti et Executricis in dicto Testamento nominato cui commissa fuit administracio omnium et singulorum bonorum jurium etc reditorum dicti defuncti de bone et fideliter administrand[um] eadem ad sancta Dei Evangelia Jurat[a]. Ex.

9. *Cal. S. P. Dom.* 6 July 1702.

Thomas Tudway.

Ever since the Reformation there have been three organists belonging to the Chapel Royal, to attend that duty by turns. The petitioner was bred up in that Chapel, and had a promise in '82 from King Charles II that he should have the next place which fell vacant. This occurred when Mr. Purcell died in 1696 [*sic*]; but his place has never been filled. Prays for it.

10. Anonymous. *Orpheus Britannicus*, book 1, 3d ed. (London, 1721).

> "Another Ode on the Same Occasion,
> by a Person of Quality"[4]
> Accord thy blessing to my bold design,
> Thou best inspirer of harmonious grief;
> Thou, who among the tuneful Nine,
> In mournful melody art chief.
> In music, wing'd with sighs, I soar,
> A second Orpheus to deplore;
> Second in time, but first in fame;
> To him blind fiction gave a name.
> The truthless tales, which frantic poets tell
> Of Thebes, and moving stones, and journeys down to Hell,
> Were only prophecies of music's force, which we
> Have wonderfully seen fulfill'd in thee.
> What mortal harmony cou'd do
> No mortal ever knew,
> Till thy transcendent genius came
> Whose strength surpass'd the praises of poetic flame:
> Whose raptures will for ever want a name.
> Out of thy orb a while
> (Content to wander here below)
> Thou did'st vouchsafe to bless our Isle,
> (With high commands from heav'n for ought we know)
> To try seditious jars to reconcile.
> But discord in a frightful form,
> With all her retinue of war,
> The drum, the pulpit, and the bar,
> The croaking crowds' tumultuous noise,
> And ev'ry hoarse outlandish voice,
> Proclaim'd so loud th'impending storm,
> That frighted hence, thou didst for refuge fly,
> To reassume thy station in the sky:

---

4. See Dryden's "Mark how the lark," no. 18 below.

There heavenly carols to compose and sing,
To heaven's harmonious King.
Where rapt in transports of ecstatic song,
Amidst th'inspir'd seraphic throng,
Crown'd with celestial ever-blooming bays,
Thou sitt'st dissolv'd in *Hallelujahs.*

11. Anonymous. "To his esteemed friend, Dr. Blow, upon publishing his book of songs, *Amphion Anglicus,*" p. iii.

(Beginning "Amphion's lute of old with magic art.")

. . . . .

Thus has our isle been long oblig'd by Blow
Who first with decent modesty did show
In blooming Purcell what himself cou'd do.
On Purcell his whole genius he bestow'd,
And all the Master's graces in the pupil flow'd;
But he unable long to bear the load,
Opprest with rapture, sunk beneath the god.
Home then the welcome deity returns,
And Blow again with youthful transports burns.

Whitehall, 20 May 1700

12. Anonymous. *Harmonia Sacra,* book 2, 3d ed. (1726).

Music and verse have been abus'd too long,
Idly to furnish out some wanton song;
To varnish vice, to make loose folly shine,
And gild the vain delights of love, or wine:
Both heav'nly-born, but both constrain'd to fall
So far below their great original,
The erring world, not knowing how to trace
Thro' vile employments their celestial race,
Suppos'd their birth was, as their office, base.
Rescu'd by you, they have again put on
Those glorious rays with which at first they shone;
Assert their native honour; and excite,
With awful pleasure, rev'rence and delight:
Here no loud rant, no wild ungovern'd strain,
Invokes plump Bacchus, and his sordid train;
Here no fond couplet kindles am'rous fires,
No melting note gives birth to loose desires:
Each air, each line, which in this work appear,
Angels may fitly sing, and saints may hear.
Go on my friend; set sacred music free
From scandal, and move sacred poetry:

Publish'd by you, with double grace they shine,
Lovely and grave, harmonious and divine.

By an unknown hand

13. Anonymous. "A Poem Occasioned on the Death of Mr. Henry Purcell, late Musician-in-Ordinary to His Majesty. Quocunque choros agitat mors Musica dormit." *Bat.* [*sic.*] By a Lover of Music (London, 1695), with a note added in a contemporary hand: "18. Decemb." in the copy in the Yale University Library: K/Foxwell/ 26835d.

I

Ye gentle spheres
Cease now your wonted melody,
Rest and ever silent be—
Nought now remains for comfort or relief,
But a free vent to our just source of grief.
An untaught groan best language is,
For such a dismal scene as this.
Yet like our dying swans you first may tell,
In softest music to attending ears,
How the lov'd Strephon liv'd, and how lamented fell:
Tell then th'admiring world how often he,
Has ev'n charm'd you to extasie,
How oft you've envy'd at the praise he won,
Yet smil'd to see yourselves outdone.
Tell this in different notes, in such as he,
Was used to charm us here below, that make one Harmony.

II

The little birds throughout the plains,
Repeat their notes in doleful strain.
In doleful strains they all complain
As if they never were to sing again.
Sad Philomel amongst the rest
As if some story she'd relate,
Not of her own but of her master's cruel Fate.
In mournful notes her grief exprest,
In careless melancholy lays
She sung his praise.
Now all her art she tries,
Now all her strength applies,
To warble forth an elegy
Sacred to his memory.
She sings, alas her songs are all in vain,
Nothing can alter destiny,
The swain can ne'er return to life again.

III

What do I hear, what dismal groans,
What sighs, what shrieks, what melancholy moans,
Now spread themselves o'er all the pensive plains,
And tears the breasts of all the tender swains,
'Tis for Strephon dead and gone.
Mourn all ye shepherds, mourn with me your master's fate.
With me attend his funeral,
With me adorn his hearse
With never fading garland, never dying verse.
Alas! no sounds will now prevail,
To tell their melancholy tale,
Since dead he is who made their songs to live,
He their dull numbers could inspire,
With charming voice, and tuneful lyre,
He life to all but to himself could give.
No longer now the swains unto each other play,
Their arms across, their heads hung down,
Their oaten pipes, beside them thrown,
Their flocks neglected stray,
Ev'n Pan himself o'erwhelm'd with grief
    has thrown his pipe away.

IV

See Love himself all bath'd in tears,
His bow he breaks, away his dart he flings,
Then folds his arms and hangs his drooping wings,
Venus herself close mourner here appears.
No longer now she thinks herself secure,
But sighing from her throne looks down,
Her greatness cannot long endure
Since its supporter's dead and gone;
Since that the tuneful Strephon's fall'n—
Now silent lies his lyre,
No longer warms our hearts into desire,
For dead is he who could our passions move,
Who best could gentle thoughts inspire,
Who best could fan the amorous fire,
Make us at once submit and own the pow'r of love.

V

Gone is the glory of our Age,
The pride and darling of the stage
The theatre his worth well knew,
Saw how by him its greatness grew.

In him their honour, pride and glory liv'd,
For as his soul they now are fled,
And scarce can sooner be retriev'd,
For all their hopes in him are dead.
Whilst he vouchsaf'd to stay below
They were too blest long to continue so.
But oh! no more the tuneful Strephon's songs they'll hear,
No more his joyful notes will glad the wond'ring theatre.

                              VI

Ye sons of Phoebus, write his elegy
But let it be
Great as the subject, sad as your calamity,
Let every Muse his praise aloud proclaim,
And to the distant poles, let Echo spread his fame.
Write epitaphs that so
The world may know,
How much to him ev'n poetry did owe,
For you but say, 'tis he that makes you sing,
His Art the embryo words to perfection bring.
By us the Muse at first conceives, 'tis true,
He makes it fit to see the light, that gift to him we owe:
Naked at first, and rugged they appear,
But when by him adorn'd they be,
Assume a pomp and bravery,
Nor need they longer blush to reach a Prince's ear.

                              VII

How rigid are the laws of fate,
And how severe the black decree,
For nothing, nothing here is free,
But all must enter th'Adamantine gate.
The great, the good, the just, nay all must come,
To Nature's dark retiring room.
He! he! alas is gone,
Whose gentle airs did make our numbers live,
Who immortality could give,
His soul to 'ts first abode is flown,
Blasted are all our glories now,
Our laurels wither as they grow,
The Muse herself forsakes us too.
Come then, come quickly come,
Let's pay our tears for off'rings at his tomb.

Let us not strive who best deserves the bays,
He that grieves most best claims the highest praise.

VIII

Arise, ye blest inhabitants above,
From your immortal seats arise,
And on our wonder, on our love,
Gaze with astonish'd eyes;
Arise, arise, make room,
The wish'd for shade is come;
Haste, and yourselves prepare
To me [*sic*] the joyful chorister,
Meet him halfway with songs, such as you sing
Before the throne of the Eternal King,
With welcomes let th'aetherial palace ring,
Welcome the guardian angel says,
Full of songs and full of bays,
Welcome thou art to me,
And to these regions of serenity;
Welcome the winged choir resounds,
While with loud Fugues all the sacred place abounds
Lo now above he chants eternal lays
Above our wonder and our praise.

FINIS

14. (?)Rev. J. Bowen. *Orpheus Britannicus*, book 1, 2d ed. (1706) [U.C.L.A. Library "Seminar Room" M 1616.P97.0 (on flyleaf in contemporary hand) with "Rev. J. Bowen" written on front cover].

Great soul of music, if we right devine
Thy wondrous worth, thou of the muses nine
Art diapason, harmony divine.
Shown to the world, to teach them how to sing
Then summon'd to attend the heavenly choirs
Thy harp the seraphs with new mirth inspires
Who in thy strains hymn the eternal King.

15. Tom Brown. *Harmonia Sacra*, book 2, 1st ed. (1693).

To his unknown friend, Mr. Henry Purcell, upon
his excellent compositions in the first and
second books of *Harmonia Sacra*

Long had dark ignorance our Isle o'erspread,
Our music and our poetry lay dead:
But the dull malice of a barb'rous age,

Fell most severe on David's sacred page;
To wound his sense, and quench his heav'n-born fire,
Three dull translators lewdly did conspire.
In holy dogg'rel and low-chiming prose;
The king and poet they at once depose.
Vainly he did th'unrighteous change bemoan,
And languish'd in vile numbers not his own:
Nor stop'd his usage here—
For what escap'd in wisdom's ancient rhymes,
Was murder'd o'er and o'er by the composer's chimes.
   What praises, Purcell, to thy skill are due;
Who hast to Judah's monarch been so true?
By thee he moves our hearts, by thee he reigns,
By thee shakes off his old inglorious chains,
And sees new honours done to his immortal strains.

Not Italy, the mother of each art,
Did e'er a juster, happier son impart.
In thy performance we with wonder find
Bassani's genius to Corelli's joyn'd.
Sweetness combin'd with majesty, prepares
To raise devotion with inspiring airs.
   Thus I unknown my gratitude express,
And conscious gratitude could pay no less.
This tribute from each British Muse is due,
Our whole poetic tribe's oblig'd to you.
For where the author's scanty words have fail'd,
Your happier graces, Purcell, have prevail'd.
And surely none but you with equal ease
Could add to David, and make D'Urfey please.[5]

16. From the *Diverting Post*, for February 1706. (Burney Coll., vol. 131b)

    The Force of Music: to the memory of the late famous
           Henry Purcell, a Pindaric Ode

While tow'ring with seraphic wings,
   The mighty Purcell heights unknown explores,
Sublime on music's force he upward springs,
   Till to divinity he soars.
Mankind lies ravish't with his lays,
And all in vain attempts his praise;
Still while our grov'ling thoughts aspire
To reach the raptures we admire;

5. Cf. Cummings, p. 83, for a version published in the *Gentleman's Journal*, June 1693, which differs from the above in several details.

We but degrade the name we meant to raise.
  Boundless and free thy numbers move
  With native fury fir'd;
And with diffusive raptures rove
  By none but thy great self inspir'd,
The gods themselves, thy lays attend,
To thee their ravisht ears they bend.
A while their heav'nly rapture they decline,
And tune their own imperfect notes by thine.
Now godlike Nassaw feels thy sov'reign power,
And conquests o'er his soul, unknown before:
  Prostrate the vanquish't Hero lies,
And with each vary'd note unwillingly complies.

2

See, see, the mighty Purcell comes,
(Sound the trumpets beat the drums)
He leaves his triumphs in the skies
  Attempts a greater prize.
Th'angelic choir his absence mourn,
Repeat past joys and long for his return,
High in seraphic state he stands,
And with insulting force, the pliant hero bends.
His song began with Dioclesian's fame,
The trembling notes resound his mighty name.
And to the list'ning world his glorious deeds proclaim;
  Descending angels crowd around,
  And join their heav'nly lays!
The vaulted roofs improve the sound,
  And propagate his praise.
When to redeem a sinking world,
  The daring hero rose,
Around his scatter'd rage he hurl'd,
  And quell'd his numerous foes.
In vain conspiring nations join,
In vain oppose his bold design;
Himself alone subdu'd their weaker aid,
Himself alone reveng'd the injur'd maid,
And from th'insulting monarch's brow pull'd down the violated shade.

3

Nor earth nor sea can stop his course,
Nor Tyber's more impetuous force,
  When swelling with its weight,
Around the mighty ruin lay,
And men and arms promiscuous fill'd the way,

And thwart his envy'd fate.
Unmov'd the dauntless hero view'd
Millions of foes and fought and swam in blood.
    Widely he dealt destruction round,
And hew'd his dreadful passage down,
And cut his mangled way and clove the purple flood.
In Virtue's just defence he rose,
And gave the troubled world repose,
At once their peace and freedom he restor'd
While grateful nations in return obey'd,
Obey'd their just, their rightful lord.
And gave him but the laurels he had won,
    the conquests he had made,
A present Dioclesian all resound;
A present Dioclesian all the vaulted roofs rebound,
The trembling strings untoucht repeat the name
    and swell his praise around,
Sooth'd with the sound the monarch rose,
To troubled nations gave a fresh repose,
And thrice he swam the Boyne and thrice he slew his foes.

                              4
The mighty Purcell smil'd to see
The wondrous force of harmony;
Chang'd his hand, left the lyre,
Checkt his rage and kindled softer fire.
    The mournful flute he chose
    Soft passion to infuse
    Such as parting lovers use
Such as lab'ring sighs disclose,
Such as Maria's death requires, as reaches all our woes.
    Maria's harder fate he sung,
    Maria fair and young,
In bloom of youth and beauty's pride,
Snatch'd from the trembling monarch's side,
While panting in his arms she lay,
And in soft kisses breath'd her soul away.
In vain the hero rushes to her aid,
Alas! a stronger power does invade;
With all the laurels thou hast won,
And level with the common dust, an undistinguisht shade,
The breathing notes unwillingly complain,
    And gently tell th'unwelcome news around;
Bemoaning Echo imitates in vain,
    And falters in the sound.
With down-cast eyes the monarch view'd

All his flatt'ring hopes destroy'd,
Afresh her image he renew'd,
  Afresh his tears employ'd.
To heav'n again the tuneful conqu'ror flies,
Resumes his triumphs in the skies,
There to the blest seraphic choir
  Relates the conquest of his lays;
His wondrous skill they all admire,
And through the vocal heav'ns resound his praise.
  Th'unwelcome news Maria heard,
Much for her vanquish't lord she fear'd,
Yet knew no human force cou'd him confine,
  Nor less than harmony divine.
Much she enquires of things below,
And longs to hear her lov'd Britannia's state;
  At that the tears began to flow,
(Tears such as angels shed if they can sorrows know)
And with indulgent grief she mourn'd,
    th'unhappy Gloucester's Fate.

GRAND CHORUS

  Meanwhile th'angelic choir prepare,
To rear him trophies, and reward his care,
His brows with myrtle wreaths they bound,
(So shou'd his vast desert be crown'd)
And through the wond'ring skies aloft the conqu'ror bear.
Around his triumphs they proclaim,
  And with his conquests swell the mouth of fame.
Henceforth let Purcell and Nassau be prais'd,
Or Nassau yield the crown,
A sinking world the monarch rais'd
  He pull'd that monarch down.

17. Henry Carey, "The Poet's Resentment," *Poems on Several Occasions* (1729).

    Ev'n heaven-born Purcell now is held in scorn,
    Purcell who did a brighter age adorn. . . .

18. John Dryden. *Orpheus Britannicus*, book 2, 3d ed. (1721), p. iv.

An Ode on the death of Mr. Henry Purcell
by Mr. Dryden

I

Mark how the lark and linnet sing,
With rival notes

They strain their warbling throats,
To welcome in the Spring.
But in the close of night,
When Philomel begins her heav'nly lay,
They cease their mutual spite,
Drink in her music with delight,
And list'ning and silent, and silent and list'ning,
    and list'ning and silent obey.

II

So ceas'd the rival crew when Purcell came,
They sung no more, or only sung his fame.
Struck dumb, they all admir'd the godlike man:
    The godlike man
Alas! too soon retir'd,
    As he too late began.
We beg not hell our Orpheus to restore;
    Had he been there,
    Their sov'reign's fear
    Had sent him back before.
The pow'r of harmony too well they knew,
He long ere this had tun'd their jarring sphere,
    And left no hell below.

III

The heavenly choir, who heard his notes from high,
Let down the scale of music from the sky:
    They handed him along
And all the way he taught, and all the way they sung.
    Ye brethren of the lyre, and tuneful voice,
    Lament his lot, but at your own rejoice.
    Now live secure and linger out your days,
    The gods are pleas'd alone with Purcell's lays,
    Nor know to mend their choice.

(This ode is set to music by Dr. Blow, and may be bound up with this
collection.)

19. John Gilbert. *Orpheus Britannicus*, book 1, 3d ed., p. v. The following
lines were design'd for Mr. Purcell's monument; which being supply'd by a
better hand, the author of this inscription, in veneration to the memory of
that great master, prefixes it to his golden remains.

Memoriae Sacrum H.P.
En! marmor loquax
(Vix, heu! prae dolore)
Lacrymas stillatim sudat;

Manes Purcelli sacros,
Quisquis es, viator,
Siste ac venerare.
Eheu! quam subito orbis harmonici
Procubuit columen!
Angliacus ille Amphion, Orpheus, Apollo,
Deus Harmoniae Italo-Anglus,
Certe Corellius;
Artis musicae
Perquam difficilis
Facile Coryphaeus.
Per acuta musicae victor ibat ovans.
Et placida animam compede alligavit.
Eheu! quam brevi
Praecox marcescit ingenium!
Invida quippe natura juvenem,
Arte senescentem, corripuit.
At—desine tendem,
Miserantis quaerimoniae:
Non omnis moritur,
Vivunt symphoniae immortales.
Angelorum chori Purcellum stipantes,
Nectaris immemores,
Mellitiores istos bibunt aure sonos:
Et plaudentes recinunt.
Vivent, in aeternum
Aeternumque placebunt.
Abi, viator, &, si musicus, aemulare:
Sed calcibus humum leviter preme,
Ne nascentes atteras rosas.

Johannes Gilbert A. M. Coll. Christ. Cantab.

20. R.G. *Orpheus Britannicus*, book 2, 3d ed., p. i.

> On the death of the late famous Mr. Henry Purcell,
> author of the first and second books of
> *Orpheus Britannicus*

Make room ye happy natives of the sky,
Room for a soul, all love and harmony;
A soul that rose to such perfection here,
It scarce will be advanc'd by being there.
Whether (to us by transmigration given)
He once was an inhabitant of heav'n,
And form'd for music, with diviner fire

Endu'd, compos'd for the celestial choir;
Not for the vulgar race of light to hear,
But on high-days to glad th'immortal ear.
So in some leisure hour was sent away,
(Their hour is here a life, a thousand years their day)
Sent what th'aetherial music was to show,
And teach the wonders of that art below.
Whether this might not be, the muse appeals
To his composures, where such magic dwells,
As rivals heav'nly skill, and human pow'r excels.

Vile as a sign-post dauber's painting shows,
Compar'd with Titian's work, or Angelo's;
Languid and low, as modern rhyme appears,
When Virgil's matchless strain has tun'd our ears,
So seem to him the masters of our isle,
His inspiration, theirs but mortal toil:
They to the ear, he to the soul does dive,
From anger save, and from despair revive:
Not the smooth spheres in their eternal rounds,
The work of angels, warble softer sounds.

What is that heav'n of which so much we hear
(The happy region gain'd with praise and pray'r)
What but one unmolested transport, which
No notion, or idea e'er cou'd reach?
As it appears in vision, 'tis but this,
To be opprest with joy, and strive with bliss!
Confounded with the rays of ceaseless day,
We know not what we think, or see, or say!
Endless profusion! joy without decay!
So, when his harmony arrests the ear,
We lose all thought of what, or how, or where!
Like love it warms, like beauty does control,
Like hidden magic seizes on the whole,
And while we hear, the body turns to soul!

From what blest spring did he derive the art,
To soothe our cares, and thus command the heart!
Time list'ning stands to hear his artful strain,
And death does at the dying, throw his shafts in vain;
Fast to th'immortal part of the mortal cleaves,
Nor, till he leave to charm, the body leaves.
Less harmony than this did raise of old
The Theban wall, and made an age of gold.
How in that mystic order cou'd he join

So different notes! make contraries combine,
And out of discord, cull such sounds divine.
How did the seeds lie quick'ning in his brain!
How were they born without a parent's pain?
He did but think, and music wou'd arise,
Dilating joy, as light o'erspreads the skies;
From an immortal source, like that it came;
But light we know,—this wonder wants a name!

What art thou? From what causes dost thou spring
O Music! thou divine mysterious thing?
Let me but know, and knowing, give me voice to sing.
Art thou the warmth in spring that Zephire breathes,
Painting the meads, and whistling thro' the leaves?
The happy season that all grief exiles,
When God is pleas'd, and the creation smiles?
Or art thou love, that mind to mind imparts,
The endless concord of agreeing hearts?
Or art thou friendship, yet a nobler flame,
That can a dearer way make souls the same?
Or art thou rather, which does all transcend,
The centre where at last the blest ascend;
The seat where Hallelujahs never end?
Corporeal eyes won't let us clearly view,
But either thou art heav'n, or heav'n is you!

And thou my Muse (how e'er the critics blame)
Pleas'd with his worth, and faithful to his fame,
Art music while y'are hallowing Purcell's name.
On other subjects you applause might miss,
But envy will itself be charm'd with this,
How oft has envy at his airs been found
T'admire, enchanted with the blissful sound?
Ah! cou'd you quite forget his early doom,
I wou'd not from the rapture call you home:
But gently from your steepy height descend,
You've prais'd the artist, and now mourn the friend!
Ah most unworthy! shou'd we leave unsung
Such wond'rous goodness in a life so young.
In spite of practice, he this truth has shown,
That harmony and vertue shou'd be one.
So true to Nature, and so just to wit,
His music was the very sense you writ.
Nor were his beauties to his art confin'd;
So justly were his soul and body join'd,
You'd think his form the product of his mind.

A conqu'ring sweetness in his visage dwelt,
His eyes wou'd warm, his wit like lightning melt,
But those no more must now be seen, and that no more be felt.
Pride was the sole aversion of his eye,
Himself as humble as his art was high.
Ah! let him heav'n (in life so much ador'd)
Be now as universally deplor'd!
The muses sigh'd at his approaching doom,
Amaz'd and raving, as their own were come!
Art try'd the last efforts, but cou'd not save—
But sleep, O sleep, in an unenvy'd grave!
In life and death the noblest fate you share;
Poets and princes thy companions are,
And both of 'em were thy admirers here.
There rest thy ashes—but thy nobler name
Shall soar aloft, and last as long as Fame.

Nor shall thy worth be to our isle confin'd,
But fly and leave the lagging day behind.
Rome that did once extend its arms so far,
Y'ave conquer'd in a nobler art than war:
To its proud sons but only earth was giv'n,
But thou hast triumph'd both in earth and heav'n.

And now farewell! nor fame, nor love, nor art,
Nor tears avail!—we must for ever part!
For ever! dismal accent! what alone!
But that can tell our loss, or reach our moan!
What term of sorrow preference dare contend?
What? but the tenderest dearest name of—friend!

Hail him ye angels to the Elysian shore,
The noblest freight that ever Charon bore,
Tho' Orpheus and Amphion pass'd before.
His skill as far exceeds, as had his name
Been known as long, he wou'd have done in fame.
Tho' the wide globe for tuneful souls you cull,
Hope no more such—the happy choir is full.
The sacred art can here arrive no higher,
And heaven itself no further will inspire.

21. Henry Hall. *Orpheus Britannicus*, book 1, 3d ed., p vi.

To the memory of my dear friend
Mr. Henry Purcell

Music, the chiefest good the gods have giv'n,
And what below still antedates our heav'n,
Just like a spirit, by a lasting spell,
Confin'd to Italy, did ages dwell.
Long there remain'd a pleas'd and welcome guest,
Lov'd best to live where best she was exprest.
By glory led, at length to France she came,
And there immortaliz'd great Lully's name;
As yet a stranger to the British shore,
Till Lock, and Blow, deep learn'd in all her lore,
And happy artful Gibbons, forc'd her o'er.
Where with young Humphries she acquainted grew,
(Our first reforming music's Richelieu)
Who dying left the goddess all to you.
There are, I own, a num'rous tuneful throng,
Composing still, though often in the wrong,
And with old air, set forth a fine new song.
These to thy juster art have no pretence,
For if they make a tune they mar the sense.
If sparkling Air the taking treble grace,
'Tis murder'd quite by the ungodly bass.
These to old Morley's maxims counter run;
In overtures rejoice, in jigs they mourn:
Whilst their too great example, mighty you,
That you might still impartial justice do,
At once to music, and the muses too;
Each syllable first weigh'd, or short, or long,
That it might too be sense, as well as song.
Where e'er thy well-known name with theirs is found,
Is as if Cowley, up with Quarles were bound.
Purcell! the pride and wonder of the age,
The glory of the temple, and the stage.
When I thy happy compositions view,
The parts so proper find, the air so new,
Your cadence just, your accent ever true;
How can I e'er enough the man admire,
Who's rais'd the British o'er the Thracian lyre!
That bard cou'd make the savage-kind obey,
But thou has't tam'd yet greater brutes than they:
Who e'er like Purcell cou'd our passions move!
Whoever sang so feelingly of love!

When Thyrsis does in dying notes complain
His hapless love and Phillis' cold disdain;
Brib'd by the magic sounds that strike the ear,
We parties turn, and blame the cruel fair;
But when you tune your lyre to martial lays,
In songs immortal, mortal hero's praise;
Each song its hearers does to hero's raise.

Hail! and for ever hail harmonious shade!
I lov'd thee living, and admire thee dead.
Apollo's harp at once our souls did strike,
We learnt together, but not learnt alike,
Though equal care our master might bestow,
Yet only Purcell e'er shall equal Blow:
For thou, by heaven for wond'rous things design'd,
Left'st thy companion lagging far behind.
Sometimes a hero in an age appears;
But scarce a Purcell in a thousand years.

H. Hall, Organist of Hereford

22. Henry Hall. *Orpheus Britannicus*, book 1, 3d ed., p. ii.

To Mr. Henry Playford, on his publishing the
second part of *Orpheus Britannicus*

Next to the man who so divinely sung,
Our praise, kind Playford, does to thee belong,
For what you gave us of the bards before,
Vast thanks were due, and now you merit more,
Tho' Purcell living, had our utmost praise,
And dead, almost does adoration raise,
Yet he, ev'n he, had scarce preserv'd a name,
Did not your press perpetuate his fame,
And shew'd the coming age as in a glass,
What our all-pleasing Britain's Orpheus was.
Go on my friend, nor spare no pains nor cost,
Let not the least motet of his be lost;
Whose meanest labours your collections show,
Excells our very best performance now.

Duly each day, our young composers bait us,
With most insipid songs, and sad sonata's.
Well were it, if the world would lay embargo's
On such Allegro's and such Poco Largo's:
And would enact it, there presume not any,
To tease Corelli, or burlesque Bassani;

Nor with division, and ungainly graces,
Eclipse good sense, as weighty wigs do faces.
Then honest Cross might copper cut in vain,
And half our sonnet-sellers starve again:
Thus while they print their prick'd-lampoons to live
Do you the world some piece of Purcell's give,
Such as the nicest critic must commend,
For none dare censure that which none can mend.
By this, my friend, you'll get immortal fame,
When still with Purcell we read Playford's name.

H. Hall, Organist of Hereford

23. Mr. Herbert. *Orpheus Britannicus*, book 1, 3d ed., p. vii.

A Pindaric Ode on Dr. Blow's excellency
in the art of music
By Mr. Herbert

[Stanza I begins: "The Liberal arts . . ."
Stanza II begins: "Thus Bird, a British Worthy . . ."]

III

Great master of the instrument divine,
Descended of inspir'd Jubal's line!
How many plants of art, set by his hand,
Have spread, and still are spreading o'er the land!
Cedars in Libanus could not thicker stand.
    One hopeful stripling soon grew very tall,
Higher than all the rest, like goodly Saul;
And, if the Muses late sorrows don't recall,
Nor we disturb a soul at rest,
T'was Purcell, Purcell—Harry the great, the blest!
His labours highly of the Muse deserve;
And she as tenderly will ever them preserve.
His fam'd Te Deum, all the world admires,
Perform'd in those renown'd Italian choirs.
The master's, which he knew to be sublime
The scholar often wished to hear
Desiring here below no longer time.
But Providence, which granted not that pray'r,
Took him away, and left us here to grieve,
And doleful sounds were heard on St. Cecilia's Eve.
Thus Orpheus fell; the hills and valleys groan,
The nymphs lament, his lyre changes tone,
Makes a most sad, most gruesome moan
When in the troubl'd river Hebras thrown.

24. P. K. *Orpheus Britannicus*, book 2, 2d ed. (London, 1702).

"To my friend, Mr. Henry Playford, on his publication of Mr. Henry Purcell's *Orpheus Britannicus*; which is now render'd complete, by the addition of this second book."

As when the god of numbers charms the throng,
And gives melodious tunes to every song,
The voice deals inspiration and desire
To ev'ry Muse, to fill the sacred choir;
Each of the Nine, appears with her applause,
And justifies the god and music's cause;
As ev'ry tender accent gently moves,
And shews their duty, as it shews their loves;
Ev'n so must I with infant notes repair,
And wanting judgement, prove I want no care.

What great Apollo does to us deny,
He let this chosen son of his enjoy:
We poets sow the seed of Fame in vain,
T'expect a crop while we alive remain;
He puts us off till death, and then will give,
When we are not permitted to receive.

Ah! who'd be pleas'd to have these temples crown'd
Whose brains are lost, and heads are underground?
But Purcell's privilege was vastly more,
He planted all the laurels which he wore,
And heard his wide applause fly all around,
For still his fame did with his music sound.

    All this to Purcell, but there's something due
To Purcell's and Apollo's friend, to you,
From injuries of time you save his lays,
And rescue him from Fate, to claim our praise.
Oh! cou'd you but the like return receive,
And have our gratitude for what you give,
Rewarded for your toil, exchange your pains,
Not only for our thanks, but for your gains,
While interloping French and Dutch oppose,
And shew themselves both your and music's foes.

But it's in vain to hope, we're all abus'd,
Fond of the riff-raff, which the world refus'd:
Each foreign fool sits wheedling in his shop,
And grinning entertains the thoughtless fop,
Whose love for trifles, makes him rove from home,
And even hug diseases brought from Rome.

Let these, my friend, a while pursue their trade,
Your province and your right alone invade,
Their feeble malice but your fame secures,
And publishes both Purcell's works, and yours.

25. Nat. Oldham. British Museum, Add. MS. 23,076. "1732. George White. Verses at his last work and death—a print Mezzotint of a boy playing on a fiddle, painted by Fr. Hals."

(Col. 1)   Boy turn thy laughter into floods of tears.
And tune the instrument to mournful airs.
Play to the numbers of my broken verse
Whilst I the loss of friend and art rehearse.
A friend whom none in friendship could surpass,
An artist worth all monuments of brass.

(Col. 2)   O Shakespeare for thy soul to raise my flame
Thy music Purcell to resound his fame.
But what can verse or music raise so high
As this his last & silent harmony?
On him nor verse nor music need be spent
Read but George White and that's his monument.

                           Nat. Oldham arm—1732

"Vertue Note Books," vol. 3, *The Twenty-Second Volume of the Walpole Society* (1933–34) (Oxford, 1934).

26. (?)Henry Playford. *Orpheus Britannicus*, book 1, 3d ed., p. vi.

    To the memory of his much lamented friend
             Mr. H. Purcell

Hark! what deep groans torment the air,
Is nature sunk into despair;
Or does the trembling earth descry
A fit of falling-sickness nigh?
O my prophetic fears! he's gone!
'Twas nature's diapason'd groan.

Harmonious soul! took'st thou offence
At discords here, and fled'st from hence?
Or in thy sacred raptures hear
The music of heaven's warbling sphere?
Then mounted strait where angels sing,
And love does dance on every string.

For balms thou need'st not rob the East,
Nor strip the Phoenix spicy nest:

For, O my friend, thy charming strains
Perfume the skies with sweeter grains.
Touch but thy lyre, the stones will come,
And dance themselves into a tomb.

27. Henry Sacheverell, of Magdalen College, Oxford. *Harmonia Sacra*, book
2, 3d ed.

To Dr. John Blow and Mr. Henry Purcell, upon the
first and second books of *Harmonia Sacra*

When sacred numbers and immortal lays,
Join'd to record the great Almighty's praise,
Indulgent heav'n the poet did inspire
With lofty song to fill the tuneful lyre.
Thus when of old from Egypt's fruitful land
God brought forth Moses by a mighty hand,
His joyful tongue with untaught numbers flow'd,
Th'unusual harmony its author show'd.
The sea divided as he pass'd along,
Retreating back at his triumphant song.
When David's hand upon his harp was found,
Heav'n soon repeating, listen'd to the sound.
And struggling nature chang'd her wonted course,
Unable to resist his music's sacred force.
His prince's rage this taught him to control,
And tune the discords of his troubled soul.
Not fabled Orpheus, or Amphion's verse,
Can such amazing prodigies rehearse.
We here the mystic art may learn t'unfold,
And feel the wonders which we there are told.
No cloudy passions can our breasts invade,
When sacred harmony dispels the shade.
Here sprightly numbers raise our heighten'd zeal,
And charming sounds seraphic joys reveal.
Each skilful hand and tongue at once conspire
With strings and voice to make a tuneful choir:
Whilst mighty joys the ravish'd senses wound,
And the soul labours with th'inspiring sound.
Whither aloft it tow'rs Isaiah's flight,
Wing'd by devotion to the greatest height;
Or mourning with the royal prophet lies,
And weeps Jerusalem's just miseries;
Or loves sweet Sion's beauteous joys to tell,
Where God himself chiefly delights to dwell;
Such lofty measures, notes so sweet, so strong,

Exalt the numbers and improve the song.
Hail mighty pair! of Jubal's sacred art,
The greatest glory!—
Not skilful Asaph understood so well,
And Heman vainly labour'd to excel.
Where e'er the Gospel's sacred page is sung
Where e'er great David's tuneful harp is strung,
Each sacred verse shall your just glories raise,
Each dancing string shall echo forth your praise.
The church as yet could never boast but two
Of all the tuneful race, from Jubal down to you.

Dr. John Blow and Mr. Henry Purcell.

28. John Sheffield, Duke of Buckingham: a son of the Earl of Mulgrave, born 1650 (cf. *Musical Times* 37 (1 Feb. 1896): 85, article by A. Hughes-Hughes).

Ode on the death of Purcell

Good angels snatched him eagerly on high:
Joyfully they flew, singing and soaring through the sky,
Teaching his new-fledg'd soul to fly,
While we, alas! lamenting lie.
    He went musing all along,
    Composing new their heavenly song.
Awhile his skilful notes loud Hallelujahs drown'd,
But soon they ceas'd their own to catch his pleasing sound.
    David himself improved the harmony
    David in sacred story so renown'd,
    No less for music than for poetry;
    Genius sublime in either art,
Crown'd with applause surpassing all desert
    A man just after God's own heart.
    If human cares are awful to the blest
    Already settled in eternal rest,
Needs must he wish that Purcell only might
Have liv'd to see what he vouchsaf'd to write:
    For sure the noblest thirst of fame
    With the frail body never dies
    But with the soul ascends the skies,
From whence at first it came.
'Tis no little proof we have
That part of us survives the grave,
And in our fame below still bears a share.
Why is the future else so much our care,
Ev'n in our last moments of despair,
And death despised for fame by all wise and brave?

Oh! all ye blest harmonious choir,
Who pow'r almighty only love, and only that admire
Look down with pity from your peaceful bow'r
   On this sad isle perplex'd
   And even vex'd
With anxious care of trifles, wealth and pow'r.
In our rough minds due reverence infuse,
For sweet melodious sounds and each harmonious Muse.
Music exalts man's nature, and inspires
High elevated thoughts, or gentle kind desires.

29. J. Talbot, *Orpheus Britannicus*, book 1, 3d ed., p. v.

An Ode for the consort at York Buildings,
upon the death of Mr. H. P.
by J. Talbot, Fellow of Trinity College in Cambridge[6]

I

Weep, all ye Muses, weep o'er Damon's hearse,
And pay the greatful honours of your verse;
Each mournful strain in saddest accents dress,
His praises, and your sorrows to express.
Ye sons of art, lament your learned chief
With all the skill and harmony of grief;
To Damon's hearse your tuneful tribute bring,
Who taught each note to speak, and ev'ry Muse to
   sing.

II

	Hark! how the warlike trumpet groans,
1st Accompaniment	The warlike trumpet sadly moans,
Flat Trumpet	Instructed once by Damon's art
	To warm the active soldier's heart,
Sharp trumpet	To soften danger, sweeten care,
	And smooth the rugged toils of war,
	Now with shrill grief, and melancholy strains
Flat trumpet	Of Damon's death, and Albion's loss complains.
	The sprightly hautboys, and gay violin,
	By Damon taught to charm the list'ning ear,
	To fill the echoing theatre,
2nd Accompaniment	And with rich melody adorn each scene;
Hautbois and violins	Forgot their native cheerfulness,
	Their wonted air and vigour to express,
	And in dead doleful sounds a tuneless grief confess.

6. This ode was also published separately with the inscription "Set by Mr. Finger," with marginal notes and instructions for repetition of the last stanza as a grand chorus.

Chorus	{ Weep all ye Muses, weep o'er Damon's hearse, And pay the grateful honours of your verse.

III

3rd Accompaniment *Flute and theorbo*	{ Mark how the melancholy flute, Joins in sad consort with the amorous lute, Lamenting Damon's hopeless fate: From him they learn'd to tell the lover's care, With soft complaints to move the cruel fair, To calm her anger, and to change her hate.
4th Accompaniment *Organ*	{ The various organ taught by Damon's hand A holier passion to command, The roving fancy to refine, And fill the ravish'd soul with charms divine; Now in loud sighs employs its tuneful breath, And bids each secret sound conspire To mourn its darling Damon's death. And with consenting grief to form one num'rous choir.
Chorus	{ Weep all ye Muses, weep o'er Damon's hearse, And pay the grateful honours of your verse.

IV

Cease, cease, ye sons of art, forbear
To aggravate your own despair:
Cease to lament your learned chief
   With fruitless skill, and hopeless grief,
   For sure, if mortals here below
   Ought of diviner beings know,
Damon's large mind informs some active sphere,
And circles in melodious raptures there;
Mix'd with his fellow-choristers above,
In the bright orbs of harmony and love.

Grand Chorus   Cease, cease, ye sons of Art, etc.

[Printed for Francis Saunders, at the Blue Anchor in the Lower Walk of the New Exchange. 1695 (Yale University Library: Press mark K/Foxwell/26835d).]

30. Nahum Tate. *Orpheus Britannicus*, book 1, 3d ed., pp. iv–v.

A lamentation for the death of Mr. H. Purcell.
Set to music by his brother, Mr. Daniel Purcell.
   The words by N. Tate, Esq.

I

A gloomy mist o'erspreads the plains,
More gloomy grief the nymphs and swains;
The shepherd breaks his tuneful reed,

His pining flocks refuse to feed.
Silent are the lawns and glades,
The hills, the vales, the groves, the dales,
All silent as Elysian shades.
No more they sing, no more rejoice,
Echo herself has lost her voice.

II

A sighing wind, a murm'ring rill,
Our ears with doleful accents fill:
They are heard, and only they,
For sadly thus they seem to say,
The joy, the pride of Spring is dead,
The soul of harmony is fled.
Pleasure's flown from Albion's shore,
Wit and mirth's bright reign is o'er,
Strephon and music are no more!
   Since Nature thus pays tribute to his urn,
   How should a sad, forsaken brother mourn!

31. From R. J. S. Stevens, *Anecdotes*. MS. in Pendlebury Library, Cambridge University, fo. 18.

When Handel was blind, and attending a performance of the oratorio of "Jephtha," Mr. Savage (my master) who sat next him, said, "This movement, sir, reminds me of some of old Purcell's music." "O got te teffel" (said Handel). "If Purcell had lived, he would have composed better music than this."

[*Related by*] *Mr. Savage in 1775*

32. *Sixth Report of the Royal Commission on Historical Manuscripts* (London, 1877), part 1, p. 395.

Eulogium—Henricus Purcell, Corellius Britannicus. (15 lines of Latin)

[Letters to Ripley Castle, to the County Record Office, York and elsewhere have as yet brought no results.]

XIV ?THE THIRD HENRY PURCELL (son)

All Hallows the Less: Marriage, Burial, and Baptism Registers: College of Arms.

Baptisms: 9 July 1681.
   Henry, son of Henry and Frances Pursell.
Burials: 18 July 1681.
   Purssall, Henry.

xv ?THE FOURTH HENRY PURCELL (son)

Westminster Abbey Reg., p. 219.

Burial: 23 Sept. 1687.
Henry Purcell, a child: in the east cloister.

[Baptized at St. Margaret's, Westminster, 9 June 1687.]

xvi JOHN PURCELL (?grandfather)

Margaret M. Verney, *Memoirs of the Verney Family during the
Commonwealth, 1650–1660*, vol. 3 (London, 1894), p. 278. (Letter to Sir
Ralph Verney from Mun, housekeeper for the Verneys, 9 June 1656.)

Sir, this last week came Pursill the carpenter and his men, he only himself
sat in the house, but all his men came in for their beer, and that nor seldom
nor in small proportions; and by their example all the workmen do so
worry me for drink, that though I many times anger them, and hourly vex
myself, with denying one or other or them, yet we spend a great deal of
beer—three barrels last week. . . .

xvii JOHN BAPTISTA PURCELL (son)

1. *Westminster Abbey Reg.*, p. 72.

Baptisms: 9 Aug. 1682.
John-Baptista, son of Mr. Henry Purcell.

2. Ibid., p. 206.

Burials: 17 Oct. 1682.
John-Baptista Purcell, a child (cloisters).

xviii JOSEPH PURCELL (brother)

1. Marriage Licences: St. James's, Duke's Place. MS. 7894, Guildhall
Library.

9 Jan. 1693/4. Joseph Purcell, Bachelor [and]
Sarah Dormer, Spinster
Frances Jackman [Witness]

2. *Christchurch, Aldersgate Street* (Greyfriars: Harl. Soc. Reg. 21), p. 110.

Baptisms: 20 Jan. 1707/8.
Ann, daughter of Joseph and Sarah Purcell (born 26th Dec. 1707).

[See also under Daniel Purcell, III, 7(*a*) and (*b*).]

XIX KATHERINE PURCELL (sister)

1. *Westminster Abbey Reg.*, p. 67.

Baptisms: 13 March 1661/2.
Katherine, daughter of Mr. Henry Purcell.

[See also XII, 3.]

2. St. Mary Magdalen Registers (typescript of marriages, made by W. H. Challen, in the Guildhall Library).

18 June 1691.
William Sale of Seldwick in Kent and Katherine Pursall of St. Margaret's, Westminster.

XX MARY PETERS PURCELL (daughter)

Westminster Abbey Reg., p. 76.

Baptisms: 10 Dec. 1693.
Mary-Peters, daughter of Henry and Frances Purcell.

[Not mentioned in her mother's will; perhaps died before 1706.]

XXI MATTHEW PURCELL (cousin)

Charles Dalton, *English Army Lists and Commission Registers, 1661–1714*, vol. 2, p. 161.

Matthew Purcell, Ensign to Captain Scudamore, in Prince George of Denmark's Regiment of Foot. (Also under Colonel Sir Charles Littleton.) July 21st, 1688.

Ibid., vol. 4, p. 17.

For the Bomb Vessels, [A list of Officers, Gunners, etc., appointed for the present train and for the Bomb and Machine Vessels in the year 1694] . . . Commissary and Paymaster: Matthew Purcell. £0. 10. 0. *per diem*.

Ibid., vol. 4, p. 200 (1 May 1698).

Regimental Train of Artillery to be kept in time of peace. [Gentlemen of the Ordinance] Matthew Purcell.

[In entry for Feb. 1698/9 his wages are listed as £40 per annum.]

XXII THOMAS PURCELL (uncle)

1. British Museum, Add. MS. 5751B.
Westminster, no. 12, 22 Jan.—a penciled note—?1660; however, a similar warrant in PRO (LC 5/52, p. 38) is dated 22 Jan. 12 Ch. II, i.e. 1661.

Charles R/ We will and command that immediately upon sight hereof you deliver or cause to be delivered to our well-beloved servants Lancelot Thorneton, Clerk of our Wardrobes of Robes and Beads, John Duncomber, Paule Ferine, and Thomas Pursill, grooms of our robes, the several parcels hereafter mentioned for their liveries as hath been accustomed; that is to say to each of them fourteen yards of black satin for a gown, ten shillings the yard, three yards of black velvet to guard the same gown at eighteen shillings the yard, one fur of budge for the same gown price eight pounds, for furring of the same gown three shillings four pence, and for making of the same gowns six shillings eight pence. Item for eight yards of velvet for a coat at twenty shillings the yard, two dozen of silk buttons for the said coat at eight pence the dozen, two ounces of silk to it at two shillings the ounce, eight yards of cotton to line the same coat at eight pence the yard, and for making of the same coat six shillings and eight pence. Item three yards of velvet for a doublet at twenty shillings the yard, two dozen of silk buttons to it at eight pence the dozen, one ounce of silk to it, price two shillings. Three yards of fustian to line it at eight pence the yard, and for making of the same doublet three shillings and four pence. Item two yards and an half of marble cloth for a coat at twelve shillings the yard, two yards and an half of russet velvet to guard the same coat at eighteen shillings the yard, six yards of cotton to line the same coat at eight pence the yard, four ounces of silk at two shillings the ounce, two dozen of silk buttons at eight pence the dozen, and for making of the same coat six shillings eight pence. Item to each of them two yards and a half of green cloth for a summer coat etc. . . . . during their natural lives . . . Thomas Purcill and the others. . . . May it please your excellent Majesty: this containeth your Majesty's warrant . . . amounting to £40 per annum . . . signed

Will. Rumbold

2. *KM*, p. 121 (1660).

Mentioned as the first of ten musicians "that do service in the Chapel Royal whose salaries are payable in the Treasury of His Majesty's Chamber."

3. PRO: *Cal. S. P. Dom.* 1665—66 (no. 63), 28 May 1666.

Whitehall: The king to the Lord Treasurer.

Henry Cook, Thomas Purcell and other gentlemen of the Chapel Royal petition, on behalf of themselves, the pages of the Chapel, and boys whose voices have changed, for payment, there being no money assigned to the Treasurer of the Chamber for those purposes. Thinks his honour concerned therein and therefore wishes full and punctual payment of all that is due to them on the next assignment of moneys to the Treasurer of the Chamber.

4(*a*). *Cal. S. P. Dom.* 16 Feb. 1662/3.

Warrant to the Master of the Great Wardrobe . . . to deliver to Thos. Purcell, musician in place of Henry Lawes, materials for a camlet gown, guarded with black velvet, and furred; for a damask jacket and velvet doublet, and to pay for the lining and furring thereof. . . .

4(*b*). PRO: Pipe Office Declared Account (E 351) 547.

To Thomas Purcell, another of His Majesty's said musicians in the room and place of Henry Lawes, deceased, for his like wages and livery, payable as before, by virtue of His Majesty's warrant under the signet dated the 19th of November, Anno XIIIj^{to} Regni Regis Caroli Secundi, and due to him for IIIj^r years and a half ended at Midsummer 1667. £162. 11. 3.

5. Cheque-book, p. 85 (20 May 1671).

It is ordered that the old books and surplices shall be to the use of the Gentlemen of His Majesty's Chapel Royal, paying to the Sergeant of the Vestry twelve pence for the old book, and ten shillings apiece for their old surplices. Upon the testimony of Mr. John Harding, Gentleman for 30 years standing. As also Mr. Thomas Purcell, Mr. Alfonso Marsh and Mr. William Tucker, who aver they have often heard Mr. Nightingalle to testify the same, as an ancient privilege belonging to the said gentlemen.

6. *KM*, p. 235 (Oct. 1671).

Petition from John Clement, Thomas Purcell, and William Child, musicians of His Majesty's Private Music, that the arrears due to them from His Majesty's great wardrobe for the years 1669, 1670, and 1671, may be assigned to their fellow musician, Humphrey Madge.

7. *KM*, 245 (2 July 1672).

Whereas His Majesty is displeased that the violins neglect their duty in attending in his Chapel Royal, it is ordered that if any of the violins shall neglect to attend, either to practice or to wait in the Chapel, whensoever they have received notice from Mr. Purcell or Mr. Humphryes, that for such fault they shall be suspended from their places.

8. PRO: Audit Office Declared Account A.O.1/397/90 (1672).

Paid to Thomas Pursell at xx^{li} per annum for wages, and xvj^{li} ij^{s} vj^{d} per annum for a livery—due for four years and 3 quarters ended at Mic'mas 1672. clxxj^{li} xj^{s} x^{d} ob.

9. *Cal. S. P. Dom.* 1 Sept. 1673.

Warrant for payment to W. Ashburnham of £400 a year, to be paid to Thomas Purcell for the 20 musicians who attend the service in the Chapel Royal.

10. PRO: SP 29/360, no. 128.

For his Excellency Sir Joseph Williamson, Jan. 2nd [1673/4].

Sir, I am very glad of a command from you, because I must give you an answer, which I would to your first, and all your other kind letters, but you know I cannot compliment, and I should say very many kind things to you from the kitching [*sic*] but I cannot express them,—Sir, Mr. Stefkings was joined in patten with his father and is now settled in his place. Mr. [Thomas] Purcell hath been very kind to him and would be very glad to serve you in anything, and hath desired me to present his humble service to you, so doth Mr. Rogers and very many more of your good friends, pray be pleased to present my most humble service to Sir Lionall Jenkins; [and, (erased)] Sir you know you have a most faithful friend and humble servant of William Chiffinch.

[Endorsed:] London. Feb. 6, 1673/4. R $\frac{15}{25}$ Mr. Chiffinch.

11. *Cal. S. P. Dom.* 28 Sept. 1676.

Warrant to Sir Edward Griffin and the Treasurer of the Chamber for the time being for payment yearly during pleasure by equal quarterly payments to commence from Midsummer 1673 of £46. 10s. 10d. to Thomas Purcill, one of the Gentlemen of the Chapel Royal, to be disposed of to such uses as the King shall direct.

12. Edward Chamberlayne, *Angliae Notitia*, 12th ed. (1679), p. 171.

In the office of the Robes, besides the Master above mentioned one Yeoman Tobias Rustat, three grooms, Thomas Purcell and two more.

13. Ibid., 14th ed. (1682), p. 178.

Three grooms of the robes. Thomas Purcell, Gilbert Spencer, Robert Rustat.

14. British Museum, Harl. MS. 1911: Orders of a Musical Corporation, fo. 5*v*.

9 July 1664.

Ordered that Mr. Thomas Purcell be and is hereby chosen one of the Assistants to this Corporation of Music in the room and place of Dr. Charles Coleman, deceased. Signed, Nicholas Lanier.

11 July 1664.

Ordered that all His Majesty's music do give their attendance at the chamber at Durham Yard for practice of music when the Master of the Music shall appoint them upon for feature of 5*d*. each neglect. Signed Nich. Lanier, etc.

21 Jan. 1670.

Ordered that Mr. Pelham Humfrey be and is hereby chosen one of the assistants of the corporation of music in the room and place of Gregory Thorundon, deceased. These being present: Henry Cooke, Marshall, John Hingeston, George Hudson, John Lillie, wardens.

Monday, 24 June 1672 (fo. 10).

Whereas Henry Cooke, Esquire, being Marshal of the Corporation of Music in Westminster in the County of Middlesex hath requested the said Corporation to make choice of a fit person to succeed him in the said office of Marshal, he being by reason of sickness unable to attend the business of the said Corporation, it is therefore ordered by the said corporation that Thomas Purcell, gentleman, be Marshal and that he the said Thomas Purcell is hereby chosen and appointed Marshal of the said Corporation accordingly. John Hingeston, Deputy Marshall, Humfrey Madge and Pelham Humfrey, wardens, Antoni Robert, George Hudson, John Strong, John Lillie, John Rogers, Alphonso Marsh, John Harding.

15. PRO: LC "Miscellanea," 5/14, p. 80 (13 Dec. 1671).

A warrant to the Treasurer of the Chamber to pay unto Paul Ferine, Thomas Purcell and James Watson, grooms of His Majesty's robes, the sum of two and fifty pounds for their lodging out of Court fifty-two weeks, from the 20th of Aug. 1666, to the 20th of Aug. 1667, at the rate of twenty shillings by the week.

16(*a*). PRO: S.P. Dom. Entry Books (S.P. 44) 334, p. 208.

Our will and pleasure is that out of such our treasure as now is or hereafter shall be remaining in your hands you pay or cause to be paid yearly by quarterly payments the sum of forty six pounds ten shillings and ten pence unto our Tr. etc. [trusty and well-beloved?] Thomas Purcill one of the Gentlemen of Our Chapel to be by him disposed of and paid to such use as we shall direct without any further or other account to be by him given for the same. The first payment to commence from the Feast of St. John Baptist 1673 and to continue during our pleasure. And for etc. Whitehall, Sept. 28th, 1676. By His Majesty's command, J. W. To our etc. Sir Edward Griffin, Knight, Treasurer of our Chamber and to the Treasurer of our Chamber for the time being.

16(*b*). PRO: Pipe Office Declared Account (E 351) 2835: "Account of Henry Sidney, Esq., Gentleman and Master of His Majesty's robes . . . 1680–1681," fo. 4*v*.

Shoes, galoshes, boots and buskins with tennis shoes for His Majesty's use: £110. 13. 0. Seven pair of boots, viz. for Tobias Rustat, Yeoman of the Robes, Robert Rustat, Thomas Purcell etc. . . . at 35/ each pair: £12. 5. 0.

17. Testamentum Thomas Purcell. PCC: 138 Cottle (Somerset House). Nov. 1682.

In the name of God Amen. I, Thomas Purcell, of the parish of St. Martin-in-the-Fields in the county of Middlesex, Esq., being of sound mind and memory do make my last Will and Testament in manner following, revoking all other Wills by me formerly made. My soul I surrender up unto Almighty God, my Creator, in the merits of Jesus Christ, my Redeemer. My body I desire may have decent burial at the discretion of my executrix. My worldly estate I do dispose in this manner, viz.: I do give and bequeath unto my dear and loving wife Mrs. Katherine Purcell the messuage and house wherein I now dwell situate in the parish of St. Martin-in-the-Fields aforesaid in a street called the Pell Mell street with all the building and appurtenances thereunto belonging for all my terms and terms of years therein now to come and unexpired. I do likewise give and devise unto my said dear wife all and every my furniture, household stuff, household goods, plate, linen, and goods whatsoever in my said house and also all sum and sums of money, debts, and other things whatsoever any ways due or owing unto me from the King's Majesty, my Royal Master, or any of his officers or any other person or persons whatsoever, and also all other my personal estate of what nature or kind soever the same may be and do recommend unto her the payment of all and every my debts which I shall owe at the time of my death. I desire my children may have five pounds a piece given them out of the arrears of my salary and pension when the same can be received. I do make my said dear wife sole executor of this my last Will and in testimony that is my last Will, I have hereunto set my hand and seal this fourth day of June, one thousand six hundred eighty one, Annoque Regni Regis Caroli secundi Tricesimo tertio. Thomas Purcell. Signed sealed and published by the said Thomas Purcell for his last Will and Testament (the same being first read unto him) in the presence of Giles Channpneys, Andrew Card. Probatum fuit [huiusmodi] testimentum Londini[um] coram venerabili viro Henrico Fauconberge legum Doctore Surrogato venerabilis

et egregi viri Domini Leolini Jenkins Militis legum etiam Doctoris Curiae
Praerogativae cantuariensis Magistri Custodis sive commissarij Legitime
constituti octavo die mensis Novembris Anno Domini Millesimo Sexcen-
tesimo Octogesimo secundo Juramento Catherine Purcell Relictae et Executricis in dicto testamento nominato cui commissa fuit Administratio
omnium et singulorum bonorum jurium et creditorum dicti defuncti. De
bene et fideliter Administrando eadem ad sancta Dei Evangelia Jurat[a].
Exec.

18. PRO: Treasury Disposition Book (T 61) 2, pp. 194–95 (2 Dec. 1682).

Mistress Purcell, widow of Thomas Purcell [paid] £50.0.0.

19. Ibid., pp. 222–23.

£100 to Mistress Purcell.

20. Ibid., pp. 260–62.

£100 to Mistress Purcell.

21. Ibid., p. 1420.

£10.15.11 to Widow Pursell in part of £302.18.9 [arrears due] on [her
late husband's fee of] £426.5.10. £11.12.8½ to same in part of £244.6.10½
arrears [on his fee of] £46.10.10; £11.10.7½ to the same in part of
£144.10.0 arrears on [his fee of] £46.2.6.

22. PRO: Treasury Money Book (T 53) 4, p. 254 (22 Aug. 1683).

Money warrant for £100 to the executors of Thomas Purcell for half a
year to 1678, Sept. 29th.

[A similar payment is entered for 17 April 1683.]

XXIII THOMAS PURCELL (?son)

Westminster Abbey Reg., p. 216.

Burials: 3 Aug. 1686.
Thomas Purcell, a child (cloisters).

[Another Thomas Purcell is named in Sir Wasey Sterry's *The Eton College Register* (Eton, 1943,
p. 273): "Purcell, Thomas: 1672–1673, b. in London; k.s. 1672 aged 11. He may well be the
Thomas Purcell recorded by Foster in *Alumnae Oxoniensis*, q.v."]

XXIV PETERS FAMILY

1. Sir Bernard Burke, *The General Armory of England, Scotland and Wales* (London, 1684).

> *Peter*, Devon & Essex: Gu on a bend or. betw. 2 escallops ar. a cornish chough ppr. inter as many cinquefoils az; on a chief of the second, a rose between a fleur de lis, of the first, sceded or, barbed and leaved vest—Frest two lions heads erased, conjoined and endorsed, the dexter or, the sinister az, collared ringed and counterchanged.

> *Peter* (Canterland, Scotland) or, three boars' heads, couped gu.

2. J. L. Chester (ed. J. Foster), *London Marriage Licenses*, p. 1049.

> Thomas Peters, gentleman, of St. Clement Danes, 26, and Frances West, of St. Andrew, Holborn, widow, 25, at St. Mary Savoy, 17 Oct. 1627.

[In the actual register]: 18th Oct. 1627, Thomas Petre [*sic*] and Franncis West married by licence.

3. PCC: 66 Leeds (Somerset House). Will of John Baptist Peters of St. Mary-le-Bow, gentleman, 26 Feb. 10 Anne, 1711/12.

> To his wife, remainder of an unexpired lease of the house in Jermain [*sic*] St., St. James's, Westminster, and 2 houses at Richmond, Surrey, and 1 house in Cicill Court, St. Martin's Lane, and 1 in Great Carter Lane. To his son Richard, £100 and the diamond "which I constantly wear (which was my father's)." To his son John Baptist, house on the corner of Duffolk Lane, in the parish of All Hallows the Great. To his son Bryan, another house in All Hallows. Bequests to other children: son Ellis, daughter Martha, daughter Elizabeth, daughter Mary, daughter Frances. [All daughters apparently under 18.] Executrix was his wife. Proved 19th March 1711/12.

XXV SAMUEL WALL AND TEMPERANCE PURCELL (*née* Wall)

1. Mickleham parish records, book 1, p. 23.

> 26 March 1671.
> Collected on a brief for the redemption of captives lately taken by Turkish pirates, the sum of   £4.2.0.
> Samuel Wall, Gentleman   £0.5.0
> Miss Temperance Wall   £0.1.6

[N.B. Her marriage to Edward Purcell therefore probably took place in 1671 or 1672, since she was a maiden still in 1671, and gave birth to a child in 1673.]

2. Ibid., book 2, p. 88.

Baptisms: 1673.
Samuel, son of Mr. Edward Persill and Temperance, wife, was baptized December 22, 1673. [Book 2, p. 109 shows that he was buried a few days later, on 27 December.]

Baptisms: 1675.
Catherine Purcell, daughter of Mr. Edward Purcell and Temperance his wife was baptized July 1st, 1675.

3. Ibid., book 1, p. 30.

Towards the rebuilding of the Cathedral Church of St. Paul, London, there was collected in this parish of Mickleham, Septembris 9, 1678 . . . Mrs. Pursill £0. 1. 0. . . . The two richest men of the Parish viz. Mr. Sam Wall, an attorney of Staple Inn; and Mr. Thomas Tooth, a Courier, contributing nothing among us.

4. Ibid., book 1, p. 33.

Collected in the parish of Mickleham in the county of Surrey, October 11th, 12th, and 13th, 1680, towards the redemption of captives lately taken by Turkish pirates: Mrs. Purcell £00.02.06.

5. Book of Accounts kept for the Parish of Mickleham, book 3, pp. 1, 4, 5, and 18.

A tax by virtue of an Act of Parliament for the raising of 688 001^{li}. 09^{s} 01^{d} by the month for 6 months payable at quarterly payments.

1689. Mr. Wall in his own compution	00	07	08
More for Mr. Wall's land	00	10	00
30 May 1689. Mr. Wall for land in his own possession for half a year	00	02	06
5 Aug. 1689. Mr. Wall for land in his own possession	00	00	08
Tho. Turner for Mr. Wall's land	0	0	4
Tho. Arnold for Mr. Wall's land	0	0	1
John Arnold for Mr. Wall's land	0	0	1
Mrs. Richards for Mr. Wall's land	0	0	3

(Same payments for other quarters to 1689, 1690.)

1 Aug. 1690. Mr. Wall for his own land	00	02	00
Thomas Turner for Mr. Wall's land	00	04	02

1 March 1691/2. Further payments.

6. Mickleham parish records, book 1, p. 115.

Mr. Samuel Wall buried Aprilis 23mo, 1692.

7. PCC: Fane (Somerset House) 1692, fo. 76 (abstract from the will of Samuel Wall).

. . . the last will and testament of Samuel Wall of Mickleham in the county of Surrey. . . . I give and bequeath unto my niece [*sic*] Katherine Purcell all those my ten tenements in lying and being in White Lyon Court near Charterhouse Lane in the parish of St. Sepulchre's . . . (and) my tenement called Juniper House with the appurtenances together with all the fields and grounds and coppin woods thereunto belonging. . . .

All Mickleham lands to Temperance Purcell, [daughter] . . . [mentions] £43 remaining from far greater sum taken up to pay and discharge imprudent and extravagant debts contracted by . . . said daughter . . . [hence] executrixship granted (*pro tem.*) to Temperance Saintbarbe (niece) . . . who is to satisfy son-in-law Edward Purcell (husband [of] Temperance Purcell, *née* Wall). [Executrixship to be granted to Edward and Temperance Purcell upon discharge of above-mentioned debts. However, such a grant does not seem to have been recorded, but rather:] Probate April Vitesimo nono die, 1692/Samuel Wall vitesimo nono die probatum fuit testamentum Samuelis Wall . . . de Mickleham. . . .

8. Abstract of Indenture drawn up between Edward and Temperance Purcell and others on behalf of daughter Katherine Purcell, relating to ten tenements at White Lyon Court, mentioned above.

This indenture made the nineteenth day of September Anno Domini One thousand six hundred and ninety-eight . . . between Edward Purcell of Mickleham . . . and Temperance his wife, only daughter and heir of Samuel Wall . . . deceased, and John West. . . . Richard Badham, of West Smithfield, butcher [et al.—followed by long description of legal history of six of the ten tenements mentioned above] . . . now this indenture witnesseth that the said Edward Purcell and Temperance his wife for and in consideration of twelve pence apiece of lawful money of England to them in hand paid by . . . John West . . . (at the request and by the direction of Katherine Purcell . . .) have bargained, sold, assigned, and set over . . . to the said Richard Badham and Robert Browne . . . (above-mentioned tenements). (Signed and sealed by Edward, Temperance, and Katherine Purcell, witnessed by Daniel Purcell [authentic signature of the composer, verified by signatures in the British Museum], Edward Hobart, and Ph. Bird.)

APPENDIX TWO

Henry Purcell's Origins: A Genealogical Puzzle

To some who know of the delights and mysteries of Purcell's music, the intricate genealogical puzzle surrounding his life story seems neither very interesting nor important. Indeed, its solution might well have awaited a general revival of interest in the musical legacy he left.

However unimportant it may be, the task of sorting out various relationships in the Westminster Purcell families *is* extremely complicated. Moreover, Purcell genealogy has been sheltered from critical inquiry for several decades, because the solution seemed to have been worked out satisfactorily. It now appears, however, that the status quo in Purcell genealogical research may be other than satisfactory. The following account of my own recent investigations can be considered as nothing more than an interim report. But it is worth setting out in detail here, I think, if only to facilitate the discovery of further relevant information. When I may travel to England again, I hope to follow promising lines of investigation which can only be mooted here.

Most problems of tracing Purcell's family origins still remain to be solved. As is true of other aspects of his biography, scarcity of fact has left room for conjecture and confusion. First of all, no one knows exactly where he was born. The consensus of opinion, for what it is worth, has it that he was born in England (probably in London). Some go so far as to specify Westminster. Cummings even hazarded an exact address: St. Ann's Lane, Old Pye Street, Westminster. But surely this was a rash and improbable guess, for that is where Purcell lived after his marriage. Cummings's statement is questioned in the account in *Grove's* (2d ed.), which says that after the death of the elder Henry Purcell, the house in Great Almonry South became the family home. Dennis Arundell, in his excellent biography of Purcell, after citing a legendary invader named Purcell, who was the first Norman to land at Pevensey in 1066 and first to win guerdon land, identifies a "Mr. Purcell who was a ratepayer in Westminster in 1641, 1651, 1656 and 1659." He intimates that this person may have been Henry Purcell the elder, but warns that without a Christian name there can be no certainty. He also identifies a William and Thomas Purcell.[1]

One far-fetched legend, which would have it that he was born in France, has several impressive supporters. In Ernst Ludwig Gerber's *Historisch-biographisches Lexikon der Tonkünstler* (Leipzig, 1790–92), Purcell's name is entered as "Pourcell," with "Purcell" as an alternative spelling, and followed by the statement that he was born in France about the middle of the seventeenth century. This entry no doubt was based upon that published by another musical lexicographer, Johann Gottfrid Walther, who, in his *Musicalisches Lexicon* of 1732,[2] quoted Mattheson (*Critica Musica*, vol. 2, p. 148) to the effect that Purcell was born in France. Mattheson himself not only said that Purcell was French by birth, but also attacked an unknown opponent who could not accept his statement.

All this sounds quite implausible, and any solid piece of contrary evidence would outweigh it all. One may scoff at the notion of French origin, but an unsupported scoff is not more valid than an unsupported statement. And Mattheson did have the advantage of being alive at least fourteen years before Purcell died. What is more, it is not beyond possibility that Purcell may have been born in France. His birth took place during the Commonwealth period when any number of loyal Englishmen were residing abroad. Nor is it unthinkable (though it is improbable) that his parents, or at least his mother, may have been living away from England at the time of his birth. But the notion that he was actually a native Frenchman whose immediate family was French is, I think, nonsensical.

Walther's French spelling raises another interesting point. In France the word "pourcelle" (now obsolete, from the Latin *porcellus*) meant "boar." And Purcell's coat-of-arms shows three boars' heads—a Gallic device, which adds another mite, however insignificant, to the evidence that Purcell did have French connections of later provenance than those he inherited from Hugh Porcel, the Norman ancestor who came to England with William the Conqueror.[3] However, these "canting coats-of-arms" came into vogue in England in the sixteenth century. Westrup is probably right in assuming that Purcell had descended from

1. *Henry Purcell* (London, 1927), p. 9.

2. He also confused Henry with Daniel, as the beginning of the entry shows: "Pourcel (Daniel) ein an. 1696 verstorbener Componist, liegt zu London in der Westmünster-Kirche mit einer zwar kurzen, aber sehr schmeichelhaften Engländischen Grobschrift, welche auf Teutsch also lautet: 'Hier liegt Heinrich Purcell. . . .'"

3. John O'Hart, *Irish Pedigrees*, vol. 2, pp. 347 ff., as quoted in Westrup, p. 3.

an English family. But that he sprang from either the Shropshire, the Kilkenny, or the London branch of the family is, very likely, an erroneous conjecture, as we shall see.

There has also been a claim that Purcel was of Welsh extraction, according to the Cardiff *Western Mail* of 27 September 1930:

> It may not be generally known that Purcell, the famous musician, although born in London, was a descendant of the Purcells, for many years a leading family of the then little-known town of Cardiff, and one leading old writer mentions that several of Purcell's most popular productions are only alterations or improvements of ancient Welsh melodies, among which may be reckoned his "Joy to Great Caesar" which is very much in the Welsh style and adapted to a versification very common in the Welsh tongue.

Further inquires have at last brought further light on this matter. Here I can do no better than to quote the letter sent to me by Mr. J. E. Thomas, F.L.A., City Librarian of Cardiff Public Libraries, whose archivist prepared the following:

> The only basis for connecting the Purcell family of Cardiff with Henry Purcell, the great musician, seems to be the remarks made by Benjamin Heath Malkin in his work *The Scenery, Antiquities and Biography of South Wales* (2nd ed., London, 1807, vol. 1, pp. 222–3). "I have been told," Malkin writes "that Wilson the painter was born in the town of Cardiff, and that he was brother to Alexander Wilson, late surveyor of the customs in that port, as well as that he was brought up by his maternal uncle, Alexander Purcell, to the trade of a goldsmith, which he quitted on going to London for the profession of a painter. The celebrated musician Purcell was claimed as an ancestor, though not in direct line, by the Purcell's of Cardiff. Henry Purcell was probably born in London; as his father and uncle were both gentlemen of the chapel at the restoration of Charles the Second when he was only two years old. But there seems reason to think from his compositions that the principality may claim the honour of connecting itself with this great master, and probably through his relations in this town. Several among the most favourite of his productions are only alterations or improvements of ancient Welsh melodies, among which may be reckoned his Grounds. His 'Joy to Great Caesar' is very much in the Welsh style, and adapted to a versification very common in the Welsh language, but never, I believe, naturalized with the English, excepting in the loyal song written by Tom D'Urfey to the measure of that fine melody. Of his very favourite cantata, *From Rosy Bowers*, many of the parts or stanzas are on the most prevalent principles of Welsh versification, and such as both look and sound very uncouth in English poetry. From all these musical and poetical predilections, which could scarcely have been the work of chance, or

of accidentally meeting with a Welsh air, it is probable that he was introduced to his intimacy with this national style of melody and rhythm by family connection. There are no Purcells now remaining at Cardiff." We have never seen any other references to the Welsh connections of Henry Purcell and his music, and with regard to the latter our own music librarian is of the opinion that Malkin had very little ground for his assertions.

There are numerous references to members of the Purcell family of Cardiff in John Hobson Matthew's *Cardiff Records* (6 vols., Cardiff, 1898–1911), a work which will be available in the British Museum and probably at some of the larger London reference libraries, e.g. Westminster. The references can easily be traced by means of the comprehensive index in volume 6. They show that the Cardiff Purcells were a substantial and well-to-do family, but they contain no information which can be used in support of Malkin's statements.

Although Benjamin Heath Malkin was headmaster of Bury St. Edmunds Grammar School and later became the first professor of history in London University, he does not seem to have been very critical of the information given to him by his friends and acquaintances in South Wales. It is interesting to note that just before treating of Cardiff and the Purcells he eulogizes Edward Williams (Iolo Morganwg), and it would be still more interesting to know whether it was Edward Williams who supplied him with information about the Purcells of Cardiff, the connection with Henry Purcell and the "Welsh flavour" of the latter's music.

Biographies of Benjamin Heath Malkin and Edward Williams appear in the *Dictionary of Welsh Biography* (London, Honourable Society of Cymmrodorion, 1959).

18 January 1965

Apart from the fact that Purcell wrote no such song as "Joy to Great Caesar," the lack of evidence in support of his theoretical Welsh origins brings this theory also into serious doubt.

On this same subject Sir Frederick Bridge included in his *Twelve Good Musicians* (London, 1920, pp. 121–22) an interesting extract from a letter written by his brother, Chester. The lack of a first name for "Mr. Purcell" and the absence of any supporting evidence detract somewhat from the value of this communication, which nevertheless needs to be taken into account:

In 1661 the family had gone up to London and we find the Steward there and recording

Dec. 24, Paid for a quart of Purle with Mr. Purcell . . . 2d.

As a rule only the names of important personages are put in the accounts. As the Steward did not *live* in London, it looks as if Mr. Purcell was a former acquaintance from somewhere near Chirk. This place is on the borders of three counties of which Shropshire is one, and as the Purcells probably came from Salop, their birthplace or place of residence may have been at the Chirk end of the county. Possibly Mr. Purcell was an old friend of the Steward's. (Chirk Castle Accounts, kept by the steward of Sir Thomas Myddelton)

Sir Frederick goes on to say that the elder Henry Purcell (to whom the above quotation presumably refers) no doubt "lived in the place called the Almonry, where the 'singing men' had houses. These stood where the well-known Westminster Palace Hotel now stands. And here his distinguished son was born."

So much for a few of many extant hypotheses. A solider, though as yet not fully documented, case can be made for the establishment of Buckinghamshire as the county in England of which Purcell's father, Henry, and uncle, Thomas, were native. In Thornborough, Bucks., there flourished for a century or more before the Restoration a numerous colony of Purcells (mainly carpenters and artisans) who seem to be related not only to similar colonies elsewhere in the county (particularly at Water Eaton, near Oxford; near Bletchley, Bucks.; and at Buckingham), but also to some of the Purcell families in London.

As the reader will have noted, the first names of these Thornborough Purcells (see branches "B" and "C" of the family tree in Table 2) frequently correspond to the first names of London Purcells. Such correspondences are particularly noticeable in the families of Henry the elder and Thomas Purcell, traceable in London from about 1653 onward. The implied connection is described in the following excerpt from a letter of the late Mr. F. G. Gurney (of Egginton, Beds.) to Mr. A. Vere Woodman, F.S.A., of Wing, Bucks., written on 22 February 1939 and transmitted to me on 14 February 1961:

> There is hardly the slightest doubt that the great musician was a Bucks. man. His father, Henry, used for his sons the names used by the Oving[4] Purcells throughout. Henry Purcell, the father, was married by 1652 and was probably born between *c.* 1622 and 1631 (a statement according well with the fact that Henry Purcell of Thornborough was baptized in 1627, and Thomas Purcell in 1629/30).

All this might seem merely an interesting but wholly unsubstantiated hypothesis except for positive proof of a direct connection between the Buckinghamshire and London Purcells, in the form of an inscription on a stone in St. Katherine's chapel, at the east end of the south aisle in the parish church in Wing:

4. Oving is a small village in Buckinghamshire, near Wing, which lies between Aylesbury and Leighton Buzzard.

Here lies [the body of] Elizabeth, the wife of Henry Redman late of Ascot [and daughter of] Catherine and Thomas Purcell, yeoman of the robes and one of the Gentlemen of the Chapel Royal to Charles the 2nd [she died] Oct. 29 1733, Aged 73.

This inscription warrants, I believe, the recounting of a local Buckinghamshire legend, which otherwise might best be dismissed as just that and nothing more. According to this tale both Henry the elder and Thomas had been kidnapped to serve as choristers in the Chapel Royal in Westminster. There they settled in the early 1640s, founding the two families shown on branches "D" and "E" in Table 2, and founding also the family's musical fame, which was to be brought to its highest point by the younger Henry Purcell. The phrases in the above quotation shown in square brackets have been effaced by time since Mr. Gurney transcribed them some sixty years ago; however, the remaining lines can still be read. The parish register shows that Elizabeth Redman was buried on 30 October 1733, and other records reveal that from the early sixteenth century onward the Redmans and Purcells had lived side by side for over a hundred years in Oving. Both families disappear from the records about the beginning of the seventeenth century, but the names of the Redmans reappear around 1650, when they served as superior domestics in the household of the earl of Carnarvon.

The discovery of the inscription quoted above has brought to light a numerous family of Purcells in Thornborough, headed by one John Purcell, a carpenter in the employ of the Verneys, among whose sons were Thomas and Henry Purcell, both born in just about the right years to have emerged in Westminster society as mature citizens at the Restoration, as both the musicians by these names actually did. Moreover, this discovery has also brought to light a number of interesting connections between members of the Purcell families of Westminster and several prominent Buckinghamshire families, which connections upon investigation may well shed further light on the matter. Certainly it would be too much to explain all these relationships as coincidental. Before leaving London in 1682, Charles Purcell made a will, which was witnessed by Sarah Fynes—very probably the same young lady by that name who was buried in Wing parish church that May. A dozen years later Joseph Purcell married Sarah Dormer, as may be confirmed by an entry in the marriage register for St. James's, Duke's Place, dated 9 January 1693/4. Colonel Edward Purcell retired to the country residence of the earl of Abingdon (Montagu Bertie) near Wytham, Berks., whose daughter Catherine married Robert Dormer, possibly he of Dorton, also with connections in the area.[5] Another prominent person with strong connections in the Thornborough area was Dr. Richard Busby, a friend of young Henry Purcell's (as we know from his having bequeathed Henry a mourning ring). Finally, dwelling in Frances Purcell's neighborhood in Richmond at the time of her death were Peregrine Bertie, Ann Eeles—a William Eeles witnessed Henry Purcell's will—Amy Howlett, and several Dormers, all of whom had family connections in this very same area. These circumstances, it seems to me, plead for further investigation, even though the evidence they afford is circumstantial.

Whatever further investigations in Buckinghamshire records may bring to light, there is merit still in the accounts given by the earliest biographers (mainly Burney and Hawkins), who described Henry Purcell as the son of the elder Henry and the nephew of Thomas Purcell, who had adopted him upon his father's death early in August 1664. Supporting documents establish other members of the young composer's immediate family quite clearly. Elizabeth Purcell was his mother, Katherine his sister; and he had at least three brothers, two of whom may have been older than he (Edward and Joseph) and one (Daniel) who was certainly younger, despite Cummings's statement to the contrary.[6]

Then in 1937 Sir Jack Westrup, one of the pioneers of scientific "musicology" in England, pointed out in his brilliant, never-to-be-surpassed life of Purcell that he may well have been the son of Thomas, like the elder Henry a Gentleman of the Chapel Royal and, moreover, a very prominent member of the famous four-and-twenty fiddlers of Charles II. Sir Jack's arguments were as discerning as they were convincing, with the result that most modern books of reference and practically all subsequent biographical accounts discuss Thomas as father. To be sure, he did write to the celebrated bass singer John Gostling in 1679 refering to young Henry as his son. But such would naturally have been his habit if, as is likely, he had been acting in loco parentis for fifteen years. And it may be true that Thomas had a son named Edward, just as it is *certain* that young Henry had a brother by that name. But the assumption that Thomas's son and Henry's brother were one and the same cannot continue to be accepted tacitly (as it has been for nearly three decades now, with mischievous results to Purcell genealogy). It must be either proved, disproved, or labeled hypothesis.

The two opposing genealogies are given together (tables 1 and 2) for ease of reference.

5. Letter of A. Vere Woodman, 4 Sept. 1964.
6. In his article "On Henry Purcell and His Family," *PMA*, 1876–77, p. 8.

At first glance the various branches of either version of this Purcell family tree present a bewildering, indeed a Shakespearian, variety of possible mistaken identities. In the younger Henry Purcell's generation alone, the names Edward, Katherine, and Charles each appear twice, as if to imply that both families had soon run through a slender stock of suitable family Christian names. The confusion naturally arising from these has caused most of the trouble. It is not enough, for instance, to prove the notion that Henry Purcell had a brother by the name of Edward; it is necessary if he had a cousin by that name to show which is which—not an easy demonstration, since extant records seldom furnish anything beyond the minimum of information called for in any particular kind of account.

Proving that Purcell did have a brother named Edward is a fairly simple and straightforward exercise. The brother's career can be followed in detail through various court and military records, more or less as it is outlined in his epitaph, still to be read in its original state in the chancel at the Wytham parish church (see App. One, IV, 13).[7] Other records verify the data given on the stone, which prove to be correct, or nearly so throughout. In fact, only the statement that an Edward was a gentleman usher to Charles II appears to be unverifiable. Edward Chamberlayne recorded an Edward Purcell among those employed at court as gentleman usher in waiting, assistant, to come in at the first vacancy in the 1679 and 1682 editions of *Angliae Notitia* (pp. 162 and 166 respectively). But in the fifteenth edition, of 1684, Edward Purcell's name is nowhere to be found, although the appearance of four new persons who held the position shows that vacancies *had* occurred in the interim. On the other hand, Chamberlayne may merely have been careless in keeping up with promotions at court, for another account mentions Edward Purcell as gentleman usher, as does the gravestone, without the qualification "assistant."[8]

It may be that this Edward Purcell had begun his military career by this time. At any rate, in *English Army Lists and Commission Registers 1661–1714*, Dalton records for an Edward Purcell a fairly rapid rise from the lieutenancy to which he was commissioned in February 1685 to a captaincy by November 1687. On 8 June 1702 he was promoted to major, and on 1 March 1704 to the high rank of lieutenant-colonel (*vice* Lt.-Col. Rook) to Brigadier-General Seymour. Then on 1 May

7. The erroneous transcript published by Sir John Hawkins in his *A General History of the Science and Practice of Music*, vol. 2 (London, 1853), p. 749, has been followed by all subsequent scholars with mischievous results, since Edward Purcell's age at death reads "61," *not* "64."
8. See App. One, IV, 4 and 13.

TABLE I. (After Westrup, p. 307) Showing Henry as son of Thomas

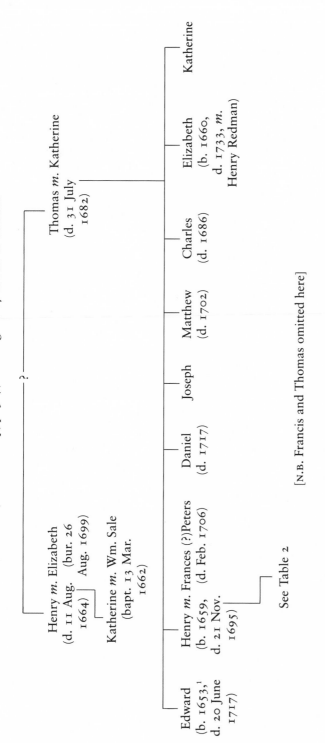

?

Thomas *m.* Katherine
(d. 31 July
1682)

Henry *m.* Elizabeth
(d. 11 Aug.   (bur. 26
1664)   Aug. 1699)

Katherine *m.* Wm. Sale
(bapt. 13 Mar.
1662)

Edward
(b. 1653,[1]
d. 20 June
1717)

Henry *m.* Frances (?)Peters
(b. 1659,   (d. Feb. 1706)
d. 21 Nov.
1695)

See Table 2

Daniel
(d. 1717)

Joseph

Matthew
(d. 1702)

Charles
(d. 1686)

Elizabeth
(b. 1660,
d. 1733, *m.*
Henry Redman)

Katherine

[N.B. Francis and Thomas omitted here]

1. As dated from Hawkins's erroneous transcription.

TABLE 2. Showing Henry as Son of Henry

Possible ancestors: *Sir Hugh Porcell*, who landed at Pevensey in 1066; *Roger Purcell* of Oxfordshire; or *Henry Purcell* of Fulham House.[1]

(A)

(B) John Purcell *m.* Sarah[2]
(will made 11 Aug. 1658, in Thornborough)

(C) William[3]   Edward   Elizabeth   Ann   Sarah   Stephen   Thomas *m.* Katherine   Henry *m.* Elizabeth   John   (etc.?)
[*m.* Hotton]   [*m.* Horne]   [*m.* Howe]   (W.A.R., 205)   (will adm. 7 Sept. 1699)

(D) Matthew[4]   Edward *m.* Temperance Wall   Francis[5]   Charles[6]   Elizabeth[7] *m.* Henry Redman   Katherine   Thomas
(b. ca. 1650, d. or mvd. to London bef. 4 June 1686)   (b. ca. 1653; app. Groom of Privy Ch. 1673)   (app. Capt. 1684; d. Guinea, Mar. 1686; will admin. May 1686)   (b. ca. 1660; bur. Wing Parish Church, 30 Oct. 1733, age 73)

(E) Edward[8]   Charles[9] *m.* ?   Henry *m.* Frances (?)Peters[10]   Katherine[11] *m.* Wm. Sale   Joseph[12] *m.* Sarah Dormer   Daniel[13]
(b. ca. 1657–58)   (b. ca. 1659; d. 21 Nov. 1695)   (bur. 14 Feb. 1706)   (20 June 1691; executed mother's will 7 Sept. 1699)   (b. ca. 1663)

(F) Henry[14]   Elizabeth   Ann[15] (b. 26 Dec. 1707)
(both minors as of 27 June 1695, when they were made wards of Eliz. Purcell, widow)

(G) Henry[16]   John Baptista[17]   Thomas[18]   Henry[19]   Frances[20] *m.* L. Welstead   Edward[21] *m.* Anne   Mary-Peters[22]
(bapt. 9 July 1681)   (bapt. 9 Aug. 1682)   (bur. 3 Aug. 1686)   (bapt. 9 June 1687, bur. 23 Sept. 1687)   (b. 30 May 1688)   (b. 6 Sept. 1689)   (bapt. 10 Dec. 1693)

(H) Frances[24] (bapt. 2 Sept. 1708)   Frances (b. 19 Apr. 1711)   Edw. Henry[23] *m.* Abigail (b. ?26 Nov. 1716)   Frances[25] (b. 12 Apr. 1761)

1. See Arundell, *Henry Purcell*, p. 9; Westrup, p. 3; and London County Record Office (BRA 203/102) in connection with Fulham House, 4 Jan. 1326/7.

2. Bucks. County Record Office, Aylesbury.

3. Arundell, p. 9.

4. Possibly the Matthew Purcell registered as an ensign 21 July 1688 (Dalton, *English Army Lists*, vol. 2, p. 161).

5. PRO: LC "Miscellanea," 5/53, fo. 50v, passim.

6. PCC 63 Lloyd.

7. Wing Parish Registers.

8. Gravestone, Wytham Parish Church; W.P.L. Acct. Will exec. by Mary Williams.

9. Admin. Act. 1695, fo. 115[v]. Listed as a Bishop's Boy in 1672, when he was at least fourteen years of age, he probably was born ca. 1657–58.

10. See coat of arms, plate 13 (PCC 11 July 1706).

11. Westrup, p. 307.

12. St. James's, Duke's Place, marriage license: Guildhall Library MS. 7894.

13. A Chapel Royal choir boy as late as 8 Apr. 1679, he could have been no older than sixteen. Notice of the candidacy of Edward Purcell for organist's place in the room of his uncle Mr. Daniel Purcell, deceased, in the *Daily Courant*, 11 Dec. 1717. Will adm. by brother Joseph Purcell, 17 Jan. 1718.

14. Admin. Act 1605, fo. 115[v].

15. Christchurch, Aldegate St. (Harl. Soc. Reg, vol. 21, p. 110).

16. All Hallows the Less: Marriage, Burial, and Baptism Registers: Royal College of Arms, MS 5160/2, n. 12 (baptism) and p. 17 (burial) respectively.

17. *Westminster Abbey Reg.*, pp. 72 and 206 respectively.

18. Ibid., p. 216.

19. Ibid., p. 219.

20. Ibid., p. 74.

21. Ibid.

22. *Westminster Abbey Records*, p. 76.

23. PRO: LC "Miscellanea," 5/70, p. 175.

24. Westrup, p. 307.

25. *The Register of St. Clements, Eastcheap and St. Martin Orgar.* Transcribed and edited by A. W. Hughes Clarke (1937).

1711 he sold his commission to a German officer, Kempenfeldt, but did not leave the regiment, according to official record, until May 1716, slightly more than a year before he died. (The details of the sale of the commission have not come to light, but it is difficult to imagine that within a year he would have been destitute, as some have been led to conjecture from the poetic phrases on the stone: "decayed with age, and broken with misfortunes.") At any rate this Edward Purcell, who can be identified in the lively miniature portrait (probably by Thomas Forster) now in the Holburne Museum at Bath (see plate 43), is certainly the brother of the younger Henry Purcell, and hence is also brother of Daniel and the son of the elder Henry Purcell.

But what of the Edward Purcell who took part in the legal proceedings attendant upon the administration of the will of Charles Purcell who died in 1686 off the coast of Guinea?[9] He is named as brother and executor of Charles's will (drawn up on 4 June 1682), which specifies Katherine Purcell as his mother and Elizabeth and Katherine as his sisters. Moreover, in the Chancery Proceedings he is referred to as Edward Purcell of Mickleham, gentleman,[10] and not as Lieutenant Edward Purcell—a significant difference. The proving of the will gave rise to a trying situation, which got Edward Purcell into the Courts of Chancery.

Charles, when he died, had had in his cabin on His Majesty's sloop *Le George* considerable bullion, brandy, and other valuable portable property. After his death, one William Bayley, a mate of Captain Charles Purcell, who sailed also on the companion ship, the *Orange Tree*, acquired the lot. But he also died at sea, so that these goods fell at last into the hands of his wife, Anne Bayley, who thus acquired considerable wealth and achieved widowhood all at once. The wealth she was unwilling to part with, hence Edward Purcell's taking her to court. In any event, this Edward, referred to as Mr. Edward Purcell of Mickleham, was probably very busy with this case all through the latter part of 1686 and most of 1687. Hence it is unlikely that he should be identified as the newly fledged Lieutenant Edward Purcell, who ought to have been fully occupied discharging new responsibilities involved in various military affairs in the west of England, in Ireland, and elsewhere.

The name Mr. Edward Purcell of Mickleham provides an important lead, for it appears in the Mickleham parish records in connection with

9. App. One, I, 1.
10. App. One, I, 4.

the birth in 1673 of a son, Samuel Purcell (buried that same year on 27 December), and the baptism of a daughter, Katherine Purcell, in 1675. This Edward therefore must have married his wife, Temperance (*née* Wall) at least as early as 1672, when Edward Purcell of Westminster would have been between fourteen and sixteen years old, for Temperance Wall is last mentioned as a maiden in an entry for 26 March 1671. This is not an impossible age for marriage in those days, but somewhat improbable, in view of the fact that Temperance Wall was the daughter of one of the chief citizens—at least one of the wealthiest —of Mickleham, as is known from another entry in the parish registers (see App. One, XXV, 3). No record of the marriage itself has come to light, so that a more precise date is unobtainable at present. However, Lieutenant Edward Purcell's youth, his military preoccupation, and the fact that he died a bachelor, neither his will nor his epitaph making mention of relatives other than his father and famous brother, all rule against his being the husband of Temperance Wall or the father of this Katherine Purcell.

At any rate, old Samuel Wall died in 1692, leaving his Mickleham estate to one Edward Purcell and Temperance (his only daughter) and ten messuages, tenements, etc., to their child, Katherine Purcell, his only granddaughter. However, she did not come into possession of all of these. At least six were relinquished by Edward and Temperance Purcell, who were paid twelve pence apiece for their interest, according to the terms of an indenture drawn up, signed, sealed, and delivered on 19 September 1698. (Actually the Purcells may have lost out altogether here, for the names of Edward, Temperance, and Katherine are nowhere to be found in contemporary records.)[11]

At any rate, the evidence appears to establish the identity of two Edward Purcells who were in and about London during the last quarter of the seventeenth century and the first decade of the eighteenth. Proof positive may never be found, but to relate to one Edward Purcell all the records listed in Appendix One, IV, involves so many difficulties that the case is indeed improbable, if not totally impossible:

1. Edward Purcell would have had to marry at the age of fourteen or fifteen, or possibly sixteen.

---

11. An "Edward Purcell of St. Sepulchers" appears in the testamentary records now housed in Somerset House (PCC: 29 Irby), but he cannot be the same man, having died in Feb. 1695 and left a widow named Sarah Purcell. Temperance is likewise unrecorded, or only elusively so. But Katherine's name turns up again at the bottom of Matthew Purcell's will, which she witnessed in 1702. Her signature on this document and that made four years earlier on the indenture discussed above are precisely, unquestionably identical.

2. Captain Edward Purcell would have alternatively been styled by his military rank and as Mr. Edward Purcell of Mickleham.

3. He would have taken a great deal of time off from military duties for litigation attendant upon the execution of Charles Purcell's will.

4. Lieutenant-Colonel Edward Purcell would have died a bachelor, away from the properties in Mickleham (and elsewhere), which he and his wife, Temperance, had inherited in 1698, with no mention of his daughter or wife.

5. In the codicil to his will (see App. One, IX, 11, above) and elsewhere, Lieutenant-Colonel Edward Purcell is mentioned as "of the parish of St. Margaret's, Westminster," whereas the putative cousin is consistently referred to as Mr. Edward Purcell, gentleman, of Mickleham.

6. Edward Purcell would have had to be son to both Henry and Thomas Purcell at one and the same time, for an Edward Purcell is definitely referred to as both brother to the younger Henry Purcell and brother to Matthew Purcell, son of Thomas.

7. Edward Purcell would have been charged with heavy responsibilities in Charles II's Secret Service at a very tender age, hence my belief that Edward Purcell, son of Thomas, was very likely he who is mentioned in the *Calendar of Treasury Books* as receiving a warrant on 25 March 1673 for "100 marks per an. . . . to be for preventing uncertain charges (by bills) which he shall be put to for His Majesty's service about making ready of standing houses and progress houses in the [King's] removes and other services as Gentleman Usher *Daily Waiter Assistant*." [Italics mine] It is unlikely that such heavy responsibility would have been entrusted to Edward, son of Henry, then but sixteen or seventeen. However, other records of an Edward Purcell serving as gentleman usher at the court of Charles II probably refer to the son of Henry Purcell. Thomas, incidentally, placed another son, Francis, in similar employment, as groom of the Privy Chamber, then groom of the robes to Charles II, and also as housekeeper at Somerset House, Queen Catherine of Braganza's abode.[12]

If Colonel Edward was the son of Henry and Elizabeth, then the question also arises, why was he not chosen to administer his mother's estate in 1699 instead of Katherine, who is actually named as executrix?[13] Quite simply, Edward, then still an officer in Colonel Henry Trelawney's 4th Regiment of Foot (1692–1702), would have been very busily occupied and far from the scene, either in the Low Countries,

---

12. See Genealogical Table 2, under Thomas Purcell, and n. 5. See also App. One, XI passim.
13. App. One, IX, 3.

where the regiment was on intermittent duty from 1689 until 1715, or in Ireland, where the unit was often called, or perhaps elsewhere on the continent.

Nor is it surprising to find that Daniel Purcell could not afford the time to act as his mother's executor, since he would have been busy preparing for the London theatrical season; it would therefore have been more logical for Katherine Sale (*née* Purcell) to undertake the business. Whatever the truth of the matter might be with regard to this small detail, it is in a document having to do with Daniel Purcell that we find the final, clinching evidence, which shows both Daniel and Henry the younger to have been the sons of Henry Purcell the elder. First though, to corroborate their relationship as brothers, in the *Daily Courant* for 12 December 1717, Edward Purcell (son of Henry the younger) advertised his application for the post of organist "in the room of his *uncle* [italics mine], Dr. Daniel Purcell, deceased."

Proof that Daniel and also, therefore, Henry were sons of Henry Purcell turns up in the likeliest of all places. Daniel Purcell was organist at Magdalen College, Oxford, from 1689 to 1696 (for which latter year, having moved to London in May of 1695, he shared his pay with Benjamin Hecht). In the Magdalen College registers he is entered thus:

> 1688. Purcell, Daniel, res. 1695. Son of Henry Purcell, Gentleman of the Chapel Royal *obiit* 1718. He was brother of Henry Purcell. . . .[14]

This leaves little room for doubt that Henry was also son of Henry, and this little room is seriously diminished by another piece of evidence brought to light recently by the researches of Rev. John A. Fitch (vicar of Reydon) into the history of the Hingeston family. He discovered the information—and passed it on to Sir Jack Westrup, who gave it to me—that John Hingeston had in December of 1683 willed £5 to his godson "Henry Pursall (son of Elizabeth Pursall)."

There remain two small grains of doubt to be removed, however. Could there have been a second young Henry Purcell who was Hingeston's godson, but not to be identified as his apprentice? On legal as well as logical grounds the answer must be "No." Hingeston's will was carefully drawn up, and possible confusion on this score would have been cleared up, especially where one of the Henry Purcells would have been so famous already. Then, accordingly, one might well ask why so

---

14. J. R. Bloxham, ed., *A Register of the Presidents, Fellows, Demies . . . of St. Mary Magdalen College*, vol. 2, p. 203 (see also App. One, III, 5). The fact pointed out by Westrup that Anthony à Wood first entered Daniel Purcell as "son of Henry Purcell" later crossing out "son" and replacing it with the word "brother" does not indicate that he had discovered his own mistake, but only that young Henry had become famous meanwhile (see App. One, III, 1).

small a gift and such scant reference to a composer already gaining national recognition. Why indeed? we inquire from our present vantage point, knowing what Henry Purcell was to become. But to Hingeston he may well have seemed a tiresome young assistant, too ambitious and newfangled, and too talented for comfort. Was he not just then composing sonatas in the Italian vein, brashly turning his back on the somber English instrumental polyphony that Hingeston knew and loved? Perhaps it is a wonder that Hingeston mentioned him at all. Whatever the case as concerns Hingeston versus Purcell, this statement definitely establishes Henry Purcell's parentage on the distaff side and, presumably, affirms that the elder Henry was his father.

The information that has led to the setting up of the second genealogical table shown above may be summarized quickly. That the famous composer's father was Henry and his uncle was Thomas seems much more tenable than the contrary theory. However, it is quite probable that all the younger members of both families referred to one another as brothers and sisters, at least after 11 August 1664, when the elder Henry died. This possibility, all the more probable in view of Thomas Purcell's reference in 1679 to Henry as his son, suggests an interesting, possibly valid, solution to the strange duplication of first names. That there were two Charles Purcells seems undeniably true. But given the looseness of reference suggested above, there is no reason to insist that there were really two Edwards (although the contrary case raises many difficulties, none is insuperable) or two Katherines, sons and daughters of Henry and Thomas respectively. However, there were undoubtedly two Charleses.

To summarize by way of conclusion, then, it seems fairly certain that two families of Purcells moved to London, settling in or near Westminster during the Commonwealth period, and that young Henry, named after his father, was born in the shadow of Westminster Abbey, where he later was to be established as organist and England's most celebrated musical genius. After his father's death, he may have moved to live with his widowed mother in South Tuttle (i.e., Tothill) Street, or he may have moved into the more fashionable area (which was to become the parish of St. Martin-in-the-Fields) where his uncle Thomas held property in Pall Mall. Even though the traditional assumption that Thomas adopted him in 1664 or 1665 cannot be proved (or disproved), it is safe to assume that he would have taken interest in the rearing of his nephew, in his schooling, and, particularly, in his musical training. After fifteen years he would have been entirely justified in referring to Henry as his son, without qualification, both by force of habit and contemporary custom.

At any rate, this mention of Henry as his son by Thomas dwindles into relative insignificance in the face of all the new solid evidence that has come to light—not to mention the fact that the source for this statement has been neither examined nor evaluated for over fifty years now.

APPENDIX THREE

Iconography: Purcell Portraiture

ACCORDING TO THOMAS CARLYLE, a biographer finds most valuable assistance to his literary efforts in "a good portrait if one exists; failing that, even an indifferent if sincere one." But what is to be done about the situation prevailing in Purcell portraiture, where some of the best portraits portray the wrong person, one of which appeared recently on the front cover of a Purcell Society Edition publication and still turns up from time to time? Of the correctly identified, authentic portraits of Henry Purcell, only a few are good or even sincere, and many are poor copies unskillfully executed, or engravings that have descended through too many generations to be of much value.

Thus, we begin with a situation in which portraits of two or more different persons are actually taken to represent one and the same famous composer. Fortunately there is little doubt about which of the persons so variously represented is the real Henry Purcell. Several portrait engravings published during or immediately after his lifetime bear the stamp of authenticity to full satisfaction. Because we know that they were widely accepted either while he was alive or later, by many who had known him intimately, we may regard them with confidence. Thus there can be no question about the engraving published with the *Sonatas of III Parts* in 1683 or that appearing in *Orpheus Britannicus* in 1698. (See items 4, 5, 20, 21, 24, and 25 in the following list of portraits for further information on these and other authentic likenesses. Other items on the list that at least represent the right person include nos. 2, 3, 6, 7, 9, 13, 14, and most of the engravings, although many of the latter suffer from the ailment mentioned at the end of the first paragraph above.)

Of the forty-two items in the list of portraits, twenty-four of which are reproduced below, twelve are lost; nine identify the wrong person;

seven are authentic and good, or at least sincere; thirteen are authentic but poor (in my opinion); and one is corrupt or possibly forged. As a first step toward creating order out of this confusion, here is a list of extant paintings, drawings, and engravings; each entry is followed by commentary regarding location and cross-references to the Portrait List and plates.

PORTRAIT LIST

I. Paintings

A. Portraits of Purcell That Are More or Less Authentic

1. 1683?: Original painting for the engraved frontispiece in the *Sonatas* of 1683.
—Unknown. Possibly the *Purcell's Head Tavern* sign. See nos. 12, 24, 26.

2. 1685?: Painting said by W. A. Shaw in 1920 to be a portrait of Purcell, age 22. Inscription: "Henry Purcell, 1685." Size 29 × 23 inches. Oils on canvas (plate I.A).
—Source and present location unknown. Reproduced from *Musical Times*, Sept. 1920.

3. 1689?: Painting also said by W. A. Shaw to be a portrait of Purcell, age 31. Inscription: "Henry Purcell, *aetat.* 31, *An.* 1689." Size 9 × 6 inches. Oils on panel (plate I.B).
—Source and present location unknown. Reproduced from *Musical Times*, Sept. 1920.

4. Before 1695?: Rectangular version resembling no. 5, probably derived from no. 19, also attributed to Godfrey Kneller.
—In possession of Mr. H. M. Calmann in 1948. Present location unknown.

5. Before 1695?: Painting traditionally ascribed to Godfrey Kneller, now removed to category "anonymous" by authorities in the National Portrait Gallery, London. Inscription: Mr. "Henry Purcell." Size 23 × 21 inches. Oils on canvas (plate III.H).
—National Portrait Gallery no. 2150.

6. 1695?: Painting by, or after, Johann Baptist Closterman, supposed to have been done from a bust copied from a death mask taken by Sir Christopher Wren. Size 29 × 24 inches. Oils on canvas (plate IV.P).
—National Portrait Gallery no. 1352.

7. 1695–98?: Painting said by W. A. Shaw to be a portrait of Purcell and ascribed to Closterman (plate IV.Q).

—Source and present location unknown. Reproduced from *Musical Times*, Sept. 1920.

8. 1695–98?: A replica, reputedly related to the two preceding items, mentioned in the article on Purcell in Grove V.
—Dyrham Park, Chippenham. Lost.

9. ?: Painting of Purcell said to have belonged to Dulwich College, and supposed to have disappeared about 1794. From the engraved reproduction (see no. 29), it would appear to have been roughly contemporaneous with the two preceding portraits.
—Lost.

10. ?: An undated, unsigned painting last seen in Stroud, Gloucestershire. It is unlike Purcell as he appears in the authentic portraits and is probably spurious.
—Source and present location unknown.

11. ?: A painting that appears to be either a copy from no. 5 above or a retouched portrait of someone other than Purcell. It is probably the same portrait as that reported by Cummings in the A. F. Hill collection.
—Source and present location unknown.

12. ?: The *Purcell's Head Tavern* sign.
—Lost. Possibly the same as no. 1. This painting belonged to one Kennedy, keeper of the Purcell Head Tavern in Wych Street, bassoonist and member of the opera band at Covent Garden.

13. After 1698: A still life by E. Collier (?), depicting several musical instruments, two MS music books, and two printed music books opened to their title pages. One of these is the *Violin Primo* part of *A Collection of Ayres compos'd for the Theatre* of 1697, with an engraved portrait of Purcell showing as the frontispiece. No extant copy of this publication has this engraving, which appears to be the same as that used for the frontispiece of the 1698 edition of *Orpheus Britannicus* (see no. 25). Size 27½ × 47 inches. Oils on canvas (plate IV.S).
—Now in the private collection of Mrs. E. Croft-Murray.

14. Before 1695?: A painting similar to National Portrait Gallery no. 2150 (see no. 5).
—Now in the private collection of Jeremy Lemon.

B. *Works in Which the Subject Is Not to Be Identified with Henry Purcell*

15. Ca. 1695–1700?: Painting of Daniel Purcell (?) by Closterman (?). Almost full length–close up. Size 22 × 18½ inches. Oils on canvas (plate V.V).
—National Portrait Gallery no. 1463.

27. ?: Engraving preserved in Burney: *Theatrical Portraits;* vol. 7, p. 50

16. Ca. 1695–1700?: Another almost full-length painting very similar to the preceding one except for minor details. Size 22½ × 18 inches. Oils on canvas.
—Worcester Cathedral.

17. 1705?: Half-length painting of Daniel Purcell (?) by Closterman (?), which has a pedigree reaching back to Henry Purcell's grandson, Edward. Traditionally described as a portrait of Henry Purcell, early owners having explained the obvious incompatibility with other Purcell portraits as being the result of his last illness. Size 28½ × 24 inches. Oils on canvas (plate V.X).
—Royal Society of Musicians, London.

18. Thomas Clark portrait said to be of Purcell by writer of the Purcell article in *DNB*, but it is certainly not.
—Dulwich College board room.

19. 1693: Painting reported to have been in the Royal College of Music, London. Inscription: "Henry Purcell 1693." Erroneous identification. (The painting, a copy of which is shown in plate V.W, was in RCM all along, being effectively hidden above the entryway to a rather dark room. Because it resembles neither the authentic nor any of the other mistaken identifications, this painting has escaped notice for nearly a century.)
—Royal College of Music, London.

II. Drawings

A. *Henry Purcell*

20. Portrait of Henry Purcell, inscribed "Purcell"—black chalk heightened with white, bearing the inscription of William Seward: "Purcell the musician / dra(wn) some have supposed by Sir Godfrey / Kneller." There is a dedicatory letter: "Carolus Burney / Artis Musicae Doctori / Viro / Orphei Britannica nil exemplum / Arte suae praestantissimo necnon bonis literis excultissimo / Moribus ingenuis / Ac orationis lepore, ac gratia ornatissimi / Hanc Purcelli Imaginem / dd / Illuius Amantissimus / W.S. / 1791." Both the inscription and the letter formerly were on the backing (plate III.F).
—National Portrait Gallery no. 4994.

21. Before 1695?: A drawing traditionally ascribed to Kneller; although this ascription is probably as doubtful as that for no. 5, as it appears to be very closely related to it. It has been suggested that this may have been a study for the painting. Black chalk on lilac paper heightened with white. Size 15¾ × 10⅝ inches (plate III.G).
—British Museum, Prints and Drawings Room.

B. *Daniel Purcell (?)*

22. ?: Drawing in which the subject is clearly identifiable as the sitter for portraits nos. 15–17. It would appear that this drawing is in fact a copy from either no. 15 or 16, because it agrees with these in practically all details; study for the portrait (? Daniel Purcell) in the National Portrait Gallery attributed to Closterman. Size 8⅞ × 6⅛ inches. Black and white chalk on brown paper.
—Christ Church College Library, Oxford.

III. Bust

23*a*. Before 26 November 1695. Bust of Henry Purcell, reported to have been done from a death mask taken by Sir Christopher Wren. For some time there was a bust of Purcell in the Music School at Oxford, which may have been one and the same.
—Lost.

23*b*. Death mask.
—Lost.

IV. Engravings

A. *Henry Purcell*

24. 1683: Published as the frontispiece to the *SONNATA'S / OF III PARTS: / TWO VIOLLINS AND BASSE: / To the Organ or Harpsecord . . . Printed for the AUTHOR: / And Sold by I. Playford and I. Carr . . . 1683. / Tho. Cross Junior Sculpt. /* and labeled: "*HENRICI PURCELL, / Aetat: Suae* 24 . . ." (with scutcheon) (plate II.C).
—Original unknown. Possibly from *Purcell's Head Tavern* sign. See nos. 1, 12, 24.

25. 1698: Published as the frontispiece to *ORPHEUS BRITTANICUS, / A / COLLECTION OF ALL / The Choisest SONGS / FOR / One, Two, and Three Voices. / COMPOS'D By. Mr. Henry Purcell. / . . . J. Heptinstall for Henry Playford . . . MDCXCVIII* and labeled: *Henricus Purcell / Aetat. Suae,* 37. 95. *I. Closterman pinx / R. White Sculp* . . . (with Purcell coat of arms). The same engraving (?) appears in the painting listed as no. 13, where it is shown as the frontispiece to *A / COLLECTION / OF / AYRES, / Compos'd / For the Theatre . . . J. Heptinstall, for Frances Purcell . . . 1697* (plate IV.R).
—Originally traditionally held to be the painting no. 6 (plate IV.P).

26. 1776: Engraving by C. Grignion in Hawkin's *General History of the Science and Practice of Music,* London, 1776.
—From *Purcell's Head Tavern* sign (?). See nos. 1, 12, 22.

(British Museum, Prints and Drawings Room). The sculpturesque quality of this engraving suggests that if not copied from a painting, it might possibly have been copied from the missing bust (plate III.J).
—From the painting no. 8?

28. 1777: Engraving for *Universal Magazine* for December. Printed for J. Kinton at the *King's Arms* in Paternoster Row (plate II.D).
—From the paintings nos. 1 or 22?

29. 1794: "Henry Purcell / Musician & Actor." S. Harding del., W. N. Gardiner sculpt. Published 1794 by E. & S. Harding, in *Biographical Mirrour.* "From an original picture in Dulwich College" (plate III.K).
—From the painting no. 9?

30. 1798: "Purcell." Engraved by T. Holloway from a drawing by Sir Godfrey Kneller in the possession of Dr. Burney. "Published as the Act directs by I. Johnson—St. Paul's Churchyard" (plate III.I).
—From the drawing no. 19.

31. 1801: "Purcell" on a sheet of medallions with miniatures of Blow, Croft, Arne, and Boyce, drawn by "R. Smirke," engraved by "Drayton."
—Purcell miniature from the Closterman painting, listed as no. 5 above (see plate IV.T, cf. plate IV.R).

32. 1823: Engraving by W. Pinnock, said to be from no. 5 (see Grove V, p. 1002), but more likely from the previous engraving (no. 29), because it is turned the other way round and appears to be at least once more removed from the original, although otherwise almost identical (plate III.L).

33. 1846: "Purcell. Engraved by W. Humphrys from a drawing by Edw. Novello after the original picture by Sir Godfrey Kneller in the possession of Edward Bates, Esq." (plate III.M).
—From nos. 9 or 27?

34. ?: Engraving by H. Adlard, which may have been taken from the original drawing, or may have been copied from the frontispiece to *Orpheus Britannicus* listed as no. 25 (plate IV.U).
—From nos. 6 or 23.

35. ?: Henry Purcell and Geminiani. Date, source, and provenance unknown. The portrait of Purcell appears to be a crude copy of no. 23 (plate II.E).
—From no. 22?

36. ?: "Purcell." An engraving appearing as part of a decorative title ornament for *What shall I do to show how much I love her?* Engraved by

W. J. Linton from a drawing by H. Avelay. Date, source, provenance, and authenticity most uncertain (plate III.N).

37. 1815: *Six figures design'd and etch'd by Edward Purcell*

B. *Engravings from the Portraits of Daniel Purcell (?)*

38. An engraved photo-mezzo by E. Gilbert.
—From no. 21.

39. A mezzotint by G. Zobel.
—From no. 17

40. An engraving published by Hardy & Page.
—From no. 17.

41. Portrait of Henry Purcell (?) oil, attributed to Volders (plate III.O).
—Only photostat available.

In searching, classifying, verifying, and discussing both genuine and spurious portraits of Henry Purcell, the need for clarity, order, and extensibility have best been served by medium, material, and technique, which have provided the basis of organization for the foregoing list of portraits. However, reproductions of these portraits in this Iconography will be grouped according to similarities of subject and style of portrayal, cutting across medial boundaries between paintings, drawings, engravings, and so forth. Sorting out reproductions of the main portraits now extant, we discover five distinct categories: boyhood and early youth (plates I.A–B); Purcell as a rising young composer (plates II.C–E); Purcell as an established figure on the English musical scene (plates III.F–O); post-mortem paintings and engravings (plates IV.P–U); and portraits that do not portray Henry Purcell (plates V.V–X).

PLATE I.A. Henry Purcell holding a tenor violin, age ?16. Source and present location unknown (see Portrait List, no. 2)

PLATE I.B. Henry Purcell composing at a table, age ?20. Source and present
location unknown (see Portrait List, no.'3)

PLATE II.C. Henry Purcell (Henrici Purcell), frontispiece to *Sonatas of III Parts*, published 1683, age ?24 (see Portrait List, no. 24)

HENRY PURCELL.

PLATE II.D. Henry Purcell, engraving, *Universal Magazine*,
1777 (see Portrait List, no. 28). (British Museum)

PLATE II.E. Henry Purcell and Francesco Geminiani. Date, source, and provenance unknown (see Portrait List, no. 35). (British Museum)

PLATE III.F. Henry Purcell, ca. 1690. "Skillikorn" drawing of Purcell. (National Portrait Gallery, London)

PLATE III.G. Henry Purcell, charcoal sketch on lilac paper, a possible study for III.F (see Portrait List no. 21). (British Museum)

PLATE III.H. Oval portrait of Henry Purcell (see Portrait List, no. 5). (National Portrait Gallery, London, no. 2150)

PURCELL

Engraved by T. Holloway from a drawing by S.' Godfrey Kneller in the possession of D.' Burney.

PLATE III.I. Purcell, from a drawing by Sir Godfrey Kneller "in the possession of Dr. Burney." Engraving by T. Holloway, 1798 (see Portrait List, no. 30). (British Museum)

PLATE III.J. Henry Purcell, engraving from Burney Theatrical Portraits (see Portrait List, no. 27). (British Museum)

PLATE III.K. Henry Purcell, "Musician & Actor," from an original picture in Dulwich College. Engraving by W. N. Gardiner, 1794 (see Portrait List, no. 29). (British Museum)

PLATE III.L. Henry Purcell, engraving by W. Pinnock, 1823 (see Portrait
List, no. 32). (British Museum)

PLATE III.M. Purcell, from a drawing by Edward Novello after the original by Sir Godfrey Kneller. Engraving by W. Humphreys, 1846 (see Portrait List, no. 33). (British Museum)

PLATE III.N. Purcell, from a drawing by H. Avelay. Engraving by W. J. Linton (see Portrait List, no. 36). (British Museum, Prints and Drawings Room)

PLATE III.O. Portrait said to be of Henry Purcell, by Volders(?) (see Portrait List, no. 41). (National Portrait Gallery, London)

PLATE IV.P. Henry Purcell (see Portrait List, no. 6). (National Portrait Gallery, London, no. 1352)

PLATE IV.Q. Henry Purcell, reproduced in W. A. Shaw's article in the *Musical Times*, September 1920 (see Portrait List, no. 3)

PLATE IV.R. Henricus Purcell, frontispiece from *Orpheus Britannicus I*.
Engraved from IV.P. by R. White (see Portrait List, no. 25)

PLATE IV.S. Musical Still Life. An engraved portrait of Henry Purcell is shown as the frontispiece in "A Collection of Ayres compos'd for the Theatre." Engraving by Edward Collier (?) (see Portrait List, no. 13). (from the private collection of the late Edward Croft-Murray)

PLATE IV.T. Purcell, Croft, Blow, Arne, and Boyce. Engraving by Drayton for medallions (see Portrait List, no. 31)

PLATE IV.U. Purcell. Engraving by H. Adlard (see Portrait List, no. 34). (British Museum)

PLATE V.V. Portrait of Daniel Purcell (?), by Johann Baptist Closterman (?) (see Portrait List, no. 15). (National Portrait Gallery, London, no. 1463)

PLATE v.w. Portrait of Daniel Purcell (?) (see Portrait List, no. 19). (Royal College of Music)

PLATE V.X. Portrait of Daniel Purcell (?) at a more advanced age, Royal
Society of Musicians (see Portrait List, no. 17). (British Museum)

COMMENTARY AND ANALYSIS

The foregoing list of portraits of Henry Purcell is, at best, a finding list that will perhaps pose as many questions as it answers. However, if it accomplishes no more than to define better the problems relating to Purcell portraiture (the study of which as a whole has so far suffered from lack of attention), it will have served some purpose. There is no certain knowledge of the existence of the first painting on the above list, not to mention any facts concerning the artist, date, or location of the work. It is unlikely that Thomas Cross, Jr., sculpted the engraving for the frontispiece to Purcell's *Sonatas* of 1683 "*a mente*," but there is only the shakiest of evidence to indicate that he may have worked from a model. However, evidence is evidence, and this is all that is available at present.

The early Purcell scholar Dr. W. H. Cummings (1831–1915) relates the legend that Grignion's engraving printed in Hawkins's *General History* was modeled after the *Purcell's Head Tavern* sign then in the author's possession. This engraving is very like the engraving printed as the frontispiece to the 1683 *Sonatas*, except that it is a much finer and livelier representation of Purcell. This difference suggests that Grignion's engraving may have been copied from an original, which in turn may also have served as the model for the earlier engraving. Grignion's engraving may therefore have been copied from the Tavern sign, as the tradition suggests.

The status of the second of the portraits (no. 2) is also somewhat uncertain. Although positively identified as a portrait of Henry Purcell by W. A. Shaw (*Musical Times*, Sept. 1920), the plate and description given are not accompanied by any mention of the provenance or location of the painting, not to mention any substantiating evidence for the identification.

For these reasons, it is not hard to agree with the authoritative view that the information given in Mr. Shaw's article is to be used with caution. Still, the painting shown in the plate is extremely interesting, and not at all unlike what we may imagine of Purcell as a youth from his portraits of later years. It seems authentic in that it shows the dress and circumstances of a king's musician-in-ordinary, ca. 1685. We see a young composer seated at a handsomely draped table on which rest a viol and bow, an inkwell with pen, and a full sheet of manuscript paper. From his fixed, distant gaze it appears that a musical idea has begun to take shape in his mind, and that he is recasting it before writing it down. In short, the details of the painting (particularly the aura of intense concentration surrounding the face and the tense figure of the subject) and the few facts presented accord well with what we know of Purcell's circumstances around 1685. If, after allowing Mr. Shaw to beg the question altogether as to the authenticity of this portrait, one were tempted to quarrel with any of the statements made, that giving the age of the subject as twenty-six would seem most debatable. For, judging on appearance alone, the young man portrayed would seem nearer twenty than twenty-six.

On this score, Mr. Shaw's second portrait (no. 3) is even more suppositious. The face of the subject here shows the soft outlines of adolescence, not the set contours of the "thirties." So, unless the portrayer may have been intentionally falsifying his sitter's age, we must suppose either that the assigned date is wrong, or that the subject was a grown man of uncommonly immature appearance. Mr. Shaw's third portrait (no. 7) seems to remove this latter possibility at once. For it is inconceivable that the six years that are supposed to have intervened between these two portraits could have altered and remodeled so completely the lineaments and contours of a man's face. That the latter is a portrait of Purcell very similar to the well-known Closterman (?) portrait now in the National Portrait Gallery can scarcely be doubted. So the former, if it is, indeed, a portrait of Purcell, can hardly show him as he was at the age of thirty-one. Incidentally, the inclusion of organ pipes in the backgrounds of these two paintings strengthens the case for Mr. Shaw's identification, at least in the measure that it limits the field for the identification of other possible subjects; for between the three portraits, we see the subject as composer, violist, and organist—qualifications with which few besides Purcell were equipped at that time.

The next painting on the list (no. 5) is perhaps the happiest of the lot, both with regard to the artist's conception and execution, and to the record of facts relating to its history. According to a signed statement by Joah Bates (1741–1799), Purcell gave this portrait to his friend John Church, whose granddaughter gave it to Bates. From the latter's descendants it passed into the possession of A. H. Littleton, then to that of William Barclay Squire, who donated it to the National Portrait Gallery.

It shows the head of the composer turned three-quarters to the left, his large and expressive grey eyes looking straight ahead. In their level gaze, and in the air of composure lent by the rest of the features, we catch a glimpse of the character of a man of genius who has known and tested his powers with full confidence. With all this, we are instinctively drawn to like the man represented here. It may be the fair, open brow, the positive chin, or the hint of good humor in the set of the mouth—or perhaps all these enlivened by the painter's sense of character—but here, we feel, is a man that it would have been good to know.

Somehow this quality is missing in painting no. 6, which though more authentic and even more fully documented, is less appealing. In this work the artist seems to have sought to portray Purcell in the grandest and most impressive manner possible. From the high wig, dressed in the latest style of fin de siècle, to the set features, to the plum-colored robe, to the loose ribbon in the full shirt, the eye travels from detail to detail without encountering anything truly arresting or convincing. The painting is perhaps more monumental than any other, but, at the same time, it seems to have less life.

It is this lifelessness that lends credence to Cummings's account (*Musical Times*, Nov. 1895) of the origin of this painting—an account that is, at best, conjectural and obviously fallacious on at least one point. While Purcell lay in state, Sir Christopher Wren is supposed to have taken a death mask of his face at the request of Sir John Dolben, Dean of Westminster.[1] From this mask an unknown sculptor is said to have produced a portrait bust, which, in turn, served as the model for the portrait. There is some circumstantial evidence to support this theory but nothing conclusive. There was a portrait bust of Purcell in the Music School at Oxford for some time, and the Closterman portrait seems lifeless enough to have originated in such a way. But these facts in themselves prove nothing without better evidence.

Although the date of origin, the source, and the present location of the painting listed as no. 7 are all unknown, it seems obvious that this painting is closely related to the previous ones. In fact W. A. Shaw states that this version served as the model for the National Portrait Gallery painting. This statement is based on Mr. Shaw's opinion that Purcell's appearance in this missing portrait is young enough for a man of thirty-seven, whereas his appearance in the National Portrait Gallery painting is "too old." But this, surely, would be something very like pure speculation, even if we had the two portraits side by side for comparison. Otherwise, the paintings seem very much alike, except that the version Mr. Shaw has described has two ranks of organ pipes showing in the background. According to the *Grove* article, another painting closely related to these is to be found at Dyrham Park, Chippenham (no. 8).

The tenth item listed above—an undated, unsigned painting last seen in Stroud, Gloucestershire—is probably a spurious work. It bears extremely little resemblance to any of the known Purcell portraits, although it appears to have been retouched with the aim of increasing what little resemblance there was. The succeeding item (no. 11) is in much the same category and can very well be dismissed as far as any real significance to the problem in hand is concerned.

No. 12, the *Purcell's Head Tavern* sign painting, which once hung in Wych Street to the view of all passers-by, has been missing since about the end of the eighteenth century, when it was in Hawkins's collection. It is another of those paintings that raises questions that are at present unanswerable. In the *Grove* article it is related to the "two Closterman portraits." But this is pure conjecture, as is the suggestion given earlier in this study, relating it to the 1683 engraving, and to the engraving by Grignion in Hawkins's *History of Music.* Cummings has reproduced the following description of the painting, which may be useful one day if it ever reappears: "half-length; the dress a brown full-bottomed wig, and a green night-gown, very finely executed." Owned by the bassoonist, Kennedy, the sign since somehow has become lost.

The last of the genuine portraits listed (no. 13) is an unusual painting in which the ordinary relation between engraved and painted versions of a portrait is reversed. This portrait was painted after the engraving by R. White, which appeared as the frontispiece of *Orpheus Britannicus*, Book I, published in 1698. As may be seen from plate IV.S, the painting is a still life showing an

---

1. It is on this point, as C. J. Holmes has pointed out, that Cummings's account is not in accord with the facts. John Dolben the elder died in 1686, and Sir John Dolben the younger was ill at the time of Purcell's death.

arrangement of musical instruments and music books resting on a tapestry-covered table. The familiar engraved portrait of Purcell is shown here bound in with *A Collection of Ayres composed for the Theatre*, which was published in 1697. This does not necessarily imply that this particular engraving was published in 1697 rather than in 1698, the year to which it is generally ascribed; for, as the late E. Croft-Murray has pointed out, music collections of the times were often thus bound together with the frontispieces from other collections.

Possibly the best portrait of all is the drawing recently acquired by the National Portrait Gallery from W. G. Skillicorn, Esq., of Liverpool (see no. 20 in the list above). Croft-Murray identified this drawing as the original portrait from life from which derived portraits listed above as nos. 4, 5, 9, and 33. It appears also to be the immediate original for no. 21.

A better-known portrait drawing of Henry Purcell is to be found in the British Museum, Collection of Prints and Drawings (no. 21 on the list). In the past, it has been attributed both to Kneller and to Closterman. At present the consensus of opinion is, for want of conclusive evidence, that it should be considered anonymous. As a portrait, the drawing is a sympathetic presentation of the composer when young. It is something like the painting in the National Portrait Gallery shown in plate III.H. Some authorities have gone so far as to say that the drawing was in fact a study for the painting.

But if one may believe the testimony of one's eyes, any such direct relationship between these two is largely theoretical. In the drawing, the shape of the eyes and their expression, the modeling of the nose, and the set of the chin differ so completely from these features as shown in the painting that the differences between the two works outweigh their similarities at least as far as the general impression each gives is concerned. The drawing seems a far more intimate and subjective realization than the painting and gives us a glimpse of Purcell in meditation—a mood not suggested in any other authentic portrait, although there is something of the same quality to be seen in the portrait (no. 2) supposedly showing the young composer at the age of twenty-two. Here the artist has captured for us a glimpse of Purcell the dreamer, which adds yet another facet to the knowledge of his character that can be surmised, if not known, from other authentic portraits.

Relevant information on the engravings may be quickly summarized. As for modern reproductions of these engravings, little need be said but that these have, for the most part, only further confused the situation.

Of the engraved portraits, that which was published with the *Sonatas* of 1683 (no. 24) appears to be the earliest of the extant engravings. By comparison with later engravings—particularly that published in 1698—it seems crude and somewhat lifeless. It portrays Purcell as a gross and complacent person—perhaps even a little surly. As Westrup remarks, the subject would seem better fitted for some mundane calling like cheese merchantry than for the role of a gifted and imaginative young musician. The later engravings, which, ostensibly, have been taken from this, are much the same (plates nos. II.D and II.E).

No. 25, the engraving published with the first book of *Orpheus Britannicus* in 1698, is so like the Closterman painting (no. 6) that further comment seems unnecessary. W. A. Shaw has introduced some doubt as to the relationship between these two by claiming that the third of his three portraits of Purcell served as the model for this engraving. However, as well as can be judged from the poor reproduction accompanying his article, this claim seems biased. The resemblance is not at all close. It is possible that this engraving was first reproduced in 1697 rather than in 1698, since it was shown by E. Collier (?) as the frontispiece to *Ayres for the Theatre*, which was published in the earlier year. A final decision on this matter will have to await the accumulation of further evidence.

For the rest, further comment is warranted only for the engravings from Hawkins's *General History* (no. 26) and from the *Universal Magazine* of December 1777 (no. 28). The former is said to have been copied from the *Purcell's Head Tavern* sign, which statement, if true, provides us with the only clue we have as to the appearance of that painting, aside from Hawkins's verbal description as quoted above. It appears to be the same in almost every detail as the engraving published with the *Sonatas* of 1683. If Hawkins did indeed have this engraving made from the Tavern sign, it must have been that painting that served as the model for the 1683 engraving. The fact that Grignion's portrait is a much warmer and more sensitive representation than that appearing with the *Sonatas* of 1683 strengthens the possibility that there was an original model for both, since it seems unlikely that he worked from the earlier engraving. The engraving in the December 1777 issue of the *Universal Magazine* appears to be a copy from this earlier engraving, however, for it is equally crude and lifeless.

Finally, the engraved title page (no. 37) from the *Six figures design'd & Etch'd by Edw. Purcell* is listed purely in the spirit of speculation. Whether these etchings included any likenesses of Edward's famous grandfather, or where these may be now, are yet other questions which cannot be answered at present.

One other group of portraits (nos. 15–18, 22, 38–40; plates V.X, V.V) remains to be discussed. These all portray a man who is clearly not the Henry Purcell shown in the portraits discussed so far. C. J. Holmes has developed a convincing hypothesis ("The Portraits of Arne and Purcell" in *The Burlington Magazine*, April to September 1915) that the man shown in this group is Daniel Purcell, Henry's younger brother. Since the pedigree of one of the paintings may be traced back to Purcell's grandson, it is likely that these portraits are of some member of the family. A certain family resemblance about the eyes of the two men shown in these portraits strengthens this possibility, and, since Daniel Purcell's circumstances about the time these portraits were painted are not inconsistent with the facts that may be deduced from the paintings themselves, Holmes's identification seems the best so far provided. The two different portraits listed as nos. 15 and 17 below seem to represent two different persons. Yet given the passing of several years between the times of origin of the two, and given also the fact that they were painted by different artists, the details on which they vary are not so significant as those on which they agree. The brows, the shape of the nose in each, and general resemblance in bone structure are enough to suggest that the same sitter is shown in each.

The first of these paintings (no. 15) shows, almost full length, a young man seated cross-legged at the harpsichord. With his left elbow resting on top of the harpsichord, he points with his left forefinger to a miniature showing a lady elsewhere described as "stout." He wears a long, brown wig, a lace cravat, and a white shirt with full puffed sleeves. A crimson shawl is draped across his lap and around his torso, covering also the stool on which he sits. His face reveals little of his character except that he appears to have been well provided for, perhaps a little too well. It certainly gives not the slightest hint of the "greatness of soul" that Longinus tells us to expect in men who do great things—a quality of which we catch a glimpse in some of the authentic portraits of Henry Purcell. This in itself is sufficient evidence to confute the traditional identification with Henry Purcell, but there is more, which may be summarized briefly.

On the harpsichord, which stands open, is a stack of some nine or ten books, the bottom one of which lies opened to a composition bearing the title *Sonata Settima*. At present, the most that can be said of the notation shown is that it is the beginning of the bass part of some instrumental sonata either by an Italian composer, or by an English composer addicted to Italian titles. It is not from any of Henry Purcell's sonatas, and, since Daniel Purcell published only six, it is probably not from any of his known works.

On the spine of the second book from the top of the stack is to be seen the shelf-mark: O 22, no doubt indicating that it belonged to some contemporary library. The walls of the room are richly panelled, suggesting that the portrait was done in the Senior Common Room of some well-to-do college, or perhaps in the music room of a wealthy club.

The very similar portrait now in Worcester Cathedral (no. 16) is the same in almost all details, except that the lady in the miniature appears to be another person, and the piece showing in the open book is Henry Purcell's own *Britons strike home* (in a slightly altered version). Both these portraits were generally regarded as portraits of Henry Purcell up to the time of Holmes's article, in spite of their obvious incompatibility with the genuine portraits. The National Portrait Gallery painting was described in the catalogue for the Archdeacon Burney sale in 1814 as "a very fine original portrait of Henry Purcell; in his hand is a miniature of Queen Mary." Neither the identification of Purcell nor that of Queen Mary has any apparent basis. The Worcester picture is similarly identified, again, it would seem, more in the interests of sales promotion in the auction room than out of any regard for fact.

The same person appears a third time in the painting (no. 17) now in the possession of the *Royal Society of Musicians*, and in the early engraving (probably taken from this) now in the British Museum. The false identification of this painting as a portrait of Henry Purcell has been rendered more persistent by the fact that its pedigree extends back to Purcell's grandson. Cummings's preservation of the following hearsay evidence in his article on Purcell's portraits has done nothing to lessen the confusion: "Purcell's son, and also his pupil, Henry Needler, declared the portrait was extremely like Purcell, and that during the latter years of his life he had rapidly changed appearance in consequence of bad health." We are not told by what means this information came to be preserved, or on what grounds it was attached to this portrait. Nor are we given any explanation as to what process it could have been that caused a man to appear healthier and more prosperous with the progress of a fatal disease.

Obviously, this is another portrait of the person shown in the two paintings discussed immediately above. Several features of this portrait further substantiate the possibility that Daniel Purcell is indeed the subject. The later style of wig and dress fashion (indicative of a period sometime within the first decade or so of the eighteenth century) and the "conductor's attitude" of the sitter point to the period in which Daniel Purcell had moved from Oxford to London and established something of a reputation in the musical world there. It is further significant in this connection, as Holmes has pointed out, that Daniel Purcell is recorded to have given a concert of vocal and instrumental music in Stationer's Hall in April 1712.

A drawing discovered at Christ Church, Oxford, referred to by C. F. Bell, is yet a fourth portrait of this same person. Although it has been described as a study for one of the first two oils discussed above, Mr. David Piper of the National Portrait Gallery is of the opinion that it is quite possible that the drawing was done from one of the paintings.

At this time all that can definitely be said of the last four items discussed is that they are almost certainly portraits of one and the same person, and that this person, even more certainly, is not Henry Purcell. Exactly who this person may be, if not, as suggested, Daniel Purcell, must remain yet another of those questions which this essay will leave unanswered for the time being.

Fifthly, there is the portrait in the Royal College of Music discussed in the fourth edition of *Grove's Dictionary*, which has been supposed lost for over a half century. Actually the portrait said to represent Henry Purcell never left the premises but hung all the while over a rather dark doorway in a dimly lit room. The portrait was well disguised, as it resembles no other genuine portrait of Henry Purcell in any way, and it seems at first glance not to resemble those that may represent Daniel Purcell. Once again, however, it is quite possible that given the passage of time and change of artists, the two portraits show more in the way of family resemblance than coincidence might explain. The portrayal of the sitter's right profile, rather than three-quarters full, creates differences more apparent than real, particularly given the upward tilt in the face of the sitter for no. 19. Confusion is, of course, augmented by the fact that the painting is clearly labeled "Henry Purcell," an identification indicating care-lessness on the part of either the original painter or someone through whose hands it passed later on.

BIBLIOGRAPHY AND ACKNOWLEDGMENTS

1. Literature on Purcell's Portraits

Arundell, Dennis. *Henry Purcell*. London, 1927.

Bell, C. F. "English Seventeenth-Century Portrait Drawings in Oxford Collections." *Walpole Society Journal* 5 (1917).

Binyon, Laurence. *Catalogue of Prints and Drawings in the British Museum*. London, Longman, 1902.

Colles, H. G. et al., eds. "Henry Purcell." in *Grove's Dictionary of Music and Musicians*, 5th ed. London, Macmillan, 1954.

Croft-Murray, Edward. *Catalogue of Prints and Drawings of the British School by Foreigners in England Preserved in the Department of Prints and Drawings in the British Museum*. Vol. 1 (in press).

Cummings, W. H. "Portraits of Purcell." *Musical Times*, November 1895.

———. *Purcell*. London, 1887.

Dupre, Henry. *Purcell*. Paris, 1927.

Granger, The Rev. J. *A Biographical History of England*. 2d ed. London, 1824.

Holland, Arthur Keith. *Henry Purcell, The English Musical Tradition*. London, 1932.

Holst, Gustav. "Henry Purcell." In *The Heritage of Music*, vol. 1. Oxford, 1927.

Howes, Frank Stewart. "Purcell." In *Chamber's Encyclopedia*. London, 1950.

Jacob, Mons. *Collectanea Biographica*. London, 1853 (now in the Anderson Collection, British Museum).

O'Donoghue, Freeman. *Catalogue of Engraved British Portraits in the British Museum*. Vol. 3. London, 1912.

Piper, David. *Catalogue Raisonné of Seventeenth Century Portraits in the National Portrait Gallery*. In press.

Runciman, John F. *Purcell*. London, 1909.

Scholes, Percy A. *The Oxford Companion to Music*. 9th ed. London, 1955.

Shaw, W. A. "Three Unpublished Portraits of Henry Purcell." *Musical Times*, September 1920.

Sietz, R. *Henry Purcell: Zeit, Leben, Werk*. Leipzig, 1955.

Westrup, Jack Allen. *Purcell*. London, 1947.

———. "Fact and Fiction about Henry Purcell." *Proceedings of the Musical Association*, 1935–36.

2. Sources of Engravings

Burney, Charles. *Theatrical Portraits*. Vol. 7, no. 50.
Harding, S. *Biographical Mirror*. London, 1794.
Hawkins, John. *General History of the Science and Practice of Music*. 1st ed. London, 1776. Vol. 1, p. 495.
Purcell, Henry. *A Collection of Ayres compos'd for the Theatre*. London, 1697.
————. *Orpheus Britannicus*. London, 1698.
————. *Sonatas of III Parts*. London, 1683.

3. Acknowledgments

Among many others there are several persons, to whom I owe a special debt of gratitude for assistance with the task of gathering together the photographic reproductions and the information upon which this article is based. First of all, I must thank Mr. Edward Croft-Murray, Keeper of Prints and Drawings in the British Museum, for his valuable and generous help in several matters. To him, and also to the members of his staff in the "Prints and Drawings" Room, acknowledgments are due for cooperation and service exceeding the demands of official courtesy. I must also thank Mr. Croft-Murray for showing me his own private collection, for furnishing the photograph from which the accompanying plate of the Collier "Still-life" was made, and for advising me on numerous matters of which my own knowledge was inadequate.

It is my pleasure also to render thanks to Mr. David Piper of the National Portrait Gallery, for allowing me to take away sections pertinent to this article from his "Catalogue Raisonné of 17th Century Portraits in the National Portrait Gallery," which is now in the press. To Mr. Piper also, I am indebted for a great deal of helpful and very expert advice.

Finally, I must thank Mr. Thomas Manning, Director's Secretary at the Royal College of Music, Miss Barbara Banner, Librarian, Miss Gillian Squire, her assistant, and the several other members of the Royal College staff who helped (and were so patient with my persistence) in the search for the missing Purcell portrait.

Notes

NOTES TO CHAPTER 1

1. Bodleian, MS. Wood D 19(4), fo. 104. Denis Arundell, in *Henry Purcell*, p. 9, fn. 2, alludes to a rate-payer named "Purcell" in Westminster rate-books for 1641, 1651, 1656, and 1659, presuming him to be Henry Purcell the elder. He also mentions a Thomas Purcell of the precinct of the Tower of London, who died in 1635, and a brother, William, who died in 1645.

2. Pulver, p. 387.

3. For Wood's entry, see note 1; otherwise, St. Margaret's, Westminster, *Overseers' Accounts* (hereafter "Overseers' Accounts"), in the Westminster Public Library, Buckingham Palace Road.

4. In *Roscius Anglicanus*, pp. 20–21. In his essay on *Heroic Drama*, John Dryden intimates that William D'Avenant dropped his operatic pretentions at the restoration of Charles II in 1660. With the Puritans no longer in power, the pretext of musical entertainment was no longer necessary, and D'Avenant had not intended really to establish opera in any case:

> . . . it being forbidden him in the Rebellion times to act tragedies and comedies, because they contained some matter of scandal to those good people who could more easily dispossess their lawful sovereign than endure a wanton jest, he was forced to turn his thoughts another way and to introduce the examples of moral virture writ in verse and performed in recitative music. The original of this music and of the scenes which adorned this work he had from the Italian operas, but he heightened his characters (as I may properly imagine) from the example of Corneille and some French poets.
>
> In this condition did this part of poetry remain at His Majesty's return, when, growing bolder, as being now owned by a public authority, he reviewed his *Siege of Rhodes* and caused it to be acted as a *just drama*. (italics mine)

To be sure, there is no mention of either music or musicians in Downes's entry or in the various entries in *The London Stage*, vol. 1, p. 29, which ends with a verse on the *Siege of Rhodes* corroborating that the 1661 revival was a play:

> For the Siege of Rhodes all say
> It is an everlasting play. . . .

5. I discount the putative signature of the elder Purcell in the *Book of Common Prayer*, which does not appear authentic.

6. See "Overseers' Accounts" for 1654 to 1664 (E 168 to E 177 respectively). There is no volume for 1660, and that for 1662 (E 185) was destroyed during the Second World War. However, final proof that the 1656 performance of *The Siege of Rhodes* ever actually took place is wanting.

7. See Genealogical Table 2. Very little is known of the second son, Charles. The only document referring to him (PCC: 63 Lloyd) makes it clear that he cannot have been the Charles Purcell, a cousin, who died off Guinea in 1686. This source mentions Elizabeth Purcell as his mother, so he must have been Henry Purcell's brother.

8. *Henry Purcell: Zeit, Leben, Werk*, p. 35.

9. From the part book for "Violino Primo" in Purcell's *Sonnatas of III Parts* (London: Playford and Carr, for the author, 1683) (British Museum, K.4.g.10).

10. Important as the musician who established the first entrepreneurial concert series in London.

11. According to the Rev. Canon Overton, in *DNB*.

12. J. E. Smith, *A Catalogue of Westminster Records* (London, 1900), p. 56.

13. *DNB*.

14. St. Margaret's, Westminster: Parish Church Records, "Weddings," 1645–81.

15. Ibid.

16. *Memoirs of Samuel Pepys*, vol. 1, p. 18. Pepys (M), vol. 1, p. 62.

17. WAM 33695. At Michaelmas (29 Sept. 1661) Henry was retroactively paid £7.10s. for three quarters as master of the choristers. Therefore, it is clear that he had taken up his duties sometime during the previous January. Even earlier, Purcell's name is recorded, along with a list of choristers, in various accounts of fees received for singing at funerals and other ceremonial occasions that took place in the Abbey.

18. *KM*, p. 122; Cheque-book, p. 128. See also App. One, XXII, 3.

19. *KM*, p. 124.

20. Angelo Notari was one of the eldest of the musicians who returned to court positions after the restoration of Charles II. As Lafontaine points out, he also represented the oldest strata of direct Italian influence in England, having published his *Prime musiche nuove* in 1616, in London.

21. WAM 61228A (Precentor's Book, 1660–71, fo. 3).

22. Ibid., fo. 6. As is often true in Restoration records, the figures are out. Payments recorded add up to £6 5s. 4d., leaving 8s. unaccounted for in the sum said to be available, £6. 13s. 4d. Or, counting in the 8d. still due Mr. Finnell, the discrepancy would amount only to 7s. 4d.

23. See Westrup, p. 7, n. 3, for a discussion of the probable effects of inflation on the economic situation at court.

24. See App. One, XII, 7 and 12.

25. Cf. *KM*, p. 131, where warrants are recorded for musicians' liveries; see also p. 136, where remuneration to Captain Cooke for "torches and lights for practising the music against his Majesty's coronation" is belatedly entered for 16 Sept. 1661.

26. Cheque-book, p. 128. See also Eric Halfpenny, "The Entertainment of Charles II," pp. 32–44.

27. Evelyn, 22 and 23 April 1661.

28. Pepys, 22 April 1661.

29. Baker, pp. 760–61. For other detailed information on these ceremonies, see John Ogilby's *The Entertainment of His Most Excellent Majestie Charles II, in His Passage through the City of London to His Coronation*; and Halfpenny, "The Entertainment of Charles II," pp. 32–44.

30. Baker, p. 767.

31. Ibid.

32. Reported by Pepys (W) (15 Nov. 1661) and Evelyn (9 Jan. 1661/2).

33. London (?), 1662. See plate 7.

34. *Westminster Abbey Reg.*, p. 67; quoted in App. One, XIX, 1.

35. *KM*, p. 121.

36. Grove V, vol. 6, p. 997.

37. *KM*, p. 151.

38. He was appointed to Angelo Notari's place on St. Thomas's Day and also was one of the few chosen to be exempted from payment of various subsidies required by act of Parliament (*KM*, p. 165).

39. *MGG*, vol. 10, col. 1770. The death of Henry Purcell on 11 Aug. 1664 establishes April 1665 as the latest month in which Daniel's birth can have occurred. Joseph was probably Daniel's elder brother—cf. App. One and Genealogical Table 2—but no records have been found to establish his birthdate.

40. *KM*, pp. 160, 162.

41. Wood, vol. 1, p. 94.

42. Treasurer's Rept., 23 Dec. 1661.

43. Ibid.

44. Pepys (W), 26 Nov. 1663: "The plague, it seems, grows more and more at Amsterdam; and we are going upon making of all ships coming from thence and Hambrough, or any other infected places, to perform their Quarantine. . . ."

45. Westrup, p. 39.

46. Cheque-book, p. 13: "Mr. Henry Purcell, one of His Majesty's Gentlemen of the Chapel died the eleventh day of August, 1664, in whose place came Mr. Thomas Richardson." See also App. One, XII, 16, for the record of his burial in Westminster Abbey cloisters.

47. See accounts for 1665–69 at Westminster Public Library, Buckingham Palace Road. Information from missing volumes of the rate-book series often may be found in the Poor Ledger for the corresponding year. The chapter showed unusual dilatoriness, even by its standards, in ratifying Elizabeth Purcell's change of residence. Papers were not drawn up until 31 December 1669: "Ordered that a lease be made to Mrs. Purcell of a tenement in Tothill Street for 40 years under the old rent and the usual covenant" (W.A. Chapter Minutes, 1662–85).

48. St. Margaret's, Westminster, Churchwarden's Accounts, vol. 80.

49. See App. One, VIII, passim, and various entries in WAM 61228A (Precentor's Book, 1660–71, fols. 56ᵛ, 57ᵛ, 58, and 61, for instance).

50. 1674–93, fo. 42.

51. A thorough search of related records produced no evidence to explain the suspicious attitude reflected in the closing admonition.

52. See App. One and App. Two for information on the children.

NOTES TO CHAPTER 2

1. Pepys (M), 30 Apr. 1665.

2. Nathaniel Hodges, *Loimologia; or An Historical Account of the Plague in London in 1665*, pp. 1–2. See also J. W. Ebsworth, ed., *The Bagford Ballads*, I, 39, for a lugubrious ballad on the plague.

3. *KM*, pp. 178–79.

4. Westrup, p. 17. However, see Nanki Mus. Libr. MS N-5/10, where the "Club Anthem" is identified as the work of these three. It is the last anthem copied into this very authentic, contemporary part-book.

5. See Evelyn's entry for 2 Aug., also a Wednesday.

6. Hodges, *Loimologia*, pp. 16–17, 18, 19.

7. WAM 61228A, fo. 138.

8. *DNB*.

9. W. G. Bell, *The Great Fire of London in 1666*, p. 129. The mention of "22 musicians on the violin" is doubly misleading. Possibly Bell intended to refer to "the 24 violins of the King," all of whom, of course, were not violinists, and of whom there were twenty-six, all told.

10. Pepys (M) 10 Oct. and 20 Nov. 1666.

11. *Cal. S. P. Dom.*, 7 Nov. 1666; (see also the entry for 2 June 1669).

12. *Cal. S. P. Dom.*, 12 Nov. 1666.

13. *KM*, p. 191.

14. *Cal. S. P. Dom.*, 7 Nov. 1666. See also *KM*, p. 193.

15. Pepys (M), 1 Oct. 1667.

16. Evelyn, 23 April 1667.

17. Evelyn, 4 April 1667.

18. Pepys (M), 29 July 1667.

19. Ibid.

20. See plate 12, "The Cabal," by J. B. Medina. The topical title for this conversation piece is probably only accidentally relevant here. However, it is still of interest in the biography of a musician. In fact, of the figures shown, that on the far right is not unlike Matthew Locke, and the central figure bears more than passing resemblance to Henry Purcell. (See also J. W. Ebsworth, *The Roxburghe Ballads*, vol. 4, p. 582.)

21. See Pepys (M) for 12 Aug., 9 Sept., and 30 Dec. that year.

22. Ibid., 1 Nov. 1667. According to the article in Grove V, vol. 4, p. 404, Humfrey had been sworn in on 26 Oct. 1667, as a gentleman of the Chapel Royal.

23. WAM 61228A (Precentor's Book, 1660–71), passim and 20 May 1668: "Money warrant for £20 to Elizabeth, relict of Henry Purcell, late (one of the King's Music)," and, for 8 July 1668: "Signature by Treasury Lords of Order on the hearth money for £20 to Elizabeth, relict of Henry Purcell, of the King's Music."

24. See the inscription transcribed by the present writer, who *did* "get down on all fours," from his memorial tablet in Wytham Church, App. One, IV, 13. However, there may have been two men named "Edward Purcell" at court about this time.

25. *Cal. Tr. Bks.*, 15 Sept. 1673. His appointment probably preceded that of one Francis Purcell, appointed one of the grooms of the Privy Chamber (in-ordinary, assistant) on 8 Aug. 1673. Francis was son to Thomas Purcell.

26. P.R.O. *Admin. Act*, 1695, fo. 115ᵛ. His relationship to the family is established by this document, which is an official record of the "Wardship granted to Elizabeth Purcell, widow, grandmother of Henry and Elizabeth Purcell, minors." These were his children, and he was brother to Edward, Henry, Daniel, and Joseph, and son of the elder Henry Purcell. He is not to be confused with the Charles Purcell discussed in chapter 3, who was probably his cousin.

27. The first entry in *The King's Musick* is that for 8 Apr. 1679, which refers back to Sept. 1678. By then Daniel was at least fourteen or fifteen years old and near the end of his days as a choirboy.

28. Westminster Abbey, Treasurer's Reports, 20 May 1668.

29. See Grove V, under "Académie de Musique."

30. See *Cal. S. P. Dom.* for these dates. This was not Cooke's first recourse to such desperate remedies; witness the similar entries for 24 Jan. 1668 and 7 Dec. 1669. See

Westrup, pp. 9–16, for a discussion of the daily activities of the choristers and for an account of Cooke's difficult responsibilities.

    31. Cummings, p. 20, states that E. Rimbault owned a manuscript copy "in the handwriting of Pelham Humphreys." Rosamund McGuiness, fo. 39, suggests that the ode, "See, Mighty Sir, the Day Appears" (attributed to Humfrey in Br. Mus. Add. MS 33287, fo. 69ᵛ) may represent the piece in question. This is quite possible. However, her suggestion that the copy in question might be Humfrey's autograph weakens the case for Purcell's authorship, since Humfrey obviously would not have claimed Purcell's well-advertised ode for himself. My own view of the matter is as follows: (a) the music in question would indeed be creditable for a boy of eleven; and (b) the copy looks very similar to a hand discussed by A. Hughes-Hughes as an anonymous copyist working closely with Purcell. (See "Henry Purcell's Handwriting," p. 81.) The peculiar G-clef and end-of-stave design are idiosyncratic. See Add. MS 33287, a manuscript, moreover, which Hughes-Hughes discusses.

    32. *Analytical Catalogue*, no. D120.

    33. WAM 33703 (Treasurer's Account, 1670), fo. 4.

    34. See p. 50 below.

    35. See J. L. Hotson, *The Commonwealth and Restoration Stage*, p. 232. D'Avenant had died on 7 Apr. 1668 (*DNB*). See also *The London Stage*, vol. 1, p. 189.

    36. M. Summers, *The Playhouse of Pepys*, pp. 40, 105, and *Analytical Catalogue*, commentaries and entries in App. 4 for nos. 631, 632, and S100. The two remaining Shakespeare adaptations were performed elsewhere: *King Richard II* at the Theatre Royal (Laurie, fo. 165) and *The Fairy Queen* at the Queen's Theatre (see *Analytical Catalogue*, no. 629).

    37. *KM*, p. 485.

    38. See *KM*, pp. 271, 318ff.

    39. *KM*, p. 231.

    40. *KM*, p. 230. See also entries for 8 Feb., 13 Mar., and 21 Mar. 1671.

    41. *KM*, p. 235. See also entries for 8 Feb., 13 Mar.

    42. *KM*, p. 245 passim.

    43. *KM*, p. 240; however, the date in the *Cal. Tr. Bks.* is given as 1673.

    44. *Cal Tr. Bks.*: entries for 15 Sept. 1672 (or 73?); 17 Oct. 1673; 31 Dec. 1673; 30 Nov. 1674, etc.

    45. Grove V, vol. 2, p. 240. See plate 6 for an account of a contemporary event.

    46. *KM*, p. 247.

    47. *MGG*, vol. 10, col. 1777.

    48. *Cal Tr. Bks.*, 15 Sept. 1673.

    49. Pepys (M), 10 Aug. and 5 Oct. 1664.

NOTES TO CHAPTER 3

    1. *KM*, p. 251; 1672–73, 17 Jan. "Warrant to provide and deliver to Pelham Humphreys, master of the children of his Majesty's Chapel Royal, for the use of Henry Hall, late child of the Chapel, whose voice is changed and is gone from the Chapel, two suits of plain cloth, two hats and hat-bands, four whole shirts, four half shirts, six bands, six pairs of cuffs, six handkerchiefs, four pairs of stockings, four pairs of shoes, and four pairs of gloves."

    2. *KM*, p. 251; see App. One, XIII, 20, for Hall's eulogy to Purcell in a dedicatory

printed in *Orpheus Brittanicus*, 3d ed., 1721. Though four years older than Purcell, Hall evidently had great respect for his young colleague. Hall's compositions reveal a certain talent, which apparently did not flourish in the provinces.

3. *KM*, p. 263; see App. One, XIII, 4, for a warrant of this same date providing clothing for Purcell upon his leaving the Chapel.

4. *KM*, p. 251; as if by afterthought, Purcell's allotment was augmented by a supply of handkerchiefs shortly after the beginning of the new year (*KM*, p. 265, 2 Feb. 1673/4). On the twentieth "fine cloth for 2 suites for a chappell boy whose voice is changed" also was entered. Purcell was probably the boy.

5. *KM*, p. 255.

6. *KM*, p. 260 (29 Sept. 1673). "Articles of agreement between Pelham Humfrey of Westminster, Master of the Children of His Majesty's Chapel Royal, and John Lilly of the parish of St. Andrew's, Holbourn, one of His Majesty's musicians-in-ordinary."

7. *DNB*. "Transmogrified" means "adapted as an opera."

8. Grove V, vol. 9, p. 312. Stephen Crespion, later a close friend, near neighbor, and deathbed companion of Henry Purcell, signed Wilson's burial order on 27 Feb.

9. *KM*, p. 268.

10. Thomas Purcell was named as the first of ten musicians "that do service in *the Chapel Royal*." He was a tenor, as we know from an entry in *KM*, p. 269, 14 Apr. 1674, although the entry merely lists a "Mr. Purcell," who may have been young Henry, whose voice had broken a year or more earlier. Thomas was also named among the musicians for "lutes and voices, theorbos and virginals" (*KM*, pp. 121–22); this position may have duplicated that to which he succeeded on the death of Henry Lawes on 10 Nov. 1662. On 16 November, he also inherited Lawes's place in the Private Music for Lutes, Viols, and Voices, and as musician-in-ordinary (*KM*, p. 151). He also shared with Pelham Humfrey the place of George Hudson when the latter died in 1672 (*KM*, p. 240). His position as groom of the robes was his fifth, and the acquisition of Wilson's place brought the total to six, or possibly seven if the above-mentioned pair were not duplicates. In addition, he contracted Bernhardt Smith to install an organ in the private chapel at Whitehall (see Arundell, *Henry Purcell*, p. 13).

11. See plate 2.

12. *MGG*, vol. 2, col. 691.

13. *KM*, p. 269. Grabu evidently did not live up to his part of the agreement, for more than a month later on 27 Apr., the lord chamberlain had to sign a "warrant to deliver to Sir Christopher Wren, His Majesty's Surveyor-General of the works, the scenes belonging to His Majesty's Theatre at Whitehall, which were formerly delivered to Mr. Grabu for the use of the French opera in Bridges Street" (*KM*, p. 270).

14. Ibid., p. 273.

15. Ibid., p. 283.

16. Grove V, vol. 3, p. 270 (Grabu), and vol. 2, p. 25 (Cambert), respectively. Grove VI does not include the reference to Grabu and the Papal Nuncio.

17. 5 Jan. 1673/4. E. S. de Beer, in his edition of Evelyn's *Diary*, p. 48, suggests that the opera may have been Perrin's *Ariane*. However, Evelyn could scarcely have mistaken this for an Italian opera. Very likely the production Evelyn witnessed was a rival affair, possibly arranged for Mary of Modena, who had been persuaded—some said by Louis XIV himself—to take up residence in London, as duchess of York, in preference to taking the veil in Italy.

18. Grove V, vol. 2, p. 766.

19. Downes, p. 43; for Reggio's authorship, see Westrup, p. 93.

20. *KM*, p. 271. So much for the royal order prohibiting choristers from appearing in public theaters.

21. Evelyn, 19 Nov. 1674; see also Roger North, *The Musical Grammarian*, pp. 25, 34–37, and *Memoirs of Musick* (ed. E. F. Rimbault), pp. 122–23, for accounts of his success as a teacher, of his intemperate arrogance upon first arrival in England, and of his later tractability.

22. Evelyn. The concert took place at the house of Henry Slingsby, master of the mint. "Signor Francesco" was probably Francesco Galli (cf. Westrup, p. 91 and n. 2).

23. Grove V, vol. 4, p. 404; see also *KM*, p. 273; also Grove VI, vol. 8, p. 776.

24. The inscription on Blow's memorial at Westminster Abbey reads "Master of the famous Mr. H. Purcell." His becoming master of the children of the Chapel Royal in 1674 would automatically have brought Henry Purcell under his tutelage, even though his voice had broken. See also Grove V, vol. 1, pp. 768–75, and Grove VI, vol. 2, pp. 805–12.

25. *KM*, p. 273.

26. Grove VI, vol. 2, pp. 805–12.

27. Ibid. Blow gained what for all practical purposes must have been a seventh preferment later in 1674, when he married Elizabeth, daughter of Edward Braddock, then master of the children in Westminster Abbey, and later clerk of the cheque of the Chapel Royal. Add to this Blow's annual liveries as musician-in-ordinary in the place of Giles Tomkins, and he becomes master pluralist of them all (*KM*, p. 276).

28. *KM*, p. 288, recording a warrant for £30 to Blow for the maintenance of Holder dated 1 Apr. 1675, but made retroactive to 29 Sept. 1674.

29. British Museum, Harleian MSS. 7338–42.

30. British Museum, Add. MS. 34072, fo. 1–5. See also F. T. Arnold, *The Art of Accompaniment from a Thorough Bass*, pp. 163–72. According to Arnold, the ms is probably in Blow's handwriting.

31. British Museum, Add. MS. 30933, fo. 163–73ᵛ.

32. Grove V, vol. 2, p. 766; see also the *Musical Times* for Sept. 1936, p. 835.

33. *KM*, p. 275.

34. Evelyn, 15 Dec. 1674. See also E. Boswell, *The Restoration Court Stage 1660–1702*, pp. 177ff.; and A. Nicoll, *The Stuart Masques and the Renaissance Stage* (London, 1964), passim.

35. Only the last of the seven settings from *Calisto*, in Br. Mus. Add. MS 19759 (fo. 18, 18ᵛ) bears the ascription to "Staggins." However, on stylistic grounds, if indeed style has anything at all to do with these songs, all seven appear to be the work of one man.

36. Roger North coined this term; it appears in *Memoirs of Musick*, pp. 115–16.

37. According to an announcement in the *London Gazette* for 10 Jan. 1673/4. Banister's concerts had been resumed "until Michaelmas next." A later advertisement in the same journal for 24 Sept. advised of their continuance from 29 Sept. (i.e., "Michaelmas next") onward. The concerts seem to have gone on throughout the year.

38. *KM*, p. 288; the agreement, with another musician, John Hill, was drawn up on 3 Apr. 1675.

39. *KM*, p. 290.

40. See p. 34 above.

41. Pepys (W), 15 Nov. 1667.

42. WAM 33709 (Treasurer's Account, 1675), fo. 5 (see App. One, XIII, 5). How-ever, Westrup was wrong, I think, in assuming that the £2 represented payment for an entire year. Purcell's appointment was "in-ordinary without fee" rather than "ordinary with fee," as would have applied had he had a regular annual stipend. He could depend on occasional payments such as this, but had no guarantee.

43. See *KM*, p. 202, where it is recorded that Grabu was paid £165. 9s. 6d. for duties as copyist, from 4 Nov. 1666 to 25 Mar. 1668. This impressive sum was paid him in addition to his regular salary as master of the King's Music.

44. See his autograph score in Fitzwilliam Museum Library, Cambridge (MS. 88), copied ca. 1677, if the deductions of Dr. Nigel Fortune be correct. See "Purcell's Au-tographs," in *Henry Purcell 1659–1695: Essays on His Music*, ed. Imogen Holst, App. A. Here Purcell had copied dozens of anthems written by his English contempo-raries and predecessors, including compositions by Orlando Gibbons, Tallis, Byrd, Wil-liam Mundy, Thomas Tomkins, and Adrian Batten, among others, before beginning to compose regularly for Westminster Abbey and the Chapel Royal.

45. Bryant, p. 244.

46. *KM*, p. 294.

47. Ibid., p. 292.

48. Ibid., p. 288, recording a warrant for £30 to Blow for maintenance of Holder, dated 1 Apr. 1675 but made retroactive to 29 Sept. 1674.

49. British Museum, Harleian MSS. 7338–42.

50. See p. 38 above.

51. Grove V, vol. 4, p. 322; see also the *Musical Times*, Sept. 1936, p. 835.

52. *Westminster Abbey Reg.*, p. 189.

53. Pulver, p. 198.

54. Fellowes was probably wrong in assuming, in his article on Christopher Gib-bons for Grove V, that he was Matthew Locke's companion at Exeter. Not only was he Locke's senior by fifteen years, but he took up his appointment as organist at Winches-ter in 1638, the year Locke first went to Exeter Cathedral as a chorister. The error has been corrected in Grove VI.

55. Pulver, p. 198.

56. MS. 88, Fitzwilliam Museum Library, Cambridge, fo. 136^v, 124^v, and 112^v. An-other work by Gibbons—a "Gloria in G," copied anonymously into Fitzwilliam MS. 152, on p. 55—has been described as being in Purcell's autograph. It is not.

57. See p. 42 above.

58. Cummings, p. 27. For instance, it is unlikely that Locke would have used both polite and familiar form ("thee" and "you") in addressing the same person within the body of one letter.

59. To be sure, Pepys did record an occasion on which an anthem was "tried over"—clearly a rehearsal and not merely a musical gathering (see Pepys [W], 23 Feb. 1660/61).

60. Bodleian Library, MS. Wood D 19(4), fo. 86^v: "Lock (Matthew) was bred a chorister in the Cathedral Church of Exeter (being, as I presume, a Devonian born) while William Wake was Master of the choristers there—Organist to Queen Catharine of Portugal—Afterwards turned Papist."

61. See the entry in *KM* for 22 May 1677 (p. 318); but more important, the follow-ing entry from *Cal. S. P. Dom.* for 26 Feb. 1675/6: "Pass for Nicholas Staggins, Master of the King's Music, having leave to go and remain in Italy and other foreign parts for a year, with his servants, etc., to embark for his transportation and to return."

62. He composed the vocal music for the fourth entry in the *Siege of Rhodes* and was involved in the musical event recorded by Pepys for 21 Feb. 1659/60.

63. For further discussion of this work, see *Analytical Catalogue*. no. 472. The first line of the poem is that which suggests Purcell's authorship of the elegy (as H. C. Colles has remarked in *Voice and Verse*, p. 78): "What hope for *us* remains now he is gone?" (my italics). It is tempting to interpret the use of first-person plural to mean that Purcell wrote as spokesman for the younger generation of composers, all suitably impressed by Locke's virtuosity, as described in the balance of the poem. However, poetic license certainly would have allowed for such usage even if some anonymous poet had written these lines. Certainly the prosodic and rhyming skills would do Purcell credit, were he the poet. As composer, Purcell adhered to a long-standing tradition among great composers of the past, who frequently wrote laments for esteemed colleagues. For a few well-known examples, see Nicolas Gombert's *Musae Jovis*, composed in memory of Josquin Deprès; Josquin's *Nymphes des bois*, in honor of Ockeghem; and Ockeghem's "Mort, tu as navré," written in honor of Gilles Binchois. (These works are discussed in Gustav Reese, *Music in the Renaissance*, rev. ed. [New York, 1959].) Within just over two decades, Purcell would be the subject of similar tributes from his contemporaries in England.

Notes to Chapter 4

1. *KM*, p. 322; see also p. 282, where Purcell's name has been inserted for that of Matthew Locke as recipient of livery fees of £16. 2s. 6d. per annum.

2. Edward Dyer, who replaced Locke as composer-in-ordinary to the Private Music, had earlier been admitted musician-in-ordinary on 10 Sept. 1672 (*KM*, p. 247) and therefore was probably Purcell's senior by several years. Locke's successor as composer for the wind music has not been identified, but presumably the office continued. G. B. Draghi succeeded to Locke's post as organist to the queen, a promotion that must have pleased those Italian masters who, as Roger North observed "did not approve of his (Locke's) manner of play, but must be attended by more polite hands" (*Memoirs of Musick*, p. 95).

3. *Cal. S. P. Dom.*, as quoted in Westrup, p. 42, n.4.

4. *KM*, p. 317.

5. *KM*, p. 319. Grabu apparently gave up shortly after this exchange. On 31 Mar. 1679, according to an entry in *Cal S. P. Dom.*, there was issued a "Pass to France for Lewis Grabu, late master of the King's Music, native of France, with his wife and three small children." *MGG*, vol. 5, col. 617, further reports that he was unsuccessful among four competitors for the place of master of music in the French Chapel Royal.

6. HMC, Bath MSS. vol. 2, fo. 165.

7. *KM*, p. 318. According to McGuiness, fo. 43, Blow's "The Birth of Jove" was written for the same occasion. Locke probably filled in for Staggins during the latter's trip to Italy.

8. *KM*, p. 315.

9. WAM 33712 (Treasurer's Account, 1677), fo. 5.

10. See *Analytical Catalogue*, nos. 26, 732, 733, 363, 387, 397, 418, and 433. The chamber works are also discussed later (see pp. 76–770). As for the songs, I have as yet been unable to discover anything more solid than stylistic evidence for approaching the problem of authenticity in connection with the six pieces ascribed to Henry Purcell in Banister's and Low's *New Ayres and Dialogues Composed for Voices and Viols* of

1678. The date 10 Sept. may be significant in connection with a mysterious inscription by Purcell in the flyleaf of Fitzwilliam MS 88.

11. MS. 88, Fitzwilliam Museum Library, Cambridge. For a discussion of the inscribed date and a full list of contents, see Nigel Fortune and F. B. Zimmerman, "Purcell's Autographs," p. 108.

12. Fitzwilliam Museum Library, Cambridge, MS. 88. See plate 14.

13. WAM 33703 (Treasurer's Account, 1670), fo. 3. The account for this year, which reads the same as for each year following except for the changes of scholarship holders, includes Charles Purcell's name for the first time, along with the names of Jacob Leisely, Thomas Neeve, and Robert Radford. Neeve was replaced by John Antrobuspo in 1671, and Robert Radford by one of the three new scholars, John Cooper, Daniel de Lyn, and Wildbore Ellis in 1672, there being six scholars this year. From 1673 until 1677 other changes occurred, but Charles Purcell stayed on.

14. The names of both Charles and Henry Purcell are listed in the Westminster School rolls for these years. See G. F. Russel Barker and Alan H. Stenning, eds., *The Record of Old Westminsters*, vol. 2 (London, 1928), entries for Charles and Henry Purcell, respectively.

15. Cf. Frances Purcell's nuncupative will, App. One, IX, 3.

16. Preface "To the ingenuous reader," from Purcell's *Trio Sonatas of 1683*, from the facsimile in the modern practical edition published by the Lyrebird Press (Paris, 1936).

17. WAM 33713 (Treasurer's Account, 1678), fo. 5; see also 33714 and 33715.

18. See pp. 73–75 below.

19. *The Record of Old Westminsters*, vol. 2, pp. 1109–10.

20. Ibid., p. 1109.

21. See above, p. 2.

22. *The Lover*, 27 Apr. 1714 (no. 27), as quoted in R. Blanchard, ed., *Richard Steele's Periodic Journalism, 1714–16* (Oxford, 1959), p. 99.

23. As quoted in G. F. R. Barker, *Memoirs of Richard Busby (1606–95)*, p. 122.

24. *KM*, p. 337.

25. Grove V, vol. 4, p. 610.

26. Burney, vol. 2, pp. 183–85.

27. Cf. E. H. Meyer, *English Chamber Music* (London, 1946), pp. 217ff.

28. Thomas Mace, *Musick's Monument; or, A Remembrancer of the Best Practical Music*, p. 234.

29. Cf. Robert A. Warner's "The Fantasia in the Works of John Jenkins." Warner revises and corrects E. H. Meyer's earlier incomplete list, as given in *Die mehrstimmige Spielmusik des 17. Jahrhunderts in Nord- und Mitteleuropa*.

30. See all references for Scholes, Pulver, and Tilmouth.

31. Wood, vol. 1, p. 209.

NOTES TO CHAPTER 5

1. Bryant, p. 270.

2. See *Analytical Catalogue*, nos. 606/5, 8, and 9.

3. Luttrell, vol. 1, p. 5.

4. *London Gazette*, 31 Oct.–4 Nov. 1678.

5. *Analytical Catalogue*, no. 261.

6. Bryant, pp. 246 and 252, respectively.

7. Vol. 1, p. 462.

8. See Bryant, pp. 270–74, for a discussion of the wave of fear of English Catholics that swept the country at this time.

9. Evelyn, 21 Sept. 1662.

10. Pepys (M), 14 Sept. 1662.

11. But such innovations are not, as is sometimes said, to be attributed solely to Charles II's tastes, or even to the style-conscious borrowings from modernistic Italian and French fashion on the part of English composers. Before the Cromwellian period, both Byrd and Gibbons (in their respective anthems "Christ Rising" and "This Is the Record of John") had opened the way for such developments.

12. 12 Aug. 1660; see also entries for 2 Sept., 7 Oct., etc.

13. Those of the St. Cecilia Society, the Sons of the Clergy, and the Yorkshire Society are best known. But other groups, like the Eton Scholars, the Hampshire, the Herefordshire, Wiltshire, and Worcestershire Societies, as well as the Artillerymen and Loyal Livery Men, were quite active and are worth investigating. The following, quoted from a typical notice, was printed in the *London Gazette* for 23–26 Oct. 1682: "The Stewards for the Annual Meeting of the Clergymen's Sons do hereby give notice that they intend to have the Sermon at St. Mary-le-Bow church . . . and from thence to Merchant Taylors' Hall to dinner."

14. Charles Duff, *England and the English* (New York, 1959), p. 145.

15. As Bryant, pp. 282–87, explains, Charles II was well aware of the need to effect this transition slowly.

16. "Anthem" was first used as a term in Charles II's *Prayer Book* of 1662, at the end of the third collect: "In choirs and places where they sing here followeth the anthem . . ." (a second was sung after the sermon).

17. So much so that one of the most obvious identifying marks of the occasional piece is its textual source outside the Psalms (cf. the funeral sentences, the collects, and especially the anthems like Purcell's "O Sing unto the Lord").

18. Witness the fact that among Purcell's sixty-nine anthems, no fewer than fifteen are topical in origin (see *Analytical Catalogue*, nos. 2, 4, 5, 9, 10, 17, 19, 24, 30, 44[?], 45[?], 56, 57, and N67).

19. David Hume, *The History of England to 1688*, vol. 7, pp. 69–70.

20. *Analytical Catalogue*, no. 62.

21. Ibid., no. 26.

22. Ibid., no. 64.

23. Reprinted in Cummings, p. 28. He claims that the original of the letter was in his possession—a claim that is verified by the presence of the letter in the Nanki Music Library, Japan, which the present writer has used to verify this transcript. The remark at the end of the postscript is still to be clarified. Westrup explains that "F faut" and "E lamy" refer to very low notes in the gamut. But these are not low notes—at least they would not seem so to a bass soloist of Gostling's ability—but actually correspond either to the "E and F" just above middle C or the same notes an octave lower.

24. Grove V, vol. 3, p. 722 (not mentioned in Grove VI).

25. *Analytical Catalogue*, no. N67. For further information concerning this anthem, see the author's "A Newly Discovered Anthem by Purcell," pp. 302–11.

26. See the later discussion of some of the omitted verses from the same psalm, which represent a royal figure of totally different aspect. Similar editorial methods there produce a stern, warlike hero, representing William III, of course. The contrast could not be more striking, either in texts or musical settings.

27. See the exemplar of Dryden's political allegory in the Huntington Library, San Marino, Calif.

28. Reprinted as one of the "Bagford Ballads" in J. W. Ebsworth's edition, part 1, p. 95.

29. This quotation, which confirms the identifications discussed above, also gives the key to scriptural names attached to other prominent persons on the political scene, namely, "Achitophel" for Shaftesbury, "Zimri" for the duke of Buckingham, etc. Robert Bell remarked: "The characters assigned to the persons introduced clung to them for the rest of their lives; the same scriptural titles were employed by hosts of poetasters and pamphleteers; and even the clergy volunteered to give increased notoriety to their application by bringing them into their discourses from the pulpit." Again: "The characters hit home; the names passed glibly into the ballads, lampoons, and political tracts of the day; and Charles and David remained convertible terms to the end of the reign" (*viz.* Feb. 1684/5).

30. *Analytical Catalogue*, no. 135.

31. Bryant, p. 286, records a bill brought in by the House of Commons against popery and the succession to the throne by James, duke of York, and discusses Charles II's efforts to parry their thrusts.

32. John K. Galbraith, *The Affluent Society* (Boston, 1958), chap. 2.

33. Cf. E. Wind, "Julian the Apostate at Hampton Court," pp. 127–37, where a similar propagandistic purpose is shown to have governed the choice of Verrio's subjects for the painting of these allegorical murals above the king's staircase at Hampton Court. In this instance, however, the propaganda was directed against a Stuart, namely, James II, who already had been satirized in a pamphlet as "Julian the Apostate" as early as 1682, while he was still James, duke of York. King William III figured as the hero, shown in various guises, in this instance.

34. According to Anthony à Wood, Oxford, Bodleian MS. Wood D 19(4), fo. 14, who also mentions his earning some money by playing on the "Flagillet," perhaps remembering the concert he himself had reported hearing on 11 Jan. 1665/6: "Mr. Banister of London and divers of the King's musicians gave us a very good meeting at the Schools in music, where he played on a little pipe or flageolet in consort . . ." (Wood, vol. 2, p. 69).

35. *London Gazette*, 14–18 Nov. 1678. As William van Lennep has pointed out in *The London Stage*, vol. 1, p. 274, 22 Nov. 1678 actually fell on Friday, not Thursday.

36. *Westminster Abbey Reg.*, p. 197. (He was buried in the cloisters the following day.)

37. *KM*, p. 340.

38. François Marie Arouet de Voltaire, *Le siècle de Louis XIV*, p. 383.

39. Hawkins, vol. 2, p. 700, erroneously calls it the first such concert series, but Robert Elkins, in *The Old Concert Rooms of London*, sets the matter straight (see pp. 22ff.).

40. British Museum, Add. MS. 24889, passim. This manuscript consists of arrangements for strings (in parts) copied by Britton himself. The works it contains, which have been ascribed to Purcell, include transcriptions of the songs "No, No, Poor Suff'ring Heart," from *Cleomenes*; "Twas Within a Furlong of Edinboro Town," from *The Mock Marriage*; sections from "Behold the Man That with Gigantic Might," from *The Richmond Heiress*; of "Let the Soldiers Rejoice," from *Dioclesian*; and some of the songs from the *Indian Queen* (*Analytical Catalogue*, nos. 576, 605, 608, 627, and 630, re-

spectively). Purcell's instrumental works are represented by the "Trumpet Tune" from *Dioclesian* (*Analytical Catalogue*, no. 627/21) and by an arrangement for strings of the little harpsichord piece "Lilliburlero," which figured in the downfall of James II. In other words, Britton gathered together in his library a potpourri of Purcell's most popular tunes.

41. *Analytical Catalogue*, nos. 731–32, 745–52.

42. Roger North, *Memoirs of Musick*, p. 103.

43. "Since the Pox," "Amintas to My Grief," "Scarce Had the Rising Sun," and "I Resolve Against Cringing," *Analytical Catalogue*, nos. 471, 356, 469, and 386.

44. *Analytical Catalogue*, no. 606.

45. Downes, p. 38. See *Analytical Catalogue*, no. 606.

46. *KM*, p. 337, vol. 2, p. 337; Burney, vol. 2, p. 382n, states that Purcell had already provided music for the stage in writing an overture and set of act-tunes for Aphra Behn's *Abdelazer*, and the Masque in Shadwell's *Timon of Athens* in 1678. Both dates are wrong (see commentaries, *Analytical Catalogue* for nos. 570 and 632, respectively).

47. As quoted in McGuiness, fo. 44.

48. Bryant, pp. 278–80; see also Evelyn's entry for 25 Jan. 1678/9. Danby (Sir Thomas Osborne) was Charles II's lord high treasurer until the time of his impeachment, after which he spent some five years in the Tower (*DNB*).

49. *Cal S. P. Dom.*, 31 Mar. 1679.

50. *KM*, p. 339.

51. Evelyn.

52. *KM*, p. 340.

53. Bryant, p. 287.

54. *KM*, p. 346.

55. Bryant, p. 292.

NOTES TO CHAPTER 6

1. Roger North, *The Musicall Grammarian*, pp. 33–34.

2. *Analytical Catalogue*, nos. 735–43.

3. Ibid., no. 626.

4. Ibid., no. 328.

5. Luttrell, vol. 1, p. 41.

6. Ibid., p. 46.

7. Ibid., p. 54. See also *Analytical Catalogue*, no. 340.

8. Nicoll, p. 419, says the original production began in September, without explaining why the play should have been mounted before the opening of the season. Dr. Laurie, fo. 162, dates the first performance after the second week in October, but finds no evidence that the works might not have been performed at the end of summer as well. Downes and Montague Summers (*The Playhouse of Pepys*) give no dates. See also Term Catalogues, Mich., 1680, which indicates an earlier date.

9. Downes, p. 38.

10. Nicoll, pp. 133n and 225. On pp. 310 and 311 he also records performances for 17 Nov. 1674 (prices doubled); 18 Nov. 1677, and 28 Nov. 1677.

11. *Analytical Catalogue*, nos. 413 and 508, respectively.

12. See *Register of Baptisms*, All-Hallows-the-Less: "July 9th, Purssell, Henry S. of

Henry and Frances" and the *Register of Burials*, in the same location, for 18 July: "Purssall, Henry." No other Purcells are mentioned anywhere in extant records of the parish of All-Hallows-the-Less or for All-Hallows-the-Great, with which the former merged shortly after the Great Fire in 1666. At least, none of the parish registers, rate books, etc., now preserved in the Guildhall Library, shows any reference to the Purcell family. Hence it would seem Henry and Frances Purcell would have come into the parish especially for the event. Could this pair be any other than the young composer and his bride? Possibly. But probability scarcely allows for two Henry Purcells marrying two Franceses within so short a period. Moreover, the lack of any record of Henry Purcell's residence or domestic affairs in or around Westminster Abbey about this time makes it all the more likely that this record does indeed refer to the composer.

13. I.e., Henry Purcell m. Rachel Purcell, 1653; another Henry Pursill, son of John of Thornborough, Bucks (see App. Two); Henry Pursell, poulterer, Norton Folgate, Middlesex (d. Buckingham), will proved Mar. 1689 (wife, Alice); Henry Purcell, (d. ca. 1695), son of the bursar of the Royal Navy, Charles Purcell.

14. Westrup, p. 262.

15. Unfortunately, both the rate-books and their duplicates for St. Margaret's, Westminster, are missing for 1681. It is therefore impossible to say when Purcell moved into his residence in St. Ann's Lane, where he is listed as the twenty-fourth of the rate-payers canvased in the following year (1682).

16. Westrup, p. 45.

17. See my "Purcell Iconography: Missing Items," p. 369.

18. As shown in plate 13.

19. *Westminster Abbey Reg.*, 10 Dec. 1693.

20. *Analytical Catalogue*, no. 131.

21. However, there is evidence indicating another possible date of origin for "Beati omnes." In Tenbury Library, Ms. 17c has the following annotation on p. 247, at the end of the copy of this work: "The foregoing was undoubtedly composed by command of James the 2d on the supposed pregnancy of the Queen, which was proclaimed in 1688." The lateness of the annotation, the obvious confusion of this work with "Blessed Are They" (the same psalm in English), the prejudice with regard to the famous pregnancy, and, above all, the early stylistic character of the Latin setting—all these factors convince me that the writer of the note had confused the two works.

22. Br. Mus. Add. MS. 30930.

23. *Analytical Catalogue*, no. 130.

24. Ibid., nos. 17AB, etc.

25. Ibid., no. 581. See also *The London Stage*, vol. 1, p. 293, which suggests 8, 9, and 10 Dec. as actual dates of performance.

26. Bryant, pp. 306–8.

27. *DNB*.

28. *Analytical Catalogue*, no. 264.

29. *Venus and Adonis*, ed. Anthony Lewis, *L'Oisean Lyre*, pp. 53–63.

30. From the typescript of an article, "Blow's Court Odes," fo. 6, lent by Rosamond McGuiness. Similar sentiments were expressed in Blow's birthday ode for 29 May, following "Up, Shepherds, Up."

31. Bryant, p. 308.

32. Wood, vol. 2, p. 511.

33. Ibid.

34. Luttrell, vol. 1, p. 68.

35. As suggested above.

36. At least Nicoll records no royal visits for that part of the year.

37. Whips loaded with lead weights.

38. Accompanied by the Catholic and already politically, as well as musically, discredited Grabu, of all people.

39. Huntington Library (San Marino, Calif.), Bindley Pamphlets.

40. Ibid.

41. Bryant, p. 311.

42. *KM*, p. 352. Hingeston's name is added in a later list (see p. 353) but Purcell's does not appear.

43. See App. One, XI, for the text of the documents involved.

44. See App. One, XX, 16, for information on Francis Purcell, and XXII, 17, for a transcript of Thomas Purcell's will.

45. See App. One, IV/V, 1–4.

46. See pp. 73–74 above.

47. *Analytical Catalogue*, no. 336.

48. Vaughan Williams, editor of the Purcell Society edition of this work, suggested that the occasion was Charles II's return from Newmarket on 12 Oct. 1681; since the text of the ode and Purcell's setting are concerned with an elaborate metaphor involving the river Isis—an old name for the higher reaches of the Thames—a return along the river from Windsor seems the more plausible occasion.

49. See Wood, *Life and Times*, vol. 2, p. 552, for the ghastly details.

50. *Analytical Catalogue*, nos. 230 and 35, respectively.

51. WAM 33717 (Treasurer's Account, 1681), fo. 5ᵛ. The amount paid suggests that the work in question was the massive B-flat Major service, not the smaller G-Minor service. This suggestion is strengthened by additional reference to an anthem, which probably was the five-part "O God, Thou Art My God." (See my "Purcell's 'Service Anthem,' 'O God, Thou art my God' and the B-flat Major Service," p. 207.)

52. See Bodleian MS. Mus. A–1; also my article "Purcell and Monteverdi," pp. 368–69.

53. For an English translation, see Strunk, *Source Readings in Music History* (London, 1952), pp. 394–95ff.

54. In the personal collection of the late R. Thurston Dart, who very kindly allowed me to make a copy.

55. *Analytical Catalogue*, no. 589.

56. Laurie, fo. 167.

57. Luttrell, vol. 1, p. 144.

NOTES TO CHAPTER 7

1. As quoted in R. McGuiness, "Blow's Court Odes," fo. 8.

2. *London Gazette*, 30 Jan.–2 Feb. 1681/2:
Whereas an indignity hath lately been offered to the picture of His Royal Highness the Duke of York, in the Guildhall of the said city, which cannot be understood otherwise than an effect of malice against his person; the Lord Mayor and Court of Aldermen of the said city, out of a just and due regard to the honour of His Royal

Highness, and their deep resentment of that indolent and villainous act (to be abhorred by every good man and loyal subject) and being greatly concerned, and desirous to find out the author thereof, do unamimously publish and declare that if any person know of, or can discover the person who committed the fact; the said Lord Mayor and Aldermen will not only kindly receive, and acknowledge his or their discovery, as a most acceptable service to the said city, but the person or persons that shall make the said discovery, either to the Lord Mayor or the said Court, so as the person be apprehended and convicted therof, he or they shall thereupon receive a reward of five hundred pounds. Dated this 27th day of January, in the 33 year of His Majesty's reign.

Wagstaffe.

3. Evelyn, 24 Jan. 1681/2.

4. St. Margaret's, Westminster, *Overseers Accounts of poor-rates* for 1681, passim. The names of Blow and John Wilson are to be found in the duplicate book, though missing in the rate books.

5. Purcell's daily journey may still be retraced, along St. Ann's Lane to Orchard Street, then through a rather narrow lane, leading to a small gate at the back of the Dean's Yard, and then into a rear entrance of Westminster Abbey, which still leads to the organ loft. Today, however, one must enter through the muniments room and Abbey library.

6. 17 May 1682.

7. *Analytical Catalogue*, no. 341.

8. Etymological progenitor of the modern term "mob" (*OED*).

9. Bryant, p. 330.

10. Quoted from McGuiness, fo. 47.

11. WAM 33717 (Treasurer's Account, 1682), fo. 6. The copyist—probably John Needham himself—has confused the trips from Newmarket and Windsor. But his meaning is fairly clear, and can be corroborated in Luttrell.

12. Bryant, p. 329.

13. Maitland, vol. 1, p. 473.

14. Ibid.

15. *Analytical Catalogue*, no. 10. Though biblical, the text is not from the Authorized Version.

16. Providentially undone, the plot's undoing called for yet another celebration. For this, Purcell composed the royal ode "Fly, Bold Rebellion" (*Analytical Catalogue*, no. 324) in 1683.

17. *Analytical Catalogue*, no. 337.

18. See App. One, I, 2.

19. Cheque-book, p. 17.

20. In his article for *PMA* (1876–77), Cummings raises the point that Thomas may have been a close friend of Matthew Locke, indeed so close that Thomas named his eldest son after him.

21. Cummings, pp. 34–35, claimed that the original was in his possession. F. Purcell may have been either Francis, son of Thomas, or Frances, Henry's wife. It is now in the Nanki Music Collection, in Shirakawa, Fujiwara Prefecture, Japan.

22. See App. One, XXII, 17.

23. Cf. Westrup's discussion of the death of young Henry Purcell, "Fact and Fiction About Purcell."

24. Cheque-book, p. 17.

25. *KM*, p. 358.

26. *KM*, p. 360.

27. Not mentioned in Edward Chamberlayne, *Angliae Notitiae* . . . (15th ed., 1684), but see App. One, XI, 2, where Francis's succession is documented, and XI, 3 and 4, concerning his position at Somerset House.

28. *Westminster Abbey Reg.*, p. 72 (also Westrup, p. 45). A younger J. B. Peters died in the parish of St. Mary-le-Bow on 26 Feb. 1710/11 (PCC 66 Leeds). But since all the daughters mentioned in the will were under eighteen at the time of his death, he cannot have been the father of Purcell's wife, though possibly the brother. Perhaps his father, who gave him the diamond ring he thus passed on to his son, Richard, was also named John Baptist. Among his children was a daughter, Frances, possibly the niece of Purcell's wife.

29. *Westminster Abbey Reg.*, p. 206.

30. MS. 88, flyleaf, verso. See plate 14.

31. Henry Purcell III. See App. One, XIV. Westrup, p. 263, indicates that the death took place in October.

32. *KM*, p. 372.

33. See p. 90 above.

34. *Henry Purcell: Zeit, Leben, Werk*, p. 35.

35. Luttrell, vol. 1, p. 218. However, the *London Gazette* (7–11 Sept. 1682) gives 10 Sept. as the day of return.

36. Charles II had championed Pritchard (?1632–1705) mainly out of regard for his anti-Whig sentiments. Pritchard did not disappoint the king in this regard, and continued to persecute Whigs throughout his tour of duty (see *DNB* article on William Pritchard).

37. J. W. Ebsworth, ed., *The Roxburghe Ballads*, vol. 5, p. 22.

38. Ibid., p. 166; a dozen such examples could easily be cited. See also pp. 234, 274, 279.

39. London, 1682, p. 4 (cf. *Analytical Catalogue*, no. 606/5). Although the title page definitely refers to the lord mayor's inauguration, it is possible that Purcell may have written other songs for festivities the previous day.

40. Ibid., p. 6 (cf. *Analytical Catalogue*, no. D571/9).

41. Grove V, vol. 6, p. 998. The event is not mentioned in the article on Purcell in the sixth edition.

42. See *Analytical Catalogue*, no. 271.

43. 15th ed. (1684), part 2, p. 202.

44. Ibid.

45. As quoted in R. McGuiness, "Blow's Court Odes," fo. 9.

46. See *Analytical Catalogue*, nos. 195, 370, 390, 411, 413, 415, 435, and 581.

47. See p. 73 above.

48. See Westrup, pp. 51–53, and Edmund Macrory, *Notes on the Temple Organ*.

49. *KM*, pp. 393 and 436.

50. Perhaps related to Edward Wormall, a musician who had served under James I and Charles I but was replaced soon after the Restoration by John Harding (*KM*, p. 150). The churchwarden is probably to be identified with the Giles Borrowdell whose name appears on the covers of several of the St. Margaret's "Overseers' Accounts."

51. *Middlesex County Records*: Sacrament Certificate 4/13, the original of which is reproduced as plate 16.

52. As Douglas Newton has indicated in his book *Catholic London*, unfortunately without substantiating documentation.

53. Suspicion was aroused already, even though the Anabaptist oil-merchant Keeling did not reveal the details of the plot until 12 Apr. (see Bryant, p. 334, for an account of the plotters' plan to establish a strong republic under the "dogeship of Monmouth").

54. Cheque-book, p. 17.

55. See *KM*, pp. 361–62.

56. Michael Tilmouth, "A Calendar of References to Music in Newspapers Published in London and the Provinces (1660–1719)," pp. 5–6.

57. Ibid., p. 6.

58. Purcell, meticulous soul that he was, probably did make all the corrections in his own hand, as J. A. Fuller-Maitland has suggested in his preface to the *Purcell Society Edition* (vol. 5, p. iii).

59. "From Hardy Climes," *Analytical Catalogue*, no. 325.

60. Tilmouth, "Calendar of References," p. 6. Another such advertisement for music in the Italian style was made by August Kühnel, a German composer, who advertised his works in the *London Gazette* for 23 Nov. 1684.

61. Purcell's obvious interest in Lelio Colista, Monteverdi, Bassano, Carissimi, and others notwithstanding, his basic inspiration, or at least the impression one gains from his music, remains English in nature.

62. See p. 131 below.

63. Quoted in *Roger North on Music*, ed. John Wilson, p. 47. Roger North waxed enthusiastic on the subject of sonatas, writing in an earlier notebook: "Then rose up the noble Purcell, the Jenkins of his time, or more. He was a match for all sorts of designs in music. Nothing came amiss to him. He imitated the Italian sonata and (bating a little too much of the labour) outdid them. And raised up operas and music in the theatres, to a credit, even of fame as far as Italy, where Sigr. Purcell was courted no less than at home" (ibid., p. 307n). North also wrote very highly of the sonatas in the *Musicall Grammarian*, pp. 36–37, and in "An Essay on Musical Ayre," as quoted above.

64. *London Gazette*, 26–30 July 1683.

65. Luttrell, vol. 1, p. 284.

66. Grove V, vol. 1, p. 769; Grove VI, vol. 2, p. 805.

67. Luttrell, vol. 1, p. 285.

68. WAM 33718 (Treasurer's Account, 1683), fo. 6.

69. *Analytical Catalogue*, nos. 329 and 339, respectively.

70. Playford's general statement is corroborated by Maitland (vol. 1, p. 484). The latter reported, more precisely, a violent frost, which froze the Thames over and "created a new city on ice," lasting until 5 Feb.

71. *KM*, p. 361. However, Lafontaine earlier lists one Thomas Hingeston as the keeper and repairer of His Majesty's organs and other instruments (*KM*, p. 128).

72. Ibid., p. 159.

73. Ibid., p. 207.

74. Ibid., p. 255.

NOTES TO CHAPTER 8

1. The days on which knights wore the collars of their orders (*OED*).

2. E. Chamberlayne, *Angliae Notitiae*, 15th ed. (1684), part 1, pp. 142, 147, and 180.

3. *KM*, pp. 364–65.

4. Ibid., pp. 173 and 200, respectively. See also pp. 214, 223, 231, 235, 253, 298, etc.

5. Ibid., p. 160.

6. *Analytical Catalogue*, no. 339.

7. Though advertised in the *London Gazette* for 12 May, the publication had no doubt been in preparation earlier in the year. Purcell's references to "these compositions" may perhaps be taken as a sign that he had originally intended to publish more works for St. Cecilia than the one that appears in print. The Stewards named are those for 1684, not 1683. See also *The London Stage*, vol. 1, pp. 324–25.

8. *Analytical Catalogue*, no. 329.

9. Ibid., no. 334.

10. See Luttrell, vol. 1, p. 304; also *London Gazette*, 3–7 Apr. and 15–19 Sept. 1684. (The latter records the return of the court to Whitehall.)

11. Luttrell, entries for 1 Jan. and 8 Apr. 1684, respectively (vol. 1, pp. 295 and 304).

12. As Boswell, after Lawrence, points out.

13. Ibid.

14. *Analytical Catalogue*, no. 594.

15. Purcell's music for the play was dated 1685 until recently, when Dr. Laurie (fos. 167–68), following a lead provided by William Barclay Squire, demonstrated that it may have been composed in 1684 or perhaps in 1683 or even for the original production in 1677. Squire was wrong in saying that there was no place in the play where three voices could have been introduced naturally and easily. See also *The London Stage*, vol. 1, p. 322.

16. *Analytical Catalogue*, no. 246.

17. Hawkins, vol. 2, p. 691; Burney, vol. 2, p. 344. Burney's summary of the affair is as comprehensive and accurate as any, although he did confuse G. B. Draghi with J. B. Lully.

18. Grove IV, vol. 3, p. 751.

19. E. Macrory, *Notes on the Temple Organ*, pp. 30–31. The list given in Grove IV is defective and incomplete. Note that the cromorne and double courtall stops, which Harris challenged Smith to make within a given time, are not listed here. Presumably Smith did not install these permanently but only during the contest.

20. An unspecified payment of £8. 19s. 4d. is recorded in the *Cal. Tr. Bks.* for 13 Aug.: "To Mr. Purcell, one of the King's musicians." The sum is unusual, and probably represents remuneration for some special service, such as this. As we know from a note to Jacob Tonson (see *The London Stage*, vol. 1, p. 328–29), his play, *The Conquest of Granada*, and "the singing opera," *The Tempest*, were in readiness toward the end of Aug. 1684.

21. *Analytical Catalogue*, no. 326.

22. See *PRO Chancery Roll* C5/64/74.

23. See the "Warrant to make the theatre ready for dancing on the Queen's birthday, 10 Nov. 1684," Boswell, p. 238.

24. Luttrell, vol. 1, p. 320.

25. Ibid.

26. See my "Handel's Purcellian Borrowings in His Later Operas and Oratorios," p. 22. See also *The London Stage*, vol. 1, p. 334. Handel, of course, did not merely quote Blow's invention. He used the themes to construct a much more impressive piece.

27. See *Analytical Catalogue*, App. 5, which lists twenty-one works in all for the period from the end of 1683 to the beginning of 1685.

28. HMC, vol. 7, Rutland MSS. II, p. 85. See also *The London Stage*, vol. 1, pp. 337 and 386.

29. *Analytical Catalogue*, no. 380.

30. Fo. 22, with "Gone" written in the margin.

31. See "Overseers' Accounts," E 197–98, for years 1684 and 1685, respectively.

32. See the account of the organ-loft incident, pp. 161–69 below, and App. One, XIII, 7, for Purcell's will, witnessed by Crespion, living at this address since 1678.

33. McGuiness, fo. 50.

34. *KM*, p. 369.

35. Evelyn, 27 Jan. 1684/5.

36. Ibid., 28 Jan. 1684/5.

37. *DNB*.

38. See, especially, those by Tate and Thomas.

39. Evelyn, 6 Feb. 1684/5.

40. *Analytical Catalogue*, nos. 393 and 368, respectively.

NOTES TO CHAPTER 9

1. Luttrell, vol. 1, p. 338, mentioning the opening of the playhouse on 27 Apr.

2. *The History of the Coronation of . . . James II*, pp. 65ff. These lists apparently identify the various musicians shown in the magnificent plates published by Sandford. (See plates 22–25.) The total number of musicians who took part was considerably greater than the thirty-six performers, Purcell among them, as listed in the *Cal. Tr. Bks.* for 14 Apr. 1685.

3. The names "Jacob" and "George" appearing together in the list here may be those mentioned as performers for *Timon of Athens*.

4. Sandford, *History of the Coronation*, pp. 69ff. A marginal note identifies Purcell as "Organist of St. Margaret's, Westminster." As Westrup has pointed out (p. 54), Bernard Smith, not Purcell, held that post officially. But it does not follow with absolute certainty that Sandford made a slip in associating Purcell with St. Margaret's. He may well have been performing there from time to time, as Mackenzie Walcott has suggested in *Westminster: Memorials of the City* (Westminster, 1848), p. 322. He states that Purcell and Blow both attended St. Margaret's Church, playing the anthem when the Abbey choir came to sing in the afternoon service upon the great festivals of Nativity, Easter, and Whit Sunday. To many, Purcell may have seemed one of the chief figures at St. Margaret's, even though he appeared there only occasionally. Obviously, Staggins, Purcell, and Forcer were listed under "Basses" because they were at the end of the line.

5. Sandford, *History of the Coronation*, p. 80. The wording may indicate that Child had composed this anthem for earlier coronations, not for this one. Perhaps Purcell's setting was used for this occasion.

6. Carola Oman. *Mary of Modena*, pp. 7–9. See also *Encyclopedia Brittanica Micropaedia*, vol. 6, p. 664.

7. For a view of the enthronization in Westminster Abbey showing the positions of musicians, trumpeters, and drummers, as well as other persons participating, see plate 9 in Franklin B. Zimmerman, *Henry Purcell*, 1st ed.

8. *History of the Coronation*, pp. 82ff.

9. *Analytical Catalogue*, no. 19.

10. Ibid., no. 30.

11. *KM*, p. 380. See also Franklin B. Zimmerman, "Anthems of Purcell and Contemporaries in a Newly Rediscovered 'Gostling Manuscript,'" p. 62.

12. Luttrell, vol. 1, p. 339; see also plate 30 for a later fireworks celebration.

13. Bodleian, Rawl MS. D 872; Secret Services, p. 124.

14. Nicoll, p. 406. See also *The London Stage*, vol. 1, p. 124.

15. *DNB*. See also Maitland, vol. 1, p. 485, for a full account of the grisly scene.

16. *Analytical Catalogue*, no. 481.

17. Just the year before, Vitali had dedicated to the queen his *Balli in stile francese à cinque stromenti, consecrati alla Sacra Real Maestà di Maria Beatrice d'Este Stuarda, Regina della Gran Bretagna . . .* Opera duodecima . . . (Modena, 1685). Eleven years before he had entered the service of Duke Francisco II, her brother.

18. "Ambition Brought Low: or, The Downfall of Monmouth."

19. *Analytical Catalogue*, no. 494. See also *The London Stage*, vol. 1, p. 338.

20. Cf. Laurie, fo. 168.

21. *Analytical Catalogue*, no. 590; see also *The London Stage*, vol. 1, p. 413 and p. 332.

22. In *Orpheus Britannicus*, Book 2 (1702), as Dr. Laurie points out on fo. 169.

23. Laurie, fo. 169.

24. *Analytical Catalogue*, no. 575. However, see *The London Stage*, vol. 1, p. 332.

25. Ibid., no. 575, Commentary.

26. *KM*, p. 369.

27. *KM*, p. 371–72. Checking these entries against certificates of appointments following upon the above warrant within the next few weeks, we find that "Monsieur Mario" was probably a misreading for "Monsieur Mariens." Lafontaine records no certificate for Charles Staggins, appointed tenor oboist on 27 Jan., upon the death of his father, Isaac, although his name continues to appear on warrants during the remainder of James II's reign; nor is there a certificate for Edward Hooton, of whom the same may be said. The appearance of the names of these two instrumentalists among those of the "Counter tenors" no doubt explains the disproportionate number appearing under this heading.

28. *KM*, p. 372; see also HMC, vol. 8, p. 12b.

29. Vol. 1, p. 358.

30. *Analytical Catalogue*, no. 343.

31. Vol. 1, p. 359.

32. See Jeffrey Pulver, "The English St. Cecilia Celebrations of the Seventeenth Century," p. 346.

33. Husk, pp. 20–22.

34. Michael Tilmouth, *RMA Research Chronicle*, no. 1, p. 7.

35. See J. A. Westrup, "Foreign Musicians in Stuart England," p. 76.

36. HMC, vol. 2, p. 99.

37. McGuiness, fo. 51.

38. W. J. Lawrence, "The French Opera in London: A Riddle of 1686," *Times Literary Supplement*, 28 Mar. 1936, p. 268. See also *The London Stage*, vol. 1, p. 347, where the date 11 Feb. 1686 is given.

39. HMC, Rutland MSS., vol. 2, pp. 102–4.

40. *Analytical Catalogue*, no. 631.

41. *Cadmus et Hermione, Tragédie mise en musique par Monsieur de Lully* . . . Representée pour la premiere fois devant le Roy, à Saint-Germain-en-Laye, en l'Année 1674 (Paris, 1719). The "Entrée de l'Envie," from which the melody—but the melody only—appears in *The Tempest*, is printed on p. 21 of Lully's edition.

42. See App. One, I, 3.

43. See App. One, I, 4, for a full account of this matter.

44. *Analytical Catalogue*, no. 437.

45. *Analytical Catalogue*, no. 438.

46. Ibid., no. 646.

47. Ibid., no. 253.

48. Westrup, p. 65.

49. Tilmouth, *RMA Research Chronicle*, no. 1, p. 7.

50. *KM*, p. 379, entry for 9 Nov., which lists riding charges, paid to Staggins, for musicians for 141 days from 14 May to 1 Oct. See also Luttrell, vol. 1, p. 385, who records the return of James II and Queen Mary on that date.

51. Vestry minutes of St. Katherine Cree (now in London, Guildhall Library, MS 1196/1), as quoted in *Churches, Their Organists and Musical Associations*.

52. Ibid.

53. Guildhall MS. 1198/1.

54. Husk, p. 29.

55. *Analytical Catalogue*, no. 344.

56. Luttrell, vol. 1, p. 415.

57. *Analytical Catalogue*, no. 344/5ab.

58. Reproduced in facsimile, Westrup, opposite p. 236.

59. Luttrell, vol. 1, p. 320.

60. *London Gazette*, 20–23 Dec. 1686.

61. *Analytical Catalogue*, no. 610.

62. Nicoll, p. 10. See also *The London Stage*, vol. 1, p. 356.

63. Secret Services, pp. 144, 169, 189, and 196, respectively.

64. Duly ushered in by the usual New Year's celebrations at court. Blow's "Is It a Dream" was the work performed on the occasion.

65. See *The London Stage*, vol. 1, p. 357.

66. Luttrell, vol. 1, pp. 398–99.

67. 19 Apr. 1687.

68. *MGG*, vol. 5, col. 955. See also Evelyn's entries for 30 Jan. 1687 and 19 Apr. 1687.

69. Grove V, vol. 9, p. 21. See also Grove VI, vol. 20, p. 18.

70. A. Liess, "Materialen zur römischen Musikgeschichte des Seicento: Musikerlisten des Oratorio San Marcello 1664–1725," pp. 137–71.

71. *Cal. Tr. Bks.*, 26 Apr. 1687.
72. Ibid., 5 July 1687. (Cf. *KM*, pp. 384 and 389.)
73. *Analytical Catalogue*, no. 656.
74. The list of those with whom he worked included such notable figures as Carlo Caproli, Ercole Bernabei, and perhaps, more significantly in view of Purcell's Italianate tendencies, Lelio Colista (cf. Liess, "Materialen zur römischen Musikgeschichte," passim).
75. *Westminster Abbey Reg.*, p. 219.
76. *Cal. Tr. Bks.*, 10 June 1687.
77. Wood, vol. 3, p. 217, and especially pp. 222ff.
78. Luttrell, vol. 1, p. 410.
79. Ibid., p. 411.

NOTES TO CHAPTER 10

1. *Westminster Abbey Reg.*, p. 219. He was buried on 23 Sept. in the east cloister of Westminster Abbey (according to the unofficial register), slightly more than a week after Mr. Gervais Price, sergeant-trumpeter, had been buried in the Abbey proper.
2. *Analytical Catalogue*, no. 335.
3. *KM*, p. 383.
4. Vol. 2, p. 422.
5. Purcell furnished twelve compositions, all told; Blow seven and a half—he had collaborated with Humfrey in the composition of one dialogue; Locke, four; Humfrey three and a half; and Johnson and Turner, one each. In addition there are two songs doubtfully ascribed to Purcell. Locke and Humfrey were the masters who had died, to whom Playford made reference in the preface.
6. John Wilson, ed., *Roger North on Music*, p. 110.
7. *Gentleman's Journal*, Apr. 1693, p. 107.
8. *Analytical Catalogue*, no. 430.
9. Though not generally regarded as a song composer, Shadwell is listed by Day and Murrie as the composer of five songs.
10. *Analytical Catalogue*, no. 282.
11. Of fifty-three songs printed in the collection, Purcell was responsible for ten; with other settings for solo voice by Ackroyde, Aleworth, Blow, R. Courteville, Damascene, Draghi, Farmer, Gore, G. Hart, J. Hart, Hawnay, Jackson, R. King, Locke, Marsh, Reading, Roffey, Snow, and Turner (see *Day and Murrie*, p. 72).
12. *Analytical Catalogue*, no. 543.
13. Husk, pp. 20–21. See also *The London Stage*, vol. 1, p. 361. The cast *is* known and is listed by Husk. The importance of the famous basso John Gostling is commemorated in the composer's autograph in Chichester Cathedral, where, at a bottom C in the bass solo, "(Gostling)" is written under the musical staff, in Draghi's hand.
14. Recorded for 28 Nov. 1687 in PRO Chancery Roll C5/90/90, addressed, "To the Right Honourable George Lord Jeffreys." See App. One, I, 4.
15. *Cal. Tr. Bks.*, 12 Dec. 1687. Treasury warrant to the bishop of Durham to report on the petition of Henry Purcell, praying payment of £20. 10s. appearing to be due him.
16. *Analytical Catalogue*, no. 5.

17. 15 Jan. 1688. See also E. S. de Beer's note for the entry for this date.

18. Luttrell, vol. 1, p. 430.

19. Burney, vol. 2, p. 379.

20. *Analytical Catalogue*, no. 593. See also *The London Stage*, vol. 1, p. 362.

21. Luttrell, vol. 1, p. 431.

22. P. 351; see also *The London Stage*, vol. 1, p. 362.

23. Pp. 173–74.

24. P. 40.

25. 1699 ed.

26. See p. 140 above.

27. *Cal. Tr. Bks.*, 5 Mar. 1687/8.

28. As recorded in *Cal. Tr. Bks.*

29. *Analytical Catalogue*, no. 571. See also *The London Stage*, vol. 1, p. 362. In addition to the songs listed there, the libretto includes texts for three stanzas from Purcell's "mad-song," "From silent shades": (1) "In yonder cow-slip"; (2) "I'll lay me down"; and (3) "I'll mount to yon coelum" (see *Analytical Catalogue*, no. 371).

30. Laurie, fo. 175.

31. P. 275; see also *The London Stage*, vol. 1, pp. 362–63.

32. Laurie, fos. 175–77. It is fairly certain that he did not sing all the songs, as Westrup suggests (p. 60).

33. *Wit for Money* (London, 1691), p. 26.

34. *Analytical Catalogue*, nos. 260, 262, 275. Interestingly, the collection also contains "The last new Scotch song: 'Cold and raw.'"

35. Evelyn, 20 May 1688, and Th. Smith in HMC, LeFleming MSS, p. 210.

36. *Westminster Abbey Reg.*, p. 174.

37. Ibid., p. 74.

38. *Analytical Catalogue*, no. 284.

39. John Walsh, *The Second Book of the Catch Club* (London, 1689), no. 298.

40. As quoted by E. J. van der Straeten in *The Romance of the Fiddle*, pp. 124–25. Signor Fede is also recorded in *KM* (pp. 384 and 388) as master of His Majesty's Chapel Royal musicians. The lists in which his name appears are noteworthy for the large number of foreign names they contain—including Seignor Grande, Seignor Sansoni, Mr. Anatean, Seignor Albreis, Seignor Francisco, Seignor Bernardo, et al.—and for the absence everywhere of Henry Purcell's name. However, he may be represented in one instance by the anonymous entry "one organist" in the latter list.

41. *KM*, p. 388.

42. Ibid., pp. 388–89. The foreign musicians named above in note 40 were listed here along with several English masters, to make a total of seventy-two in the musical establishment, including Blow (also unnamed), eight children of the Chapel Royal, two sacristans, two vergers, one "keeper of the tribune," and one "cushion man." In addition, there were seventeen trumpeters and kettledrummers under Sergeant Trumpeter, Gervais Price. The following represents a conflation of these lists, rearranged in one alphabetical order:

John Abel	Seignor Filiber	Alphonso Marsh, Jr.
Samuel Akeroyde	Gottfried Finger	Mr. Merchants
Seignor Albreis	Theophilus Fitz	Edward G. Morton
Mr. Anatean	Edmund Flower	Mr. Neydenhanger
Mr. Arnould	Seignor Francisco	Mr. Nicholson

James Bannister
John Banister
Rev. Samuel Bentham
Seignor Bernardo
John Blow
Josias Bouchier
Henry Brockwell
Thomas Browne
Robert Carr
William Clayton
Charles Coleman, Jr.
Stephen Crespion
John Crouch
Mr. Curkaw
William Davis
Mr. Desabay
Henry Eccles
Solomon Eccles
Thomas Farmer
Joseph Fashion, Jr.
Seignor Fede

Nathaniel French
John Gostling
Seignor Grande
Edward Greeting
William Hall
Morgan Harris
James Hart
Richard Hart
Henry Heale
Thomas Heywood
Ed Hooten
Richard Jones
Rev. William Hopwood
Mr. Keelin
Robert King
Mr. La Grange
John Lenton
Francis Le Rich
Richard Lewis
François Mariens

James Paisible
——— Pawmeister
Mr. Pordage
Charles Powell
Rev. William Powell
Henry Purcell
Balthazar Reading
Thomas Richardson
Seignor Sansoni
Rev. J. C. Sharole
Rev. Henry Smith
Charles Staggins, Jr.
Nicholas Staggins
Richard Tomlinson
Rev. Andrew Trebeck
William Tucker
Nathaniel Vestment
Rev. Blase White
Michael Wise
Leonard Woodson

(See also *The London Stage*, vol. 1, p. 163.)

Notes to Chapter 11

1. Wood, vol. 3, p. 281.
2. T. Macaulay, *The History of England*, vol. 1, p. 151.
3. *Analytical Catalogue*, no. 255.
4. Ibid., no. 517.
5. See Westrup, p. 65.
6. For which, see W. Chappell's *Old English Popular Music*, vol. 2, p. 58.
7. *Notes and Queries*, 3d ser. (July 1965), p. 13.
8. J. Dalrymple, *Memoirs of Great Britain and Ireland*, p. 291.
9. Tilmouth, fo. 23.
10. Luttrell, vol. 1, p. 498 (see also McGuiness, fo. 52).
11. Scholes, p. 45. See the portrait of Judge Sewall opposite p. 48.
12. Luttrell, vol. 1, p. 501.
13. *KM*, pp. 390–91.
14. Ibid., p. 391.
15. Ibid., p. 394.
16. P. 74.
17. "Overseers' Accounts" (Poor Rate Ledger E. 307, p. 80).
18. Luttrell, vol. 1, p. 520; however, see also plate 31, involving music by Purcell.
19. WAM 51117 (Coronation Papers, 1661). Colonel Chester, in *Westminster Abbey Reg.*, p. 177, no. 5, records Osgood's burial in the north cloister of the Abbey on 22 Aug. 1672 and speaks of his first mention as a clerk of the works as an entry in the

Chapter Books for 26 Apr. 1662. The document quoted above shows that his appointment had begun at least one year before that date.

20. WAM 61228A (Precentor's Book, 1660–71), fo. 15ᵛ.

21. WAM 51147 (Coronation Papers, 1714).

22. WAM 51128 (Coronation Papers, 1689). In the original the last phrase has been struck out, as if its possible effect were called into doubt.

23. WAM 51125 (Coronation Papers, 1689).

24. Vol. 2, p. 745.

25. WAM 51164 (Coronation Papers, 1714).

26. *Westminster Abbey Chapter Minutes*, 1683–1714, fo. 25 (18 Apr. 1689). I have followed Sir Jack Westrup's transcription of Needham's almost illegible hand.

27. WAM 51126 (Coronation Papers, 1689).

28. WAM 61228A (Precentor's Book, 1660–71), fo. 119ᵛ.

29. WAM 51137 (Coronation Papers, 1689).

30. Ibid.

31. Ibid.

32. For a few instances, chosen more or less at random, see *KM*, p. 378 (where the staggering sum of £2,484. 16s. 3d. owed to various musicians at court was more than a year in arrears); p. 381 (where we find a memorandum to the effect that £220. 12s. 6d. was still due Thomas Purcell's executrix nearly five years after his death); and p. 399 (reproducing a warrant dated 15 Apr. 1690, to pay John Blow £30. 13s. 4d., which sum had been owing to him since the time of his service to King Charles II). In the first instance actual payments came to a total of £2,757. 5s. 11d.

33. Westrup, p. 57. Part of the bill had been owing for two years when he finally collected the money.

34. Bodleian, Rawl. MS. D 872, fo. 99.

35. From Receipt Book for payments by William Jackson, out of Secret Service Money, William III, 20 Apr. 1689 until June 1691. Oxford, MS. Bodl. Rawl. A.306, p. 170.

36. *The London Stage*, vol. 1, p. 371. For Frances Purcell's birth, see *Westminster Abbey Records*, p. 74.

37. *The London Stage*, vol. 1, p. 371.

38. *Poems on Affairs of State*, vol. 2 (1697); see *Analytical Catalogue*, no. 332.

39. A. S. Borgman, *Thomas Shadwell*, p. 81.

NOTES TO CHAPTER 12

1. For instance, see John Evelyn's account of his daughter Mary's musical accomplishments (vol. 4, pp. 271, 421–22, 427, etc.), which he discusses in various entries in his diary. See also the account below of Purcell's having been hired to instruct Miss Katherine Howard on the harpsichord, and John Weldon, then still a student at Eton, who took lessons with Purcell on organ for a considerable period. See also the account of Purcell's experience with one "Mr. Hodg," who lived in his home.

2. *Analytical Catalogue*, no. 322. See also *The London Stage*, vol. 1, p. 371.

3. See Purcell's autograph in British Museum, Royal Manuscript 20.h.8, fo. 125ᵛ. Rev. Lewis Maidwell was master of a school in King Street, Westminster, just a short way from the Abbey, and also quite near Purcell's residence. See F. H. W. Sheppard, ed.,

Survey of London, vol. 31, p. 178; apparently he had been rejected upon applying for the position of master at St. Peter's in 1668 and, consequently, had set up his own school. (See John Sargeaunt, *Annals of Westminster School*, p. 106.)

4. See J. Max Patrick's introduction to L. Maidwell's *An Essay upon the Necessity and Excellency of Education* (1705).

5. P. 50.

6. RMA Research Chronicle, no. 1, p. 4.

7. See William Barclay Squire, "'Beauties Triumph' at Mr. Priest's School," p. 250.

8. *Westminster Abbey Reg.*, p. 74.

9. Cf. Laurie, fos. 51ff., for a concise summary of the evidence.

10. Music Library, Royal College of Music, London.

11. See, however, E. W. White, "New Light on *Dido and Aeneas*," p. 14, and Laurie, fos. 53ff., for further discussion.

12. As reprinted in Thurston Dart's and A. Margaret Laurie's edition of *Dido and Aeneas* (London, 1961), p. 106.

13. As quoted in McGuiness, fos. 57 and 116. The similarity suggests that Nahum Tate may have written the birthday ode ("Welcome, Welcome, Genial Day"), which hitherto has been listed as an anonymous work. Note also the correspondence with the line "To celebrate this genial day," as quoted above.

14. John Blow, *Venus and Adonis*, composed 1682.

15. William D'Avenant, *Siege of Rhodes* (1656, 1661) and *The Cruelty of the Spaniards in Peru* (1567).

16. Richard Flecknoe, *Love's Dominion* (1654, unacted) and *Love's Kingdom* (L.I.F., 1664).

17. Matthew Locke, *Psyche* (D.G., 1674/5).

18. Luttrell, vol. 2, p. 57 (June 1690).

19. Ibid., p. 595.

20. Thomas D'Urfey's *Pills to Purge Melancholy*, vol. 2 (New York, 1959), p. 289.

21. Boswell, p. 238.

22. *Cal. S. P. Dom. 1689*, as quoted in R. Elkin, *The Old Concert Rooms of London*, pp. 38–39.

23. Husk, p. 25.

24. Vol. 2, p. 1; see also McGuiness, fo. 53.

25. *Analytical Catalogue*, no. 333.

26. J. Dalrymple, *Memoirs of Great Britain and Ireland*, p. 414.

27. D'Urfey's *Songs Compleat, Pleasant and Divertive* (1719), vol. 1, pp. 114–16.

28. Luttrell, vol. 2, p. 263.

29. Ibid., p. 16 (2 Feb. 1689/90).

30. Luttrell, vol. 3, p. 488 (25 June 1695). "Mr. Storey" may have been either George Walter Storey, author of *An Impartial History of the War in Ireland* (1691), or his brother, Thomas Story, friend of William Penn (*DNB*).

31. *Analytical Catalogue*, no. 320. See also *The London Stage*, vol. 1, p. 381.

32. *Analytical Catalogue*, no. 465.

33. As published in D'Urfey's *Songs Compleat, Pleasant and Divertive* (1719), p. 62. Purcell also disregarded D'Urfey's formal divisions and instructions for choral performances in that portion of the poem he did not set.

34. P. 238.

35. P. 352.

36. *Cal. Tr. Bks.*, 2 May 1690; William Jephson to the lord chamberlain.

37. That is to say, one more than the twenty-five allowed in the retrenchment discussed above; see *KM*, p. 397.

38. *Analytical Catalogue*, no. 627. See also *The London Stage*, vol. 1, pp. 382, 390, where *The Spanish Fryar* and *The Tempest* both are listed.

39. Downes, p. 42.

40. London, 1690.

41. Cf. Dryden's preface to *Amphitryon*.

42. *Analytical Catalogue*, no. 577. See also, *The London Stage*, vol. 1, p. 382.

43. *Analytical Catalogue*, no. 525, and Laurie, fo. 181. Laurie points out that this dialogue may have been intended for *The Gordion Knot Unty'd*.

44. *Analytical Catalogue*, no. 597, and Laurie, fo. 180. However, see arguments below regarding the probable date. See *The London Stage*, vol. 1, p. 390.

45. *Analytical Catalogue*, no. 588.

46. Ibid., no. 599; see also *The London Stage*, vol. 1, pp. 386.

47. *Gentleman's Journal*, Jan. 1690/91, p. 23.

48. London, 1691.

49. Ibid.

50. "The Gordian Knot Unty'd," *The Times Literary Supplement*, 4 June 1925, p. 384. Dr. Laurie (fo. 181) finds flaws in his reasoning.

51. Laurie, fo. 181.

52. McGuiness, fo. 54. See plate 30 for a description of the "Firework," by Bernard Lens.

53. Husk, pp. 24–25.

54. Ibid., p. 25.

55. J. W. Ebsworth, ed., *The Bagford Ballads*, part 2, p. 365.

56. See Ebsworth's edition, part 2, pp. 369, 373, and 426, respectively, for other military victories for which Purcell's tune was called into service.

NOTES TO CHAPTER 13

1. *An Exact Relation of the Entertainment of His Most Sacred Majesty, William III.* . . .

2. See, for instance, Govard Bidloo, *Komst van . . . Willem III, Koning van Groot Britanje, enz. in Holland*, pp. 176ff. See also Romeinde Hooge, *Relation du voyage de Sa Majesté Brittanique en Hollande . . . 31 Janvier-April 1691* (The Hague: Arnaut Leers, 1692).

3. See Lady Susi Jeans's article on the Sackville papers in the *Monthly Musical Record* for Sept.-Oct. 1958.

4. P. 401.

5. As in the case of Lully's famed "Vingt-quatre Violons du Roi," the number of musicians employed varied from time to time. But these were seldom less than twenty-six, in either orchestra, not counting auxiliary winds.

6. Cf. Rosamund McGuiness, *English Court Odes, 1660–1820*, pp. 16–22.

7. Review in *Music and Letters* 48 (1697):366–70.

8. *KM*, p. 403.

9. Ibid.

10. Ibid.

11. Ibid., p. 404; frequent other references. *Cal Tr. Bks.*, vol. 9, part 3, pp. 902, 912, 916—3 new silver trumpets—935, 940, 967, 978, etc. These show how very extensive and expensive were preparations for the trip.

12. *London Gazette*, 9 Oct. 1690.

13. *Analytical Catalogue*, no. 628. See also *The London Stage*, vol. 1, p. 395.

14. *The Listener*, 29 Apr. 1943.

15. P. 407.

16. See *Analytical Catalogue*, no. 335/7.

17. Ibid., no. 320/lab.

18. Ed. J. C. Winning (London, 1894), p. 20.

19. As quoted by Bucinator in *Musical Antiquary*, Jan. 1911, p. 124.

20. Nicoll, p. 47.

21. Laurie, fo. 87.

22. Moore, p. 72.

23. Downes, p. 42.

24. Luttrell (vol. 2, p. 31) records a performance attended by the queen and dowager queen on 7 Jan. 1691/2.

25. See the genealogical tables and explanatory matter in App. Two for further details.

26. *KM*, p. 404.

27. *Analytical Catalogue*, no. 259.

28. Ibid., no. 278.

29. *London Gazette*, 26–29 Oct. 1691.

30. Maitland, vol. 1, p. 494. For additional information on the lord mayor's show, see also *The London Stage*, vol. 1, p. 401.

31. Vol. 2, p. 302.

32. Husk, p. 26.

33. Ibid., p. 159. See also *The London Stage*, vol. 1, p. 402.

34. London, 1700, pp. 86 and 79, respectively. The first occurs in the first stanza, while the second is to be found in the fourth (Husk, p. 159).

35. *Analytical Catalogue*, nos. 328/10 and 630/4h, respectively.

36. *Gentleman's Journal*, p. 6. By "flat tunes," Motteux means "tunes in minor modes" and by "sharp key," major mode. A replica of a ticket to such St. Cecilia's festivities, held in London in 1697, is shown as plate 32.

37. *Analytical Catalogue*, no. 598. See also *The London Stage*, vol. 1, p. 402.

38. London, Gresham College Library, MS. VI.5.6.

39. Laurie, fo. 185.

40. *Analytical Catalogue*, no. 612; Motteux, in the *Gentleman's Journal* for Jan. 1691, p. 33, pointed out that Southerne's play had been given the month before. See also *The London Stage*, vol. 1, pp. 402–3.

41. This essay reveals that Motteux, like Dryden, may have been slow to recognize Purcell's true worth. Incidentally, his reference to several performances of *King Arthur* in December supplies us with new information on the popularity of the work with contemporary music goers.

42. P. 104.

43. P. 117.

44. *Gentleman's Journal*, Jan. 1691/2, pp. 7–8.

45. *Analytical Catalogue*, no. 602. See also *The London Stage*, vol. 1, p. 404.
46. McGuiness, fo. 55.
47. Feb. 1691/2, p. 26. See also *The London Stage*, vol. 1, p. 408.
48. See *Analytical Catalogue*, no. 629, and Commentary.
49. Vol. 2, p. 378, referring to Sunday, 6 Mar.
50. Nicoll, p. 160.
51. "And all that we espect, is but to find
    Equal to our expence, the audience kind."
52. Downes, p. 42. The "other two" operas were *King Arthur* and *Dioclesian*, in both of which the "score" also was composed by Purcell, the choreography by Priest.
53. Laurie, fo. 189. See also *The London Stage*, vol. 1, p. 409. In his edition for Aug. 1692, Motteux singled out Purcell's song for special commentary.
54. *Analytical Catalogue*, no. 586.
55. Luttrell, vol. 2, pp. 327 and 331.
56. Ibid., p. 374, records his departure for Flanders on 4 Mar. "without leave of prince or princess."
57. Luttrell, vol. 2, p. 355.
58. Ibid., p. 369.
59. See Luttrell, vol. 2, pp. 352ff., 374, 375, 379, 382, for various postponements, and 403 for leave-taking, at last, with weeping.
60. P. 9.
61. *Analytical Catalogue*, no. 576.
62. See also Luttrell, vol. 2, p. 413, who makes it clear that the play was politically offensive.
63. P. 17.
64. Vol. 2, p. 422.
65. Quoted by Westrup, pp. 74–75.
66. Now in Westminster Public Library, no. E 2415, fo. 19ᵛ.
67. Cf. St. Margaret's, Westminster, "Overseers' Accounts," E. 307, p. 118.
68. Cf. J. W. Ebsworth's edition of *The Bagford Ballads*, part 2, pp. 292–99.
69. *Analytical Catalogue*, no. 627/9b.
70. *Angliae Notitiae*, 17th ed., p. 172.
71. *Analytical Catalogue*, no. 134.
72. Cf. H. D. Traill, *William the Third*, pp. 84–90.
73. *Analytical Catalogue*, no. 328.
74. *Gentleman's Journal*, Nov. 1692, p. 18.
75. Cf. *London Gazette*, 22–25 Jan. 1693/4, and Husk, pp. 29ff.
76. McGuiness, fo. 55.
77. *The London Stage*, vol. 1, p. 416.

NOTES TO CHAPTER 14

1. See C. Cibber, *An Apology for the Life of Mr. Colley Cibber . . . Written by Himself*, p. 106, for a brief character sketch. It seemed an unlucky season for actors. In October Sandford had mistakenly stabbed Powell, having picked up a real dagger, mistaking it for the false dagger he should have been using. The victim's life was despaired of for a time. (See also Luttrell, vol. 2, p. 593; Nicoll, passim; and *The London Stage*, vol. 1, p. 416.)

2. For a fuller account of this shocking incident, illustrated by maps, diagrams, etc., see Albert S. Borgman, *The Life and Death of William Mountfort*, Harvard Studies in English, vol. 15 (Cambridge, Mass., 1935), pp. 123–210.

3. Ibid., p. 145.

4. Vol. 2, p. 641.

5. Borgman, *The Life and Death*. See also the *London Gazette* for 12–15 Dec., and Evelyn's entry for 4 Feb. 1692/3, including n. 2 in E. S. de Beer's edition. Luttrell's entry (vol. 2, p. 641) is terse: "Mr. Mountfort was on Tuesday night interred at St. Clement's, where were 1000 persons present; some of the choristers at Whitehall and King's organist were there, and sung an anthem."

6. Dec. 1692, p. 15; Southern's play was *The Maid's Last Prayer*.

7. Evelyn, 2 Jan. 1692/3.

8. McGuiness, fo. 57.

9. *Analytical Catalogue*, nos. 600, 583, 580, 601, 607, 596, 608, and 580, respectively.

10. Fo. 214. However, see *The London Stage*, vol. 1, p. 399, for an earlier version.

11. Laurie, fos. 216–17. See also *The London Stage*, vol. 1, p. 399.

12. *Oedipus* was first performed at Dorset Garden about Nov. 1678, Dryden being called to account for having thus violated his contractual obligations to the Theatre Royal Company (Nicoll, p. 329). Being most successful on that occasion, according to Downes (p. 37), it was performed again in 1682 and repeated also in 1687 and 1692, then revised several times after Purcell's death. I concur in the view of Barclay Squire ("Purcell's Dramatic Music," *SIMG* 5:541), of Laurie, fo. 190, and of other authorities who accept Burney's choice of the 1692 revival as that for which Purcell provided music. This seems a logical date to me not only because of the unusual success of that production, due in no small part to the addition of Purcell's music, but because of certain stylistic features of the music that are characteristic of his very late style. See also *The London Stage*, vol. 1, p. 413.

13. Vol. 2, p. 593.

14. Dryden and Lee, *Oedipus*, epilogue.

15. Vol. 2, p. 593.

16. Burney, vol. 2, p. 390.

17. Laurie, fo. 191.

18. See *Analytical Catalogue*, no. 580/Commentary.

19. *The Gentleman's Journal*, Oct. 1692, p. 24. (The issue was not published until November.)

20. Laurie, fo. 199. See also *The London Stage*, vol. 1, p. 412.

21. Nicoll, p. 433, gives Feb. 1692/3; but I agree with Laurie, fo. 192, who states that early March is the more likely date. See also *The London Stage*, vol. 1, p. 418.

22. *Analytical Catalogue*, no. 601/1.

23. Ibid., 601/Commentary.

24. Ibid., no. 601/3. The attribution to Congreve is definite in *The London Stage*, vol. 1, p. 418.

25. Laurie, fo. 194. *The London Stage*, vol. 1, p. 418.

26. See *Analytical Catalogue*, no. 243.

27. Also sung in D'Urfey's *The Marriage-Hater Match'd* (see *Analytical Catalogue*, no. 602/2, and Commentary).

28. Both quoted in Laurie, fo. 196. See also *The London Stage*, vol. 1, p. 421.

29. Luttrell, vol. 3, p. 60.

30. There are several small, insignificant changes in the *Canzona.*
31. As quoted in Robert Elkin's *The Old Concert Rooms of London,* p. 14.
32. See Westrup, pp. 88, 92; Elkin, *Old Concert Rooms,* p. 13.
33. I.e., *The Mitre,* as quoted in Elkin, *Old Concert Rooms,* pp. 15—16.
34. As Tilmouth points out, fo. 11.
35. *Memoirs of Musicke,* pp. 110—12.
36. Ibid., p. 114.
37. Roger North, *Memoirs of Musick,* p. 126. See also Roger North, *The Musicall Grammarian,* p. 35.
38. As quoted and translated in Michael Tilmouth, fo. 11.
39. Elkin, *Old Concert Rooms,* passim; but see, especially, pp. 17, 20, and 31.
40. Also known as "Greber's Peg" and, due to her dark complexion, as "the tawney Tuscan." For her plain looks, she was also given the name "Hecate," which Dr. John Pepusch apparently had the courage to use as a term of endearment, presumably after the marriage.
41. 5—9 Jan. 1692/3.
42. *London Gazette,* 23 Jan. 1691/2.
43. Ibid., 3 Apr. and 26 Oct. 1692, for advertisements of Tosi's concerts.
44. Nicoll, p. 352. See also *The London Stage,* vol. 1, p. 418.

Notes to Chapter 15

1. *Cal. Tr. Papers,* 24 May 1693. The entry is minuted, "To be respited till the establishment is altered."
2. Ibid.
3. Luttrell, vol. 3, p. 88. See also *The London Stage,* vol. 1, p. 421.
4. *Cal. Tr. Papers,* 17 Aug. 1693.
5. See *The London Stage,* vol. 1, p. 421.
6. See below, p. 299. See also Brown, *Amusements Serious and Comical.*
7. *Day and Murrie,* no. 119.
8. *The Letters of John Dryden,* ed. Charles E. Ward, pp. 62—63. Walsh was the reputed author of *The Dialogue Concerning Women, Being a Defence of the Fair Sex,* and therefore author of the lost play, *The Gordian Knot Unty'd.* See *The London Stage,* vol. 1, p. 428.
9. "Purcell's Dramatic Music," p. 499.
10. *Gentleman's Journal,* Nov. 1693, p. 374.
11. This is probably the son of Vincenzo Albericci, whose name would be Germanized as "Alberrich," a form close enough to "Alberrix" by the lights of seventeenth-century orthography. Given the general feelings against Italians current in official circles in England at this time, the deception is perhaps understandable. According to Matthesonn, *Grundlage einer Ehren-Pforte,* p. 156, Vincenzo Albrici, who had been active as a musician at Dresden, had a son who was "dem Evangelische Gottesdienst Aufsätzig."
12. *The Letters of John Dryden,* p. 62.
13. As quoted in *The London Stage,* vol. 1, p. 433: "The second play is Mr. Dryden's, called *Love Triumphant, or Nature will prevail.* It is a tragi-comedy, but in my opinion one of the worst he ever writt, if not the very worst: the comical part descends

beneath the style and shew of a Bartholomew-fair droll. It was damn'd by the universal cry of the town, *nemine contradicente*, but the conceited poet. He says in the prologue, that this is the last the town must expect from him; he had done himself a kindness had he taken his leave before."

14. *Gentleman's Journal*, Jan.-Feb. 1693/4, p. 26.

15. See *Analytical Catalogue*, no. 582/Commentary.

16. Ibid., nos. 582 and 597/5, respectively.

17. *The London Stage*, vol. 1, p. 430.

18. *Analytical Catalogue*, no. 595.

19. P. 135; the note was probably entered by Gildon.

20. See *Analytical Catalogue*, passim.

21. Laurie, fo. 202.

22. Ibid., with a discussion of chronological evidence.

23. *Gentleman's Journal*, May 1694, p. 134.

24. Ibid., June 1694.

25. Laurie, fos. 205–7. (Abbreviations: DG = Dorset Garden; DP = dramatis personae; S = soprano; CT = countertenor; T = tenor; B = bass; DQS = *Don Quixote*, Part 2; TsM3 = *Thesaurus Musicus*, book 3; Tpt = trumpet.)

26. *KM*, pp. 390–437.

27. The signatures are autograph. An incorrect transcription was published by H. F. Westlake in the *Daily Telegraph*, 20 Dec. 1924, with notes by Sydney Nicholson, who wrote: "Of the stops mentioned, two, the 'Stopped Diapason' and the 'Nasen' are still in the Abbey organ, and are perhaps the most beautiful stops in the instrument."

28. Quoted by permission of the provost of Eton College. John Walter was organist at the college until about 1681 (cf. Albert Mellor, *A Record of the Music and Musicians of Eton College*, pp. 6–7).

29. Luttrell, vol. 3, pp. 302ff.

30. Ashtead Manor Accounts (Muniments Room, Guildford Museum), passim.

31. See the present author's edition of John Playford's *Introduction to the Skill of Music*, 12th ed. (London, 1694), with introduction, glossary, and index published in facsimile (New York, 1973).

32. Husk, p. 32.

33. *London Gazette*, 11 Jan. 1693/4.

34. Ibid., 1 Feb. 1693/4. Various similarities to the text composed by Handel several decades later are quite interesting.

35. Cf. Br. Mus. Add. MS 30934, fo. 58, where a performance at Stationers' Hall is indicated. See also Husk, p. 170.

36. 22–25 Jan. 1693/4.

37. See Michael Tilmouth, "The Technique and Forms of Purcell's Sonatas," p. 109.

38. For dimensions of the room, see Michael Tilmouth's "English Chamber Music 1675–1720," p. 19, giving a plan of the Great Room at York Buildings.

39. S. A. O. Fitzpatrick, *Dublin, a Historical and Topographical Account of the City*, pp. 114–15.

40. Ibid.

41. Evelyn, 14 Oct. 1691, and n. 2.

42. Fitzpatrick, *Dublin*, pp. 114–15; 9 Jan. 1694, incidentally, was the date upon which Joseph Purcell, brother to Daniel and Henry, was married to Sarah Dormer, at St. James's, in Duke's Place (see App. One, XVIII, 1).

43. Fitzpatrick, *Dublin*, pp. 118–19.

44. *Dunciad*, IV, 348, ed. James Sutherland (London, 1953).

45. *The London Stage*, vol. 1, p. 430.

46. Evelyn, however, exclaimed, "Never more glorious and steady summer weather." See entry in *Diary* for 8 July; also Luttrell, vol. 3, p. 342.

47. It looked as if music would have to be got out of the way to make room for various merchandise; on 24 May, a "sale of Indian goods" was advertised "at the Music Room in York Buildings." But conflict was averted through postponement of the sale until 25 May. Concerning concerts at "the Vendu," see the *London Gazette* for 28 May and 11 June, also Tilmouth, fo. 41.

48. See *Analytical Catalogue*, no. 364. See also D'Urfey's *Rivals*, as commented upon in Downes, p. 23.

49. Westminster Abbey, Chapter Minutes, 1683–1714, fo. 47ᵛ.

50. WAM 9834.

51. Apparently the first and second payments were made at the same time, however, for a payment of £100 to Smith is recorded in WAM 33728 (Treasurer's Account, 1695), fo. 5.

Notes to Chapter 16

1. *Analytical Catalogue*, no. 591. Laurie (fo. 208) points out that Nicoll was probably wrong in suggesting September for a date of the first performance. Motteux referred to the performance as "recent" in the *Gentleman's Journal* for Oct.-Nov. Since the issue was late, as usual, it is quite likely that the play was produced in November. See also *The London Stage*, vol. 1, p. 442.

2. *Analytical Catalogue*, no. 574; in *The London Stage*, vol. 1, pp. 452–53, the date of first performance is argued to have taken place not later than Oct. 1695, and probably no later than the month of September.

3. See *Analytical Catalogue*, no. 631. *The London Stage* records no revival of Shadwell's adaptation of Shakespeare's play for 1695; however, Purcell's song "Dear pretty youth" was described as "A New Song in *The Tempest*, sung by Miss Cross to her lover who is supposed Dead," in *Deliciae Musicae*, Book 3, dated 1696, but probably published the year before.

4. See *Analytical Catalogue*, no. 632; *The London Stage* records dates of performances for only 1694 (unspecified) and 1697 (2 Feb.) but discusses publications of Purcell's music that appeared in 1695.

5. See *Analytical Catalogue*, no. 630. *The London Stage* examines all the evidence and limits the date of first performance of the operatic version to the period between mid-April and late autumn.

6. It has even been suggested that part of the cause of the split between Betterton's crew and the Patentees, who stayed with Christopher Rich, arose from dissatisfactions arising from the former's procrastinations of the operatic revival of *The Indian Queen*, for which funds apparently had been received well before the break.

7. Genest, vol. 2, p. 58 (and, after him, Nicoll, p. 426, and Laurie, fo. 208).

8. See *Analytical Catalogue*, no. 57.

9. Ibid., no. N67.

10. Luttrell, vol. 3, p. 400.

11. *Analytical Catalogue*, no. 232. See also *The London Stage*, vol. 1, p. 443.

12. P. 34.

13. Neither Mr. Picket nor Mrs. Robart were well-known figures at the time, however.

14. We are indebted to Sir Frederick Bridge for preserving the anecdote. A letter published by M. Fetis recounts that his own dissatisfaction with the *Te Deum* was not less than Mendelssohn-Bartholdy's, though his patience was greater. He stayed through the *Jubilate*, while his companion unceremoniously left (see J. Frederick Bridge, *Twelve Good Musicians*, pp. 135–36).

15. Luttrell, vol. 3, p. 410. I assume that the king and queen would have heard the original performance.

16. As E. S. de Beer points out in his footnote to Evelyn's entry in his edition of the *Diary*.

17. Luttrell, vol. 3, p. 423.

18. Ibid., p. 418.

19. Ibid., p. 421.

20. Ibid., p. 442.

21. Ibid., p. 444. Luttrell also reports that each had had weekly maintenance plus £5 during the prolonged period of preparation.

22. Ibid., pp. 420–21.

23. Consensus of expert opinion would have it that these were trombones and slide trumpets. See W. Barclay Squire, "Purcell's Music for the Funeral of Mary II," pp. 225–33.

24. As the late R. Thurston Dart has shown in his excellent performing edition, which includes the unscored parts for kettledrums. See also the entry in *KM*, p. 418, for Jan. 1694/5. Although contemporary prints and editions do not prescribe drums in company with trumpets for the most part, plate 23 does show them together, and the above-quoted entry in the lord chamberlain's accounts can scarcely be interpreted to mean that drums were used for anything other than the queen's funeral.

25. Among them, young William Croft, evidently so impressed by Purcell's composition of "Thou Knowest, Lord" that he incorporated the whole into his own setting of the burial service, as published in *Musica Sacra* (1724). Croft acknowledged in his preface both Purcell's authorship of this setting and his general stylistic indebtedness to his former master in the expressive style of his setting of the other funeral sentences (see below, n. 67).

26. J. L. Chester (*Westminster Abbey Reg.*, p. 236) explains the apparent discrepancy between the dates given for Busby's death (on 5 Apr.) and his burial (also 5 Apr.) by pointing out that actually Busby probably was buried on the eleventh. Barker also indicates that the burial register is wrong.

27. For other allusions to "Tityrus" and "Galatea," see also *Vota Oxoniensis pro Serenissimus Guilhelmo Rege et Maria Regina*: Oxonii: E Theatro Sheldoniano, 1689, sig. G^v; and Pietas Oxoniensis, 1695, sig. Pz^v.

28. Possibly, the author of these verses was George Herbert, the well-known poet. But the presence of a lesser-known "Mr. Herbert," who also had poetic aspirations, leaves room for doubt. Since the poems are printed without first names and do not appear among George Herbert's complete works in any modern edition, it is at present impossible to say with certainty which of these men, if either, actually wrote them.

29. Several accounts in Magdalen Library (under the general heading "Liber Com-

puti S. M. Magd. Coll.") provide precise information on Daniel Purcell's tour of duty at Oxford. Although accounts for 1688 are missing, and those of 1689 as well, this series shows that Daniel received his yearly stipends right up to the year 1696, when he shared the organist's salary of £80 per annum with Benjamin Hecht. After that date, Hecht received the whole salary.

30. *A Register of the Presidents, Fellows, Demis . . . of Saint Mary Magdalen College*, ed. J. R. Bloxham, vol. 2, pp. 203–4n., gives the following account of Daniel Purcell's move: "The occasion of his coming to London was as follows: Dr. Sacheverell, Fellow of Magdalen College, 1701–1713, who had been a friend of his brother Henry, having been presented to the Living of St. Andrew, Holborn, found an organ in the church, of Harris's building, which having never been paid for, had from the time of its erection in 1699 been shut up. The doctor upon his coming to the living, by a collection from the parishioners, raised money to pay for it, but his title to the place of organist was litigious, the right of election being in question between the rector, the vestry, and the parish at large; nevertheless, he invited Daniel Purcell to London, and he accepted it; but in February, 1717, the vestry, which in that parish is a select one, thought proper to elect Mr. Maurice Greene in preference to Purcell, who submitted to stand as candidate. In the year following, Greene was made organist of St. Paul's, and, Daniel Purcell being then dead, his nephew Edward was a candidate for the place; but it was conferred upon Mr. John Ishum, who died in June, 1726."

31. See below, p. 314.

32. See *Analytical Catalogue*, no. 610. See also Laurie, fo. 210. Luttrell, however, did not record that the players were commanded not to act until 27 Dec. (vol. 3, p. 418). *The London Stage* does not mention a revival in 1695.

33. See *Analytical Catalogue*, no. 467; in *The Songs of D'Urfey* (p. 21), Cyrus L. Day dates this play as early as 1685, but Nicoll (p. 160) more logically places it in 1694, pointing out that its scheduled opening performance was canceled because of Queen Mary's death. In *The London Stage*, pp. 471 and 477, performances are recorded only for late December 1696 and April 1697.

34. *An Apology for the Life of Mr. Colley Cibber . . . Written by Himself*, pp. 158–59.

35. See *Analytical Catalogue*, no. 632/6–9.

36. Br. Mus. Add. MS 35043, fo. 66ᵛ. ("Mr. Paisibles (*sic*) T. in Timon of Athens.") The pieces also appear anonymously in the set of four part-books, Add. MSS. 30839 and 39565–7. See also Squire, W. B., pp. 554–58, and Laurie, fos. 219–23.

37. Grabu's setting of "Hark how the songsters" was printed in full in Playford's *Choice Ayres and Songs*, Bk. 2 (1679), p. 56.

38. R.M. 24.e.13; see also *Analytical Catalogue*, no. 632/Commentary; also no. 342.

39. *Analytical Catalogue*, no. T691; no. 632/Commentary.

40. *KM*, p. 424, for reference to Jacob Woods. George Rogers was listed by Sandford.

41. Cibber, *Apology*, vol. 1, pp. 196–97, as quoted in *The London Stage*, vol. 1, p. 445.

42. Luttrell, vol. 3, p. 471.

43. Ibid., vol. 1, p. 561.

44. *Abdelazer* in April; *The Mock Marriage* in July; *Pausanias* in May; and *Timon of Athens* between April and June (dates taken from Laurie, passim); in *The London*

Stage dates are given more tentatively for these performances, and generally the ones given are later.

45. Luttrell, vol. 3, p. 519 (Sat., 31 Aug. 1695). "This day was published a proclamation for a public thanksgiving . . . for the success in taking the town and castle of Namur, to be observed on Sunday the 8th of September here in London . . . and on Sunday the 22nd of September in all other places." The thanksgiving for the surrender of Kassel (Piedmont), another siege and another time and place, is recorded by Evelyn.

46. *Analytical Catalogue*, no. 609; *The London Stage*, vol. 1, p. 453.

47. Ibid., no. 609. See *The London Stage*, vol. 1, p. 453.

48. Ibid., no. 605; see also *The London Stage*, vol. 1, p. 452.

49. Ibid., no. 584; see also *The London Stage*, vol. 1, p. 454.

50. Ibid., no. 578; see also *The London Stage*, vol. 1, p. 453.

51. Cf. Laurie, fo. 227.

52. Ibid., fo. 217.

53. See *Analytical Catalogue*, no. 605/Commentary.

54. Laurie, fo. 229, cites RCM MS. 1172 as the source for these.

55. Ibid., fo. 228.

56. See D'Urfey's comments in the dedication, as partially reproduced by Laurie, fo. 230.

57. See *The London Stage*, vol. 1, p. 444.

58. Ibid.

59. See *Analytical Catalogue*, no. 630/Commentary.

60. Add. MS., 31453.

61. *Analytical Catalogue*, no. 631/5ab and Commentary. Cf. also D'Urfey's *Wit and Mirth*, vol. 5 (1719) and Laurie, fo. 138.

62. See *The London Stage*, vol. 1, passim.

63. See *Analytical Catalogue*, no. 394.

64. *The London Stage*, vol. 1, p. 456.

65. He also inherited, with Bernard Smith, Purcell's duties as "Tuner of the regals, organs, virginals, flutes and recorders" (see Grove V).

66. 26–28 Nov. 1695; see also the *Flying Post* (23–26 Nov.); *Westminster Abbey Reg.*, p. 238; and Luttrell, who for this occasion wrote one of the few entries in his massive chronicle having anything to do directly with music.

67. W. H. Cummings, "Purcell Portraiture," p. 286.

68. W. H. Cummings, *Henry Purcell*, p. 77.

69. Transcription and translation by "W. D. M." in *Notes and Queries*, 5th ser., 4 (30 Oct. 1875): 359.

70. Cummings, *Henry Purcell*, p. 78.

71. Ibid., p. 77.

72. *Analytical Catalogue*, nos. 27, 17AB, and 58C, respectively. The well-known account of Croft's borrowing the latter for his own setting of the burial service will perhaps bear repetition here. In his preface to *Musica Sacra* (1724), he explained: "The reason why I did not compose that verse anew (so as to render the whole service of my own composition) is obvious to every artist; in the rest of that service composed by me, I have endeavoured as near as I could to imitate that great master and celebrated composer—whose name will for ever stand high in the rank of those who have laboured to improve the English style in his so happily adapting his compositions to Eng-

lish words in that elegant and judicious manner as was unknown to many of his predecessors. . . ."

73. Cummings, *Henry Purcell*, p. 89. He also quotes from *Mackay's Journey Through England* (1722–23) the following critique of the musical reputation Purcell enjoyed a generation after his death: "The English affect more the Italian than the French music, and their own compositions are between the gravity of the first and the levity of the other. They have had several great masters of their own. *Henry Purcell's* works in that kind are esteemed beyond *Lully's* everywhere, and they have now a good many very eminent masters; but the taste of the town being at this day all Italian, it is a great discouragement to them."

Bibliography

[Addison, J.] *The Letters of Joseph Addison.* Edited by W. Graham. Oxford, 1941.

Addleshaw, G. W. O. *The High Church Tradition: A Study of Liturgical Thought in the Seventeenth Century.* London, 1941.

* Akerman, John Y. *Moneys Received and Paid for Secret Services of Charles II and James II.* London, 1851.

Anderton, Howard Orsmond. "Henry Purcell." *Musical Opinion* 32(April 1915).

Andrews, H. "Purcell and Seventeenth-Century Chamber Music." *Music Teacher*, July 1927.

Angoff, Charles. "Jean Baptiste Lully, Jean Phillipe Rameau, François Couperin, Henry Purcell, Giovanni Baptista Pergoles." In *Fathers of Classical Music*, edited by Charles Angoff. New York, 1947.

Antcliffe, H. "The Naiveté of Purcell." *Chesterian*, n.s., no. 35(1923).

Arkwright, G. E. P. "Purcell's Church Music: Bibliography." *Musical Antiquary* 1(1910).

———. "Purcell's Church Music." *Musical Antiquary* 3(1912).

———. "An English Pupil of Monteverdi." *Musical Antiquary* 4(1913).

———. "A Note on Purcell's Music." *Music and Letters* 2(1921).

Armstrong, A. Joseph. "Operatic Performances in England Before Handel." Ph.D. diss., Baylor University, 1918.

Arnold, C., and Johnson, M. "The English Fantasy Suite." *PRMA* 82(1955–56).

Arnold, F. T. *The Art of Accompaniment from a Thorough Bass.* London, 1911.

Arts Council of Great Britain. *Eight Concerts of Henry Purcell's Music . . . With a Foreword by Ralph Vaughan Williams.* Edited by Watkins Shaw. London, 1959.

Arundell, Dennis. *Henry Purcell.* London, 1927 (German translation by H. W. Draber, Leipzig, 1929).

———. "Purcell's Father." *New Statesman and Nation* 13(19 June 1937).

———. "Masterpiece in Miniature." *Radio Times*, 27 December 1947.

———. *Henry Purcell.* London, 1957.

———. *The Critic at the Opera.* London, 1957.

———. "Purcell and Natural Speech." *Musical Times* 100(June 1959).

———. "New Light on Dido and Aeneas." *Opera*, 13 July 1962.

———. "The Tragedy of Henry Purcell." *London Mercury*, 23 January 1965.

Ashbee, Anthony. "The Four-Part Consort Music of John Jenkins." *PRMA* 96(1969).

Ashley, M. *England in the Seventeenth Century.* Pelican History of England, no. 6. London, 1952.

Aston, Peter. "Tradition and Experiment in the Devotional Music of George Jeffreys." *PRMA* 94(1972–73).

Aubrey, J. *Brief Lives.* Edited by A. Clark. Oxford, 1898.

Audit Office Declared Accounts. Extracts printed in *Musical Antiquary*, passim.

Avery, E. A. *A Tentative Calendar of Daily Theatrical Performances*. Pullman, Wash.: Research Studies of the State College of Washington, 1945.

———. *The London Stage 1600–1800: A Calendar of Plays, Entertainments, and Afterpieces*. Part I: 1660–1700. Edited by William van Lennep. Carbondale, Ill., 1960.

Ayres, J. C. "The Influence of French Composers on the Work of Purcell." Ph.D. diss., Battersea College of Technology, London, 1963–64.

Azulay, G. *Purcell, the Boy Who Became England's Great Composer*. London, 1931.

Backus, E. N. *Catalogue of Music in the Huntington Library Printed Before 1801*. San Marino, Calif., 1949.

Baines, Anthony. *Woodwind Instruments and Their History*. London, 1943.

———. "James Talbot's Manuscript." *Galpin Society Journal* 1 (March 1948).

Bakeless, Katherine Little. "Henry Purcell." In *Lives of the Great Composers*, edited by Alfred L. Bacharach. Philadelphia, 1940.

Baker, H. B. *History of the London Stage and Its Famous Players (1576–1903)*. London, 1904.

* Baker, R. *A Chronicle of the Kings of England*. 6th ed. London, 1674.

Baldwin, Olive, and Wilson, Thelma. "Alfred Deller, John Freeman, and Mr. Pate." *Music and Letters* 50 (January 1969).

Barker, E., ed. *The Character of England*. London, 1947.

Barker, G. F. R. *Memoirs of Richard Busby (1606–95)*. London, 1895.

Barrett, W. A. *English Church Composers*. London, 1882.

Becking, Gustave. "Englische Musik." In *Handbuch der Englandkunde*, edited by Gustave Becking. Frankfurt am Main, 1929.

Bedford, Arthur. *The Temple of Musick*. London, 1704.

———. *The Evil and Danger of Stage Plays*. London, 1706.

———. *The Great Abuse of Musick*. London, 1711.

———. *The Hereditary Right of the Crown of England Asserted*. London, 1713.

———. *The Excellency of Divine Musick*. London, 1733.

Beeverell, J. *Les delices de la Grand' Bretagne*. Leiden, 1709.

Bell, C. E. "English Seventeenth-Century Portrait Drawings in Oxford Collections." *Walpole Society* 5 (1917).

Bell, Hamilton. "Contributions to the History of the English Playhouse." *Architectural Record* 33 (1913).

Bell, W. G. *The Great Fire of London in 1666*. London, 1920.

Bennett, J. "Henry Purcell: An Appreciation." *Musical Times* 36 (November 1895).

Bentley, G. E. *The Jacobean and Caroline Stage*. Oxford, 1941–56.

Bergmann, Walter. "Three Pieces of Music on Henry Purcell's Death." *The Consort*, no. 17 (1960).

Besant, Sir Walter. *London in the Time of the Stuarts*. London, 1903.

Beswick, D. M. "The Problem of Tonality in Seventeenth-Century Music." Ph.D. diss., University of North Carolina, 1951.

Betterton, T. *The History of the English Stage*. London, 1741.

Bevan, Maurice. *Evening Service in G-minor*. London, 1741.

Bevin, E. *A Brief and Short Instruction of the Art of Musicke*. London, 1631.

Bicknell, Joan Colleen. "Interdependence of Word and Tone in the Dramatic Music of Henry Purcell." Ph.D. diss., Stanford University, 1960.

———. "On Performing Purcell's Vocal Music: Some Neglected Evidence." *Music Review* 25 (1964).

Bidloo, G. *Komste van . . . Willem III. Koning van Groot Britanje, enz. in Holland.* The Hague, 1691.

Binyon, L. *Catalogue of Prints and Drawings in the British Museum.* London, 1902.

Birch, G. H. *London Churches of the XVIIth and XVIIIth Centuries.* London, 1896.

Blaikley, D. J. "Notes on the Trumpet Scale." *PMA* 19(1894).

Bliss, Sir Arthur. "Henry Purcell." *The Chesterian,* n.s., no. 21(1921).

Blom, Eric. *Music in England.* Hamburg, 1947.

———. "Purcell." In *Some Great Composers,* edited by Eric Blom. London, 1949.

———, ed. *Grove's Dictionary of Music and Musicians.* 5th ed. London, 1954.

Blow, John. "Rules for Composition." British Library Add. MS 30933.

———. "Rules for Playing of a Through Bass upon Organ and Harpsicon." British Library Add. MS 34072.

Bloxam, J. R., ed. *A Register of the Presidents, Fellows, Demis . . . of St. Mary Magdalen College.* Oxford, 1853–55.

Bluemantle, J. P. *An Alphabetical Index of the Streets, Squares, Alleys, Etc. of the Cities of London and Westminster.* London, 1747.

*Blume, F., ed. *Die Musik in Geschichte und Gegenwart.* 15 vols. Kassel, 1949.

Bocca, Tratelli. "Henry Purcell." *Revista Musicale Italiana* 2(1895).

Bodansky, Artur. "Dido and Aeneas." *Zeitschrift für Musikwissenschaft* 7(1925).

Bonavia, M. "Purcell and the Birth of English Opera." *Everyman,* 1931.

Bond, Richard Warwick. "King Arthur on the Stage." *Fortnightly Review* 63(May 1895).

Borgman, A. S. *Thomas Shadwell.* New York, 1928.

Boston, J. L. "Purcell's Father." *Music and Letters* 36(October 1955).

*Boswell, E. *The Restoration Court Stage 1660–1702.* Cambridge, Mass., 1932.

Brent, Smith, A. "Henry Purcell." *Music and Letters* 18(April 1937).

Bridge, J. C. "A Great English Choir-Trainer: Captain Henry Cooke." *Musical Antiquary* 2(January 1911).

Bridge, J. Frederick. "Gresham Lecture." *Musical Times* 36(February 1895).

———. "Purcell's Birthplace and Residences." *Musical Times* 36(November 1895).

———. "Purcell and Niccola Matteis." *SIMG,* July-September 1900.

———. "The Recently Discovered Violin Sonata." *Musical News,* March 1903.

———. "Purcell's Editors." *Musical News,* May 1903.

———. *Samuel Pepys, Lover of Music.* London, 1903.

———. "Purcell's Fantazias and Sonatas." *PMA* 42(1915–16).

———. *Twelve Good Musicians, from John Bull to Henry Purcell.* London, 1920.

Bridgeman, Nanie. "Purcell Dramaturge." *Musique de Tous les Temps,* no. 28, 1963.

Bridges, R. S. *Ode for the Bicentenary Commemoration of Henry Purcell and Other Poems.* London, 1896.

British Museum. *Catalogue of a Commemorative Exhibition: Henry Purcell 1659(?)–1695; George Frideric Handel.* London, 1959.

Britten, Benjamin. "Dido and Aeneas." *The Times,* 27 April 1951.

———. "On Realizing the Continuo in Purcell's Songs." In *Henry Purcell (1659–1695): Essays on His Music,* edited by Imogen Holst. London, 1959.

Brockmeier, H. F. "The Theatre Music of Henry Purcell: A Study of Songs and Instrumental Music for English Plays from 1680 to 1695." Master's thesis, University of Southern California, Los Angeles, 1947.

Brown, J. D., and Stratton, S. *British Musical Biography.* Birmingham, 1897.

Brown, Tom, *Amusements Serious and Comical.* Edited by Arthur L. Hayward, London, 1927.

Browning, Alan. "Purcell's 'Stairre Case Overture.'" *Musical Times* 121 (December 1980).

* Bryant, A. *King Charles II.* London, 1931.

———. *The Letters and Speeches and Declarations of King Charles II.* London, 1935.

———. *Samuel Pepys, the Saviour of the Navy.* London, 1949.

Bucchi, V. "Aci e Galatea di Haendel: Didone ed Enea di Purcell." *Scenario,* 1940.

Bucht, Gunnar. "Purcell och den engelska Fancyn." *Musikrevy,* 1958.

Bucinator. "Purcell's 'Come if you dare, the trumpet sound.'" *Musical Antiquary,* January 1911.

Bukofzer, M. "Allegory in Baroque Music." *Journal of the Warbourg Institute* 3 (1947).

———. *Music in the Baroque Era from Monteverdi to Bach.* New York, 1947.

Bumpas, J. S. *A History of English Cathedral Music 1549–1889.* London, n.d.

Burkhart, R. E. "The Trumpet in England in the Seventeenth Century with Emphasis on Its Treatment in the Works of Henry Purcell." D.M.A. diss., University of Wisconsin, 1972.

Burnet, G. *Bishop Burnet's History of His Own Times.* London, 1753; with *A Supplement . . .* by C. Foxcroft. Oxford, 1902.

* Burney, Charles. *A General History of Music.* Edited by F. Mercer. New York, 1935.

Busby, Thomas. *A General History of Music, from the Earliest Times to the Present, Condensed from the Works of Sir John Hawkins and Charles Burney . . . with Essays on the Lives and Works of Purcell, Handel, etc. . . . .* London, 1819.

Butler, Gregory G. "Music and Rhetoric in Early Seventeenth-Century English Sources." *Musical Quarterly* 66 (January 1980).

Buttrey, John. "The Evolution of English Opera Between 1656 and 1695: A Reinvestigation." Ph.D. diss., University of Cambridge, 1967.

———. "Dating Purcell's Dido and Aeneas." *PRMA* 94 (1967–68).

———. "Did Purcell Go to Holland in 1691?" *Musical Times* 110 (September 1969).

* *Calendar of State Papers: Domestic Series.*

* *Calendar of Treasury Books.*

* *Calendar of Treasury Papers.*

"Centenary of Purcell." *American Architect and Building News* 51 (1927).

Chamberlayne, E. *Angliae Notitiae: or The Present State of England.* 12th ed. London, 1679; 14th ed., 1682; 15th ed., 1684; 17th ed., 1692.

Chapin, Anna A. "Purcell, Master of Music." In *Makers of Song,* edited by Anna A. Chapin. New York, 1904.

Chapman, Hester W. *Mary II, Queen of England.* London, 1953.

Chappell, W., ed. *Old English Popular Music.* Rev. ed. edited by H. Wooldridge. London, 1893.

Charles II. *An Account of the Preservation of King Charles II.* London, 1803 [dictated to Samuel Pepys in 1681].

Chazanoff, D. "Early English Chamber Music from William Byrd to Henry Purcell." Ph.D. diss., Columbia University, 1964.

* Chester, J. L. *The Marriage, Baptismal, and Burial Registers of the Collegiate Church or Abbey of St. Peter, Westminster.* London, 1876.

———. *London Marriage Licenses, 1521–1869.* London, 1887.

Chissell, J. "St. Cecilia: Purcell and Britten." *Monthly Musical Record* 73 (1943).

Cibber, C. *An Apology for the Life of Mr. Colley Cibber, Comedian, Written by Himself.* London, 1740 (with a supplement by Anthony Aston, in the edition by Lowe, London, 1889).

Clark, Willington. *Purcell and Handel in Bickham's Musical Entertainer.* Cambridge, 1943.

Clarke, Henry. "John Blow." Ph.D. diss., Harvard University, 1947.

Clercx, S. *Le Baroque et la musique.* Brussels, 1948.

Clifford, James. *The Divine Services and Anthems Usually Sung in the Cathedrals and Collegiate Choirs in the Church of England.* London, 1663.

————. *The Divine Services and Anthems Usually Sung in His Majesties Chapel, and in all Cathedrals and Collegiate Choirs in England and Ireland.* 2d ed. London, 1664.

Cogan, R. "Toward a Theory of Verbal Timbre and Musical Line in Purcell, Sessions, and Stravinsky." *Perspectives of New Music* 8 (1969–70).

Colles, H. C. *The Growth of Music: A Study for Musical History for Schools.* Oxford, 1912.

————. *Voice and Verse: A Study in English Song.* London, 1928.

————. "Some Musical Instruction Books of the Seventeenth Century." *PRMA* 55 (1928–29).

————. "Lully and Purcell." In *Essays and Lectures*, edited by H. C. Colles. London, 1945.

————. "Musical London from the Restoration to Handel." In *Essays and Lectures*, edited by H. C. Colles. London, 1945.

————. "Purcell Restored." In *Essays and Lectures*, edited by H. C. Colles. London, 1945.

————, et al. "Henry Purcell." Grove V. London, 1954.

Collier, Jeremy. *Essays upon Several Moral Subjects.* 2 parts. London, 1697.

————. *A Short View of the Immorality and Profaneness of the English Stage.* London, 1698.

————. *Great Historical, Geographical, Genealogical and Poetical Dictionary.* London, 1701 (with supplements in 1705 and 1721).

Congreve, William. *The Complete Works.* Edited by M. Summers. London, 1923.

Conley, P. R. "The Use of the Trumpet in the Music of Purcell. *Brass Quarterly* 3 (Fall 1959).

Conly, J. M. "Sound the Trumpet." *Atlantic* 203 (February 1959).

Cooper, B. A. R. "English Solo Keyboard Music of the Middle and Late Baroque." Ph.D. diss., Indiana University, 1974.

————. "Did Purcell Write a Trumpet Voluntary?" *Musical Times* 119 (1978).

Cooper, G. M. "Italian Instrumental Music of the Sixteenth Century." *PMA* 55 (1929–30).

————. "The Chronology of Purcell's Works." *Musical Times* 84 (July–December 1943).

Coral, Leonore. "A John Playford Advertisement." *RMA Research Chronicle*, no. 5 (1965).

————. "Music in English Auction Sales." Ph.D. diss., University of London, 1974.

Corder, F. "Major *versus* Minor: Some Curious Statistics." *Musical Quarterly* 5 (July 1919).

Cosmo the Third. *Travels Through England during the Reign of King Charles II.* Translated from the Italian ms. in the Laurentian Library at Florence, with a memoir of his life. London, 1669.

Covell, R. "Seventeenth-Century Music for the Tempest." *SMA* 2(1968).

Cowley, Abraham. *The Works of Abraham Cowley.* London, 1668.

Cox, D. "Henry Purcell, the British Orpheus." *Gramaphone,* June 1959.

Coxon, Carolyn. "A Handlist of the Sources of John Jenkins's Vocal and Instrumental Music." *RMA Research Chronicle,* no. 8(1968).

Croft, William. *Musica Sacra.* London, 1724.

Crosby, Brian. "An Early Restoration Liturgical Manuscript." *Music and Letters* 55 (October 1974).

Crowell, F. J. "Purcell." *Blackwell's Magazine,* 1895.

———. "Purcell and the Making of Musical England." *Blackwell's Magazine* 158 (December 1895).

Cudworth, C. L. "Some New Facts About the Trumpet Voluntary." *Musical Times* 94 (September 1953).

———. "Ye Olde Spuriosity Shoppe, or 'Put It in the Anhang.'" *Notes* 12(1954–55).

———. "Baptist's Vein: French Orchestral Music and Its Influence, from 1650–1750." *PRMA* 83(1956–57).

Cummings, W. H. "On Henry Purcell and His Family." *PMA* 3(1876–77).

*———. *Purcell.* London, 1887, 1903 (facsimile ed. 1962).

———. "Purcell's Death." *Musical Times* 30(July 1889).

———. "A Brief Life of Purcell." *Musical Times* 36(November 1895).

———. "Portraits of Purcell." *Musical Times* 36(November 1895).

———. "Purcell and Dr. Arne." *Musical Times* 36(November 1895).

———. "Purcell's Music for the Funeral of Mary II." *Zeitschrift der internationalen Gesselschaft für Musikwissenschaft* 4(1903).

———. "The Mutilation of a Masterpiece." *PMA* 29(1903–4).

———. "Dr. John Blow." *PMA* 35(1908–9).

———. "Dido and Aeneas." *Musical Times* 51(June 1910).

Cunningham, Peter, and Wheatley, Henry B. *London Past and Present.* 3 vols. London, 1891.

Cutts, John P. "Seventeenth-Century Lyrics: Oxford Bodleian MS Mus. B1." *Musica Disciplina* 10(1956).

———. "An Unpublished Purcell Setting." *Music and Letters* 38(January 1957). (See also N. Fortune's letter in *Music and Letters* 38 [April 1957].)

———. "Music and the Supernatural in 'The Tempest': A Study in Interpretation." *Music and Letters* 39(October 1958).

Dalrymple, J. *Memoirs of Great Britain and Ireland.* London, 1790.

Dart, R. Thurston. "The Cibell." *Revue Belge de Musicologie* 6(1952).

———. *The Interpretation of Music.* London, 1954.

———. *March and Canzona for the Funeral of Queen Mary, 1695.* London, 1955.

———. "Purcell's Chamber Music." *PRMA* 83(1958–59).

———. [Purcell's] *Fantazias and In nomines.* Purcell Society Edition, vol. 31. London, 1959.

———. "Purcell's Harpsichord Music." *Musical Times* 100(June 1959).

———. *Trio-Sonata for Violin, Bass-Viol and Continuo.* London, 1959.

———. "Dido and Aeneas." *Music and Letters* 42(January 1961).

———. "Purcell and Bull." *Musical Times* 104(January 1963).

Davey, Henry. *A History of English Music.* London, 1895.

Davidson, L. C. *Catharine of Bragança, Infanta of Portugal and Queen Consort of England.* London, 1908.

Day, C. L., ed. *The Songs of Thomas D'Urfey.* Cambridge, Mass., 1933.

* Day, C. L., and Murrie, E. B. *English Song-Books 1651–1702.* London, 1940.

Dean, Winton B. "The Fairy Queen, Covent Garden." *Opera* 2 (September 1951).

Deane, C. V. *Dramatic Theory and the Rhymed Heroic Play.* London, 1931.

Dean-Smith, Margaret. "English Tunes Common to Playford's Dancing Master, the Keyboard Books and Traditional Songs and Dances." *PRMA* 79 (1952–53).

Dearnley, Christopher. *English Chamber Music 1650–1750.* London, 1970.

Defoe, Daniel. *The Novels and Miscellaneous Works.* Oxford, 1841.

Demarquez, S. *Purcell: la vie, l'oeuvre, la discographie.* Paris, 1951.

Demmery, M. "The Hybrid Critic." *Music and Letters* 37 (April 1956).

Dennis, John. *An Essay on the Operas after the Italian Manner.* London, 1706.

Dennison, Peter. "The Church Music of Pelham Humfrey." *PRMA* 98 (1971–72).

————. "The Stylistic Origins of the Early Church Music [of Purcell]." In *Essays on Opera and English Music in Honour of Sir Jack Westrup,* edited by F. W. Sternfeld, Nigel Fortune, and Edward Olleson. Oxford, 1975.

————. "The Sacred Music of Matthew Locke." *Music and Letters* 60 (1979).

————, ed. *Pelham Humfrey, Complete Church Music.* Musica Britannica, vols. 34–35. London, 1972.

Dent, E. J. "The Earliest String Quartets." *Monthly Musical Record* 33 (1903).

————. "The Baroque Opera." *Musical Antiquary,* January 1910.

————. "Italian Chamber Cantatas." *Musical Antiquary,* April 1911.

————. "Purcell on the Stage." *Athenaeum,* January 1920.

————. "Purcell in the Open Air." *Nation,* July 1921.

————. "Purcell in Church." *Nation,* August 1921.

————. "National Duty." *Nation and the Athenaeum* 32 (9 December 1922).

————. "America Discovers Purcell." *Nation,* January 1924.

————. *Dido and Aeneas.* London, 1925.

————. "Purcell's Dido and Aeneas." *Deutsche Kunstschau,* 1934.

————. "Purcell's King Arthur." *Deutsche Kunstschau,* 1934.

————. "Italian Operas in London." *PRMA* 80 (1944–45).

————. *Foundations of English Opera.* London, 1951.

————. "Purcell's King Arthur." In *Essays on Music,* edited by F. Aprahamian. London, 1967.

Descartes, René. *Renatus Des-Cartes excellent compendium of musick: with necessary and judicious animadversions thereupon, by a person of honour.* London, 1653.

Dezo, L. *Purcell.* Budapest, 1959.

* *Dictionary of National Biography.*

"Dido and Aeneas." *PRMA* 51 (1925).

"*Dido and Aeneas:* An Opera by Henry Purcell." Performed by Members of the Purcell Operatic Society, May 1900 and March 1901. Program, with a preface by J. A. Fuller-Maitland. London, 1902.

"Dido and Aeneas." *Catholic World,* no. 749 (May 1939).

"Dido and Aeneas." *New Republic,* no. 126 (11 February 1952).

"Dido and Aeneas." *Musical America,* no. 76 (15 November 1956).

"Didone et Enee." *Revue de Musicologie,* no. 11 (May 1927).

"Dr. Purcell-Taylor's Wild Story." *Musical Times* 57 (August 1918).

Dodwell, H. *Treatise Concerning the Lawfulness of Instrumental Music in Holy Office.* 2d ed. London, 1700.

Dolmetsch, A. *The Interpretation of Music of the XVII and XVIII Centuries.* London, 1946.

Donington, R. "Further Seventeenth- and Eighteenth-Century Evidence Bearing on the Performance of Purcell's Works." In *Henry Purcell (1659–1695): Essays on His Music,* edited by Imogen Holst. London, 1959.

———. "Performing Purcell's Music Today." in *Henry Purcell (1659–1695): Essays on His Music,* edited by Imogen Holst. London, 1959.

———. *The Interpretation of Early Music.* London, 1963.

——— and Emery, Walter. *Sonata No. 6 in G-Minor.* London, 1959.

———. *Sonata No. 9 in F-Major.* London, 1959.

*Downes, John. *Roscius Anglicanus.* Edited by M. Summers. London, 1928.

"The Dryden-Davenant-Purcell 'Tempest.'" *Musical Review* 20 (August 1959).

Dryden, John. *The Works of John Dryden.* Vols. 13–15. Edited by H. T. Swedenborg. Berkeley and Los Angeles, 1966–70.

Duckles, Vincent. "The Curious Art of John Wilson: An Introduction to His Songs and Lute Music." *Journal of the American Musicological Society* 7 (Summer 1954).

———. "English Songs and the Challenge of Italian Monody." In *Words to Music: Papers on English Seventeenth-Century Song, Read at Clark Memorial Library, December 11, 1965.* Los Angeles, 1970.

Duffet, T. *Beauties' Triumph, A Masque.* London, 1676.

Duncan, E. "The Songs of Henry Purcell." *Monthly Musical Record* 30 (1903).

Dunkin, P. "Issues of the Fairy Queen." *Library* 24 (1946).

Dupre, H. *Purcell.* Paris, 1927.

Dussauze, H. "Captain Cooke and His Choirboys." Doctoral thesis, Paris, 1911.

Dzhekobs, A. "O Genri Perselle." *Soviet Muzik* 23 (November 1959).

Eaglefield-Hull, A. "A New Light on Purcell." *Musical Times* 68 (December 1927).

Early English Church Music. The Sources of English Church Music 1549–1660. Compiled by Ralph Daniel and Peter Le Huray. London, 1972.

Ebsworth, J. W., ed. *The Roxburghe Ballads.* Hertford, 1871–99.

———. *The Bagford Ballads.* Hertford, 1876.

"Edward Henry Purcell." *Musical Times* 72 (June 1931).

Edwards, F. G. "Three Royal Funeral Anthems." *Musical Times* 42 (March 1901).

———. "A Master Organ Builder: Father Smith." *Musical Times* 46 (August 1905).

Egerton, J. *The Theatrical Remembrancer.* London, 1788.

Eggebrecht, H. H. "Walthers musikalische Lexikon in seinen terminologischen Partien." *Acta Musicologica* 29 (1957).

"An Eighteenth-Century Directory of London Musicians." *The Galpin Society Journal* 1 (March 1949).

Elkin, Robert. *The Old Concert Rooms of London.* London, 1955.

"The English Bach." *British Musician and Musical News* 8 (December 1933).

Epstein, P. "Gegen die Verbalhornung von Purcells Dido durch Bodansky." *Zeitschrift für Musikwissenschaft,* 1924.

Espinos, V. "Las realizaciones musicales del Quijote: Enrique Purcell y su comical 'Comical History of Don Quixote.'" *Revista de la Biblioteca,* 1933.

———. *El Quijote en la Musica.* Barcelona, 1947.

Estwick, Sampson. *The Usefulness of Church Music. A Sermon Preach'd at Christ Church, Novemb. 27. 1696. Upon occasion of the Anniversary Meeting of the Lovers, on St. Cecilia's Day.* London, 1696.

Evans, B. I. *A Short History of English Drama.* London, 1948.

* Evelyn, J. *Memoires of John Evelyn.* Edited by W. Bray. London, 1818.

* ———. *Diary.* 6 vols. Edited by E. de Beer. Oxford, 1955.

An Exact Relation of the Entertainment of His Most Sacred Majesty, William III . . . at the Hague (translated from the Dutch). London, 1691.

"Fairy Queen." *Musical America* 71 (September 1951).

"Fairy Queen." *Musical America* 78 (March 1958).

"Fairy Queen at Covent Garden." *Musical Times* 92 (September 1951).

"Fantazias and Other Instrumental Music." *Music and Letters* 40 (October 1959).

Farmer, H. G. "Music from Down Below." *Musical Times* 90 (September 1949).

Farquhar, George. "A Discourse upon Comedy in Reference to the English Stage." In *The Works of the Late Ingenious Mr. George Farquhar.* London, 1760.

Favre-Lingorow, S. *Der Instrumentalstil von Purcell.* Berne, 1949.

Fellowes, E. H. *English Cathedral Music.* London, 1941. Rev. ed. by Westrup in 1969.

Fenlon, Iain. *Catalogue of the Printed Music and Music Manuscripts before 1801 in the Music Library of the University of Birmingham Barber Institute of Fine Arts.* Munich, 1976.

Fenney, W. "Short Study." *Musical Opinion* 37 (June 1920).

Ferguson, Howard. "Purcell's Harpsichord Music." *PRMA* 91 (November 1964).

———. "Two Purcell Discoveries." *Piano Quarterly,* Winter 1968–69.

———, ed. *Purcell's Sonata in G-minor for Solo Violin.* London, 1958.

Finney, Theodore. "Review of Newly Discovered Purcell Anthem: 'The Lord is King.'" *American Organist* 42 (May 1959).

Fiske, Roger. "The Macbeth Music." *Music and Letters* 45 (1964).

Fitzgerald, Percy. *A New History of the English Stage.* London, 1882.

Fitzpatrick, S. A. O. *Dublin, a Historical and Topographical Account of the City.* London, 1907.

Flood, W. H. Grattan. "Irish Origin of the Tune of 'Lilliburlero' Usually Attributed to Purcell." *Musical Opinion* 39 (June 1915).

———. "Tempest Music" [ca. 1690, attribution to Henry Purcell confirmed from *Dublin Courant,* 7 January 1748, p. 3]. *Times Literary Supplement,* 22 August 1918.

———. "Purcell's *Dido and Aeneas:* Who Was Lady Dorothy Burke?" *Musical Times* 59 (November 1918).

———. "Irish Ancestry of Garland, Dowland, Campion and Purcell." *Music and Letters* 3 (January 1922).

———. "Quelques precisions nouvelles sur Cambert et Grabu à Londres." *Revue de Musicologie* 9 (1927).

Flothius, M. "Purcell, Strawinsky en de Vooruitang." *Mens en Melodie* 4 (February 1949).

Ford, W. K. "The Chapel Royal in the Time of Purcell." *Musical Times* 100 (1959).

Fortune, Nigel. "An Unpublished Purcell Setting." *Music and Letters* 38 (April 1957).

———. "Purcell's Life and Background." *Purcell-Handel Festival* (Arts Council of Great Britain, et al.), June 1959. London.

———. *Henry Purcell: Sacred Music, Part III.* Vol. 17. London 1964.

———. "A New Purcell Source." *Music Review* 25 (May 1964).

———. "Sacred Music, Part III." *Music and Letters* 46 (November 1965).

———. "The Domestic Sacred Music [of Henry Purcell]." In *Essays on Opera and English Music in Honour of Sir Jack Westrup*. Oxford, 1975.

———, and Zimmerman, Franklin B. "Purcell's Autographs." In *Henry Purcell 1659–1695: Essays on His Music*, edited by Imogen Holst. London, 1959.

Foss, H. "Music and the Festival of Britain." *Music Teacher* 30 (1951).

Foster, Joseph. *Alumnae Oxoniensis: The Members of the University of Oxford, 1500–1714*. 4 vols. Oxford, 1891.

Foster, Myles B. *Anthems and Anthem Composers*. London, 1901.

Frotscher, G. *Geschichte des Orgelspiels und der Orgelkomposition*. Berlin, 1935.

Fuller-Maitland, J. A. "Henry Purcell, 1658–1696." *Rivista Musicale Italiana* 2 (1895).

———. "Foreign Influences on Henry Purcell." *Musical Times* 37 (January 1896).

———. "A German Compliment to Purcell." *Musical Times* 37 (August 1896).

———. "Purcell's Twelve Sonatas of Three Parts." *Monatsheft für Musikgeschichte* 29 (1897).

———. "Purcell's King Arthur." In *Studies in Music*, edited by R. Grey. New York, 1901.

———, and Mann, A. H. *Catalogue of the Music in the Fitzwilliam Museum, Cambridge*. London, 1893.

Galpin, F. W. "The Sackbut, Its Evolution and History." *PMA* 31 (1906–7).

Garnett, R. *The Age of Dryden*. London, 1901.

Gavalda, Miguel Querol. *La musica en las obras de Cervantes*. Barcelona, 1948.

*Genest, J. *Some Account of the English Stage . . . 1660–1830*. Bath, 1832.

Georgii, Walter. *Klaviermusik; Geschichte der Musik für Klavier*. Vol. 2. Zürich, 1950.

Gheust, J. "'Didon et Enee' de Purcell." *Musique* 129 (December 1964).

Gieglung, F. *Giuseppe Torelli*. Kassel and Basel, 1949.

Gilbert, John [of Christ's College, Cambridge]. *Damon: A Pastoral Lamenting the Death of that Incomparable Master of Musick, Mr. Henry Purcell*. London, 1696.

Gildon, Charles. *The Life of Mr. Thomas Betterton*. London, 1710.

Goldschmidt-Jentner, R. K. *Genius der Jugend*. Berlin, 1960.

Gombosi, Otto. "Some Musical Aspects of the English Court Masque." *Journal of the American Musicological Society* 1 (Fall 1948).

Gooch, B. N. S. "Poetry and Music in England, 1660–1760: A Comparison Based on the Works of Dryden, Purcell, Pope and Handel." Ph.D. diss., University of British Columbia, 1962.

Goodison, Benjamin. *The Works of Henry Purcell in Five Classes*. London, ca. 1788–90.

Goralt, M., ed. "The Bible in English Music: W. Byrd-H. Purcell." *A.M.L.I. Studies in Music Bibliography*, 1970.

Grabau, C. "Nachwirken Purcells Shakespeare Musik." *Jahrbuch der deutschen Shakespeare Gesellschaft* 55 (1919).

Grace, Harvey. "Henry Purcell, 1659–1695." *Radio Television Nacional de Colombia, Boletin de Pragramas*. Bogota, November 1959.

———. "English Organ Music from Purcell to the Wesleys." *Musical Times* 72 (June 1981).

Graham, C. "King Arthur Revised and Revived." *Opera* 21 (1970).

Granger, J. *A Biographical History of England*. 2d ed. London, 1824.

Grassineau, James. *A Musical Dictionary: Being a Collection of Terms and Characters. . . .* London, 1740.

Gray, A. "Purcell's Dramatic Music." *PMA* 43 (1916–17).

Great Britain Arts Council. *Eight Concerts of Henry Purcell's Music—Commemorative Book of Programs, Notes and Texts.* London, 1951.

Greg, W. W. *A Bibliography of the English Printed Drama to the Restoration.* London, 1939–59.

Gresham Music Library. *A Catalogue of the Printed Books and Manuscripts . . . Guild-hall Library.* London, 1965.

Grew, Eva Maria. "Childhood of Purcell." *British Musician and Musical News* 6 (October 1933).

Grout, S. J. "Seventeenth-Century Parodies of French Opera." *Musical Quarterly,* April 1941 (part 1) and October 1941 (part 2).

* *Grove's Dictionary of Music and Musicians.* 4th ed. Edited by H. C. Colles. London, 1940.

* *Grove's Dictionary of Music and Musicians.* 5th ed. Edited by E. Blom. London, 1954.

* *Grove's Dictionary of Music and Musicians.* 6th ed. Edited by S. Sadie. London, 1981.

Haas, R. *Die Musik des Barocks.* Handbuch der Musikwissenschaft. Wildpark-Potsdam, 1928.

Halbreich, H. "La musique instrumentale d'Henry Purcell." *Musique de tous les temps* 28 (1963).

Halfpenny, Eric. "Musicians at James II's Coronation." *Music and Letters* 32 (April 1951).

———. "The Entertainment of Charles II." *Music and Letters* 38 (January 1957).

———. "A Seventeenth-Century Oboe Consort." *Galpin Society Journal,* May 1957.

Ham, R. D. "Dryden's Dedication for the Music of the Prophetess, 1691." *PMLA,* December 1935.

Harding, R. "A Thematic Catalogue of the Works of Matthew Locke." Unpublished ms. Cambridge, 1954.

———. *A Thematic Catalogue of the Works of Matthew Locke, with a Calendar of the Main Events of His Life.* Oxford, 1971.

Hardwicke, Peter. "Foreign Influences in the Verse Anthems of Henry Purcell." M.M. diss., University of Alberta, 1973.

Harley, John. "Music and Musicians in Restoration London." *Musical Quarterly* 40 (October 1954).

———. *Music in Purcell's London: The Social Background.* London, 1968.

Harman, R. Alec. *A Catalogue of the Printed Music and Books on Music in Durham Cathedral Library.* London, 1968.

"Harpsichord Works, Vol. I: Eight Suites; Vol. 2: Miscellaneous Pieces." *Musical Times* 106 (February 1965).

Harris, Ellen. *Handel and the Pastoral Tradition.* London, 1980.

Harrison, P. "A Tempest with Music." *Twentieth Century,* July 1959.

Hart, E. F. "The Restoration Catch." *Music and Letters* 34 (October 1953).

Haun, Eugene. *But Hark! More Harmony: The Libretti of Restoration Operas in English.* Ypsilanti, Mich., 1971.

* Hawkins, John. *A General History of the Science and Practice of Music.* 5 vols. London, 1873.

Hayes, G. B. *Musical Instruments and Their Music, 1500–1700.* Vol. 1: *The Treatment of Instrumental Music;* vol. 2: *The Viols and Other Bowed Instruments.* Oxford, 1930.

Heinlein, F. "Henry Purcell." *Revue Musical Chileana* 12 (May-June 1959).

"Henry Purcell." *Masters in Music* 3 (1905).

"Henry Purcell." *Universal Musical Encyclopedia.* New York, 1910.

"Henry Purcell and Italian Music." *Musical Times* 58 (April 1917).

"Henry Purcell: Twelve Sonatas of Three Parts." *Music and Letters* 20 (1939).

Herbage, J. L. "The Purcell Welcome Songs." *The Listener*, 5 May 1937.

———. "Dryden's 'King Arthur' Composed by Purcell." *Radio Times*, 6 December 1946.

* Highfill, Phillip H.; Burnim, Kalman A.; and Langhans, Edward A. *A Biographical Dictionary of Actors, Actresses, Musicians, Dancers, Managers and Other Stage Personnel.*

Hinrichsen, Max, ed. *Organ and Choral Aspects and Prospects.* London, 1958.

Hirshowitz, Betty. "The Bible in the Works of Henry Purcell." *American Literary Institute* (Haifa Museum) 10 (1970).

Hitchman, Percy. "The 'Fairy Queen' at Nottingham." *Theatre Notebook* 14 (1959–60).

Hodges, N. *Loimologia: or A Historical Account of the Plague in London in 1665.* London, 1720.

Holland, A. K. *Henry Purcell: The English Musical Tradition.* London, 1932, 1949.

———. "Purcell's Instrumental Music." *The Listener* 26 (1 September 1955).

———. "The British Worthy." *The Listener* 61 (11 June 1959).

Hollander, H. "Henry Purcell." *Neue Zeitschrift für Musik* 120 (June 1959).

Holmes, C. J. "The Portraits of Arne and Purcell." *The Burlington Magazine*, April-September 1915.

Holst, Gustav. "Henry Purcell: The Dramatic Composer of England." In *The Heritage of Music*, edited by Hubert J. Foss. London, 1924.

———. "Purcell." In *The Heritage of Music.* Vol. 1. Oxford, 1927.

Holst, Imogen. "A Note on the Nanki Collection of Purcell's Works." In *Henry Purcell 1659–1695: Essays on His Music*, edited by Imogen Holst. London, 1959.

———. "Purcell's Dances." In *Henry Purcell, 1659–1695: Essays on His Music*, edited by Imogen Holst. London, 1959.

———. "Purcell's Librettist, Nahum Tate." In *Henry Purcell 1659–1695: Essays on His Music*, edited by Imogen Holst. London, 1959.

———. *Henry Purcell, the Theory of His Life and Work.* London, 1961.

———. *Henry Purcell, the Story of His Life and Work.* London, 1969.

———, ed. *Henry Purcell, 1659–1695: Essays on His Music.* London, 1959.

Honolka, K. [*King Arthur*, Stuttgart Opera.] *Musica* 18 (1964).

———. [*King Arthur*, Stuttgart Opera.] *Opera* 15 (May 1968).

Hook, Lucile. "Portraits of Elizabeth Barry and Anne Bracegirdle." *Theatre Notebook* 15 (1961).

Hotson, S. L. *The Commonwealth and Restoration Stage.* Cambridge, Mass., 1928.

Howard, H. W. "The English Orpheus." *National Association of Teachers of Singing Bulletin* 29 (December 1972).

Howard, M. "An Anthem by Henry Purcell." *Monthly Musical Record* 833 (March-April 1953).

"How to Give a Purcell Evening." *Music Student*, 13 April 1920.

Hoyle, John. *Dictionarium Musica, being a Complete Dictionary: or, Treasury of Music.* London, 1770.

Hughes-Hughes, A. "Henry Purcell's Handwriting." *Musical Times* 37 (February 1896).
———. *Catalogue of Manuscript Music in the British Museum.* 3 vols. London, 1906–10.
———. "A Purcell Album and a Few Thoughts About It." *Monthly Musical Record* 48 (1918).
———. "Forerunners: I. Purcell and Zachau." *Monthly Musical Record* 52 (1922).
Hull, Eaglefield A. "New Light on Purcell." *Musical Times* 64 (December 1927).
———. "The Earliest Known String Quartet." *Musical Quarterly* 15 (1929).
Hume, D. *The History of England to 1688.* 8 vols. London, 1813.
Hume, R. D. *The Development of English Drama in the Late Seventeenth Century.* Oxford, 1976.
Humphries, C., and Smith, W. C. *Music Publishers in the British Isles.* London, 1954.
Hunt, J. E. *Cranmer's First Litany, and Merbecke's Book of Common Prayer Noted, 1550.* London, 1939.
* Husk, W. H. *An Account of the Musical Celebrations on St. Cecilia's Day.* London, 1857.
———. "Purcell." In *Grove's Dictionary of Music and Musicians.* 1st ed. London, 1883.
Hussey, Dyneley. "British Worthy." *Spectator,* 27 December 1935, no. 155.
Hutchinson, Hubbard. "Young Mr. Purcell [*Dido and Aeneas* at the Mecca Temple]." *Nation,* no. 130 (23 April 1930).
Illing, Robert. *Henry Purcell: Sonata in G Minor for Violin and Continuo: An Account of Its Survival from Both the Historical and Technical Points of View.* Flanders University, 1975.
"Index to the Songs and Allusions in the 'Gentleman's Journal, 1692–94.'" *Musical Antiquary,* July 1911.
"The Indian Queen Festival Orchestra." *Musical America* 84 (November 1964).
Johnson, Jane Troy. "How to 'Humour' John Jenkins' Three-Part Dances: Performance Directions in a Newberry Library MS." *Journal of the American Musicological Society* 20 (Summer 1967).
Johnstone, H. D. "English Solo Song, c. 1710–1760." *PRMA* 95 (1968–69).
Jones, George K. "Life and Work [of Henry Purcell]." *School Music Review,* no. 34 (January 1926).
"Josiah Priest's School." *Musical Times* 5 (December 1863).
Just, H. "Henry Purcell." *Musikantengilde* 7 (1929).
———. "Henry Purcell zu seinem 300. Geburtstag in diesem Jahre." *Hausmusik* 23 (March/April 1959).
Kaufman, Schimer. "Also Rans of Music." *American Mercury* 34 (February 1935).
Keddie, Henrietta. *Musical Composers and their Works; for the Use of Schools and Students of Music.* London, 1875; Boston, 1876.
Kerman, Joseph. *Opera as Drama.* New York, 1956.
Kays, Ivor. *Texture of Music: Purcell to Brahms.* London, 1961.
King, A. Hyatt. "The First Complete Edition of Purcell." *Monthly Musical Record* 80 (March/April 1951).
———. "Benjamin Goodison and the First 'Complete Edition' of Purcell." *Vötterle Festschrift.* Kassel, 1968.
"'King Arthur.'" *New Statesman and Nation* 10 (21 December 1935).
"King Arthur." *Musical Review* 20 (August-November 1959).

"'King Arthur; or The British Worthy.'" *Saturday Review* 145 (February 1928).

Kinsky, George, ed. *A History of Music in Pictures*. London, 1923.

Klenz, William. "The Church Sonatas of Henry Purcell." Ph.D. diss., University of North Carolina, 1948.

Klessmann, E. "Von Wesen der Musik Henry Purcells." *Musica* 13 (October 1959).

Koelizsch, H. "Henry Purcells Gambenfantasien." *Musica* 8 (August 1955).

Kolneder, Walter. "Zur Vorgeschichte des Streichquartetts." *HiFi-Stereophonic* 13 (1974).

Konen, V. D. "Brittanskijorfej." *Soviet Muzik* 23 (November 1959).

Konen, Valentina. "Etjudy o Zarubeznoi Muzyke." *Studies in Foreign Music*. Moskow, 1975.

Krull, Erwin. "Purcell's 'Fairy Queen.'" *Neue Zeitschrift für Musikwissenschaft* 122 (June 1961).

Kushner, D. Z. "Henry Purcell's *Dido and Aeneas:* An Analytical Discussion." *Radford* 23 (Spring 1959).

*Lafontaine, Henry Cart de. *The King's Musick*. London, 1909.

Lam, Basil. "Purcell and the Trio Sonata." *The Listener*, 20 May 1959.

Lamson, R. "Henry Purcell's Dramatic Songs and the English Broadside Ballad." *Modern Language Association of America* 53 (1938).

Landormy, Paul. "Didon et Enee de Purcell, 1689." *Menestral* (Paris) 89 (1927).

———. "Purcell's 'Dido and Aeneas' (1689)." Translated by F. Rothwell. *Musical Opinion* 51 (1928).

Lang, Paul H. *Music in Western Civilization*. New York, 1941.

*Langbaine, G. *The Lives and Characters of English Dramatick Poets*. London, 1699.

*Laurie, Margaret. "Purcell's Stage Works." Ph.D. diss., University of Cambridge, 1962.

———. "The Works of Henry Purcell." *Music Library Association Notes* 19 (3 November 1962).

———. "Fairest Isle." *Musical Times* 105 (March 1964).

———. "Did Purcell Set The Tempest?" *PRMA* 90 (1964–65).

———. "Henry Purcell's 'Dioclesian.'" *Purcell Complete Edition*. London, 1969.

———, and Arundell, Dennis. "Dido and Aeneas." *Opera* 13 (1962).

———. "King Arthur." *Purcell Complete Edition*. London, 1971.

———, and Dart, Thurston. "Dido and Aeneas." *Musical Times* 102 (September 1961).

Lawrence, W. J. "Italian Opera in London." *Musical Antiquary*, October 1910.

———. "Rare en Tout, 1677; and James Paisible." *Musical Antiquary*, October 1910.

———. *The Elizabethan Playhouse and Other Studies*. 2 vols. Stratford-upon-Avon, 1912–13.

———. "Music and Song in the Eighteenth Century Theatre." *Musical Quarterly* 2 (1916).

———. "The English Theatre Orchestra." *Musical Quarterly* 3 (1917).

———. "Foreign Singers and Musicians at the Court of Charles II." *Musical Quarterly* 9 (April 1923).

Leach, A. F. *English Schools at the Reformation (1546–8)*. Westminster, 1896.

Le Fanu, Joseph Sheridan. *Purcell Papers*. London, 1880.

Lee, Nathaniel. *The Works*. Edited by Thomas B. Stroup and Arthur Cooke. New Brunswick, N.J., 1954–55.

Lefkowitz, Murray. *William Lawes*. London, ca. 1960.

———. "Shadwell and Locke's *Psyche:* The French Connection." *PRMA* 106 (1979–80).

Leganij, Dezso. *Henry Purcell.* Budapest, 1959.

Le Huray, Peter. *Music and Reformation in England (1549–1660).* London, 1967.

———, ed. *Matthew Locke: Anthems and Motets.* Musica Britannica, vol. 38. London, 1976.

Leiris, C. "Henry Purcell." *Musica* 68 (1969).

* Lennep, William van, ed. *The London Stage 1660–1800. A Calendar of Plays, Entertainments and Afterpieces.* 6 vols. Carbondale, Ill., 1959.

Lester, Joel. "Major-Minor Concepts and Modal Theory in Germany: 1592–1680." *Journal of the American Musicological Society* 30 (1977).

Lewiński, W. E. "Ein Festspiel mit Sinn [The Fairy Queen]." *Musica* 13 (September 1959).

Lewis, Anthony. "Purcellian Manuscripts at Cambridge." *Monthly Musical Record* 65 (March 1935).

———. "Matthew Locke: A Dynamic Figure in English Music." *PRMA* 74 (1948).

———. "A Newly-Discovered Song by Purcell: The Meditation." *Score* 4 (1951).

———. "The Purcell Tercentenary." *English Church Music* 29 (February 1959).

———. "Purcell's Music for 'The Tempest.'" *Musical Times* 100 (June 1959).

———. "Purcell and Blow's 'Venus and Adonis.'" *Music and Letters* 44 (July 1963).

———. "Notes and Reflections on a New Edition of Purcell's 'The Fairy Queen.'" *Music Review* 25 (May 1964).

———. *The Language of Purcell: National Idiom or Local Dialect?* Inaugural lecture delivered in the University of Hull, 20 January 1967. Hull, 1968.

———. "The Fairy Queen." *Purcell Complete Edition.* Vol. 29. London, 1960.

———, and Fortune, Nigel. "Sacred Music, Part IV." *Purcell Complete Edition.* Vol. 29. London, 1960.

"Liber Computi S. M. Magd. Coll." Manuscript in Magdalen College, Oxford.

Liess, A. "Materialen zur römischen Musikgeschichte des Seicento: Musikerlisten des Oratorio San Marcello, 1664–1725." *Acta Musicologica* 29 (1957).

Limbert, K. E. "A Biographical Sketch [of Henry Purcell]." *Parent's Review,* September 1949.

Lincoln, Stoddard. "John Eccles: The Last of a Tradition." Ph.D. diss., Oxford, 1965.

———. "A Congreve Masque." *Musical Times* 113 (1972).

Littleton, A. H. *Purcell's Portraits.* London, n.d.

Locke, Matthew. *Melothesia: Or Certain General Rules for Playing upon a Continued-Bass.* London, 1673.

———. *The English Opera, or The Vocal Musick in Psyche.* London, 1675.

Lohr, I. "Henry Purcell und seine Bearbeiten." *Schweizerische Musik-Zeitung* (Zürich), 1951.

Long, Kenneth R. *The Music of the English Church.* New York, 1971.

Lorenz, M. "Henry Purcell, der englische Orpheus." *Neue Zeitschrift für Musik* 70 (1904).

"Lost Anthem Found ['The Lord is King']." *Musical Courier,* March 1959.

Loveless, R. E. "Yorkshiremen in London." *Yorkshire Post,* 17 February 1949 (discusses Purcell's "Of Old When Heroes Thought It Bold. The Yorkshire Feast Song").

Lowe, Edward. *A Review of Some Short Direction for Performance of Cathedral Service.* Oxford, 1664.

Lucas, C. "With Purcell in Westminster." *Musical Courier*, 27 June 1931.

Luckett, Richard. "St. Cecilia and Music." *PRMA* 99 (1972–73).

Ludman, J. "Henry Purcell: A New Look at the Great Master of English Song." *Bulletin*, 15 May 1957.

* Luttrell, N. *A Brief Historical Relation of State Affairs from September, 1678 to April, 1714*. Vols. 1–3. Oxford, 1857.

Macaulay, T. *The History of England*. London, 1870.

McCabe, W. H. "Music and the Dance on a Seventeenth-Century College Stage." *Musical Quarterly* 24 (July 1938).

McCutcheon, R. P. "Dryden's Prologue in the Prophetess." *Modern Language Notes* 39 (1924).

Mace, D. "English Musical Thought in the Seventeenth Century." Ph.D. diss., Columbia University, 1952.

———. "Musical Humanism, the Doctrine of Rhythmus, and the Saint Cecilia Odes of Dryden." *Journal of the Warburg and Courtauld Institutes* 27 (1964).

Mace, Thomas. *Musick's Monument; or a Remembrancer of the Best Practical Music*. London, 1676.

McGrady, R. J. "Henry Lawes and the Concept of 'Just Note and Accent.'" *Music and Letters* 50 (1969).

McGuiness, Rosamond. "Blow's Court Odes." Typescript. 1960.

———. "The Ground Bass in the English Court Ode." *Music and Letters* 51 (1970).

* ———. *English Court Odes, 1660–1820*. Oxford, 1971.

Maclean, Charles. "Purcell by Two Methods." *Zeitschrift der internationalen Musikgesellschaft* 11 (1910).

McLean, Hugh. "Blow and Purcell in Japan." *Musical Times* 104 (October 1963).

Macrory, E. *Notes on the Temple Organ*. 3d ed. London, 1911.

Madan, Falconer, M.A. *Stuart Papers Relating Chiefly to Queen Mary of Modena and the exiled Court of James II*. 2 vols. London, 1888.

Magalotti, L. *Travels of Cosmo the Third, Grand Duke of Tuscany, through England during the Reign of King Charles II (1669)*. London, 1821.

Mahy, K. W. "The Problem of Thorough-Bass Realization in Selected Songs of Henry Purcell: A Critical Comparison of Available Editions." Ph.D. diss., Indiana University, 1974.

Maidwell, L. *An Essay upon the Necessity and Excellency of Education*. Los Angeles: Augustan Society, 1951.

Maine, Basil S. "Neglect of Purcell." *Spectator* 149 (16 December 1932).

———. "Notes." *Musical Opinion* 69 (April-June 1936).

* Maitland, W. *The History of London from Its Foundation to the Present Time*, 2d ed. 2 vols. London, 1769.

Malcolm, Alexander. *A Treatise of Muṣick, Speculative, Practical and Historical*. Edinburgh, 1721.

Mandinian, Edward. *Purcell's "The Fairy Queen" as Presented at the Royal Opera House by the Sadler's Wells Ballet and the Covent Garden Opera*. London, 1948.

Mangeot, Andre. "The Purcell Fantasias and Their Influence on Modern Music." *Music and Letters* 7 (April 1926).

———. *Fantasias for Strings*. Transcribed by Peter Warlock. London, 1927.

Manifold, J. S. *The Music in English Drama from Shakespeare to Purcell*. London, 1956.

Mann, Alfred, ed. *Behold I Bring You Glad Tidings* [A Christmas Anthem]. New Brunswick, N.J., 1953.

Mann, W. "Dido and Aeneas." *Opera* 2 (August 1951).

Marco, G. "The Variety in Purcell's Word Painting." *The Music Review* 18 (February 1957).

Mark, J. "Dryden and the Beginning of Opera in England." *Music and Letters*, July 1924.

Mason, C. "Skimpy Honors for Purcell." *New York Times*, 12 July 1959.

Mason, D. G., ed. "Henry Purcell." In *Masters in Musick*, edited by D. G. Mason. London, 1904.

Mason, E. "Occasional Song." *Music and Musicians* 11 (September 1962).

Mason, William A. *A Copious Collection of Those Portions of the Psalms of David, Bible and Liturgy which Have Been Set to Musick, and Sung as anthems. . . .* York, 1782.

Matas, J. R. *Diccionario biografico de la musica.* Barcelona, n.d.

Mattheson, J. *Grundlage einer Ehren-Pforte.* Berlin, 1910.

Mauer, Miriam, and Peyser, Ethel. *How Music Grew from Prehistoric Times to the Present Day.* New York, 1925.

Maugars, A. *Response faite à un curieux sur le sentiment de la musique d'Italie.* Rome, 1 October 1639.

Mayer, G. L. "The Vocal Works of Henry Purcell: A Discography." *American Record Guide*, May 1959.

Mayer, H. "Purcell's Orgelmuziek." *Het Orgel* 8 (1962).

Meinardus, W. "Die Technik des Basso ostinato bei Henry Purcell." Ph.D. diss., Cologne, 1950.

Meffen, J. "A Question of Temperament: Purcell and Croft." *Musical Times* 119 1978.

Mellers, W. "The Tragic Heroine and the Un-Hero, 'Henry Purcell: Dido and Aeneas.'" *Harmonious Meeting.* London, 1965.

Mellor, Albert. *A Record of the Music and Musicians of Eton College.* Windsor, 1929.

Meltzer, E. "Henry Purcell's Secular Solo Songs: A Stylistic Analysis." Ph.D. diss., University of California at Los Angeles, 1958.

Menestrier, C. F. *Des representations en musique anciennes et modernes.* Paris, 1681.

Meyer, E. H. *Die mehrstimmige Spielmusik des 17. Jahrhunderts in Nord- und Mitteleuropa.* Kassel, 1934.

———. "The 'In nomine' and the Birth of Instrumental Style." *Music and Letters* 7 (1936).

———. *English Chamber Music.* London, 1946.

———. "Locke-Blow-Purcell: Drei Vorgänger Handels." *Handel Jahrbuch* 3 (1957).

———. *Die Kammermusik Alt-Englands vom Mittelalter bis zum Tod Henry Purcells.* Leipzig, 1958.

———. "Handel and Purcell." *Handel Jahrbuch* 5 (1959).

Miller, Hugh. "Purcell and [His Use of] the Ground Bass." *Music and Letters* 29 (October 1948).

Montague, G. "Dido and Aeneas." *London Musical Events* 6 (May 1961).

* Moore, Robert E. *Henry Purcell and the Restoration Theatre.* Cambridge, Mass., 1961.

———. "The Music to Macbeth." *Musical Quarterly* 47 (January 1961).

Moore, Stephen Sidney. *Purcell Theme Book.* London, 1953.

Moorman, John R. H. *A History of the Church in England.* 2d ed. London, 1967.

Moreley, Thomas. *A Plain and Easy Introduction to Practical Music.* London, 1597.

Motteux, P. A., ed. *The Gentleman's Journal; or The Monthly Miscellany*. January 1692–November 1694.

Muddiman, J. G. *The King's Journalist, 1659–1689*. London, 1923.

"A Musical Pilgrimage in Vanishing London." *Musical Opinion*, April 1928.

"The Music Library of Mr. T. W. Taphouse." *Musical Times* 45 (October 1904).

Myers, Clara C. "Opera in England from 1656 to 1728." *Western Reserve University Bulletin* 10 (November 1906).

Myers, R. H. "Henry Purcell: A Tribute from France." *The Chesterian*, January 1952.

Nagel, W. *Geschichte der Musik in England*. Strassburg, 1894–97.

Nelson, Everett E. "Studies in the Development of the English Fancy from John Taverner to Henry Purcell." Ph.D. diss., Cornell University, 1958.

Nettl, P. "An English Musician at the Court of Charles VI in Vienna." *Musical Quarterly* 28 (July 1942).

Newman, William S. *The Sonata in the Baroque Era*. 3d ed. New York, 1972.

Newmarch, R. "Purcell's 'Fairy Queen' at Cambridge." *The Chesterian*, n.s. no. 6 (1920).

Newton, D. *Catholic London*. London, 1950.

Newton, John. *The English Academy, or A Brief Introduction to the Seven Liberal Arts*. London, 1677.

New York Philharmonic Symphony Society. "Prelude and Death of Dido." *Program Notes*, 1 April 1953.

Nichols, J. B. and Sons. *London Pageants*. London, 1837.

*Nicoll, Allardyce. A History of English Drama: I: *Restoration Drama, 1660–1700*. II: *Early Eighteenth-Century Drama*. . . . VI. *A Short Title Alphabetical Catalog of Plays . . . 1600–1900*. Cambridge, 1952–59.

———. *Restoration Drama, 1660–1700*. 4th ed. Cambridge, 1952.

Noble, Jeremy. "The Music of Purcell." *Music in Schools*, July 1940.

———. "Festival Legacy: Music of Purcell and Handel." *London Musical Events* 14 (August 1959).

———. "Purcell and the Chapel Royal." In *Henry Purcell 1659–1695: Essays on His Music*, edited by Imogen Holst. London, 1959.

North, Roger. *A Philosophical Essay of Musick Directed to A Friend*. London, 1677.

———. "Some Notes on An Essay of Musick, printed 1677, by Way of Comment and Amendment." British Library Add. MS 32531.

———. "An Essay of Musical Ayre. Tending Chiefly to Shew the Foundations of Melody Joined with Harmony." British Museum Add. MS 32536.

———. "Some Memorandums Concerning Musick." British Museum Add. MS 32532.

———. "The Theory of Sounds." British Library Add. MS 32534.

———. *The Lives of the Right Honorable Francis North, Baron Guilford*. Rev. ed. 3 vols. London, 1826.

———. *Memoirs of Musick*. Edited by E. F. Rimbault. London, 1846.

———. *Autobiography*. Edited by A. Jessopp. London, 1887.

———. *The Musicall Grammarian*. Edited by Hilda Andrews. London, 1925.

Novello, V. *Purcell's Sacred Music*. 5 vols., with a biographical account in the prefatory volume. London, 1842.

Noyes, R. G. "A Manuscript Restoration Prologue for Volpone." *Modern Language Notes* 17 (1937).

———. "Conventions of Song in Restoration Tragedy." *PMLA* 52 (1938).

O'Donohue, F. *Catalogue of Engraved British Portraits in the British Museum.* London, 1912.

Ogilby, J. *The Relation of His Majestie's Entertainment Passing through the City of London to His Coronation.* London, 1661.

———. *The Entertainment of his Most Excellent Majestie Charles II, in His Passage through the City of London to His Coronation.* London, 1662.

Oldmeadow, E. J. *Great Musicians.* Philadelphia, 1908.

Oman, Carola. *Mary of Modena.* London, 1962.

Osborne, C. L. "Purcell's *Dido and Aeneas* Freshly Achieved." *High Fidelity* 13 (February 1963).

"O Sing unto the Lord a New Song: Verse Anthem for Four Voices, Chorus, Strings and Organ." *Musical Opinion* 89 (March 1957).

* *Oxford English Dictionary.*

Parry, C. H. H. "Purcell." *National Review,* 1895.

———. *The Music of the Seventeenth Century.* 2d ed. Oxford History of Music, vol. 3. Oxford, 1938.

Pattison, Bruce. *Music and Poetry of the English Renaissance.* London, 1948.

Pears, Peter. "Homage to the British Orpheus." In *Henry Purcell 1659–1695: Essays on His Music,* edited by Imogen Holst. London, 1959.

Pepys, Samuel. *Memoires of Samuel Pepys.* Edited by Lord Braybrook. London, 1825.

* ———. *Diary.* Edited by H. B. Wheatley. 8 vols. London, 1904.

* ———. *Memoirs of Samuel Pepys.* Edited by Robert Latham and William Matthews. 10 vols. London, 1963.

Pereyra, M. L. "La musique écrite sûr La Tempete d'apres Shakespeare par Pelham Humfrey." *Bulletin de la Société Française de la Musicologie,* October 1920.

Petre, R. "A New Piece by Henry Purcell." *Early Music* 6 (1978).

Phillips, Charles Henry. *The Singing Church: An Outline History of the Music Sung by Choir and People.* London, 1943.

Phillips, Katherine. *Poems.* London, 1669.

Pincherle, Marc. *Vivaldi.* Paris, 1955.

Playford, John. *The English Dancing Master.* Edited by M. Dean-Smith. London, 1957.

———. *An Introduction to the Skill of Music.* 12th ed. Reprint ed. with an introduction, glossary, and index by F. B. Zimmerman. New York, 1972.

Poole, H. Edward. "The Printing of William Holder's 'Principles of Harmony.'" *PRMA* 101 (1975).

Prendergast, A. H. "Masques and Early Operas." In *English Music,* edited by F. J. Crowest. London, 1906.

Price, Curtis. "Musical Practices in Restoration Plays." Ph.D. diss., Harvard University, 1974.

———. "Restoration Stage Fiddlers and Their Music." *Early Music* 7 (July 1979).

———. *Music in the Restoration Theatre: With A Catalogue of Instrumental Music in the Plays, 1665–1713.* U.M.I. Research Press, ca. 1979.

Pritchard, William. *The Lord Mayor's Show: Being a Description of the Solemnity at the Inauguration of . . . Sir W. Pritchard, Kt., Lord Mayor of London . . . Performed on Monday, Sept XXX 1682, with Several New Loyal Songs and Catches.* London, 1682.

———. *An Exact Account of the Trial Between Sir W. Pritchard . . . and Tho. Papillon,*

Esq. in an Action upon the Case 6 Nov. 1684. To which is Added, the Matter of Fact Relating to Election of Sheriffs . . . in 1682. London, 1689.

* *Proceedings of the Musical Association.*

* *Proceedings of the Royal Musical Association.*

Prunieres, H. *L'opera Italien en France avant Lulli.* Paris, 1913.

* *Publications of the Modern Language Association.*

* *Public Record Office.*

Pulver, J. *A Dictionary of English Music and Musical Instruments.* London, 1923.

*———. *A Biographical Dictionary of Old English Music.* London, 1927.

———. "The Chapel of Catherine of Braganza." *Musical Opinion,* February 1927.

———. "The English St. Cecilia Celebrations of the Seventeenth Century." *Sackbut,* July 1927.

———. "Music in England During the Commonwealth." *Acta Musicologica* 6 (1934).

———. "Purcell and Dryden." *Musical Opinion,* April 1936.

Purcell, Henry. *The Works of Henry Purcell.* 33 vols. Edited under the supervision of The Purcell Society. London, 1878–1962.

"Purcell and Handel at British Museum." *Musical Journal* 59 (December 1959).

"Purcell and Handel Festival." *London Musical Events* 14 (February 1959).

"Purcell and His Times." *Saturday Review* 80 (1935).

"Purcell Commemoration in Westminster Abbey, on Thursday, November 21, 1895 . . . Being the 200th Anniversary of the Death of Henry Purcell." London, 1895.

"The Purcell Exhibits at British Museum." *Musical Times* 36 (December 1895).

"Purcell Explored." *The Times,* 11 December 1957.

"Purcell Fantazias." *PMA* 40 (1915).

"Purcell-Handel Festival." *Musical Times* 100 (March 1959).

Purcell-Handel Festival. Edited by Nigel Fortune. London, 1959.

"Purcell Manuscript Discovered in Japan" [*Dido and Aeneas*]. *London Musical Events* 14 (July 1959).

"Purcell's Dido and Aeneas." *Neue züricher Zeitung,* 8 March 1962.

Purcell's Fairy Queen as Represented by the Sadler's Wells Ballet and the Covent Garden Opera; A Photographic Record by Edward Mandinian with the Preface Arranged by Professor Edward Dent, and Articles by Constance Lambert and Michael Ayrton. London, 1948.

"Purcell's Father." *Music and Letters* 36 (October 1955).

"The Purcell Society Edition, Volume 31." *Musical Times* 100 (September 1959).

"The Purcell Society Edition, Volumes 9 and 29." *Musical Times* 102 (June 1961).

"Purcell's Sonatas." *PMA* 40 (1915).

Purcell-Taylor, C. "A Neglected Musical Genius." *Radio,* 4 September 1925.

Quervain, F. de. *Der Chorstil Henry Purcells.* Bern and Leipzig, 1935.

Raguenet, Fr. *A Comparison of the French and Italian Musick and Operas.* London, 1709 (Reprint ed., Introduction by Charles Cudworth. Farnborough, Hants, 1968).

Rare Prologues and Dialogues, 1642–1700. Edited by Aubrey N. Wiley. London, 1940.

Ravenzwaaij, G. van. "Henry Purcell's Muzikale Synthese in Engelands Restaratie-Period." *Miscellanea Musicologica Floris van der Mueren.*

———. *Purcell.* Gottmer, Haarlem, Antwerpen, 1954.

Rawlinson, H. "Fantasia upon One Note for Strings." *Strad,* January 1948.

———. "Purcell's Music for String Orchestra." *Strad* 70 (June 1959).

Reese, Gustav. "The Origin of the English 'In nomine.'" *Journal of the American Musicological Society* 2 (1949).

Rehyer, P. *Les Masque Anglaise; Etude sur les ballets et la vie de cour in Angleterre, 1512–1640.* Paris, 1909.

Reichlin, Gerhart. "Continental Influences on the Work of Henry Purcell." Ph.D. diss., Princeton University, in progress.

Rendall, E. D. "The Influence of Henry Purcell on Handel, Traced in *Acis and Galatea.*" *Musical Times* 36 (May 1895).

———. "Some Notes on Purcell's Dramatic Music, with Especial Reference to 'The Fairy Queen.'" *Music and Letters* 1 (April 1920).

Rimbault, E. F. "An Historical Sketch of the History of Dramatick Music in England from the Earliest Time to the Death of Purcell, Anno. Dom. 1695. Introduction to *Bonduca.*" *The Musical Antiquary* 2 (1841).

———. "Robert Smith." *Musical Antiquary*, April 1911.

*———, ed. *The Old Cheque-Book, or Book of Remembrance of the Chapel Royal, from 1561 to 1774.* London, 1872.

Roberts, George. *The Life, Progresses and Rebellion of James, Duke of Monmouth.* 2 vols. London, 1844.

Robertson, Alec. *Henry Purcell* [jacket notes to accompany gramaphone records of his fantasias for strings]. London, 1937.

Robinson, T. W. *The Poetry of the Old Testament.* London, 1947.

Rohrer, Katherine T. "The Energy of English Words. A Linguistic Approach to Henry Purcell's Methods of Setting Texts." Ph.D. diss., Princeton, 1980.

Roper, E. S. "Music at the English Chapels Royal." *PMA* 33 (1927–28).

Rose, Bernard. "Some Further Observations on the Performance of Purcell's Music." *Musical Times* 100 (July 1959).

Rose, G. "Purcell, Michelangelo Rossi and J. S. Bach: Problems of Authorship." *Acta Musicologica* 40 (1968).

———. "A New Purcell Source." *Journal of the American Musicological Society* 25 (1972): 230–36.

Roseberry, E. "Britten's Purcell Realizations and Folksong Arrangements." *Tempo*, no. 57 (1968).

Rosen, W. "Der Sommernachtstraum mit Purcell-Musik." *Allgemeine Musik-Zeitung* 64 (January 1937).

———. "Theatre Music in the Sixteenth and Seventeenth Centuries." *Allgemeine Musik-Zeitung* 29 (October 1948).

Rothstein, E. *Restoration Tragedy.* Madison, Wis., 1967.

Rowen, Ruth H. *Early Chamber Music.* New York, 1949.

Ruff, Lillian M. "Fairest Isle." *Musical Times* 105 (March 1964).

Runciman, J. F. *Old Scores and New Readings.* London, 1899.

———. *Purcell.* London, 1909.

Rychlik, J. "Henry Purcell." *Tempo: Hudebni Mesticnik* (Prague), 1956.

Rylands, G. "The Tempest or the Enchanted Island." *Musical Times* 100 (1959).

"St. Andrew's Church, Holborne." *Musical Times* 46 (1905).

St. Margaret's, Westminster. *Parish Church Records.*

St. Katherine Cree Church, Vestry Minutes. Guildhall Library, London, MS 1196/T.

Sammelbände der internationalen Musikgesellschaft.

Sandford, F. *The History of the Coronation of the Most High, Most Mighty and Most*

Excellent Monarch, James II . . . and Queen Mary. London, 1687–88.

Sargeaunt, J. *Annals of Westminster School*. London, 1898.

Savage, R. "Producing 'Dido and Aeneas': An Investigation into Sixteen Problems." *Early Music* 4 (October 1973).

———. "The Shakespeare-Purcell Fairy Queen: A Defence and Recommendation." *Early Music* 4 (October 1973).

Sayle, Charles Edward. "Purcell, 'The Fairy Queen' [the Cambridge performance, 10 February 1920]." Reprinted for *The Eagle* (with plates). Cambridge, 1920.

Schjelderup-Ebbe, Dag. *Purcell's Cadences*. Stockholm, 1962.

Schmitz, E. *Geschichte der weltlichen Solokantate*. Leipzig, 1955.

Scholes, Percy A. "The Chapel Royal." *Musical Times* 42 (1 February 1902).

———. *In Purcell's Time: A Brief Sketch of Politics, Society, Literature and Religion*. London, 1913.

———. "Purcell in Praise of Princes." *Musical Times* 71 (October 1915) (odes to Charles II, James II, and Mary, with chronological list).

———. "Purcell's Orchestration, His Scheme of Orchestration." *Musical Opinion* 33 (April 1916).

———. "Henry Purcell—A Sketch of a Busy Life." *Musical Quarterly* 2 (July 1916).

———. "Great Englishman." In *Everyman and His Music: Simple Papers on Varied Subjects*. London, 1917.

*———. *The Puritans and Music in England and New England*. London, 1934.

———. *The Oxford Companion to Music*. 9th ed. London, 1955.

Schroder, F. "Henry Purcell und seine 'Feenkonigin.'" *Schweitzinger Festspiele*, 1959.

Scott, H. A. "Purcell at Chelsea." *Daily Telegraph*, 26 June 1927.

———. "London's Earliest Public Concerts." *Musical Quarterly* 22 (October 1936).

Sharp, J. W. "The Golden Sonata." *Strad*, vol. 20, nos. 223 and 224 (1909).

Shaw, H. Watkins. "Extracts from Anthony à Wood's 'Notes on the Lives of Musicians,' Hitherto Unpublished." *Music and Letters* 15 (April 1934).

———. "The Secular Music of John Blow." *PRMA* 63 (1936–37).

———. "Blow's Use of the Ground Bass." *Musical Quarterly* 24 (January 1938).

———. "A Tribute to John Blow's Music, and Comparison with That of Henry Purcell." *Musical Times* 99 (October 1958).

———. "The British Museum Purcell-Handel Exhibition." *Musical Times* 100 (1959).

———. "A Collection of Musical Manuscripts in the Autograph of Henry Purcell and Other English Composers, c. 1665–85." *The Library*, 5th ser. 14 (1959).

———. "A Contemporary Source of English Music of the Purcellian Period." *Acta Musicologica* 31 (1959).

———. "Purcell's 'Bell Anthem' and Its Performance." *Musical Times* 100 (May 1959).

———. "A Cambridge Manuscript from the English Chapel Royal." *Music and Letters* 42 (1961).

———. "The Works of Henry Purcell, Volume 29: Anthems." *Notes* 19 (1962).

———. "The Autographs of John Blow (1649–1708)." *Music Review* 25 (1964).

———. "Blow, Purcell and the Exeter Choristers." *Musical Opinion* 87 (May 1964).

———, ed. *Eight Concerts of Henry Purcell's Music: Commemorative Book of Programmes, Notes and Texts*. London: The Arts Council of Great Britain, 1951.

Shaw, W. A. "Three Unpublished Portraits of Henry Purcell." *Musical Times* 61 (September 1920).

Shaw-Taylor, Desmond. "Anniversaries." *New Statesman and Nation* 30 (1 December 1945).

Shedlock, J. S. "Purcell." *Academy*, 1895.

Sheppard, F. H. W., ed. *Survey of London*. London, 1963.

Siedentopf, H. "Eine Komposition Purcells im Klavier-Buch eine wurtemburgischen Prinzessin." *Musik Forschung* 31(1978).

Siegfried, E. "Dido and Aeneas von Henry Purcell." *Musikalisches Wochenblatt* (Leipzig), vol. 41, nos. 17–19 (1910).

Sietz, Reinhold. "Englands grösster Komponist." *Musikleben* 4(October 1951).

———. *Henry Purcell: Zeit, Leben, Werk*. Leipzig, 1959.

Silberer, H. "Why Not Try Some Purcell?" *Repertoire* 1(October 1951).

Simpson, Adrienne. "A Short-Title List of Printed English Instrumental Tutors up to 1800, Held in British Libraries." *RMA Research Chronicle*, no. 6, 1966.

Simpson, Christopher. *The Principles of Practical Musick Delivered in a Compendious, Easie and New Method: for the Instruction of Beginners, Either in Singing or Playing upon Instruments*. To which are added *Some short and Easie Ayres Designed for Learners*. London, 1665.

Smart, J. S. "The Italian Singer in Milton's Sonnets." *Musical Antiquary*, January 1913.

Smith, Alexander Brent. "Henry Purcell." *Music and Letters* 18(1937).

———. *An Index of the Works of Henry Purcell*. London, ?1970.

Smith, Cecil. "Jersey City Hears Purcell's 'King Arthur.'" *Musical America* 72(June 1972).

Smith, F. M. *Purcell*. New York, 1901.

Smith, L. *Music of the Seventeenth and Eighteenth Centuries*. London, 1931.

Smith, W. C. *A Bibliography of the Musical Works Published by John Walsh During the Years 1695–1720*. London, 1948.

Smithers, Don L. *The Music and History of the Baroque Trumpet Before 1721*. Syracuse, London, 1973.

Sorbiere, Samuel de. *Relation d'un voyage en Angleterre*. Paris, 1664. Translated as *A Voyage to England*. Edited by Thomas Sprat. London, 1709.

Souers, P. W. *The Matchless Orinda*. Cambridge, Mass., 1931.

Spink, I. *English Song: Dowland to Purcell*. London, 1974.

Squire, J. C. "Shakespeare Improved." *Observer*, 12 February 1922.

Squire, William Barclay. "An Elegy on Henry Purcell." *International Musicological Society Zeitschrift* (Leipzig) 2(1900).

———. "Purcell's Music for the Funeral of Mary II." *SIMG* 4(1904).

———. "Purcell as Theorist." *Quarterly Magazine of the International Musical Society*, July-September 1905.

*———. "Purcell's Dramatic Music." *SIMG* 5(1905). (See also *Zeitschrift der internationalen Gesellschaft für Musikwissenschaft* 6[October 1904], relating to "The Loves of Dido and Aeneas, a Masque in Four Musical Entertainments, with Prologue also set to Music.")

———. "'Beauties Triumph' at Mr. Priest's School." *Musical Times* 47 (April 1906).

———. "An Index of Tunes in the Ballad Operas." *Musical Antiquary* 2(October 1910).

———. "An Unknown Autograph of Henry Purcell." *Musical Antiquary* 3(October 1911).

———. *Catalogue of Printed Music Published Between 1487 and 1800 Now in the British Museum*. 2 vols. London, 1912.

———. "J. W. Franck in England." *Musical Antiquary*, July 1912.

———. "Purcell's Dido and Aeneas." *Musical Times* 59(June 1918).

――――. "Purcell's Fairy Queen." *Musical Times* 61(January 1920).

――――. "The Music of Shadwell's 'Tempest.'" *Musical Quarterly* 7(October 1921).

Statham, H. D. "Purcell's Church Music." *Musical Times* 65(May-June 1924).

Steele, Joshua. *An Essay towards Establishing the Melody and Measure of Speech*. London, 1775.

Steglich, Rudolph. "Die Oper in England bis 1740." In *Handbuch der Musikgeschichte*, edited by G. Adler. Frankfurt am Main, 1929.

Steinbert, Michael. "Dido and Aeneas." *Notes* 20(1963).

Sternfeld, Frederick, et al. *Essays on Opera and English Music: In Honour of Sir Jack Westrup*. Oxford, 1975.

Stevens, Denis. "Purcell's Art of Fantasia." *Music and Letters* 33(October 1952).

――――. *Thomas Tomkins*. London, 1957.

――――. "Purcell on the Gramophone." *Music and Letters* 40(1959).

――――, and Dart, Thurston, eds. *Fantazia: Three Parts upon a Ground*. London, 1963.

Stevenson, Robert Murrell. *Music Before the Classic Era: An Introduction*. London, 1955.

Stieber, H. *Henry Purcells Opernmusik "The Fairy Queen als festliche Begleitsmusik zu Shakespeare's "Sommernachtstraum."* Leipzig, 1936–37.

Straeten, E. J. van der. *The Romance of the Fiddle*. London, 1911.

Streatfield, R. A. "Life and Work of Henry Purcell." In *Modern Music and Musicians*, edited by R. A. Streatfield. London, 1906.

Summers, M. *The Playhouse of Pepys*. London, 1935.

Sumner, W. L. "The Baroque Organ." *PRMA* 31(1954–55).

Svanepol, P. E. *Das dramatische Schaffen Purcells*. Vienna, 1926.

Swalin, B. F. "Purcell's Masque in Timon of Athens." *American Musicological Society Papers*. Oberlin, 1946.

Talbot, John. "Notes on Musical Instruments, c. 1695." Christ Church Oxford MS 1187.

Tanner, L. E. *Westminster School, Its Buildings and Their Associations*. London, 1923.

Teahan, F. T. "The Literary Criticism of Music in England, 1660–1789." Ph.D. diss., Trinity College, Dublin, 1957.

Tellart, Roger. "Purcell et les influences continentales." *Musique de tous les temps* 28(1963).

Temperley, Nicholas. "John Playford and the Metrical Psalms." *JAMS* 25(Fall 1972).

* *Term Catalogues*.

Thiele, E. "Die Kirchenmusik Henry Purcells." *Musik und Gottesdienst* 12(12 January 1958).

Thieman, S. *An Index of the Purcell Society Edition*. New York Music Library Association, 1963.

Thorp, Willard. *Songs from the Restoration Theatre*. Princeton, 1934.

Tiggers, P. "King Arthur van Henry Purcell." *Mens en Melodie* 9(1954).

Tilmouth, Michael. "Some Early London Concerts and Music Clubs, 1670–1720." *PRMA* 84(1957–58).

――――. "The Technique and Forms of Purcell's Sonatas." *Music and Letters* 40(April 1959).

――――. "Henry Purcell, Assistant Lexicographer." *Musical Times* 100(June 1959).

*――――. "English Chamber Music (1675–1720)." Ph.D. diss., Cambridge University, 1960.

――――. "A Calendar of References to Music in Newspapers Published in London and the Provinces (1660–1719)." *RMA Research Chronicle*, no. 1(1961); no. 2(1962).

Towers, J. *Purcell*. Boston, 1891.

Traill, H. D. *William the Third*. London, 1888.

Trevelyan, G. M. *England Under the Stuarts*. Vol. 5 of *A History of England in Seven Volumes*, edited by Sir Charles Oman. New York, 1925.

Turner, Joseph W. "'The Fairy Queen' at Cambridge." *New Statesman* 14(28 February 1920).

Turner, William. *Sound Anatomiz'd, in a Philosophical Essay on Music wherein is Explained the Nature of Sound*. London, 1724.

Van Tassell, Eric. "Two Purcell Discoveries—I: 'Give sentence.'" *Musical Times* 118 (May 1977).

———. "English Church Music, c. 1660–1700." *Early Music* 7(January 1979).

Verney, Margaret M. *Memoires of the Verney Family*. London, 1899.

Vipont, E. *Henry Purcell and His Times*. London, 1959.

Voltaire, François Marie Arouet de. *Le siècle de Louis XIV*. Paris, 1714.

Wailes, M. "Four Short Fantasies by Henry Purcell." *Score*, June 1957.

Wallis, John. *Johannis Wallis . . . Operum Mathematicorum*. Oxford, 1699.

———. *Grammar of the English Language*. Translated and with commentary by J. A. Kemp. London, 1972.

Walker, E. *History of Music in England*. 3d ed. Oxford, 1952.

Walker, F. H. "Purcell's Handwriting." *Monthly Musical Record* 72(1942).

Walsh, T. J. "Opera in Dublin—1705–1797, the Social Scene." Ph.D. diss., University of Dublin, 1972.

Walther, J. G. *Musikalisches Lexikon oder musikalische Bibliothek*. Leipzig, 1732.

Ward, Charles E., ed. *The Letters of John Dryden*. Durham, N.C., 1962.

Warlock, P. "Purcell's Fantasias for Strings." *Sackbut* 7(1927).

Warner, Robert A. "The Fantasia in the Works of John Jenkins." 2 vols. Ph.D. diss., University of Michigan, 1951.

Welch, J. *A List of Scholars of St. Peter's College, Westminster, as they Were Elected to Christ Church College, Oxford, and Trinity College, Cambridge*. London, 1788.

Wessely-Kropik, H. "Henry Purcell als Instrumentalkomponist." *Studien zur Musikwissenschaft* 22 (1955): 85–141.

———. *Lelio Colista: Ein romischer Meister vor Corelli*. Vienna, 1961.

West. J. E. *Cathedral Organists, Past and Present*. 2d ed. London, 1921.

Westrup, J. A. "Fact and Fiction About Purcell." *PMA* 62(1935–36).

———. "Reply to D. Arundell, 'Purcell's Father.'" *New Statesman and Nation* 13 (26 June 1937).

———. "Purcell and His Operatic Style." *Listener*, 22 August 1940.

———. "Foreign Musicians in Stuart England." *Musical Quarterly* 27(January 1941).

———. "Church Music at the Restoration." *Monthly Musical Record*, July-August 1941.

———. "Domestic Music Under the Stuarts." *PRMA* 68(1942).

———. "Purcell and Dryden." *Listener*, 29 April 1943.

———. "No. 300 Anniversario de Henry Purcell." *Arte Musical* 48(February 1959).

———. "Das Englisches in Henry Purcells Musik." *Musica*, March 1959.

———. "Henry Purcell." *Musical America* 79(August 1959).

———. "Purcell's Reputation." *Musical Times* 100(1959).

———. *Purcell*. Great Composer Series. Collier, N.Y., 1962.

———. "Purcell's Music for Timon of Athens." In *Festschrift K. G. Fellerer*, edited by

Heinrich Huschen. Regensburg, 1962.

———. "Purcell's Parentage." *Music Review* 25(25 May 1964).

*———. *Purcell*. Master Musicians Series. London, 1965; rev. ed. 1975 (first published 1936; French translation by Ammettee Drendorme in La Flute de Pan Series, Paris, 1947).

———. "Purcell and Handel." *Music and Letters* 40(April 1969).

White, E. W. *The Rise of English Opera*. London, 1951.

———. "Early Performances of Purcell's Operas." *Theatre Notebook* 13(1958–59).

———. "New Light on *Dido and Aeneas*." In *Henry Purcell 1659–1695: Essays on His Music*, edited by Imogen Holst. London, 1959.

Whittaker, W. G. "Some Observations on Purcell's Harmony." *Musical Times* 75(October 1934).

———. *The First Set of Twelve Sonatas* [by Henry Purcell]. Paris, 1936.

Williams, G. F. "The Concord of This Discord." *Music in the Stage History of A Midsummernight's Dream*. Yale Theatre. Spring 1973.

Williams, J. G. "The Influence of English Music and Society on G. F. Handel." Ph.D. diss., University of Leeds, 1969.

Wilson, John, ed. *Roger North on Music*. London, 1959.

Wind, E. "Julian the Apostate at Hampton Court." *Journal of the Warburg and Courtauld Institutes* 3(1939–40).

Wolf, Johannes. "Early English Musical Theorists from 1200 to the Death of Purcell." *Musical Quarterly* 25(1939).

Wood, Anthony à. *The History and Antiquities of the Colleges and Halls in the University of Oxford*. . . . Edited by John Gutch, M.A., from manuscripts of Anthony à Wood. Oxford, 1786.

———. *The History and Antiquities of the University of Oxford*. 2 vols. Oxford, 1796.

———. *Athenae Oxoniensis* (with *Fasti*). Edited by P. Bliss. Oxford, 1813–20.

*———. *The Life and Times of Anthony Wood, antiquary of Oxford, 1632–1695, described by Himself*. Edited by A. Clark. 5 vols. Oxford, 1891–1900.

———. "Notes on English Musicians." Bodleian Library, Oxford, MS Wood D 19(4).

Wood, B. "A Note on Two Cambridge Manuscripts and Their Copyists." *Music and Letters* 56(1975).

———. "John Blow's Anthems with Orchestra." Ph.D. diss., University of Cambridge, 1976.

———. "Two Purcell Discoveries—2: A Coronation Anthem Lost and Found." *Musical Times* 118(1977).

———. "A Newly Identified Purcell Autograph." *Music and Letters* 59(1978).

Woodward, G. L., and McManaway, J. G. *A Check-List of English Plays 1641–1700*. Chicago, 1945.

"The Works of Henry Purcell: An Index of the Purcell Society Edition." *Music Library Association* (New York Chapter), 1963.

Wright, H. B., and Spear, M. K. *The Literary Works of Matthew Prior*. Oxford, 1955.

Yamamoto, H. "The Dramaturgy of Purcell's 'Dido and Aeneas.'" B.A. thesis in Musicology, Tokyo, 1967.

Young, P. M. "Henry Purcell (1659–1695)." *Musik und Gesellschaft* 9(1959).

Zimmerman, C. *Alte Meister der Musik*. Basel-Ammerbach, 1948.

Zimmerman, Franklin B. "Purcell and Monteverdi." *Musical Times* 99(July 1958).

———. "Purcell Portraiture." In *Organ and Choral Aspects and Prospects*, edited by Max Hinrichsen. Vol. 8. London, 1958.

————. "A Newly Discovered Anthem by Purcell." *Musical Quarterly* 45(July 1959).

————. "Poets in Praise of Purcell." *Musical Times* 100(October 1959).

————. "Purcell's Handwriting." In *Henry Purcell 1659–1695: Essays on His Music*, edited by Imogen Holst. London, 1959.

————. "Restoration Music Manuscripts at Lincoln Cathedral." *Musical Times* 101 (February 1960).

————. "Purcell Iconography: Missing Items." *Musical Times* 101(June 1960).

————. "Purcell and the Dean of Westminster—Some New Evidence." *Music and Letters* 43(January 1962).

————. "Musical Styles and Practices in Purcell's Anthems." *American Choral Review* 4(July 1962).

————. "Purcell's Polyphonic Anthems: Styles, Media, Interpretation." *American Choral Review* 4(October 1962).

————. "Purcell's Concerted Anthems: New Aesthetic Concepts." *American Choral Review* 5(April 1963).

————. "Thematic Integration in Purcell's Concertato Anthems." *American Choral Review* 6(July 1963), part 1; (October 1963), part 2.

————. "Handel's Purcellian Borrowings in His Later Operas and Oratorios." In *Festschrift O. E. Deutsch*, edited by Walter Gerstenberg. Kassel, 1963.

*————. *Henry Purcell (1659–1695): An Analytical Catalogue of His Music*. London, 1963.

————. "Purcell's 'Service Anthem: O God, Thou art my God,' and the B-Flat Major Service." *Musical Quarterly* 50(January 1964).

————. "Musical Borrowings in the English Baroque." *Musical Quarterly* 52(1966).

————. *Henry Purcell (1659–1695): His Life and Times*. 1st ed. London, 1967.

————. "Sound and Sense in Purcell's 'Single Songs.'" *William Clark Memorial Library Seminar*. Los Angeles, 1967.

————. "Anthems of Purcell and Contemporaries in a Newly Rediscovered 'Gostling Manuscript.'" *Acta Musicologica* 41(January-June 1969).

————. "Purcell's Family Circle Revisited and Revised." *Journal of the American Musicological Society* 16(Fall 1969).

————. *The Anthems of Henry Purcell*. New York, 1971.

————. *The William Kennedy Gostling Manuscript: A Primary Source for the Anthems of Henry Purcell, John Blow, and Their Contemporaries*. Austin, Tex., 1977.

————. "Purcell's Court Odes." *Musical Heritage Review* 4(October 1980).

————. "Purcell's Music for 'The Tempest.'" *Musical Heritage Review* 5(October 1981).

————. "Purcellian Passages in the Compositions of G. F. Handel." In *Music in Eighteenth-Century England: Essays in Memory of Charles Cudworth*, edited by Chr. Hogwood and Richard Luckett. Cambridge, 1982.

————, and Cudworth, Charles. "Jeremiah Clarke's 'Trumpet Voluntary.'" *Music and Letters* 40(October 1960).

Index